International Women
in Science

International Women in Science

A Biographical Dictionary to 1950

Catharine M. C. Haines
with Helen M. Stevens

A B C ⬥ C L I O

Santa Barbara, California   Denver, Colorado   Oxford, England

Library of Congress Cataloging-in-Publication Data

Haines, Catharine M. C.
    International women in science : a biographical dictionary to 1950 / Catharine
M. C. Haines.
        p. cm.
Includes bibliographical references and index.
    ISBN 1-57607-090-5 (acid-free paper)
    1. Women scientists—Biography. I. Title.
Q141.H2167 2001
509.2'2—dc21   2001004557

06 05 04 03 02 01   10 9 8 7 6 5 4 3 2 1

This book is also available on the World Wide Web as an e-book.
Visit abc-clio.com for details.

ABC-CLIO, Inc.
130 Cremona Drive, P.O. Box 1911
Santa Barbara, California 93116-1911

This book is printed on acid-free paper ∞.

Manufactured in the United States of America

Contents

Women by Profession, xi
Preface, xvii

International Women in Science

Abercrombie, Minnie Louie (Jane) née Johnson, 1
Adam, Madge Gertrude, 2
Adams, Jacqueline Nancy Mary née Whittaker, 2
Adams, Mary Grace Agnes née Campin, 3
Adamson, Joy (Friedericke Victoria) née Gessner, 3
Agnesi, Maria Gaetana, 4
Aitkin, Yvonne, 5
Alcock, Nora Lilian née Scott, 6
Anderson, Margaret Dampier née Whetham, 7
Anning, Mary, 7
Arber, Agnes née Robertson, 8
Armitage, Ella Sophia née Bulley, 9
Atkins, Anna née Children, 10
Auerbach, Charlotte, 10
Ayrton, Phoebe Sarah (Hertha) née Marks, 12

Bacon, Gertrude, 15
Balfour, (Lady Eve) Evelyn Barbara, 16
Balfour, (Elizabeth) Jean née Drew, 16
Ball, Anne Elizabeth, 17
Baly, Monica E., 17
Barber, Mary, 18
Barclay-Smith, Phyllis Ida, 19
Bari, Nina Karlovna, 20
Barnes, Alice Josephine (Mary Taylor; Dame Josephine Warren), 20
Barry, James Miranda Steuart, 22
Basford, Kathleen, 22
Bassi, Laura Maria Catarina, 23

Bate, Dorothea Minola Alice, 24
Beale, Dorothea, 24
Becker, Lydia Ernestine, 25
Beeton, Isabella Mary née Mayson, 26
Bell, Gertrude Margaret Lowthian, 27
Bennett, Isobel Ada, 28
Bentham, Ethel, 29
Bidder, Anna McClean, 29
Bidder, Marion née Greenwood, 31
Biheron, Marie-Catherine, 32
Bird, Isabella Lucy, 32
Bishop, Ann, 33
Blackburn, Kathleen Bever, 34
Blackburne, Anna, 35
Blackwell, Elizabeth, 36
Blackwood, Margaret, 36
Blagg, Mary Adela, 37
Bleeker, Caroline Emilie (Lili), 38
Bobath, Berta Othilie, 38
Bonheur, Rosalie Marie (Rosa), 39
Bonnevie, Kristine Elisabeth Heuch, 40
Booth, Evelyn Mary, 41
Borrowman, Agnes Thompson, 41
Boyle, Alice Helen Anne, 42
Brenchley, Winifred Elsie, 43
Bromhall, Margaret Ann, 44
Brook, Lady Helen Grace Mary née Knewstub, 44
Brown, Edith Mary, 45
Brown, Margaret Elizabeth (Mrs. Varley), 45
Bryan, Margaret, 46
Buchanan, Dorothy Donaldson (Mrs. Fleming), 47
Buchanan, Margaret Elizabeth, 47

Contents

Buckland, Mary née Morland, 48

Bülbring, Edith, 48

Burbidge, (Eleanor) Margaret née Peachey, 50

Byron, Augusta (Ada), Countess of Lovelace, 51

Cable, Alice Mildred, 53

Cadbury, Dorothy Adlington, 54

Canter-Lund, Hilda M. née Canter, 54

Cartwright, Mary Lucy, 56

Cassie Cooper, Una Vivienne née Dellow, 57

Casson, Lady Margaret née MacDonald, 58

Cheesman, Lucy Evelyn, 58

Chick, Harriette, 60

Chitty, Letitia, 61

Choquet-Bruhat, Yvonne, 62

Clarke, Patricia Hannah née Green, 62

Clay, Theresa Rachael, 64

Clayton, Barbara Evelyn, 64

Clerke, Agnes Mary, 66

Clerke, Ellen Mary, 67

Clubb, Elizabeth Mary Fitz-Simon née Thomas, 67

Cockburn, Patricia Evangeline Ann née Arbuthnot, 69

Conway, Verona Margaret, 69

Cookson, Isabel Clifton, 70

Corradi, Doris, 71

Courtauld, Katherine, 71

Courtauld, Louisa Perina née Ogier, 72

Courtenay-Latimer, Marjorie Eileen Doris, 72

Crane, Eva née Widdowson, 73

Cunliffe, Stella Vivian, 74

Curie, Marya (Manya; Marie) née Sklodowska, 75

Currie, Ethel Dobbie, 79

Cust, Aleen, 79

Dal, Ingerid Blanca Juell, 81

Dalton, Katharina Dorothea née Kuipers, 82

Datta, Naomi née Goddard, 82

Davies, Margaret, 83

Déjerine Klumpke, Augusta née Klumpke, 84

Denman, Gertrude Mary née Pearson, 84

Dent, Edith Vere née Annesley, 85

Dony, Christina Mayne née Goodman, 86

Downie, Dorothy G., 86

Drew-Baker, Kathleen M. née Drew, 87

Drower, Margaret Stephana, 87

du Châtelet-Lomont, Emilie Gabrielle née le Tonnelier de Breteuil, 88

Dunn, Barbara, 88

Dunscombe, Adaliza Amelia Clara Mary Elizabeth Emma Frances, 88

Durham, Mary Edith, 89

Eales, Nellie B., 91

Edwards, Amelia Blandford, 92

Ehrlich, Aline née Buchbinder, 92

Eyles, Joan Mary née Biggs, 93

Eymers, Johanna Geertruid (Truus), 93

Farquharson, Marian Sarah Ogilvie née Ridley, 95

Farrer, Margaret Irene, 95

Fawcett, Philippa, 96

Fell, Honor Bridget, 97

Fergusson, Mary (Molly) Isolen, 98

Flint, Elizabeth Alice, 98

Fountaine, Margaret Elizabeth, 99

Franklin, Lady Jane née Griffin, 100

Franklin, Rosalind Elsie, 100

Fraser, Roslin Margaret Ferguson, 101

Freeman, Joan, 102

Fretter, Vera, 103

Freud, Anna, 104

Frost, Winifred Evelyn, 104

Fulhame, Elizabeth, 105

Fulton, Margaret Barr, 105

Furness, Vera I., 107

Garrett Anderson, Elizabeth née Garrett, 109

Garrod, Dorothy Annie Elizabeth, 110

Gatty, Margaret née Scott, 111

Germain, Sophie, 112

Gibbons, E. Joan, 112

Gleditsch, Ellen, 113

Gordon, Isabella, 114

Gordon, Maria Matilda née Ogilvie, 115

Goss, Olga May, 115

Goulandris, Niki née Kephalia, 116

Gowing, Margaret Mary née Elliott, 117

Greig, Dorothy Margaret née Hannah, 118

Grierson, Mary Anderson, 119

Gromova, Vera Issacovna, 119

Guppy, Eileen M., 119

Gwynne-Vaughan, Helen Charlotte Isabella née Fraser, 120

Contents

Halicka, Antonina née Jaroszewicz, 123

Hanson, Emmeline Jean, 124

Harding, Jan née Ansell, 125

Harker, Margaret Florence, 126

Haslett, Caroline, 127

Hawker, Lilian E., 129

Herschel, Caroline Lucretia, 129

Heslop, Mary Kingdon, 130

Hesse, Fanny Angelina (Lina) née Eilshemius, 130

Heywood, Joan, 131

Hickling, Grace née Watt, 131

Hill, Dorothy, 132

Hindmarsh, Mary Maclean, 133

Hodgkin, Dorothy Mary née Crowfoot, 134

Hodgson, Elizabeth, 136

Hofmann, Elise, 137

Holden, Edith Blackwell, 137

Holford, Ingrid née Bianchi, 138

Holst, Clara, 139

Huggins, Lady Margaret Lindsay née Murray, 140

Humphrey, Edith Ellen, 141

Humphries, Carmel Frances, 141

Hutchison, Isobel Wylie, 142

Inglis, Elsie Maud, 143

Irvine, Jean Kennedy, 144

Isaacs, Susan Sutherland née Fairhurst, 145

Jahoda, Marie, 147

Janovskaja, Sof'ja Aleksandrovna née Neimark, 148

Jefferys, Margot née Davies, 148

Jeffrey, Carol, 149

Jekyll, Gertrude, 150

Jenkin, Penelope M., 151

Jérémine, Elisabeth née Tschernaieff, 151

Jex-Blake, Sophia, 152

Johnson, Amy, 153

Joliot-Curie, Irène née Curie, 154

Joshua, Joan Olive, 156

Kann, Edith, 157

Kennard, Olga née Weisz, 157

Kingsley, Mary Henrietta, 159

Kipling, Charlotte née Harrison, 160

Kirkaldy, Jane Willis, 160

Klein, Melanie née Reizes, 161

Knox, Elizabeth May née Henderson, 162

Kovalevskaya, Sonya (Sofya) Vasilyevna née Korvin-Krukovsky, 162

Kuroda, Chika, 164

Laby, Jean, 165

Lathbury, Kathleen née Culhane, 165

Laverick, Elizabeth, 166

Lavoisier, Marie Anne Pierrette née Paulze, 167

Lawrie, Jean Eileen née Grant, 168

Le Sueur, Frances Adams née Ross, 169

Leakey, Mary Douglas née Nicol, 170

Lebour, Marie Victoire, 171

Lee, Alma Theodora née Melvaine, 172

Lehmann, Inge, 172

Lemon, Margaretta Louisa née Smith, 174

Lepaute, Nicole-Reine Etable de la Brière, 174

Leslie, May Sybil, 175

Levi-Montalcini, Rita, 176

Leyel, Hilda Winifred Ivy née Wauton, 177

Lindsay, Lilian née Murray, 177

Lloyd, Dorothy Jordan, 178

Longfield, Cynthia, 179

Longstaff, Mary Jane née Donald, 181

Lonsdale, Kathleen née Yardley, 181

Lowe-McConnell, Rosemary Helen née Lowe, 183

Lyon, Mary Frances, 185

MacGillavry, Carolina Henriette, 189

Maclean, Ida née Smedley, 189

MacLeod, Anna Macgillivray, 190

McMillan, Margaret, 191

Macphail, Katherine Stewart, 192

MacRobert, Lady Rachael née Workman, 192

Malleson, Joan Graeme née Billson, 193

Mann, Ida Caroline (Mrs. Gye), 194

Manton, Irene, 196

Manton, Sidnie Milana (Mrs. Harding), 197

Manzolini, Anna née Morandi, 198

Marcet, Jane née Haldimand, 199

Markham, Beryl née Clutterbuck, 200

Marshall, Sheina Macalister, 201

Mary, Countess of Rosse née Field, 203

Massy, Annie Letitia, 203

May, Valerie, 204

Mee, Margaret Ursula née Brown, 205

Meitner, Lise, 206

Mellanby, Helen, 209

Mellanby, Lady May née Tweedy, 209

Merian, Maria Sibylla, 210

Millis, Nancy Fannie, 211

Contents

Milner, Marion, 212

Montagu, Lady Mary Wortley née Pierrepont, 213

Montessori, Maria, 214

Muir, Isabella Helen Mary, 216

Muir-Wood, Helen Marguerite, 217

Murray, Alice Rosemary, 217

Murray, Margaret Alice D., 218

Nashar, Beryl née Scott, 221

Needham, Dorothy Mary née Moyle, 222

Nevill, Lady Dorothy Fanny née Walpole, 223

Newbigin, Marion Isobel, 223

Newton, Lily née Batten, 224

Nicholas, Charlotte, 225

Nightingale, Florence, 225

Nihell, Elizabeth, 227

Noach, Ilse née Hellman, 228

Noble, Mary, 229

Noddack, Ida Eva née Tacke, 230

North, Marianne, 231

Ormerod, Eleanor Anne, 233

Parke, Mary, 237

Partridge, Margaret Mary, 238

Patten, Marguerite, 238

Payne-Scott, Ruby Violet, 240

Peirce, Mary Sophie Catherine Teresa, 240

Pennington, Winifred Anne, 241

Perey, Marguerite, 242

Perry, Frances Mary née Everett, 243

Petrie, Hilda Mary Isobel née Urlin, 244

Philbin, Eva Maria née Ryder, 245

Pickford, Lillian Mary, 245

Pirie, Antoinette (Tony) née Patey, 246

Pitt-Rivers, Rosalind Venetia née Henley, 247

Platt of Writtle, Baroness née Beryl Catherine Myatt, 248

Pockels, Agnes, 249

Porter, Annie (Mrs. H. B. Fantham), 250

Porter, Helen Kemp née Archbold, 252

Porter, Mary (Polly) Winearls, 253

Potter, Helen Beatrix, 253

Raisin, Catherine Alice, 257

Ratcliffe, Edna Jane, 258

Rayner, Mabel Mary Cheveley, 258

Rees, Florence Gwendolen, 259

Resvoll, Thekla Susanne Ragnhild, 260

Richards, Audrey Isabel, 260

Richter, Emma née Hüther, 262

Rickett, Mary Ellen, 262

Robb, Mary Anne née Boulton, 263

Roberts, Mary, 263

Robertson, Dorothea, 264

Robertson, Muriel, 264

Ross-Craig, Stella, 265

Rosser, Celia Elizabeth née Prince, 265

Rothschild, The Honourable Miriam Louisa, 265

Rowan, Marian Ellis née Ryan, 267

Rozhanskaya, Mariam née Mikhaylovna, 268

Rule, Margaret Helen née Martin, 269

Russell, Annie Scott Dill, 269

Russell, Dorothy Stuart, 270

Ruttner-Kolisko, Agnes née Kolisko, 272

Ryman, Brenda Edith, 272

Sackville-West, Victoria May (Vita; Lady Nicholson), 275

Salmons, Josephine Edna, 276

Sampson, Kathleen, 276

Sandars, Nancy Katharine, 277

Sanger, Ruth Ann, 277

Sansome, Eva née Richardson, 278

Sargant, Ethel, 279

Saunders, Cicely Mary Strode, 280

Saunders, Edith Rebecca, 281

Sayer, Ettie, 282

Scharlieb, Mary Ann Dacomb née Bird, 282

Schuster, Norah Henriette, 283

Schütte-Lihotsky, Margarete née Lihotsky, 284

Scudder, Ida Sophia, 285

Sexton, Alice (Elsie) Wilkins née Wing, 286

Shakespear, Ethel Mary Reader née Wood, 287

Shilling, Beatrice (Tilly), 288

Shorten, Monica Ruth, 288

Singer, Eleanor, 289

Slávíkova, Ludmila née Kaplanova, 290

Smith, Annie Lorrain, 290

Snelling, Lilian, 290

Sohonie, Kamala née Bhagwat, 290

Somerville, Mary Grieg née Fairfax, 291

Sponer, Hertha, 293

Spooner, Mary Florence (Molly) née Mare, 293

Staveley, Dulcie, 294

Stephansen, Mary Ann Elizabeth, 295

Contents

Stephenson, Marjory, 296
Stewart, Alice Mary née Naish, 298
Stewart, Olga Margaret née Mounsey, 301
Stjernstedt, Rosemary, 301
Stones, Margaret, 302
Stopes, Marie Charlotte Carmichael, 303

Tammes, Jantine (Tine), 307
Taylor, Janet, 307
Taylor, Mary, 308
Tonolli, Livia née Pirocchi, 308
Trewavas, Ethelwynn, 309
Turner, Emma Louisa, 310
Turner, Helen Alma Newton, 310
Turner-Warwick, Margaret née Moore,
    311

Uvarov, Olga Nikolaevna, 313

Vachell, Eleanor, 315
Van Heyningen, Ruth Eleanor née
    Treverton, 316
Vansittart, Henrietta née Lowe, 317
Vaughan, Janet Maria, 317
Vickery, Joyce Winifred, 319

Wakefield, Priscilla née Bell, 321
Ward, Mary née King, 321
Warington, Katherine, 322
Watson, Janet Vida, 322
Webster, Mary McCallum, 324
Welch, Ann Courtenay, 325
Welch, Barbara née Gullick, 325
White, Margaret, 326
Widdowson, Elsie May, 326
Wiggins, Philippa Marion, 328
Wijnberg, Rosalie, 329
Williams, Cicely Delphine, 329
Williams, Ethel May Nucella, 331
Willmott, Ellen, 332
Wilman, Maria, 332
Wilson, Fiammetta née Worthington, 333
Winch, Hope Constance Monica, 333
Wood, Audrey, 334

Xie, Xide (Hsieh Hsi-teh), 337

Yasui, Kono, 339
Yoshioka, Yoyoi née Washiyama, 340
Young, Grace née Chisholm, 340
Yuasa, Toshiko, 341

Select Bibliography, 343
Index, 347
About the Authors, 385

Women by Profession

Agriculture
Aitkin, Yvonne
Balfour, (Lady Eve) Evelyn Barbara
Balfour, (Elizabeth) Jean née Drew
Courtauld, Katherine

Anthropology
Durham, Mary Edith
Kingsley, Mary Henrietta
Leakey, Mary Douglas née Nicol
Richards, Audrey Isabel
Salmons, Josephine Edna

Apiculture
Crane, Eva née Widdowson

Archaeology
Armitage, Ella Sophia née Bulley
Bell, Gertrude Margaret Lowthian
Davies, Margaret
Drower, Margaret Stephana
Edwards, Amelia Ann Blandford
Garrod, Dorothy Annie Elizabeth
Murray, Margaret Alice D.
Petrie, Hilda Mary Isobel née Urlin
Rule, Margaret Helen née Martin
Sandars, Nancy Katharine

Architecture
Casson, Lady Margaret née
    MacDonald
Schütte-Lihotsky, Margarete née
    Lihotsky
Stjernstedt, Rosemary

Art
Adamson, Joy (Friedericke Victoria)
    née Gessner
Bonheur, Rosalie Marie (Rosa)

Cockburn, Patricia Evangeline Ann
    née Arbuthnot
Durham, Mary Edith
Goulandris, Niki née Kephalia
Grierson, Mary Anderson
Hesse, Fanny Angelina (Lina)
    née Eilshemius
Holden, Edith Blackwell
Mee, Margaret Ursula née Brown
Merian, Maria Sibylla
North, Marianne
Potter, Helen Beatrix
Ross-Craig, Stella
Rosser, Celia Elizabeth née Prince
Rowan, Marian Ellis née Ryan
Sexton, Alice (Elsie) Wilkins
    née Wing
Snelling, Lilian
Stewart, Olga Margaret
Stones, Margaret

Astronomy
Adam, Madge Gertrude
Blagg, Mary Adela
Burbidge, (Eleanor) Margaret née
    Peachey
Herschel, Caroline Lucretia
Huggins, Lady Margaret Lindsay
    née Murray
Lepaute, Nicole-Reine Etable de la
    Brière
Russell, Annie Scott Dill
Ward, Mary née King
Wilson, Fiammetta née Worthington

Aviation
Bacon, Gertrude
Johnson, Amy
Markham, Beryl née Clutterbuck

Peirce, Mary Sophie Catherine Teresa
Welch, Ann Courtenay

Biology

Bennett, Isobel Ada
Bishop, Ann
Brown, Margaret Elizabeth (Mrs. Varley)
Courtenay-Latimer, Marjorie Eileen
   Doris
Ehrlich, Aline née Buchbinder
Fell, Honor Bridget
Frost, Winifred Evelyn
Humphries, Carmel Frances
Kann, Edith
Kipling, Charlotte née Harrison
Lebour, Marie Victoire
Lowe-McConnell, Rosemary Helen
   née Lowe
Marshall, Sheina Macalister
Massy, Annie Letitia
Millis, Nancy Fannie
Newbigin, Marion Isobel
Parke, Mary
Pennington, Winifred Anne
Porter, Annie (Mrs. H. B. Fantham)
Ruttner-Kolisko, Agnes née Kolisko
Sampson, Kathleen
Sansome, Eva née Richardson
Spooner, Mary Florence (Molly) née
   Mare
Stephenson, Marjory
Tonolli, Livia née Pirocchi
Trewavas, Ethelwynn
Vaughan, Janet Maria
Yasui, Kono

Botany

Adams, Jacqueline Nancy Mary
   née Whittaker
Arber, Agnes née Robertson
Basford, Kathleen
Becker, Lydia Ernestine
Blackburn, Kathleen Bever
Booth, Evelyn Mary
Brenchley, Winifred Elsie
Cadbury, Dorothy Adlington
Canter-Lund, Hilda M. née Canter
Cassie Cooper, Una Vivienne née Dellow
Conway, Verona Margaret
Cookson, Isabel Clifton
Dent, Edith Vere née Annesley
Dony, Christina Mayne née Goodman

Downie, Dorothy G.
Drew-Baker, Kathleen M. née Drew
Farquharson, Marian Sarah Ogilvie
   née Ridley
Flint, Elizabeth Alice
Gibbons, E. Joan
Gwynne-Vaughan, Helen Charlotte
   Isabella née Fraser
Hawker, Lilian E.
Hindmarsh, Mary Maclean
Hodgson, Elizabeth
Hutchison, Isobel Wylie
Le Sueur, Frances Adams née Ross
Lee, Alma Theodora née Melvaine
Leyel, Hilda Winifred Ivy née Wauton
MacLeod, Anna Macgillivray
Manton, Irene
May, Valerie
Newton, Lily née Batten
Rayner, Mabel Mary Cheveley
Resvoll, Thekla Susanne Ragnhild
Robb, Mary Anne née Boulton
Sampson, Kathleen
Sargant, Ethel
Saunders, Edith Rebecca
Smith, Annie Lorrain
Stewart, Olga Margaret
Stopes, Marie Charlotte Carmichael
Vachell, Eleanor
Vickery, Joyce Winifred
Warington, Katherine
Webster, Mary McCallum
Welch, Barbara née Gullick
Wilman, Maria

Chemistry

Anderson, Margaret Dampier
   née Whetham
Borrowman, Agnes Thompson
Buchanan, Margaret Elizabeth
Chick, Harriette
Clarke, Patricia Hannah née Green
Fulhame, Elizabeth
Furness, Vera I.
Humphrey, Edith Ellen
Kuroda, Chika
Lathbury, Kathleen née Culhane
Lavoisier, Marie Anne Pierrette
   née Paulze
Leslie, May Sybil
Lloyd, Dorothy Jordan
Maclean, Ida née Smedley

Muir, Isabella Helen Mary
Murray, Alice Rosemary
Needham, Dorothy Mary née Moyle
Noddack, Ida Eva née Tacke
Perey, Marguerite
Philbin, Eva Maria née Ryder
Pockels, Agnes
Ryman, Brenda Edith
Sohonie, Kamala née Bhagwat
Wiggins, Philippa Marion

Communications
Adams, Mary Grace Agnes née Campin
Corradi, Doris
Dunn, Barbara
Heywood, Joan
Taylor, Mary

Conservation
Adamson, Joy (Friedericke Victoria)
    née Gessner
Balfour, (Elizabeth) Jean née Drew
Davies, Margaret
Goulandris, Niki née Kephalia
Lemon, Margaretta Louisa née Smith
Mee, Margaret Ursula née Brown
Rothschild, The Honourable Miriam
    Louisa

Crystallography
Hodgkin, Dorothy Mary née
    Crowfoot
Kennard, Olga née Weisz
Lonsdale, Kathleen née Yardley
MacGillavry, Carolina Henriette
Porter, Mary (Polly) Winearls

Dentistry
Lindsay, Lilian née Murray
Mellanby, Lady May née Tweedy

Education
Beale, Dorothea
Brook, Lady Helen Grace Mary née
    Knewstub
Denman, Gertrude Mary née Pearson
Fawcett, Philippa
Harding, Jan née Ansell
Heslop, Mary Kingdon
Holford, Ingrid née Bianchi
Isaacs, Susan Sutherland née
    Fairhurst

Jefferys, Margot née Davies
Manzolini, Anna née Morandi
McMillan, Margaret
Montessori, Maria
Murray, Alice Rosemary
Newton, Lily née Batten
Rickett, Mary Ellen
Robertson, Dorothea
Stopes, Marie Charlotte Carmichael
Taylor, Janet

Engineering
Buchanan, Dorothy Donaldson
    (Mrs. Fleming)
Chitty, Letitia
Fergusson, Mary (Molly) Isolen
Haslett, Caroline
Laverick, Elizabeth
Partridge, Margaret Mary
Platt of Writtle, Baroness née Beryl
    Catherine Myatt
Shilling, Beatrice (Tilly)
Vansittart, Henrietta née Lowe

Entomology
Cheesman, Lucy Evelyn
Clay, Theresa Rachael
Fountaine, Margaret Elizabeth
Longfield, Cynthia
Merian, Maria Sibylla
Ormerod, Eleanor Anne
Rothschild, The Honourable Miriam
    Louisa

Exploration
Bird, Isabella Lucy (Mrs. Bishop)
Cheesman, Lucy Evelyn
Cockburn, Patricia Evangeline Ann
    née Arbuthnot
Durham, Mary Edith
Edwards, Amelia Ann Blandford
Franklin, Lady Jane née Griffin
Kingsley, Mary Henrietta
Longfield, Cynthia

Genetics
Auerbach, Charlotte
Blackwood, Margaret
Datta, Naomi née Goddard
Lyon, Mary Frances
Tammes, Jantine (Tine)
Turner, Helen Alma Newton

Geography
Bird, Isabella Lucy (Mrs. Bishop)
Cable, Alice Mildred
Heslop, Mary Kingdon
Newbigin, Marion Isobel

Geology
Bate, Dorothea Minola Alice
Currie, Ethel Dobbie
Ehrlich, Aline née Buchbinder
Eyles, Joan Mary née Biggs
Gordon, Maria Matilda née Ogilvie
Guppy, Eileen M.
Halicka, Antonina née Jaroszewicz
Heslop, Mary Kingdon
Hill, Dorothy
Hodgson, Elizabeth
Hofmann, Elise
Jérémine, Elisabeth née Tschernaieff
MacRobert, Lady Rachael née Workman
Nashar, Beryl née Scott
Raisin, Catherine Alice
Shakespear, Ethel Mary Reader
  née Wood
Slávíkova, Ludmila née Kaplanova
Watson, Janet Vida
Welch, Barbara née Gullick
Wilman, Maria

History of Science
Baly, Monica E.
Clerke, Agnes Mary
Eyles, Joan Mary née Biggs
Gowing, Margaret Mary née Elliott
Rozhanskaya, Mariam née Mikhaylovna
Welch, Ann Courtenay

Home Economics
Beeton, Isabella Mary née Mayson
Patten, Marguerite

Horticulture
Jekyll, Gertrude
Nevill, Lady Dorothy Fanny née
  Walpole
Perry, Frances Mary née Everett
Sackville-West, Victoria May (Vita;
  Lady Nicholson)
Willmott, Ellen

Invention
Nicholas, Charlotte

Linguistics
Dal, Ingerid Blanca Juell
Holst, Clara

Mathematics
Agnesi, Maria Gaetana
Bari, Nina Karlovna
Beale, Dorothea
Byron, Augusta (Ada), Countess of
  Lovelace
Cartwright, Mary Lucy
Choquet-Bruhat, Yvonne
Cunliffe, Stella Vivian
Fawcett, Philippa
Germain, Sophie
Greig, Dorothy Margaret née Hannah
Janovskaja, Sof'ja Aleksandrovna
  née Neimark
Kipling, Charlotte née Harrison
Kovalevskaya, Sonya (Sofya) Vasilyevna
  née Korvin-Krukovsky
Nightingale, Florence
Rickett, Mary Ellen
Stephansen, Mary Ann Elizabeth
Taylor, Mary
Young, Grace née Chisholm

Medicine
Barnes, Alice Josephine (Mary Taylor;
  Dame Josephine Warren)
Barry, James Miranda Steuart
Bentham, Ethel
Blackwell, Elizabeth
Boyle, Alice Helen Anne
Brown, Edith Mary
Clubb, Elizabeth Mary Fitz-Simon née
  Thomas
Dalton, Katharina Dorothea née Kuipers
Déjerine-Klumpke, Augusta née
  Klumpke
Garrett Anderson, Elizabeth née Garrett
Inglis, Elsie Maud
Jex-Blake, Sophia
Lawrie, Jean Eileen née Grant
Macphail, Katherine Stewart
Malleson, Joan Graeme née Billson
Sanger, Ruth Ann
Saunders, Cicely Mary Strode
Sayer, Ettie
Scharlieb, Mary Ann Dacomb née Bird
Scudder, Ida Sophia
Singer, Eleanor

Stewart, Alice Mary née Naish
Turner-Warwick, Margaret née Moore
Vaughan, Janet Maria
Wijnberg, Rosalie
Williams, Cicely Delphine
Williams, Ethel May Nucella
Yoshioka, Yoyoi née Washiyama

Metallurgy
Courtauld, Louisa Perina née Ogier

Meteorology
Holford, Ingrid née Bianchi
White, Margaret

Natural Science
Ball, Anne Elizabeth
Blackburne, Anna
Bryan, Margaret
Buckland, Mary née Morland
Gatty, Margaret née Scott
Holden, Edith Blackwell
Ratcliffe, Edna Jane

Nursing and Therapy
Baly, Monica E.
Bobath, Berta Othilie
Bromhall, Margaret Ann
Farrer, Margaret Irene
Fraser, Roslin Margaret Ferguson
Fulton, Margaret Barr
Montagu, Lady Mary Wortley
  née Pierrepont
Nightingale, Florence
Nihell, Elizabeth
Robertson, Dorothea
Staveley, Dulcie
Wood, Audrey

Nutrition
Chick, Harriette
Patten, Marguerite
Widdowson, Elsie May
Williams, Cicely Delphine

Opthalmology
Dunscombe, Adaliza Amelia Clara
  Mary Elizabeth Emma Frances
Mann, Ida Caroline (Mrs. Gye)
Pirie, Antoinette (Tony) née Patey
Van Heyningen, Ruth Eleanor
  née Treverton

Ornithology
Barclay-Smith, Phyllis Ida
Hickling, Grace née Watt
Le Sueur, Frances Adams née Ross
Lemon, Margaretta Louisa née Smith
Turner, Emma Louisa

Paleontology
Anning, Mary
Gromova, Vera Issacovna
Hill, Dorothy
Hofmann, Elise
Knox, Elizabeth May née Henderson
Leakey, Mary Douglas née Nicol
Longstaff, Mary Jane née Donald
Muir-Wood, Helen Marguerite
Richter, Emma née Hüther
Stopes, Marie Charlotte Carmichael

Pathology
Alcock, Nora Lilian née Scott
Barber, Mary
Clayton, Barbara Evelyn
Goss, Olga May
Noble, Mary
Russell, Dorothy Stuart
Sampson, Kathleen
Schuster, Norah Henriette
Vaughan, Janet Maria

Pharmacology
Borrowman, Agnes Thompson
Buchanan, Margaret Elizabeth
Bülbring, Edith
Irvine, Jean Kennedy
Winch, Hope Constance Monica

Photography
Atkins, Anna née Children
Canter-Lund, Hilda M. née Canter
Harker, Margaret Florence
Mary, Countess of Rosse née Fiel
Turner, Emma Louisa

Physics
Ayrton, Phoebe Sarah (Hertha) née Marks
Bassi, Laura Maria Catarina
Bleeker, Caroline Emilie (Lili)
Choquet-Bruhat, Yvonne
Curie, Marya (Manya; Marie) née
  Sklodowska
Eymers, Johanna Geertruid (Truus)

Franklin, Rosalind Elsie
Freeman, Joan
Gleditsch, Ellen
Hanson, Emmeline Jean
Huggins, Lady Margaret Lindsay
    née Murray
Heywood, Joan
Joliot-Curie, Irène née Curie
Laby, Jean
Meitner, Lise
Payne-Scott, Ruby Violet
Sponer, Hertha
Xie, Xide (Hsieh Hsi-teh)
Yuasa, Toshiko

Physiology
Bidder, Marion née Greenwood
Biheron, Marie-Catherine
Bülbring, Edith
Levi-Montalcini, Rita
Manzolini, Anna née Morandi
Pickford, Lillian Mary
Pitt-Rivers, Rosalind Venetia née
    Henley
Porter, Helen Kemp née Archbold

Psychology
Freud, Anna
Isaacs, Susan Sutherland née Fairhurst
Jahoda, Marie
Jefferys, Margot née Davies
Jeffrey, Carol
Klein, Melanie née Reizes
Milner, Marion
Montessori, Maria
Noach, Ilse née Hellman

Science Writing
Bacon, Gertrude
Baly, Monica E.
Basford, Kathleen
Bird, Isabella Lucy (Mrs. Bishop)
Bryan, Margaret
Clerke, Agnes Mary
Clerke, Ellen Mary
Cockburn, Patricia Evangeline Ann
    née Arbuthnot
du Châtelet-Lomont, Emilie Gabrielle
    née le Tonnelier de Breteuil

Edwards, Amelia Ann Blandford
Gatty, Margaret née Scott
Haslett, Caroline
Holford, Ingrid née Bianchi
Jekyll, Gertrude
Lavoisier, Marie Anne Pierrette
    née Paulze
Marcet, Jane née Haldimand
Merian, Maria Sibylla
Milner, Marion
Newbigin, Marion Isobel
Ratcliffe, Edna Jane
Roberts, Mary
Sackville-West, Victoria May (Vita)
Somerville, Mary Grieg née Fairfax
Stopes, Marie Charlotte Carmichael
Taylor, Janet
Wakefield, Priscilla née Bell
Ward, Mary née King
Welch, Ann Courtenay

Seismology
Lehmann, Inge

Veterinary Science
Cust, Aleen
Joshua, Joan Olive
Uvarov, Olga Nikolaevna

Zoology
Abercrombie, Minnie Louie (Jane)
    née Johnson
Bidder, Anna McClean
Bishop, Ann
Bonnevie, Kristine Elisabeth Heuch
Canter-Lund, Hilda M. née Canter
Eales, Nellie B.
Fretter, Vera
Gordon, Isabella
Hanson, Emmeline Jean
Jenkin, Penelope M.
Kirkaldy, Jane Willis
Manton, Sidnie Milana (Mrs. Harding)
Mellanby, Helen
Rees, Florence Gwendolen
Robertson, Muriel
Sexton, Alice (Elsie) Wilkins
    née Wing
Shorten, Monica Ruth

Preface

This book focuses on women who were involved with science in a memorable way at some time in their lives. All were pioneers, to large or small effect, some in dramatic fashion and others in quiet persistence.

A scientist is a person searching for the truth. The women whose lives are detailed here worked within a broad range of scientific disciplines. They were either caught up in original research or applied the discoveries of others to further the well-being of the world. Many left full-time work when they married or had children and later used their experience in administration, communication, and encouraging the study of science. All showed considerable determination in their work, overcoming numerous obstacles and making the best of difficult situations.

The majority of the women included here were born in Britain; the remainder were from other countries in Europe, Australia, China, India, Kenya, Japan, New Zealand, and South Africa. A number of the British women lived abroad for part of their working lives. Several of the women from Australia, New Zealand, and South Africa went to Britain for postgraduate study, particularly after World War II, and some stayed there. Although some of these women worked or studied for a time in North America, women born in North America are excluded from this book, as their lives have already been detailed in *American Women in Science* (1994).

This book covers women within a wide time frame, from those who flourished around 1600 to those who started their careers by 1950. Many of those who are still active have contributed to their entries.

Each entry is intended to be both complete in itself and a starting point for further research. It was not always possible to fill in all the personal details about an individual or her education or employment.

Because of variations in the education systems at secondary and tertiary levels, it was difficult to compare the achievements of students in different countries. Progress in the academic world has almost always been slower and harder for women than it has been for men with equivalent qualifications. To be appointed to a professorial chair was thus a tremendous honor in Britain. Those who pursued academic careers usually came from middle- or upper-class backgrounds in which there was a tradition of education and funding available from within the family. Of course there were exceptions, and sometimes it was only with the help of a mentor that a university education was possible for these women. Gradually, more scholarships became available for academically talented but financially constrained students.

For students in Australia and New Zealand, the shortage of postgraduate facilities presented a problem; numerous students came to Britain on scholarship to do postgraduate work. Some returned to their home country, and others continued their careers in Britain.

The two world wars had a considerable effect on women's work. Certain jobs were opened to women when men were called away to active service. For some women, war work brought them into contact with new fields, and their career paths shifted. Training in male-dominated professions such as engineering became more widely accessible. Some women took up particularly dangerous roles, such as flying planes on hazardous missions. The women showed how well they could cope with responsibility. Those women already started on careers in science had to be available to do whatever work the government required and could not return to their own work until after the war. Jewish scientists were not allowed to hold positions in universities in Nazi-occupied countries; many fled to other countries to continue their work and, sadly, some were deported to concentration camps.

Up to the start of World War I, women actively campaigned as a group to obtain the right to vote. After the war the tendency was for each profession to fight its individual battles; thus groups such as the Women's Veterinary Association were set up. Women lobbied with determination for admission to professional societies, but for some time many such associations held out against admitting women. The Royal Society did not elect women as fellows until 1946.

The women described in this volume achieved a great deal, but those who worked full time did rely on domestic help, often hiring housekeepers and nannies to free them from domestic duties. Some of the single women lived in the university halls of residences; although they may have taken on responsibilities for the well-being of students, they, too, essentially escaped housework. Many women were fortunate in having husbands who were sufficiently well paid to allow their wives to carry out unsalaried jobs. A number of them helped their husbands a great deal in their work and were not always given credit for their contributions until long afterward. Others worked almost entirely on their own. Still others, through their charisma or the nature of their work, attracted fellow researchers from around the world and thus both garnered funding and published prodigious amounts of research.

There was considerably more freedom for academic staff than there is now. An appointment to a university post was generally until retirement. The direction of research was not stipulated, though there were usually some lecturing and tutoring

obligations. Today it is more common for appointments to be of shorter tenure, for research to be contingent on funding, and for the requirement that results be published.

On reaching retirement many of the women who had academic appointments were given emeritus or honorary status and had access to offices and laboratories so that they could go on with their research. Others in government or industrial posts were able to continue in an honorary capacity but with grants to provide equipment and clerical assistance. Some who started their careers after having children made up for lost time on the job by working long after they had retired. Some, particularly freelancers, never stopped working, even when they were well into their eighties or nineties.

We are indebted to many of these women not only for their groundbreaking work within their fields but for seeing to the needs of future generations of women in science: Many left generous bequests to fund further research, and several charities were started as the result of the work of these women.

Acknowledgments

Many people have helped in the compilation of this book; others have taken an interest in the project. I am very grateful to each of them, especially Sheila Beck, Judith Gain, and D. G. Humphreys.

Helen Stevens cowrote some of the entries and provided valuable secretarial help. Jonathan Ainsworth advised on computing. Jenny Hall, Jenny-Anne Dexter, and Rebecca Proctor assisted with research. Christiane Bruns and Brigitte Theunissen-Hughes aided with translation. Joan Mason gave general encouragement and, specifically, information about the Bidder family. Joan Bird, librarian at the British Geological Survey, supplied information about geologists. Helene Martin sent me articles about Australian women scientists.

A number of the living scientists included here kindly read their proposed entries and added information.

I researched information at several libraries, and I am grateful for the help given by archivists and librarians at the British Library; Girton College, Cambridge; Imperial War Museum; Linnean Society; Marine Biological Association, Plymouth; Natural History Museum, London; Newnham College, Cambridge; Public Record Office; Royal Botanic Gardens, Kew; University of Cambridge Library; and the Zoological Society, Regent's Park.

I am grateful to the librarians in the northwest at Arnitt Library, Ambleside; Freshwater Biological Association, The Ferry House, Windermere; John Rylands Library, University of Manchester; Lancaster Public Library; Lancaster University; Myer-

scough Agricultural College; Post-graduate Medical Centre, Royal Lancaster Infirmary; Preston Public Library; St. Martin's College; and the University of Central Lancashire, Preston. Many other librarians, archivists, and secretaries of societies responded to requests for information; these are detailed within the bibliographies of the individual entries.

Tony Sloggett, manager for ABC-CLIO in Oxford, encouraged me to persevere.

Catharine M. C. Haines
Lancaster, England

A

Abercrombie, Minnie Louie (Jane) née Johnson
14 November 1909–25 November 1984
zoologist

Education: Waverley Road Secondary School (Sparkbrook), Birmingham; University of Birmingham: B.S., 1930; Ph.D., 1932.

Employment: lecturer, Zoology Department, University of Birmingham, 1932–1946; Department of Anatomy, University College, London.

Married: Michael Abercrombie, director of Strangeways Research Laboratory, in 1939.

Minnie Louie (Jane) Johnson and her husband, Michael Abercrombie, were well known for their *Dictionary of Biology*. They also started and published *New Biology*.

Besides chemistry, zoology, and botany, Abercrombie took history for her higher school certificate. She entered the University of Birmingham in the second year and gained her B.S. in two years, going on to do zoology honors (first class). For her M.S. and Ph.D. theses, she studied the chemical control of respiratory movements in invertebrates. Abercrombie joined the staff of the University of Birmingham as a lecturer and was acting head of the Zoology Department during World War II.

Some of Abercrombie's research was published (under her maiden name) in the *Journal of Experimental Biology*, including "Colorimetric Method for Estimation of Dissolved Oxygen in the Field" (with R. J.

Whitney; 16, 1 [January 1939]: 56–59) and "The Respiratory Function of the Haemoglobin of the Earthworm" (18, 3 [January 1942]: 266–277). She and her husband coauthored "The Effect of Temperature on the Respiratory Movements and Viability of a Cold-Water Prawn, *Pandalus borealis*" (3, series A [1941]: 87–99 in the *Proceedings of the Zoological Society of London*).

With her husband, Abercrombie founded *New Biology*, a collection of essays aimed at sixth-formers and first-year university students. The publication was very successful and influenced many young people in deciding to become professional biologists. The first edition was published in 1945 and sold 100,000 copies. For this first volume, the publishers paid £75, which was shared among the contributors. *New Biology* ran for thirty-one volumes; by the end of its run it competed with similar publications and sold only 20,000 copies. The Abercrombies produced a glossary for *New Biology* that eventually became the *Penguin Dictionary of Biology* (1971).

Abercrombie continued to write on a wide range of topics, particularly those relating to education, as she was a respected authority on the teaching of medical students. In 1967 the Society for Research into Higher Education published her *Selection and Academic Performance of Students in a University School of Architecture* (coauthored with S. Hunt and P. Stringer). As a member of the society's Working Party on Teaching Methods, she wrote *Aims and Techniques of Group Teaching* (1970).

Bibliography: Bassett, P., Archivist, Special

1

Collections, University of Birmingham, personal communication to author, 6 May 1998; Medawar, Peter, "Michael Abercrombie, 14 August 1912–28 May 1979," in *Biographical Memoirs of Fellows of the Royal Society* 26 (1980): 1–15.

Adam, Madge Gertrude
6 March 1912–25 August 2001
astronomer

Education: Municipal High School, Doncaster; St. Hugh's College, Oxford, 1931–1934; M.A.; Lady Margaret Hall, Oxford, 1935–1937; D. Phil.

Employment: assistant tutor in science, 1937–1957 (fellow, 1941–1957); research fellow, senior research fellow, 1957–1980, St. Hugh's College, Oxford; lecturer, Department of Astrophysics, University of Oxford, 1937–1979.

Madge Adam carried out research on sunspots and interferometry.

After graduating from St. Hugh's College, Oxford, Adam did research in astrophysics and held a Junior British Scholarship at Lady Margaret Hall, Oxford. In 1937 she became a lecturer at the Department of Astrophysics at the University of Oxford Observatory.

Her early research concerned center-to-limb changes in the Fraunhofer lines of the sun, and their strengths and wavelengths. She published her research in *Monthly Notices of the Royal Astronomical Society (MN)* (see, for example, vol. 98, 1938). Much of this early work was based on observations made using two solar telescopes and associated spectroscopes at the Dominion Observatory, Ottawa, Canada, installed at the University of Oxford Observatory.

Adam investigated solar wavelengths, publishing her results in *MN* (including vol. 118, 1958), then studied the magnetic vectors and velocity fields in sunspots (*MN* vol. 155, 1971). In her later work she made use of a new interferometric measuring technique developed by Dr. P. Treanor. From 1963 to 1964 she worked at Mt. Stromlo Observatory in Australia, primarily studying magnetic stars.

Around 1980, she was made an emeritus fellow of St. Hugh's College, Oxford. She is a fellow of the Royal Astronomical Society and at one time served on its council.

Bibliography: Adam, Madge, personal communications to author 1998, 1999; *Who's Who, 2001*, London: Adam and Charles Black, 2001; Williams, K., "Madge Adam: Solar Physicist Acclaimed for Her Work on Sunspots and Magnetic Fields," *Guardian* (10 September 2001): 16.

Adams, Jacqueline Nancy Mary née Whittaker
19 May 1926–
botanist

Education: Brooklyn School, Wellington; Wellington Girls' College; Victoria University.

Employment: assistant to Dr. Lucy B. Moore and botanical artist, Plant Research Bureau, Department of Scientific and Industrial Research, from 1942; assistant curator and artist, Botany Department, National Museum, Wellington, 1956–1987; research associate after retirement.

Nancy Adams is a botanical illustrator and an expert on seaweeds.

In 1964 Adams received the Loder Cup for her part in preparing publications about New Zealand's national parks; in 1989 she was awarded the Queen's Service Order and in 1990 the Commemoration Medal for her work in botany in New Zealand. She has had several exhibitions of her drawings and published papers on early New Zealand botanical collectors. Her *Mountain Flowers in New Zealand* and *Wild Flowers in New Zealand* both appeared in 1980.

Bibliography: Lambert, M., ed., *Who's Who in New Zealand*, twelfth edition, Auckland, New Zealand: Octopus Publishing, 1991; Martin, P., *Lives with Science: Profiles of Senior New Zealand Women in Science*, Wellington: Museum of New Zealand/Te Papa Tongarewa, 1993.

Adams, Mary Grace Agnes née Campin
10 March 1898–15 May 1984
pioneer in broadcasting and television

Education: Godolphin School, Salisbury; University College, Cardiff; B.S. with honors in botany, 1921; Newnham College, Cambridge (Bathurst student), 1921–1925; M.S.

Employment: tutor and lecturer, extramural studies and Board of Civil Service studies in Cambridge, 1925–1930; British Broadcasting Corporation (BBC) from 1930: adult education officer, 1936–1939; director of Home Intelligence, Ministry of Information, 1939–1941; North American Service broadcasting, 1942–1945; BBC-TV from 1946: head of television talks and current affairs, 1948–1954; assistant to the controller of TV programs, 1954–1958 (retirement); deputy chairman, Consumers' Association, 1958–1970; member of the Independent Television Authority, 1965–1970.

Married: (Samuel) Vyvyan (Trerice) Adams, Conservative MP for West Leeds (1931–1945), on 23 February 1925. He died in 1951.

In 1936 *Mary Adams* was the first woman to be appointed as a television producer.

Adams was born in Berkshire, where her father was a farmer. When he died of tuberculosis in 1910, the family moved to Penarth in North Wales. Adams won a scholarship to the Godolphin School, an independent Church of England girls' boarding school in Salisbury. She went on to study botany at Cardiff and cytology at Cambridge. As a tutor in the Extramural Department in Cambridge, she gave a series of radio talks published as *Six Talks on Heredity* (1929). She recognized the great educational possibilities of the BBC, and as adult education officer she worked with BBC creator Sir John Reith (who became Baron Reith in 1940) to combine information with an informal approach.

In 1936 Adams moved from radio to television and persuaded eminent personalities to participate in programs. When the television service closed with the outbreak of World War II, she switched to the Ministry of Information and later the North American Service broadcasting, producing programs such as *Transatlantic Quiz.*

In 1946 she returned to BBC-TV and as head of television talks was responsible for programs such as *Animal, Vegetable, Mineral* (1952–1959, 1971); *Your Life in Their Hands* (1958–1964); and such children's programs as *Muffin the Mule* (1946–1955) and *Andy Pandy* (1950–1969, 1970–1976). She visited the Soviet Union in 1954 and traveled to Prague, Paris, and Milan in 1956.

Adams and Julian Huxley conceived of the Consumers' Association in 1937, which would help consumers compare products, but it was not established until 1957. After she retired she served as its deputy chairman for twelve years. She was fully involved in writing and campaigning on a wide variety of issues ranging from eugenics to Anglo-Chinese understanding. She had a magnetic personality and was not afraid to express daring or outlandish ideas.

She was awarded an Order of the British Empire in 1953 and made an honorary fellow of Cardiff University in 1983.

Bibliography: Dictionary of National Biography, 1981–1985, Oxford: Oxford University Press, 1990; "Mary Adams," Obituary, *Times,* 18 May 1984; *Who Was Who, 1981–1990,* London: Adam and Charles Black, 1991.

Adamson, Joy (Friedericke Victoria) née Gessner
20 January 1910–3 January 1980
botanical artist, conservationist

Education: boarding school in Austria.
Employment: self-employed artist and conservationist.
Married: Viktor von Klarwill, on 28 July 1935 (divorced); Peter Bally, artist, on 4 July 1938 (divorced); George Adamson, on 17 January 1944.

A noted botanical artist, *Joy Adamson* achieved international fame through her conservation work with lions in Kenya.

Joy Adamson (Express Newspapers/Archive Photos)

Joy Adamson was born in Troppau, Silesia (now Opava, Czech Republic), and educated in Austria. Joy met Viktor von Klarwill at a party in her hometown. He was very well off, and they traveled in Austria. However he was a Jew, so he decided it might be safer to leave Austria and live in Kenya, so he went there. Joy had a miscarriage so Viktor suggested she convalesce on the boat to Mombasa. On the boat she met Peter Bally, a botanist, and was so attracted to him that she divorced Viktor, and married Peter, living in Kenya with him.

Adamson began painting the specimens Peter Bally collected on his expeditions, then started collecting her own plants. Her work included illustrations for *Gardening in East Africa* by A. Jex-Blake (1939) and *Some Wild Flowers of Kenya* by Muriel Jex-Blake (1948). In 1941, after visiting an exhibition of Adamson's flower paintings, the wife of the governor of Kenya commissioned her to produce twenty flower paintings for the Prime Minister of South Africa General Smuts and eight for table mats in the Royal Lodge in Kenya. In 1947 Adamson's work was exhibited at the Royal Horticultural Society in London and she received the society's Grenfell Gold Medal.

Between 1947 and 1955 Adamson turned her attention to tribal portraits and continued to create both paintings and drawings, published in 1967 in *The Peoples of Kenya*. From 1937 until she died, she produced more than 500 paintings and line drawings. Many of the plants she illustrated had not been photographed in color or accurately painted before. She was said to have combined artistic layout with scientific accuracy to a degree not seen since the days of the great Dutch herbalists.

In 1944 she married George Adamson, and joined him in working for the conservation of lions in Kenya. She published several books on one particular family of lions, Elsa and her cubs. The first of these, *Born Free* (1960), was later made into a film. The books were translated into many languages, and Adamson became very well known.

Adamson was murdered in 1980 by a servant with whom she had had an argument. Her husband died in 1989 as a result of an ambush by Somali poachers.

Bibliography: Adamson, G., *My Pride and Joy,* London: Collins Harvill, 1986; Adamson, J., *Forever Free: Elsa's Pride,* London: Collins and Harvill, 1963; Blunt, W., and W. T. Stearn, *The Art of Botanical Illustration,* London: Antique Collectors' Club, Royal Botanic Gardens, Kew, 1994; House, A., *The Great Safari: The Lives of George and Joy Adamson,* London: Harvill, 1993.

Agnesi, Maria Gaetana
6 May 1718–9 January 1799
mathematician

Education: at home, from visiting professors.
Employment: honorary professor of mathematics and natural philosophy at the University of Bologna, 1750–1752; director of Pio Albergo Trivulzio, Milan, 1771–1799.

Maria Agnesi was the first European woman to be considered a mathematician.

Agnesi's father, a professor of mathematics at the University of Bologna, arranged for fellow professors to act as tutors for her. She became an expert linguist, mastering French, German, and Spanish and learning to read Greek, Latin, and Hebrew. At her father's cultural salon, Agnesi regularly presented and defended theses. In 1738 some 190 of these were published as *Propositiones philosophicae*.

When Agnesi tired of these salons, her father allowed the meetings to stop. Agnesi

Maria Gaetana Agnesi (Corbis)

father's three marriages. Once her siblings' schooling was complete, Agnesi became director at a home for the elderly and took up religious studies and social work.

Bibliography: Daintith, J., S. Mitchell, and E. Toothill, eds., *Biographical Encyclopaedia of Scientists,* vol. 1, second edition. Bristol: Institute of Physics Publishing, 1994.

Aitkin, Yvonne
1911–
agriculturalist

Education: Convent of Mercy, Horsham, Victoria, Australia; Sacred Heart College, Ballarat; University of Melbourne, Faculty of Agricultural Science, 1930–1932, 1934–1936; B.S. with honors, 1936; M.S., 1939.

Employment: Faculty of Agricultural Science, University of Melbourne: demonstrator, 1936–1945; lecturer, 1945–1956 (sabbatical year 1955 at the University of Cambridge); senior lecturer, 1957–1974 (sabbatical year 1963 in California and Wales); reader, 1975–1976.

In 1970 *Yvonne Aitkin* became the first woman to be made a doctor of agricultural science at the University of Melbourne. She was awarded the Medal of the Order of Australia in 1989 for her contributions to agricultural science.

Aitkin was born in Horsham, a country town in Victoria, Australia. After attending Sacred Heart College in Ballarat, she won a government free place to the University of Melbourne to study agricultural science. She completed the first two years, interrupted her studies for two years because of illness, then returned and graduated in 1936. She received a small research grant from Samuel Wadham, a professor of agriculture at Melbourne.

For her M.S. thesis, Aitkin studied the problem of the hard seed case of the subterranean clover, *Trifolium subterraneum,* a native of dry parts of the Mediterranean that had been accidentally introduced to Australia. A reseeding winter annual, the clover

withdrew from social life and spent a decade immersing herself in mathematical theory. In 1748 her book *Istituzoni analitiche ad uso della gioventi italiana* was published. This two-volume work with over 1,000 quarto pages aimed to give a complete, integrated treatment of algebra and mathematical analysis emphasizing concepts relatively new at the time. She wrote in Italian rather than Latin so that young people would be able to understand her explanations. The second volume was translated into French in 1749, and the entire book into English in 1801. Pope Benedict XIV congratulated Agnesi on her book, sending her a gold medal and a bejeweled gold wreath and later appointing her to the chair of mathematics and natural philosophy at Bologna. Agnesi never actually taught there but held the position for two years.

When her father died in 1752, Agnesi gradually became less involved with mathematics, concentrating instead on the education of the twenty-one children from her can grow in areas with less than 500 mm of annual rainfall, but only about 1 percent of the seeds germinate because of their hard case. Aitkin discovered ways of overcoming this problem, thereby increasing the germination rate.

Her next challenge was to find a pea plant that had a high rate of fixing nitrogen by means of the bacteria in its root nodules. When the pea plant dies, the nitrate in the nodules is available in the soil for the next crop, thus reducing the need for commercial fertilizers. Aitkin also found the characteristics that made peas most suitable for canning and eating fresh. For her work in breeding a commercial pea, and because she spent so much time in fields of peas, she became known as "Miss Peabody."

Aitkin was interested as well in the effect of day length on flowering time and was well ahead of others in her thinking and observations. In 1955 she took a sabbatical to work on different pea varieties at the University of Cambridge and visit agricultural stations from northern Sweden to Greece. In 1974 she published *Flowering Time, Climate, and Genotype,* which summarized her conclusions from data on patterns of flowering for different varieties of well-known agricultural species over a wide range of climatic zones. Aitkin analyzed the ways in which inherited differences in the rate of reproductive development affected a plant's performance in various climates.

She wrote forty research papers and coauthored *Agricultural Science—An Introduction for Australian Students and Farmers* (1962). The year before she retired she was a reader at the University of Melbourne.

Bibliography: Allen, N., "The Contribution to Agricultural Research of an Australian Woman Scientist," *Agricultural History Review* 45, 1 (1997): 73–85.

Alcock, Nora Lilian née Scott
1874–31 March 1972
plant pathologist

Employment: laboratory work, Department of Physiology, University of London; laboratory work, Plant Pathology Laboratory, Ministry of Agriculture, Kew Gardens (later Harpenden), 1913–1924; plant pathologist, Department of Agriculture for Scotland, Royal Botanic Garden, Edinburgh, 1924–1937.
Married: Alcock, professor of medicine, McGill University, Montreal, in 1905. He died in 1913.

Nora Lilian Alcock was the first government plant pathologist to be appointed in Scotland.

Alcock spent her childhood in Egypt, where her father, Sir John Scott, was judicial adviser to the khedive of Egypt. She married in 1905 and moved to Canada. When her husband died in 1913, Alcock returned to Britain with her four children. Because she had worked in the laboratory of the Department of Physiology at the University of London, she was able to obtain a post in the Plant Pathology Laboratory of the Ministry of Agriculture. Alcock worked under Sir John Fryer, who became secretary to the Agricultural Research Council. In 1924 she left to become plant pathologist for the Department of Agriculture for Scotland, a new post aimed at helping horticulturalists by investigating plant diseases. She found that red core disease in strawberries was caused by the fungus later named *Phytophthora fragariae.* She carried out research into the development of disease-resistant varieties of strawberries and supervised a breeding program. Alcock pioneered the study of seed pathology, producing a comprehensive list of seed-borne diseases. Among her numerous papers is "Notes on Common Diseases Sometimes Seed-Borne" (*Transactions of the Botanical Society of Edinburgh* 30 [1931]: 232–234).

A fellow of the Linnean Society and the Botanical Society of Edinburgh, she was made a Member of the Order of the British Empire (MBE) in 1935. She was an active member of the National Federation of Business and Professional Women and the Edinburgh branch of the Soroptimists service club.

Bibliography: Foister, C. E., "Mrs. N. L. Alcock," *Bulletin of the British Mycological Society* 6, 2 (October 1972); Foister, C. E., "Mrs.

Nora Alcock," *Botanical Society of Edinburgh News* (1972): 11; Gault, R., Botanical Society of Scotland, personal communication to the author, 15 March 2000; Noble, M., "N. L. Alcock," *Seed Pathology News* 4 (September 1972): 7.

Anderson, Margaret Dampier née Whetham
21 April 1900–1997
biochemist, indexer

Education: at home; University College, Exeter; Newnham College, Cambridge, 1918–1921; M.A., 1926.
Employment: biochemical researcher, Newnham College, Cambridge, 1920–1927; abstractor, *British Chemical Abstracts*, 1948–1951; abstractor, *Food Science Abstracts*, 1950–1957; freelance indexer from 1960.
Married: Dr. Alan Bruce Anderson, clinical pathologist, on 12 September 1927.

Margaret Anderson brought her skills as a scientist to the field of publishing.

From 1920 to 1927 Anderson did research in biochemistry with Marjory Stephenson, including pioneering work on the washed cell suspensions technique for analyzing cells. She coauthored (under her maiden name) four papers with Stephenson, two published in the *Proceedings of the Royal Society* and two in the *Biochemical Journal.* From 1926 to 1927 she held the Old Students (of Newnham College) Jubilee Research Fellowship.

For several years, Anderson wrote abstracts of scientific articles, and when she was sixty began working as a freelance scientific indexer, compiling indexes for a wide range of books, nonscientific as well as scientific, 567 in all. She joined the Society of Indexers in 1962 and was one of the first registered indexers. She was the society's treasurer from 1965 to 1972 and later served as membership secretary, member of the board of assessors, and vice president. In 1975 she was awarded the Wheatley Medal for her index to *Copy-editing: The Cambridge Handbook,* and in 1983 she won the Carey Award for her indexing. Anderson wrote *Book Indexing* (1971) and numerous journal, magazine, and newspaper articles. With W. C. D. Whetham she compiled *Cambridge Readings in the Literature of Science* (1924); she also created *Reformers and Rebels* (1946), a calendar of anniversaries.

She was secretary of the Children's Care Committee in Cambridge and a manager of St. Philip's Church School, Cambridge.

Bibliography: *Newnham College Register, 1871–1923,* vol. 1, Cambridge: Newnham College, 1963; Wallis, E., "Margaret Dampier Anderson," *Indexer* 20, 4 (October 1997): 218.

Anning, Mary
1799–9 March 1847
paleontologist

Education: Charmouth village school.
Employment: self-employed, selling fossils she collected.

Mary Anning discovered several fossils of vertebrates previously unknown in Britain, such as an almost complete skeleton of *Plesiosaurus* in 1824.

Anning was born in Lyme Regis in Dorset. Her father, a carpenter, collected fossils and sold them from a stand outside his home. After his death in 1810, Anning essentially took over her father's fossil-selling business.

In 1811 she found the skeleton of an *Icthyosaurus*, a land reptile adapted to marine life. She paid workers to extract it and sold it to a Mr. Henley for £23. Henley donated the skeleton to Bullock's Museum at the Egyptian Hall in Piccadilly; eventually it was bought by the British Museum.

In 1824 Anning discovered embedded in shale the skeleton of another extinct reptile, a *Plesiosaurus*. It was 10 feet long and 6 feet wide. She sold it to the duke of Buckingham for 150 guineas. Her next discovery, in December 1828, was the first British example of a Pterosaur, or flying reptile; in the same month she found a young *Plesiosaurus*. She also uncovered a ganoid fish, *Dapedius*.

Besides carrying out her own excavations, Anning guided geologists to suitable sites to search for fossils themselves. Although Anning made accurate drawings of the fossils she unearthed, she rarely wrote about them. Still, she became quite famous after her discoveries were publicized and was given a small annuity by the Geological Society. She suffered from rheumatism, and died of breast cancer at age forty-eight. A stained glass window in Lyme Parish Church honors her memory.

Bibliography: Lang, W. D., "Mary Anning and the Pioneer Geologists of Lyme," *Proceedings of the Dorset Natural History and Archaeological Society* 60 (1939): 142–164; Swinnerton, H. H., *Fossils*, New Naturalist Library Series, London: Collins, 1960; Van Riper, A. B., "Did You Know? Mary Anning, Fossil Hunter," *BSHS Education Forum* 29 (October 1999): 6–7.

Arber, Agnes née Robertson
23 February 1879–22 March 1960
botanist

Education: North London Collegiate School, 1887–1897; University College, London, 1897–1899; B.S. with honors; Newnham College, Cambridge, 1899–1902; University College, London, 1902–1908; D.Sc., London, 1905.

Employment: research assistant to Ethel Sargant, Reigate, 1902–1903; lecturer in botany, University College, London, 1908–1909; demonstrator, Balfour Laboratory, Cambridge, 1911–1913; research fellowship, Newnham College, Cambridge, 1912–1913.

Married: E. A. N. Arber, demonstrator in paleobotany, University of Cambridge, on 5 August 1909. He died in 1918.

Agnes Arber was the first woman botanist to be elected as a fellow of the Royal Society (1946) and the first woman to be awarded a gold medal from the Linnean Society (1948).

Arber was born in London. Her father, an artist, taught her to draw, and her mother interested her in plants. She attended the North London Collegiate School from the age of eight and went on to University College, London, where in two years she earned her B.S. with honors. At Newnham College she excelled in botany, chemistry, geology, and physics.

After studying at Cambridge, she became research assistant to the plant anatomist Ethel Sargant in her garden-shed laboratory in Reigate. Arber became a skilled microscopist. She was awarded a Quain scholarship at University College, London, for five years' research, after which she lectured in botany for a year. She wrote several papers, mostly on paleobotany. On the strength of these, she was awarded a doctorate in science from University College.

After her marriage she lived in Cambridge, where her husband was both a demonstrator in paleobotany and in charge of the collection of fossil plants in the Sedgwick Museum. The Arbers had domestic help, so Agnes could concentrate on her research. When her husband died in 1918, Arber brought up their daughter, Muriel, alone. (Muriel Arber later became a geologist.)

Arber published her first book, *Herbals: Their Origin and Evolution. A Chapter in the History of Botany, 1470–1670,* in 1912. As a fellow of Newnham College, Arber was allowed to work at its Balfour Laboratory rent-free and to use the existing equipment for her research on plant anatomy. She took over the publication of *The Monocotyledons* (1925), started by Ethel Sargant, and wrote *Water Plants* (1920) and *The Graminae* (1934). When the college sold the Balfour laboratory in 1927, she set up a laboratory in her home, but she was given the equipment she needed on long-term loan and once settled in seems to have welcomed the chance to work undisturbed. Most of her studies were self-funded, but she did have a Leverhulme research fellowship from 1936 to 1938.

During her working life, Arber wrote more than seventy papers on various aspects of botany and science. She gradually moved away from practical work to a more philosophical approach. Interested in Goethe since she was young, she translated his *Botany: The Metamorphosis of Plants*, publishing it in *Chronica Botanica* (1946). She also wrote *The Natural Philosophy of Plant Form* (1950), which linked her laboratory experience with her ideas on plant morphology. In *The Mind and the Eye* (1954), she looked at the nature of biological research and the bases of biological thinking; it was what she called an attempt at a "more generalised analysis of the biologist's approach to his own subject and to philosophy." Her last book, *The Manifold and the Eye* (1957), an exploration of a wide variety of world faiths, showed the astonishing amount of reading Arber had done.

Arber was made a corresponding member of the Botanical Society of America. In 1921 she was proposed as president of the botany section of the British Association for the Advancement of Science, making her the second woman president two years in succession. The notion was too progressive for the committee: Arber had to resign in spite of her considerable contributions to botanical knowledge.

Bibliography: Daintith, J., et al., eds., *Biographical Encyclopaedia of Scientists*, vol. 1, second edition, Bristol: Institute of Physics Publishing, 1994; Desmond, R., *Dictionary of British and Irish Botanists and Horticulturalists, Including Plant Collectors and Botanical Artists*, London: Taylor and Francis, 1977; *Dictionary of National Biography, 1951–1960*, Oxford: Oxford University Press, 1971; *Newnham College Register, 1871–1923*, vol. 1, Cambridge: Newnham College, 1963; Packer, K., "A Laboratory of One's Own: The Life and Works of Agnes Arber FRS (1879–1960)," *Notes and Records of the Royal Society of London* 51, 1 (1997): 87–104; Thomas, H. H., "Agnes Arber 1879–1960, F.R.S.," *Biographical Memoirs of Fellows of the Royal Society* 6 (1960); *Who Was Who, 1951–1960*, London: Adam and Charles Black, 1961.

Armitage, Ella Sophia
née Bulley
3 March 1841–20 March 1931
archaeologist

Education: at home; Newnham College, Cambridge, 1871–1872.

Employment: history lecturer, Women's Department, Owen's College, Manchester, 1874–1884.

Married: Rev. Elkanah Armitage, a nonconformist minister, in 1874. He died in 1929.

Ella Armitage was one of the first five students at Newnham College, Cambridge, and was the college's first research student. In 1887 she was elected as the first and only woman on the school board at Rotherham.

Armitage was born in Liverpool, one of fourteen children. She had to teach her younger brothers and sisters at home and wrote in her diary that she would "overcome the accursed thraldom of womanhood." She was a competent linguist, but her main interest was archaeology. After completing her studies at Newnham, she taught history at Owen's College in Manchester (later Manchester University).

G. T. Clarke's *Mediaeval Military Architecture in England* (1884) spurred Armitage to her own research. She was sure that Clarke's ideas about the origins of the mottes, or mounds, in Anglo-Saxon Britain were wrong, she set about proving that none had appeared until after the Norman invasion. She worked with G. H. Round, George Neilson in Scotland, and Goddard Orpen in Ireland, all well known scholars at the time. She wrote several controversial articles on the subject and in 1912, after eleven years of research, published *The Early Norman Castles of the British Isles*, which set forth the theory that all castles in the British Isles were Norman in origin.

Armitage was awarded an honorary M.A. in 1919 by Manchester University for her work in archaeology. She was an honorary fellow of the Society of Antiquaries of Scotland and founder and first president of the Yorkshire Congregational Women's Guild of Christian Service. She held numerous voluntary posts, serving on the Rotherham School Board (1884–1890); the Bradford School Board, West Riding Education Committee (1890); and as assistant commissioner to the Royal Commission on Secondary Education (1894).

Bibliography: Nicholls, C. S., ed., *Dictionary of National Biography: Missing Persons,* Oxford: Oxford University Press, 1993; *Newnham College Register, 1871–1923,* vol. 1, Cambridge: Newnham College, 1963; *Who Was Who, 1929–1940,* London: Adam and Charles Black, 1947.

Atkins, Anna née Children
16 March 1799–9 June 1871
botanist, photographic artist

Married: John Pelly Atkins, sheriff, railway promoter, and owner of coffee plantations in Jamaica, in 1825.

Anna Atkins was a pioneer in photography, using the medium for scientific illustration. She published the first book to be illustrated with photographs, *British Algae: Cyanotype Impressions,* privately published in parts from 1843 to 1853.

Atkins was born in Tonbridge, Kent. Her mother died when Atkins was only twenty months old, and she was brought up by her father, John George Children, a keeper of zoology at the British Museum. She developed a close bond with her father, who encouraged her in her early scientific interests. She met other leading scientists of the day and developed her artistic skills, making over 250 drawings of shells to illustrate the translation of Lamarck's *Genera of Shells* (1823) that her father published. In 1938 Atkins's father was vice president of the Botanical Society of London (later the Botanical Society of the British Isles), and a year later Atkins, herself a keen student of botany, was elected a member; she was active in the society for many years.

In 1839, Louis Daguerre publicized his photographic techniques in France, and William Henry Fox Talbot publicized his methods in England. Talbot presented his findings at a Royal Society meeting chaired by John Children. Atkins developed an interest in photography and performed experiments with her father. Talbot's process involved coating sensitized paper with silver compounds, drying and ironing these, then exposing them to sunlight—a difficult and time-consuming procedure. Atkins decided instead to investigate the use of the cyanotype, developed by John Herschel, which involved placing objects directly onto light-sensitive paper and exposing the paper to sunlight. She used this process for *British Algae: Cyanotype Impressions,* which also included photographic copies of her own handwritten text.

In 1852, when Atkins's father died, she was comforted by her childhood friend Anne Dixon, who then became interested in cyanotypes. The two women often worked together to produce plates. Atkins turned her attention to ferns, and in 1854 she presented her friend with the book *Cyanotypes of British and Foreign Ferns.* She collected many botanical specimens and in 1865 donated her large collection to the British Museum.

Bibliography: Nicholls, C. S., ed., *Dictionary of National Biography: Missing Persons,* Oxford: Oxford University Press, 1993; Rosenblum, N., *A History of Women Photographers,* London: Abbeville, 1994; Schaaf, L. J., *Sun Gardens: Victorian Photograms by Anna Atkins,* Oxford: Phaidon, 1985.

Auerbach, Charlotte
14 May 1899–17 March 1994
geneticist

Education: Auguste-Viktoria Schule, Berlin-Charlottenburg, Germany; University of Berlin, 1919–1920, 1921–1922, and 1924; University of Würzburg, 1920–1921; University of Freiburg, 1922–1923; postgraduate research, Kaiser-Wilhelm Institut für Biologie, Berlin-Dahlem, 1928–1929; Institute of Animal Genetics, University of Edinburgh, 1933–1935; Ph.D., 1935; D.Sc., 1947.
Employment: teacher, private school, Heidelberg, Germany, 1924–1925; teacher,

Schiller Schule, Frankfurt; teacher, various girls' secondary schools, Berlin, 1929–1933; Institute of Animal Genetics, University of Edinburgh: research assistant, 1935–1937; lecturer (later reader), 1947–1967; personal chair, 1967–1969.

Charlotte Auerbach discovered that mustard gas could induce mutations in the chromosomes of living cells.

Auerbach was born in Krefeld am Rhein, Germany, the only child of a chemist. She later moved with her family to Berlin, where she was inspired by an hourlong talk on chromosomes and mitosis given by her biology teacher. Her father encouraged her interest in science, particularly in natural history, and also instilled in his daughter a love of music.

Auerbach studied biology at university, taking a range of courses at the Universities of Berlin, Würzburg, and Freiburg. She passed her final examinations with flying colors in 1925 and wrote a thesis on thermoregulation. She trained as a teacher, and passed this exam with distinction as well, but did not get far in her teaching career: She was dismissed from her second job because of her Jewish ancestry.

In 1928 she started postgraduate research in developmental biology under Otto Mangold at the Kaiser-Wilhelm Institut für Biologie in Berlin-Dahlem, financing her work with a small inheritance. When her money ran out in 1929, she returned to teaching, only to be summarily dismissed once the Nazis came to power in 1933.

The situation for Jews in Germany became so serious that Auerbach decided to travel to Britain. She was eventually accepted as a Ph.D. student at the Institute of Animal Genetics in Edinburgh, working under F. A. E. Crew. Although she had no previous experience in genetics, she persevered and wrote her thesis on genetic variations in the legs of *Drosophila*, the fruit fly. She then continued her research at the institute, taking many poorly paid jobs in order to support herself. H. J. Muller, an internationally renowned geneticist, worked at the institute from 1938 to 1940. Under his tutelage, Auerbach studied the mutagenic ac-

tion of carcinogens in *Drosophila*. Although this line of research was not fruitful, Auerbach was greatly influenced by her work with Muller.

Having become a naturalized British citizen in 1939, Auerbach avoided being classed as an alien during World War II. Shortly before the war, her mother arrived in Edinburgh with no money or possessions, and the two women lived in poverty, supported by Auerbach's limited salary.

In 1940 Auerbach began one of her most important research projects. Professor A. J. Clark of the Pharmacology Department was studying the biological effects of mustard gas for the War Office. Auerbach and J. M. Robson, who worked for Clark, looked at gene mutations in *Drosophila* exposed to mustard gas. The experiments were hazardous, but it appears that Auerbach avoided most of the dangerous tasks. Preliminary findings suggested that the mustard gas did have mutagenic effects; a series of further experiments over several months confirmed these results. Muller, who was by this time in the United States, sent a congratulatory telegram after Auerbach informed him of their initial success; she considered this "her greatest reward."

Although their results could not be published until after the war, Auerbach and Robson wrote a letter to *Nature* in 1944 (15 July) reporting their findings without specifying the substance involved. In 1946 (9 March) they again wrote to the journal, giving more details and naming mustard gas as the substance they had tested. They published a full account in 1947 in the *Proceedings of the Royal Society of Edinburgh*, and in 1948 Auerbach presented the paper "Chemical Induction of Mutations" at the Eighth International Congress of Genetics in Stockholm. In 1948 Auerbach received the Royal Society of Edinburgh's Keith Prize, much to the chagrin of Robson, who felt that he should have shared the award. Although Auerbach tried to appease him, the issue brought about a permanent rift between the two scientists.

Auerbach summarized progress in the field of chemical mutagenesis in *Biological Reviews* 24 (1949): 355–391. She continued to use *Drosophila* in her experiments on mutagenic substances but stopped testing mustard gas because of its hazardous nature. She resisted calls to test a wide range of substances on the grounds that her knowledge of chemistry was inadequate for her to specialize in this field.

During the 1950s she began to study microorganisms such as *Neurospora* and later *Schizosaccharomyces pombe.* She investigated the phenomenon of mosaics, in which a mixture of mutant and nonmutant cells occurs within an organism. She also worked on replicating instabilities, mosaics that themselves produce more mosaics in subsequent generations, and studied the delayed effects of chemical mutagens.

From 1959 to 1969 Auerbach was honorary director of the Medical Research Council's Unit of Mutagenesis Research in Edinburgh. She became an emeritus professor when she retired in 1969 and continued to take a keen interest in her area of research, though in later years her eyesight failed and her general health deteriorated.

As well as many articles in scientific journals, she wrote several textbooks, including *Notes for Introductory Courses in Genetics* (1942), *The Science of Genetics* (1962), and *Mutation Research* (1976). She received honorary degrees from the University of Leiden (1975); Trinity College, Dublin (1977); the University of Cambridge (1977); and the University of Indiana (1984). She was made a fellow of the Royal Society of Edinburgh in 1949 and of the Royal Society in 1957. She was also a member of the Danish Academy of Science (1968) and the U.S. National Academy of Sciences and an honorary member of the Genetics Society of Japan. She received the Darwin Medal of the Royal Society and the Gregor Mendel Prize of the German Genetics Society.

Bibliography: Beale, G. H., "Charlotte Auerbach," *Biographical Memoirs of Fellows of the Royal Society* (1995); Uglow, J. S., ed., *The Macmillan Dictionary of Women's Biography,* third edition, London: Macmillan, 1998; *Who Was Who, 1897–200_.* CD-ROM version, London: Adam and Charles Black.

Ayrton, Phoebe Sarah (Hertha) née Marks
28 April 1854–26 August 1923
physicist

Education: at home; Girton College, Cambridge, 1877–1881; Finsbury Technical College, 1884–1885.

Employment: teacher, 1870–1877; mathematics teacher, 1881–1885; part-time teacher, 1885–1889.

Married: William E. Ayrton, professor of applied physics, Finsbury Technical College, in 1885. He died in 1908.

Hertha Ayrton was elected as the first woman member of the Institution of Electrical Engineers. No more women were elected until 1959, except as student members.

Ayrton was born in Petworth, Sussex, the third of eight children. Her father, a watchmaker and jeweler, died when she was seven years old. Despite the difficulties of bringing up the family alone, Ayrton's mother was determined that her children, especially the girls, should receive a proper education, and she sent Ayrton to an aunt's school in London from the age of nine. When she was sixteen, Ayrton began to earn a living teaching in London. She studied mathematics at Girton College, Cambridge, encouraged by the novelist George Eliot and Barbara Bodichon, one of the cofounders of Girton.

While at Cambridge she invented a sphymograph to record pulse beats and later patented a device that was able to divide a line into any number of equal parts. She also set up the Girton Fire Brigade and was leader of the College Choral Society. She returned to London in 1881 and taught mathematics. In 1884 she went to evening classes in science at Finsbury Technical College. Her instructor was William Ayrton, an electrical engineer who had worked in India and Japan on practical and educational projects and had helped found Finsbury Technical College in 1879. After her marriage, Ayrton lectured to women on electricity, but it was not until she received a legacy from Barbara Bodichon in 1891 that she was able to employ a housekeeper and start on her own research.

Both Ayrton and her husband worked on improving electric arc lighting. When her husband went to a congress in Chicago in 1893, Ayrton posted the results of her work to him every week. After a maid used some of the papers to light a fire, Ayrton repeated all the research on her own. She presented "The Hissing of the Electric Arc" at the Institution of Electrical Engineers (IEE) meeting of 23 March 1899, the first time a woman had been allowed to speak at a meeting of the group. With the support of her husband, who had been president of the IEE in 1892, she was elected a member of the IEE two days later.

By the "hissing arc," Ayrton meant "the sudden change from purple to green of a part of the arc vapor, and as sudden a diminution in P.D. [potential difference] between the carbons." In 1902 she published *The Electric Arc,* based on papers she had prepared for the Annual Meetings of the British Association for the Advancement of Science in 1895, 1897, and 1898 and the Royal Society and articles published in *The Electrician.*

She presented a paper at the International Electrical Congress in Paris in 1900, and the following year her paper on the mechanism of the electric arc was read by John Perry at the Royal Society. On 21 June 1899 she was the only woman demonstrator at the Royal Society conversazione, an exhibition where scientists met with the public to talk about their work. Her work on the electric arc helped to improve antiaircraft searchlights, lighthouses, cinemas, and street lighting before incandescent lighting was developed. She took out six patents for carbons and carbon holders in 1913–1914.

In 1904 she was the first woman to read a paper at the Royal Society. Her topic on that occasion was ripples in sand, which she had become interested in while staying in the English coastal town of Margate in 1901. Her research in this area was widely reported to the engineering section of the British Association for the Advancement of Science (1904) and the Physical Society (1907) and in further papers to the Royal Society (1908 and 1911).

In 1902 the Royal Society debated the possibility of Ayrton's election to fellowship. It was eventually decided that she could not be elected, not simply because she was a woman but because she was a married woman and thus had no status in law. Other women scientists at this time were similarly struggling to gain admittance to learned societies. Around this time Ayrton became involved in the women's suffrage movement and took part in a number of marches for the cause. In 1912 her daughter, Barbara, was arrested during a demonstration at which Ayrton was present. Ayrton assisted leading suffragettes who were released from prison in 1912–1913 following hunger strikes, her home in Norfolk Square becoming a recovery center.

Following the first gas attack, using chlorine, by the Germans at Ypres in April 1915, Ayrton applied her knowledge of air movement to develop the Ayrton flapper fan to drive the heavy gases away from the men in the trenches. The authorities were skeptical but finally agreed to try it out. Eventually 104,000 of these motorized fans were made and issued to 5 million soldiers in France. Ayrton did not take out a patent but gave this invention to the country, publishing details in the *Proceedings of the Royal Society* (96, series A [1919]: 256). After the war she continued to perfect the fan to improve the ventilation of mines, sewers, and military pillboxes.

Hertha Ayrton was awarded the Hughes Medal by the Royal Society in 1906 for her work on the electric arc and sand ripples. She was the first woman to receive this medal. In 1920, in response to the Sex Disqualification (Removal) Act of 1919, the Royal Society, together with other learned societies, changed its statutes to allow women to be elected as members. But because only one of the members who had originally supported her bid for membership in 1902 was still alive in 1920, Ayrton did not apply again.

The Hertha Ayrton Science Fellowship at Girton College was founded in her memory.

Bibliography: "Anti-Gas Fans in the Trenches," *Times,* 5 January 1920; "The Ayrton Anti-gas Fans: A Woman's War Invention Revealed," *Illustrated London News* (9 August 1919); Bernhard, S., archivist, Institution of Electrical Engineers, personal communication to author, 4 November 1997; "Hertha Ayrton," obituary, *Journal of the Institution of Electrical Engineers* 61 (1923): 1151; Mason, J. "Hertha Ayrton (1854–1923) and the Admission of Women to the Royal Society of London," *Notes and Records of the Royal Society of London* 45, 2 (1991): 201–220; Nicholls, C. S., ed., *Dictionary of National Biography: Missing Persons*, Oxford: Oxford University Press, 1993; Sharp, E., *Hertha Ayrton*, London: Edward Arnold, 1926; Symons, E. D. P., "Hertha Ayrton—A Forgotten Pioneer," *Electric Living* (Winter 1981): 13; Trotter, A. P., "Reminiscences of Alexander Pelham Trotter," archives, Insititution of Electrical Engineers (SC Mss 66, paragraphs 569–591).

B

Bacon, Gertrude
19 April 1874–22 December 1949
aeronaut, writer, lecturer

Education: at home.
Employment: freelance writer and lecturer.
Married: Thomas J. Foggitt, a chemist and botanist, in 1929.

Gertrude Bacon was the first woman to fly in an airship, in August 1904; the first English woman to fly in an airplane, on 29 August 1909; and the first to fly in a hydroplane, on Windermere in 1912.

Bacon was the daughter of Rev. John Mackenzie Bacon, a keen balloonist and scientist who conducted numerous experiments on sound transmission. Gertrude Bacon accompanied him on most of his expeditions and lecture tours. In August 1896 Bacon traveled to Norway with her father and a group of scientists to witness the total eclipse of the sun from the Veranger Fjord on the Arctic Circle. After the astronomers set up elaborate equipment to photograph the eclipse, which was due to last 106 seconds, the sky clouded over. Not to be defeated, she and her father traveled to India for another total eclipse in January 1898 and successfully photographed and described it. Two years later they went to the United States to observe another solar eclipse.

Bacon became fascinated by flying and as a journalist reported on the various airships and planes being built. In August 1904 she was a passenger in the initial flight of an 84-foot-long airship designed and piloted by Stanley Spencer. The craft almost crashed into the watching crowd on takeoff but managed to escape with minimal damage to the airship, rising to 2,000 feet and eventually landing on a hedge near a railway line, just missing an excursion train.

From 22 to 29 August 1909, the world's first aviation meeting was held at Rheims, France. Bacon was determined to go for a ride in one of the new machines. On the last day she was taken up in a Farman plane, squeezed between the radiator and the pilot. She described the takeoff: "The motion was wonderfully smooth—smoother yet—and then—! Suddenly there had come into it a new indescribable quality—a lift—a lightness—a life!" Thus she became the first Englishwoman to fly. Her second flight was in 1910 at Brooklands with D. G. Gilmour in "The Big Bat" monoplane.

In July 1912 she became the first passenger to be taken out in a hydroplane; she made a complete circuit of Lake Windermere, which lasted forty-two minutes. Later she was the first woman to fly in a hydromonoplane, a Depurdussin monoplane being tested by the Admiralty, based at Barrow-in-Furness. The plane went 70 mph and took fifteen minutes to fly up Windermere and back.

Bacon's last "terrifying" experience was in 1927. During an excursion at the annual meeting of the British Association for the Advancement of Science, she was lowered 360 feet into the caverns of Gaping Ghyll in the Yorkshire Dales.

She wrote several books about flying and lectured around the country. She was a member of the British Association for the Advancement of Science, and an original member of the British Astronomy Association.

Bacon and her husband were keen botanists, and she joined the Wildflower Society in 1901. She played an active part in the society for over forty years and codiscovered a species of rush new to Britain, *Carex microglochin*, in 1923.

Bibliography: Bacon, G., *Memories of Land and Sky,* London: Methuen, 1928; Bacon, G., *The Record of an Aeronaut: Being the Life of John M. Bacon,* London: John Long, 1907; "Mrs. Gertrude Foggitt, JP," *Wildflower Magazine* 407 (Autumn 1986): 34, 44.

Balfour, (Lady Eve) Evelyn Barbara
16 July 1898–16 January 1990
agriculturalist

Education: private tuition at home; Department of Agriculture, University of Reading, 1915–1918; diploma in agriculture, 1918.

Lady Eve Balfour founded the Soil Association in 1946 and launched the organic movement in British farming.

Balfour decided to become a farmer when she was twelve and went to the University of Reading to take a diploma in agriculture when she was seventeen. In 1918 she trained girls to work on farms with the Land Army, which replaced male agricultural workers conscripted for military service with female workers.

In 1919, after the war, she bought New Bells Farm at Haughley, near Bury St. Edmunds, Suffolk. In 1939 she started what she called the Haughley Experiment, designed to compare organic and inorganic farming methods; she eventually published the final results of the experiment in 1975. Balfour was interested in the relationships between farming methods and the health-giving properties of the resulting crops, an issue she explored in *The Living Soil*, first published in 1943.

Balfour was also a saxophone player, pilot, and sailor. She wrote three detective novels, *Paper Chase* (1927) being the most successful. She was made an Officer of the Order of the British Empire (OBE) in 1990.

Bibliography: Balfour, Evelyn Barbara, *The Living Soil,* revised edition, London: Faber and Faber, 1949; Balfour, Hearnden (a pseudonym for Balfour, Eve), *The Paper Chase,* London: Hodder and Stoughton, 1927; Massingberd, H., ed., *The Daily Telegraph Book of Obituaries: A Celebration of Eccentric Lives,* London: Macmillan, 1995.

Balfour, (Elizabeth) Jean née Drew
4 November 1927–
forester, conservationist, land manager

Education: University of Edinburgh, B.S. with honors, 1949.
Employment: partner/owner, Balbirnie Home Farms and Balbirnie Dairy Farm; director, A. & J. Bowen and Company, 1960–1997; Chieftain Industries, 1983–1985; chair, Loch Dueart Ltd., from 1999.
Married: John Charles Balfour, in 1950.

Jean Balfour was chair of the Countryside Commission for Scotland from 1972 to 1983.

Balfour has been involved in forestry, agriculture, and land management and is interested in arctic alpine vegetation. She has been on botanical expeditions to Greenland, Ellesmere Island, Spitzbergen, Franz Joseph Land, Novaya Zemlya, Severnaya Zemlya, and arctic Siberia. She and Professor R. M. M. Crawford at St. Andrews University, who is studying the problems of population dynamics in changing climatic conditions, have used her field data to collaborate on several papers, including "Female Predominant Sex Ratios and Physiological Differentiation in Arctic Willows" (*Journal of Ecology* 71 [1983]: 149–160) and "Potential Impact of Climatic Warming on Arctic Vegetation" (*Flora* [1993]: 188f.).

In 1984, at the government's request, she wrote *A New Look at the Northern Ireland Countryside* (1984), a report that listed more than twenty recommendations for restructuring the legislation and arrangements for countryside management and nature conservation in Northern Ireland. Most of her suggestions were acted upon.

Besides being a company director and farm owner, since 1958 Balfour has held a wide range of public appointments, mainly linked to her interest in land management. She was governor of the East Scotland College of Agriculture for thirty years, and vice-president from 1982 to 1988; member of the Scottish Agriculture Development Council, 1972–1977, and the Nature Conservancy Council, 1973–1980; vice-chairman of the Scottish Wildlife Trust, 1968–1972, and of the West Sutherland Fisheries Trust from 1996. She is chairman of the Seafish Industry Authority (SIA), which promotes fisheries research and is particularly concerned with whitefish and herring. Balfour was a deputy chair of the Committee on Women in Science, Engineering, and Technology (Office of Science and Technology, Cabinet Office) in 1993–1994, which published a report entitled *The Rising Tide* regarding women in traditionally male-dominated fields. She is also an honorary vice-president of the Scottish Youth Hostels Association. She has been a justice of the peace for Fife since 1963.

Balfour is a fellow of the Institute of Chartered Foresters, the Royal Society of Arts, the Royal Society of Edinburgh, the Royal Zoological Society for Scotland, and the Institute of Biology and an honorary fellow of the Royal Scottish Geographical Society. She was made a Commander of the Order of the British Empire (CBE) in 1981 and awarded honorary doctorates from the Universities of St. Andrews (1977) and Stirling (1991). She was awarded the Order of the Falcon (Iceland) in 1994 and the Institute of Chartered Foresters Medal for services to British Forestry in 1996, one of only two women to receive this honor.

Bibliography: Balfour, Jean, personal communication to the author, 18 February 2000; Committee on Women in Science, Engineering, and Technology, *The Rising Tide,* London: Her Majesty's Stationery Office (HMSO), 1994; *Who's Who, 1999,* London: Adam and Charles Black, 1999.

Ball, Anne Elizabeth
1808–1872
naturalist

Anne Elizabeth Ball collected seaweeds, flowering plants, and butterflies along the Irish coast.

Ball gathered specimens for Dr. W. H. Harvey, a seaweed expert. He named two after her, *Ballia callitricha* and *Cladophora balliana* (the latter she had found at Clontarf on 16 May 1843).

The seaweeds she collected between 1834 and 1836 are in the herbarium at University College, Cork. The herbarium of the National Museum in Dublin has ninety-six drawings by Ball that appear to have been copied from plates already published.

Bibliography: Wilson, M. A., "Anne Elizabeth Ball of Youghal," *Irish Naturalists' Journal* 11, 8 (1954): 1–3.

Baly, Monica E.
24 May 1914–12 November 1998
nurse, historian, writer

Education: St. Hilda's School for Girls, London; London County Council Fever Hospital; Middlesex Hospital, S.R.N., 1938; S.C.M., 1939; Royal College of Nursing, health visitor, 1945; Open University, B.A., 1979; London University, Ph.D., 1983.

Employment: Princess Mary's Royal Air Force Nursing Service 1939–1944; health visitor, 1945–1949; chief nursing officer, Foreign Office, Displaced Persons Division, British Occupation Zone, Germany, 1949–1952; Western Area Officer, Royal College of Nursing, 1952–1974; lecturer in nursing, London University; lecturer in social policy and history of nursing, Bristol Polytechnic.

Monica Baly was a leading nurse historian. Under the aegis of the Royal College of Nursing, she founded the History of Nursing Society and edited its journal, now the *International History of Nursing Journal.*

After leaving school, Baly trained in a fever hospital, moving to the Middlesex

Hospital for her professional nursing training, followed by a year of midwifery. During World War II she worked for Princess Mary's Royal Air Force Nursing Service in the Middle East and Italy, where she set up a burns unit.

Baly trained as a health visitor at the Royal College of Nursing (RCN); after holding posts in clinics in Surrey, in 1949 she became chief nursing officer, working with displaced persons in Germany. She persuaded the British government to employ German nurses and set up a nursing school in Hannover.

With the establishment of the National Health Service in 1948, it became clear that the RCN needed to act as a trade union to ensure fair rates of pay. While she had trained at the college, Baly had calculated a cost-of-living index that showed that it was impossible to live on the salary a health visitor received in the initial year of employment. Baly was the first to be appointed as an area coordinator to deal with personal problems of nurses in their employment. She was responsible for a huge region stretching from Cornwall to the Midlands, with half of Wales.

Baly organized the first lobby of MPs by nurses and addressed meetings throughout the UK as part of what was called the "Raise the Roof" campaign intended to improve the salaries of the top personnel in nursing, the thinking being that those in the lower ranks would subsequently receive more too. Nurses received a 22 percent pay rise as a result of the campaign.

In 1960 Baly saw through the amalgamation of the National Council of Nurses with the RCN. She lectured in social policy and the history of nursing and wrote *Nursing and Social Change* (1973).

When she retired, Baly studied for an Open University degree, choosing courses slanted toward history. On a grant from the Nightingale Fund, she wrote her doctoral dissertation on the life of Florence Nightingale, providing a much wider picture of Nightingale than previously available. Her thesis was published as *Florence Nightingale and the Nursing Legacy* (1986). Baly also wrote a history of the Queen's Nursing In-

stitute and was made centenary fellow in 1985. A fellowship from the RCN was conferred on her in 1985 as well.

Bibliography: Baly, M. E., *Florence Nightingale and the Nursing Legacy,* London: Croom Helm, 1986; Dopson, L., S. Kirkby, C. Maggs, P. Nuttall, and E. R. Parker, "Monica Baly," *International History of Nursing Journal* 4, 2 (1998/1999): 41–45; Hancock, C., "Monica Baly: The Lady of the Lamp," *Guardian* (20 November 1998).

Barber, Mary
3 April 1911–11 September 1965
pathologist

Education: London School of Medicine for Women and Royal Free Hospital, conjoint diploma, 1934; M.B. and B.S., 1936; M.D., 1940.

Employment: Royal Free Hospital: resident assistant, Pathology Unit, 1936–1937; A. M. Bird Scholar in pathology, 1937–1938; assistant pathologist, Archway Group Laboratory, 1938–1939; Hill End and the City Hospitals, St. Albans, 1939–1940; assistant pathologist and lecturer in bacteriology, British Postgraduate Medical School (BPMS), Hammersmith, 1940–1948; reader in bacteriology, St. Thomas's Hospital, 1948–1958; BPMS, Hammersmith: reader in clinical bacteriology, 1958–1963; professor, 1963–1965.

Mary Barber was one of the first pathologists to document the development of penicillin-resistant bacteria. Her main interests were in the behavior of the staphylococci bacteria, cross-infection, and the use and development of antibiotics.

After her initial medical training, Barber specialized in pathology and published her first paper on *Listeria* meningitis in 1937. She studied penicillin resistance in staphylococci and showed that it was increasing, publishing her results in 1947. When she was at St. Thomas's Hospital, she investigated cross-infection by staphylococci at a nearby maternity hospital. She found the infection was due to a penicillin-resistant strain and that the nurses became nasal carriers soon after working on the wards.

She continued with this research at Hammersmith Hospital and developed a policy restricting the use of antibiotics and suggested that antibacterial drugs should not be used singly but combined with one another. These measures reduced the level of antibiotic resistance among the hospital population.

Barber received funding from the Medical Research Council to investigate semisynthetic penicillins, cephalosporins, fucidin, lincomycin, and pristinamycin. Her work was published in many journals, and with L. P. Garrod she coauthored *Antibiotic and Chemotherapy* (1963), at the time a useful book for anyone starting off in the subject and still interesting from a historical perspective for its long lists of references.

Barber was an active member of several academic societies and had strong religious and political convictions. She was killed in a road accident at the age of fifty-five.

Bibliography: "Mary Barber, MD, MRCP." *British Medical Journal,* 19 September 1965, p. 707.

Barclay-Smith, Phyllis Ida
1903–2 January 1980
ornithologist

Education: Church House School, Worthing; Blackheath High School, London; King's College, London.

Employment: Royal Society for the Protection of Birds: assistant secretary, 1924–1935; honorary secretary of British section, 1935; International Council for Bird Preservation: assistant secretary, 1935–1946; secretary, 1946–1974; secretary-general, 1974–; work in Foreign Office, 1939; secretary to business manager, Bristol Aeroplane Factory, 1939–1942; editor, *Avicultural Magazine,* 1939–1973; specialist local welfare officer (southwest region), Ministry of Labour, 1943–1945; honorary secretary and treasurer, British Ornithologists' Union, 1945–1951; honorary secretary, International Wildfowl Research Bureau (now the International Waterfowl Research Bureau), from 1948.

In 1958 *Phyllis Barclay-Smith* became the first woman to be named a Member of the Order of the British Empire (MBE) for work in conservation. In 1971 she was made a Commander of the Order of the British Empire (CBE). She built up the International Council for Bird Preservation to its present importance.

Barclay-Smith's father was professor of anatomy at Cambridge University and encouraged his daughter's interest in birds. After graduating, she served as secretary at the Royal Society for the Protection of Birds (RSPB) until she moved to the International Council for Bird Preservation (ICBP) in 1935, becoming secretary in 1946. During World War II she worked initially in a secretarial post, moving to social welfare work. After the war she was secretary of the British Ornithologists' Union as it began to expand. She was involved in setting up the International Wildfowl Research Bureau, with Professor Edward Hindle, in liaison with the Wildfowl Trust.

She co-opted Jim Callaghan, a member of Parliament who later became prime minister of the United Kingdom, to be chairman of the Advisory Committee on Oil Pollution of the Sea, organized three major conferences on oil pollution, and edited the resultant proceedings.

Barclay-Smith was one of the first members of the RSPB to have written a scientific paper. As editor of the *Avicultural Magazine,* she accepted articles on a wide variety of subjects related to birds. She used her linguistic skills to translate several books on ornithology from French and German, such as P. Barvel's *Birds of the World* (1954) and G. Hess's *The Bird* (1951). She wrote several books about birds (all under the surname "Smith"): *British and American Game Birds* (1939); *Birds of Lake, River, and Stream* (1939); *Garden Birds* (1945); *A Book of Ducks* (1951); and *Woodland Birds* (1955).

She received many honors, including the RSPB's Gold Medal, the Delacour Medal from the ICBP, and the Netherlands Order of the Golden Ark. She was a corresponding member of several ornithological unions abroad, including the Hungarian Institute of Ornithology.

Bibliography: "Miss Phyllis Barclay-Smith," *Times* (5 January 1980); Bourne, W. R. P., "Phyllis Barclay-Smith, CBE," *Birds* 8 (1980): 13; Delacour, J., "Miss Phyllis Barclay-Smith, CBE," *Aviculture Magazine* 86 (1980): 46–48; Nicholson, E. M., "Miss Phyllis Ida Barclay-Smith, CBE, MBOU (1903–1980)," *British Birds* 73 (1980): 215–216; Thorpe, W. H., "Phyllis Barclay-Smith," *Ibis* 122, 3 (1980): 274–275.

Bari, Nina Karlovna
19 November 1901–15 July 1961
mathematician

Education: L. O. Vyazemska's School for Girls; Moscow State University, 1918–1921; Research Institute of Mathematics, Moscow State University, Ph.D., 1926.

Employment: teaching from 1921; research assistant, Institute of Mathematics and Mechanics, Moscow, from 1926; professor, Moscow State University, 1932.

Married: V. V. Nemytski.

Nina Bari, a noted researcher and academic, made an important contribution to the study of mathematics in Russia.

Bari was born in Moscow, the daughter of a doctor. At school she was found to have an aptitude for mathematics, and she studied at the Faculty of Mathematics and Physics at Moscow State University. After graduation she taught and did research at the newly established Research Institute of Mathematics of Moscow State University. It was around this time that she met V. V. Nemytski, a fellow student, whom she later married.

In 1926 she was awarded a doctorate for work on trigonometrical series and obtained a position as a research assistant at Moscow's Institute of Mathematics and Mechanics. For the next few years, she spent time abroad, particularly in Paris. She was appointed professor at Moscow State University in 1932, the year in which her first textbook, *Higher Algebra,* was published. A second book, *The Theory of Series,* appeared

in 1936. She wrote more than fifty articles and edited two mathematical journals. She also edited the complete works of Luzin, who had been her teacher and mentor at Moscow State University.

Bibliography: "Nina Karlovna Bari." At http://www-history.mcs.st-andrews.ac.uk/mathematicians/bari/html.

Barnes, Alice Josephine (Mary Taylor; Dame Josephine Warren)
18 August 1912–28 December 1999
obstetrician, gynecologist

Education: Oxford High School, 1921–1930; Lady Margaret Hall, Oxford, 1930–1934; B.A. with honors in physiology; M.A., B.M., B.Ch., 1937; University College Hospital Medical School, M.D., 1941.

Employment: Various posts, University College Hospital (UCH); Samaritan Hospital, Marylebone and Hammersmith, Queen Charlotte's Hospital, Radcliffe Infirmary, Oxford, 1939–1945; Elizabeth Garrett Anderson Hospital, 1945–1977; deputy academic head, Obstetric Unit, UCH, 1947–1952; surgeon, Marie Curie Hospital, 1947–1967; consulting obstetrician and gynecologist, Charing Cross Hospital and Elizabeth Garrett Anderson Hospital, 1977–; private practice, London, until 1995.

Married: Sir Brian Warren, a lieutenant in the Royal Army Medical Corps, in 1942.

Josephine Barnes was the first woman president of the British Medical Association, a post she held in 1979–1980. In 1954 she was appointed as the first female consultant gynecologist at Charing Cross Hospital.

Barnes was born in Sheringham, Norfolk. Her father, a Methodist minister, served as an army chaplain in World War I. Her mother was a gifted pianist. In 1921 her mother inherited some money from her grandfather, one of the founders of the Midland Bank. The family settled in Oxford and Barnes's father enrolled as an undergraduate at Oxford University while Barnes went to Oxford High School. At thirteen she decided to train for medicine; five years later, in 1930, she won a scholarship to Lady Margaret Hall, one of only five women reading medicine. Because at the time it was not considered acceptable for women to dissect cadavers in the same room as men, Barnes had to work on her own in another room, going by the dissection manual. She gained a first-class degree in physiology from Oxford and won a Goldschmid scholarship, which enabled her to continue her medical studies at University College, London. After qualifying in 1937, she specialized in obstetrics and gynecology, working at University College Hospital (UCH).

With the outbreak of World War II, many doctors were called up for national service. This gave Barnes an opportunity to obtain a proper post, and from 1939 she worked at the Samaritan Hospital. Because the hospital's location near Marylebone Station was considered dangerous, the entire hospital was moved in one day to Queen Charlotte's in Hammersmith.

In 1942 Barnes married Dr. Brian Warren. A lieutenant in the Royal Army Medical Corps, he went on overseas service; it was not until the end of the war that the couple was able to settle into a home in Chester Square, Belgravia, which they slowly restored from its near derelict condition. Barnes's first child, Penny, was born in 1943, but she enlisted the help of her parents and went back to work two weeks after Penny's birth, as she did for her other two children. She remarked that at one time she employed six people to allow her to work full time so her training would not be wasted.

Barnes delivered many babies during the bombing in London. From 1947, based at UCH, she ran an obstetric flying squad that went out to people's homes and became convinced that it was safer for women to have their babies in hospitals. She was in charge of the steering committee for two government maternity surveys set up between 1948 and 1970. For this, a cohort of babies born in 1948 was followed through their lives to see the effect of premature birth, social status, and other factors on their development.

Barnes was appointed to the Elizabeth Garrett Anderson Hospital for women, initially only temporarily but then as a permanent consultant from 1947. Barnes was part of a successful campaign to prevent the hospital's closure by Prime Minister Margaret Thatcher.

Barnes was elected an honorary fellow of the Royal College of Physicians (1977) and the Royal College of Obstetricians and Gynaecologists (1994). Her reputation as a competent surgeon grew, and she held posts at several hospitals besides running a private practice in London. She enjoyed traveling and used to time her family holidays so that she could participate in gynecological conferences worldwide.

From 1971 to 1973 Barnes was involved with the committee that investigated how well the Abortion Act 1967 was functioning. She was also on Dame Mary Warnock's Committee in 1981; the results of their findings were the basis of the Human Embryology Bill, which defined conditions for experiments on embryos.

Barnes was made a Dame Commander of the Order of the British Empire (DBE) in 1974 and was awarded honorary doctorates by many universities, including Leicester (1980) and Oxford (1990). She was elected an honorary fellow of numerous societies and was invited to give lectures throughout Britain, serving as the Hunterian Orator for the Hunterian Society in 1994.

President of a wide range of organizations, such as the Medical Women's Federation (1966–1967), the National Association of Family Planning Nurses, and the Friends of the Girls' Public Day School Trust and vice-president of the National Union of Townswomen's Guilds (1979–1982), Barnes also published several books, including *Gynaecological Histology* (1948) and *Essentials of Family Planning* (1976), and wrote numerous articles for medical journals.

Bibliography: Barnes, J. Interview on *Woman's Hour*, Radio 4, 14 September 1998; "Dame Josephine Barnes," *Daily Telegraph* (30 December 1999); "Dame Josephine Barnes," *Times* (29 December 1999): 19;

Neustatter, A., "Dame Josephine Barnes," *Guardian* (29 December 1999): 16; *Who's Who, 1997*, London: Adam and Charles Black, 1997.

Barry, James Miranda Steuart
1795–25 July 1865
army doctor, social reformer

Education: Edinburgh University, 1810–1812; Guys Hospital, London, 1813.

Employment: army doctor from June 1813; assistant surgeon and surgeon major, 1827; deputy inspector general, 1851; inspector general, 1858; half pay from July 1859.

In 1812 *James Barry* became, strictly speaking, the first woman in the United Kingdom to qualify as a doctor. Throughout her training and in her career, however, Barry masqueraded as a man.

Barry studied medicine as a young "man" in Edinburgh and qualified as a doctor there. In London she wrote a thesis on hernia of the groin (1811). She studied surgery at Guy's Hospital with Sir Astley Cooper and learned to dress wounds at St. Thomas's Hospital.

After joining the army in June 1813 at Chatham, Barry was sent to Plymouth as a doctor's assistant. In 1816 she was transferred to Cape Colony (Cape Town), where she served as both army doctor and director of the Vaccine Board. She was also personal physician to the governor of Cape Colony, Lord Somerset. In 1819 she was sent to Mauritius for two months to deal with a cholera outbreak. In 1826 Barry performed the first completely successful cesarean section in South Africa and only the second successful one in the Western world.

She returned to England in 1829 to nurse Lord Somerset until he died in 1831, when she was posted to Jamaica. She also worked in St. Helena (1836). Though considered a good and an especially gentle doctor, she upset several people by her outspokenness. Many suspected that Barry was a woman, but no one appears to have made that opinion public during her lifetime.

Barry became principal medical officer in Malta in 1846. In 1855 she went to the Crimea to observe the wartime conditions. Her final posting abroad was to Quebec, a harsh change from the tropical climates to which she was accustomed.

After her discharge from the army, she lived in Marylebone until her death. One Sally Bishop laid her out, and when the army hesitated to pay her dues, Bishop told the army that James Barry was a woman and had even been pregnant. On learning this, the army refused to give Barry a military funeral.

Bibliography: Dictionary of National Biography, vol. I, Oxford: Oxford University Press, 1885; Longford, E., *Eminent Victorian Women*, London: Weidenfeld and Nicholson, 1981; Prasad, R., "Prisoner of Gender," *Guardian* (31 May 1999): 8–9.

Basford, Kathleen
6 September 1916–20 December 1998
botanist, writer

Education: Harrogate Ladies College; art school, Nottingham; evening classes in botany, University of Manchester, M.S. (following a period of full-time research).

Employment: research post, University of Manchester, from 1952; post in Department of Diagnostic Cytology, Christie Cancer Hospital, Manchester, until retirement; freelance research and writing.

Married: Dr. Freddie Basford, in 1936.

Kathleen Basford worked as a botanist; her main area of interest was genetics. After she retired she researched the architectural and cultural significance of the Green Man, a mythical figure whose head sprouted foliage.

Basford was born in Grantham, Lincolnshire. Though she had not studied much biology at school, she took a course in botanical drawing at art school in Nottingham. It was at this time that she met her future husband. The couple had three children and lived in Manchester.

In the late 1940s Basford became interested in the cultivation of fuchsias, experimenting with crosses of different types. She took evening classes in botany at Manchester University and in 1952 wrote a paper for the *Journal of the Fuchsia Society* detailing a cross between a New Zealand and a Mexican fuchsia. Apparently this type of fuchsia had existed 20–30 million years ago, before the continents had separated. The importance of the finding was recognized by the geneticist S. C. Harland, who offered Basford a job in the Botany Department at the University of Manchester. For her M.S., she researched the genetic and morphogenetic effects of radiation, using groundsel as her plant material. With Harland she carried out research on breeding maize in Peru before taking up a post in the Department of Diagnostic Cytology at Christie Cancer Hospital in Manchester, where she stayed until her retirement.

A visit to Fountains Abbey in Yorkshire aroused Basford's interest in the Green Man, who appeared in medieval architecture not just in Britain but also in Turkey, France, and Germany. During her retirement she was able to research the phenomenon and wrote *The Green Man* (1978), in which she theorized that the motif symbolized "the spiritual dimension of nature" and that it had relevance in modern society. She donated her photographs of the Green Man to the charity Common Ground, an organization concerned with the relationship between culture and nature.

Bibliography: Darnley, P., Hon. Secretary, the British Fuchsia Society, personal communication to the author, 13 May 2001; "Fuchsia Research at Manchester University," *The Fuchsia Annual* (1956): 18–23; King, A., and S. Clifford, "Kathleen Basford: The Green Man Lives," *Guardian* (15 January 1999).

Bassi, Laura Maria Catarina
1711–1778
physicist

Education: taught by Dr. Gaetano Tacconi, professor at the College of Medicine; University of Bologna, doctor of philosophy, 1732.

Employment: University of Bologna: lecturer in experimental physics, 1745–1778; professor of physics, 1776–1778.
Married: Dr. Giovanni Giuseppe Veratti, a scientist, in 1738.

In 1776 **Laura Bassi** became the first woman in the world to be appointed as a professor of physics. The length of her career, spanning her entire adult life, was unique for a woman in the eighteenth century.

Born in Bologna, Bassi was the daughter of a lawyer. She was educated at home in a range of subjects and was said to be a brilliant student. She was elected to membership of the Academy of the Institute for Science in March 1732. The archbishop of Bologna, Cardinal Prospero Lambertini, heard about her skill in philosophical argument and invited her to take part in a public debate with her teacher, Gaetano Tacconi, and four other professors on 17 April 1732. She was awarded a doctorate by the University of Bologna the same year. Although the university subsequently employed her, she initially had limited duties and so campaigned for greater responsibility. The allowance she received did at least enable her to continue her studies.

There was some public disapproval of Bassi's marriage in 1738, as people thought it would detract from her role at the university. She went on to have eight children but held lectures at home. Despite her modest salary, she was expected to purchase her own equipment; her salary was eventually raised thanks to the influence of her patrons.

Lambertini continued to use his power to assist Bassi's career even after he became pope in 1740. In 1745, as Pope Benedict XIV, he selected an elite group of twenty-four scientists, the Benedetti, or Benedictines, of the Academy of Science. Again with the help of her supporters, Bassi was able to join this group as its twenty-fifth member.

Throughout her career she was a proponent of Newton's ideas and published papers on physics, hydraulics, mechanics, chemistry, and mathematics. She carried out research on electricity in her own laboratory. The microbiologist Lazzaro Spallanzani "liberalized his education" under her influence;

some of her work confirmed Spallanzani's theories on animal reproduction.

Bassi was appointed to the University of Bologna's chair of experimental physics when she was sixty-five years old, two years before her death.

Bibliography: Alic, M., *Hypatia's Heritage: A History of Women in Science from Antiquity to the Late Nineteenth Century*, London: Women's Press, 1986; Millar, D., et al., *The Cambridge Dictionary of Scientists*, Cambridge: Cambridge University Press, 1996; Cavazza, M., "Und sie fürchtet sich vor niemandem," (Review of Beate Ceranski), *Die Physikerin Laura Bassi (1711–1778)*, Frankfurt/New York: Campus, 1996, available at http://cis.almo.unibo.it/NewsLetter/101997/Nw/bassi.htm; Nies, K. A., "Laura Bassi: A Physicist Supported by the Church," available at www.geocities.com/Athens/Delphi/1836/laura/bassi.html; Ogilvie, M. B., *Women in Science: Antiquity through the Nineteenth Century*, New York: MIT Press, 1986.

Bate, Dorothea Minola Alice
8 November 1879–13 January 1951
geologist

Education: self-educated, working in the British Museum (Natural History).
Employment: freelance geologist; officer in charge of Natural History Museum, Tring, Hertfordshire, 1947–1951.

Dorothea Bate was an authority on the Pleistocene mammals and birds of Mediterranean islands.

Bate became interested in natural history during her childhood in Carmarthenshire, Wales. On moving to London in her teens, she was given permission to work in the bird room at the Natural History Museum and trained herself in anatomy. In 1901 she published her first paper, about a bone cave she had excavated in the Forest of Dean, in the *Geological Magazine*.

Also in 1901 she explored the caves in Cyprus, where she unearthed numerous fossils, including those of a newly discov-

ered pigmy elephant, *Elephas cypriotes*, and a dwarf hippopotamus, *Hippopotamus minutus*. She went on to Crete in 1904 and found the fossil of another pigmy elephant, *E. creticus*. In the Balaeric Islands she uncovered the fossilized remains of *Myotragus*, a specialized antelope. Bate traveled to Gibraltar, Corsica, Sardinia, Malta, and Palestine, writing up her discoveries for each locale.

Under the direction of Professor Dorothy Garrod, Bate worked on the animal remains excavated from the Wady el-Mughara Caves, Mount Carmel. Bate's monograph *The Fossil Fauna of the Wady el-Mughara Caves* (1937) discusses the change in climatic conditions in relation to the changes in the distribution of species in the various layers. She went on to study fossils in Africa, in particular in the Sudan. At sixty-eight she traveled to Rusinga Island, Lake Victoria, to work with Dr. Louis S. B. Leakey. For the last few years of her life she served as officer in charge of the Tring branch of the Natural History Museum.

Bate published over eighty papers, including several on archaeology. She joined the Geological Society in 1915 and was elected a fellow in 1940. The Wollaston Fund honored her with an award for her research in mammalian paleontology.

Bibliography: "Edwards, W. N.," Obituary, *Proceedings Geological Association* 106, 3 (1952): 56–58; "Edwards, W. N.," Obituary, *Annual Report of the Council of the Geological Association* (1952): 106–107.

Beale, Dorothea
21 March 1831–9 November 1906
mathematician, educator

Education: Stratford, Essex; attended lectures at Gresham College and Crosby Hall Literary Institution; Mrs. Bray's School, Paris, 1847–1848; Queen's College, Harley Street, London, 1848–1849.
Employment: Queen's College, Harley Street, London: mathematics tutor, 1849–1854; head teacher, 1854–1856; headmistress, Clergy Daughters' School,

Casterton, Cumbria, 1857; principal, Cheltenham Ladies College, 1858–1906.

From 1858 to 1906 **Dorothea Beale** was principal of Cheltenham Ladies College. In 1885 she founded the first residential training college for women in secondary education, St. Hilda's College in Cheltenham.

Beale was born in London, one of eleven children. Her father was a surgeon, and her mother was from a Huguenot family. Beale had a varied education, finally ending up at Queen's College, Harley Street, London, where she received leaving certificates in mathematics, English, Latin, French, German, and geography. She worked as a tutor, first in mathematics and then in Latin, and was appointed head teacher at Queen's College. Because she felt that the authority of women tutors was being undermined and that students admitted to the college had lower standards of educational achievement than previously, she resigned in 1856.

Her next appointment, as head teacher at Casterton School, was of short duration. Beale was dismayed at conditions in the school (portrayed as Lowood in Charlotte Brontë's novel *Jane Eyre*). The school governors were reluctant to implement the changes she proposed and did not accept her religious beliefs. They dismissed her in December 1857. For a brief time, she lived at home in southwest London, taught locally, and wrote *Student's Text-book of English and General History* (1858). Less than a year after her dismissal from Casterton, Beale was chosen from among fifty candidates to be principal of Cheltenham Ladies College; she remained there for the rest of her life.

When Beale took over as principal, the college had only sixty-nine pupils and its finances were in dire straits. She improved standards, making the college one of the top girls' public schools, where many future leaders were educated. She spurred her students to seek knowledge rather than learn passively, encouraging the young women to be involved in extracurricular activities and inviting prominent scholars to speak at the college. "It is such a great thing for the girls to have things explained by those who have the enthusiasm of original obsessions,"

Beale wrote in 1896 to G. P. Bidder, a marine biologist.

In 1865 she gave evidence to the Endowed Schools Inquiry; the resulting report highlighted the poor standards of teaching in most girls' secondary schools. Seeing the need for training of secondary school teachers, Beale founded St. Hilda's College in Cheltenham. In 1892 she bought Cowley House, Oxford, to be St. Hilda's hall of residence for women. Later this became St. Hilda's College and was accepted as a college of Oxford University.

Beale was president of the Headmistresses' Association from 1895 to 1897 and was involved with other educational groups. She was awarded an honorary LL.D. by Edinburgh University in 1902, only the second woman to be so recognized. She died of cancer in 1906, and her ashes were placed in the Lady Chapel in Gloucester Cathedral.

Bibliography: Cambridge University Library Archives 9227, Box 2 of G. P. Bidder III, letter from D. Beale to G. P. Bidder, 1 September 1896; *Dictionary of National Biography*, Oxford: Oxford University Press, 1912; Johnson, J., librarian, Cheltenham Ladies College, personal communication to the author, 1 February, 2000; Kamm, J., *How Different from Us: A Biography of Miss Buss and Miss Beale*, London: Bodley Head, 1958.

Becker, Lydia Ernestine
24 February 1827–18 July 1890
botanist, campaigner for women's suffrage

Education: boarding school, Everton, Liverpool.

Lydia Becker was a keen botanist who was committed to scientific education for women and women's suffrage.

Becker was born in central Manchester, the eldest of fifteen children. By the age of two, she knew her alphabet and showed great promise. She soon became interested in the natural sciences, particularly botany, and sent specimens to Charles Darwin. In

1864 she published *Botany for Novices: A Short Outline of the Natural System of the Classification of Plants*, illustrating it herself with engravings. In 1865 she was awarded the Royal Horticultural Society's Gold Medal for the best collection of wild plants in a year.

In 1867 Becker founded the Manchester Ladies' Literary Society, which was intended for women who were interested in science and literature. They met at the Royal Institute in Mosley Street. Despite support from Charles Darwin, who sent a paper to be read at the society, the group did not flourish.

She became involved in women's suffrage in October 1866, when she went to a meeting of the Social Science Association at which a paper on the subject was read. In 1867 she became secretary of the Manchester Women's Suffrage Society and in 1868 spoke on women's suffrage at the Free Trade Hall in Manchester, the first woman in the area to do so. She was a member of the British Association for the Advancement of Science, and at its annual meeting in 1868 gave a talk "On Some Supposed Differences in the Minds of Men and Women with Regard to Educational Necessities," which caused quite a stir and made it clear she was committed to the cause of women's suffrage. From 1870 to 1890 she was editor of the *Women's Suffrage Journal*, and during this time she worked for the National Society for Women's Suffrage, acting as its representative at meetings around the country.

In 1870 Becker was one of the first women elected to serve on a school board in Manchester. She always retained her interest in botany and sometimes gave botanical lectures. Throughout her life she suffered from chronic back problems due to rheumatoid arthritis and osteoarthritis. She died of diphtheria in Geneva.

Bibliography: Desmond, R., *Dictionary of British and Irish Botanists and Horticulturalists, Including Plant Collectors and Botanical Artists*, London: Taylor and Francis, 1977; *Dictionary of National Biography*, vol. 1, Oxford: Oxford University Press, 1912; Kelly, A., *Lydia Becker and the Cause*, Lancaster: Centre for North-west Regional Studies, University of Lancaster, 1992; Uglow, J. S., ed., *The Macmillan Dictionary of Women's Biography,* second edition, London: Macmillan, 1991; *Women's Suffrage Journal* (1 August 1874): 112–113; *Women's Suffrage Journal* (2 November 1874): 148.

Beeton, Isabella Mary née Mayson
12 March 1836–5 February 1865
home economics writer

Education: schools in Islington and Heidelberg.
Employment: self-employment as a writer.
Married: Samuel Orchart Beeton, on 10 July 1856.

In 1861 **Isabella Beeton** compiled the *Book of Household Management*, a detailed and comprehensive manual covering all aspects of home economics for the general reader.

Beeton spent much of her childhood at the Epsom race course, as her stepfather was clerk of the course. She went to a dame's private school in Islington and then to a school in Heidelberg, Germany, where she learned French, German, piano, and cookery. She was better educated than most women of her time.

Soon after her marriage, she started writing articles on fashion and domestic subjects for the *Englishwoman's Domestic Magazine*, started in 1852 by her husband, Samuel Beeton, who also had the idea of the *Book of Household Management*. Isabella Beeton compiled but did not write the entire book, which initially appeared in parts between 1859 and 1861. The book was published as a single 1,112-page volume in October 1861. Among other things it clearly set out ways of both managing the household economy and cooking nutritious food. As the book was sold in parts, it was easily affordable, and it had a considerable influence on home economy for many years. The updated *Book of Household Management* continues to sell.

Beeton died at twenty-nine of puerperal fever contracted after the birth of her fourth child.

Bibliography: Foreman, A., "Delia Smith and Mrs. Beeton (1837–1865)," *Saturday Express* (22 November 1997): 7; Freeman, S., *Isabella and Sam*, London: Victor Gollancz, 1977; Garner, C., "Mrs. Beeton's Recipe for Happiness Sold for £8,600," *Independent* (11 April 1997); "Pass Notes," No. 1338, *Guardian* (1 February 1999): 3; Sotheby's, *Printed Books and Maps,* Catalogue entry 294, 10 and 11 April 1997; Wintle, J., *Makers of Nineteenth Century Culture, 1800–1914,* London: Routledge and Kegan Paul, 1982.

Bell, Gertrude Margaret Lowthian
14 July 1868–12 July 1926
archaeologist, diplomat

Education: at home; Queen's College, Harley Street, London; Lady Margaret Hall, Oxford, 1886–1889; modern history.

Employment: war work, France, 1914–1915; work with Colonel T. E. Lawrence, Cairo, 1915–1916; oriental secretary, Basrah, Iraq, 1916; director of archaeology, National Museum of Antiquities, Baghdad, 1923–1926.

An archaeologist, *Gertrude Bell* was Sir Percy Cox's oriental secretary when Iraq was established as a new Arab state in 1916.

Bell was born at Washington Hall, County Durham. Her father, Sir Hugh Bell, was an ironmaster and steel manufacturer. She was taught at home initially but later went to Queen's College, where her mother's friend was principal. At Lady Margaret Hall, Oxford, she became the first woman to receive a first-class honors degree in modern history.

After graduating, she traveled in Europe. She studied Persian, and published *Safar Nameh: Persian Pictures—A Book of Travel* (1894) and translated *Poems from the Divan of Hafiz* from Persian to English (1897). On her return to England, she learned Arabic, and in 1899 she went to live in Jerusalem, where she continued studying Arabic. Throughout her travels she wrote detailed letters to family and friends; many of these letters are held in the special collections of the Robin-

Gertrude Margaret Lowthian Bell (Corbis)

son Library at the University of Newcastle upon Tyne.

Bell was an avid climber of the Alps. Her most remarkable ascent was on the Finsteraarhorn in the Bernese Oberland from 31 July to 2 August 1902. She and her guides were out on the mountain for fifty-seven hours, fifty-three of them attached to their ropes. Although the party did not reach the summit, the climb was recorded as an outstanding achievement.

Bell continued to travel in the Middle East and India. She wrote about Syria in *The Desert and the Sown* (1907) and, with Sir William Ramsey, about the churches and ruins in Lycaonia in *The Thousand and One Churches* (1909).

In 1914 Bell was sent to France to help organize a special branch to trace the missing and wounded. She went to Cairo in 1915 and worked with Colonel T. E. Lawrence ("Lawrence of Arabia") collecting and summarizing information about the tribes and sheikhs of North Africa. After a short time in Delhi, she went to Baghdad in 1916 to work for Sir Percy Cox, using her knowledge of the local area to sort out information for him. She also edited *Al Arab*, an Arabic newspaper published by the British administration. She was made a commander of the British Empire (CBE) in 1917 and in 1919 took part in the Allied conference in Paris before the signing of the peace treaties that made Iraq and Palestine mandated territory run by the British.

Bell pushed hard to establish the National Museum of Antiquities in Baghdad, and from 1923 she was its director of archaeology. She worked with Sir Leonard Woolley on the excavation of Ur. In 1926 she died in Baghdad and was given a state funeral.

Bibliography: Bell, G., *The Letters of Gertrude Bell,* London: Penguin Books, 1953; Bozman, E. F., ed., *Everyman's Encyclopaedia,* vol. 2, fourth edition, London: Dent, 1958; "Gertrude Bell Project Goes On-line," University of Newcastle upon Tyne *Alumni Association News* (July 1999): 5 available at: www.gerty. ncl.ac.uk/home/index. htm; Kamm, J., *Daughter of the Desert: The Story of Gertrude Bell,* London: Bodley Head, 1956.

Bennett, Isobel Ada
9 July 1909–
marine biologist

Education: Somerville House, Brisbane, 1923–1925.
Employment: secretary, patent attorney's office, Brisbane; secretary, Associated Board of the Royal Schools of Music, Sydney; research assistant, Department of Zoology, University of Sydney, 1932–1971; honorary research associate, Australian Museum, 1971–.

Isobel Bennett became a prominent marine biologist, renowned in her native Australia and beyond, despite her lack of academic degrees.

Bennett was the eldest of four children, born in Brisbane, Australia. After her mother's death, her father remarried, and Bennett's stepmother insisted that she receive a good education. But she left school at the age of sixteen without having been taught science and, after completing a secretarial course, took a job in an office in Brisbane. She then moved to Sydney with her family, where she worked for four years in the office of the Associated Board of the Royal Schools of Music before it was closed because of the depression.

In 1932, with one of her sisters, Bennett took a cruise to Norfolk Island, where by chance she met Professor W. J. Dakin. He invited her to assist him with his research on whaling, and she agreed. He later offered her a temporary position as his general assistant in the Department of Zoology at the University of Sydney. Her duties included research and secretarial work, proofreading, and, more unusual, crewing the research vessel owned by the university. Under Dakin's supervision and through her own efforts, Bennett learned a range of scientific techniques and expanded her knowledge. While Dakin was on sabbatical in 1935, she attended first-year zoology practical classes, the only formal course she took in her whole professional life. On the final examination she earned a mark of 98 percent, the highest ever awarded. Bennett carried out other valuable work at this time, cataloguing the department library and demonstrating to students.

In 1942 Dakin went to Canberra to become technical director of camouflage at the Department of Home Security; Bennett accompanied him as his research assistant. Back in Sydney after the war, Dakin asked her to undertake surveying work on the coastline of New South Wales. She worked with Elizabeth Pope, a zoologist, and Helen Newton Turner, a statistician, cataloguing animal species. For one part of the project, Dakin and his wife joined them on the coast. The paper that resulted from this work was the basis of Dakin's important book *Australian Seashores* (1952). On Dakin's retirement in 1948, Bennett continued to help him with his work. The professors who succeeded Dakin had very different research interests but allowed her to continue in marine biology for some of her time.

In 1958 she began to lead the annual biology excursions to the Great Barrier Reef, since she was the only member of staff who knew the area well. Her first scientific paper as sole author was published in 1958. She wrote *The Fringe of the Sea* (1967), her first book, while she was still employed full time at the university.

In the course of her work, Bennett undertook many research expeditions, often as one of few women, to remote and inhospitable destinations. She traveled four times to Macquarie Island in the Antarctic, which she described in *Shores of Macquarie Island* (1971). In 1963 she sailed on Stanford University's research vessel and was made a temporary associate professor for the duration of the trip. She lectured to students on the voyage, and acted as "dean of women." She also traveled abroad to attend scientific conferences and give lectures.

In 1962 Bennett was awarded an honorary master of science degree by the University of Sydney, the first it had ever given. She was also awarded an honorary D.Sc. from the University of New South Wales. Despite her growing reputation and tireless efforts in all aspects of the department's work, she was not considered an academic. Her pay was poor in relation to her achievements, and when she retired in 1971 she was still officially classified only as a technical officer. After retirement she continued to carry out research, lecture, and travel. Her books, including *The Great Barrier Reef* (1971), brought her wide recognition.

She served as a councillor on the Great Barrier Reef Committee for a number of years and became one of its first honorary life members. She was only the second woman to be honored with the Mueller Medal of the Australia and New Zealand Association for the Advancement of Science, in 1982. Several species of marine animal and one coral reef were named after her, and she was awarded the Order of Australia in 1984.

Bibliography: Allen, N., "Australian Women in Science: Two Unorthodox Careers [Isobel Bennett and Helen Newton Turner]," *Women's Studies International Forum* 15, no. 5/6 (1992): 551–562; *Who's Who in Australasia and the Far East*, second edition, Cambridge: Melrose Press, 1991.

Bentham, Ethel
?–19 January 1931
doctor, specialist in child health

Education: Alexandra School and College, Dublin; London School of Medicine for Women, 1890–1894; Rotunda Hospital in Dublin; M.D., University of Brussels, 1895.
Employment: general practitioner, Newcastle upon Tyne and Gateshead; general practitioner, North Kensington; organizer and consultant medical officer, Margaret O. MacDonald Memorial Clinic for Children under School Age.

Ethel Bentham was a pioneer in working to provide for the needs of preschool children and the health of their mothers.

Bentham was a member of the Metropolitan Asylums Board. After World War I she became a justice of the peace and a member of the Children's Court, acting under the Lunacy and Mental Deficiency Acts. She was a member of Kensington Borough Council for thirteen years and was active in the women's suffrage campaign. She stood as Labour Party candidate in East Islington in 1922 and was eventually successful in 1929.

Bibliography: Crawford, A., et al., eds., *The Europa Biographical Dictionary of British Women: Over a Thousand Notable Women from Britain's Past*, London: Europa Publications, 1923; *Who Was Who, 1929–1940*, London: Adam and Charles Black, 1947.

Bidder, Anna McClean
4 May 1903–1 October 2001
zoologist

Education: at home; Pearse Girls' School, Cambridge, 1915–1921; University College, London, 1921–1922; Newnham College, Cambridge, 1922–1926, 1928–1931; Ph.D., 1934; University of Basel, winter sessions, 1926–1928.
Employment: teaching, Zoology Department, Cambridge University, 1929–1965; curator of mollusks, Zoology Department, Cambridge University, 1963–1970.

Anna McClean Bidder (Julia Hedgecoe)

Anna Bidder, a marine biologist, specialized in squids, cuttlefish, and the pearly nautilus. She was the cofounder and from 1965 to 1970 the first president of Lucy Cavendish College, Cambridge.

Bidder was born in Cambridge, the younger of two daughters. Her father, George Parker Bidder III, was a well-known zoologist and an expert on sponges; her mother, Marion Greenwood Bidder, a physiologist, organized the Balfour Laboratory in Cambridge until she married.

Bidder went to lectures in mathematics and zoology at University College, London, and from there entered Newnham College, Cambridge, where she read mathematics, physics, and zoology, concentrating on marine zoology. At the University of Basel, Switzerland, she did research on yolk absorption in the squid, *Loligo;* her report on the results, coauthored with A. D. Portmann, appeared in the *Quarterly Journal of Microscopical Science* in 1928.

During the summers of 1927 and 1929 and in September 1930, Bidder worked at the Marine Laboratory, Plymouth, rearing squid larvae and investigating ciliary currents in the squid gut. In the summers of 1928 and 1930, she occupied the Cambridge table at the Stazione Zoologica in Naples. Her father had conducted much of his research on sponges there and owned a hotel in Naples. During April 1929 she did marine fieldwork at Banyuls-sur-Mer. She was based at Newnham College and in 1934 completed her Ph.D. thesis, "The Functional Morphology of the Cephalopod Digestive System."

Bidder taught physiology and botany at Newnham and Girton Colleges and did research on cephalopods, publishing several articles and contributing to the volume on cephalopods in Pierre P. Grassé's *Traité de zoologie* (1989). At the annual meeting of the British Association for the Advancement of Science in 1933, Bidder gave a talk on the alimentary canal of the cephalopod the day after her father, who was president of the zoology section, gave his address. Bidder herself became president of the zoology section in 1973.

Bidder was the first president of Lucy Cavendish College and gave the college much of the Bidder family silver, her collection of children's books, her house in Cavendish Avenue (later converted into flats), and £80,000 as a nucleus to establish the Greenwood Bidder Research Fellowship. Bidder was elected a fellow of the Linnean Society in 1928 and made an honorary fellow in 1991.

Anna joined the Society of Friends in the 1920s as a reaction to the horrors of World War I. She was a member of several Quaker committees until her death 1 October 2001.

Bibliography: Davies, K., archivist, Lucy Cavendish College, Cambridge, personal communication to the author, July 2000; Bidder, Anna, personal communication to the author via Dr. Joan Mason (History and Philosophy of Science Department, University of Cambridge), 1999; Cambridge University Library Archives, Add MS9227, Box 3 and Box 18, accessed by the author December 1997; "Down Your Street," (Cambridge) *Weekly News* (18 September 1986): 6–7; Heaton, M., "A Tale That Is Told," *Oc-*

casional Local Publications No. 5, City of Bradford Metropolitan Council, Libraries Division, Local Studies Department, 1983.

Bidder, Marion née Greenwood
24 August 1862–25 September 1932
physiologist

Education: Bradford Girls' Grammar School; Girton College, Cambridge, 1879–1883; postgraduate student, 1883–1884.

Employment: Lecturer in physiology, Balfour Laboratory, University of Cambridge, 1885–1887; head of the laboratory, 1890–1899; lecturer and director of studies in biology for Newnham and Girton Colleges, Cambridge, 1888–1899; examiner in cookery, Gloucestershire School of Cookery and Domestic Economy.

Married: Dr. George Parker Bidder III, on 8 June 1899.

From 1890 to 1899 **Marion Greenwood Bidder** was in charge of the Balfour Laboratory in Cambridge, where the Newnham College students had their practical classes in biology. She was one of the first women at Cambridge to do independent research. In 1895 she was the first woman to give her own paper at a meeting of the Royal Society.

Bidder was born at Myton, Hull, where her father was a shipping agent and a Baptist lay preacher. The family moved to Oxenhope, near Haworth, Yorkshire, in 1869, because Marion's uncles owned Brook's Meeting Worsted Mill, established there by the Greenwood family in 1761. She went to Bradford Girls' Grammar School, and when she was seventeen won a school scholarship to Girton College, winning honors in the natural sciences.

She held a Bathurst research studentship from Newnham College and in 1889 was awarded the Gamble Prize by Girton College for her dissertation. A demonstrator in physiology, she also pursued her own research under the direction of Michael Foster. Her papers on the gastric glands of the pig, the action of nicotine on certain invertebrates, and the physiology of protozoa appeared in the *Journal of Physiology.* From

1888 she lived at Newnham College, where she was both lecturer and director of studies in biology and tutor for the women physiology students. She also tutored and lectured at Girton College. Bidder took her responsibilities for the Newnham students very seriously, telling them in her introductory talk how important it was for science students to maintain an interest in literature and to present clear and accurate written work.

When she married George Parker Bidder in 1899, she gave up her post at the Balfour Laboratory and indeed her professional work. It took four people to replace her. Initially the Bidders lived in Plymouth while her husband was doing research on sponges at the laboratory of the Marine Biological Association; in 1902 they moved back to Cambridge, living at Cavendish Corner, Hills Road, from then on.

Bidder was keen on cooking and with Florence Baddeley wrote *Domestic Economy in Theory and Practice* (1901), intended as a textbook for teachers and students. Bidder wrote the part that dealt with theoretical and scientific aspects of the subject, whereas Baddeley wrote about the practice and teaching of domestic economy. The foreword stated that "the scientific portion of the book comes from the pen of an author who has lived in the clear atmosphere of scientific truth."

The Bidders had two children, Caroline, born in 1900, and Anna, born in 1903. George Bidder developed tuberculosis and beginning in 1905 had to stay in a sanatorium for some time and then live quietly for a few years thereafter. Although he eventually made a complete recovery, remaining out of circulation at what should have been his most active time in terms of his zoological career was unfortunate. He did keep his mind engaged, but he developed the habit of getting up late and working into the small hours of the morning, which was often difficult for the rest of the family.

Bidder was president of the Cambridge Women's Liberal Association and encouraged women to become members of town and county councils. She was a Poor Law guardian and vice-chairman of the Cambridgeshire Voluntary Association for Mental Welfare. For eighteen years, she was a governor of Homerton Teacher Training College in Cambridge, chair of trustees from 1925, and a governor of Girton College from 1924 to 1932. She died of tuberculosis.

Bibliography: Bidder, Anna, personal communication with author via Dr. Joan Mason (History and Philosophy of Science Department, University of Cambridge), 1999; Cambridge University Library Archives, Add MS9227, Box 3, accessed by the author December, 1997; Greenwood, M. "Address to Students," 1888, Newnham College Archives, in M. Greenwood's papers; Hardy, W. B., "Mrs G. P. Bidder," *Nature* 130, 3288 (1932): 689; Heaton, M., "A Tale That Is Told," *Occasional Local Publications No. 5*, City of Bradford Metropolitan Council, Libraries Division, Local Studies Department, 1983; *Newnham College Register, 1871–1923*, vol. 1, Cambridge: Newnham College, 1963; "Noted Student at Cambridge," *Keighley News* (1 October 1932).

Biheron, Marie-Catherine
1719–1786
anatomist

Education: studied illustration.
Employment: freelance anatomist and modeler; teacher.

The anatomist *Marie-Catherine Biheron* became well known for the wax models she produced and exhibited.

Biheron was born in France, an apothecary's daughter. She studied illustration under Madeleine Basseport, who from 1735 to 1780 was illustrator at the Jardin Royal des Herbes Médicinales and encouraged her to begin modeling in wax. Wax anatomical models were used at this time for medical teaching, particularly in gynecology. Biheron became highly skilled, her work acknowledged as extremely lifelike. In 1759 she was invited to present her work to the academics at the French court.

In 1770 she demonstrated her working model of a pregnant woman in different stages of labor to the Académie Royale des Sciences. It was found to be invaluable for teaching students about difficult births. As late as 1830 the academy still considered Biheron's models to be the best of their kind. Indeed they were famous throughout Europe: She displayed them to the crown prince of Sweden, and Catherine the Great acquired a number of works for the St. Petersburg Academy of Sciences.

Despite her renown, Biheron was not considered part of the official medical establishment. She earned her living by exhibiting her models once a week for anyone who wanted to pay to see them and teaching students at home. This latter activity was not welcomed by Parisian doctors, who saw her as a rival. The bodies she required to make her models were said to be stolen from the army by people she hired, presumably because she was not in a position to obtain them through official channels. She was eventually forced to travel to London to look for work, without success.

Bibliography: Ogilvie, M. B., *Women in Science: Antiquity through the Nineteenth Century*, New York: MIT Press, 1986; Schiebinger, L., *The Mind Has No Sex?* Cambridge: Harvard University Press, 1991.

Bird, Isabella Lucy
(Mrs. Bishop)
15 October 1832–October 1904
geographer, explorer, writer

Education: privately at home; medicine in London (from 1886).
Employment: self-employed writer.
Married: Dr. John Bishop, on 8 March 1881. He died on 6 March 1886.

In 1892 *Isabella Bird* became the first woman to be elected a fellow of the Royal Geographic Society.

Bird was born at Boroughbridge Hall, Yorkshire, the daughter of a clergyman. From the age of twenty-two, she traveled in North America, followed by eight years in Asia. She lived in Edinburgh in 1860 then moved to Tobermory on Mull to look after a sister.

At forty-nine she married Dr. John Bishop, who had tended her sister. When he died, she decided to train as a doctor. Bird went to India as a medical missionary, founding two hospitals, one in the Punjab and one in Kashmir. From 1894 to 1897 she traveled alone over 8,000 miles in China and eventually set up three hospitals there. In 1901 she made a 1,000-mile trip to Morocco, crossing the Atlas Mountains. An avid photographer and microscopist, Bird wrote numerous articles and books, ranging from *An Englishwoman in America* (1856) to *Pictures from China* (1900). She was an honorary member of the Oriental Society of Pekin.

Bibliography: Archives of the Royal Geographical Society, RGS Correspondence Block, 1881–1910; Barr, P., *A Curious Life for a Lady,* London: Martin, Secker, and Warburg, 1985; *Who Was Who, 1897–1916,* London: Adam and Charles Black, 1920.

Ann Bishop (Godfrey Argent Studio)

Bishop, Ann
19 December 1899–7 May 1990
protozoologist, parasitologist

Education: Fielden School, Manchester, 1909–1912; Manchester High School for Girls, 1912–1918; Manchester University, B.S. with honors, 1921; M.S., 1922; D.Sc., 1932; Cambridge University, Ph.D., 1926; D.Sc., 1941.

Employment: part-time lecturer, Zoology Department, University of Cambridge; Molteno Institute of Parasitology, Cambridge (Medical Research Council): staff member, 1942–1948; director, 1948–1964.

Ann Bishop was a leading protozoologist and parasitologist. Her most important work was investigating the development of drug resistance in the parasites that cause malaria.

Ann Bishop was home-schooled until she was seven, when she went to a small private school. From 1909 to 1912 she attended Fielden School, an experimental school where much of the work was project-based. Her father, a furniture maker, deciding she was capable of going to university, transferred her to Manchester High School for Girls so that she would receive a more conventional education.

Bishop considered studying history, but at that time the only posts available for women history graduates were in teaching, so instead she opted for science, which seemed to offer more career options. As she had not studied physics at school, she had to enroll for a general B.S. rather than an honors degree in chemistry. In her first year she studied chemistry, botany, and zoology. She had developed an interest in biology through reading about the work of Charles Darwin, and she found zoology the most absorbing of her three subjects. She did so well that she was able to transfer to the Honors School of Zoology for her final two years. She was awarded the John Dalton Natural History Prize at the end of her second year.

Bishop turned her attention to protozoa and collected samples from the ponds in the Cheshire countryside. She was allowed bench space at Manchester so that she could study and identify them. Professor S. J. Hickson at Manchester asked her to stay on as an honorary research fellow after she graduated. Besides helping with the zoology classes, she cultivated the ciliate *Spirostomum ambiguum,* the subject of her M.S. thesis.

Bishop was determined to find a university post where she could do research. She was given an unofficial part-time teaching post in the Zoology Department at Cambridge, which was, like most departments at that time, male dominated. At tea the men sat at a table while she and the only other woman, Sidnie Manton, perched on the first-aid box—happy at least to be allowed in the same room.

Bishop continued her research on *Spirostomum,* gaining a Ph.D. in 1926. Clifford Dobell, a protozoologist with the Medical Research Council at Mount Vernon, Hampstead, took an interest in her work, and she acted as his scientific assistant for three years, giving her a thorough grounding in technique.

In 1929 she was awarded a Beit Memorial Fellowship, which she held at the Molteno Institute in Cambridge. She remained there for the rest of her working life. She used the culture techniques she had learned from Dobell to culture various protozoa and published several papers detailing her discoveries, which she presented for her D.Sc. from Manchester University. In 1941 she received a D.Sc. in title only from Cambridge for her papers on flagellates and protozoa (at that time women were barred from earning official Cambridge degrees).

Bishop's next challenge involved the chemotherapy of malaria and the biology of malarial parasites. In World War II the Japanese captured the Dutch West Indies. This area was the source of quinine used in antimalarial treatment, so an alternative chemical was needed. With three different coworkers, Bishop worked on the development of resistance with the drugs pamaquin, atebrin, and paludrine in chicks infected with *Plasmodium gallinaceum.* Paludrine stimulated resistance in the parasite, as reports of using the drug on humans in Malaya confirmed.

In the 1950s a parasitology group led by Bishop was founded within the Institute of Biology. Because the group had limited funding, Bishop used to pass the hat—in the form of a pudding basin—after every meeting. Eventually it was decided that a separate parasitology society was needed, and in 1960 the British Society for Parasitology was founded with Bishop as chair. Bishop was asked to be president of the Institute of Biology in the 1960s but felt unsuited to the public role of the office. (By 2001 the Chartered Institute of Biology still had not had a woman president.)

Bishop was elected a fellow of the Royal Society in 1959 on the basis of her thorough research in several areas. When she retired in 1967, Bishop was made a life fellow of Girton College, where she had lived since 1932. She was on the college council several times and a college governor, and was remembered for her quirky habit of wearing a hat to breakfast, since her room was a long way from the dining hall, and after breakfast she would set off for the three-mile walk to the Molteno Institute. A memorial plaque to Bishop in the chapel of Girton College is inscribed with the phrase *Felix qui potuit rerum cognoscere causas,* "Happy is the one who has been able to get to know the causes of things."

Bibliography: Girton College Register, 1869–1946, vol. 1. Cambridge: Girton College, 1948; Goodwin, L. G., and K. Vickerman, "Ann Bishop, 19 December 1899–7 May 1990," *Biographical Memoirs of Fellows of the Royal Society* 38 (1992); *Who Was Who, 1981–1990,* London: Adam and Charles Black, 1991.

Blackburn, Kathleen Bever
23 February 1892–20 August 1968
botanist

Education: Bedford College, London, 1910–1914 and 1915–1916; B.S. with honors, 1913; M.S., 1916; D.Sc., 1924.
Employment: lecturer in botany, Southlands Training College, Battersea, 1914–1918; Armstrong College, Newcastle-upon-Tyne

(now Newcastle University): lecturer, 1918–1947; reader in cytology from 1947.

Kathleen Blackburn was a pioneer in the teaching of practical plant cytology.

Blackburn's most important research was in collaboration with Professor Heslop Harrison when she was a lecturer at Armstrong College. Harrison and Blackburn researched the cytotaxonomy of the Salicaceae (willows) and of the genus *Rosa;* they were also the first to record sex chromosomes in flowering plants. Later Blackburn became interested in pollen analysis. She was awarded a D.Sc. from London University in 1924.

Blackburn was a council member of the Natural History Society of Northumbria, 1938–1957; a member of the Hancock Museum Management committee, 1945–1957; and president of the Northern Naturalists Union in 1935.

Bibliography: Blackburn, Kathleen, archives, Hancock Museum, Newcastle upon Tyne, accessed by author in 1986; Desmond, R., *Dictionary of British and Irish Botanists and Horticulturalists, Including Plant Collectors and Botanical Artists,* London: Taylor and Francis, 1977; Dyer, L., archives assistant, Royal Holloway/Bedford College, University of London, personal communication to the author, January 2000; Valentine, D. H., "Kathleen Bever Blackburn," *Watsonia* 8 (1970): 69–74.

Blackburne, Anna
1726–30 December 1793
naturalist, collector

Anna Blackburne built up a significant collection of natural specimens from a number of countries. Several species were named in her honor.

Blackburne was born near Warrington, near Manchester (now in Cheshire), one of nine children, the daughter of a wealthy landowner. Her father established an extensive collection of plants at the family home, Orford Hall. When her mother died, Blackburne assumed the role of lady of the manor.

Blackburne began her own collection, obtaining specimens from a number of sources. Her brother, who lived in North America, was able to supply her with birds and insects. She was also in contact with several scientists, including the Swedish taxonomist Linnaeus, to whom she sent some of her North American specimens for identification. One of Linnaeus's students, Johann Fabricus, visited Blackburne in order to study her collection of insects and named a beetle after her *(Scarabaeus blackburnii,* now *Geotrupes blackburnii).* Blackburne's North American specimens, particularly the birds, were also of great interest to the naturalist Thomas Pennant, who was able to use them as the basis of some of the descriptions in his *Arctic Zoology.* Pennant named the Blackburnian warbler, *Dendroica fusca,* in her honor.

The German naturalist Johann Forster, a tutor in natural sciences at Warrington Academy from 1767 to 1770, taught Blackburne entomology. He named a genus of plants in honor of Blackburne and her father *(Blackburnia,* specifically *Blackburnia pinnata,* reclassified under a different genus as *Zanthoxylum blackburnia).* Peter Pallas, another German naturalist, had traveled widely in Siberia and exchanged many specimens, particularly birds, minerals, and plants, with Blackburne.

Blackburne lived at Orford Hall until her father died in 1786. She then had a house, Fairfield, built for her nearby, which included a room designed to accommodate her collection. Her health deteriorated in her later years, and she was unable to complete her plan to arrange the garden according to Linneaus's classification. Following her death in 1793, her nephew inherited her collection. By the early 1900s it had been dispersed.

Bibliography: Dictionary of National Biography, vol. 2, Oxford: Oxford University Press, 1885–1886; Wystrach, V. P., "Anna Blackburne (1726–1793)—a Neglected Patroness of Natural History," *Journal of the Society for Bibliography Natural History* 8, 2 (1977): 148–168.

Blackwell, Elizabeth
3 February 1821–31 May 1910
doctor

Education: private schools in Bristol and New York; medicine at the Geneva Medical School (now Hobart and William Smith Colleges) of Western New York; M.D., 1849; La Maternité and Hotel Dieu, Paris; St. Bartholemew's Hospital, London.

Employment: teacher, Kentucky and North and South Carolina; New York Infirmary for Women and Children, from 1853; Women's Medical College, 1868; hospitals in London and Hastings from 1869; professor of gynecology, London School of Medicine for Women, 1875–1907.

Elizabeth Blackwell was a pioneer in medical training for women. She was the first woman to qualify as a doctor in the United States and the first woman to be entered on the Medical Register in Britain.

Blackwell began her education in her birthplace of Bristol. Her family emigrated to New York when she was eleven, and she completed her schooling there. After a succession of teaching posts, she decided she would rather pursue a career in medicine. She applied to the Geneva Medical School in New York and was accepted because her application was assumed to be a joke. She was nevertheless allowed to take up her place and graduated in 1849.

Blackwell then studied in Paris and London, returning to New York in 1851. Not permitted to practice medicine, she began lecturing. In 1853 she set up a dispensary that became the New York Infirmary for Indigent Women and Children (later the New York Infirmary). She planned to establish a medical school but was prevented from doing so by the Civil War; instead she traveled to Europe to lecture on the opportunities for women in medicine. She was admitted to the Medical Register in Britain in 1859 and subsequently returned to the United States. She was able to set up a medical school attached to the hospital she had founded in New York.

In 1869 Blackwell traveled back to London and began to practice medicine. She

Elizabeth Blackwell (Museum of the City of New York/Archive Photos)

was involved in the establishment of the National Health Society of London and the London School of Medicine for Women, where she was professor of gynecology for over thirty years. After retiring from her post, she moved to Scotland.

During her lifetime she published a number of works, including *The Physical Education of Girls* (1852) and *Pioneer Work in Opening the Medical Profession to Women* (1895).

Bibliography: Guthrie, D., *A History of Medicine,* London: Nelson, 1945; Millar, D., et al., *The Cambridge Dictionary of Scientists,* Cambridge: Cambridge University Press, 1996; *Who Was Who, 1897–1915,* London: Adam and Charles Black, 1920.

Blackwood, Margaret
26 April 1909–1986
geneticist

Education: Melbourne Church of England Girls' Grammar School; Melbourne University, B.S., 1937; M.S., 1941; University of Cambridge, 1948–1951, Ph.D.

Employment: teacher in Melbourne schools; Women's Australian Auxiliary Airforce from 1941; promoted to position of wing officer, 1948; Botany Department, University of Melbourne, 1952–1974: lecturer, senior lecturer, reader.

Margaret Blackwood pioneered research in cytogenetics in Australia.

A grammar school teacher inspired Blackwood to become a botanist and geneticist. Because she had to support herself while she studied for her degree, she taught in girls' schools around Melbourne. In 1937 she won a scholarship for postgraduate work to examine dieback in *Pinus radiata* and taught herself the techniques of cytogenetics. She was beginning to establish herself as a scientist when she suddenly decided to enlist in the Women's Australian Auxiliary Airforce. When she was discharged, she went back to the Botany Department at the University of Melbourne, but her professor made it clear that she would have to take further training overseas. In 1948 she went to Cambridge and worked toward her doctorate on the B chromosomes of maize. Upon her return to Melbourne, she was appointed to a permanent lectureship. She published only five papers between 1953 to 1968 because of the heavy teaching load she had as the only geneticist in the department. She was made a Member of the Order of the British Empire (MBE). The Margaret Blackwood collection is at the University of Melbourne Archives in Australia.

Bibliography: Cary, J., "Margaret Blackwood (1909–1986)," *Australasian Science* (April 1999): 46; *Who's Who in Australia,* Melbourne: Herald and Weekly Times, 1971.

Blagg, Mary Adela
17 May 1858–14 April 1944
astronomer

Education: at home; private boarding school, London.

Mary Blagg was an amateur astronomer who collated an important list of lunar for-

mations. She also studied variable stars and was joint author of a number of papers on the subject.

Blagg, the eldest daughter of a solicitor, was born in Staffordshire in central England. After leaving school, she returned home and did volunteer community work. For mental stimulation, she read her brother's schoolbooks on mathematics and developed skills that proved useful in her later astronomical work.

After attending university extension astronomy lectures in Cheadle by J. A. Hardcastle, Blagg began to study astronomy. She was particularly interested in lunar formations, which at that time were given different names by different astronomers. In 1907 she was asked to collate these names by an international committee set up to tackle the issue. Her list was published by the International Association of Academies in 1913. A definitive list, which subsequently became the standard reference on the names of lunar formations, was prepared by a subcommittee of the International Astronomical Union's Lunar Commission, to which Blagg had been appointed in 1920.

As well as this and other astronomical work, Blagg continued with community activities, such as caring for Belgian refugee children in World War I. Her other main astronomical interest at this time was variable stars. She volunteered to assist the astronomer H. H. Turner in interpreting the data on variable stars in a manuscript by Joseph Baxendell. She and Turner jointly authored ten papers on their findings (*Monthly Records* 73–78, 1912–1918).

Blagg was a member of the British Astronomical Association and was elected to the Royal Astronomical Society in 1915. The International Lunar Committee named a small lunar crater after her following her death in 1944.

Bibliography: Kinder, A., honorary librarian, British Astronomical Association, personal communication to the author, July 2001; Millar, D., et al., *The Cambridge Dictionary of Scientists,* Cambridge: Cambridge University Press, 1996; Ogilvie, M. B., "Obligatory Amateurs: Annie Maunder

(1868–1947) and British Women Astronomers at the Dawn of Professional Astronomy," *British Journal for the History of Science* 33 (2000): 67–84; Ogilvie, M. B., *Women in Science: Antiquity through the Nineteenth Century,* New York: MIT Press, 1986; Ryves, P. M., "Mary Adela Blagg," *Monthly Notices of the Royal Astronomical Society* 105 (2) (1945): 65–66.

Bleeker, Caroline Emilie (Lili)
17 January 1897–12 November 1985
physicist

Education: Lange Sint high school, Pietersstraat, Middelburg, the Netherlands; University of Utrecht (mathematics, physics) from 1916; Ph.D., 1928.
Employment: teaching in girls' secondary school; assistant in the Physics Department, Utrecht University, from 1919; founder of consultancy and factory, Utrecht, 1930–1944; director of Ned-Optifa, Zeist, 1949–1964.
Married: Adrian W. P. Keg.

Lili Bleeker worked on the design and production of scientific instruments.

Bleeker was a top student, but because her mother was not keen for her to go to university, Bleeker taught at a secondary school in order to pay for her astronomy and physics courses at Utrecht University. From 1919 she worked as an assistant in the physics laboratory in Utrecht; she was the head assistant there from 1926. She was awarded a Ph.D. in 1928 for her thesis on measurements of emissions and dispersion in the series spectra of alkaloids.

Bleeker started a consultancy in 1930 then opened a small factory for making scientific apparatus. The factory did well, and she moved into the production of optical equipment, supported in her venture by Professor Frits Zernike. During World War II Bleeker was involved with the Dutch resistance, and when her activities were discovered, the factory was closed down. Bleeker was awarded a royal distinction for her wartime activities. In November 1949 a new NED-OPTIFA factory opened

in Zeist, near Utrecht, with Bleeker as its director. This was the first factory in the world to make the phase contrast microscope invented by Zernike. He received the Nobel Prize for physics in 1953 for this work.

Some years after Bleeker's death, a building was named in her honor at Utrecht University.

Bibliography: Offereins, M. I. C., "Caroline Emilie Bleeker (1897–1985): een vrouw in een fysisch bedrijf," *Gewina* 20 (1997): 297–308; Offereins, M., and G. van Ginkel, information supplied to "Women in Science" conference, Newnham College, Cambridge, 10–12 September 1999.

Bobath, Berta Othilie
5 December 1907–20 January 1991
physiotherapist

Education: remedial physical therapy training in Berlin; Diploma of Chartered Society of Physiotherapy 1950; fellowship, 1954.
Employment: therapist, Princess Louise Hospital, 1944–1951; Western Cerebral Centre (private clinic), founded 1951 (renamed the Bobath Centre in 1975 and moved to Hampstead, London).
Married: Karel Bobath, 1941.

Berta Bobath was a pioneer in the treatment of cerebral palsy and adult hemiphlegics.

Bobath trained as a remedial physical therapist, with a special interest in movement and relaxation. She came to Britain from Germany in 1938 and married Karel Bobath, a refugee from Czechoslovakia whom she had known in Berlin.

At the Princess Louise Hospital, Bobath treated a well-known portrait painter, Simon Elwes, who had had a stroke on his right side. Her relatively unorthodox therapy alleviated his spasticity, and eventually he was able to continue painting. Bobath trained as a physiotherapist, obtaining her diploma in physiotherapy in 1950 and a fellowship in 1951.

In 1951 she set up a private clinic, initially known as the Western Cerebral Centre. Her husband was the honorary consultant physician. Bobath ran postgraduate courses for doctors, physiotherapists, and occupational and speech therapists and went on lecture tours abroad. In 1975 the center moved to larger premises in Hampstead and became known as the Bobath Centre. Bobath was named a Member of the Order of the British Empire (MBE) in 1978 and received an honorary doctorate of humane letters from Boston University in 1981. She and her husband were the first couple to be given the Harding Award "for outstanding work of benefit to the disabled."

Bibliography: Bryce, J., "Berta and Karel Bobath," *Physiotherapy* 77, 2 (February 1991): 99; Jary, S., Chair of the British Association of Bobath-Trained Therapists, personal communication to the author, July 2001.

Bonheur, Rosalie Marie (Rosa)
1822–1899
animal painter

Rosalie Marie (Rosa) Bonheur (Hulton-Deutsch Collection/Corbis)

Education: trained by her father in his studio.
Employment: self-employed artist.

Rosa Bonheur painted domestic animals, mainly horses, creating an "irreplaceable guide to the evolution of Western Europe's farmyard stock," in much the same way as a botanical artist accurately records the evolution of plants.

Bonheur was born in Bordeaux into a family of Swedish origin and considerable talent. Her father, Raymond Bonheur, trained her at his salon. Her painting *Ploughing the Nivernais* (1848) was bought by the French government for the Luxembourg Gallery in Paris. Bonheur had official police permission to attend the horse market in Paris dressed as a man. Her best-known work, *Horse Fair* (1853), is now in the Metropolitan Museum of Art in New York City. When *Horse Fair* was taken on tour in Europe and the United States, it attracted large crowds; it was even displayed at Buckingham Palace so that Queen Victoria could see it. Her Belgian agent, Earnest Gambert, obtained hundreds of orders for her "country scenes."

Bonheur's studio near Barbizon, France, is preserved. Her last companion and legatee was the artist Anna Klumpke. Bonheur was the first woman officer of the Legion of Honor (1894).

Bibliography: Bozman, E. F., ed. *Everyman's Encyclopaedia*, vol. 2, fourth edition, London: Dent, 1958; Klumpke, Anna, *The Artist's (Auto)biography: Rosa Bonheur*, translated by G. van Slyke, Ann Arbor: University of Michigan Press, 1997; Murray, P., and L. Murray, *A Dictionary of Art and Artists*, fourth edition, Harmondsworth, England: Penguin, 1976; Webster, P., "France Honours Pioneer Feminist and Painter of a Lost Animal World," *The Guardian* (27 October 1997): 20.

Bonnevie, Kristine Elisabeth Heuch
8 October 1872–30 August 1948
zoologist

Education: University of Kristiania (later Oslo), zoology, 1892–1898, doctorate 1906; Zurich University 1898–1899; Wurzberg University 1900–1901; Columbia University, New York 1906–1907.

Employment: curator, zoology museum, Kristiania, 1900–1912; Extraordinary professor, Kristiania University, full professor 1919–1938; director, Institute for Genetic Research, Oslo, 1916–1938.

Kristine Bonnevie was the first woman professor at the university in Kristiania (Oslo), the first woman elected to the Norwegian Academy of Science and Letters in 1911, and the first president of the Norwegian Federation of University Women (1922–1925).

She was born in Trondheim, but when she was 14 her family moved to Kristiania. She began by studying medicine, but soon changed to zoology, and was taught by Johan Hjorts.

Her initial interest was marine biology and she explored the intertidal areas. In 1896 while still an undergraduate she published a paper on ascidians (sea squirts) that had been collected on the North Sea Expedition (1876–1878). She wrote about new species of hydroids found in Norway (1898), hydroids from the expedition (1899), and hydroids from Bergen (1901). She did some research at the marine laboratory in Naples. In 1910 she was the first woman in Norway to become an "external examiner" when Hjalmar Broch defended his thesis on arctic hydroids. He named the hydroid *Bonneviella grandis* after her.

In 1902 she published a zoology textbook for high school students that ran into seven editions, the last in 1929. Throughout her life she believed in the importance of biology in the school curriculum.

She became interested in cytology and studied abroad, learning from experts such as Arnold Lang in Zurich, Theodor Boveri in Wurzburg, and later E. B. Wilson at Columbia University. For her doctorate, which she successfully defended in 1906, she studied the development of the gametes in a parasitic slug.

In 1900 she became the curator at the zoology museum in Kristiania. G. O. Sars and Robert Collett, who were zoology professors, allowed her to do some teaching and administrative work in the zoology department. In 1910 she applied for a professorship at the University of Bergen. She was not appointed, partly because the staff in Kristiania did not want to lose her. In the spring of 1912, parliamentary legislation allowed women to be appointed to official posts, and Bonnevie was made an extraordinary professor. She became a full professor in 1919 and stayed in this position until she retired.

Bonnevie also did research in heredity, and in 1916 was appointed as director of what later became the Genetics Institute. She developed family trees for the inheritance of polyploidy, a condition found in some members of isolated fell communities in Norway at that time. She spent a decade studying the genetics of human fingerprint patterns, and did a considerable amount of genetics research using mice. Throughout her life she continued identifying and publishing the results of the North Sea expedition.

Bonnevie was concerned with the welfare of women students and academics and founded the Norwegian branch of the Federation of University Women; she was elected as president of the International Federation when it met in Kristiania in 1922. She helped set up student housing. During World War I she and her students helped with the potato harvest and with cooking meals for the needy; and during World War II she gave out food from her own home.

In 1911 she was the first woman to be elected to the Norwegian Academy of Science and Letters (Det Norse Videnskaps Akademie), and she was a corresponding member of several scientific societies abroad. In 1920 she was awarded King Olav's Gold Medal, in 1935 Fridtjof Nansen's Prize, and in 1946 she was made a member of the St. Olav's Order (first class). She was interested in radio broadcasting and gave several talks about biological subjects in the 1930s.

She was well known for the interest she took in her students. Thor Heyerdahl, famous for his voyage in the raft *Kon-tiki* in 1947, studied zoology in her department. She suggested that he could get his doctorate by studying the origin of species on the Marquesas Islands in Polynesia, which led to his epic voyage.

The biology and biochemistry building at the University of Oslo is named the "Kristine Bonnevie hus."

Bibliography: Aschehoug og Gyldendals Store Norske Leksikon, vol. 2 (1998): 522. Oslo: Kunnskapsforlegt; Heggen, Liv, librarian, the National Library, Oslo, and librarians at the University of Oslo (translation help from V. Jansson), personal communication to author, July 2001; Heyerdahl, T., *In the Footsteps of Adam: An Autobiography,* translated by A. Zwick, London: Little, Brown and Company, 2000 [*I Adams Fotspor: En Erindringsreise,* Oslo: J. M. Stenersens Forlag, 1998]; *Norsk Biografisk Leksikon,* vol. 2 (1925), Oslo: H. Aschehoug & Co. (W. Nygaard); *Norske Biografisk Leksikon,* vol. 1. Oslo: Kunnskapsforlegt, 2000; Semb-Johansson A., 1999, "Kristine Bonnevie—vår forste kvinnelige professor" [Kristine Bonnevie—our first woman professor], www.nifu.no/Fpol/ 4–99/art.10. html [published in *Forskingspolitikk* nr.4/99, in Norwegian]; http://anart. no/Lydia/scarlets/24html.

Booth, Evelyn Mary
30 October 1897–13 December 1988
botanist

Employment: nurse, Essex, during World War II.

Evelyn Booth compiled the *Flora of County Carlow* (1979), the first Irish county flora book to be written by a woman.

Booth was born in Ireland and spent most of her life there. During World War II she served as a nurse in Essex but returned to Ireland to look after her sick mother. After meeting Edith Rawlins, an enthusiastic

botanist and a member of the Wild Flower Society, Booth became devoted to observing and recording plants. She collected information on the plants of Carlow and Wexford, eventually producing the *Flora of County Carlow* in 1979.

Bibliography: Fitzgerald, R., "Evelyn Mary Booth," *Watsonia* 18 (1990): 238–239; Scannell, M., "Evelyn Mary Booth," in *Stars, Shells, and Bluebells,* Dublin: Women in Technology and Science, 1997.

Borrowman, Agnes Thompson
1881–20 August 1955
pharmaceutical chemist

Education: pharmacy apprenticeship, Melrose, followed by one year in Edinburgh; part-time and full-time studies, qualified at York Place, 1903; passed examination to become pharmaceutical chemist, 1909.

Employment: pharmacy manager, Runcorn, 1903–1906; work on soil and water analysis, Dorking, 1906–1909; researcher, Pharmaceutical Society School of Pharmacy, London, from 1909; research chemist, Rubber Growers' Association of Malaya and Ceylon (based in London), 1909–1913; pharmacist, Slough, 1913–1914; joint proprietor of retail pharmacy, Clapham, London, 1914–1945.

Agnes Borrowman was the first woman to be appointed to the board of examiners of the Pharmaceutical Society. In her role as proprietor of a pharmacy business, she contributed to the training of women pharmacists.

Borrowman was born near Melrose, Scotland, and served her pharmaceutical apprenticeship in Melrose (four years) and subsequently in Edinburgh (one year). During this latter period she attended part-time pharmacy classes, eventually qualifying in 1903 as a registered chemist and pharmacist. She worked as a pharmacy manager in Runcorn while preparing for her examination to become a pharmaceutical chemist; she also undertook soil and water analysis in Dorking. After passing the examination in 1909, she remained at the Pharmaceutical Society's

School of Pharmacy in London. Her first research paper was published in the *Pharmaceutical Journal* in 1909. She then worked as a research chemist but returned to retail pharmacy because of her family's financial circumstances following her father's death.

With Margaret Buchanan and two other women, she took over the pharmacy in Clapham, London, established by Henry Deane, who had been president of the Pharmaceutical Society from 1853 until 1855. Margaret Buchanan had founded a School of Pharmacy for Women, and students were able to spend time in the pharmacy at Clapham to further their practical training and business skills. Soon after World War I, Borrowman became sole proprietor of the business and began improving it. She devoted herself to this work, which took a toll on her health. When the pharmacy was badly damaged by a V2 bomb in January 1945, she was affected to such an extent that she was forced to take a period of rest. During 1945 she changed the business into a limited company with Miss H. F. Wells.

Borrowman made several other notable contributions to the field of pharmacy. She helped compile *Pharmocopedia* with Edmund White and John Humphrey and was involved in practical work relating to two editions of the *British Pharmaceutical Codex* (1911 and 1923). From 1924 she served on the Pharmaceutical Society's board of examiners, the first woman to hold such an appointment. She was president of the South-West London Chemists' Association from 1929 to 1931 and took part in the establishment of the National Association of Women Pharmacists. She was a fellow of the Pharmaceutical Society.

Bibliography: "Miss A. T. Borrowman," Obituary, *Pharmaceutical Journal* (27 August 1955): 155; "Miss Agnes Thomson Borrowman," *Pharmaceutical Journal and Pharmacist* (15 December 1923): 625; "Miss Borrowman," *Pharmaceutical Journal* (3 September 1955): 191; Jones, L., assistant curator, Museum of the Royal Pharmaceutical Society, letter to author, July 2001; Shellard, P. J., Notes on Women Pharmacists (unpublished), Museum ref. IR1996.40.

Boyle, Alice Helen Anne
1869–20 November 1957
psychiatrist

Education: London School of Medicine for Women, M.D., 1893; Brussels University, M.D., 1984.

Employment: assistant medical officer, Claybury Asylum, London County Council; medical superintendent, Canning Town Mission Hospital; private dispensary for women, Brighton; honorary senior physician, Lady Chichester Hospital for Early Nervous Cases, Hove, 1905–1955; war service in Serbia, 1915–1918; honorary medical officer, Royal Sussex County Hospital, Brighton, from 1930.

In 1939 **Helen Boyle** became the first woman president of the Royal Medico-Psychological Association (now the Royal College of Psychiatrists).

Boyle was born in Dublin and educated in Ireland, Germany, and Belgium. She did her medical training at the Royal Free Hospital School of Medicine for Women and at Brussels University, where she earned an M.D. with distinction.

Her first appointment was at Claybury Asylum, with Sir Robert Armstrong Jones as her supervisor. Her next post was as medical superintendent of the Canning Town Mission Hospital. She realized that nervous and mental disorders were rarely recognized in their initial stages, and at that time it was possible for patients to be treated only when they had been certified and admitted to mental hospitals. Boyle became determined to make people aware of the need for the diagnosis and early treatment of mental disorders.

She and her friend Dr. Mabel Jones ran a private clinic in Brighton for women and children. They decided that more extensive accommodation was needed, and with only £200 set up the Lady Chichester Hospital for the Treatment of Early Nervous Disorders in 1905. Boyle was in charge of the hospital for fifty years. It expanded considerably and treated those who had suffered from the traumas of World War I, in active service or at home. During the war, Boyle worked with a unit in Serbia and was awarded the Order of St. Sava and the Serbian Red Cross Medal.

In 1920 she went on a lecture tour of Canada and the United States and met Clifford Beers, who had founded the American National Committee for Mental Hygiene. Boyle came back to Britain convinced that more could be done for the mental health of the community. In 1923, with Sir Maurice Craig, she founded the National Council for Mental Hygiene, now the National Council for Mental Health.

After the war, the Lady Chichester Hospital moved to larger premises, and in 1930 the management committee of the Royal Sussex County Hospital agreed to a liaison between the two hospitals. Boyle was appointed the first woman honorary medical officer and was in charge of the Department of Early Nervous Disorders.

In 1939, as president of the Royal Medico-Psychological Association, she advocated the treatment of voluntary patients in mental hospitals (without waiting for certification) and suggested that doctors from all specialities should visit mental hospitals to become aware of the current treatments.

Boyle was one of the original members of the Churches' Council on Healing. In 1953 she was elected a member of the committee of honor of the World Federation for Mental Health. In her role as consulting physician, she opened a new therapy unit for the Lady Chichester Hospital in 1955.

She inspired many students with her lectures and gave both time and money to numerous causes she considered worthwhile.

Bibliography: Nokes, E. M., archivist, Royal College of Psychiatrists, personal communication to the author, 28 November 1999; Riding, N., archivist, Royal Free Hospital, personal communication to author, 2000; "Report of Meeting of Medical Women's Federation on 16 March 1920," *Magazine of the London (Royal Free Hospital) School of Medicine for Women* 15, 116 (1920): 113–114.

Brenchley, Winifred Elsie
10 August 1883–27 October 1953
botanist

Education: James Allen's School, Dulwich; Swanley Horticultural College; University College London, B.S., 1905; D.Sc., 1911.

Employment: head of Botanical Department, Rothamsted Experimental Station, 1907–1948.

In 1906 **Winifred Brenchley** was the first woman scientist to be appointed to the staff of Rothamsted Experimental Station, Harpenden, Hertfordshire, and indeed the first to be appointed at any agricultural station.

Brenchley was brought up in Camberwell, London, where her father was a teacher. As a result of measles, she was deaf, but this did not hinder her in her activities.

After training in horticulture at Swanley, Kent, she went to University College, London, to study botany. She was awarded a Gilchrist Scholarship for postgraduate studies at University College in 1906–1907. She then held a temporary post at Rothamsted, which was made permanent, and she was head of the Botany Department until she retired at sixty-five. One of the innovations accompanying her arrival was the institution of a tea club, which proved to be useful in bringing together members of different departments to exchange ideas over tea.

Brenchley did research on weeds, ecology, plant physiology, and nutrition, publishing numerous papers, many in the *Annals of Botany*. In the summer she collected weeds from farms before the grain was cut. She wrote several books, including *Inorganic Plant Poisons and Stimulants* (1914), *The Weeds of Farmland* (1920), and *Manuring of Grass Land for Hay* (1924).

Brenchley was elected a fellow of the Linnean Society in 1910 and was a fellow of University College, London. She was named an Officer of the Order of the British Empire (OBE) in 1948.

Bibliography: Allsopp, S. E., librarian, Rothamsted Library, Harpenden, personal communication with author, July 1999;

Brenchley, W. E., "Twenty-five Years of Rothamsted Life," *Records of the Rothamsted Staff Harpenden* 3 (1931): 34–37; Russell, E. J., "Dr. Winifred Brenchley OBE," *Nature* 172 (1953): 936; "The Weed Hunter: Woman's Striking Work for English Farmers," *Daily News and Leader* (8 July 1913): 10; *Who Was Who, 1951–1960*, London: Adam and Charles Black, 1961.

Bromhall, Margaret Ann
7 November 1890–5 January 1967
radiotherapist

Education: Manchester University, M.B., Ch.B., 1924; diploma in medical radiology and electrotherapy (DMRE), 1932.
Employment: radium officer, North of England Radium Institute, Newcastle upon Tyne; resident radiotherapist, Perth, Australia; radiotherapist, North Middlesex Hospital, London, 1934–1954.

Margaret Bromhall was the first radiotherapist to be appointed to North Middlesex Hospital, London, which had one of the first radiotherapy departments in Britain.

After medical training at Manchester University, Bromhall worked for a time at the North of England Radium Institute. Her lifelong desire to travel led her to Perth, Australia, where she worked for several years as a radiotherapist. After obtaining her diploma in medical radiology and electrotherapy in 1932, she started work at the North Middlesex Hospital in 1934, in charge of the newly established radiotherapy department. Throughout her thirty-year career there, she demonstrated a clear vision of what could be achieved in this new area of treatment, and she was known for her thorough and methodical approach.

Bibliography: J. F. H., "Margaret A. Bromhall, M.B., Ch.B., D.M.R.E.," *British Medical Journal* (28 January 1967).

Brook, Lady Helen Grace Mary née Knewstub
12 October 1907–3 October 1997
family planning campaigner

Education: Convent of the Holy Child Jesus, Mark Cross, Sussex.
Employment: volunteer, Family Planning Association, 1949–1997; vice-president, 1987; Family Planning sales, 1972; chairman, 1972–1981; director of Marie Stopes Memorial Clinic, 1959–1964; vice-president, National Association Family Planning Nurses, from 1980.
Married: George Whittaker, in 1925 (divorced); Sir Robin Brook, in 1937.

Helen Brook founded the Brook Advisory Centre for Young People in 1964.

Educated as a Catholic, Brook joined the Church of England as an adult. After the war she volunteered in a family planning clinic in Islington, London, a formative experience for her. Beginning in 1959 she was responsible for the Marie Stopes Clinic in Whitfield Street, London. At that time only married women were allowed family planning advice, but Brook felt that unmarried women, too, should be given help, so she quietly broke the rules. As word of her services spread, her client list grew. Eventually she left the Marie Stopes Clinic to open the first Brook Advisory Centre in London in 1964, with financial backing from her husband. She saw so many unhappy girls that she started giving advice to the unmarried under-sixteens who came to the clinic, causing public outrage. But Brook believed in the family and felt a child should be brought up by both parents. Thus she did not welcome the increase in single parents.

Brook was made a freeman of the City of London in 1993 and was awarded an honorary D.Sc. from the City University in the same year. In 1994 she received the Galton Institute Medal and in 1995 was made a Commander of the Order of the British Empire (CBE).

Bibliography: Knewstub, N., "Helen Brook: Mother of the Free," *Guardian* (7 October

1997): 14; *Who's Who, 1997,* London: Adam and Charles Black, 1997.

Brown, Edith Mary
24 March 1864–6 December 1956
doctor

Education: Manchester High School; Croydon High School; Girton College, Cambridge, 1882–1885; London School of Medicine for Women and Royal Free Hospital, 1886–1891; Licenciate of the Royal College of Physicians and Surgeons, 1891; M.D., 1891.

Employment: teacher, Exeter High School, 1885–1886; doctor in charge of small hospital, Ludhiana, Punjab, 1891–1892; doctor in villages near Delhi, India, 1892–1894; North India Medical School for Christian Women (later Women's Christian Medical College), Ludhiana: founder and principal, 1894–1942; principal emeritus, honorary treasurer, and lecturer in surgery, 1942–1948.

Edith Brown set up and ran the first medical college for women in India. Her energy and dedication led to great improvements in the health of the population.

Brown was born in Whitehaven, Cumbria, the daughter of a bank manager. After leaving Girton College, she took a teaching post in Exeter, Devon, unable to afford to begin her medical studies immediately. Through assistance from a friend, however, she soon started her medical training. After periods in London, Edinburgh, and Brussels, she qualified in 1891 and subsequently traveled to India for medical study.

The conditions that Brown found in India came as a great shock to her, and she was determined to help as much as she could. The position of women in Indian society was a particular concern. As a doctor, Brown saw that she could assist individuals, but it soon became apparent to her that wider intervention was needed, and she hit upon the idea of giving medical training to Indian women. She established the North India Medical School for Christian Women in Ludhiana. The local midwives were unimpressed and did not attend her lectures until Brown offered them a fee for their attendance. This eventually extended to paying the midwives fees if they called her in to assist with difficult cases, and this in itself led to a dramatic fall in the childbirth mortality rate.

The college hospital won government recognition after two years and received encouragement from the University of Lahore, which put forward the possibility of affiliation. On more than one occasion over the years, however, the staff had to struggle against closure because of a whole range of problems, not least the lack of support from the state authorities. Despite the difficulties, thousands have been trained as doctors, nurses, dispensers, and midwives since the establishment of the college.

Brown wrote a handbook for midwives that was published in Urdu, Hindi, and Punjabi. In 1922 she was awarded the Gold Kaiser-I-Hund medal. She was made a Dame Commander of the Order of the British Empire (DBE) in 1932 and continued to contribute to the running of the hospital after her retirement in 1942. She died in Srinagar, Kashmir. In 1994 the Friends of Ludhiana published a book of her meditations, prayers, and poems, *My Work Is for a King.*

Bibliography: Duk, A., archivist, Cumbria Record Office, Whitehaven, Cumbria, letter to Mrs. S. Oldfield, 5 November 1998; French, F., *Miss Brown's Hospital: The Story of the Ludhiana Medical College and Dame Edith Brown, D.B.E., Its Founder,* London: Hodder and Stoughton, 1954; *Girton College Register, 1869–1946,* vol. 1, Cambridge: Girton College, 1948.

Brown, Margaret Elizabeth
(Mrs. Varley)
28 September 1918–
fish biologist

Education: Hilders School, Haslemere; Malvern Girls' College; Girton College, Cambridge, 1937–1945; M.A., 1944; Ph.D., 1945; M.A., Oxford, 1959.

Employment: Girton College, assistant lecturer, 1942–1946; lecturer in natural sciences, 1946–1950; Zoology Department, University of Cambridge, demonstrator, 1945–1950; visiting scientist, East African Fisheries Research Organisation, Jinja, Uganda, 1950–1951; lecturer, King's College, London, 1951–1955; demonstrator in zoology, University of Oxford, 1959–1965; St. Hilda's College, Oxford: lecturer in zoology, 1959–1961; tutor in zoology, 1961–1969; Open University: senior lecturer in biology, 1969–1974; reader in biology, 1974–1983.

Married: Professor George Copley Varley, in 1955.

Margaret Brown, a leading expert on fish biology, has published several books on the subject and has been a member of many societies and committees on fisheries and conservation.

Brown was born at Mussoorie in the Punjab, where her father served in the Indian Civil Service. She won a scholarship to Girton College and studied zoology. She was awarded the Crewdson Prize in 1939 and 1941. She stayed on at Cambridge and for her doctorate studied the growth of brown trout, *Salmo trutta.* Her interest in trout began as a result of a wartime project relating to fish production. She and Winifred Frost collaborated on the New Naturalist volume *The Trout,* finally published in 1967. While at Cambridge she coauthored *A Manual of Practical Vertebrate Morphology* (1949), which was widely used as a textbook.

She spent a formative year at the new research center of the East African Fisheries Research Organisation in Uganda, returning to Britain to lecture in vertebrate zoology at King's College. She stayed there until her marriage, when she moved to Oxford.

From 1957 to 1971 she was a biological consultant to the Salmon and Trout Association. She continued her research and lecturing at Oxford University, based at St. Hilda's College, then moved to the Open University in 1969 and was chair of four course teams and a writer for second- and third-level biology courses, besides serving as senior lecturer and then reader. As well as numerous articles, Brown edited the two-volume *Physiology of Fishes* (1957), which was used as a textbook in universities worldwide. Her *British Freshwater Fishes: Factors Affecting Their Distribution* (1967) was based on her lectures as visiting Buckland Professor.

She was a member of the Councils of the Freshwater Biological Association, the Institute of Biology, the Institute of Fisheries Management, and the Linnean Society; she was vice-president of the Linnean Society in 1982.

Bibliography: *Girton College Register, 1944–1969,* vol. 2, Cambridge: Girton College, 1991; Marren, P., *The New Naturalists,* London: HarperCollins, 1995.

Bryan, Margaret
fl. 1815
natural scientist, writer

Employment: science writer; schoolmistress.
Married: Mr. Bryan.

Margaret Bryan published several works on scientific topics and ran a school for girls.

Bryan published a *Compendious System of Astronomy* in 1797, dedicating it to her pupils. In the front of the book was an engraving of herself and two daughters, indicating that she had married and had children by this time. In 1806 she published lectures on various topics, including acoustics and pneumatics. *Conversations on Chemistry* appeared in 1806, published anonymously but widely thought to have been written by Bryan. She also wrote *An Astronomical and Geographical Class Book for Schools* (1815).

She founded a school for girls called Bryan House in Blackheath, London; it apparently moved near Hyde Park Corner at some point and later to Margate, Kent.

Bibliography: *Dictionary of National Biography,* Oxford: Oxford University Press, 1885–1886.

Buchanan, Dorothy Donaldson (Mrs. Fleming)
8 October 1899–1985
civil engineer

Education: Langholm Academy until 1918; Edinburgh University, 1918–1922; B.S. in civil engineering.

Employment: Dorman Long, Sydney Harbour Bridge project, 1923(?)–1926; S. Pearson and Sons, Belfast, 1926–1927; Dorman Long, Bridge Department, 1927–1930.

Married: Mr. Fleming, 1930.

In 1927 **Dorothy Buchanan** was the first woman to become a corporate member of the Institution of Civil Engineers.

Buchanan was born in Dumfriesshire, Scotland, not far from where the engineer Thomas Telford was born. It seemed to Buchanan that she was always finding new bridges he had built. By the time she was a teenager, she had decided to train as a civil engineer. She used to make scale models in clay and practice drawing to scale.

After graduating in 1922, and with a testimonial from Professor Hudson Beare, her supervisor in Edinburgh, Buchanan looked for work in London while recovering from pneumonia. Ralph Freeman, a consultant for Dorman Long, admired her determination and decided to employ her on the design staff for the Sydney Harbour Bridge. She was paid £4 a week plus overtime. After a year in this department, she moved to the drawing office to work on the southern approach spans to the bridge. People used to come into her office just to see what a woman engineer looked like.

Her next move was to S. Pearson and Sons to work on a gravity dam for Belfast's waterworks, in the Mourne Mountains of Northern Ireland. Initially she had to endure the company of a chaperone, but she soon solved that problem by consistently leaving before her chaperone arrived. After a year she returned to England, once more taking a job in Dorman Long's bridge design department; she worked on the George V Bridge, spanning the River Tyne at Newcastle and on the Lambeth Bridge in London.

In 1927 Buchanan took the admission examination for the Institution of Civil Engineers (ICE), hoping to become its first woman member. As she took the exam, another woman sat in the room with her; fearing she was a rival, Buchanan asked her what she was doing. To Buchanan's great relief, she turned out to be a chaperone. Buchanan did indeed become the only woman of the 9,979 members of ICE. "I felt that I represented all the women in the world," she said. "It was my hope that I would be followed up by many others."

In 1930 she married and left Dorman Long, thinking she could not be both a successful wife and a civil engineer.

Bibliography: Lucas, S., "Meet Dot Buchanan, ICE's First Lady," *New Civil Engineer* (6 July 1978): 15–16.

Buchanan, Margaret Elizabeth
1864–1 January 1940
pharmaceutical chemist

Education: North London Collegiate School for Girls; trained with father (a doctor) and Mr. and Mrs. Kerr, Bruton Street, London; qualified as registered chemist and druggist, 1886; qualified as pharmaceutical chemist, 1887.

Employment: hospital pharmacist from 1888; joint proprietor of pharmacy business, Clapham, London; founder and principal, School of Pharmacy for Women, Gordon Hall, London, 1908–1925; instructor in pharmacy, London School of Medicine for Women.

Margaret Buchanan founded the School of Pharmacy for Women. She established the Women Pharmacists' Association in 1905 and was its first president; in 1918 she became the first woman member of the Pharmaceutical Society's Council.

Buchanan began her pharmaceutical training under her father, who was a doctor, and continued with a husband-and-wife team named Kerr in London. After qualifying and working as a hospital pharmacist, she became joint proprietor, with Agnes

Borrowman and two other women, of a pharmacy business in Clapham, with the intention of offering training for women in pharmacy and business practices.

As a member of the council of the Pharmaceutical Society, she traveled to Canada in 1922, collecting information on the pharmaceutical profession there and the qualification and registration requirements in each province. The detailed report she prepared led to a reciprocity agreement between the province of Ontario and the Pharmaceutical Society.

Bibliography: "Association Presidents," *Chemist and Druggist* (6 March 1909): 377; "Buchanan," *Chemist and Druggist* (13 January 1940): 27; Jones, L., assistant curator, Museum of the Royal Pharmaceutical Society, personal communication to the author, July 2001; "Margaret Elizabeth Buchanan, M.P.S.," Obituary, *Pharmaceutical Journal* (6 January 1940): 10.

Buckland, Mary née Morland
?–1857
naturalist

Married: William Buckland, in 1825.

Mary Buckland provided invaluable assistance to her husband, who was professor of geology at Oxford University.

Buckland was born near Abingdon, Berkshire, and spent much of her childhood in Oxford. Little is known about her, except that she lived with Sir Christopher Pegge, a physician, and his wife, and was encouraged by them in her interests, including her love of nature.

Although Buckland assisted her husband, illustrating his books, helping him with his writing, and taking notes on his observations, he was not much in favor of women scientists. William Buckland, did, however, acknowledge the help of his wife in compiling *The Bridgewater Treatise* (1836), a mixture of geological and paleontological science and philosophical reflections.

Buckland also did drawings for William Conybeare, a geologist. She combined her enthusiasm for natural history with an interest in social problems and a love of family life.

Bibliography: Dictionary of National Biography, vol. 3, Oxford: Oxford University Press, 1886–1887; Ogilvie, M. B., *Women in Science: Antiquity through the Nineteenth Century,* New York: MIT Press, 1986.

Bülbring, Edith
27 December 1903–5 July 1990
pharmacologist, physiologist

Education: Klostermann Lyzeum, Bonn, 1910–1920; private tuition, 1920–1922; Bonn Gymnasium, 1922–1923; University of Bonn, 1923–1925; medical training: Munich, Freiburg, and Bonn, 1925–1928.

Employment: house physician, Westend Hospital, Berlin, 1928–1929; voluntary assistant to Paul Trendelenburg, University of Berlin, 1929–1931; pediatrician, University of Jena, 1931–1932; clinical research assistant, Infectious Disease Unit, Virchow Hospital, Berlin, 1933; research assistant, Pharmaceutical Society, London, 1933–1937; Department of Pharmacology, University of Oxford: department demonstrator, 1937–1946; university demonstrator and lecturer, 1946–1960; reader, 1960–1967; professor, 1967–1971.

Edith Bülbring carried out research in pharmacology, and was an expert on the physiology of smooth muscle.

Bülbring was born in Bonn, Germany. Her father was professor of English at the University of Bonn; her Dutch mother came from a family of Jewish bankers. Edith was the youngest of four children. Her father died in 1917 following a fall on an icy road.

Because her school did not prepare pupils for university entrance, she was privately tutored for two years, after which she studied mathematics, chemistry, and physics at the Bonn Gymnasium. She passed the entrance examinations for the University of Bonn in 1923 and studied physiology, zoology, and anatomy. Having successfully completed the preclinical courses in 1925,

Edith Bülbring (Godfrey Argent Studio)

she started on her medical training, spending a year in Munich then six months in Freiburg, where she particularly enjoyed the lectures of the pharmacologist Paul Trendelenburg. Bülbring returned to the University of Bonn for her final year. Her doctoral thesis, on the histological technique of staining nerve fiber, was published in the *Virchow Archiv* (vol. 268).

After qualifying as a physician, Bülbring worked as a house officer in Westend Hospital in Berlin. Trendelenburg, who by then was professor of pharmacology at the University of Berlin, offered her a position as his assistant. She was not paid for this work but was able to support herself using funds established by her mother's family following the death of Bülbring's father. When Trendelenburg died of tuberculosis, Bülbring was uncertain whether she could pursue a career in pharmacology and decided to take a job as a pediatrician in Jena.

After a year she returned to Berlin to work at the Infectious Disease Unit of the Virchow Hospital with Ulrich Friedemann, an immunologist. This was in 1933, when Hitler and the Nazi Party were coming to power. Bülbring's family background did not initially cause problems, since only two of her four grandparents were Jewish. But Friedemann and several of his staff were forced out of their posts. Friedemann went to London to work with Henry Dale, with whom he had been a student.

Bülbring carried on her work at the hospital, though she, too, was soon dismissed because of her Jewish ancestry. In September 1933 she and her sister traveled to England for a holiday. Before leaving England, she visited Friedemann in London and met Dale, who, much to Bülbring's surprise, arranged for her to be given a job at the Pharmaceutical Society's biological standardization laboratory as assistant to J. H. Burn. Bülbring's English was poor. To improve it she translated Burn's book *Biological Standardisation* into German; her translation was published in 1937.

At the Pharmaceutical Society laboratories, Bülbring worked on the standardization of vitamin and hormone preparations. A well-known biochemist, Katherine Coward, supervised her standardization work. She also did experiments on animal tissues, particularly in relation to vasodilator responses in muscles, research directed by Burn.

Bülbring was still able to visit Germany because of her dual nationality (German–Dutch). Following her mother's death in 1938, the Bülbrings rented out the family home in Bonn and moved some of the family possessions to England.

In 1937 Bülbring moved to the University of Oxford with J. H. Burn, who had been appointed to the chair of pharmacology. From 1937 to 1946 she worked as a departmental demonstrator, assisting medical students with their experiments and carrying out her own research. She coauthored a number of papers on a range of subjects, including the effects of adrenaline on nerve activity (with David Whitteridge). In 1946 she was appointed university demonstrator and lecturer, and in the same year she published an important paper on the stimulation of the phrenic nerve in rat diaphragm muscle (*British Journal of Pharmacology* 1: 38–61). This was the basis of further work both by Bülbring and some of her colleagues. During the late 1940s and early 1950s, she researched the effects of adrenaline and acetylcholine. In 1949 she published a paper on the formation of adrenaline from noradrenaline in the adrenal gland by the action of adenosine triphosphate (ATP), the first time this process had been described.

After World War II Bülbring decided to pursue her own research interests. In 1949 she spent eight months at Johns Hopkins University in Baltimore, Maryland, working on various effects of anesthetics on rabbit tissues. She learned to use polarized platinum electrodes to measure oxygen tension, a technique that was important in her own subsequent work on smooth muscle.

Bülbring returned to Britain in 1950 and began research on smooth muscle, which was often used in experiments by pharmacologists but which had not itself been fully investigated. Initially she used the technique she had learned in the United States. Later, with the help of colleagues, she was able to set up the equipment necessary to enable her to use microelectrodes. From the mid-1950s she began to build up her own team of smooth-muscle researchers, and during the next seventeen years, until her retirement, around forty scientists from all over the world worked within her group. She supported her colleagues and encouraged them to work and publish independently, adding her name to research only if she had made a significant contribution to the experiments.

Bülbring and her coworkers investigated many aspects of smooth muscle, including electrical activity, oxygen consumption, response to drugs and transmitters (especially adrenaline), ion levels, response to nerve activity, and peristalsis. In 1970 she published *Smooth Muscle*.

In 1960 she was elected to a professorial fellowship at Lady Margaret Hall, University of Oxford. A bicycle accident during her early days in Oxford had left her with poor circulation in her foot, and when she was in her seventies this, together with atheroscle-rosis, forced the amputation of her leg below the knee. She eventually had an artificial limb made in Switzerland, after which she was able to lead a more or less normal life. She continued working and traveling, and for a time nursed a sister who had a slowly developing brain tumor. But Bülbring's circulation problems continued, and she underwent numerous treatments to attempt to improve matters. She had a venous graft operation in 1990 but died from complications three days later.

Bülbring was elected as a fellow of the Royal Society in 1958. She received honorary degrees from the universities of Groningen in the Netherlands (1979), Leuven in Belgium (1981), and Homburg in Germany (1988) and the Schmiedeberg-Plakette of the Deutsche Pharmakologische Gesellschaft in 1974. In 1985 she was awarded the Wellcome Gold Medal in Pharmacology. She held honorary membership in the British Pharmacological Society from 1975, the Deutsche Physiologische Gesellschaft from 1976, and the Pharmacological Society of Turin from 1957. From 1971 to 1975 she was on the British Physiological Society's Committee and in 1981 was made an honorary member of the society.

Bibliography: Bolton, T. B., and A. F. Brading, "Edith Bülbring, 27 December 1903–5 July 1990," *Biographical Memoirs of the Fellows of the Royal Society* 38 (1992); *Dictionary of National Biography, 1986–1990,* Oxford: Oxford University Press, 1996; *Who Was Who, 1981–1990,* London: Adam and Charles Black, 1991.

Burbidge, (Eleanor) Margaret née Peachey
12 August 1919–
astronomer

Education: Francis Holland School for Girls, London; University College, London, B.S., 1936–1939; University of London Observatory, Ph.D., 1943.

Employment: University of London Observatory: assistant director, 1948–1950; acting director, 1950–1951; research fellow,

Yerkes Observatory, University of Chicago, 1951–1953; research in astronomy department, University of Cambridge, 1953–1955; research fellow, California Institute of Technology, 1955–1957; associate professor, Yerkes Observatory, 1957–1962; University of California, San Diego: research astronomer, 1962–1964; professor of astronomy, 1964–1990; director, Royal Greenwich Observatory, 1972–1973; director, Centre for Astrophysics and Space Sciences, 1979–1988; emeritus and research professor at the Department of Physics, University of California, since 1990.

Married: Geoffrey Burbidge, on 2 April 1948.

Margaret Burbidge is an astronomer of international renown who has worked closely with her husband on a range of research projects. Her own research on galaxies provided the basis for the first precise estimates of their masses.

Burbidge studied physics at University College, London. In 1948 she was assistant director at the University of London Observatory while working for her doctorate; she later became acting director. Her husband had started his academic career in particle physics but switched to astrophysics after his marriage. The Burbidges formed a very successful partnership, publishing numerous research papers. Their *Quasi-Stellar Objects* (1967) was one of the first books on quasars.

Margaret Burbidge held several short-term fellowships, and her husband had junior university positions, often in the same university. She returned twice to England, once to work with Fred Hoyle in the department of astronomy at Cambridge while her husband held a two-year post there; later to serve as director at the Royal Greenwich Observatory during a leave of absence from her position at the University of California.

Burbidge has received many honors, including first woman president of the American Astronomical Society, 1976–1978; fellow of University College, London, 1967; and honorary fellow of Lucy Cavendish College Society, 1971. She has honorary doctorates from Girton College; the Universi-

ties of Sussex, Bristol, and Leicester; and the City University. She was awarded the Einstein Medal from the World Cultural Council in 1988.

Bibliography: Biographical Dictionary of Scientists, vol. 1, London: Adam and Charles Black, 1982; Burbidge, E. M., "Watcher of the Skies," *Annual Review of Astronomy and Astrophysics* 32 (1994): 1–36; Green, T., "A Great Woman Astronomer Leaves England—Again," *Smithsonian* (January 1974): 34–41; *Who's Who 1997*, London: Adam and Charles Black, 1997; Yount, L., *Twentieth-Century Women Scientists*, New York: Facts on File, 1996.

Byron, Augusta (Ada), Countess of Lovelace
10 December 1815–27 November 1852
mathematician

Education: at home, by tutors.

Married: William King (Baron King and Baron Ockham, later Earl of Lovelace), in 1835.

Augusta (Ada) Byron, Countess of Lovelace (Kean Collection/Archive Photos)

Ada Byron was a mathematician whose work with Charles Babbage, the inventor of the first "computer," was an important contribution to the field.

Byron was born in London, the daughter of the poet Lord Byron. Her parents separated when Ada was very young. She had poor health as a child and often used crutches until she was seventeen. She was educated by tutors and excelled at horseback riding and mathematics. Her social circle included famous writers and thinkers of the time, including Mary Somerville, Charles Dickens, and Sir Charles Wheatsone.

In 1833 she met Charles Babbage and observed his "difference engine," the basis of the computer, at his home. In October 1842 an Italian, General Menabrea, published a paper, in French, describing the engine in *Bibliothèque Universelle de Genève*. At Wheatstone's suggestion, Byron translated the piece into English and, under Babbage's supervision, prepared a comprehensive set of notes. Her translation was published in *Taylor's Scientific Memoirs* (3 [1843]: 666– 673).

Because the notes contained the equivalent of "programs," Byron is often credited with being the first computer programmer, though Babbage wrote much of the detailed mathematical part of the work. Byron's contribution was important in helping people to understand the concept of computing itself, aside from the technicalities of the process. In her words, "the Analytical Engine weaves algebraical patterns just as the Jacquard loom weaves flowers and leaves."

Byron had married in 1835, becoming the Countess of Lovelace when her father-in-law died in 1838. She died of uterine cancer in 1852.

Bibliography: Nicholls, C. S., ed., *Dictionary of National Biography: Missing Persons*, Oxford: Oxford University Press, 1993; Plant, S., *Zeros and Ones*, London: Fourth Estate, 1997; Woolley, B., *The Bride of Science: Romance, Reason, and Byron's Daughter*, London: Macmillan, 1999; Woolley, B., personal communication to the author, 20 January 2000.

C

Cable, Alice Mildred
1878–30 April 1952
geographer, missionary

Education: Guildford High School; medical studies, University of London.

Employment: missionary teacher with the China Inland Mission, Hwochow Girls' School, 1900–1921; traveling missionary, 1923–1941; voluntary work with the British and Foreign Bible Society, 1941–1952.

Mildred Cable traveled along trade routes across the uncharted Gobi Desert from 1926 to 1941 with Evangeline and Francesca French. Between expeditions they lectured throughout Britain and wrote about their experiences, published as *A Desert Journal: Letters from Central Asia* (1934).

Cable was born in Guildford, Surrey, where her father was a draper. She met a female missionary working with the China Inland Mission in 1893, when she was fifteen, and decided to apply to join the mission.

After studying medicine at the University of London, she left for Shanxi, northern China, in 1900. With Evangeline and Francesca French, Cable ran a girls' school for twenty-one years. Through their efforts the school expanded from one group of ten girls to an establishment with a range of classes, from nursery school to teacher training.

In 1923 the three women became itinerant missionaries. Dressed in Chinese clothes, they traveled by cart, camel, and on foot along trade routes across the Gobi Desert, evangelizing as they progressed in Chinese and Turki. On return visits to England, they lectured to universities and scientific bodies on the archaeological and geographical material they had collected on their travels. In 1939 they were expelled from the area by the Russian authorities and returned to England. They worked for the British and Foreign Bible Society, touring in Britain and abroad and lecturing on the Christian gospel.

They were awarded the Lawrence Memorial Medal of the Royal Central Asian Society for their book *The Gobi Desert* (1942). The Royal Scottish Geographical Society presented them with the Livingstone Medal in 1943. They published several books, including *Journey with a Purpose* (1950) and *Why Not for the World?* (1952).

Bibliography: Crawford, A., et al., eds., *The Europa Biographical Dictionary of British Women: Over a Thousand Notable Women from Britain's Past*, London: Europa Publications, 1983; *Dictionary of National Biography, 1951–1960*, Oxford: Oxford University Press, 1971; Thomas, H., archives assistant, Royal Geographical Society, personal communication to the author, December 1999; Uglow, J. S., ed., *The Macmillan Dictionary of Women's Biography*, third edition, London: Macmillan, 1998.

Cadbury, Dorothy Adlington
14 October 1892–21 August 1987
botanist

Employment: director, Cadbury Bros., Bournville, Birmingham, until 1952.

Dorothy Cadbury, an expert on pondweeds, made around 400 collections of *Potamogeton* from different parts of Britain for the British Museum. These included British species and natural hybrids. One rare hybrid, *Potamogeton x. cadburyae,* was named after her.

Cadbury started collecting wildflowers when she was young, coloring in the matching pictures in her *Illustrations of the British Flora* as she identified each specimen. She joined the Wild Flower Society in 1929, serving as Warwickshire recorder for many years, and became a member of the Botanical Society of the British Isles in 1936.

In 1950 she joined the Birmingham Natural History Society (BNHS). One of her first achievements was to make a complete list of the flowering plants in Edgbaston Park in Birmingham. In January 1950 she became part of the team working on the revision of *The Flora of Warwickshire,* a joint project between the BNHS and the Botany Department of Birmingham University that involved weekly meetings to identify material sent in by collectors and collate records. The results were published as *The Computer-mapped Flora of Warwickshire* in 1971.

Cadbury was a committed member of the Society of Friends.

Bibliography: Hawkes, J. G., "Dorothy Adlington Cadbury (1892–1987)," *Watsonia* 17 (1988): 208–216.

Canter-Lund, Hilda M.
née Canter
1922–
mycologist, protozoologist, photographer

Education: Drayton Park Elementary School, London, 1927–1933; Camden High School for Girls, London, 1933–1940; Bedford College, London, 1940–1944; B.S. with honors; Department of Education, University of London, 1944–1945; diploma in education, 1945; Department of Botany, Queen Mary College, London, 1945–1948; Ph.D., 1948; D.Sc., 1955.

Employment: part-time demonstrator, Botany Department, Birkbeck College, London, 1945–1946; mycologist, Freshwater Biological Association (FBA), Windermere, 1948–1987 (honorary appointment, 1956–1962; senior principal scientific officer, 1976–1987); honorary research fellow, FBA, from 1990.

Married: Dr. John W. G. Lund, phycologist, Freshwater Biological Association, in 1949.

Hilda Canter-Lund is an expert on the fungi that parasitize freshwater algae; she has also studied other protozoan parasites that kill algae and made hundreds of photographs of microscopic organisms.

Canter-Lund was born in Highbury, London. Her father was a gas fitter who was assigned to the Royal Engineers in World War I. She went to Camden High School for Girls in London, which was evacuated to Grantham and then to Stamford during World War II. She gained her intermediate B.S. in botany, zoology, physics, and geography from Bedford College (based in Cambridge for the duration of the war). She graduated with an honors degree in botany and returned to London to take her diploma in education.

In 1943 Canter-Lund had attended a botany course for students at Wray Castle, the first research center of the Freshwater Biological Association (FBA), on the shores of Windermere. She noticed that several of the phytoplankton they collected were infected by fungi, among them a particularly striking saprophytic chytrid on *Ceratium* that she could not identify. She contacted Professor C. T. Ingold of Birkbeck College, who studied these fungi, and sent him a sample. He replied saying that it was a new genus, which he later described as *Amphicypellus.* From then on Canter-Lund began investigating chytrids and other fungi associated with algae, initially guided by Ingold.

In 1945 she held a University of London postgraduate studentship at Queen Mary College, in F. Fritsch's Botany Department; in the evenings she was a demonstrator at Birkbeck College. A second studentship in 1946 gave her the opportunity to continue her research on fungi at Wray Castle with Ingold as her supervisor. Canter-Lund was appointed as a mycologist to the FBA staff in 1948. The FBA moved to its present site, The Ferry House, in 1950.

From 1952 onward, in order to bring up her children and attend to other family commitments and illness, she undertook part-time employment and from 1956 to 1962 had an honorary position. The Royal Society gave her a grant for a microscope so that she was able to continue her studies from home. She retired in 1987.

In 1955 Canter-Lund was awarded a D.Sc. from Queen Mary College on the basis of her published papers. She received a fellowship of the Royal Photographic Society in 1965 and an individual special merit promotion by the Civil Service Department in 1976.

With her husband, Dr. John Lund, one of the earliest research workers at the FBA and a specialist in algae, Canter-Lund did much valuable work on the algae and fungi of the Lake District. They compiled *Freshwater Algae: Their Microscopic World Explored* (1995), a collection of 387 color and 253 monochrome photographs with commentaries on each, combined with a general text. With this book, which they wrote "for everyone," they hoped "to take people into a world of great beauty and fascination, which they normally never see but which is all around them when ever they go outdoors" (xiii). They received the Prescott Award in 1997 from the American Phycological Society for publication of the best book about algae.

Many of Canter-Lund's photographs of algae have been exhibited, and they have appeared in numerous publications, including the front cover of the *Radio Times* magazine to announce the start of David Attenborough's *Life on Earth* series for BBC Television in January 1979.

Canter-Lund has published over seventy-four papers, twenty-five of them in collaboration with other colleagues. Much of her early work, describing new species of chytrids, was published in the *Transactions of the British Mycological Society* beginning in 1946.

With her husband and Dr. S. I. Heaney, Canter-Lund showed the biological importance of epidemics of parasitic fungi and protozoa in controlling populations of algae. She and G. H. M. Jaworski achieved the first successful isolation of a chytrid, *Rhizophydium planktonicum*, parasitic on a planktonic diatom. The paper describing this in *Annals of Botany* (42 [1978]: 967–979), was later selected for publication by the Phycological Society of America in a special volume detailing outstanding accomplishments in phycology from 1971 to 1981.

With G. W. Beakes, Canter-Lund performed experiments with this chytrid and grew further chytrid species in culture for ultrastructural studies. These results were published in *Annals of Botany, Mycological Research,* and other journals between 1979 and 1993.

The British Mycological Society awarded Canter-Lund their Benefactor's Medal in November 1991, and in 1996 she was elected a centennial fellow of the society. She is an honorary member of the FBA.

Bibliography: Canter, H. M. (Mrs. J. W .G. Lund), "Fungal and Protozoan Parasites and Their Importance in the Ecology of the Phytoplankton," *Freshwater Biological Association Forty-seventh Annual Report* (1979): 43–50; Canter-Lund, Hilda, personal communication to the author, April–September 2000; Canter-Lund, Hilda, "[Reports from] Honorary Research Fellows," *Freshwater Biological Association Sixty-eighth Annual Report* (2000): 33; Canter-Lund, Hilda, "Reports from Honorary Research Fellows, 1998– 1999," *Freshwater Forum* 12 (1999): 51–52; "Congratulations to Dr. Hilda Canter-Lund DSc FRPS," *Freshwater Forum* (1992): 14–15; Reynolds, C. S., "Report of the Acting Director," *Freshwater Biological Association Sixty-sixth Annual Report* (1998): 14–15.

Cartwright, Mary Lucy
17 December 1900–3 April 1998
mathematician

Education: Leamington High School; Godolphin School, Salisbury; St. Hugh's College, Oxford, 1919–1923 and 1928–1930; M.A., D. Phil., 1930; Girton College, Cambridge, 1930–1934; M.A., 1937, Sc.D., 1949.

Employment: teacher, Alice Ottley School, Worcester, 1923–1924; teacher, Wycombe Abbey School, 1924–1927; Girton College, Cambridge: fellow and lecturer in mathematics, 1934–1949; director of studies in mathematics and mechanical science, 1936–1949; mistress of Girton, 1949–1968; University of Cambridge: assistant lecturer in mathematics, 1933–1935; lecturer, 1935–1959; reader in theory of functions, 1959–1968; emeritus reader, 1968–1998.

In 1947 *Mary Cartwright* became the first woman mathematician to be elected as a fellow of the Royal Society and the first to serve on its council.

Cartwright's father was the rector of Aynho, Northamptonshire. She went to boarding school from the age of eleven and to St. Hugh's College, Oxford, in 1919. There were only five women in Oxford studying mathematics, and Cartwright was the first to complete a degree course in this subject. Her work was influenced by Dr. G. H. Hardy.

For financial reasons, Cartwright taught mathematics in two girls' boarding schools, but she missed the academic challenges she had experienced in Oxford and returned to her studies under Hardy, writing her thesis on "Zeros of Integral Functions of Special Types." Cartwright was awarded a Yarrow research scholarship, based at Girton College, Cambridge, and attended the courses of J. E. Littlewood, who had been the external examiner for her thesis. She began working on complex function theory, a branch of mathematics used in the proof of Fermat's last theorem, aircraft design, and statistical forecasts.

In a series of papers, Cartwright continued to investigate the theory of complex functions, from which modern pictures of fractals are developed. She described the deep and delicate phenomena that can develop near fractal boundaries.

In 1938 Cartwright noticed that the Radio Research Board of the Department of Scientific and Industrial Research was appealing to the London Mathematical Society for help with some of the equations used by radio engineers. During the war she worked with Littlewood on numerous permutations of the Val der Pol equation used to describe the oscillation of radio waves. Some fifteen years after they finished their studies, the mathematician Steven Smale made a detailed study of their research papers and devised the horseshoe map, the basis of the modern theory of chaos. The structures Cartwright and Littlewood found were examples of what was known as the butterfly effect, a theory that if even one butterfly is killed, all of evolution thereafter changes.

In 1940 she began planning her book *Integral Functions*, which tried to make certain parts of the theory of integral functions more easily available. In 1949 Cartwright went to the United States to lecture on her work. In the same year she was elected mistress of Girton, a position she held for nineteen years while she continued with her lectures and research. Her book was finally published in 1956.

Upon her retirement Cartwright became a visiting professor in the United States and Poland. She was president of the Mathematical Association from 1951 to 1952 and of the London Mathematical Society from 1961 to 1963. The Royal Society presented her with the Sylvester Medal in 1964, and several universities, including Edinburgh and Oxford, awarded her honorary doctorates. She was created a Dame Commander of the Order of the British Empire in 1969.

Bibliography: Cartwright, M. L., address given in the University Church, Cambridge, in *Religion and the Scientists*, London: Student Christian Movement Press, 1959; Daintith, J., et al., eds., *Biographical Encyclopaedia of Scientists*, vol. 3, second edition, Bristol: Institute of Physics Publishing, 1994; "Dame Mary Cartwright," *Daily Telegraph* (7 April 1998); "Dame Mary Cartwright," *Times* (7

April 1998); *Girton College Register, 1869–1946*, vol. 1, Cambridge: Girton College, 1948; Rees, J., "Dame Mary Cartwright," *Independent* (9 April 1998); Series, C., "Dame Mary Cartwright: On the Way to Chaos Theory," *Guardian* (9 April 1998).

Cassie Cooper, Una Vivienne née Dellow
29 September 1926–
botanist

Education: Takapuna Grammar School, 1939–1943; University of Auckland, 1944–1950; B.A., 1947; M.A., 1949; University of Wellington, Ph.D., 1955.

Employment: junior lecturer, Victoria University of Wellington, 1951–1953; researcher, New Zealand Oceanographic Institute, Department of Scientific and Industrial Research, Wellington, 1957–1960, 1962–1964; Botany Department, University of Auckland: demonstrator, 1966–1968; tutor in botany, 1968–1970; lecturer, 1972–1974; researcher, Botany Division, Department of Scientific and Industrial Research, Mt. Albert Research Centre, Auckland, 1975–1986.

Married: Richard Morrison Cassie, professor of biometry, University of Auckland, in 1953 (he died in 1974); Dr. Robert Cecil Cooper, retired botanist, Auckland Museum, in 1984.

Between 1957 and 1960, **Vivienne Cassie Cooper** made the first regional study of New Zealand marine phytoplankton.

Cassie Cooper was born in Auckland and graduated with first-class honors in botany. For her M.A. thesis, she investigated the intertidal ecology of New Zealand's Narrow Neck Reef, and for her doctorate she examined the ecology of the marine algae of the Hauraki Gulf. After three years as a junior lecturer in botany, she moved to the New Zealand Oceanographic Institute (NZOI) and started the first regional survey of New Zealand marine phytoplankton.

In 1960–1961 she had a fellowship from the American Association of University Women and with her husband was able to study at oceanographic institutions in the United States, mainly at Woods Hole, Massachusetts. She also visited over forty other institutions in the United States, Italy, and Britain. When she returned to New Zealand, she continued to work at NZOI, studying phytoplankton collected by members of the Fuchs Transarctic expedition.

Her first child was born in 1962, the second in 1963. Cassie Cooper returned to part-time research in 1964, looking into seasonal changes in phytoplankton in the Hauraki Gulf. From 1966 until 1974 she worked in the Botany Department at the University of Auckland; during this time she investigated the freshwater phytoplankton populations in Lakes Rotorua and Rotoiti.

In 1971 Cassie Cooper and her husband had leave to go to La Jolla, California, where she studied the effects of lead poisoning on algae in culture at the Scripps Institute of Oceanography.

After her husband died, Cassie Cooper was appointed as a research scientist in freshwater algae at the Botany Division, Department of Scientific and Industrial Research (DSIR), Mt. Albert Research Centre at Auckland. In 1980 and 1982, while based there, she received several grants that enabled her to travel to European institutions where diatoms were being studied; she also presented papers at conferences in Glasgow and Budapest. At St. Johns, Newfoundland, she helped with the organization of the first International Phycological Congress in 1982.

Cassie Cooper's major publications include "Marine Phytoplankton in New Zealand Waters" (*Botanica Marina* 2 [1961]), "Checklists of the Freshwater Diatoms of New Zealand" (*Bibliotheca Diatomologica* [1984]), and *Microalgae: Microscopic Marvels* (1996). She has also contributed chapters to several books and published over fifty papers.

After she retired she was awarded an honorary research associateship by the Botany Department at the University of Auckland and by the Botany Division of the DSIR. She is an honorary life member of both the New Zealand Limnological Society and the New Zealand Marine Science Society and was awarded the New Zealand

Order of Merit in 1997 for her services to marine and freshwater biology. She has been a research associate of Landcare Research NZ Ltd. since 1990 and continues to do research.

Bibliography: Cassie Cooper, Vivienne. Personal communication to the author, July–August 2000; Martin, P., *Lives with Science: Profiles of Senior New Zealand Women in Science,* Wellington: Museum of New Zealand/Te Papa Tongarewa, 1993.

Casson, Lady Margaret née MacDonald
26 September 1913–12 November 1999
architect, designer

Education: Wychwood School, Oxford; Bartlett School of Architecture, University College, London.

Employment: architect employed by Christopher Nicholson, 1937–1938; private practice, South Africa, 1938–1939; designer for Cockade Ltd., 1946–1951; senior tutor, Royal College of Art, 1952–1974; private practice as architect and designer for private and public buildings and interiors.

Married: Professor Sir Hugh Casson, architect, 19 November 1938.

Margaret Casson, a leading architect, specialized in photography, particularly sciagrams, or shadow drawings.

Casson was born in Pretoria, where her father, Dr. James MacDonald Troup, was a general practitioner and later medical advisor to the president of South Africa, General Smuts. She was one of a few women at the time who studied at the Bartlett School of Architecture of University College, London. Her initial employment was in the office of Kit Nicholson (the brother of artist Ben Nicholson), where her husband, Hugh Casson, also started his professional life.

She then worked privately as an architect in South Africa, and Hugh Casson joined her there. When World War II started, they returned to Britain. From 1951 Hugh Casson was professor of interior design at the Royal College of Art, and Margaret Casson was senior tutor, responsible for organizing the department and teaching; she shared an office with her husband for twenty years.

Casson was a member of many design committees and councils, such as the Arts Council (1972–1975), the Crafts Advisory Committee (1976–1982), and the Council of the Zoological Society of London (responsible for the London Zoo) (1983–1986). She was also closely involved with redesigning the interior of the Royal Society of Arts building in the 1970s.

When her husband was appointed as president of the Royal Academy in 1975, Casson assisted him. She was chairperson of the shop and restaurant committee and founded the Royal Academy's Country Friends. She was a senior fellow of the Royal College of Art (1980) and honorary fellow of the Royal Academy (1985).

Casson and her husband died within three months of one another and were honored with a joint memorial service at St. Paul's Cathedral.

Bibliography: Debrett's People of Today 1998; Manser, J., *Hugh Casson: The Biography,* London: Viking, 2000; McCarthy, F., "Margaret Casson," *Guardian* (23 November 1999): 24; *Who's Who, 2000,* London: Adam and Charles Black, 2000.

Cheesman, Lucy Evelyn
1881–5 April 1969
entomologist, explorer

Education: at private school; entomology course, Royal College of Science, London.

Employment: governess, Mecklenburg-Schwerin, Germany, 1904–1905; canine nurse, 1912–1914; temporary civil servant, the Admiralty, 1914–1918; assistant curator of insects, 1917–1920, curator of insects, Zoological Society of London, 1920–1925; official entomologist, St. George's Expedition, 1923–1925; volunteer, British Museum (Natural History); various independent expeditions, 1929–1955; freelance writer.

Evelyn Cheesman traveled extensively, collecting insects worldwide.

Cheesman was born in Westwell, Kent, and educated at private schools. Because of her knowledge of German and French, she was able to work as a governess. Her real ambition, however, was to train as a veterinary surgeon, and she applied to the Royal Veterinary College in London. Women were not allowed in the profession at that time, so Cheesman became a canine nurse so that she could at least work with animals. Having been interested in natural history since childhood, she joined the Zoologcial Society of London, which among other benefits offered free admission to the London Zoo.

During World War I she was a civil servant at the Admiralty. Her work involved the Neutral and Enemy Trade Index (NETI). After the war she took a typing course at the Imperial Institute, where she met Grace Lefroy. Through her, Cheesman was offered the post of curator of insects to the Zoological Society of London by Professor Maxwell Lefroy, Grace Lefroy's cousin. Cheesman held this position (which included caring for other invertebrates besides insects) from 1920 to 1926; she gave several talks on the animals at meetings of the society, which were recorded in its *Proceedings.* She also spoke about the animals on *Children's Hour* on the BBC Home Service, encouraging children to come see the insects for themselves.

In 1924 she took a leave of absence in order to work with Cynthia Longfield, another entomologist, on the St. George's Expedition, organized by Scientific Research Expeditions Ltd. They collected insects in Panama, the West Indies, the Galápagos Islands, and the South Pacific islands. While in Tahiti, Cheesman decided to travel independently and leave the expedition. She stayed on her own in Tahiti for a year and eventually had to resign from her post at the Zoological Society, having stayed away too long.

Her first publication, "Exhibits from the Caird Insect House," appeared in the *Proceedings of the Zoological Society of London* in 1917. She published over forty papers in a range of natural history and geographical journals. Her last, "Biogeographical Signifi-

cance of Aneityum Island, New Hebrides" (*Nature* 180 [1957]: 903–904), is considered to be her most important contribution to the field of biogeography.

In 1924 Cheesman published *Everyday Doings of Insects* and *The Great Little Insect,* both favorably reviewed in *Nature* (115 [1925]: 414). The first was especially addressed to "boy inquirers with the view of encouraging their interest in entomology"; the second was praised as "a fascinating [volume] for the fireside reading of winter evenings." By the time she returned to London after her first expedition, Cheesman was writing articles and short stories in her spare time in order to support herself financially. During the day she volunteered at the British Museum (Natural History), studying some of the 500 specimens she had collected on her travels. She borrowed a microscope until she could purchase her own with a small sum of money she inherited. She published several papers on the species she had come across in the South Pacific in order to build her reputation as a scientist and secure funding for further expeditions.

Cheesman organized and undertook a series of independent expeditions—to the New Hebrides (1929–1931, 1954–1955), Papua (1933–1934), the Cyclops Mountains of Dutch New Guinea (1936), Waigeu and Japan, Dutch New Guinea, and the Torricelli Mountains (1938–1939), and New Caledonia (1949–1950).

During World War II she carried out war work, including plane spotting. She also lectured to the forces in Kent and Cambridge, delivering 1,020 talks on the subject of the Pacific War. She resumed her travels in 1949, and made her final expedition when she was in her seventies. In all she presented over 50,000 specimens of insects to the British Museum (Natural History).

As well as her taxonomic and geographical papers, she wrote a number of popular books, some for children. These were mostly factual, but *Marooned in Du-Bu Cove* (1949) was an adventure story based on her own experiences. She also wrote two autobiographies, *Things Worthwhile* (1957) and *Time Well Spent* (1960). She made frequent contributions to BBC radio programs, including the Pacific program *Calling the Islands.* She continued to give talks on *Children's Hour,* including, in 1946, a series on her camping adventures in New Guinea in which she described the practical problems of setting up camp in dense forest regions, as well as the dramatic beauty of the surroundings.

Cheesman was a fellow of the Entomological Society of London from 1919 to 1939 and from 1947 and of the Zoological Society of London from 1922 to 1937. She was made an Officer of the Order of the British Empire (OBE) in 1955 and given a Civil List Pension in 1953 in recognition of her scientific work.

Bibliography: Cheesman, L. E., scripts for broadcasts on *Children's Hour,* 9 July and 2 November 1946, BBC Radio Home Service; Palmer, M., archivist, Zoological Society of London, personal communication to the author, August 2001; Smith, K. G. V., "Lucy Evelyn Cheesman, OBE, FRES," Obituary, *Entomologist's Monthly* 105 (1969): 217–219; Stearn, W. T., *The Natural History Museum at South Kensington.* London: Heinemann, 1981.

Chick, Harriette
6 January 1875–9 July 1977
biochemist, nutritionist

Education: Notting Hill High School (Girls' Public Day School Trust); Bedford College, London; University College, London, 1894–1896; B.S., 1896; D.Sc., 1904; research at Hygiene Institutes of Vienna and Munich and at Thompson-Yates Laboratory, Liverpool.
Employment: research, Lister Institute of Preventive Medicine, London, 1905–1945; honorary staff member, 1945–1975.

Harriette Chick was a leading medical research scientist who worked in nutrition and public health.

Chick was born in London, the fifth of eleven children in a strict Methodist household. Her father was a property owner and lace merchant. Chick did well at university and won the advanced-class prize in botany in 1894–1895 and the senior-class Gold Medal for botany in 1896. After graduating she studied bacteriology, traveling abroad on scholarship. On returning to Britain she did a survey of the amount of contamination by *Bacillus coli* in water supplies for large cities. She was awarded a D.Sc. from London University for her study of the function of green algae in polluted water. She was the first woman to be granted (over some opposition because of her gender) a Jenner Memorial Research Scholarship at the Lister Institute of Preventive Medicine, London.

In 1906 Chick began research on disinfectants. The work she carried out with Charles Martin (director of the Lister Institute) resulted in the Chick–Martin test for the efficacy of disinfectants. They went on to make important findings on the chemical processes involved in the heat coagulation of protein (*Journal of Hygiene* 8 [1908]).

When World War I broke out in 1914, Chick worked on testing and bottling tetanus antitoxin for the army, then on agglutinating sera so that typhoid, paratyphoid, and dysentery could be diagnosed. She next studied beri-beri, a condition caused by a lack of vitamin B, and as a result of her findings, dried egg and yeast were added to the army diet.

In 1918 she became a fellow of University College, London, and began to serve as secretary to the Accessory Food Factors committee. As a member of this committee, she traveled to Vienna in 1919 to investigate the prevalence of conditions such as rickets and scurvy. With the staff of the Universität Kinderklinik, she and her team recommended the use of ultraviolet light and cod-liver oil for the prevention of rickets. Her work on the committee also included contributions to several publications on vitamins between 1919 and 1932.

From 1922 she studied pellagra, a condition caused by lack of nicotamide, part of the vitamin B complex. She lectured in the United States in 1932 on maize diets and pellagra. During World War II the nutrition section of the Lister Institute moved from London to Cambridge and was based in Charles Martin's house. Chick carried out research into wartime diets and was involved in planning "the National Loaf," which was bread intended to supply optimum nutrition.

In 1941 she and ten other scientists founded the Nutrition Society. She retired from her post at the Lister Institute in 1945, though she remained active, serving as a member of the institute's governing body. She was president of the Nutrition Society from 1956 to 1959 and in 1974 received the British Nutrition Foundation's annual prize.

The University of Manchester awarded her an honorary D.Sc. in 1933. She was made a Commander of the Order of the British Empire (CBE) in 1932 and a Dame Commander of the Order of the British Empire (DBE) in 1949. She died at the age of 102.

Bibliography: Creese, M. R. S., *Ladies in the Laboratory? American and British Women in Science, 1800–1900: A Survey of Their Contributions to Research,* Lanham, Maryland: Scarecrow Press, 1998; *Dictionary of National Biography, 1971–1980,* Oxford: Oxford University Press, 1986.

Chitty, Letitia
15 July 1897–October 1982
civil engineer

Education: private tuition; Newnham College, Cambridge, 1916–1917, 1919–1921; mathematics tripos, 1917; mechanical science tripos, 1921; M.A., 1926.

Employment: Admiralty Air Department, 1917–1918; Aircraft Stressing Panel of the Air Ministry, with Professor R. V. Southwell at Oxford University; assistant, Bristol Aeroplane Company, 1923–1924; government research worker in engineering mathematics, Cambridge, 1926–1934; research assistant and lecturer in civil engineering, Imperial College, London, 1934–1962.

In 1921 *Letitia Chitty* became the first woman to obtain first-class honors in the mechanical sciences tripos at Cambridge University. She was the first woman member of the Technical Committee of the Insti-

tution of Civil Engineers, and she was a member of the research committee set up in 1958 to review designs for arch dams.

Chitty's initial interest was in aircraft structure, and after completing the mathematics tripos at Newnham she was allowed leave from her course of study to work for the Admiralty Air Department on the stress analysis of experimental airplanes. Later she worked with the group analyzing the crash of the R58, at the time the world's largest airship. In the 1930s her findings on stresses and strains in airship structures appeared in a number of papers produced by the Air Ministry.

From 1934 Chitty was employed at Imperial College, London, initially as a research assistant and then as a lecturer. During World War II she worked on issues relating to the safety of shelters, bridges, and buildings. She spent several years on experimental and analytical studies for the Dokan Dam in Iraq, an arched dam, and in 1968 contributed to an Institution of Civil Engineers international symposium on arched dams. She published a wide range of scientific and technical papers. Throughout her career she had a reputation for meticulous accuracy.

In 1971 Chitty was made a fellow of Imperial College and in 1969 became the first woman to receive the Telford Gold Medal. She was an honorary fellow of the Royal Aeronautical Society.

Bibliography: Baroness Platt of Writtle, "Women in Technology," Leggett Lecture, University of Surrey, 1984, 2–3; Institution of Civil Engineers, archivist, information about Chitty dated 6 August 1969; *Newnham College Register, 1871–1923,* vol. 1, Cambridge: Newnham College, 1963; Sinclair, R. B., "Letitia Chitty," *Times* (8 October 1982); "There Are Only Five," *Times* (15 December 1958).

Yvonne Choquet-Bruhat (Pictorial Parade/Archive Photos)

Choquet-Bruhat, Yvonne
1923–
mathematical physicist

Education: D.Sc., 1951.

Employment: teaching assistant, Ecole Normale Supérieure, 1946–1949; research assistant, then research associate, Centre Nationale de la Recherche Scientifique, 1949–1951; researcher, Institute for Advanced Study, Princeton, New Jersey, 1951–1952; Faculté des Sciences de Marseilles, 1953–1958; lecturer, Université de Reims, 1953–1959; professor, Faculté des Sciences de Paris, from 1960; professor and emeritus professor, Université Pierre et Marie Curie, Paris.

Yvonne Choquet-Bruhat is a mathematician of international renown.

Choquet-Bruhat's main research is in the field of mathematical physics, which includes partial differential equations on manifolds and the applications of problems derived from fundamental physics such as general relativity, super gravities, and gauge theories. She has published almost 200 papers and a research monograph, *Graded Bundles and Super Manifolds.* She has also written several textbooks, such as *Analysis, Manifolds, and Physics* (1977), coauthored with Cécile Dewitt-Morette and Margaret Dillard-Bleick. She was elected to the French Academy of Sciences in 1979 and to the American Academy of Sciences in 1985.

Bibliography: "Yvonne Choquet-Bruhat on Partial Differential Equation of Gauge Theories and General Relativity," available at http://awm-math.org/noetherbrochure/Choquet86.html.

Clarke, Patricia Hannah née Green
29 July 1919–
biochemist

Education: Coedpenmaen Girls' Elementary School, 1924–1930; Howells School, Llandaff, 1930–7; Girton College, Cambridge, 1937–1940; B.A. (Cantab), 1940; D.Sc. (London), 1966.

Employment: Armament Research Department, Ministry of Supply, 1941–1944; Wellcome Research Laboratories, Beckenham, Kent, 1944–1947; National Collection of Type Cultures, Public Health Laboratory Service, Colindale, London, 1951–1953; Department of Biochemistry, University College, London: lecturer, 1953–1966; reader, 1966–1974; professor of microbial biochemistry, 1974–1984.

Married: Michael Clarke, on 7 June 1940.

Patricia Clarke researched the properties and evolution of bacterial enzymes. She also collaborated with biochemical engineers in research on methods for producing and purifying bacterial enzymes for industrial use and became involved in developments in biotechnology.

After attending a local school, Clarke obtained a scholarship to Howells School, Llandaff, Wales. She was a Sparke scholar at Girton College, Cambridge, where she studied natural science. She was particularly in-

Patricia Hannah Clarke (Godfrey Argent Studio)

terested in biological chemistry. Rather than staying at Cambridge to do research, Clarke did war work, carrying out experiments on explosives in Swansea and Woolwich Arsenal for several years before going to the Wellcome Research Laboratories in Beckenham to join B.C.J.G. Knight in a group working on pathogenic *Clostridia*. The objective of their research on growth and toxin production was to improve methods for immunizing against these anaerobic bacteria, which cause serious infections in war wounds. Clarke worked mainly with laboratory cultures of *Clostridium oedomatiens* and strains isolated from casualties in the Western Desert. The results were published in the *Journal of General Microbiology* (1, [1947]: 91–107).

After World War II Clarke spent several years at the National Collection of Type Cultures, working with S. T. Cowan. They developed a series of micromethods for the identification of bacteria based on enzyme reactions. Again, findings were published in the *Journal of General Microbiology* (12 [1955]: 37–43).

In 1953 Clarke was appointed to a lectureship at University College, London. At this time there was renewed interest in bacterial adaptation, a subject to which she had been introduced by Marjorie Stephenson at Cambridge in 1940. She was influenced by the work of Roger Stanier with *Pseudomonas* species, which can grow on a large number of organic compounds. At the time it was difficult to interpret some of those findings because of the long lag before bacterial suspensions began to oxidize certain compounds unless the compound had been present in the growth medium. Clarke showed that for certain substrates of the tricarboxylic acid cycle the lag was due to the time taken to synthesize specific inducible permeases (*Journal of General Microbiology* 20 [1959]: 144–155). This led to a series of studies on the synthesis of novel enzymes and permeases.

The metabolic versatility of the pseudomonads made them suitable subjects for research on experimental enzyme evolution. The essential requirements for a model system were to start with a compound used for growth, such as acetamide, which could be easily modified chemically, and an enzyme assay that was convenient to use. The enzyme used for research on experimental evolution was the aliphatic amidase of *Pseudomonas aeruginosa*. The general procedure involved devising growth media on which the parent strain could not grow but on which a mutant arising spontaneously, or after mutagenic treatment, could do so. Clarke and her colleagues subjected the mutants to genetic analysis and the mutant enzymes isolated and purified. The wild type amidase gene and enzyme were sequenced and mutations identified; later research established the mechanism of gene regulation (*BioScience Reports* 8 [1988]: 103–120).

Clarke and Malcolm Lilly, one of her research students, collaborated in experiments on the regulation of enzyme synthesis in continuous culture. Later they worked together using amidase regulatory mutants as model systems for producing high yields of enzymes on an industrial scale (*Proceedings of the Royal Society* 207, series B [1980]: 385–404). The two also worked together in teaching microbial biochemistry and genetics to students taking the biochemical engineering M.S. course.

Clarke was elected a fellow of the Royal Society in 1976 and was a council member and vice-president from 1981 to 1982. After retiring from her chair at University College, she was appointed professor emeritus, held a Leverhulme Fellowship (1984–1986), and was an honorary professorial fellow at the University of Wales (1984–1987). She was appointed Royal Society Kan Tong-Po Professor at the Chinese University of Hong Kong in 1986 to help set up teaching and research on biotechnology and was a member of the advisory committee of the Palm Oil Research Institute of Malaysia (1990–1993).

Clarke received honorary doctorates from the University of Kent (1988) and the Council for National Academic Awards (1990). She was invited to give the Royal Society Leeuwenhoek Lecture in 1979, the Society for General Microbiology Marjorie Stephenson Memorial Lecture in 1981, and the Birkbeck College Bernal Lecture in 1988.

An advocate for the advancement of women in science, Clarke was a member of the committee set up by the British government to produce the report *Women in Science and Technology* (1994). She has also been concerned with promoting science education in schools.

Bibliography: Clarke, P. H., personal communications to the author, July and November 2000; Clarke, P. H., "Regulation of Expression of Microbial Genes," in M. G. Ord and L. Stocken, eds., *Further Milestones in Biochemistry*, Oxford: Department of Biochemistry, University of Oxford, 1997, 239–275.

Clay, Theresa Rachael
7 February 1911–1995
entomologist

Education: St. Paul's Girls' School, London; University of Edinburgh, D.Sc., 1955.
Employment: own research and collecting until 1938; British Museum (Natural History), London: unofficial worker, 1938–1949; temporary staff member,

1949–1952; senior scientific officer, 1952–1955; principal of Apterygote collection from 1955; deputy keeper of entomology, 1970–1975.
Married: R. G. Searight, in 1975.

Theresa Clay, a world authority on bird lice, was coauthor, with Miriam Rothschild, of *Fleas, Flukes and Cuckoos* (1952).

Clay worked as an entomologist on scientific expeditions to Africa, the Middle East, and the Arctic in 1935–1938 and 1946–1949. She was a volunteer at the British Museum (Natural History) beginning in 1938 until she was appointed as a full-time staff member eleven years later. Clay was in charge of the Natural History Museum's *Phthiraptera* and *Apterygota* section, which consisted of bird and mammal lice, springtails, and other wingless insects. She collected specimens from several different countries, including India and Pakistan (1951), the western Himalayas (1957), Trinidad and British Guiana (1961), and Malaysia (1974). She published over forty papers.

After her marriage in 1975, she retired from the museum; her papers, drawings, and correspondence are held there.

Bibliography: Gocke, C., librarian, Entomology Department, British Museum (Natural History), London, personal communication to the author, 1999; Marren, P., *The New Naturalists*, London: HarperCollins, 1995.

Clayton, Barbara Evelyn
2 September 1922–
chemical pathologist

Education: University of Edinburgh, M.B., Ch.B., 1946; Ph.D., 1949; M.D., 1953, fellow of the Royal College of Pathologists, 1971; fellow of the Royal College of Physicians, London, 1972; fellow of the Royal College of Physicians, Edinburgh, 1985.
Employment: house physician, Edinburgh Royal Infirmary; consultant and then honorary consultant, Hospital for Sick Children, Great Ormond Street, London, 1959–1978; professor of chemical pathology, Institute of Child Health, University

of London, 1968–1978; professor of chemical pathology and human metabolism, University of Southampton, 1979–1987; dean of the Faculty of Medicine, University of Southampton, 1983–1986.

Married: William Klyne, in 1949. He died in 1977.

Barbara Clayton, a chemical pathologist, has been involved in several aspects of health, ranging from nutrition to geriatrics.

Clayton's research was originally in endocrinology, but when she moved into pediatrics she became concerned with nutrition and environmental problems. In 1964 she copublished a major paper that suggested that exposure to lead, then commonly used in paint, might be harmful to children's neurological development (Moncrieff, et al. 1964). In the following years she investigated many lead-containing substances, including old and new paints, contaminated foodstuffs, nursery furniture, and gasoline. She served as a member of the Royal Commission on Environmental Pollution (1981–1996), which studied the effects of lead and other pollutants. Partly because of Clayton's work, the levels of lead in British children today are, with rare exception, very low. She described her service on the Royal Commission in the *Southampton Health Journal* (Clayton 1997, 27–29).

Clayton contributed to the development of a national screening program to check infants for phenylketonuria (PKU), an inherited metabolic disorder that prevents the body from properly using phenylalanine (present in all proteins), which then accumulates in the body and causes severe brain damage. PKU was previously not detected until the child was obviously retarded; now all infants in the United Kingdom are tested for the disorder between the sixth and fourteenth days of life. Such early detection and treatment, with a special diet Clayton helped develop in which most protein is replaced with amino acids, prevents mental retardation (Clayton, et al. 1966, 267–272). Just before Clayton left the Hospital for Sick Children, Great Ormond Street she set up tests for hypothyroidism in infants born in north London (see *British Medical Journal* 1 [1980]: 675–678). Screening for this is now done for all children in Britain, thus preventing brain damage from poor thyroid function.

Clayton's interest in nutrition led her to study various gastrointestinal disorders in infants and children and develop supplements of vitamins and trace elements; she then moved on to study nutrition in those over seventy-five.

Clayton has written widely about her work, including contributions to *The Treatment of Inherited Metabolic Disease* (1975, ed. D. N. Raine), and she coauthored *Chemical Pathology and the Sick Child* (1984), with J. M. Round.

When she retired from the University of Southampton, she was able to continue her research there. For two years, she had a Leverhulme Research Fellowship and is now honorary research professor in metabolism in the Faculty of Medicine at the University of Southampton. Currently she is based in the Department of Geriatric Medicine.

Clayton was president of the Royal College of Pathologists, 1984–1987; the Association of Clinical Biochemists, 1977–1978; the Biomedical Sciences Section of the British Association for the Advancement of Science, 1981–1982; the Society for the Study of Inborn Errors of Metabolism, 1981–1982; and the National Society for Clean Air and Environmental Pollution, 1995–1997. She has been honorary president of the British Dietetic Association since 1989 and of the British Nutrition Foundation since 1999, and she is vice-president of the Caroline Walker Trust. She has been on several committees for the Medical Research Council and the Department of Health, especially those related to problems of nutrition and the environment.

She was chairperson of the Standing Committee on Postgraduate Medical and Dental Education from 1988 to 1998 and on the General Medical Council from 1983 to 1987. She led the Nutrition Task Force (NTF) for the Health of the Nation (1993–1996) on behalf of the Department of Health and the Ministry of Agriculture, Fisheries, and Food. As chair of the NTF, Clayton gave the

British Nutrition Foundation annual lecture in 1996, entitled "Nutrition Tasks: Achievments and challenges for the Future" (Clayton 1997, 32–46). The nutritional program the task force developed is still being used, and gradually the British population is changing its diet to lessen the chance of cardiovascular disease.

Clayton was made a Commander of the Order of the British Empire (CBE) in 1983 and a Dame Commander of the Order of the British Empire (DBE) in 1988; she has been awarded honorary degrees by the University of Edinburgh (1985), the University of Southampton (1992), and the University of London (Medicine) (2000). The British Medical Association presented her with its Gold Medal in 1999. In April 2000 she was given an honorary fellowship of the Institute of Biology.

Bibliography: Clayton, B. E., "Benefits Arising from Studies of an Inherited Metabolic Disorder," inaugural lecture delivered on 5 February 1980 at the University of Southampton; Clayton, B. E., "Improving Public Awareness of Nutrition Issues" *Nutrition* 16, 7/8 (2000): 637–639; Clayton, B. E., personal communications to the author, October and November 2000, January and May 2001; Clayton, Barbara E., A. A. Moncrieff, G. Pampiglione, and Jean Shepherd, "Biochemical and EEG Studies in Phenal Ketonuria Children during Phenal Alanine Tolerance Tests," *Archives of Disease in Childhood* 41 (1966): 267–272; "Honorary Degrees on Foundation Day 2000," *Convocation Newsletter 2000,* University College, London; *The Medical Directory 1998,* London: F. T. Healthcare, 1998; Moncrieff, A. A., et al., "Lead Poisoning in Children," *Archives of Disease in Childhood* 39, 203 (1964): 1–13; Snell, E., "Honours Award for Lifetime Contributions to Biology," *Biobits,* July 2000; *Who's Who, 2000,* London: Adam and Charles Black, 2000.

Clerke, Agnes Mary
10 February 1842–20 January 1907
writer on astronomy and the history of science

Education: at home; in Italy, 1867–1877.

Agnes Clerke was considered the leading popular writer on astronomy in her day.

Clerke was born in Skibbereen, County Cork, Ireland. Her father, an amateur astronomer, had a telescope set up in his garden, and his interest influenced both his daughters. When she was fifteen, Agnes Clerke went to live in Italy with her sister and mother in the hope of improving her poor health. For the next ten years, the sisters studied hard, Agnes Clerke focusing on the history of science and her sister on Italian literature.

In 1877 the sisters moved to London. Clerke had two articles accepted for publication in 1877 in the *Edinburgh Review,* one on the Sicilian Mafia and the other on Copernicus in Italy; she contributed more than fifty pieces on diverse topics over the next thirty years. Writing one of the articles, "The Chemistry of the Stars," made her realize she wanted to concentrate on astronomy. After a publisher accepted her proposal for a history of astronomy, she set to work in earnest on the project. *A Popular History of Astronomy* was published in 1885, with three further editions. In 1888 Sir David Gill invited Clerke to spend three months at the Royal Observatory at the Cape of Good Hope, allowing her for the first time to do long-term practical astronomy. As a result of this visit, she wrote several articles for the *Observatory.* She also wrote about astronomy for *Nature.*

Her second major work was *The System of the Stars* (1890), which dealt with sidereal astronomy, including many unsolved problems. Clerke also published *The Herschels and Modern Astronomy* (1895), *The Concise Knowledge of Astronomy* (1898; with J. E. Gore and A. Fowler), and *Problems in Astrophysics* (1903). In this last book she put forward her ideas for future work on the sun, stars, and nebulae. After the book's publication, she was elected an honorary member of the Royal Astronomical Society. She was offered a post as a computer at Greenwich Observatory but declined in order to continue writing.

Clerke was a prodigious researcher, producing 149 entries for the *Dictionary of National Biography (1885–1901)* and articles on astronomy and astronomers for the ninth edition of the *Encyclopaedia Britannica.*

She was a founding member of the British Astronomical Association in 1890 and was the first non-American corresponding member of the Astronomical Society of the Pacific. She was awarded the Actonian Prize for science writing in 1893 by the Royal Institution. In 1901 she was asked to write an essay on the research on low temperatures, conducted mainly by Sir James Dewar, done at the Royal Institution between 1893 and 1901 . She was elected a member of the Royal Institution in 1903.

A crater on the moon near the place where *Apollo 12* landed on 11 December 1972 is named after Clerke.

Bibliography: Brück, M. T., "Bringing the Heavens Down to Earth," in *Stars, Shells, and Bluebells,* Dublin: Women in Technology and Science, 1997, 66–77; Creese, M. R. S. *Ladies in the Laboratory? American and British Women in Science, 1800–1900: A Survey of Their Contributions to Research,* Lanham, Maryland: Scarecrow Press, 1998; Crone, J. S., *A Concise Dictionary of Irish Biography,* Dublin: Talbot, 1928; McKenna-Lawlor, S., *Whatever Shines Should Be Observed: Quicquid Nited Notandum,* Blackrock, Dublin: Samton, 1998; Ogilvie, M. B., *Women in Science: Antiquity through the Nineteenth Century,* New York: MIT Press, 1986.

Clerke, Ellen Mary
20 September 1840–2 March 1906
science writer, poet

Education: at home; in Italy, 1867–1877.

Ellen Clerke, an accomplished linguist, wrote articles in both German and Italian, translated Italian poetry and composed her own, wrote well-researched travel articles,

and published a monograph on Jupiter (1892) and one on Venus (1893).

Clerke was born in Skibbereen, Ireland. In 1867 she accompanied her mother and sister, Agnes, to Italy, a move spurred by her sister's poor health. While in Italy Clerke developed her linguistic skills and her talent for writing, learning to read Arabic and contributing to both German and Italian periodicals. In 1877 she moved to London.

Clerke wrote a leader in the *Tablet* for twenty years and travel pieces for the *Dublin Review* for twenty-five. She also contributed to the *Observatory,* an astronomy journal. Clerke's "Madagascar Past and Present" (*Dublin Review* 1884) was based on eight contemporary accounts of explorers. "The Crisis in Rhodesia" (*Dublin Review* 1896) reflected her fascination with Africa; her political interests were apparent in "Maritime Canals" (*Dublin Review* 1885) and "A Review of Worldwide Petroleum Resources" (*Dublin Review* 1886). Her novel *Flowers of Fire* (1902) had as its main theme her observations of the eruption of Vesuvius in 1872.

Bibliography: Creese, M. R. S., *Ladies in the Laboratory? American and British Women in Science, 1800–1900: A Survey of Their Contributions to Research,* Lanham, Maryland: Scarecrow Press, 1998; Crone, J. S., *A Concise Dictionary of Irish Biography,* Dublin: Talbot, 1928; McKenna-Lawlor, S., *Whatever Shines Should Be Observed: Quicquid Nited Notandum,* Blackrock, Dublin: Samton, 1998.

Clubb, Elizabeth Mary Fitz-Simon née Thomas
18 December 1922–
doctor, expert in natural family planning

Education: Blackheath High School, London; St. Mary's Convent, Ascot; Medical School, King's College, London, and West London Hospital; M.B., B.S., 1947.

Employment: principal in general practice in Oxford, with her husband, Dr. John Clubb (joined by their daughter, Dr. Cecilia Pyper, in 1977), 1948–1988; medical adviser to the Natural Family Planning Service of the Catholic Marriage Advisory Council (CMAC), 1953–1990; scriptwriter for health education programs in the Department of Medical Illustration, John Radcliffe Hospital, Oxford, 1978–1998; medical director, Natural Family Planning Service of CMAC (renamed Marriage Care), 1990–1997.

Married: Dr. John Clubb, in 1948.

Elizabeth Clubb was a general practitioner in Oxford for forty years. She has worked in natural family planning and continues to lecture and write on the subject.

Clubb and her husband bought a small practice in Cowley, Oxford, in April 1948, just before the National Health Service was launched. In 1950 they joined with Dr. Robert Harvard in St. Giles, Oxford, and the practice grew until it was one of the largest in Oxford, with almost 15,000 patients.

Harvard retired in 1968. Seven years later the practice was amicably divided, leaving the Cowley area to Clubbs' partners, the Clubbs centering their practice on Bury Knowle Park in Headington and St. Giles, Oxford. With fewer patients they were able to introduce counseling and do more preventive medicine.

From the beginning of her time as a GP, Elizabeth Clubb, a committed Catholic, was aware of the problems experienced by her patients, Catholics and others, who had conscientious objections to the use of contraception. So she sought to find effective ways of natural family planning that were both easy to keep to and reliable. At the same time, Catholic doctors in the Catholic Marriage Advisory Council (CMAC) in the UK and internationally were researching methods of natural family planning that would be safe, efficient, and acceptable to people of all cultures and religions. They developed the temperature method and later the ovulation, or cervical mucus, method; together these were combined to produce the symptothermal method. By the 1980s this method had been researched under the auspices of the World Health Organization and found as efficient as other forms of contraception, with the exception of hormonal methods.

Clubb taught her patients how to know when their own fertility was at its peak by using the symptothermal method. Many patients with infertility problems also benefited from this knowledge. There was such a need for education that within her practice Clubb employed a fertility nurse, Jane Knight. Together they published *Fertility— Fertility Awareness and Natural Planning* (1987), which explains both basic biology and techniques.

In 1978 John Marshall, one of the originators of the temperature method, held a course in Oxford for teachers of natural methods of family planning. Clubb invited a family planning nurse, a health visitor, a midwife, and a district nurse, helping to bring natural family planning to the attention of those in the National Health Service (NHS). From that date onward, lecturers on natural family planning were invited to speak at NHS family planning courses. In 1997 Clubb, Dr. Cynthia Pyper (Clubb's daughter), and Knight obtained university accreditation for the fertility and natural family planning training course for nurses.

In the early 1980s Clubb had sabbatical leave to work with Dr. Serena Parenteau-Carreau in Canada, developing breastfeeding programs. Research was being carried out to help women identify the weeks of infertility after childbirth and during lactation.

Clubb became involved with scriptwriting for health education programs with Oxford Medical Illustration, based at the John Radcliffe Hospital, Oxford. She published a number of tape-slide programs on women's health, menopause, breast-feeding, fertility, and natural family planning. With Knight she produced a six-part video *Fertility—A Guide to Natural Family Planning*, to accompany their book with the same title (1987).

Since 1990 Clubb has been responsible for *Fertility File*, a newsletter for teachers of natural family planning, which now has an international circulation. She has spoken at many international conferences and published numerous articles in medical journals.

She was a founding member of the Royal College of General Practitioners in 1953 and elected a fellow in 1986.

Bibliography: "Changes at National Office," *News from the Mews*, 1997; Clubb, Elizabeth, personal communications to the author, 1998–2000; *Medical Register 1998;* Ponting, L., *Public Health in Oxfordshire: The Past*, Oxford: Oxfordshire Health Authority, 1998.

Cockburn, Patricia Evangeline Ann née Arbuthnot
17 March 1914–6 October 1989
artist, conchologist, writer, traveler

Education: governesses at home; Westminster College of Art.

Married: Arthur Byron, a Lloyds underwriter, in October 1932 (divorced in 1939); Claud Cockburn, a Communist agent and journalist, in 1940. He died in 1981.

Patricia Cockburn was an intrepid traveler. Just before World War II she went to equatorial Africa on behalf of the Royal Geographical Society and mapped the languages spoken by the various groups of Pygmies.

Cockburn was born in Rosscarbery, County Cork. Her father was a merchant banker who also served in the Scots Guards and was the first writer of the "Beachcomber" column in the *Daily Express*. Cockburn was educated by governesses at home and presented at court. For a time, the family lived at Myrtle Court, Youghal, her mother's home.

Cockburn was an avid equestrian. After a serious riding accident on her sixteenth birthday, she was sent to Algeria to recover; this experience spurred her interest in travel.

She married Arthur Byron in 1932, leaving art college in London to do so. Byron took a year's leave from his job at Lloyds, and the couple traveled around the world. Cockburn wrote up their adventures, among them finding a python in their hut and narrowly escaping death from a volcanic eruption. Admiral Sir William Goodenough from the Royal Geographical Society, who had suggested a route for their trip, was so pleased with the report Cockburn submitted on her return that he asked her to

travel across Africa, mainly to live among the true Pygmies in the Ituri Forest in the Congo, to find out about their language and its relationship to the languages of other tribes in the area.

Cockburn and her husband left their son, Darrell, with his grandparents and set out again. Cockburn wrote up full accounts of her observations of the Pygmies, and her photographs were exhibited when she returned to Britain.

Soon after they returned, their son died of blood poisoning. Cockburn and her husband separated, then divorced; in 1940 she married Claud Cockburn. Horrified that her new husband was a Communist, her family disinherited Cockburn. For the first time in her life, she had to survive on what she and her husband earned, about £9 weekly. When her first child from this marriage was born, family relations were restored.

Both Cockburn and her husband worked as journalists, living in Ireland. Their three sons all became journalists as well. Cockburn edited the *Week*, a scandal sheet that later developed into *Private Eye*, and published excerpts from the magazine in *The Years of the Week* (1968). She also created beautiful shell pictures and was a competent horse-trader. Her autobiography *Figures of Eight* came out in 1985.

Bibliography: Andrews, D., ed., *The Annual Obituary 1989*, London: St. James Press, 1990; Thomas, H., archives assistant, Royal Geographical Society, personal communication to the author, December 1999; "Patricia Cockburn," *Daily Telegraph* (11 October 1989).

Conway, Verona Margaret
13 January 1910–19 December 1986
botanist

Education: Newnham College, Cambridge, 1929–1933; Girton College, Cambridge, 1933–1936; Ph.D., 1937; Unitarian College, Manchester, 1961–1963.

Employment: demonstrator and assistant lecturer in Botany, Westfield College, London, 1936–1939; London Volunteer Ambulance Service, 1939–1941; West of Scotland Agricultural College, 1941; assistant lecturer, Botany Department, University of Sheffield, 1941–1946, 1947–1949; University of Minnesota, 1946–1947; Nature Conservancy, 1949–1955; director of Nature Conservancy Research Centre, Merlewood, Grange-over-Sands, Cumbria, 1955–1961; Unitarian minister, Lancaster, 1963–1973.

Married: Eric Swale, in 1969.

Verona Conway gained international recognition for her work on the ecology of the sedge, *Cladium mariscus,* and her studies on the blanket bogs of the Pennines.

Conway's father was professor of Latin at the University of Manchester. After attending school in Manchester, Conway became the third member of her family to go to Cambridge, where she studied botany and was awarded a Yarrow Research Scholarship. She did doctoral work under Dr. Harry Godwin, who was well known for his studies on Wicken Fen. Conway studied the anatomy of *C. mariscus* at this fen in relation to the environmental conditions there, explaining why the sedge did not survive when it was cut annually. Her results were published in *New Phytologist.*

After an initial appointment at Westfield College and two years as a volunteer driving ambulances in London through the blitz, she moved to the Botany Department at the University of Sheffield. There Professor W. H. Pearsall, an authority on the flora of mountains and moorlands, suggested that Conway investigate the blanket bogs on the nearby Hallam Moors. She took peat borings and was able to establish from a study of the pollen types when and what vegetation changes had taken place in the area. Her findings appeared in the *Journal of Ecology.* During a year's study leave in the United States, made possible by the American Association of University Women, she studied the bogs of central Minnesota. She worked at Sheffield for two more years, then transferred to the Nature Conservancy. In 1955 she was appointed director of Merlewood. She also was responsible for Moorhouse research station on the North Pennine moors.

In 1961, when she was in her early fifties, Conway decided to leave science and train as a minister in the Unitarian Church. She was the Unitarian minister in Lancaster for a decade and married while she held this post. She retired in April 1973.

Bibliography: Pigott, D., "Obituary: Verona Margaret Conway (1910–1986)," *Journal of Ecology* 76 (1988): 288–291.

Cookson, Isabel Clifton
25 December 1893–1 July 1973
botanist, paleobotanist

Education: Methodist Ladies College, Melbourne; University of Melbourne, 1913–1916; B.S., 1916; D.Sc., 1932.

Employment: Botany Department, University of Melbourne: demonstrator, 1916–1925; lecturer, 1930–1947; researcher, Imperial College, London, 1925–1926; researcher, University of Manchester, 1926–1927 and 1948–1949; head of Pollen Research Unit, University of Melbourne, 1949–1952; research fellow in botany, 1952–1959; honorary associate in paleontology, National Museum of Victoria, 1959–1962.

Isabel Cookson was a world expert on paleobotany and pioneered the study of fossil pollen grains (palynology) in Australia.

After graduating in zoology and botany at the University of Melbourne, Cookson was a demonstrator in botany while she did research on the flora of the Northern Territory. She had a government scholarship in 1917 to study the longevity of cut flowers and crown rot in walnuts. In the mid-1920s she carried out research at Imperial College, London, and the University of Manchester.

Cookson was responsible for teaching the evening course in botany at Melbourne for first-year students from 1930. She was fascinated by fossil plants and began collecting samples and publishing her findings.

In 1940 she started work on microscopic plant fossil remains; these gave useful evidence about past Australian vegetation. She also showed how fossil remains could help both in correlating geological strata and in oil exploration. In 1948–1949 a Leverhulme research grant enabled her to study at the University of Manchester. When she returned to Australia, she founded a pollen research unit at the University of Melbourne.

During her fifty-eight years of research, Cookson published eighty-five papers, fifty-two of them coauthored with other scientists. She was a life member of the Royal Society of Victoria. She donated her collection of fossil plants to the National Museum of Victoria in 1950.

Bibliography: Baker, G., "Dr. Isabel Clifton Cookson: A Preface to Special Publication No. 4," *Geological Society of Australia* (1973): v–x; Ritchie, J., ed., *Australian Dictionary of Biography,* vol. 13 (1940–1980), Melbourne: Melbourne University Press, 1993.

Corradi, Doris
1922–
wireless operator, cipher operator

Employment: Royal Air Force base, Ruislip; Women's Auxiliary Air Force Compton Bassett wireless operator; Chicksands, morse slip reader; Government Communications Headquarters Eastcote, cipher operator, teleprinter operator; Government Communications Headquarters Cheltenham, teleprinter operator.
Married: Guy Corradi, British Merchant Navy Service, in 1949.

Doris Corradi was a wireless operator and Morse slip reader during World War II.

Corradi lived in central London until January 1940, when her home was demolished in an air raid. The family then stayed with relatives before finding a house in Ruislip, Middlesex.

Corradi worked at the Royal Air Force (RAF) base in Ruislip and with the encouragement of the wing commander decided to join the Women's Auxiliary Air Force (WAAF), where she learned how to operate the wireless and read Morse code. One night the building in which she was taking her Morse slip (ticker tape containing code)

reading class was bombed. Eight people were killed and seventy injured. Corradi had to wait over four hours before she was rescued from the rubble; she was hospitalized for four days with a cut on her head. Following three weeks' leave, she completed her class and went to Chicksands in the Bedfordshire countryside, where she worked until the end of the war. After the war she volunteered with the returning ex-prisoners of war from Japan.

Corradi worked as a cipher operator at Eastcote for over two years. When she married, she was vetted by Government Communications Headquarters (GCHQ), as her husband's father was Italian; she had to transfer from cipher operator to teleprinter operator. The family moved to Cheltenham, where she worked for three years as a part-time teleprinter operator at GCHQ.

She and her husband were keen amateur radio operators, and she belonged to the Radio Society of Great Britain.

Bibliography: Corradi, D., personal communications to the author, February, March, April 2000; Smith, M., *Station X: The Codebreakers of Bletchley Park,* London: Channel 4 Books, Macmillan, 1998.

Courtauld, Katherine
13 July 1856–5 July 1935
agriculturalist

Employment: farming assistant; self-employed farmer from 1878.

Katherine Courtauld, a renowned fruit grower, ran her own farm from the age of twenty-one and became an advocate for women in agriculture.

The Courtaulds, originally Huguenots, made their fortune in the rayon industry. Katherine Courtauld helped manage one of her father's farms, the only way a woman could learn about agriculture at the time. When she was twenty-one, her father bought her the 243-acre Knights Farm in Colne Engaine, Essex. She raised cattle, sheep, pigs, and poultry, purchasing the livestock herself. One of her main interests was her orchard, and she became known as a fruit grower. She eventually expanded her farm to 2,000 acres.

Courtauld promoted the training of women in agriculture and took on several pupils at Knights Farm. She was a member of the Women's Farming and Gardening Union (WFGU), on its council from 1900, and chair in 1907. In 1920 she and Louisa Wilkins, a pioneer of the smallholdings movement, bought 98 acres to set up Small Holding Colony near Lingfield in Surrey. They rented out cottages and smallholdings to women and trained them in agriculture. In 1932 Courtauld gave the freehold of Courtauld House near Gower Street in London to the WFGU for use as its headquarters.

Courtauld was a keen horsewoman, an interest she shared with her long-time companion, Mary Gladstone. Katherine enjoyed hunting and sailing, and she had her own yacht. She had her hair cut short and wore a waistcoat, jacket, collar, and tie.

Bibliography: Courtauld, Sir S. L., *The Huguenot Family of Courtauld*, vol. III, London: n.p., 1957; King, P., *Women Rule the Plot*, London: Duckworth, 1999.

Courtauld, Louisa Perina née Ogier
1729–12 January 1807
silversmith

Employment: silversmith, 1765–1780.
Married: Samuel Courtauld.

Louisa Perina Courtauld was a silversmith, which required considerable knowledge of chemistry.

Her family were Huguenots, originally from Poitou, France. Her father was a silk weaver. Louisa Ogier married Samuel Courtauld, a Huguenot goldsmith, and lived in London. Samuel's father Augustin, and later Samuel, made silver toys such as tea sets, along with bedwarmers, candlesticks, and furniture. He and Louisa had eight children.

When her husband died in 1765, Courtauld carried on the business in her name until 1769. She made several fine pieces and

had her own mark, which was registered at the Goldsmiths' Company, in 1766–1767. Her son Samuel, also a silversmith, helped her from 1777 to 1780, and in 1780 the business was sold to John Henderson, who later became prime warden of the Goldsmiths' Company. Courtauld died in London in 1807.

Bibliography: Coleman, D. C., *Courtaulds: An Economic and Social History*, vol. 1, *The Nineteenth Century—Silk and Crepe*, Oxford: Oxford University Press, 1969; Courtauld, Sir S. L., *The Huguenot Family of Courtauld*, vol. 1, London, n.p., 1957; Evans, J., "Huguenot Goldsmiths in England and Ireland," *Proceedings of the Huguenot Society of London* 14 (4) (1933): 496–554; Hughes, B., and T. Hughes, *Three Centuries of English Domestic Silver, 1500–1820*, London: Lutterworth, 1952.

Courtenay-Latimer, Marjorie Eileen Doris
24 February 1907–
ichthyologist, museum curator

Education: convent school, South Africa.
Employment: curator, later director, East London Museum, South Africa, from August 1931.

On 22 December 1938 *Marjorie Courtenay-Latimer* discovered a freshly caught coelacanth, a fish that previously had been known only from fossils.

From an early age, Courtenay-Latimer was interested in nature, particularly birds, in her native South Africa. After leaving school she decided to become a nurse, but before she started her training, she was offered the chance to apply for the job of curator at the new East London Museum. She was successful, and in August 1931 started work at £2 a month. The museum had only a few poor exhibits; Courtenay-Latimer cleared most of them out and made a fresh start. She dedicated much time and effort to filling the museum with natural specimens from the local area, such as birds' eggs, seaweeds, and insects. The museum's reputation grew, and Courtenay-Latimer developed her own skills and knowledge.

In 1932 she spent six months working in the museum in Durban and a year later worked for six months at the South African Museum in Cape Town. In 1936 she fulfilled a long-held ambition to visit the remote Bird Island. She spent three months there collecting specimens of birds, plants, and shells for the museum.

On 22 December 1938, Courtenay-Latimer noticed an unusual fish in the catch of a local fisherman who regularly offered her specimens for the museum. A strange blue, the fish was 5 feet long and weighed 127 lbs. She recognized it as an important find and contacted J. L. B. Smith, a leading ichthyologist at Rhodes University, Grahamstown, asking him to identify it. She sent Smith a rough but accurate sketch of the fish, then, with the help of a local taxidermist, wrapped the fish in cloth and newspaper soaked with formalin. Smith suspected that the fish was of a type thought to be extinct and asked Courtenay-Latimer to preserve the internal organs; by the time he contacted her, these had been disposed of and the specimen mounted.

On 9 January 1939 Smith wrote to Courtenay-Latimer announcing that he had provisionally named the fish *Latimeria chalumnae* in her honor (*chalumnae* because it was found at the mouth of the Chalumna River). Smith was thrilled when he actually saw the coelacanth. The study of the coelacanth and the search for further specimens virtually took over his life. He reported the find in *Nature* in 1939.

Extensive searches were made for more living coelacanths, and by the end of the twentieth century over 200 had been found, mainly by fishermen around the Comoro Islands and in Indonesia. Some films were made of living coelacanths as well. "It was the energy and determination of Miss Latimer which saved so much, and scientific workers have good cause to be grateful," said Smith. "The genus *Latimeria* stands as my tribute" (Smith 1939, vol. 3627, 748–750).

Courtenay-Latimer continued to work at the East London Museum, eventually becoming its director. On the fiftieth anniversary of her discovery of the coelacanth, a ceremony was held at the museum on the Comoro Islands. In 1998 the South African mint produced a limited-edition set of gold coins with a coelacanth design. Courtenay-Latimer was guest of honor at the launch ceremony and was presented with a commemorative coin.

Bibliography: Bone, Q., and G. M. Hughes, "Coelacanth Stories," *MBA (Marine Biological Association of the UK) News* 20 (November 1973): 5; Hughes, G. M., "Coelacanths and Conservation," *MBA News* 21 (March 1999): 4; Lowenstein, Celia, producer, "The Fish That Time Forgot," aired on Channel 4, 24 June 2001; Smith, J. L. B., "The Living Coelacanthed Fish from South Africa," *Nature* 143, no. 3627 (1939): 748–750; Smith, J. L. B., "A Living Fish of Mesozoic Type," *Nature* 143, no. 3620 (1939): 455–456; Weinberg, S., *A Fish Caught in Time,* London: Fourth Estate, 1999.

Crane, Eva née Widdowson
c. 1911–
apiculturalist

Education: King's College, University of London, B.S. in mathematics, 1932; B.S. in physics, 1933; M.S. in quantum mechanics, 1935; Ph.D. in nuclear physics, 1938.

Employment: lecturer in physics, Universities of Hull and Sheffield, 1936–1945; Medical Research Council, part-time, 1945–1948; director, International Bee Research Association (IBRA), 1949–1983; editor of *Apicultural Abstracts,* 1950–1983; of *Bee World,* 1950–1983; of *Journal of Apicultural Research,* 1963–1982; scientific consultant to the Council of IBRA from 1983.

Married: James Alfred Crane, an officer in the Royal Naval Volunteer Reserve, in 1942. He died in 1978.

Eva Crane was the first director of the Bee Research Association (BRA) when it was founded in 1949.

Crane initially worked as a physicist. Having been given a swarm of bees as a wedding present, she decided to learn as much as she could about beekeeping. Because she and her husband were financially secure, Crane could pursue her vocation full time.

She joined the Beekeepers' Association in Sheffield but found that there were no scientific journals or abstracting services for beekeepers. She was elected to the British Beekeepers' Association Research Committee, out of which the Bee Research Association was founded, with Crane as its first director. The Cranes' home at Chalfont St. Peter in Buckinghamshire was the headquarters of the BRA until 1966. (In 1976 the BRA became the IBRA—the International Bee Research Association.) The main ofice of IBRA was later moved to Cardiff, where Crane donated her books and they established an Eva Crane Library.

Crane decided that beekeeping needed to be put on a more scientific footing. When the BRA took over publication of *Bee World*, Crane became editor and started a section with abstracts of published research on bees. Beginning in 1961 *Apicultural Abstracts* was published separately at quarterly intervals; a cumulative index (1950–1972), said to be the first computerized abstract index, appeared in 1976.

Bee World continued as a journal for the general reader, but from 1963 the *Journal of Apicultural Research* published articles documenting original research. Crane transmitted her own enthusiasm for bees in both general interest and specialist books, such as *Honey: A Comprehensive Survey* (1975), *The Archaeology of Beekeeping* (1983), and *Bees and Beekeeping: Science, Practice and World Resources* (1990). In 1999 she published *The World History of Beekeeping and Honey Hunting: Bees as a World Resource* (1999), which explores humans' use of bees from prehistoric times to the present.

Crane has traveled widely and acted as adviser in many countries. Some of her visits abroad were arranged by the British Executive Services Overseas (BESO), for whom she was still volunteering at the age of eighty. In 1992 she worked in Thailand, Nepal, Trinidad, and North Vietnam. She was also involved with the publication of the IBRA's dictionary of beekeeping terms

in nineteen languages. She has compiled numerous bibliographies of research into beekeeping throughout the world and updated lists of research workers. Her articles have been published in many countries and cover a wide variety of topics related to beekeeping.

In 1984 Crane was named an Officer of the Order of the British Empire (OBE) and in 1985 was awarded an honorary doctorate from Ohio State University, an important center for bee research. She is an honorary life president of IBRA, an honorary member of Apimondia (International Federation of Beekeepers' Associations), and an honorary fellow of the British Beekeepers' Association.

Bibliography: Connor, L., "A Conversation with Eva Crane, the First Lady of Beekeeping," *Speedy Bee* (June 1986): 11–12; Crane, E., personal communications to the author, 1998, 1999; Forristal, L. J., "Queen of the Bees," *The World and I* (March 1993): 208–215.

Cunliffe, Stella Vivian
12 January 1917–
statistician

Education: Parsons Mead School, Ashtead; London School of Economics, B.S. in economics, 1938.

Employment: Danish Bacon Company, 1939–1944; voluntary relief work in Europe, 1945–1947; statistician, Arthur Guinness Son and Company, 1947–1970; head of research unit, Home Office, 1970–1972; director of statistics, Home Office, 1972–1977.

Stella Cunliffe was the first woman to be president of the Royal Statistical Society.

Cunliffe took a degree from the London School of Economics prior to the start of World War II; her first job was with the Danish Bacon Company, where she was involved with wartime food allocation. From 1945 to 1947 she did voluntary relief work, first in Rotterdam, helping with the emergency feeding of starving people, then in Belsen and in displaced persons' camps west of Berlin.

When she returned to Britain, she was employed as a statistician at Guinness, the well-known brewery firm, and was later head of the statistical department at their Park Royal Brewery. Experiments by workers at Guinness were subjected to statistical analysis. Cunliffe always felt she should go to the site of the experiments (for example, the hop garden) to understand the enthusiasm of the experimenter and often to advise on the design and analysis of the experiments.

Cunliffe moved to the Home Office, a government department, as head of the research unit and was mainly concerned with criminological problems. She found that sociologists were not used to setting up a null hypothesis, designing their experiments carefully, or using statistics to analyze their results, and she tried to show them the value of using statistics. In almost all areas of experimental science, the role of statistics is now accepted, but there is a long way to go in using statistics to interpret human behavior. Cunliffe was constantly on the lookout for anomalies or unexpected correlations when examining collected data and interpreting them for government ministers.

As president of the Royal Statistical Society (RSS), Cunliffe worked hard to increase the involvement of the RSS in public affairs. In 1976–1977 the RSS gave evidence and a formal opinion on fluoridation to the Data Protection Committee and submitted views on traffic forecasting to the Department of the Environment. During her tenure, for the first time in the history of the RSS, the council's recommendation for the her successor as the president was disputed, testing Cunliffe's skills in diplomacy. At that time the position of president alternated between a well-known public figure (usually a nonstatistician) and a fellow of the RSS. In the end the question was put to the vote, and the proposed public figure lost (though only 42 percent of the members took part in the election). After this situation the election procedures of the RSS were altered.

Cunliffe retired from the Home Office in 1977. She was statistical adviser to the Finniston Committee of Enquiry into the Engineering Profession, which published the report *Engineering Our Future* in 1980. In 1984, at the request of the chairman of the Statistical Users Council, she wrote a discussion document, "The Need for a National Statistical Council"; her research was funded by the Social Science Research Council.

She was named a Member of the Order of the British Empire (MBE) in 1993, mainly for her volunteer work with the Girl Guides and with prisoners.

Bibliography: Cunliffe, S. V., personal communication to the author, August 2000; Cunliffe, S. V., "The President's Address, Given on November 12th, 1975," *Journal of the Royal Statistical Society,* series A, 139 (1976): 1–19; Cunliffe, S. V., "President's Report," *Journal of the Royal Statistical Society* 140 (1977): 518–521; Foster, J., archives consultant, Royal Statistical Society, personal communication to author, 23 June 2000; "Report of the Council—Session 1976–77," *Journal of the Royal Statistical Society* 140 (1977): 527; *Who's Who, 1999,* London: Adam and Charles Black, 1999.

Curie, Marya (Manya; Marie) née Sklodowska
7 November 1867–4 July 1934
physicist

Education: school in Warsaw until 1883; Sorbonne, Paris, 1891–1894; Licencie de Physique, 1893; B.S., 1894; D.Sc. 1903.

Employment: private tutor, Warsaw, 1883–1885; governess, 1885–1889; physics teacher, Women's Teacher Training School, Sèvres, 1900–1904; laboratory manager, Ecole Supérieur de Physique et de Chimie, 1904–1906; professor of general physics, Faculté des Sciences, Sorbonne, 1906-1914; director of the Curie Laboratory, Radium Institute, Paris 1914-1934.

Married: Dr. Pierre Curie, chief of the laboratory, Ecole Supérieur de Physique et de Chimie , Paris, on 26 July 1895. He died on 19 April 1906.

Marie Curie, with her husband, Pierre, discovered the radioactive elements radium

Madame Marya (Marie) Curie (Library of Congress)

and polonium. In 1903 they shared the Nobel Prize in physics with Henri Becquerel, the first time a woman had received a Nobel Prize. In 1911 she was awarded the Nobel Prize for chemistry in her own right, becoming the only person to have been awarded the Nobel Prize twice. In 1896 she was the first to use the term "radioactivity." A unit of radioactivity, the "curie," is named after her.

Curie was born in Warsaw, the fifth and last child in the family. Her multilingual father taught physics and mathematics at a high school; her mother ran a small boarding school for girls in their home.

Warsaw was under Russian rule when Curie was at school, so the students had their lessons in Russian. Curie won a gold medal for her achievements in secondary school but overworked during her last school year and was sent to stay with relatives in the country for a few months to recover.

Curie and her older sister Bronya decided to study medicine in Paris, where women were admitted. They planned to work to save money for Bronya's education; once she was qualified and earning, she would send for Curie to start her university education. Curie became a resident governess in the village of Szczuki and ran a literacy class for the village children. By 1885, the sisters had saved enough money for Bronya to begin her studies in Paris. Five years later, Curie joined her there. Her sister was to marry Casimir, a fellow medical student; Marie could live with them. By July 1893 she took her first physics examination and was at the top of her group. In 1894, using a government scholarship from Poland, she studied for a degree in mathematics, which she achieved with distinction.

Marie set off for Paris with high hopes. In the beginning she could not understand French very well, but she persevered. Bronya's home was two hours' journey from the Sorbonne, so in March 1892, Marie moved into her own room in the Latin quarter near the Sorbonne. This meant she had extra time for studying.

In 1894 she was introduced to Pierre Curie, a physicist who with his brother Jacques had worked on piezoelectricity. Pierre's parents lived at Sceaux, on the outskirts of Paris. Marie and Pierre Curie were married on 26 July 1895 and went off for a bicycling honeymoon. Pierre Curie was a lecturer at the Ecole Supérieur de Physique et de Chimie in Paris. Marie Curie was allowed a room in the same building, as she needed space for her experiments on the magnetic properties of tempered steels; she was aided by a grant from the Society for the Advancement of National Industry, and her results were published in 1897. On 12 September that year their first daughter, Iréne, was born.

Curie's next problem was to find a suitable research project for her doctorate. In 1896 Henri Becquerel had published his investigations on radiation, which had followed from Röntgen's descriptions of the effects of X-rays in the previous year. Becquerel wanted to find out if any substances could be induced to produce radiation. He had discovered that uranium compounds were able to produce energy-containing rays, which affected a photographic plate. Using an ionization chamber, a Curie quadrant electrometer, and a piezoelectric quartz, Curie worked through samples of uranium salts and showed that the intensity of radiation was related to the quantity of the uranium in the sample (determined chemically). Next she checked the radiation levels of all known samples of minerals at her disposal and found that only ores containing uranium and thorium indicated radiation. When she tested pitchblende, a uranium-containing ore, she found a reading four times higher than anticipated. Repetition of the experiments gave similar results. She concluded that there must be another, more radioactive element in pitchblende producing this radiation.

Her husband had become interested in Curie's investigations and left his own research in order to work with her. By July 1898 they had discovered polonium, and by the end of the year they guessed there must be another element, which they called radium, whose radiation was 900 times more powerful than that of uranium. Eugene Demarcay, who worked in Pierre Curie's laboratory, tested the radium sulfate with his spectroscope and found that radium was indeed a new element with a unique spectral line. Thus the Curies could publish their discovery.

The next challenge was to extract enough radium to determine its properties. Eventually the Austrian government allowed them to have a ton of waste pitchblende from the mine at St. Joachimsthal, and the Curies paid for its transport. Pierre Curie concentrated on the physical properties of radium, whereas Marie worked on purifying the samples of radium salts. They were given a shed with a courtyard in which most of the heating could be done outside. They started the work in 1899; not until 1902 had they extracted enough radium. Both Pierre and Marie Curie were physically exhausted and suffered from lethargy; Pierre had terrible rheumatism-like pains in his legs. Neither then nor later would Marie Curie accept in public that the radiation had caused their poor health.

Curie wrote up her part of the work for her doctorate and successfully defended it on 25 June 1903. Later that year she and her husband shared the Nobel Prize for Physics with Henri Becquerel. In 1903 the Curies traveled to London to receive the Davy Medal at the Royal Society and gave a lecture at the Royal Institution.

Pierre Curie was appointed as a professor at the Sorbonne in 1904, with Marie in charge of his laboratory. She taught part time at Sèvres until their second daughter, Eve, was born in December 1904. Pierre had published twenty-one papers between 1898 and 1904, some coauthored (five with Marie), but after that he did no more experimental work, as he fell too ill; yet he continued with his teaching responsibilites. After the family had returned from a holiday in the countryside, on 19 April 1906, Pierre Curie fell in front of a pair of horses and his skull was crushed. Marie Curie stepped into her husband's position as professor, but the work she did from then on tended to be repetitive and thorough rather than creative. She gave her first lecture at the Sorbonne on 5 November 1906, the first woman to lecture there in physics. She became more aware of the need for adequate funding for her work and set up links with industry.

From 1906, Curie was head of the Radium Institute. Over the years several scientists, about a third of them women (such as May Sibyl Leslie from Britain and Ellen Gleditsch from Norway), came and worked there. Curie tended to delegate to them routine tasks rather than encourage original research. She stubbornly refused to accept the dangers of radiation, in particular radon gas, and failed to provide adequate protection for those in her laboratory; many later died young of radiation-induced illnesses.

Curie founded the journal *Le Radium* to ensure that research on radium would reach the public domain. She worked hard to establish an international radium standard, insisting that the work be carried out in her laboratory, and the results were presented at the 1911 Solvay Conference. After the acceptance of the international radium standard, her workers earned income for the laboratory by doing measurements of radium salt samples to be used in medicine and industry.

Curie compiled information about radioactivity for her *Traité de radioactivité* (Treatise on Radioactivity), published in 1910. She thought it would help her laboratory if she applied for election to the Académie des Sciences and so in 1910 set about gathering support for her application. But because she was involved with Paul Langevin, a former pupil of her husband and a married man, the media ensured that the vacant place in the academy went to her rival. Paul was separated from his wife and he had a bachelor flat near the university, to which Marie made frequent visits. This caused a public scandal, which upset Marie so much that she became ill.

Friends in Paris and the international scientific community rallied to her support and, concerned about her rejection by the Académie des Sciences, nominated her for the Nobel Prize in chemistry, which she was awarded in 1911, officially for the discovery of radium (though some scientists thought that on the basis of the work she had done between 1903 and 1911, she did not merit the prize). Soon after returning to Paris from Stockholm, she collapsed with exhaustion and did not work again until the following October.

It had been decided that a new Radium Institute would be constructed, and once back at work, Curie took a keen interest in the actual building, which was ready by 31 July 1914. Curie was to be in charge of the physical and chemical research. When World War I began, Curie took on the challenge of providing a mobile X-ray service for the troops. With the help of her daughter Irène, she toured the battlefields, X-raying the injured (Irène died prematurely from her exposure to radiation). Curie trained radiographers in her institute and raised funds to equip more radiological cars; by 1917–1918, over a million men had been X-rayed by mobile units.

When the war was over, Curie used her connections to industry to get equipment for her laboratory. In 1921 she visited the United States for an interview with Marie Meloney, an American reporter, and toured the country giving talks and meeting officials. She was awarded nine honorary doctorate degrees on her visit, along with nine honorary memberships in learned societies, and she returned to France with a gram of radium and over $160,000. Curie visited the United States again in 1929 in order to raise money for an Institute of Radium in Warsaw. Though she succeeded financially, the trip was not as productive as the first, as the effects of radiation poisoning were hitting her hard: Curie had severe cataracts, her hearing was diminished, and she was in poor health overall. In 1934 she was taken to a sanatorium at Sancellemoz, Savoy, where her condition gradually worsened. By the time she died, the adverse cumulative effects of radiation were being recognized along with its beneficial uses, especially in the short-term treatment of cancer.

Bibliography: Birch, B., *Marie Curie: The Polish Scientist Who Discovered Radium and Its Life-Saving Properties*, Watford, Herts: Exley Publications, 1988; Boudia, B., "The Curie Laboratory: Radioactivity and Metrology," *History and Technology* 13 (1997): 249–265; Cotton, E., *Les Curies*, Paris: Editions Seghers, 1963; Curie, E., *Madame Curie*, translated by V. Sheehan, London: Heinemann, 1938; Davis, J. L., "The Research School of Madame Curie in the Paris Faculty, 1907–14," *Annals of Science* 52 (1995): 321–355; Ellis, P., ed., *100 Years of Radium: Madame Curie and the History of Radiochemistry*, Hatfield, Herts: Association for Science Education, 1999; Hughes, J., "Marie Curie and the Discovery of Radium," notes for talk at Association for Science Education meeting, 9 January 1998, Liverpool, and British Association for the Advancement of Science meeting, 7 September 1998, Cardiff; Hughes, J., personal communication to the author, 29 March 2000; Nobel Foundation, *Nobel Lectures, Including Presentation Speeches and Laureates' Biographies, Physics 1901–1921*, London: Elsevier, 1967; Pflaum, R., *Grand Obsession: Marie Curie and Her World*, London: Doubleday, 1989; Reid, R., *Marie Curie*, London: Collins, 1974; Roqué, X., "Marie Curie and the Radium Industry: A Preliminary Sketch," *History and Technology* 13

(1997): 267–291; Rutherford, E. "Obituary. Mme. Curie," *Nature* (21 July 1934): 90–91.

Currie, Ethel Dobbie
4 December 1898–24 March 1963
geologist

Education: Bellahouston Academy, Glasgow; University of Glasgow, B.Sc., 1920; Ph.D. 1925, D.Sc. 1945.

Employment: assistant curator, Hunterian Museum, Glasgow, 1920–1962; senior lecturer, University of Glasgow, 1960–1962.

Ethel Currie spent her career at the Hunterian Museum in Glasgow, where she played a major role in the care and development of the geological collections; in 1952 she became the first woman to be president of the Geological Society of Glasgow.

Currie was born and educated in Glasgow, studying under Professor J. W. Gregory, who invited her to work as a demonstrator in his department and then appointed her to the post of assistant curator at the Hunterian Museum. The growing geological collections there needed to be catalogued, and Currie undertook this task with enthusiasm. She prepared exhibits on aspects of geology and did some teaching as well.

Her early work concentrated on fossil echinoids, and her Ph.D. thesis was entitled "Jurassic and Eocene Echinoidea from Somaliland." She then turned her attention to ammonites; the Royal Society of Edinburgh awarded her the Neill Prize in 1945 for her paper "Growth Stages in Some Jurassic Ammonites." She carried out key research on the fauna of Skipsey's Marine Band and published the results (with C. Duncan and H. M. Wood) in 1937. This formed the basis of one of her most important pieces of work, a comprehensive description of the Scottish carboniferous goniatites (ammonites with a simple septal structure). She also published papers relating to aspects of the Hunterian Museum's collections, such as a monograph on mammalian fossils (with J. W. Gregory), and on the museum's Begg Collection (fossils donated by James Livingstone Begg in the 1940s).

In recognition of her work, she was awarded the Wollaston Fund of the Geological Society of London; in 1949 she was one of the first three women to be admitted to fellowship of the Royal Society of Edinburgh.

Bibliography: Clark, Neil D. L., curator of palaeontology, Hunterian Museum, University of Glasgow, personal communication to the author, May, June 2001; "Ethel D. Currie, D.Sc., Ph.D., FRSE, FGS, FMA," *Transactions of the Geological Society of Glasgow* 25, pt. 1 (1963): 98–100; Weir, J., "Ethel Dobbie Currie, Ph.D., D.Sc. (Glas.), FGS," *Year Book of the Royal Society of Edinburgh* (1963): 15–17.

Cust, Aleen
1868–29 January 1937
veterinary surgeon

Education: New College, Edinburgh 1896–1900.

Employment: assistant to William Byrne, Roscommon, Ireland, 1900–1910; own practice, Roscommon, 1910–1914; veterinary inspector (part time), Galway County Council, 1905–1914; YMCA volunteer, Abbeville, France, 1915–1917; unit administrator (captain), Queen Mary's Army Auxiliary Corps (QMAAC), January 1918–July 1918.

Aleen Cust was the first woman veterinary surgeon in Britain and in 1922 became the first woman to be registered as a member of the Royal College of Veterinary Surgeons.

Cust was born the eldest of six children near Tipperary, Ireland, where her father was a land agent. Her mother, Charlotte Bridgeman, was the daughter of a vice-admiral. On 14 January 1878 her father, Leopold Cust, inherited the family fortune and the baronetcy of his father, Sir Edward Cust. Soon thereafter Sir Leopold died suddenly, and in March 1878 the family left Ireland for England. On the death of her brother in 1893, Cust received an inheritance and a year later went to Edinburgh to train as a veterinary surgeon. She enrolled in 1896 at the New Veterinary College. At the time her mother was a woman of the bedchamber to Queen Victoria, so to avoid any scandal, Cust registered as A. I. Custance (using the surname of a well-known jockey of the day). She was the only woman student and was awarded the Gold Medal for zoology.

In April 1897 she applied to the examination committee of the Royal College of Veterinary Surgeons (RCVS) to take her first professional examination. The matter was referred to counsel; the majority voted against Cust's admission. The minutes of the meeting were published in the *Veterinary Record* on 24 April 1897, resulting in considerable correspondence on the subject of admitting women. The case was eventually heard at the Court of Sessions in Edinburgh, the RCVS obtaining a ruling that the court had no jurisdiction over it as the RCVS had no domicile in Scotland (though in fact the RCVS had three of the four veterinary colleges in Scotland and an office there with its own letterhead. This last was never produced; if it had been, the RCVS would probably have lost the case). Cust did not appeal and did not try to gain entry into the profession again until 1922.

Cust continued with the remaining three years of her veterinary studies in considerable financial hardship. A vet in Dundee, Andrew Spreull, allowed Aleen to be his pupil. When she left the college in 1900, she was given a testimonial by the principal saying that she had completed the course and proved her competence. She became assistant to William Byrne in Roscommon, Ireland, and gradually built up her reputation as a vet.

Cust attended the National Veterinary Congresses at Windermere, Buxton, and Budapest and in 1906 gave a talk to the Irish Central Veterinary Association: "A Trip to the Imperial Horse Breeding Studs and Large Herds of Hungary and Serbia."

Over the objections of the RCVS, she was appointed to the part-time post of veterinary inspector for Galway County Council in 1905 and again in 1906. By this time she was widely known for her veterinary skills and well paid. (For its part, the RCVS was sliding into bankruptcy.)

Byrne died suddenly in 1910, and Cust took over his practice. She bought a house in Athleague and had four domestic helpers. She kept goats, Jersey and Derry cattle, cats, and cocker spaniels. She rode side-saddle on a white Arabian stallion to make her visits, or used a back-to-back gig if she had to take equipment. By World War I the Army Veterinary Corps had been formed and by 1917 there were eighteen hospitals for horses, each taking 250 horses.

Cust went to northeastern France in 1915 under the auspices of the Young Men's Christian Association (YMCA), where she unofficially helped the veterinary surgeons in the Remount Hospital for horses. She had her own car and was based near Abbeville in the northeast part of the country. In January 1918 she enlisted in the Queen Mary's Army Auxiliary Corps and served as a bacteriologist for five months.

On 23 December 1919 the Sex Disqualification (Removal) Act was passed, opening the way for women to be admitted to any incorporated society. Cust applied to the RCVS for permission to take the final examination in December 1922. Because of her war service, she had to take only the oral examination. She was given her RCVS diploma and was on the register from 1924.

During the Anglo-Irish war, Cust, an English aristocrat, was considered an enemy in Ireland; by 1924 she had sold her property and moved to England and lived in the New Forest, Hampshire. Although her health prevented her from setting up in general practice, she continued to treat animals when asked and to attend meetings of the National Veterinary Medical Association. She also bred Pomeranians, cocker spaniels, and ornamental pheasants.

She died in 1937 while on holiday in Jamaica, leaving the RCVS £5,000 to be invested in the Aleen Cust Research Scholarship.

Bibliography: Ford, C. M., *Aleen Cust, Veterinary Surgeon: Britain's First Woman Vet*, Bristol: Biopress, 1990; "Miss Aleen Cust: The First Woman Veterinary Surgeon," *Veterinary Record* 49, 6 (1937): 167; "Miss Aleen Cust's Death: Information from Jamaica," *Veterinary Record* 49, 9 (1937): 274.

D

Dal, Ingerid Blanca Juell
2 August 1895–17 February 1985
linguist

Education: Kristiana University, 1914–1920 and Heidelberg University, 1920–1925, philology and philosophy; University of Hamburg, Ph.D., 1925; University of Oslo, Ph.D., 1930.

Employment: University of Oslo: research assistant, 1930–1938; lecturer in German linguistics, 1938–1939; professor of German philology, 1939–1965.

Ingerid Dal was a professor of German philology at the University of Oslo. She was elected as a member of the Norwegian Academy of Sciences in 1940.

Dal was born in Drammen, near Oslo. From an early age she was interested in science, philosophy, philology, and mathematics, preferring to stay at home reading rather than go out with friends. After completing school in 1914, she moved to Oslo and following World War I went to Germany, where there was an increasing interest in culture. She studied philology and philosophy at the Universities of Hamburg and Heidelberg and in 1925 presented her thesis on Lask's *Kategorienlehre* in relation to Kant's philosophy. Five years later she finished a thesis at the University of Oslo on the origin and use of old Nordic expletive particles.

Dal worked at the University of Oslo initially as a lecturer; from 1939 she was a professor of Germanic philology. Her predecessor, Jacob Sverdrup, had a strong personality and unorthodox views; following in his footsteps presented a considerable challenge.

But Dal produced a substantial amount of research of fundamental importance in its field. She wrote a paper on the history of the weak-toned prefixes in the Nordic languages, published in the *Norsk Tidsskrift for Sprogvitenskap* and one on the origins of the present participle in the English language, in the same journal. Her brief historical study of German syntax was published in 1952 in the well-known *Sammlung kurzer Grammatiken germanischer Dialekte*, a widely used textbook for university students.

In 1940 she was made a fellow of the Norwegian Academy of Sciences and in 1954 was awarded a Nansen Foundation prize. In 1958 Dal became a fellow of the Norwegian Academy for Language and Literature and was presented the Goethe Gold Medal for her services to the German language abroad. For her seventy-fifth birthday, the Norwegian General Scientific Research Committee produced a collection of her research papers under the title *Research into the History of the German Language,* published in 1972.

Bibliography: Aschehoug og Gyuldendals Store Norske Leksikon, vol. 3, Oslo: Kunnskapsforlaget, 1998; Heggen, L., librarian, the National Library, Oslo, personal communication to the author, June 2001; Høst, G., "Aus dem Rahmen eines Bildes—Ingerid Dal," translated by Christiane Bruns, Osloer Beitrage zur Germanistik 8 (1983): 18–21; Jahr, E. H., Agder University College Kristiansand. Personal communication to the author, 20 September 1999 and August 2001; Norsk Biografisk Leksikon, vol. 2, Oslo: Kunnskapsforlaget, 2000.

Dalton, Katharina Dorothea
née Kuipers
12 November 1916–
chiropodist, doctor

Education: Norfolk House High School, London, 1922–1925; Royal Masonic School, Herts, 1926–1934; London Foot Hospital School of Chiropody, 1934–1936; Northern Polytechnic Insitutute, 1942–1943; Royal Free Hospital, 1943–?; Member of the Royal College of Surgeons, Licentiate of the Royal College of Physicians, 1948; fellow, Royal College of General Practitioners, 1982.
Employment: chiropodist; general practitioner; PMS Clinic, University College Hospital.
Married: Mr. Thomson (died 1942); Tom E. Dalton, Unitarian minister.

Katharina Dalton became known for her work on the stages of the menstrual cycle and its effects on behavior.

Dalton initially trained and worked as a chiropodist, and her textbook, *The Essentials of Chiropody for Students* (1938), went through six editions, the last in 1968. Left a war widow with four children, she studied medicine at the Royal Free Hospital and worked in general practice for twenty years.

Dalton became interested in the problems associated with premenstrual tension and started interviewing women, especially those in closed communities such as boarding schools and prisons. Her first publication on the topic, "The Pre-menstrual Syndrome," coauthored with Raymond Greene, appeared in the *British Medical Journal* in 1953. *The Menstrual Cycle* (1969) dealt with the basic biology involved and ways of coping with premenstrual pain and tension. Perhaps of greatest interest were the links Dalton made between accidents and behavior problems and the day of the menstrual cycle. In 1954 she established the first clinic dealing with premenstrual syndrome and its problems, at University College, London. She was also among the first to bring these matters to public attention. She has given talks on radio and television, and in 1991 set up a help line.

She has written many articles and books on cyclical criminal acts, premenstrual syndrome, and postnatal depression; among these works are *Depression after Childbirth* (1989) and *The Pre-menstrual Syndrome and Progesterone Therapy* (1984). She was a founding member of the Royal College of General Practitioners and in 1971 was the first woman member of the general practitioner section of the Royal Society of Medicine. Dalton has also been the honorary physician for the Royal Society of Musicians and honorary medical officer for Chorleywood College for the Blind.

She was awarded the Hawthorne Clinical British Medical Association Prize in 1954, 1966, and 1976; the Upjohn Travel Fellowship in 1960; the Charlotte Brown prize from the Royal Free Hospital in 1961; and the Migraine Prize from the Royal College of Practitioners in 1972.

Bibliography: The Medical Directory 1999, London: F. T. Healthcare, 1999; *Medical Register 1995;* Riding, N., archivist, Royal Free Hospital Archives Centre, personal communication to the author, 6 February 2001; Zita, J. N., "The Premenstrual Syndrome: Diseasing the Female Cycle," in N. Tuana, ed., *Feminism and Science,* Bloomington: Indiana University Press, 1989, 188–210.

Datta, Naomi née Goddard
17 September 1922–
bacteriologist

Education: St. Mary's School, Wantage; University College, London; West London Hospital Medical School, M.B., B.S., 1946; diploma in bacteriology (University of London), 1950; M.D. (London), 1952.
Employment: junior medical posts, 1946–1947; senior bacteriologist, Public Health Laboratory Service, 1947–1957; lecturer and professor of microbial genetics, Royal Postgraduate Medical School, London, 1957–1984 (emeritus professor from 1984); part-time researcher, Centre for Genetic Anthropology, University College, London, from 1996.
Married: S. P. Datta, in 1943.

Naomi Datta (Godfrey Argent Studio)

Naomi Datta did research on the genetics of antibiotic resistance in bacteria.

After qualifying in medicine, Datta joined the Public Health Laboratory Service as a bacteriologist, a post she held for ten years. In 1957 she was appointed lecturer at the Royal Postgraduate Medical School at Hammersmith Hospital, London, where she later became professor of microbial genetics. Datta studied the genetics and epidemiology of drug resistance in bacteria. In 1962 she demonstrated that antibiotic resistance could be transmitted between bacteria, the first time this had been achieved outside Japan. She identified and classified the plasmids that carry genes for drug resistance. In 1983 she coauthored, with Victoria Hughes, "Conjugative Plasmids in Bacteria of the 'Pre-antibiotic' Era" (*Nature* 302: 725–726).

She was elected a fellow of the Royal College of Pathologists in 1973. She retired in 1984 and became emeritus professor of microbial genetics at the University of London. In 1985 she was elected a fellow of the Royal Society.

She joined the Centre for Genetic Anthropology as a part-time researcher in 1996 and is investigating Y chromosome variation in Greeks, Turks, Greek Cypriots, and Turkish Cypriots.

Bibliography: "Professor Naomi Datta FRS M.D.," Available at www.ucl.ac.uk/tcga/people/naomi.html; *Who's Who, 1997,* London: Adam and Charles Black, 1997.

Davies, Margaret
1914–6 October 1982
conservationist, archaeologist

Education: Bury Grammar School; Manchester University, B.S., Ph.D.
Married: Elwyn Davies, later chief inspector for the Welsh Education Office, in 1940.

Margaret Davies, the first chair of the Welsh Committee of the Countryside Commission, was also president of the Cardiff Naturalists Club and on the Council of the National Museum of Wales.

Davies studied archaeology at Manchester University. She worked on Bronze Age sites in France and investigated megalithic monuments in the Irish Sea and North Channel coastlands for her Ph.D. dissertation, published in the *Antiquaries Journal.* She was elected a fellow of the Society of Antiquaries in 1943.

After World War II ended, she and her husband moved to Cardiff. She became involved in natural history and was a competent field botanist. She was on the editorial board of Collins's New Naturalist series and revised H. J. Fleur's *Natural History of Man in Britain.* She was made a Commander of the Order of the British Empire (CBE) in 1973.

Bibliography: "Dr. Margaret Davies: Conservation of the Welsh Countryside," *Times* (16 October 1982).

Déjerine-Klumpke, Augusta née Klumpke
15 October 1859–5 November 1927
doctor

Education: University of Paris, M.D. 1887.
Employment: Lourcine Hospital, 1887; Tenon Hospital 1888; Bicentre, 1888; research in neurology, Salpetrière.
Married: Jules Déjerine, neurologist at Salpetrière, Paris, in 1888.

Augusta Déjerine-Klumpke was an expert on the anatomy and physiology of the central nervous system.

Déjerine-Klumpke was born in San Francisco. The family moved to Lausanne, and later to Paris, mainly so that Déjerine-Klumpke could train as a doctor.

Although she did very well in her baccalaureate examinations in science, the medical professors made no secret of their antagonism to women doctors. She was one of eleven women who enrolled in the medical faculty; they were not welcomed by their male colleagues. For a time, she worked with Blanche Edwards, an American who led a three-year campaign to allow women to become fully qualified as doctors. Déjerine-Klumpke finally received her doctor's degree in January 1887 and worked in several hospitals, encountering great hostility from the male staff.

After her marriage she concentrated entirely on neurology, publishing *L'Anatomie des centres nerveux* (The anatomy of the nervous centers) with her husband in 1885. They developed an efficient technique of cutting brain sections, and Déjerine-Klumpke developed a reputation for her outstanding anatomical work, especially for her description of what is known as Klumpke's paralysis, in which nerves and muscles of the hand and forearm are impaired. During World War I she cared for soldiers with nerve damage. Following her husband's death in 1917, she worked with paraplegics and those with peripheral nerve damage.

She was the first woman member of the Société de Neurologie, becoming president in 1914. She was also president of the So-

ciété de Biologie in 1924, and was made an officer of the Legion of Honour in the same year.

Bibliography: Bailey, H., and W. J. Bishop, *Notable Names in Medicine and Surgery*, London: Lewis, 1964; *Dictionnaire de Biographie Française*, vol. 10, Paris: Librairie Le Touzey et âne, 1965.

Denman, Gertrude Mary née Pearson
1884–2 June 1954
educator, birth control campaigner, campaigner for rural life

Education: at home, by governess; Queen's Gate Day School; finishing school, Dresden, Germany.
Married: Lord Thomas Denman, on 26 November 1903.

Gertrude Denman was an influential figure in the development of practical education for women, particularly in rural areas. She played an important role in the growth of the Women's Institute movement in Britain.

Denman's family was wealthy and well connected, her father having been made a baronet in 1894. He owned silver mines in Bolivia, and Denman had a solid silver bicycle made by Tiffany's in New York. Denman was brought up in London, though she went to finishing school in Germany. She married in 1903, becoming Lady Denman. In 1905 she was given her own country estate, Balcombe Place, by her father.

By 1908 Denman had begun to play a role in public affairs. She was elected to the executive of the Women's National Liberal Federation. In 1911 she accompanied her husband to Australia, where he had been made governor-general. In 1913 she became involved in the Bush Nursing Association.

Women's Institutes (WI) had started in Canada in 1896 and were established in Belgium, Poland, and the United States. The organization was intended to improve rural life through activities for women from small communities. In 1915 the first WI in Britain was set up in Wales. When she returned to Britain, Denman became active in the group and was the WI chair from 1917 to 1946. The movement expanded rapidly, and by the end of 1918 there were a total of 760 Women's Institute groups.

In the late 1920s Denman chaired a committee looking into the practical education of women for rural life. The committee produced a report in 1928. In 1930 she obtained funding that enabled individuals to be trained to teach farm household management and rural domestic economy. She set up a scheme to show how to keep hens profitably in backyards and had her own farm until 1916. In 1939 she became director of the Women's Land Army, gave over Balcombe Place for its headquarters, and set up women's committees for the Women's Land Army in every county. The Land Army was set up to supply female agricultural workers to replace male workers drafted for military service.

Denman also championed family planning, serving as chair of the National Birth Control Association from 1930, later known as the Family Planning Association.

In 1946 the Women's Institute established a residential college at Marcham, Abingdon, near Berkshire, as a focus for the organization's educational activities. This was opened officially in September 1948 and was named Denman College in recognition of Denman's important contribution to the Women's Institute. She was made a Commander of the Order of the British Empire (CBE) in 1920 and a Dame Commander of the Order of the British Empire (DBE) in 1933.

Bibliography: Dictionary of National Biography 1951–1960, Oxford: Oxford University Press, 1971; Huxley, G. "Lady Denman, CBE 1884–1954," London: Chatto and Windus, 1961; King, P., *Women Rule the Plot,* London: Duckworth, 1999; Teaching center coordinator, Denman College, Abingdon, personal communication to the author, 1997.

Dent, Edith Vere née Annesley
1863–12 October 1948
botanist

Education: local school.
Married: Robert Wilkinson Dent, in 1893.

Edith Dent founded the Wild Flower Society in 1886. From very modest beginnings, the society went on to undertake serious botanical work.

Edith Dent was the eldest of six children of the vicar of Clifford Chambers, a village near Stratford-on-Avon. When she left school, she taught her youngest sister at home for eight years, doing formal lessons in the mornings and exploring the countryside in the afternoons.

Dent drew up a list of common flowers for her sister Alice to tick off when and where she found them. Five other local children joined in, and more asked if they could as well. Because it would have taken too long to write out a list of flowers for each child by hand, Dent had the first *Wild Flower Diaries* printed (based on Bentham and Hooker's *Handbook of British Flora*) and started the *Wild Flower Magazine.*

In 1893 she married Robert Dent and moved to Tunbridge Wells, where she continued to run the Wild Flower Society. In 1903 the family moved to Shap in Westmorland, now Cumbria, with their five children. From her home (and with the help of her family), Dent compiled articles, collected subscriptions, and dealt with correspondence for the *Wild Flower Magazine,* published three times a year. Many botanists contributed articles; Dent wrote the editor's letter.

During World War I, Dent was president of the Red Cross for her area and organized VAD detachments for Westmorland. Two of her sons were killed in active duty and after this tragedy, she always wore black. She was named an Officer of the Order of the British Empire (OBE) for her voluntary work.

Dent wrote her last editor's letter for the September-December 1948 magazine and died in October that year. She had seen the Wild Flower Society develop into a prominent organization associated with many eminent botanists, its members involved in vital recording work. The membership of the Wild Flower Society continued to increase and now has several regional branches. Each year members are invited to send in their diaries (now based on J. E. Dandy's *List of the Vascular Plants of the British Isles*); awards are presented to those who find the most species.

Bibliography: Norman, E., "Violet Schwerdt MBE 1900–1996," *Wild Flower Magazine* 437 (Autumn 1996): 1–5; Schwerdt, V. V. C., "The President's Letter," *Wild Flower Magazine* 407 (Autumn 1996): 1–7.

Dony, Christina Mayne
née Goodman
1910–23 May 1995
botanist

Education: Edgbaston High School for Girls, Birmingham.

Employment: work in family business (builders and coal merchants), Selly Oak, Birmingham, 1932–1962; volunteer work in Air Raid Precautions, Birmingham Service Club, and an aircraft factory during World War II.

Married: John Dony, honorary secretary of the Botanical Society of the British Isles, in 1962.

Christina Dony was membership secretary of the Botanical Society of the British Isles from 1964 to 1974 and contributed much to the study of local flora in several counties.

Dony was born in Selly Oak, Birmingham, one of five children. She spent her working life in the family business of construction and coal sales, eventually becoming a director. As a young adult she focused mainly on sports, particularly hockey, and played on England's national team three times.

Dony joined the Birmingham Natural History Society in 1947. She contributed to the *Flora of Warwickshire* (1971) and was on the society's council. She also served as secretary of the botanical section for seven years. Dony joined the Botanical Society of

the British Isles (BSBI) in 1948 and the Wild Flower Society in 1964.

She met her husband through a shared botanical interest in the "wool aliens" of Worcestershire, plants that grow particularly in areas where there is waste from woolen mills. With him she carried out a comprehensive study of the flora of Hertfordshire and Bedfordshire, completing *The Bedfordshire Plant Atlas* (1976) in a relatively short time. She and her husband also surveyed and documented important sites for flora in Bedfordshire, reporting their results in *Watsonia*. She continued studying the flora of Bedfordshire in particular and (with coauthor Adrian Rundle) published an important record of the *Taraxacum* species in the county.

In 1964 Dony became membership secretary of the BSBI, a position she held for ten years. She frequently presented exhibits at the BSBI's annual exhibition meetings. She was made an honorary member of the BSBI in 1975, the first time a wife and husband had both been recognized in this way. She recorded species until just before her death; her final total, in 1994, was 2,532.

Bibliography: Boon, C. R., "Christina Mayne Dony (1910–1995)," obituary, *Watsonia* 21 (1997): 297–299; Ellis, R. G., Honorary Secretary, Botanical Society of the British Isles, personal communication to the author, July 2001.

Downie, Dorothy G.
September 16 1894–22 August 1960
botanist

Education: University of Edinburgh, B.S. (science), 1917; B.S. (forestry), 1919; Moray House Training College, Edinburgh, 1919–1920; University of Chicago, 1925–1928, Ph.D.

Employment: University of Aberdeen: assistant, 1920–1925 and 1928–1929; lecturer, 1929–1949; reader, 1949–1960.

Dorothy Downie was the first woman to take a degree in forestry at the University of Edinburgh.

After graduation Downie worked as an assistant to W. G. Craib, Regis Chair of Botany at the University of Aberdeen. She received a Carnegie Scholarship to work toward a Ph.D. at the University of Chicago from 1925 to 1928; her thesis was on the male gametophyte of *Microcycas calocoma*. In 1927 she traveled on horseback in the western Sierras of Cuba, collecting cycads.

Downie returned to Aberdeen in 1928 and again worked as an assistant at the university. She became a lecturer the following year and a reader in 1949. Her research focused on orchid nutrition. In 1948 she presented some of her work at a meeting of the Botanical Society of Edinburgh; it was published the following year as "The Germination of *Goodyera repens* (L.) R.Br. in Fungal Extract" (*Transactions of the Botanical Society of Edinburgh* 35, 21 [1949]: 120–125). In this paper she showed that the fungal extract, as well as sugars, was a prerequisite for the germination of orchids.

Bibliography: Matthews, J. R., "Dr. Dorothy G. Downie," *Transactions of the Botanical Society of Edinburgh* 39 (1961): 245–246; Wiseman, A., archives assistant, University of Aberdeen, personal communication to the author, October 2000.

Drew-Baker, Kathleen M.
née Drew
c. 1900–c. 1958
botanist

Education: Bishop Wordsworth's School, Salisbury; University of Manchester, B.S. with honors, 1922; M.S., 1923; postgraduate studies in California; D.Sc. (Manchester), 1939.
Employment: University of Manchester: assistant lecturer, Botany Department, from 1923; research fellow, Cryptogamic Botany Department.
Married: H. Wright Baker.

Kathleen Drew-Baker was the first president of the British Phycological Society and was recognized internationally as an expert on the Rhodophyceae (red seaweeds).

Drew-Baker was born in Leigh, Lancashire. Her family moved to Salisbury, and she went to secondary school there, then studied botany on scholarship at Manchester. She worked for her M.S. and continued her research on algae while lecturing in the Botany Department. She was awarded a Commonwealth Fellowship and worked in California on seaweeds, traveling to Hawaii to collect material. On her return to Britain, she married and took up her post once again at the University of Manchester. She left her job to bring up her family but went on with her research and was awarded a D.Sc. in 1939.

She returned to the Department of Cryptogamic Botany as a research fellow. Between 1924 and 1957 she published forty-seven papers, mainly concerned with red algae. These included an article for *Biological Reviews* (1955) on life histories of the algae. With several other phycologists she was involved in the wartime survey of seaweeds suitable for the manufacture of agar for cultivating bacteria.

Bibliography: Newton, L., "Kathleen Drew-Baker," *Revue algol* 1 (1958): 3–6.

Drower, Margaret Stephana
c. 1913–
Egyptologist

Education: University College, London.
Employment: University College, London, from 1937: lecturer in ancient history, reader in ancient history, honorary research fellow in the Departments of History and Egyptology.
Married: C. Hackforth-Jones.

Margaret Drower is well known as an archaeologist and writer.

Drower studied Egyptology at University College, London, and spent two winters excavating in Egypt. She lived in Baghdad for some years.

From 1937 onward she was involved in teaching and research at University College, London. During her retirement she helped with BBC programs on archaeology. She wrote several chapters for the revised 1965 edition of the *Cambridge Ancient History* and a biography of archaeologist Flinders Petrie (1985).

Bibliography: Drower, M. S., *Flinders Petrie: A Life in Archaeology*, London: Gollancz, 1985.

du Châtelet-Lomont, Emilie Gabrielle
née le Tonnelier de Breteuil
1706–1749
writer and translator of scientific books

Education: at home.
Married: Marquis Florent-Claude du Châtelet-Lomont, in 1725.

Emilie du Châtelet-Lomont wrote and translated scientific books.

Du Châtelet-Lomont's father was Louis-Nicholas le Tonnelier de Breteuil, Baron Preuilly and chief of protocol at the court of Louis XIV. Because Emilie du Châtelet-Lomont was very tall (175 cm, or 5 feet 9 inches), her father thought she would remain single, and he provided suitable tutors for her to developed her intellect. She did marry, but her husband was often away fighting in wars.

After the birth of her third child, she studied Newtonian physics with P. L. de Maupertius and A.-C. Clairaut. She was Voltaire's mistress from 1733 and lived with him at Montjeu and later at Cirey-sur-Blaise, where she had a laboratory for simple experiments. She wrote several books, including *Institutions de physique* (Institutions of physics) in 1740.

When she was forty-two, pregnant with her fourth child, she worked long hours translating Newton's *Principia mathematica* into French. She gave the manuscript to the Bibliothéque du Roi in Paris; it was published in 1759. She died of puerperal fever soon after giving birth.

Bibliography: Millar, D. et al., *The Cambridge Dictionary of Scientists*, Cambridge: Cam-

bridge University Press, 1996; Perl, T., *Maths Equals: Biographies of Women Mathematicians and Related Activities*, Menlo Park, California: Addison-Wesley, 1978.

Dunn, Barbara
c. 1910–
amateur radio operator

Barbara Dunn is believed to be the first woman amateur licensed to transmit. She received her license in 1927 and remained the only female amateur radio operator from 1927 to 1932.

Dunn had an active low-power station at Stock in Essex; her call sign was G6YL. A member of the Radio Society of Great Britain, she was awarded the 1930 Committee Cup for her outstanding work in the first series of 1.7Mc/s tests. She was the first woman to win a Radio Society trophy.

Bibliography: Clarricoats, J., *The World at their Fingertips*, London: Radio Society of Great Britain, 1984.

Dunscombe, Adaliza Amelia Clara Mary Elizabeth Emma Frances
31 July 1867–December 1943
optician

Adaliza Dunscombe was the first woman member of the British Optical Association.

Born in London, Dunscombe was the eldest and only daughter of eight children. The family moved to Bristol, where her father, Matthew William Dunscombe, was manager for an optician, and then purchased the business in 1874. He was one of the founders of the British Optical Association (BOA) and its president from 1903 to 1935. Adaliza Dunscombe worked in the shop as an optician, and passed the examination of the BOA, gaining her certificate in 1899.

Bibliography: Bateman, N. P., Batemans Opticians, Bristol, personal communication to the author, 31 August 1999; Bradley, J., librarian, Bristol Reference Library, personal communication to the author, 31 July 1999; Dunscombe, P. (great-great nephew of Adaliza Dunscombe), personal communication to the author, 28 October 1999; "Miss Dunscombe," *Dioptric and Ophthalmometric Review* 6 (1902): 17; Mitchell, M., *History of the British Optical Association 1895–1978*, London: British Optical Association and British Optical Association Foundation, 1982.

Durham, Mary Edith
8 December 1863–15 November 1944
artist, writer, anthropologist

Education: Bedford College, 1878–1882; Royal Academy Schools.

Edith Durham was the first woman vice-president of the Royal Anthropological Institute.

Durham was born in London, the eldest of nine children. Her father was a surgeon at Guy's Hospital. After studying at Bedford College, she decided to train as an artist at Royal Academy schools. She illustrated the volume on reptiles in the *Cambridge Natural History* (1901), doing almost all of her vivid drawings from living specimens.

When she was nearly forty, Durham decided to travel in the Balkans rather than stay at home as a spinster. She did relief work during the Macedonian insurrection in 1903 and made several trips on horseback into northern Albania. In addition to writing dispatches for the *Times* and the *Manchester Guardian*, she lobbied in Parliament, drawing attention to the problems of the Albanians. With Aubrey Herbert she also founded the Anglo-Albanian Society. She was known in Albania as the "queen of the mountaineers," and some Albanian streets are still named after her.

She published *High Albania* in 1909 and after studying Balkan ethnography wrote *Some Tribal Origins, Laws and Customs of the Balkans* in 1928. She gave her Albanian artifacts to the Pitt Rivers Museum in Oxford; her collection of folk costumes to the Bankfield Museum, Halifax; and her photographs and sketches to the Royal Anthropological Institute.

Bibliography: Nicholls, C. S., ed., *Dictionary of National Biography: Missing Persons*, Oxford: Oxford University Press, 1993.

E

Eales, Nellie B.
14 April 1889–7 December 1989
zoologist

Education: University College, Reading (London University), B.S., 1907; Ph.D., 1921; D.Sc., 1926.

Employment: University College, Reading (Reading University from 1926): museum curator, 1912–1919; lecturer and senior lecturer, Zoology Department, 1919–1954; honorary research associate, Zoology Department and Cole Library, 1954–1989.

Nellie Eales, the first woman to be awarded a Ph.D. from University College, Reading, was a zoologist and an expert on the history of zoology.

Eales's first published research, in 1917 and 1918, was on the life history and economy of cheese mites. She moved onto marine biology, researching the biology of the sea hare, *Aplysia,* and publishing her findings in 1921. For this and the cheese mite research, she was presented with a Ph.D. As a fellow of the Zoological Society of London, she was offered the fetus of an African elephant to study. Most of this research was published in the *Transactions of the Royal Society of Edinburgh* (1926) and was presented for her D.Sc.

Eales was a full-time lecturer in zoology and a conscientious tutor. She ran courses at the Marine Biological Association laboratory at Plymouth and did much of her research in marine biology there. Her greatest work in the field was her compilation of *The Littoral Fauna of Great Britain: A Handbook for Collectors* (1939). With illustrations and keys to help identify specimens plus useful hints on shore collecting, the book provided a good starting point for further study. She wrote *Practical Histology and Embryology* (1940) as a textbook for her students.

Eales was president of the Malacalogical Society of London (1948–1951) and edited the society's journal from 1956 to 1969. When Eales retired, she took on the challenge of cataloguing the Cole Library of works on early medicine and zoology at Reading University. In 1969 she completed the first part of the catalogue; the second part was published when she was eighty-six.

In 1981, at age ninety-two, she gave the Reading University Library a beautifully illuminated fifteenth-century Book of Hours written at the Pedrizet School near Paris. When she reached 100, the university council formally thanked her for the contributions she had made to the university over three-quarters of a century.

The Nellie B. Eales Travel Award was founded in her memory and gives grants to students studying pure and applied zoology, allowing them to visit marine or other biological stations.

Bibliography: Ashill, C., Senate House Librarian, University of London, personal communication to the author, 21 June 1999; Bott, M., archivist, University of Reading, personal communication to author, February 1999; "Death of Dr. N. B. Eales," *University of Reading Bulletin* (January 1990): 4; D'Rourke, D., librarian, Cole Library, University of Reading, personal communication to the author, February 1999; Edwards, J. A., "A Gift and Its Donor: Some Account of MS 2087 [The Book of Hours], presented to the Library by Dr. Nellie B. Eales," 1984; "Nellie B. Eales Travel Award," *University of Reading Bulletin* (1991): 261.

Edwards, Amelia Ann Blandford
7 June 1831–15 April 1892
Egyptologist, novelist, journalist

Education: at home
Employment: freelance journalist

Amelia Edwards was responsible for setting up the Egypt Exploration Fund in 1882, and endowed the first British Chair in Egyptology in 1892.

Amelia was brought up in London and mostly taught by her mother. She was a gifted artist, musician, and writer. Both her parents died in 1860, and Edwards took up journalism as the best way to earn her living. Among other journals she wrote for *Household Words,* and she wrote eight novels, of which *Barbaras History* (1864) was the most successful.

Amelia Ann Blandford Edwards (Corbis)

In 1873–1874 Edwards went to Egypt and travelled up the Nile and went on to Syria and the Levant. From then on she devoted herself to Egyptology, learning hieroglyphics, collecting antiquities, and visiting museums. She realized that one way to reduce the number of antiquities being destoyed was to set up scientific explorations. She worked hard to interest people in this idea, and founded the Egypt Exploration Fund with Reginald Stuart Poole and herself as secretaries. The Fund sent an expedition to Egypt every winter.

Edwards traveled in United States in 1889–1890 on a successful lecture tour and was awarded honorary degrees by three American universities. When she died, the capital endowment she bequeathed to University College, London, provided income to establish a professorship of Egyptian archaeology and philology. The work of the department included the deciphering and reading of hieroglyphic and other Egyptian scripts or writings. She also bequeathed her books, photographs, and collection of Egyptian antiquities to University College, London.

Bibliography: Dictionary of National Biography, vol. 2, London: Smith Elder, 1901; Drower, M. S., *Flinders Petrie: A Life in Archaeology,* London: Gollancz, 1985.

Ehrlich, Aline née Buchbinder
26 December 1928–5 February 1991
freshwater biologist and geologist

Education: secondary school in Pau, France; Faculty of Sciences, University of Paris.
Employment: biology teacher; research in the Geological Department, University of Paris.
Married: Mr. Ehrlich.

Aline Ehrlich was known for her work on diatoms.

Ehrlich was born in Berlin. In 1938 the family emigrated, hiding in a small village in southern France during the German occupation. Ehrlich studied chemistry, geology, botany, and zoology at the University of Paris. She became particularly interested in diatoms.

Proficient in French, English, German, Russian, and Hebrew, Ehrlich left Paris in 1969 to travel to Israel, where she worked for the Geological Survey for twenty years. She investigated the distribution of diatoms and compiled a comprehensive atlas on the diatoms of Israel just before she died.

Bibliography: Moshkovitz, S., "Dr. Aline Ehrlich (1928–1991)," *Diatom Research* 8, 1 (1993): 221–225.

Eyles, Joan Mary née Biggs
15 June 1907–14 June 1986
geologist, historian of science, and book collector

Education: St. Winifride's Convent, Swansea; University College, Cardiff, 1924–1928; London University, B.S. with honors, 1929; King's College, London, Geology Department, 1930–1931.
Married: Victor Ambrose Eyles, in October 1931.

Joan Eyles was an expert on William Smith, who was known as the father of British geology. She and her husband collected books on the history of geology that are now held in the Eyles Library at the University of Bristol.

Eyles grew up in Bridgend, Wales, and went to a private school in Swansea. She studied science at University College, Cardiff, graduating in 1928 with a first-class honors degree and then completing an external B.S. with London University the following year. The next step was postgraduate work at King's College, London, from 1930, where she started research on volcanic rocks in the southern uplands of Scotland. In 1931 she joined the Geological Society.

When she met and married Victor Eyles, a geologist with the Geological Survey, then based at Newcastle upon Tyne, she abandoned her initial line of research. Her husband was transferred to London to organize the displays for the new Geological Museum. Sparked by the purchase in 1933 of a copy of William Smith's *Geological Map of*

1815, the Eyles became avid book collectors. Their library increased in spite of moves to Edinburgh in 1935 and her husband's move to Northern Ireland during World War II to assess bauxite deposits. After the war, her husband was promoted to district geologist for the Geological Survey. He retired in 1955 to Oxfordshire and the couple moved to the Cotswolds.

Joan Eyles wrote several centenary articles about geologists for *Nature*. In 1955 she started researching the life of William Smith, whose manuscripts had been found in an attic of an Oxford museum. After her husband died in 1978, she continued her work. She was a keen member of the History of the Earth Sciences Society and the Society for the History of Natural History.

Bibliography: Torrens, H. S., "Joan Mary Eyles née Biggs, 1907–1986," *British Journal of History of Science* 20 (1987): 349–369.

Eymers, Johanna Geertruid (Truus)
1903–1988
physicist and museum conservator

Education: high school for girls, Arnhem, Netherlands; University of Utrecht, 1923–1926, Ph.D., 1935.
Employment: Keuring Elektrotechnische Materialen Arnhem (KEMA) Factory, Arnhem 1927; laboratory assistant, Physics Department, University of Utrecht, 1927–1933; director, University Museum, Utrecht, from 1955.
Married: Pieter H. Van Cittert, conservator at the University Museum, Utrecht, in 1938.

Truus Eymers did research in physics and was director of the museum of the University of Utrecht.

Eymers's father was the head teacher of a primary school in Arnhem. On finishing high school, she went to the University of Utrecht and studied mathematics, physics, and chemistry.

After graduating she worked in a factory for two months, then joined Leonard Ornstein in his research at the Physics Department at the University of Utrecht. Her doctoral thesis was entitled "Fundamental Principles for the Illumination of a Picture Gallery Together with Their Application to the Illumination of the Museum at The Hague." Afterward, she did research on bioluminescence. When she married in 1938, she was not allowed to continue in paid employment, so she helped her husband in the University Museum, where he was the conservator. She was appointed as director in his place from 1955 until her retirement.

Bibliography: Stamhuis, I. M., and M. I. C. Offereins, "Twee Vrouwelijke natuurkundigen en hun promotor in het interbellum: Lili Bleeker, Truus Eymers en Leonard Ornstein," *Gewina* 20 (1997): 256–268.

F

Farquharson, Marian Sarah Ogilvie née Ridley
2 July 1846–20 April 1912
botanist

Education: at home.
Married: Robert F. Ogilvie Farquharson, in 1883. He died 3 May 1890.

Marian Farquharson was the first woman fellow of the Royal Microscopical Society, elected on 8 April 1885.

Farquharson, a keen botanist, joined the Epping Forest and Essex Naturalists' Field Club in 1881. She wrote *A Pocket Guide to British Ferns* the same year.

When she married, she moved to Haughton, near Aberdeen, and became an active member of the Alford Field Club and the East of Scotland Union of Naturalists' Societies. Although she was allowed to become a fellow of the Royal Microscopical Society in 1885, women were not permitted to attend meetings or vote on society business. In April 1900 she submitted a petition to the president and council of the Linnean Society asking that duly qualified women be made eligible for ordinary fellowship and, if elected, be admitted to meetings. Her proposal was rejected, and the following April she tried again via Zoology Secretary G. B. Howes, and F. Ducane Goodman, a council member. Again she was refused. She tried once more on 19 December 1901, via Professor J. R. Green. The matter was put to the vote at a special meeting in 1902, and it was decided women could be elected. On 17 November 1904, sixteen women were elected to become fellows of the Linnean So-ciety; Marian Farquharson was not among them. She was finally elected in March 1908 but was too ill to attend to sign the register. She died from heart disease in Nice in 1912.

Bibliography: Douglas, Gina, librarian at the Linnean Society, London, personal communication to the author, 5 November 1998; Gage, A. T., and W. T. Stearn, *A Bicentenary History of the Linnean Society of London,* London: Academic Press, 1988.

Farrer, Margaret Irene
23 February 1914–25 July 1997
midwife, nursing officer

Education: Poltimore College, Exeter; University College Hospital, London, 1933–1936 (general), 1936–1937 (midwifery).
Employment: University College Hospital, 1937; Royal Northern Hospital, 1938–1942; midwifery tutor, General Lying-In Hospital, 1942–1949; matron, St. Mary's Maternity Hospital, West Croydon, Surrey, 1949–1956; matron, Forest Gate Maternity Hospital, 1956–1971; chief nursing officer, Thames Group Management Committee, 1971–1974.

Margaret Farrer was the first midwife to be appointed deputy chair of the Central Midwives Board, previously dominated by the medical profession. She was elected chair of the board in 1973 and held this position until 1979.

Farrer was born in Rhodesia, but her family returned to England when she was thirteen, settling in Devon.

Farrer was aware of the need for midwives to be thoroughly trained, and as a member of the Central Midwives Board (CMB) she was able to make her views known. She also became involved in health policy and served on the Central Health Services Council, the North East Metropolitan Hospital Board, and the Thames Regional Health Authority. As chief nursing officer of the Thames Group hospital management committee, she was responsible for both nursing and midwifery care in the poor East End of London. (She let staff and children from the East End stay in her Devon home in the summer.)

She was on the editorial board of *Midwife and Health Visitor,* honorary treasurer of the Royal College of Midwives from 1967 to 1976, and a member of the steering committee dealing with the reorganization of the National Health Service. She was made an Officer of the Order of the British Empire (OBE) in 1970.

Bibliography: Ashton, R. "Margaret Farrer: Midwife to the Baby-Boomers." *Guardian,* 24 September 1997; Library, Royal College of Midwives; "Profile: Margaret I. Farrer, OBE, SRN, SCM, DN (Lond), RNT, MTD," *Midwife and Health Visitor* 9 (June 1973): 194; *Who's Who, 1997,* London: Adam and Charles Black, 1997.

Fawcett, Philippa
4 April 1868–10 June 1948
mathematician, educator

Education: Clapham High School; Bedford College and University College, London; Newnham College, Cambridge, 1887–1891.

Employment: lecturer in mathematics, Newnham College, 1892–1902; private secretary to acting director of education, Transvaal Education Department, 1902–1905; chief assistant to the director of education, London County Council (LCC), 1905–1920; assistant education officer for higher education for LCC, 1920–1934.

Philippa Fawcett played a key role in the development of the education systems of South Africa and London.

Fawcett was the daughter of Henry Fawcett, professor of political economy at Cambridge University and later member of Parliament and postmaster general. Her mother, Dame Millicent Fawcett (née Garrett), was a suffragette who helped set up the Cambridge lecture scheme, which eventually developed into the founding of Newnham College.

After preliminary study in London, Fawcett read mathematics at Cambridge. She won the highest honors an undergraduate at Cambridge could receive in mathematics. Although women were not awarded degrees in 1890, her success was hailed as a great achievement for the women's movement. She held a Marion Kennedy studentship in 1891 and lectured in mathematics at Newnham.

In 1901 her mother was asked to head a committee investigating conditions for women and children in the camps in South Africa after the Boer War. Fawcett accompanied her. In 1902 Fawcett started and organized elementary schools in Transvaal. Her academic experience assured her respect, and her work was important for the establishment of South Africa's education system as a whole. On the strength of this experience, she was appointed chief assistant to the director of education for the London County Council (LCC). She had a considerable influence on educational policy at all levels, especially because local education authorities, established in 1902, were responsible for setting up their own secondary schools. Fawcett carried out much of the planning for these schools and in 1920 was made responsible for higher education. Furzedown and Avery Hill teacher training colleges were founded while she was in charge.

During World War I she spent some of her summer holidays delivering mail in the north of England so that a man could be released for the forces. After the war, she was involved in setting up meetings concerned with the League of Nations. During World War II she organized sewing parties.

Bibliography: Creese, M. R. S., *Ladies in the Laboratory? American and British Women in*

Science, 1800–1900: A Survey of Their Contributions to Research, Lanham, Maryland: Scarecrow Press, 1998; "Ms. P. G. Fawcett: A Pioneer in Education," *Times* (12 June 1948): 6E; *Newnham College Register, 1871–1923,* vol. 1, Cambridge: Newnham College, 1963; *Newnham College Roll* (January 1949): 46–54; Ware, F., "Miss Philippa Fawcett," *Times* (16 June 1948); *Who Was Who, 1941–1950,* London: Adam and Charles Black, 1952.

Fell, Honor Bridget
22 May 1900–22 April 1986
cell biologist

Education: Wychwood School, Oxford; Madras College, St. Andrews; University of Edinburgh, B.S. in zoology, 1922; Ph.D., 1924, D.Sc., 1932.

Employment: scientific assistant to T.S.P. Strangeways, Cambridge Research Hospital, 1923–1926; director of this hospital, renamed Strangeways Research Laboratory, 1929–1970; researcher with R.R.A. Coombs, Immunology Division, Pathology Department, Cambridge University, 1970–1979; research worker at Strangeways, 1979–1986.

Honor Fell, an outstanding cell biologist, did important research on the development of bone and cartilage; the action of vitamin A on bone, skin, and membranes; the role of lysosymal enzymes in the breakdown of tissues; and the role of synovial tissue in the decomposition of cartilage and bone.

Fell was the youngest of nine children. Her mother designed the family home in Yorkshire; her father was a landowner. As a girl, Fell was interested in animals and was a gifted artist.

In 1921 she started doing research at Edinburgh, looking at the stages of development in the ovaries and testes of chickens. She went to Cambridge to learn Tom Strangeways's technique of observing living cells under the microscope and was thrilled to watch mitosis (cell division) actually happening rather than surmising the sequence of chromosome movement from prepared slides.

In 1923 Strangeways asked Fell to work in his Cambridge Research Hospital. Initially she was funded by the Medical Research Council; from 1924 to 1931 she held annual Beit Fellowships. When Strangeways died three years after Fell's arrival, Fell was reluctant to see the laboratory close and so the trustees decided to keep it running. She asked for funding from the Medical Research Council via Walter Fletcher, who was impressed with her enthusiasm, dedication, and ideas for the future development of the laboratory. The hospital was renamed the Strangeways Research Laboratory and gradually became known worldwide for its cell biology research.

Fell was appointed scientific director when she was twenty-nine; she continued in this post until she was seventy. From 1931 she was funded by the Royal Society with research fellowships. She was made a Royal Society research professor in 1963. In 1933 there were only thirteen staff members at Strangeways; when she retired in 1970, there were 121 laboratory staff, including sixty-two scientists and twenty-nine technicians. Fell was so successful in her own research and as an administrator that she attracted high-caliber scientists to work with her—and also major funding to expand the laboratory. Because she believed strongly in the involvement of different disciplines in a research project, a variety of specialists worked at the laboratory, exchanging ideas and expertise on aspects of cell biology, such as the effects of radiation on living cells.

Fell was appointed senior biological adviser to the Biophysics Unit at King's College, London. She visited the unit weekly from 1947 to 1968. Fell was interested in the education of young scientists and traveled abroad to learn about tissue culture. She helped set up societies for cell biology and tissue culture and was elected an honorary member of many of them. She retained her enthusiasm for biology throughout her life and was always excited about new discoveries. She continued with her research almost until her death, at eighty-six, from cancer. In her lifetime she wrote 120 papers, the first of them published in 1922.

In 1952 she was elected a fellow of the Royal Society and was made a Dame Commander of the Order of the British Empire (DBE) in 1963.

Bibliography: Dictionary of National Biography, 1986–1990, Oxford: Oxford University Press, 1996; Mason, J., "Honor Fell 1900–1986," in E. Shils and C. Blacker, eds., *Cambridge Women: Twelve Portraits,* Cambridge: Cambridge University Press, 1996.

Fergusson, Mary (Molly) Isolen
28 April 1914–30 November 1997
civil engineer

Education: York College, York; University of Edinburgh from 1933.
Employment: Blyth and Blyth, Edinburgh: civil engineer, senior partner, 1948–1978; consultant from 1978.

In 1957 **Mary Fergusson** became the first woman to be elected to fellowship of the Institution of Civil Engineers.

Fergusson was brought up in York, where her father was a pioneer in radiology and devised much of his own equipment. She graduated from the University of Edinburgh in civil engineering. To complete her training, she was indentured for two years with the Edinburgh firm of Blyth and Blyth. She was unpaid for the first year and in the second was paid thirty shillings a week. She worked on the design and construction of bridges in the highlands and islands. Fergusson eventually became senior partner at Blyth and Blyth and was responsible for various civil engineering projects, including paper mills, water purification schemes, sewers, and bridges.

When she retired from full-time work, she used her consultancy fees to set up a fund to help engineering students. A member of the Women's Engineering Society, she encouraged other women to take up engineering. At one time she was chair of the Edinburgh Soroptimists service club and a member of the Business Committee of the General Council of Edinburgh University. She was also commissioner for the Cub Scouts. She

was made an Officer of the Order of the British Empire (OBE) in 1979 and awarded an honorary doctorate from Heriot-Watt University in Edinburgh in 1985.

Bibliography: "Dr. Mary (Molly) Fergusson," obituary, Institute of Civil Engineers Archive Department.

Flint, Elizabeth Alice
26 May 1909–
botanist

Education: Sandal Dene School, New Malden, Surrey; St. Margaret's College, Christchurch, New Zealand; Canterbury College, University of New Zealand, Christchurch, M.S., 1935; King's College, University of London, one session, 1930–1931; Queen Mary College, University of London, Ph.D., 1940.
Employment: scientist, Metropolitan Water Board Laboratory, London, 1939–1943; operational research scientist, Royal Air Force, 1943–1945; lecturer in Botany, Victoria College, University of New Zealand, Wellington, 1947; lecturer in Botany, University of Leeds, 1948–1950; lecturer in Botany, University College, Hull, 1950–1955; Department of Scientific and Industrial Research (DSIR): part-time research, soil department, and later ecology section, 1956–1974; research associate, Botany division of the DSIR (now Landcare Research New Zealand).

Elizabeth Flint is an expert on freshwater algae.

Flint became interested in algae during her undergraduate studies. For her M.S. degree at the University of New Zealand, she investigated the phytoplankton in a small subalpine lake, and for her doctorate in London she studied the algae in the city's reservoirs. She has continued with her research on algae and other plants, mainly in New Zealand.

She returned to New Zealand in 1955 so that she could look after her parents. Between 1983 and 1994 she helped Professor Hannah Croasdale prepare and publish an account of the desmids of New Zealand, part of the *Flora of New Zealand.*

Flint is a fellow of the Linnean Society (1942) and of the Royal Society for the Protection of Birds (1987) and an honorary life member of the New Zealand Limnological Society. She was made an Officer of the Order of the British Empire (OBE) in 1991 and received the Prince and Princess of Wales Science Award in 1989 and the New Zealand Commemoration Medal in 1990.

Bibliography: Flint, Elizabeth, personal communications to the author, 1997; Lambert, M., ed., *Who's Who in New Zealand,* twelfth edition, Auckland, New Zealand: Octopus Publishing, 1991.

Fountaine, Margaret Elizabeth
16 May 1862–21 April 1940
entomologist (lepidopterist)

Education: at home.
Employment: freelance collector of insects.
Married: Khalil Neimy.

Margaret Fountaine collected butterflies for over forty years throughout the world, especially in the tropics; her collection of over 22,000 specimens was given to the Castle Museum in Norwich after her death.

Fountaine was born in Norfolk, where her father was a rector. She was the second in a family of eight children. In 1878 her father died and the family moved to Norwich.

Fountaine was left a legacy by an uncle, allowing her to travel. In 1891 she and her sister spent a holiday collecting butterflies in Switzerland. So fascinated was Fountaine that for the next ten years she traveled around southern and central Europe collecting butterflies and began publishing her findings. One of her earliest papers was on the butterflies of Sicily (*Entomologist* 30, 4 [1897]). She published numerous other articles during her lifetime, many in the *Entomologist,* detailing her studies in Asia Minor, Algeria, Costa Rica, the Philippines, and Greece.

In 1901, when she was thirty-nine, she traveled in the Middle East. In Damascus she hired Khalil Neimy as her interpreter and guide. They fell in love and decided to marry (though he was fifteen years her junior and already had a wife).

Fountaine and Neimy went collecting together in 1903, this time in Spain, Corsica, the Balkans, and South Africa. Later they went to the eastern United States, the Caribbean, Costa Rica, India, Ceylon, Sikkim, and the Himalayas. They tried to settle as farmers in Australia, but neither of them was used to this type of life.

In 1917 Fountaine went collecting in southern California, then rejoined Neimy in Australia. They traveled in the Far East, and Neimy returned to Damascus while Fountaine went collecting on commission in the West Indies.

Neimy died while Fountaine was in West Africa, but she continued collecting throughout the world. In autumn 1939 the ship on which she was traveling to Trinidad was attacked by a submarine. The event weakened her health, and she later collapsed while out walking in Trinidad, her butterfly net in her hand. She died soon thereafter.

On Fountaine's death, all her collecting equipment went to the youngest member of the Royal Entomological Society, which Fountaine had joined in 1898. Her sketchbook and paintings (1910–1926) were donated to the library of the British Museum (Natural History). She also left a box of manuscripts with instructions that it was not to be opened until 15 April 1978. The box contained twelve diaries, begun on 15 April 1878. Extracts from these were published as *Love among the Butterflies: The Travels and Adventures of a Victorian Lady* (1980) and *Butterflies and Late Loves: The Further Travels and Adventures of a Victorian Lady* (1986), both edited by W. F. Cater.

Bibliography: Creese, M. R. S., *Ladies in the Laboratory? American and British Women in Science, 1800–1900: A Survey of Their Contributions to Research,* Lanham, Maryland: Scarecrow Press, 1998; Monteith, G. B., "Margaret Fountaine," in J. McKay, compiler, *Brilliant Careers: Women Collectors and*

Illustrators in Queensland, Brisbane: Queensland Museum, 1997; Salmon, M. A., *The Aurelian Legacy: British Butterflies and Their Collectors*, Colchester, Essex: Harley Books, 2000; S[heldon], W. G., "Margaret Elizabeth Fountaine," *Entomologist* 73, 928 (1940): 193–195.

Franklin, Lady Jane
née Griffin
1792–1875
explorer

Education: at home.
Married: Sir John Franklin, on 5 November 1828. He died on 11 June 1847.

Lady Jane Franklin, a noted explorer, was the first white woman to climb Mount Wellington in Tasmania.

After her marriage, Franklin traveled in Syria and Asia Minor and joined her husband's ship, *The Rainbow.* In 1836 he was appointed lieutenant governor of Van Diemen's Land (now Tasmania). They arrived at the convict station of Hobart on 6 January 1837 and stayed for seven years. Franklin assisted many of the women convicts, founding the Tasmanian Society for the Reformation of Female Prisoners in 1843. She and her husband helped establish the Royal Society of Hobart Town and bought land for a botanical garden and museum and an agricultural settlement. She founded Christ's College, a state school, in 1840.

After they returned to Britain, her husband sailed on 18 May 1845 with the *Erebus* and the *Terror* to try to find the Northwest Passage. The ships were stocked with enough food for three years. When they had not returned by 1848, Franklin offered a reward of £2,000 to anyone who could find them. Over the next few years, numerous parties searched for the lost ships. It was eventually established that Sir John Franklin's ship had become trapped in the ice near King William Island. After more than a year, the crew had attempted to escape on foot, but all had died. Franklin was awarded the Founder's Medal by the Royal Geographical Society in 1860 for her zeal and self-sacrifice in searching for her husband and his companions. She later financed the outfitting of the *Pandora* in its attempt to find the Northwest Passage.

Franklin was the first white woman to travel overland from Melbourne to Sydney. She also traveled in Japan, India, the United States, and Hawaii.

Bibliography: Bozman, E. F., ed., *Everyman's Encyclopaedia*, vol. 5, fourth edition, London: Dent, 1958; *Dictionary of National Biography, 1921–1922*, Oxford: Oxford University Press, 1927; Uglow, J. S., ed., *The Macmillan Dictionary of Women's Biography*, third edition, London: Macmillan, 1998.

Franklin, Rosalind Elsie
25 July 1920–20 March 1958
biophysicist

Education: St. Paul's Girls' School, London; Newnham College, Cambridge 1938–1942; Ph.D., 1946.
Employment: researcher, British Coal Utilisation Research Association, 1942–1947; researcher, Laboratoire Centrale des Services Chimiques de L'Etat, Paris, 1947–1950; research fellow, X-ray diffraction unit, Biophysics group, King's College, London, 1951–1953; director of research team, Birkbeck College, London, 1953–1958.

Rosalind Franklin helped discover the structure of DNA and was an expert crystallographer.

Franklin enjoyed practical work from an early age and had a logical and efficient mind. She decided at fifteen that she would be a scientist, and her family encouraged her. From St. Paul's Girls' School she went to Newnham College, Cambridge, and read natural sciences. She did so well that she was awarded a scholarship by Newnham College for her fourth year. She started researching the polymerization of acetaldehyde and formic acid but found the work unsatisfying and was thankful when she was offered a job with the British Coal Research Association at Kingston in 1942. She studied the colloidal properties of cokes and chars, providing the subject for her doctoral thesis, "The Physical Chemistry of Solid Organic Colloids with Special Relation to Coal and Related Materials"; she was awarded her degree in 1946.

From 1947 to 1950 Franklin started work in the Laboratoire Centrale des Services Chimiques de L'Etat in Paris, where the technique of X-ray diffraction was being developed. She improved the technique and obtained some beautiful photographs of crystal structure. Having discovered the differences between carbons that turned into graphites when heated and those that did not, she was able to link these differences to the chemical constitution of the source molecules for the two carbons.

She returned to England in January 1951 as Turner Newall Fellow at the X-ray Diffraction Unit at King's College, London, headed by Professor John Randall. Here she worked on the structure of DNA with Raymond Gosling, building on preliminary work done by Maurice Wilkins.

Franklin was amazed to find that at King's College women were not allowed in the Men's Common Room, and that men and women had separate dining facilities. Opportunities for the friendly discussions that can lead to the development of new ideas were thus immediately reduced. She had also understood that Wilkins would have moved onto something other than DNA. He did not, and it was said that he repeated Franklin's work and then gave the results, without Franklin's permission, to James Watson and Francis Crick in Cambridge, who were working on a model to show the structure of DNA. In fact Franklin had sent her paper (based on an earlier draft, discovered only after she had died) to *Nature* before Watson and Crick sent in theirs.

In March 1953 she moved to Professor J. D. Bernal's department at Birkbeck College and, building on her work on DNA, began research on the structure of tobacco mosaic virus with a distinguished group of workers, including Aaron Klug. Franklin published seventeen papers during her time at Birkbeck. In 1956 she developed breast cancer.

Bernal considered Franklin an outstanding scientist, a clear thinker, and a perfectionist. She was also an excellent director of a research team, inspiring her coworkers to reach her own high standards. With the skills she developed for the X-ray diffraction technique, she discovered the B form of the DNA molecule and found that the A and B forms exist in different conditions and can change from one to the other. Once Watson and Crick had announced their double helix model, Franklin showed that this was consistent with the X-ray diffraction patterns she had found with both A and B forms. Her notebooks at this time indicate that she had also correctly surmised other features of the structure of DNA, such as the location of the phosphate groups on the outside of the molecules.

Bibliography: Bernal, J. D., "Dr. Rosalind E. Franklin," *Nature* (19 July 1958): 154; Glynn, J., "Rosalind Franklin, 1920–1958," in E. Shils and C. Blacker, eds., *Cambridge Women: Twelve Portraits*, Cambridge: Cambridge University Press, 1996; Hetzel, P., "In Memoriam: Rosalind Franklin (1920–1958); NC 1938–1942," *Newnham College Roll* (1994): 59–63; Klug, A., "Rosalind Franklin and the Discovery of the Structure of DNA," *Nature* (24 August 1968): 808–810, 843–844; Nicholls, C. S., ed., *Dictionary of National Biography: Missing Persons*, Oxford: Oxford University Press, 1993; Sayre, A., *Rosalind Franklin and DNA*, New York: W. W. Norton, 1975.

Fraser, Roslin Margaret Ferguson
21 May 1927–8 December 1997
psychiatric nurse

Education: Dingwall Academy; Edinburgh University (botany).
Employment: psychiatric nurse, Prudhoe Hospital, Northumberland; nursing tutor, Balderton Hospital.

In 1990 *Ros Fraser* was the first psychiatric nurse to be appointed as deputy president of the Royal College of Nursing.

Fraser left her original career as a botanist to train as a nurse when she was widowed with five children to support. She started working with patients with learning difficulties at Prudhoe Hospital, where her husband had been a consultant psychiatrist. As a tutor at Balderton Hospital, she built up a pioneering approach in mental handicap nursing. She successfully lobbied the General Nursing Council to restructure mental handicap nursing, and she championed the new 1982 syllabus for training nurses in learning disabilities. In 1985 she was the first psychiatric nurse to be appointed as a mental health commissioner. She had a particular responsibility for Rampton Hospital.

Fraser used the Royal College of Nursing (RCN) as a means of increasing awareness of the needs of people with learning disabilities and their caregivers. She was instrumental in forming the RCN Society for Mental Handicap Nursing, and she was the first RCN adviser in learning disability nursing. She campaigned for women's issues and through the RCN published guidance for nurses on female genital mutilation, the first such guidelines to be published by a health care organization. She joined the Womens' National Campaign in 1991 and from 1996 served as chair of the National Alliance of Women's Organisations. She represented the RCN at the UN Fourth World Conference on Women in 1995 in Beijing and campaigned for womens' health and against violence against women.

Bibliography: Hancock, C., "Ros Fraser: Skilled Force in Nursing," *Guardian* (18 December 1997); O'Brien, F., assistant archivist, Royal College of Nursing Archives, Edinburgh, personal communication to the author, August 2001.

Freeman, Joan
7 January 1918–18 March 1998
physicist

Education: Sydney Church of England Girls' Grammar School; Sydney Technical College (physics only); Sydney University, 1936–1940; double first-class honors, post- graduate, 1940–1941; M.S., 1942; Newnham College, Cambridge and Cavendish Laboratory from 1946; Ph.D., 1949.

Employment: Radiophysics Laboratory, Commonwealth Scientific and Industrial Research Organisation, Sydney, 1941–1946; temporary research assistant, Cavendish Laboratory, Cambridge, 1948–1951; Atomic Energy Research Establishment (AERE), Harwell: senior scientific officer, Nuclear Physics Division, 1951–1960; group leader for the Tandem Group, 1960–1978; consultant, 1978–1983.

Married: Dr. John Jelley, in February 1958. He died in 1995.

Joan Freeman was the first woman to be awarded the Rutherford Medal by the British Institute of Physics (jointly with Blin-Stoyle) for their work on the beta-radioactivity of complex nuclei.

From an early age, Freeman was fascinated by science. Having decided that she was going to study physics at university, she set about to ensure she gained a scholarship. Physics classes were inadequate at her school, so for a year she enrolled at an evening class at the Sydney Technical College, the only girl in the group—and at the top of her class. One day when inspectors came, school authorities hid her behind a screen, as they were afraid of what the inspectors might think of a girl in the class. Of course they found out about her when the examination results were announced, and no other girls were allowed for some time. But Freeman's place at Sydney University was assured.

She studied mathematics, chemistry, physics, and zoology, doing well in all her subjects. Lecture seats were allocated, and for one set of physics lectures Freeman was the only woman. (And the authorities stipulated that a seat must be left vacant between a woman student and a man.)

After graduating she was awarded a Commonwealth Research Scholarship and was able to stay on at Sydney to work for her M.S. When the radiophysics laboratory nearby advertised for staff, Freeman decided to apply; while there she worked on radar. In 1946 she had the chance to go to

Cambridge to study for her doctorate at the Cavendish Laboratory. After a slow start because of the general postwar disorganization at the university and a large influx of postgraduate students, she was able to work as a research associate until both her thesis and the magnetic spectrometer she was making were complete.

In June 1951 she was a employed at Atomic Energy Research Establishment (AERE), Harwell, as a senior scientific officer. She was paid far less than her male counterparts; it was eight years before their pay was equalized. She joined the Van de Graff accelerator group as a senior scientific officer.

In 1958 she and John Jelley, a fellow worker from Cavendish laboratory in Cambridge, were married and took a sabbatical year in the United States, Freeman working as a research fellow at the High Voltage Laboratory of the Massachusetts Institute of Technology (MIT).

It was at MIT that Freeman met Blin-Stoyle, a theoretical physicist from Oxford who later worked with her on the award-winning beta-radioactivity research. When she returned to Harwell in 1960, she was appointed group leader of the Tandem Accelerator Group, which she led until her retirement, later acting as a consultant.

Her autobiography was published in 1991. She was clearly a woman of much determination. She had at least eighty other publications to her credit, ranging from a chapter on local oscillations in a 1947 textbook on radar to a paper she gave at the International Conference on Atomic Masses and Fundamental Constants in 1975.

She was awarded an honorary doctorate by the University of Sydney.

Bibliography: Freeman, J., *A Passion for Physics: The Story of a Woman Physicist*, Bristol: Adam Hilger, 1991; *Harwell Bulletin* 7616 (13 February 1976): 1; "Joan Freeman," obituary, *Times* (10 April 1998): 25; Newnham College archivist, personal communication to the author 26 August 1998.

Fretter, Vera
5 July 1905–15 October 1992
zoologist

Education: Furzedown College, London, teacher training; Birkbeck College, University of London, B.S., 1934; Ph.D., 1936.

Employment: teacher, London County Council (LCC) primary schools in southeast London; lecturer, Royal Holloway College, 1936–1945; lecturer, Birkbeck College, 1945–1954; Department of Zoology, University of Reading: reader, 1954–1970; honorary research associate, 1970–1992.

Vera Fretter was an expert on Prosobranch mollusks.

Fretter was born and brought up in southeast London. Trained as a primary school teacher at Furzedown College, she was undecided whether to concentrate on natural history or art. While she was at her first teaching post in a school in one of London's poorest neighborhoods, a visiting inspector, aware of her interest in natural history, suggested that she study for a degree. She enrolled as a part-time student at Birkbeck College in London and continued teaching. She graduated with a first-class honors degree in zoology and was able to work full time on her doctoral thesis. In 1936 she began a part-time job teaching zoology at Royal Holloway College, pursuing her own research at the same time. When World War II ended she worked at Birkbeck College as a full-time lecturer until 1954, when she took a job as reader at the University of Reading.

Fretter's work on mollusks complemented the research of marine biologist Nellie Eales. Fretter produced numerous papers with carefully drawn illustrations while teaching full time at Reading. She wrote *British Prosobranch Molluscs* (1962) and with the collaboration of Professor Alaistair Graham, published a revised edition in 1994. She also wrote *A Functional Anatomy of Invertebrates* (1976). She took part in numerous conferences in Britain and abroad and served as president of the Malacological Society. Fretter also taught postgraduate courses and supervised research in the United States and India. An outstanding marine field naturalist, she often worked at the Marine Biological Association's Plymouth laboratory.

Bibliography: "Dr. Vera Fretter," *University of Reading Bulletin* 258 (December 1992): 4; Graham, A., "Dr. Vera Fretter," *Journal of Molluscan Studies* 59, 2 (1993): 267–268; Graham, A., "Vera Fretter," *Independent* (12 November 1992): 151.

Anna Freud (Bettmann/Corbis)

Freud, Anna
3 December 1895–9 October 1982
psychoanalyst

Education: Cottage Lyceum, Vienna; Wagner Jauregg Psychiatric Clinic during 1920s.
Employment: teacher, Cottage Lyceum, Vienna; work with deprived children, nursery, Vienna in 1920s; lecturer, writer, and practicing psychoanalyst from 1920s onward.

Anna Freud collaborated with her father, Sigmund Freud, in developing psychoanalytical theory and established her own reputation in the field, becoming known in particular for her work with children.

Freud was born in Vienna, the youngest of Sigmund Freud's six children. Although she taught school for several years, she became more and more interested in psychoanalysis through her father (who for a time even acted as her analyst). During the 1920s she began taking patients herself as well as working at a nursery for deprived children and studying at Wagner Jauregg's psychiatric clinic. She assisted her father in his work and began to lecture on psychoanalysis. In 1922 she published her first paper. One of her most influential books, *The Ego and Mechanisms of Defence*, appeared in 1936.

She escaped to London with her father in 1938. Following his death in 1939, Anna Freud continued her work in London and in 1940, with her lifelong friend and colleague Dorothy T. Burlingham, set up the Hampstead Wartime Nurseries for children from disrupted families. She subsequently founded the Hampstead Child Therapy Course and Clinic, becoming its director in 1952. Freud immersed herself in the work of the clinic while writing, lecturing in Britain and abroad, researching, and seeing clients. Her book *Normality and Pathology in Childhood* (1966) offered a comprehensive account of new and established psychoanalytical methods.

Freud took up a post as visiting lecturer at Yale Law School and carried out influential work on the law relating to children and psychoanalysis. Several papers resulted, together with two books.

In 1967 Freud was made a Commander of the Order of the British Empire (CBE). She was awarded a number of honorary degrees, including an M.D. from the University of Vienna in 1975 and a D.Phil. from the J. W. Goethe University, Frankfurt, in 1981.

Bibliography: Dictionary of National Biography, 1981–1985, Oxford: Oxford University Press, 1990; *Who Was Who, 1981–1990,* London: Adam and Charles Black 1991.

Frost, Winifred Evelyn
2 March 1902–August 1979
freshwater biologist

Education: County Secondary School, Crewe, 1913–1916; Cowley Girls' School, St. Helens, 1917–1920; Liverpool University, 1920–1923, B.S.; diploma in education, 1924; M.S. (zoology), 1926; D.Sc., 1945.
Employment: assistant inspector of fish-

eries, Dublin, from 1938; research scientist, Freshwater Biological Association, Windermere, 1938–1979.

Winifred Frost, an authority on the natural history of the fish in the Lake District, made detailed studies of minnows, eels, pike, and char. She believed strongly in observing fish in their natural habitat.

Frost's initial research was on euphausids (shrimps) with Professor James Johnstone at Liverpool University. After obtaining an M.S. she worked for the Fisheries Branch in Dublin, investigating trout in the River Liffey (and learning the art of fly fishing).

She was appointed to the staff of the Freshwater Biological Association (FBA) at Windermere in 1938. Many remembered Frost not only for her fish expertise but for her strict attitude toward students exhilarated by celebrations at the end of two-week Easter vacation courses run by the FBA.

Frost was awarded a D.Sc. by Liverpool University on the basis of her published papers. With Margaret E. Brown she wrote *The Trout,* published in 1967 in the New Naturalist series. The book took twenty-one years to prepare and write, though most of it was written during the late 1950s.

As a member of the Council of the Salmon and Trout Association and chair, then president of the Windermere and District Angling Association, Frost traveled widely to international scientific meetings and spent some time in central Africa investigating eels.

She left most of her estate to the FBA, which set up a scholarship to finance postgraduate students doing research in freshwater biology.

Bibliography: Allan, Adrian, archivist, Liverpool University, personal communication to the author, 1999; Le Cren, D., "The Windermere Perch and Pike Project: An Historical Review," *Freshwater Forum* 15 (2001): 3–34; Marren, P., *The New Naturalists,* London: HarperCollins, 1995; "Report of the Council," *Forty-eighth Annual Report,* Windermere: Freshwater Biological Association, 1980.

Fulhame, Elizabeth
fl. 1780
chemist

Married: Dr. Thomas Fulhame.

Elizabeth Fulhame carried out research into the reduction of metal salts, published a book on combustion, and is credited with the discovery of the concept of catalysis.

Few biographical details are known about Elizabeth Fulhame. In 1780, interested in the idea of using metal salts to stain cloth, she studied the reduction of metal salts, looking in particular at the presence of water in reactions. She persevered with her work despite the skepticism of her husband and friends and in 1794 published her findings as *An Essay on Combustion, with a View to a New Art of Dying and Painting, Wherein the Phlogistic and Antiphlogistic Hypotheses Are Proved Erroneous.* The book was positively received, and Fulhame's ideas were discussed by prominent scientists of the time. She gained the greatest recognition in the United States and was elected a corresponding member of the Chemical Society of Philadelphia.

Bibliography: Freemantle, M., *Chemistry in Action,* Basingstoke, UK: Macmillan, 1987; Laidler, K. J., and A. Cornish-Bowden, "Elizabeth Fulhame and the Discovery of Catalysis: 100 Years before Buchner," in Cornish-Bowden, A., ed., *New Beer in an Old Bottle: Edward Buchner and the Growth of Biochemical Knowledge,* Valéncia: Universidad de Valéncia, 1997.

Fulton, Margaret Barr
14 February 1900–1989
occupational therapist

Education: Manchester High School for Girls; Philadelphia School of Occupational Therapy, Pennsylvania.
Employment: occupational therapist, Metropolitan Hospital, New York; instructor in occupational therapy, Aberdeen Royal Asylum, 1925–1963.

Margaret Fulton was the first qualified occupational therapist employed in the United Kingdom.

Fulton was born in Manchester, the youngest of five children. She always thought of herself as a Scot, as both her parents were Scottish. Her father was a general practitioner in Salford and had trained at Glasgow University. After he died in 1919, Fulton and her mother went to the United States to visit relatives; there Fulton heard about occupational therapy and decided to study at the Philadelphia School of Occupational Therapy, founded in 1918.

During the first academic year, she went to lectures and learned various crafts. This was followed by six months in three different hospitals. When she was qualified, Fulton worked at the Metropolitan Hospital in New York for a short time before returning to Britain, where occupational therapy had not yet been developed. After seven months of searching for employment, she contacted Dr. David Henderson at the Glasgow Royal Hospital, Gartnavel, who had set up the first occupational therapy department in Britain. He contacted Dr. Dods Brown, the medical superintendent at Aberdeen Royal Asylum, urging him to appoint Fulton.

In August 1925 Fulton became the hospital's first qualified instructor in occupational therapy on a salary of £120 a year. The hospital then had 800 beds. Fulton initially worked with patients in an army hut constructed in the hospital grounds for her work. One year into her post, Fulton had over 100 patients attending an hour's class each week, and other patients were working at various crafts throughout the day in "the Hut." In 1927 she organized an exhibition of the patients' work, opened by Commissioner for Lunacy Sir Arthur Rose.

In 1929 the first occupational therapy training course in Britain was set up by Dr. Elizabeth Casson in Bristol. Fulton was asked to be second principal there in 1933, but she refused. Her salary at the Aberdeen Royal Asylum was, however, raised with word of the offer.

Fulton set high standards for the work done by the patients and firmly believed that the relationship between staff and patients was of paramount importance. Unfor-

tunately, she did not record either her philosophy or many case histories.

In 1942 a new occupational therapy department was opened within the main building at Aberdeen. Dods Brown retired then, and Fulton found his replacement, Andrew Wyllie, less easy to work with.

At a Rotary Club meeting, Fulton mentioned the lack of follow-up for psychiatric patients. In 1950 she and Dr. Mary Esslemont set up the Amity Club for women who had been patients. They met weekly in Esslemont's dining room and did craftwork. Fulton trained members of the Soroptimist service club as support workers.

In May 1932 the Scottish Association of Occupational Therapists (SAOT) was formed, with Fulton as secretary and treasurer. Meetings were suspended in 1939 because of the war, but the SAOT was reorganized, with Fulton as chairwoman, in 1946. She held this position until 1949 and served on the council from 1949 to 1960 and 1964 to 1971.

In 1952 Fulton was involved in setting up the World Federation of Occupational Therapists (WFOT) and was elected its president. The group's first international congress, held in Edinburgh in August 1954, was attended by almost 400 delegates from twenty-one countries. Fulton was made a Member of the Order of the British Empire (MBE) for this work; she was named an honorary fellow of the WFOT in 1960.

After her retirement Fulton lived in Edinburgh. She was selected for an honorary degree by the Council for National Academic Awards (CNAA) but died before she could knew of this and CNAA awards were not made posthumously.

On 12 May 1995, Her Royal Highness Princess Anne, patron of the College of Occupational Therapists, opened the Fulton Clinic and Memorial Garden in the grounds of the Royal Cornhill Hospital, previously the Royal Aberdeen Mental Hospital, where Fulton had worked tirelessly during her professional career.

Bibliography: Paterson, C. F., director, Department of Occupational Therapy, Robert Gordon University, Aberdeen, personal communication to the author, October 2000; Paterson, C. F., "Margaret Barr Fulton, MBE (1900–1989): Pioneer Occupational Therapist," in A. Adam, D. Smith, and F. Watson, eds., *To the Greit Support and Advance of Helth,* Aberdeen: Aberdeen History of Medicine Publications, 1996.

Furness, Vera I.
2 June 1921–
chemist, industrial manager

Education: teacher training college; London University, B.S., 1946; M.S., 1948; Ph.D., 1952.

Employment: teacher; development chemist, BX Plastics, Walthamstow; Birmingham College of Technology: research associate, part-time lecturer; Courtaulds, Coventry: research chemist, 1953–1962; section leader of Courtelle research project, 1962–1964; deputy head, acting head, then head of Acetate and Synthetic Fibres Laboratory, Coventry, 1964–1969; general manager of Research Division, 1970–1976; technical director of Courtaulds Knitwear, then chair of Steel Cords Ltd., 1976–1978; managing director of Courtaulds, Campsie, Northern Ireland, 1978–1981.

As head of the Research Division at Courtaulds, *Vera Furness* was responsible for 400 graduate or equivalent staff, with a total strength of around 1,400, working at nine different sites in chemistry, physics, chemical engineering, engineering, and textile technology.

Furness, originally trained as a teacher, studied for an external degree in chemistry at London University while teaching full time. After she graduated, she became the development chemist at BX Plastics, doing research for her M.S. Her thesis dealt with the preparation of fluoroquinolines monosubstituted in the benzene ring.

Furness did part-time third-level teaching at Birmingham Technical College (now the University of Aston) while doing her Ph.D. research on the reactions of hexomethylenetetramine with phenols and dialkylanilines. Although she was offered a full-time teaching post, she decided to return to industrial research. In 1953 she joined Courtaulds in Coventry, remaining there until she retired.

Furness worked on the production of the acrylic known as Courtelle. A colleague, W. Schmidt, had developed a means of producing the acrylonitrile polymer in solution ready for spinning, forgoing the multistage process of making it in an aqueous medium, separating, drying, and redissolving it. Although the new process had potentially great cost savings and was much neater, there were major problems with the product. The fiber would not accept dye and was a dirty fawn color that would not bleach using any normal bleaching process. Under pressure of time, Furness developed a copolymer that enabled the fiber to be commercially dyed. Soon afterward she incorporated a reagent into the process that gave an almost white fiber. She worked on all aspects of the process, including mechanical as well as chemical problems. The most important involved ideas for modifications for extrusion, which required a radically different jet configuration and both simplified the process and improved the quality of the final product.

All these changes and numerous minor ones were incorporated in a new plant and made the production of Courtaulds more efficient than any other acrylic process in the world. When the Soviet Union and later Poland and China were in the market to buy acrylic plants, they chose Courtelle after visits to all the major acrylic plants in the West. Furness visited these countries to explain the technical process prior to the construction of the plants.

During this period the Royal Aircraft Establishment was developing carbon fibers, which they believed would give a high-modulus, high-tensile fiber for structural components of aircraft. When they found in 1963 that Courtelle was the best precursor fiber, Furness became involved in improving the fiber and creating a process for making it on a commercial scale, which they did from 1965. She was section leader and head of the largest research laboratory, where 100 graduates were employed. No woman had held such a position in industry over professional men prior to this in England.

At the time of the oil crisis, when she had been promoted to head of the research division, Furness was asked to reduce energy consumption across all 400 sites in the United Kingdom. By setting targets based on production, which had to take account of differences between a major chemical plant and a knitting machine, the company achieved enormous savings.

Her last move was as director and general manager at Courtaulds factory in Campsie. She was appointed as a member of the Science Museum Advisory Commit-

tee in the 1970s. After she went to Northern Ireland in 1978, she served on several boards and committees, including the Western Education and Library Board, the Northern Ireland Economic Council, Enterprise Ulster, the University of Ulster Council, and Labour Relations Agency conciliator. Furness was made an Officer of the Order of the British Empire (OBE) in 1971 for her services to export.

Bibliography: Furness, V. I. Personal communications to the author, 2000; Rodden, S., archivist, Akzo Nobel (formerly Courtaulds), personal communications to the author, December 1999–May 2001.

G

Garrett Anderson, Elizabeth née Garrett
9 June 1839–17 December 1917
doctor

Education: by governess; boarding school, Blackheath, London, 1849–1851; Middlesex Hospital, London, during 1860; obtained license to practice as an apothecary, 1865; M.D., University of Paris, 1870.

Employment: founder of dispensary for women and children (later New Hospital for Women), Marylebone, London, 1866; senior physician, New Hospital for Women and Children, 1872–1892; London School of Medicine for Women: lecturer, 1874–1897; dean, 1883–1903.

Married: James George Skelton Anderson, director of the Orient Line, on 9 February 1871.

Elizabeth Garrett Anderson was the first woman to qualify in medicine in England and the founder of the first hospital staffed by medically qualified women.

Garrett Anderson was born in London, the daughter of a merchant. At school in Blackheath she was much influenced by her teachers, the Misses Browning (aunts of the poet Robert Browning), and was determined to have her own independent career. She decided to undertake medical training in 1859, after listening to three lectures by Dr. Elizabeth Blackwell, who had qualified as a doctor in the United States. As a woman, however, she was unable to enroll for formal training at the universities in London, Edinburgh, or St. Andrews, though

Elizabeth Garrett Anderson (Hulton-Deutsch Collection/Corbis)

in 1860 she did undertake some informal study at the Middlesex Hospital. Encouraged by her father, she persisted in her efforts to qualify and approached the Society of Apothecaries, who gave her permission to study privately and take their examinations. In 1865 she qualified as a medical practitioner under this arrangement, though the society subsequently altered its rules to allow only those trained at recognized medical schools to take its exams.

Garrett Anderson opened a dispensary for women and children in Marylebone in 1866. The facilities and treatments it offered were extended, and it eventually became the New Hospital for Women. She held the position of senior physician there until 1892. In 1870 she stood as a candidate for the London School Board, and such was her reputation that she polled the highest number of votes ever recorded in such elections. She married in 1871 and received great support for her work from her husband. In 1873 she became a member of the British Medical Association and for many years was the only woman member.

As well as practicing as a doctor and developing the medical facilities offered at the New Hospital for Women, Garrett Anderson was determined to help other women to qualify as doctors. With Sophia Jex-Blake, she founded the London School of Medicine for Women at the Royal Free Hospital in 1874. From 1875 to 1897 she lectured there, and she was dean of the school from 1883 to 1903.

She had a home at Aldeburgh and in 1908–1909 served as mayor of Aldeburgh, the first woman to hold such a position in Britain. In 1918 the New Hospital was renamed the Elizabeth Garrett Anderson Hospital. Garrett Anderson's daughter, Louise Garrett Anderson, trained as a doctor.

Bibliography: Dictionary of National Biography, 1912–1921, Oxford: Oxford University Press, 1927; Manton, J., *Elizabeth Garrett Anderson*, London: Methuen, 1965.

Garrod, Dorothy Annie Elizabeth
5 May 1892–18 December 1968
archaeologist

Education: Birklands School, St. Albans; Newnham College, Cambridge, 1913–1916; M.A., 1927; diploma in anthropology (Oxford University), 1922; Institut de Paléontologie Humaine, Paris, 1922–1923; B.S., Oxon, 1924; D.Sc., Oxon, 1938.

Employment: worker in C.W.L. Huts, northern France and Bonn, 1916–1919; Newnham College, Cambridge: research fellow, 1929–1931; director of studies in archaeology and anthropology, 1933–1942; Disney Professor of Archaeology, 1939–1952; section officer, Women's Auxiliary Air Force (Photographic Intelligence), 1942–1945.

In 1939 **Dorothy Garrod** became the first woman to be appointed as a professor in Cambridge, and in 1968 she was the first woman to be awarded the Gold Medal of the Society of Antiquaries of London.

Garrod was born in London, the only daughter of Sir Archibald Garrod, famous for his investigation of alkaptonuria (a genetic metabolic disorder). She read history at Newnham College, Cambridge, and after taking her final examinations worked in the C.W.L. Huts in northern France for the rest of World War I. She became interested in archaeology after meeting Dr. R. R. Maret, a French archaologist who specialized in spelunking (exploring caves). Through Maret she in turn met Abbé Henri Breuil and Comte Bégouen, and she started off by exploring the painted caves in the Pyrenees under their aegis.

Garrod obtained her diploma in anthropology at Oxford. A Mary Ewart Traveling Scholarship enabled her to work with Breuil in Paris. She presented her research for a B.S. at the University of Oxford in 1922 and published *The Upper Palaeolithic Age in Britain* four years later.

In 1926 she led an archaeological expedition to the Devil's Tower Shelter in Gibraltar and found five parts of a Neanderthaloid skull of a child and stone implements belonging to the Mousterian culture. In 1928, while based at the British School of Archaeology in Jerusalem, she investigated a limestone cave at Shukba, Palestine, and discovered fossil human bones and stone tools similar to those in Gibraltar. In the same year, the Department of Antiquities of the government of Israel asked her to look at the strata in the Athlit Cave, Mount Carmel. Garrod worked with Dorothea Bate, and together they proved that the cave was used in Paleolithic times by Neanderthal humans. They published their results jointly in 1937 as *The Stone-Age of Mount Carmel I.*

On the basis of her studies, Garrod was awarded a D.Sc. from Cambridge University and honorary doctorates from the University of Pennsylvania and Boston College. Her election to the Disney Professorship at Cambridge in 1939 meant more administrative work. Although Garrod was companionable when out excavating, as a professor she was immensely shy; she prepared her lectures carefully but did not seem to enjoy lecturing. She worked hard to alter the archaeology examinations and ensured that archaeology could be taken as a final-year specialist subject.

During World War II Garrod joined the Photographic Intelligence Service and was a section officer in the Women's Auxiliary Air Force. On returning from the war, she received her full salary from Cambridge even before classes restarted and fought successfully to ensure lecturers in her department had their salaries restored at the same time. She resigned her professorship at age sixty in order to have more time for field research.

Once she had retired, she was free to travel abroad to excavate. She moved to Chavente and spent winters in Paris. She stayed in Jerusalem, Beirut, and Saïda and was able to establish the time sequence of the Lower Paleolithic in Lebanon. With J. G. D. Clark she wrote the chapter "Primitive Egypt, Western Asia, and Europe" for the revised *Cambridge Ancient History* (1965).

She was made a Commander of the Order of the British Empire (CBE) and was a fellow of the British Academy.

When the French archaeologist Suzanne Cassou de Saint-Mathurin died in 1991, her papers were bequeathed to the Bibliothèque du Musée des Antiquités Nationales; among them were the diaries, letters, field notes, photographs, and manuscripts of Dorothy Garrod. These were rediscovered by scholar Pamela Jane Smith, who was told of their existence by Paul Bahn, a friend of the Garrod family. Until then relatively little was known about Garrod and there were few photographs of her. Now her achievements and her character are becoming more understood.

Bibliography: Cassou de St.-Mathurin, S., "Dorothy Annie Elizabeth Garrod, 1892–1968," *Newnham College Roll* (1970): 50–54; Leakey, L. S. B., and V. M. Goodall, *Unveiling Man's Origins*, Cambridge, MA: Schenkman, 1969; *Newnham College Register 1871–1923*, vol. 1, Cambridge: Newnham College, 1963; Smith, P. J., Notes for talk given at the conference "Women in Science," Newnham College, Cambridge, September 10–12, 1999.

Gatty, Margaret née Scott
3 June 1809–4 October 1873
naturalist, writer

Education: at home; self-educated.
Married: Rev. Alfred Gatty, on 8 July 1839.

Margaret Gatty was known for her children's books. She was also an expert on seaweeds.

Gatty was brought up at Burnham Rectory, in Essex. Her mother died when she was two. Her father, who had been Lord Nelson's chaplain on the *Victory,* collected books and educated his daughter at home. By the time she was ten, she was studying in the Print Room at the British Museum and learned to do etchings and calligraphy.

Gatty married the vicar of Ecclesfield, near Sheffield, when she was thirty and lived there for the rest of her life. She had eight children. Her first book for children, *The Fairy Godmothers, and Other Tales* came out in 1851. She continued to write, mainly for children, throughout her life and also edited *Aunt Judy's Magazine,* which came out monthly from 1866 until 1873.

She started to study algae while convalescing. After fourteen years of research she published *British Seaweeds* (1863), with a second, two-volume edition in 1872. She was supervised by Professor R. D. Harvey and redrew illustrations from his *Phycologica Brittannica.*

A stained glass window known as the Parable Window was placed in Ecclesfield Church in 1874 as a memorial to Gatty.

Bibliography: "Death of Mrs. Alfred Gatty,

Ecclesfield Vicarage," *Sheffield Daily Telegraph* (6 October 1873): 4; *Dictionary of National Biography*, vol. XXI, Oxford: Oxford University Press, 1889–1890; "The Late Mrs. Alfred Gatty," *Illustrated London News* (18 October 1873): 370–371.

Germain, Sophie
1 April 1776–27 June 1831
mathematician

Education: self-taught.

Sophie Germain was the first woman who was not a wife of a member to be admitted to the sessions of the French Academy of Science.

Germain was self-educated, borrowing notes from friends who were students at the École Polytechnique in Paris. Interested in number theory, she was encouraged in her studies by Joseph-Louis Lagrange and Adrien-Marie Legendre, who taught at the Polytechnique. In 1804 she wrote to the German mathematician Carl Friedrich Gauss about Fermat's equation, signing her letters "Antoine-Auguste Le Blanc." Gauss was impressed with her thinking and for some time did not know she was a woman, until in 1806 during the Napoleonic War she inquired about his well-being in a letter signed with her own name. She had been anxious that, being a scientist, he might have been killed as Archimedes was by the Romans. Germain last wrote to Gauss in 1808 but did not receive a reply, as he had changed his field of study and been appointed professor of astronomy at the University of Gottingen.

Germain moved on to try to explain Ernst F. F. Chladni's figures, patterns that formed when sand was poured onto a glass plate and the plate subjected to vibrations. After he had seen these, Napoleon offered the prize of a kilogram of gold to anyone who could explain the mathematics behind the shapes. The competition was announced in 1809 by the first-class members of the institute of France, a section of the French Academy of Sciences. By 1811 Germain was the only entrant but was not awarded the prize.

She spent another two years rethinking her ideas; though she still was not granted the prize, she did receive the academy's congratulations. She revised and resubmitted her work in 1816 after having read a paper by Simeon-Denis Poisson on elastic plates. Although she finally won the prize, she did not go to the award ceremony.

Germain was, however, at last accepted into the French scientific community and attended sessions of the French Academy of Sciences. From the 1820s she worked with Legendre revising her ideas on number theory. Gauss tried to persuade the University of Göttingen to award her an honorary doctorate in 1830 but failed. Germain died of breast cancer in 1831 at the age of fifty-five.

Bibliography: Dalmedico, A. D., "Sophie Germain," *Scientific American* (December 1991): 76–81.

Gibbons, E. Joan
1902–2 December 1988
botanist

In 1975 *Joan Gibbons* published *The Flora of Lincolnshire*, the first full flora of an English county to be written by a woman, and the county flora that covers the largest area. As a result she was elected president of the Lincolnshire Naturalists' Union for a second term, the first woman to achieve this distinction.

Gibbons was born in Essex but spent most of her life near Market Rasen in Lincolnshire, having moved there when she was five. Her father, Rev. Thomas Gibbons, took her to the first meeting of the Lincolnshire Naturalists' Union when she was eleven, and she joined the society at the age of eighteen. She held the position of botanical secretary for almost fifty years, from 1936, and was first elected as president in 1939.

She joined the Botanical Society of the British Isles (BSBI) in 1946 and soon became recorder for the two Lincolnshire vice-counties (each county was divided into vice-counties for this particular survey). By 1960 her hard work and determination had produced a thorough record of the county's flora. As well as botany, she had a keen interest in the lives of those who studied it, often recording historical details in her writings.

In 1948 Gibbons was a founding member of the Council of the Lincolnshire Naturalists' Trust, an offshoot of the Lincolnshire Naturalists' Union that focused on conservation. For forty years, she contributed her extensive knowledge to many of the trust's projects, including the rescue of *Iris spuria,* a threatened species.

Gibbons was assistant county secretary of the Girl Guide Association for twenty-eight years and was county secretary for the handicapped guides. During World War II she collected medicinal herbs such as rosehips for the Lindsay and Holland Rural Community Council. She was also involved with the Society for Lincolnshire History and Archaeology. She was a fellow of the Linnean Society from 1969 until her death in 1988.

Bibliography: Perring, F. H., and I. Weston, "E. Joan Gibbons (1902–1988)," *Watsonia* 17 (1989): 507–509.

Gleditsch, Ellen
29 December 1879–5 June 1968
physicist

Education: middle school, final examinations, 1895; pharmacy apprenticeship completed, 1898; further pharmacist examination, Kristiania 1902; Kristiania University, Ph.D., 1906; Sorbonne, Paris, Licenciée des Sciences Physiques, 1912; Yale University, 1913–1914.

Employment: pharmacy assistant, Kristiania (later Oslo), 1899–1902; University of Kristiania, chemistry laboratory assistant, 1903–1906; assistant to Madame Curie, Paris, 1907–1912; University of Kristiania, research assistant, 1911–1916; lecturer in radiochemistry 1916–1929; professor of inorganic chemistry 1929–1946.

Ellen Gleditsch was a leading expert in radioactivity who made careful measurements of the half-life of radium that con-

firmed Rutherford's measurements for the radium standard, and demonstrated that the ratio of uranium to radium varied in different radioactive minerals.

Gleditsch went to middle school in Tromsø where her father was a teacher. After taking her examinations there in 1895, she served an apprenticeship as a chemist. In 1898 she moved to Kristiania, taking her final examinations as a pharmacist in 1902.

She worked as a laboratory technician at the university while studying for her university entrance examinations and was graduated with a degree in chemistry in 1906. That same year, she published her first scientific paper, entitled "Sur quelques derives d'amylbenzene tertiare," in the *Bulletin de la Societe Chimique.* Shortly thereafter, her teacher, Eivind Bødtker, went to Paris to study, and asked Marie Curie if Gleditsch could work in her laboratory. Madame Curie agreed, and with a scholarship from Norway, Gleditsch worked there from 1907 to 1912. Initially she was Madame Curie's student, but later became her assistant, and they published some joint papers. Gleditsch graduated from the Sorbonne in 1912 and returned to Norway for a short time before attending Yale University on another scholarship to work with Bertram Boltwood.

Gleditsch returned again to Norway just before the start of World War I. Initially, she relied on research grants, but became a lecturer at the University of Oslo in 1916 and a professor there from 1929 until her retirement. She published her work in French and Norwegian journals and traveled to France for short periods, but became very aware of the dangers of radioactivity, especially after several of Madame Curie's laboratory workers died.

With Eva Ramstedt, a Swede who also worked with Madame Curie, Gleditsch published "Radium og de radioactive processor" in 1917. This paper was the foundation for Gleditsch's textbook on inorganic chemistry, published in 1928 with seven subsequent editions. Her research was recognized worldwide. She was elected as a member of the Norwegian Academy of Arts and Sciences in 1917, and after fifty years of

Ellen Gleditsch (Pictorial Parade/Archive Photos)

Bibliography: *Aschehoug og Gyldendal's Stora Norske Leksikon,* vol. 6, Oslo: Kunnskapsforlaget, 1998; "Contributions of 20th Century Women to Physics—Ellen Gleditsch": available at www.physics.ucla.edu~cwp/Phase2/Gleditsch,_Ellen@842345678.html; Heggen, Liv, librarian, National Library, Oslo (and the librarians at the science library, University of Oslo), personal communications to the author, June 2001; Kronnen, T., and A. C. Pappas, *Et liv in forskning og medmenneskelighet med et utvalg av hennes korrespondance med Madame Curie og andre forskere* [A life of research and helping humanity, with a selection of her correspondance with Madame Curie and other scientists], Oslo: Aventura Forlag, 1987; *Norsk Biografisk Leksikon,* vol. 4, Oslo: H. Aschehoug & Co. (W. Nygard), 1929; *Norsk Biografisk Leksikon,* vol. 3, Oslo: Kunnskapsvorlaget, 1999; Rayner-Canham, M. F., and G. W. Rayner-Canham, "Pioneer Women in Nuclear Science," *American Journal of Physics* 58, 11 (1990): 1036–1043.

membership, King Olav awarded her an honorary diploma.

In 1920 she was award the Fridtjof Nansen's Prize. When the International Federation of University Women met in Kristiania in 1924 she was elected as vice-president, and then president when the federation met again in Amsterdam in 1926. In 1938 she was made a Chevalier de la Legion d'Honneur in Paris, and in 1946 she was made a member of the Order of St. Olav. She was awarded honorary doctorates by Smith College (1914), the University of Strasbourg (1948), and the Sorbonne (1962).

Gleditsch remained very interested in the history of science, and particularly after her retirement wrote more than twenty biographies of physicists and chemists, including one on Irène Joliot-Curie, whom she knew well. She also wrote articles for the popular press and gave several radio talks in the 1930s. Throughout that decade she also helped political refugees, and gave several refugee scientists work in her laboratory during and after World War II. One of the lecture halls on the new university campus at Kristiansand is named after her.

Gordon, Isabella
18 May 1901–11 May 1988
zoologist

Education: Keith Grammar School, 1907–1918; Aberdeen University, 1918–1922; Aberdeen Teacher's Training College, 1923–1924; Imperial College of Science, University of London, 1924–1926, Ph.D.; Woods Hole Marine Laboratory, Woods Hole, Massachusetts, July 1926; Hopkins Marine Station, California, autumn 1926; Jamaica, January 1927; Yale University, March 1927–early 1928, D.Sc., Aberdeen University, 1928.

Employment: initially assistant keeper and finally principal scientific officer, Crustacean Section, British Museum (Natural History), London, 1928–1966.

Isabella Gordon was a world expert on crustaceans, particularly crabs (Malacostraca) and sea spiders (Pycnogonida).

Gordon started her research in Aberdeen, having been awarded the first Kilgour Research Scholarship, and studied the Alcyonaria, a type of sea anemone. For her

Ph.D., she studied sea urchin development at Imperial College, London. She was able to continue her studies at marine laboratories in North America, with the help of a Commonwealth Fund Fellowship. As a result of her publications in zoology, she was awarded a D.Sc. by Aberdeen University in 1928.

Also in 1928 Gordon started work as an assistant keeper in the Crustacean Section in the British Museum (Natural History) and worked there until her retirement. She published numerous papers and identified specimens of crabs sent to her from all over the world. She was a founding member of the Groupe d'Etudes Carcinologiques (1955), which developed into the Colloquia Crustacea Mediterranea.

The highlight of her career was her visit in April and May 1961, at the invitation of a Japanese newspaper, to celebrate the sixtieth birthday of Emperor Hirohito of Japan, a keen marine biologist. Gordon had an audience with him and later gave a talk on the crustacean collections in the British Museum. After the opening of the Odwara Carcinological Museum and the founding of the Carcinological Society of Japan, Gordon traveled throughout Japan as an honored guest of the Japanese scientific community.

She was a fellow of the Linnean Society and of the Zoological Society and was made an Officer of the Order of the British Empire (OBE) in 1961.

Bibliography: Holthuis, L. B., and Ingle, R. W., "Isabella Gordon D.Sc., O.B.E.–1901–1908," *Crustaceana* 56, 1 (1989): 93–105.

Gordon, Maria Matilda
née Ogilvie
1864–24 June 1939
geologist

Education: Ladies College (Merchant Company Schools), Edinburgh; Royal Academy of Music, London; Heriot Watt College, Edinburgh; University College, London, D.Sc., 1893; University of Munich, Ph.D., 1900.
Married: Dr. John Gordon.

Maria Gordon was the first woman to become a doctor of science, which she was awarded in 1893 by London University for her work on the geology of the Wengen and St. Cassian strata in the south Tyrol. In 1900 she became the first woman to gain a Ph.D. from Munich University; her doctorate was on recent and fossil corals.

After her marriage to Dr. John Gordon of Aberdeen, she continued her research in the Dolomites in south Tyrol. She showed that the area had been subject to considerable faulting, contrary to the contemporary belief that the area was undisturbed coral reefs. She translated Zittel's *History of Geology* and wrote a geological guide to the western Dolomites.

When her husband died in 1919, she moved to London with her three children. She was one of the first women justices of the peace and served as chair of the Marylebone Court of Justices. In 1919 she formed the Council for the Representation of Women in the League of Nations and was elected honorary life president of the National Women Citizens Association.

In 1932 Gordon was awarded the Lyell Medal by the Geological Society of London. She was made a Dame Commander of the Order of the British Empire (DBE) in 1935 and an honorary doctor of law of Edinburgh University.

Bibliography: Garwood, E. J., "Dame Maria Matilda Ogilvie Gordon," *Proceedings of the Geological Society of London* 102, 2 (1946): xi–xii.

Goss, Olga May
1916–1994
plant pathologist

Education: University of Western Australia, Perth, 1934–1937; B.S. with honors in zoology.
Employment: University of Western Australia: laboratory assistant, 1938–1939; demonstrator, 1939–1943; pathologist, Princess Margaret Hospital for Children, Perth, 1943; plant pathologist, Department of Agriculture, 1947–1980.

Olga May Goss was an expert in plant pathology and in 1978 became the first Australian woman to be named the Australian Nurseryman of the Year. She worked in the Department of Agriculture in Perth for thirty-five years on a wide spectrum of plant pathology problems and was senior plant pathologist when she retired.

Goss was born in Perth, the elder of two sisters. In 1934 she won the science exhibition awarded by the state and studied biological subjects at the University of Western Australia. After she graduated, she stayed on to work at the university in the department, both lecturing and demonstrating, but did not have as much time to concentrate on research as she had hoped.

She took up a position as a hospital pathologist but became ill. When she recovered, she was employed by the Department of Agriculture in Perth, where she worked on the seed treatment of tomatoes to control bacterial canker, culturing *Rhizobium* on a commercial basis, and the cause of apple scab. In 1951 she began to specialize in plant nematology, the study of eelworms. At this time she was the only worker in the department in this field, so she had to teach herself. She worked on nematode-resistant peach rootstocks and cereal eelworm. She also worked on producing a rust-resistant runner bean, Westralia, and found a fungicide that killed the causative agent of powdery scab in potatoes.

Goss wrote the handbook *Practical Guidelines for Nursery Hygiene* (1978) based on the work of Dr. Ralph Baker, an American. Most of the fifty articles she wrote were published by the Department of Agriculture. Some of her work was published in *Australian Plant Pathology* and the *Australian Journal of Agricultural Research*.

While employed in the Department of Agriculture, Goss was paid less than male scientists at the same grade. As a woman, she was not allowed to go on official field visits alone or to stay away overnight. Until the end of 1967, women in the department had to resign on marriage, so although she had a stable relationship, in order to continue with her work she did not marry or have children.

Bibliography: Allen, N., "Plant Pathology in Western Australia: The Contributions of an Australian Woman Scientist [Olga May Goss]," *Prometheus* 15, 3 (1997): 387–398; Crommelin, J., "Goodbye to the Plants," *West Australian,* 11 November 1980; Evans, A., reference librarian, Biological Science Library, University of Western Australia, personal communication to the author, February 2000.

Goulandris, Niki née Kephalia
1925–
botanical artist, conservationist

Married: Angelos Goulandris.

Niki Goulandris is a botanical artist and worker for conservation.

Goulandris and her husband, Angelos, founded the Goulandris Natural History Museum at Kifissia near Athens in 1965.

Goulandris has illustrated several books, including *Wild Flowers of Greece,* by C. Goulimis and W. T. Stearn (1968), and *Peonies of Greece,* by U. T. Stearn and P. H. Davies. She has held high-profile political and public positions, acting as deputy minister for social services and in 1974 becoming Greece's secretary of state for health. She has played a leading role in the media, and in 2000 became honorary deputy president of Hellenic Radio and TV. She was winner of the United Nations Environmental Programme (UNEP) Global 500 award in 1990 and was named Woman of Europe in 1991 (an award given jointly by the European Commission, the European Parliament, and the European Movement). She has continued her interest in botany and is involved in ecological issues, particularly those relating to Greece.

Bibliography: Blunt, W., and W. T. Stearn, *The Art of Botanical Illustration,* London: Antique Collectors' Club, Royal Botanic Gardens, Kew, 1994; "Profile. Greek Biotype/Wetland Centre—EKBY," available at www. ekby.gr/ekby/en/profile_main_en.html.

Gowing, Margaret Mary
née Elliott
26 April 1921–7 November 1998
historian of science

Education: Christ's Hospital; London School of Economics, B.S. (economics).

Employment: Board of Trade, 1941–1945; researcher, Cabinet Office, 1945–1959; archivist/historian, United Kingdom Atomic Energy Authority, 1959–1966; reader in contemporary history, University of Kent, 1966–1972; professor of the history of science, University of Oxford, 1973–1986; fellow of Linacre College, Oxford, 1973–1986.

Married: Donald J. G. Gowing, in 1944. He died in 1969.

Margaret Gowing was a renowned historian of science with an international reputation. In 1973 she became the first professor of the history of science at the University of Oxford.

After graduation from the London School of Economics with a first-class degree, Gowing worked at the Board of Trade. She moved to a post at the Cabinet Office, where she was involved in a project on the history of war. She coauthored two books, *British War Economy* (1949, with Keith Hancock) and *Civil Industry and Trade* (1952, with E. L. Hargreaves). In 1952 she was invited to join the committee examining government departmental records, under the leadership of Sir James Grigg. The resulting report formed the basis of legislation, particularly the Public Records Act of 1958.

Her work on this committee led to her appointment as archivist/historian to the United Kingdom Atomic Energy Authority (UKAEA) in 1959. Gowing began research on the history of atomic energy and in the course of her work met several prominent physicists, such as Sir James Chadwick, Rudolf Peierls, and Niels Bohr, and had access to records that had not previously been available for study. Her important book *Britain and Atomic Energy, 1939–1945* was published in 1964.

In 1966 she became reader in contemporary history at the University of Kent. She continued her work with the UKAEA, consulting British and U.S. records to build up a picture of the development of atomic energy after World War II. This research was published in 1974 in two volumes (coauthor Lorna Arnold), entitled *Independence and Deterrence: Britain and Atomic Energy, 1945–1952*. Her work on the history of nuclear technology highlighted several points not previously emphasized, such as the importance of the contribution made by scientists in the UK, a contribution Gowing felt had been eclipsed by the Manhattan Project in the United States.

In 1973 Gowing became honorary director of the Contemporary Scientific Archives Centre in Oxford, with the support of the Royal Society. She held this position until 1986, during which time the papers of over 100 twentieth-century scientists were catalogued. The center was moved to the University of Bath in 1976, where it is now known as the National Cataloging Unit for the Archives of Contemporary Scientists.

She held several other public appointments, including trustee of the National Portrait Gallery and member of the Imperial War Museum's governing body. She was made a fellow of the British Academy in 1975, a Commander of the Order of the British Empire (CBE) in 1981, and a fellow of the Royal Society in 1988. She received honorary doctorates from the universities of Leeds (1976), Leicester (1982), Manchester (1985), and Bath (1987). In 1988 she was a founding member of the Academia Europaea.

Bibliography: Harper, P., *Guide to the Manuscript Papers of British Scientists Catalogued by the Contemporary Scientific Archives Centre and the National Cataloging Unit for the Archives of Contemporary Scientists, 1973–1993*, Bath: University of Bath, 1993; Hewlett, R. G., "Margaret Gowing, 26 April 1921–7 November 1998," *Isis* 90, 2 (1999): 326–328; Norton-Taylor, R., "Professor Margaret Gowing: Exploding the Myth of the Bomb," *Guardian* (9 November 1998): 15; *Who's Who, 1998*, London: Adam and Charles Black, 1998.

Greig, Dorothy Margaret née Hannah
11 February 1922–10 June 1999
mathematician (applied)

Education: Central Newcastle High School (GPDST); Newnham College, Cambridge, 1940–1943, M.A.; research in textile department, University of Leeds; M.S.; Ph.D., 1950.

Employment: Air Warfare Analysis Section, Ministry of Defence, from 1943; Ministry of Works; lecturer, Department of Textile Industries, University of Leeds, 1948–1959; senior lecturer in mathematics, Constantine Technical College, Middlesborough, 1959–1964; lecturer and senior lecturer in mathematics, University of Durham, 1964–1986.

Married: W. A. Greig, in 1948.

Margaret Greig did research in applied mathematics. She received the Textile Institute's Warner Memorial Medal in 1959 for her mathematical analysis of the factors controlling the operation of the Ambler superdraft process used in spinning worsteds.

Greig went to both the junior and senior departments of the Central Newcastle High School, winning a class prize every year. On the results of her school certificate examinations, she was awarded a First Trust Scholarship and was the first girl in Newcastle to win a major scholarship at Cambridge. At Newnham College she obtained first-class honors and was classed as a Wrangler, an honor awarded at Cambridge in mathematics. She was the first person from her school to achieve this.

After graduation Greig worked for the Ministry of Defence in the Air Warfare Analysis Section, where accurate navigational information was calculated for the radar-guided bombing of targets in Europe. She also worked with Bomber Command on the scatter of bomb craters around targets. After her section was disbanded, she worked for the Ministry of Works.

She was appointed to the post of lecturer in the Department of Textile Industries at Leeds University in 1948. Her main area of research was the mathematical parameters involved in the functioning of the Ambler superdraft system used in the worsted spinning industry. The purpose of a drafting device is to make sure the fibers are moved steadily forward from the back rollers to the front ones. The superdraft unit has four parts: the twist stabilizer, a fiber guide, a pair of tension rollers, and a flume, and the unit can be clipped onto the control bar. Greig worked out the theory behind the device and developed improvements to the roller. She published her work in the *Journal of the Textile Institute* and gave lectures on the topic at several conferences, including an International Wool Conference in Australia.

Greig was appointed senior lecturer at Constantine Technical College from 1959, and while there, with T. H. Wise, published *Hydrodynamics and Vector Field Theory:* volume 1, *Examples in Elementary Methods* (1962), and volume 2, *Examples in Special Methods* (1963). Her last appointment was at the University of Durham, where she did research in numerical analysis and operational research. She wrote a textbook on optimization, published in 1980. She supervised several postgraduate students, was a member of the university senate for some time, and was on the higher degree board of the Council for National Academic Awards (CNAA) for Mathematical Sciences. She was an external examiner in mathematics for Brighton Polytechnic.

Greig was much admired for the way she combined her family life with a full-time teaching and research position. She had three sons and a daughter.

Bibliography: Ambler, G. G., and M. Hannah, "High Drafting and the Ambler Superdraft System," *Journal of the Textile Institute—Proceedings* 41, 3 (1950): 115–123; Carter, O., *History of Gateshead High School 1876–1907 and Central Newcastle High School 1895–1955*, privately published ca. 1955, 134; Greig, W. A., personal communication to the author, August 1999; Hannah, M., "Developments in the Amber Super-draft Process for Worsted Spinning," *Journal of the Textile Institute—Proceedings* 42, 6 (1951): 246–250; Hannah, M., "The Theory of High Drafting," *Journal of the Textile Institute—*

Transactions 41, 3 (1950): 57–123; Parrin, J., librarian, Central Newcastle High School, personal communications to the author, March 2000 and May 2000.

Grierson, Mary Anderson
27 September 1912–
botanical artist

Education: Bangor County School for Girls, North Wales; studied painting with John Nash, 1959–1961.
Employment: freelance botanical artist for Women's Auxiliary Air Force (WAAF) from 1940; military aerial photography interpreter, 1940–1945; cartographical draftswoman, Hunting Surveys Ltd., 1946– 1960; staff artist, Royal Botanic Gardens, Kew, 1960–1972.

Mary Grierson had a long and successful career as a botanical artist.

Grierson's freelance career began in 1940 and continued for many years, though she held a number of employed positions alongside this work. During World War II she served as an aerial photography interpreter and then was a commercial cartographical draftswoman. She worked as a botanical artist at the Royal Botanic Gardens, Kew, for twelve years.

Because one of her particular areas of interest was endangered species, Grierson depicted specimens from around the world. Her work was shown not only in Britain, including at the Royal Society, the Linnean Society, the Royal Horticultural Society, and the British Museum, but also internationally, including in South Africa, the Netherlands, the United States, and Israel. She illustrated a number of books, including *Mountain Flowers* (A. J. Huxley, 1967) and *Orchidaceae* (P. F. Hunt, 1974), and provided illustrations for a range of journals and other publications. She designed the stamps for the "British Flora" stamp issue in 1967.

Grierson was awarded the Gold Medal of the Royal Horticultural Society in 1966, 1969, and 1973 and became a fellow of the Linnean Society in 1967.

Bibliography: Buckman, D., *Dictionary of Artists in Britain since 1945*, Bristol: Art Dictionaries, 1988; *Fourth International Exhibition of Botanical Art.* (Booklet that accompanied exhibition.) London: Royal Botanic Gardens, Kew, 1977.

Gromova, Vera Issacovna
8 March 1891–21 January 1973
paleontologist

Education: St. Petersburg, higher girls' courses, 1908–1911; Moscow, higher girls' courses, 1912–1918; degree in vertebrate zoology, 1918.
Employment: head of osteology section, Zoological Museum, Academy of Sciences, Moscow, 1919–1942; Paleontological Institute, Academy of Sciences, Moscow, 1942–1960 (head of mammals laboratory from 1946).

Vera Gromova specialized in fossil ungulates.

Gromova's particular interest was the development of the horse and the relationships between climatic change and long-term skeletal changes. She was in charge of the osteological section at the Zoological Museum in Moscow. From 1946 she was in charge of the mammals laboratory at the Paleontological Institute.

Bibliography: Gabunia, L., and B. A. Trofimov, "Vera Gromova, 1891–1973," *Society of Vertebrate Palaeontology Newsletter* 9 (1973): 64–65; Sarjeant, W. A. S., *Geologists and the History of Geology,* vol. 2, London: Macmillan, 1980.

Guppy, Eileen M.
24 May 1903–8 March 1980
geologist

Education: Bedford College, University of London, 1920–1903, B.S. with honors.
Employment: assistant, Chemical Research Laboratories, Lennox Iron Foundry Co., New Cross, 1923?–1926; Geological Survey of Great Britain: assistant in the Petrographical Department, 1927–1943; assis-

tant geologist, 1943–1945; senior experimental officer, 1945–1966.

In 1943 *Eileen Guppy* became the first woman to be employed as a geologist by the Geological Survey of Great Britain and in 1966 became the first woman staff member to be made a Member of the Order of the British Empire (MBE), for her thirty-nine years of service.

Guppy published two editions of *Chemical Analyses of Igneous Rocks, Metamorphic Rocks and Minerals*, one in 1931 and the other in 1956; her book *Rock Wool* (1945) had a second edition in 1949. Although promoted to the rank of assistant geologist in the Geological Survey of Great Britain in 1943, at the end of the war she was put back into senior experimental officer grade, as it was decided she had fulfilled her wartime role.

Bibliography: Badham, S. H., archivist, Royal Holloway/Bedford College, University of London, personal communication to the author, June 1998; Bailey, E., *Geological Survey of Great Britain*, London: Thomas Murby, 1952; Plant, J. A., D. Hackett, and B. J. Taylor, "The Role of Women in the British Geological Survey," *Geology Today* (July/August 1994): 151–156.

Gwynne-Vaughan, Helen Charlotte Isabella *née Fraser*
21 January 1879–26 August 1967
botanist

Education: by governesses; Cheltenham Ladies' College; King's College, London, 1889–1904; B.S., 1904; D.Sc., 1907.

Employment: demonstrator, University College, London, 1904–1905; assistant lecturer, Royal Holloway College, 1905–1907; lecturer, University College, Nottingham, 1907–1909; head of botany, Birkbeck College, London, 1909–1917; joint chief controller, Women's Army Auxiliary Corps, 1917–1918; commandant, Women's Royal Air Force, 1918–1919; Birkbeck College, London: head of Botany Department, 1920–1944; professor of botany, 1921–1944; director, Auxiliary Territorial Service, 1939–1941.

Married: David T. Gwynne-Vaughan, professor of botany, in 1911. He died in 1915.

Helen Gwynne-Vaughan was a botanist who specialized in fungi. During the two world wars, she undertook important roles in women's service organizations.

Gwynne-Vaughan was born in London. Her father, a captain in the Scots Guards, died when she was young. Her mother married a member of the consular service. For much of her childhood, Gwynne-Vaughan lived abroad, though she spent her last year of school education at Cheltenham Ladies' College. In 1899 she went to King's College, London, to study botany and in 1902 was awarded the Carter Gold Medal. She was a demonstrator at University College, London, and in 1905 moved to Royal Holloway College, London, where she was an assistant lecturer. In 1906 and 1909 she presented papers on fungi at the annual meetings of the British Association for the Advancement of Science. In 1909, after two years as a lecturer in botany at University College, Nottingham, she was made head of the Botany Department at Birkbeck College, London. She was also a university examiner and a member of the University of London board of studies in botany.

Gwynne-Vaughan married in 1911; when her husband, a botany professor, died of tuberculosis four years later, she took over his final piece of research so that it could be published. She was keen to carry out war work and in 1917 was appointed joint chief controller of the Women's Army Auxiliary Corps. She went to France, where she was able to use her organizational abilities to the full in leading the thousands of members of the corps. In 1918 she was made a Commander of the Order of the British Empire (CBE) and was appointed as commandant of the Women's Royal Air Force. She left in 1919 after fifteen months and was made a Dame Commander of the Order of the British Empire (DBE) in the same year.

On her return to Birkbeck College in 1920, Gwynne-Vaughan resumed her position as head of the Botany Department and in 1921 was made professor of botany. She channeled her desire to perform public service into politics, standing in one local and three general elections over the next few years; she was never elected. In 1922 she published her first textbook, *Fungi: Ascomycetes, Ustilaginales, Uredinales;* five years thereafter she coauthored *The Structure and Development of the Fungi* with B. Barnes. During her career she also published twenty-five pieces of research, mainly on the reproductive system of fungi. She was chair of the botany section of the British Association for the Advancement of Science in 1928 and was president of the British Mycological Society in the same year, and vice-president the following year.

During World War II Gwynne-Vaughan was once again involved in women's service organizations, becoming the first director of the Auxiliary Territorial Service (ATS) in 1939. But disagreements within the service led her to leave in 1941, and she returned to her work at Birkbeck College. When she retired in 1944, she was made honorary secretary to the London branch of the Soldiers, Sailors, and Air Force Association (SSAFA). Although this was an unpaid role, she devoted herself to it full time.

She was elected a fellow of the Linnean Society in 1905 and was awarded the society's Trail Medal in 1920. She was awarded an honorary doctor of law by the University of Glasgow.

Bibliography: "New Woman Professor," *Daily Sketch* (30 May 1921); *Dictionary of National Biography, 1961–1970,* Oxford: Oxford University Press, 1981; Gwynne-Vaughan, Dame Helen, *Service with the Army,* London: Hutchinson, 1942; Marsh, N., *The History of Queen Elizabeth College,* London: King's College, 1986; Public Record Office, Kew, London, CW1898, 11 March 1919 AIR/2/CW528: From 3.07.1918.

H

Halicka, Antonina
née Jaroszewicz
13 February 1908–30 December 1973
geologist

Education: high school, Vilnius, Lithuania; Stefan Batory University, Vilnius, 1930–1939; M.S., 1935; Ph.D., 1939.

Employment: assistant lecturer and researcher, Stefan Batory University, Vilnius, 1930–1939; leader of prospecting group, Lithuanian Geological Service, 1940–1945; work for Polish government, Warsaw, 1945–1947; Museum of the Earth, Warsaw: deputy director, 1947; director, 1950–1973.

Antonina Halicka was director of the Museum of the Earth in Poland and a specialist in quaternary geology.

Halicka was born in Maly Loswid, near Vitebsk, Russia (now Belarus), and attended school and university in Vilnius, Lithuania. At the Stefan Batory University, her studies focused on geology and chemistry, and she was awarded her M.S. degree in 1935. Her Ph.D. thesis detailed the geology of the moraines of the Vilna region. While she pursued her studies, she was an assistant lecturer and researcher and carried out geological surveys in the area. In 1937, with a grant from the Polish National Culture Fund, she visited a number of countries, including Sweden, Finland, and Italy, and was able to study quaternary deposits and volcanic activity.

In 1940 Halicka began working for the Lithuanian Geological Service, mapping several areas of the country in relation to different commercial activities, including mineral prospecting and hydroelectric power. In 1945 she moved to Warsaw, working first for the Ministry of Food Supply and Trade and subsequently taking a job as head of the Department of Natural History Research at the Ministry of Education. Her contribution to the postwar reconstruction of Poland's economy and culture was recognized by the award of a Gold Cross by the Polish government.

Halicka became deputy director of the Museum of the Earth in Warsaw in 1947; the museum did not become fully operational until 1948. She was made its director in 1950, a position she held until her death in 1973. Under her management the museum secured improved premises and grew in importance as a center of research. In 1969 the museum became part of the Polish Academy of Sciences.

Halicka worked hard to popularize geology through exhibitions and events. She also contributed to the development of the subject in universities as a member of the Geological Commission in the Ministry of Higher Education. She edited *Transactions of the Earth Museum*, in which she had over forty papers published on quaternary deposits, the history of science, and museum management. In 1950 she was involved in preparations for the First Congress of Polish Science and subsequently organized two bilateral Soviet-Polish symposia on the history of Soviet-Polish scientific contacts in geology and geography, held in Warsaw in 1969 and Leningrad (St. Petersburg) in 1972.

Halicka was promoted to the rank of professor in 1955. She was a member of the Polish Academy of Science, the Polish Committee of the International Museal Union, and numerous other committees and scientific boards. In her later years much of her work was focused on the history of geology, and she was elected a member of the International Commission on the History of Geological Sciences in 1972.

Bibliography: "Antonina Halicka," *International Committee on the History of Geological Sciences Newsletter* 8 (1973): 14–15; Kosmowska-Ceranowicz, B., "The Work of Antonina Halicka in the Field of Geology and Petrography in the Years 1930–45," translated by Robert Skarzynski, *Prace Museum Ziemi* (*Proceedings of the Museum of the Earth*) 38 (1986); Sarjeant, W. A. S., *Geologists and the History of Geology: An International Bibliography from the Origins to 1978,* 5 vols., London: Macmillan, 1980; Popiolek, Joanna, archivist, Museum of the Earth, Polish Academy of Sciences, Warsaw, personal communication to the author, February 2000.

Hanson, Emmeline Jean
14 November 1919–10 August 1973
biophysicist, zoologist

Education: High School for Girls, Burton-on-Trent, 1930–1938; Bedford College, London, 1938–1941; B.S. with honors; postgraduate studies at Bedford College and the Strangeways Laboratory, Cambridge; Ph.D., 1951.

Employment: demonstrator in zoology, Bedford College, 1944–1948; researcher, Biophysics Research Unit, King's College, London, 1948–1953 and 1954–1966; Massachusetts Institute of Technology (MIT), 1953–1954; professor of biology, King's College, London, 1966–1973; director of Muscle Biophysics Unit, King's College, 1970–1973.

Jean Hanson was an outstanding biophysicist, known for her research on muscles. Hanson's father was in charge of the Derbyshire police; he died soon after she was born. Her mother, a primary school head teacher, encouraged her daughter in her love of music and the arts.

Hanson became interested in biology at school and was able to study zoology at Bedford College, London, with the help of scholarships. Because her college was evacuated to Cambridge during World War II, she had to postpone her original research topic. Instead she worked at the Strangeways Laboratory in Cambridge on the development of mammalian skin in tissue culture.

When the war ended she moved back to Bedford College and did research on aspects of structure and function of annelids. The Medical Research Council set up a Biophysics Research Unit at King's College, London, in 1947, and Hanson moved there in 1948 to establish the biological section. Hanson worked there on isolated myofibrils, but realizing that she needed to know how to use an electron microscope if she was to progress, she took a year's study leave at MIT. During the period from 1952 to 1953, in collaboration with Hugh Esmoor Huxley, she proposed the sliding filament theory of muscle contraction. They discovered through electron microscopy and X-rays the site of actin and myosin in the striation pattern of the filaments, which slide past each other when the muscle contracts. They thought the sliding force could be produced by moving myosin cross-bridges, a theory now widely accepted. She later worked with Dr. Jack Lowy, a physiologist, and together they provided further proof of the double filament system. She also worked on the molecular aspects of the contraction mechanism.

Hanson was elected a fellow of the Royal Society in 1967. Besides being a professor, from 1970 she was director of the Muscle Biophysics Unit at King's College. She had an immense capacity for hard work. She died at fifty-three after contracting a rare brain infection. Her archives are held at King's College in London.

Bibliography: *Dictionary of National Biography, 1971–1980,* Oxford: Oxford University Press, 1986; "Professor Jean Hanson," *Nature* 246 (November 2, 1973); Randall, J., "Emmeline Jean Hanson," *Biographical Memoirs of Fellows of the Royal Society* 21 (1975): 313–344.

Harding, Jan née Ansell
10 May 1925–
science educator

Education: Royal Holloway College, University of London, 1943–1946, B.S.; Institute of Education, University of London, diploma in education, 1947; Chelsea College, London (part-time study), 1969–1975; M.Ed., 1971; Ph.D., 1975.

Employment: science teacher, 1947–1959, at St. Elphin's School, Darley Dale; Clapham County Girls' Grammar School, Blackheath High School, and Preston Manor County School, Middlesex; tutor, Trent Park College, Middlesex (became part of Middlesex Polytechnic, now Middlesex University), 1966–1975; head of Chemistry Section, Centre for Science and Mathematics Education, Chelsea College, University of London, 1975–1985; equal opportunities consultant from 1985.

Married: Arthur Harding.

In 1981 **Jan Harding** founded the International Gender and Science and Technology Association (GASAT) in a joint venture with Professor Jan Raat of Eindhoven University in the Netherlands. GASAT is concerned about issues arising from interactions between gender and science and technology. Some of the aims of GASAT are to encourage research into gender differentiation in science and technology education and employment.

Harding studied chemistry at university and subsequently taught in several secondary schools. While bringing up her children, she worked part time in education for three years. When her children were older, she was a tutor at Trent Park College, a teachers' training college. Concurrently she studied for her master's degree and later her doctorate in science education at Chelsea College.

Harding became aware that early in their lives boys were encouraged to undertake technological activities and face practical challenges, whereas girls were not, and that boys claimed labs and workshops as their territory, elbowing out the girls and grabbing the best equipment. When girls and boys were expected to conduct practical experiments, the girls in mixed groups often ended up simply watching the boys carry out the experiments. Harding observed students in both mixed and single-sex practical science classes. She watched the teachers carefully and noticed how frequently the teachers "taught to the boys." The results were that girls felt science was not for them and opted out of the subject as soon as this was allowed. In girls-only classes, if (and only if) they were shown in lots of ways that the school expected them to do science, girls worked with competence and enjoyment.

Harding tried to make those in science education aware of the factors that have hindered girls and women electing to become engaged in science, especially the physical sciences. She has been involved with the Schools Council, which published her book, *Switched Off: The Science Education of Girls* (1983).

Harding has written many papers about gender issues and edited and contributed chapters to seminal texts, such as Alison Kelly's *Science for Girls?* (1987) and Murphy and Gipp's *Equity in the Classroom* (1996).

She has traveled widely to attend international GASAT conferences and to act as a consultant to a variety of education groups. She has been a named international consultant for the Key Centre for Science and Mathematics Education (especially for women) at Curtin University, Western Australia, and in 1994 spent three months as the first visiting scholar appointed to the newly formed Education Faculty of the University of Melbourne.

As the chair of the International GASAT Association, she traveled to Beijing in 1995 to attend the Nongovernmental Organization Forum associated with the UN Fourth World Conference on Women. She lobbied for the inclusion of stronger statements on the importance of women's involvement in science and technology.

She developed science curricula, particularly in relation to chemistry, and has helped ensure that the subject matter is more related to everyday and social issues. In 1984–1985 she was president of section X of the British Association for the Advancement of Science. In August 1985 she coordinated a five-day program at Strathclyde University on "Women and Science" at the association's annual meeting.

For four years, she acted as chair of the working group set up by the Committee on the Public Understanding of Science (COPUS) and the National Federation of Women's Institutes (NFWI) to develop the project "Science, You, and Everyday Life."

Harding argues that it is not only science education but science itself that is gender-based through the dominance of male perspectives, ways of thinking, and emotional needs. This influences the way science is practiced and the concepts and assumptions that shape its development.

In 1991 Harding was elected a fellow of the Royal Society of Arts.

Bibliography: Harding, J., *Breaking the Barrier: Girls in Science Education,* Paris: International Institute for Educational Planning/ UNESCO, 1992; Harding, J., personal communication with the author, October, 1998; Harding, J., "Science in a Masculine Straight-jacket," in L. H. Parker, L. J. Rennie, and B. J. Fraser, eds., *Gender, Science and Mathematics: Shortening the Shadow,* Dordrecht: Kluwer Academic Publishers, 1996; Harding, J., and L. H. Parker, "Agents for Change: Policy and Practice Towards a More Gender-Inclusive Science Education," *International Journal of Science Education* 17, 4 (1995): 537–553.

Harker, Margaret Florence
17 January 1920–
photographer, lecturer, historian, author

Education: Howell's School, Denbigh; Southport School of Art; Regent Street Polytechnic, London, 1940–1943.

Employment: professional architectural photographer, 1941–1959; Regent Street Polytechnic: lecturer, School of Photography, 1943–1959; head, School of Photography, 1959–1974; professor of photography from 1972; dean of the Faculty of Communication, 1974–1975; assistant director,

Margaret Florence Harker (University of Westminster Archive)

Polytechnic of Central London (formerly Regent Street Polytechnic), 1975–1980; professor emeritus from 1987.

Married: Richard George Farrand, photographer, on 20 December 1972.

Margaret Harker was the first woman professor of photography and the first woman president of the Royal Photographic Society (1958–1960); she was also president of the British Institute of Professional Photographers (1964–1965).

Harker was born in Southport, Lancashire. She studied photography at the Polytechnic in Regent Street, where she was awarded a Silver Medal for her work for the City and Guilds Final Examination in Photography.

She was particularly interested in architectural photography and from 1941–1959 had many commissions in this field, among them photographing the Royal Festival Hall in London, various Georgian houses, and John Soane's Museum. She took photographs of cathedrals in England for a series of books published by the Pitkin Press.

During this period Harker was a part-time lecturer at the Polytechnic, becoming a full-time lecturer in 1943. In the same year she was elected a fellow of the Royal Photographic Society and also of the British Institute of Professional Photographers. In 1959 she was promoted to head of the School of Photography at the Regent Street Polytechnic. The school was the first British institution to design and award degrees in photography—a B.S. in photographic sciences and a B.A. in photographic arts. In 1972 the Polytechnic was awarded university status, and Harker was one of the first six professors appointed.

Harker began publishing her works early in her career. One of her first books was *Photographing Architecture* (1951). She has published numerous articles, mainly in the *Royal Photographic Society Journal* and the *British Journal of Photography*. One of her most detailed books, *The Linked Ring* (1979), deals with the Secession movement in photography in Britain, from 1892 to 1910.

Harker has exhibited her work widely. Her first major exhibition was in 1958 at the Photokina World Fair in Cologne, and her most recent was at Petworth House, West Sussex, in 1998. She also researched material for an exhibit of the work of Henry Peach Robinson, master of photographic art, which was displayed at venues in Britain and abroad from 1988 to 1990. She wrote a book, *Henry Peach Robinson* (1988), to accompany the exhibit.

She was a member of the photography board of the Council for National Academic Awards (CNAA) from 1971 to 1983, on their council from 1977 to 1983, and chair of the photography board from 1978 to 1983. The CNAA awarded her an honorary doctorate in 1987.

Harker was president of the European Society for the History of Photography in 1985. From 1964 she was a member of the council of the Royal Society of Arts and on three of their committees. She was awarded an honorary fellowship of the Royal Photo-

graphic Society in 1942, the society's Hood Medal in 1945 and 1948, and their Fenton Medal in 1989.

She gave many public lectures on various aspects of both the history of photography and photographic techniques. On 22 January 1996 she unveiled a plaque commemorating the establishment of the Margaret Harker Photography Centre at the Harrow Campus of the University of Westminster (formerly the Polytechnic of Central London).

Bibliography: Howard, P., Secretary, Royal Photographic Society, Bath, personal communication to the author, April 1998; *Debrett's People of Today 2001*, London: Debrett's Peerage Ltd., 2001; Harker, Margaret, personal communications to the author, March 1998–July 2000; Williams, V., *Women Photographers*. London: Virago, 1986.

Haslett, Caroline
17 August 1895–4 January 1957
electrical engineer, writer

Education: Haywards Heath High School.
Employment: Cochran Boiler Company: junior clerk, then manager, 1913–1918; general and electrical engineer, 1918– 1919; secretary, Women's Engineering Society (WES), from 1919; director, Electrical Association for Women (EAW), 1924– 1956.

Caroline Haslett was the first director of the Electrical Association for Women (EAW). In 1932 she was the first woman appointed as a companion member of the Institution of Electrical Engineers and one of the first two women elected as a visitor of the Royal Institution of Great Britain. She was the first and only woman appointed as a member of the British Electrical Authority when the electrical industry was nationalized in 1947.

Haslett was born near Crawley, Sussex. Her father was a railway signal fitter and a pioneer member of the cooperative movement. After leaving school she worked as a secretary with the Cochran Boiler Company and soon was promoted to managing the clerical department. Deciding she would

Caroline Haslett (Hulton-Deutsch Collection/Corbis)

drawing room on 12 November 1924, and the EAW was formed, with Caroline Haslett as its first director. She ran both the WES and EAW, and the two organizations initially shared offices, staff, finances, and even membership. The EAW campaigned for electrical equipment to be more widely available and ran educational courses for women ranging from afternoon classes on how to change fuses and wire plugs to diploma courses. The EAW set up an all-electric flat at the 1930 Batchelor Girls' Exhibition and an all-electric house in Bristol in 1935. Such was the enthusiasm of EAW members that by 1934 there were forty-seven branches throughout Britain, and over 200 by 1981.

Haslett lectured throughout Britain and gave radio talks. Although the EAW membership was predominantly middle class, Haslett did campaign actively to help working-class people. With Margaret Partridge, she edited *The Electrical Age for Women,* which started in June 1926 with monthly editions. Her *Electrical Handbook for Women* (1934) went through nine editions before being revised and retitled *Essential Electricity, a User's Guide* (edited by Ann McMullen, 1983).

Haslett was very aware of the likelihood of accidents with electricity and always stressed safety; she was a vice-president of the Royal Society for the Prevention of Accidents. She was also involved with many other organizations and was a fellow of the Royal Society of Arts, where an annual lecture is held in her memory. She was a council member of several colleges, including Bedford College, the London School of Economics, and Queen Elizabeth College. She was a justice of the peace for the county of London.

She was made a Commander of the Order of the British Empire (CBE) in 1931 and a Dame Commander of the Order of the British Empire (DBE) in 1947. The Caroline Haslett Memorial Trust cosponsors the Girl Technician Engineer Award given annually since 1978 to focus attention on electrical and electronic engineering as a worthwhile career for women.

rather be an engineer, she first trained as a general engineer and then specialized in electrical engineering. At her request she was transferred to the Cochran works in Annan, Dumfries, and worked as an engineer there for some time.

In late 1919 Haslett applied for and was appointed to the post of secretary of the Women's Engineering Society (WES). She was their first secretary and founded and edited their journal, *The Woman Engineer.*

Haslett was the first director of the Electrical Association for Women (EAW), formed in 1924 by members of the WES and a variety of other organizations after the Institute of Electrical Engineers showed no interest in setting up a group for women. She asked the WES if they could do so. Lady Parsons, the wife of Charles Parsons (the inventor of the steam turbine, son of Mary, Countess of Rosse), who was an engineer and WES member, agreed to help. The initial meeting was held in Lady Parsons's

Bibliography: "Dame Caroline Haslett,

DBE," *Times* (5 January 1957): 8E; "Dame Caroline Haslett, Engineer and Educator 1895–1957," *Shell Times* 70 (1989/90); *Dictionary of National Biography, 1951–1960,* Oxford: Oxford University Press, 1971; Pursell, C., "Domesticating Modernity: The Electrical Association for Women, 1924–86," *British Journal for the History of Science* 32 (1999): 46–67; Sprenger, E., and P. Webb, "Persuading the Housewife to Use Electricity? An Interpretation of Material in the Electricity Council Archives," *British Journal for the History of Science* 26 (1993): 55–65; *Who Was Who, 1951–1960,* London: Adam and Charles Black, 1961.

Hawker, Lilian E.
1908–5 February 1991
mycologist

Education: University of Reading, B.S., M.S.; University of Manchester; Imperial College, London, from 1932.

Employment: Imperial College; Botany Department, University of Bristol, 1945–1973: professor of mycology, 1965–1973; dean of Faculty of Science, 1970–1973.

In 1965 *Lilian Hawker* was appointed as the first professor of mycology in Britain.

Hawker graduated with a degree in botany from the University of Reading and did research on plant physiology both at Reading and at the University of Manchester. In 1932 she had a grant to study mycology at Imperial College, London. As well as research, she was known for her work as a teacher and writer. She wrote several books, including *Fungi—An Introduction* (1966). In 1970 she became the first woman to be dean of Faculty at the University of Bristol. She played a large part in setting up the Honours School of Microbiology and promoted the biological sciences as part of the B.Ed. degree. When she retired in 1973, she was made an emeritus professor.

Bibliography: Alumni Gazette—University of Bristol (1972–1973): 20; "Professor L. E. Hawker," *University of Reading Bulletin* 242 (April 1991): 26.

Herschel, Caroline Lucretia
16 March 1750–9 January 1848
astronomer

Caroline Herschel was the first prominent woman astronomer and the first woman to be paid for this work.

Herschel was born in Hannover, Germany, into a family of musicians. She had smallpox when she was four and the disease left her badly disfigured, so she realized her chances of getting married were minimal. Her mother wanted her to be skilled in the domestic arts, but her father encouraged her in more academic pursuits. Upon her father's death in 1767, Herschel tried to learn dressmaking and to study so that she could leave home, but her mother would not let her. Then in 1772 her brother William was appointed organist at the Octagon Chapel in Bath, and Herschel moved there to be his housekeeper and to train as a singer.

William Herschel was more interested in astronomy than music. He trained his sister to be his assistant in making telescopes, and they spent most clear evenings sweeping the skies. Caroline Herschel recorded their observations as they made them and wrote them up neatly the following mornings, educating herself about astronomy in the process. William soon gave up his musician's post to become king's astronomer, and the Herschels moved to Slough, Berkshire.

The mirrors for his huge telescope had to be polished by hand by teams of twelve men working in two shifts. With their 20-foot reflecting telescope, the Herschels were able to move into sidereal astronomy—the study of objects outside the solar system. Caroline had a smaller telescope that she used when William was away. On 1 August 1786, along with calculating the positions of 100 nebulae, she discovered her first comet. Her discovery was communicated to the members of the Royal Society, and many people came to the Herschels' home to look at it.

Altogether Caroline Herschel discovered eight comets and three nebulae—this on top of having full responsibility for the household responsibilities and doing other work in astronomy. From 1787 King George III paid her £50 a year, the first time she had ever had any money of her own to spend. She was understandably upset when her brother married and she had to move to her own home. But she had an indoor observatory and continued to work both on her own and with William. When he died in 1822, she returned to Hanover for the rest of her life.

In 1828 she was given the Gold Medal of the Royal Astronomical Society, and in February 1835 she was elected an honorary member of the society.

Bibliography: Alic, M., *Hypatia's Heritage: A History of Women in Science from Antiquity to the Late Nineteenth Century,* London: Women's Press, 1986; *Dictionary of National Biography,* vol. XXVI, London: Smith, Elder & Co., 1891; *Everyman's Encyclopaedia,* vol. 6, London: Dent, 1958; Lubbock, Lady Constance Anne, ed., *The Herschel Chronicle: The Life Story of William Herschel and His Sister Caroline Herschel,* Cambridge, UK: Cambridge University Press, 1933; Raffan, S., BBC Radio Science, personal communication to the author, October 1997; Winterburn, E., curator of astronomy, Royal Observatory, Greenwich, personal communication to the author, January, 2000.

Heslop, Mary Kingdon
1885–1955
geologist, geographer, teacher

Education: Armstrong College, Newcastle upon Tyne (University of Durham), 1901–1906; B.S. in physics and geology; research fellow, 1906–1909; M.S., 1909; School of Geography, Oxford University; diploma in economic and political geography, 1916.

Employment: demonstrator, Geology Department, Armstrong College, and then at Bedford College for Women, London, 1909–1915; geography teacher, Church High School, Newcastle upon Tyne 1916–?; lecturer in geography, University of Leeds; lecturer in geography; Kenton Lodge Teacher Training College, Newcastle upon Tyne, 1923– 1950.

In December 1919 *Mary Kingdon Heslop* be-

came one of the first women to be elected a fellow of the Geological Society.

Heslop was born and educated in Egypt. After her undergraduate studies she investigated the igneous dikes in northern England, taking color photomicrographs of the rocks she studied. Her findings were published in the *Geological Magazine* in 1912. Though she worked as a demonstrator in geology, she saw that there were not many opportunities for women geologists, so she studied for a diploma in geography and switched to teaching. Her first post was at the Church High School in Newcastle upon Tyne; later she taught at Leeds University. Her final post was at Kenton Lodge Teacher Training College in Newcastle. She was committed to her students and a skilled pianist and artist.

Bibliography: Dyer, L., archives assistant, Royal Holloway/Bedford College, University of London, personal communication to the author, January 2000; Smythe, J. A., "Mary Kingdon Heslop," *Proceedings of the Geological Society of London* 1529 (1955): 139–140.

Hesse, Fanny Angelina (Lina) née Eilshemius
22 June 1850–1 December 1934
laboratory technician, medical illustrator

Married: Dr. Walther Hesse, on 16 May 1874.

In 1881 *Fanny Hesse* was responsible for suggesting that agar jelly could be used instead of gelatin for cultivating bacteria. She was working as a laboratory technician for her husband, who was studying in Robert Koch's laboratory. Koch immediately switched to agar instead of gelatin to cultivate the bacteria that cause tuberculosis.

Fanny Hesse was from New York. She was introduced to Dr. Walther Hesse, a physician who practiced in Germany, in 1872. Her family went on holiday to Europe later that year, and Fanny and her sister went to Dresden to see Dr. Hesse again. In the summer of 1873 Fanny was engaged to him, and they were married in Geneva in 1874.

Walther Hesse was a country doctor in the mining area of the Erzgebirge, the mountains bordering German and Czech lands. From 1881 to 1882 Dr. Hesse took a sabbatical from his medical post to learn about bacteriology from Robert Koch. Fanny Hesse was his unpaid laboratory technician and used to make drawings to accompany her husband's publications.

Dr. Hesse found that in the high summer temperatures not only did gelatin liquefy but also some proteolytic bacteria broke down gelatin to liquid. He asked his wife why her jellies remained solid in summer. She explained that she prepared them with agar-agar, which is widely used in the Dutch East Indies. Agar was found to be stable at varying temperatures and resistant to most microbial enzymes; it could also be sterilized and stored for a long time.

Koch mentioned that he was using agar in an 1882 paper on the tuberculosis bacilli but did not say why he had changed from using gelatin. Dr. Hesse developed a nutrient agar that was commercially manufactured; apart from this, the Hesse family did not gain financially from Fanny Hesse's suggestion.

The Hesses moved to a suburb of Dresden in 1900. Dr. Hesse died in 1911, and Fanny Hesse later moved into Dresden to be nearer to her children.

Bibliography: Bridson, E., treasurer, Medical Sciences Historical Society, personal communication to the author, September 1999; Hesse, W., and D. H. M. Gröschel, "Walther and Angelina Hesse—Early Contributors to Bacteriology," *ASM News* 58, 8 (1992): 425–428.

Heywood, Joan
1923–
wireless operator, crypt analyst

Education: training as wireless operator and crypt analyst in the Women's Auxiliary Air Force (WAAF), Edinburgh; technical training at Compton Bassett.

Employment: WAAF wireless operator, ground to air, Thornaby on Tees and Wick, 18 Group Headquarters at Pitreavie

Castle, Dunfermline, 1941–1944; Government Communications Headquarters (GCHQ), Cheltenham, crypt analyst, executive officer, 1966–1983.

Married: Stuart Heywood, on 10 January 1942.

Joan Heywood was involved in telecommunications throughout her working life.

Heywood was born in India, where her father was serving with the British Army; the regiment was posted back to Britain before World War II. She served in the Women's Auxiliary Air Force (WAAF) mainly in Scotland and worked as a ground-to-air wireless operator. Her husband was a telegraphist for thirty-one years in the Royal Air Force, and both were members of the Radio Society of Great Britain (RSGB).

After her children were grown up, Heywood joined the Government Communications Headquarters (GCHQ) in Cheltenham, where she worked for more than seventeen years as a crypt analyst. She took all the necessary examinations and was an executive officer running her own section.

On retirement Heywood took the examinations to become an amateur radio operator; her call sign is GOGZA. She and her husband were Morse code examiners for the RSGB in Gloucestershire for almost eight years. She is also a life member of the Royal Air Force Amateur Radio Society (RAFARS) and served on the council for nearly five years as the call-book editor. In 1992 she was awarded the G2LR Memorial Trophy presented for an outstanding contribution to the activity of the society in the previous year.

Bibliography: Heywood, J., personal communication to the author, April 2000.

Hickling, Grace née Watt
10 August 1908–30 December 1986
ornithologist

Education: Harrogate Ladies' College; Armstrong College, Newcastle upon Tyne; Newnham College, Cambridge, 1928–1931; M.A., 1934; teacher's diploma, 1932.

Employment: teacher, St. Margaret's School,

Bushey, 1932–1936; war room intelligence officer and regional intelligence officer (based in Newcastle), Ministry of Home Security, 1939–1945; honorary secretary, Natural History Society of Northumbria, 1948–1986.

Married: Henry George Albert Hickling, emeritus professor of geology, in 1954.

Grace Hickling was the leading expert on the wildlife of the Farne Islands in Northumberland.

Hickling started her working life as a teacher. During World War II she was called up for war service and was an intelligence officer at £400 a year until it was noticed that her name was "Grace": her salary promptly dropped to the women's rate of £300. In this post Hickling met Russell Goddard, curator at the Hancock Museum, Newcastle-upon-Tyne, and became interested in the Farne Islands, in the North Sea off Northumberland. Hickling soon became honorary secretary of the Natural History Society of Northumbria, a post she held for thirty-eight years.

Following Goddard's death in 1948, Hickling started making neat transcriptions of his notes on the Farne Island birds. Together with her own observations, this amounted to twenty-two volumes. These have been photocopied by the National Trust so that they can be used for research. Every year in April, May, and June, Hickling was in charge of the bird tagging on the Farne Islands; 187,600 birds were tagged under her guidance.

She published two books, *The Farne Islands: Their History and Wildlife* (1951) and *Grey Seals and the Farne Islands* (1962). When the Lindisfarne National Nature Reserve was set up in September 1964, Hickling became the naturalists' representative. She was on the Farne Islands local committee of the National Trust from 1949.

In 1954 she married Albert Hickling, an emeritus professor of geology at King's College, in Newcastle; he died a few weeks after their wedding.

She was made a Member of the Order of the British Empire (MBE) in 1974 in recognition of her services to natural history. Her ashes were scattered upon the sands of St. Cuthbert's Cove, Inner Farne, on 20 March 1987. This was the 1300th anniversary of St. Cuthbert's death, and a service had already been planned for that day at the cove.

Bibliography: *Newnham College Register, 1871–1923,* Cambridge: Newnham College, 1963; Shannon, D. R., "Obituary. Grace Hickling MBE MA MBOU," *Transactions of the Natural History Society of Northumbria* 55 (1987): 5–11.

Hill, Dorothy
10 September 1907–23 April 1997
geologist, paleontologist

Education: Brisbane Girls' Grammar School; University of Queensland, 1925–1930; B.S., 1928; M.S., 1930; D.Sc., 1942; Newnham College, Cambridge, 1930–1937; Ph.D., 1932.

Employment: research fellow, University of Queensland, 1937–1942; second officer, Women's Royal Australian Navy Service (WRANS), 1942–1945; University of Queensland: lecturer, 1946–1952; reader, 1955–1959; research professor, 1959–1972.

Dorothy Hill was an expert on the geology of Australia, particularly that of Queensland. She became the first woman fellow of the Australian Academy of Science in 1956, and in 1965 she became the first Australian woman to be made a fellow of the Royal Society of London.

Hill was born in Brisbane, Australia, and won a scholarship to the University of Queensland in 1925. She graduated in 1928 with a first-class honors degree in geology and mineralogy and received a university Gold Medal for outstanding merit. She continued her studies at the university with a research scholarship, investigating the Mesozoic rocks of the Brisbane valley. She became interested in paleontology, especially rugose (corrugated), corals.

From 1930 she continued her research in Cambridge, based at the Sedgwick Museum. She was a research fellow at Newnham College after she had obtained her doctorate and had a senior studentship there from 1935 to 1937. She returned to Australia in 1937, by which time she had published papers on rugose corals. As a Commonwealth research fellow at the University of Queensland, she concentrated on Australian corals. During World War II she was a second officer in the Women's Royal Australian Navy Service (WRANS) and did cipher work. She returned to the University of Queensland in 1946 as a lecturer in the Geology Department.

Hill was honorary secretary to the Great Barrier Reef Committee for nine years from 1946 and played an important role in the setting up of the Heron Island Marine Biological Station. In 1949 she became the first woman president of the Royal Society of Queensland, having been the society's honorary secretary and a member of its council.

Hill was editor of the Geological Society of Australia's journal from 1958 to 1964. She was also joint editor (with A. K. Denmead) of a comprehensive collection of papers (from sixty-two contributors) on the geology of Queensland. In 1962 she helped found the Queensland Palaeontographical Society. She contributed to Moore and Teichert's *Treatise on Invertebrate Palaeontology* (1956), writing the first volume of Part E, on the Archaeocyatha (1972).

She received the Lyell Medal of the Geological Society of London in 1964 for her research on Paleozoic corals. In 1970 she was president of the Australian Academy of Science, another first for a woman, and was also the first woman to be president of an Australian university's professorial board, a position she held from 1971 to 1972. She was made a Commander of the Order of the British Empire (CBE) in 1971 and was a life member of the Linnean Society of New South Wales. In 1993 she was made a Companion of the Order of Australia.

When Hill retired from the University of Queensland in 1972, a chair of paleontology and stratigraphy was established in her name; the Earth Sciences Library at Queensland University was named after her as well. She was emeritus professor of geology from 1973 to 1997.

Bibliography: Anderson, D. T., "Death of Dorothy Hill," *Linnean Society of New South Wales Newsletter* 84 (1997): 1–2; Denmead, A. K., "Professor Dorothy Hill," in K. S. W. Campbell, ed., *Stratigraphy and Palaeontology: Essays in Honour of Dorothy Hill,* Canberra: Australian National University Press, 1969; Jell, J. S., "Dorothy Hill," in J. McKay, comp., *Brilliant Careers: Women Collectors and Illustrators in Queensland,* Brisbane: Queensland Museum, 1997; Moore, R. C., and Teichert, C. *Treatise on Invertebrate Palaeontology,* vol. 1, part E, second edition, Lawrence: University of Kansas, 1972; *Newnham College Roll Letter* (1998): 112–114; *Who's Who in Australasia and the Far East,* second edition, Cambridge: Melrose Press, 1991.

Hindmarsh, Mary Maclean
21 July 1921–10 April 2000
botanist

Education: Lismore High School; New England University College, Armidale, Australia, 1939–1943; B.S., 1943; Sydney University, 1949–1953; Ph.D., 1953.

Employment: teacher, Ascham School, Sydney; demonstrator, University of Sydney; demonstrator and tutor, Commonwealth Reconstruction Training Scheme; research, Chester Beatty Research Institute, Royal Cancer Hospital, London, 1953–1954; New South Wales University of Technology, Ultimo, Australia (later University of New South Wales, Kensington, Sydney): lecturer, 1954–1959; senior lecturer, 1959–1972; associate professor, 1972–1978.

Mary Hindmarsh was a noted botanist, known especially for her work at the University of New South Wales.

Hindmarsh was the eldest of four girls, brought up by their grandmother after their mother's death. Hindmarsh showed an early enthusiasm for botany and in 1939 entered the recently established New England University College in Armidale, Australia, graduating in 1943 with a B.S. in botany and geology. She was a teacher for a short time, then a demonstrator in botany, this latter role including work with ex-servicemen and -women under the Commonwealth Reconstruction Training Scheme.

Hindmarsh had a Linnean Macleay Fellowship at the University of Sydney from

1949 to 1953. Her doctorate was a study of the effects of certain substances on cell division and root growth. After a year of postgraduate research at the Royal Cancer Hospital in London, she became lecturer in botany at the New South Wales University of Technology in Ultimo. While there she built up an internationally registered herbarium collection for both teaching and research. She was on the council of the Linnean Society of New South Wales between 1970 and 1974 and a foundation member of the Friends of the Royal Botanic Gardens.

Despite having systemic lupus erythematosis from the time she was in her thirties, she led an active life, both academically and in her leisure interests. She continued to carry out botanical research in her retirement, including work on a key to rainforest species south of the Macleay River watershed. (She was unable to complete this project because of the sudden death of her colleague John Waterhouse in 1983.) Later she developed motor neurone disease, from which she died.

Bibliography: Anderson, K., ed., "Trailblazer for Women in Science," *Sydney Daily Telegraph* (28 July 2000): 115; "Vale Mary Hindmarsh," *Uniken* (University of New South Wales community magazine) (August 2000): 14; "Vale Mary Maclean Hindmarsh," *Linnean Society of New South Wales Newsletter* (July 2000): 2.

Hodgkin, Dorothy Mary
née Crowfoot
12 May 1910–29 July 1994
crystallographer

Education: Parents' National Education Union School, Burgess Hill; home tuition from her mother; Sir John Leman School, Beccles, Norfolk, 1921–1927; Somerville College, University of Oxford, 1928–1931; research at Cambridge and Oxford Universities.

Employment: Somerville College, University of Oxford: university demonstrator in chemical crystallography, 1945–1955; reader in X-ray crystallography, 1955–

1960; Wolfson Professor (appointed by the Royal Society), Oxford University, 1960–1977.

Married: Thomas Lionel Hodgkin, on 16 December 1937.

On 29 October 1964 *Dorothy Hodgkin* became the first British woman to win a Nobel Prize. She was awarded the prize in chemistry for her work on the structure of vitamin B_{12} and penicillin.

Hodgkin was born in Egypt and spent her early childhood there. Her father was assistant director of education from 1903 to 1916, and then director of education from 1916 to 1926 in the Sudan. He became director of the British School of Archaeology in Jerusalem in 1927. Her mother, a talented artist and botanist, had trained as a midwife at the Clapham School of Midwifery.

Hodgkin was the first of four girls. Her mother taught the children at home until 1921, when the family moved to Celdesten near Beccles in Norfolk. Hodgkin attended the Sir John Leman School, where she did so well that she was in a class with pupils on average almost two years older than she. In 1927 she made the highest overall mark of any girl taking the Oxford local examinations and was awarded £30 as a prize.

She knew she wanted to study chemistry at university; as her mother had contacts with Somerville College in Oxford, it was decided that Hodgkin should try for a place there. This meant private tuition in Latin and botany, both essentials for entry at that time. Hodgkin obtained a place without much difficulty.

Her director of studies and moral tutor at Oxford was Jane Willis Kirkaldy, a zoologist. At first Hodgkin found chemistry disappointing, but she had plenty of opportunity for independent study and soon showed that she was exceptionally able. For her last year of undergraduate study, she was able to start research on crystallography. Her base was the X-ray crystallography laboratory on the first floor of the University Museum. She was awarded a first-class degree in chemistry in 1932, only the third woman to achieve this, and was given half of a Vernon Harcourt Scholarship.

J. D. Bernal accepted her as a postgraduate student in crystallography, and Hodgkin enrolled at Newnham College, Cambridge. Her thesis, completed in 1937, was on the chemistry and crystallography of the sterols. She had barely started and was thoroughly enjoying life in Cambridge when Somerville College wrote to offer her a research fellowship with some teaching. To the surprise of Somerville, she refused, so the offer was changed to a two-year fellowship at £200 a year, with the proviso that she could spend the first year in Cambridge and the second on research without teaching responsibilities.

Bernal soon found that Hodgkin was adept at photographing crystals; she was also good at mathematical analyses and had a particularly useful three-dimensional imagination. She photographed pepsin using X-ray diffraction techniques, producing the first X-ray diffraction photograph of a protein. Bernal cited her as coauthor for twelve of his research papers published between 1933 and 1936, which was a great help to Hodgkin in establishing herself.

In September 1934 she returned to Oxford. She used Fourier analyses to look at the structures of sterols. She had been interested in insulin for many years and on 25 October 1934 she took her first photograph of the insulin crystal. She published her results in *Nature* in 1935; it was the first article she published as sole author.

In the spring of 1937 she met Thomas Lionel Hodgkin, an Oxford graduate and something of a revolutionary. They met again by chance in Oxford soon after this and enjoyed each other's company. They married in December 1937. Dorothy Hodgkin was determined that marriage would not interfere with her research, especially as she was doing so well and had just taken on her first research student. Throughout their married life, the couple almost never seemed to be employed in the same city, and they tended to see each other only on weekends.

In February 1938, Hodgkin found she was pregnant. The Somerville authorities knew that she wanted to continue with her work after her child was born and that her husband's income was precarious. So they paid her while she was on maternity leave, the

Dorothy Mary Hodgkin (London Express/Archive Photos)

first time any Oxford college had done so. Luke Hodgkin was born on 20 December 1938, the first of three children.

When she was twenty-eight, Hodgkin had a bad attack of rheumatoid arthritis. With treatment she recovered, but her hands were never the same again, though she continued her delicate work on crystals. She applied to the Rockefeller Foundation in 1940 for a grant for equipment and was given £1,000; she received annual funding from the foundation for many years. With her research student C. H. Carlisle she worked on the crystal structure of cholesterol iodide. In 1945 their results appeared in the *Proceedings of the Royal Society*, the most complete three-dimensional crystallographic analysis of a biochemically important molecule published up to then.

During World War II Hodgkin and her colleagues worked on the structure of penicillin; the results were not published until 1949. Penicillin was the most complex molecule ever to have been analyzed by means of X-ray crystallography. Once the pharmaceutical companies knew the structure, they were able to move into developing a range of semisynthetic types of penicillin.

In spite of all her success in attracting equipment grants, the Hodgkins were not well off. Her husband's salary covered only his living expenses. In 1944 Dorothy Hodgkin applied for a university post to help financially, and a year later she was appointed as a demonstrator in chemical crystallography.

Hodgkin's proposal for election as a fellow of the Royal Society was accepted on 20 March 1947, at the same time as that of mathematician Mary Cartwright. In autumn 1947 she went to the United States on a Rockefeller Traveling Fellowship. With more financial support from the Rockefeller Foundation, the Department of Scientific and Industrial Research, and the Nuffield Foundation from 1948 onward, she was able to work on the structure of vitamin B_{12}, the essential substance needed to prevent pernicious anemia. The Royal Society awarded her the Royal Medal, their highest honor, on 30 November 1956; she was the first woman to be so recognized. In May 1960 she was appointed Wolfson Professor of the Royal Society.

On 29 October 1964, while she and her husband were in Ghana, she was told she had won the Nobel Prize for chemistry; her family traveled from all over the world to be at the ceremony in Stockholm. Her acceptance lecture was on "The X-ray Analysis of Complicated Matter."

She was elected a member of the Ghana Academy of Sciences in 1964. In 1965 she was given the Order of Merit (OM), the first woman to be honored in this way since Florence Nightingale received it in 1907, and the Freedom of Beccles.

In July 1965 Hodgkin at last clearly established the structure of insulin. She did not retire from the Wolfson Professorship until 1977 and thereafter continued to take an active interest in research. Her final paper, on insulin, was published in 1988 in the *Philosophical Transactions of the Royal Society*.

In 1970 she was appointed chancellor of Bristol University, becoming the first woman other than members of the royal family to hold such a position in Britain. In the same year she was made a member of the commission of inquiry into U.S. war crimes in Vietnam and vice-president and then president of the Medical Aid Foundation for Vietnam. From 1972 to 1975 she was president of the International Union of Crystallography. She was president of the Pugwash Conferences on Science and World Affairs from 1975. She was awarded the Lenin Peace Prize in 1987. The Royal Society awards

four-year fellowships named in her honor in natural sciences, including mathematics and engineering.

Bibliography: Baker, E., et al., "The Structure of 2 Zn Pig Insulin Crystals at 1.5 Å Resolution," *Philosophical Transactions of the Royal Society of London,* series B, 319 (1988): 369–456; Carlisle, C. H., and D. Crowfoot, "The Crystal Structure of Cholesteryl Iodide," *Proceedings of the Royal Society,* series A, 239 (1945): 135–182; Crowfoot, D., "X-ray Single Photographs of Insulin," *Nature* 135 (1935): 591–592; "Dorothy Crowfoot Hodgkin," *Shell Times* 74 (1991); "Dorothy Hodgkin Fellowships," Available at http://www.royalsoc.ac.uk/gr_dhf.htm; Ferry, G., *Dorothy Hodgkin: A Life,* London: Granta Books, 1998; Opfell, O. S., *The Lady Laureates: Women Who Have Won the Nobel Prize,* Metuchen, New Jersey: Scarecrow Press, 1978; Uglow, J. S., ed., *The Macmillan Dictionary of Women's Biography,* third edition, London: Macmillan, 1998.

Hodgson, Elizabeth
1814–26 December 1877
botanist, geologist

Education: at home.

Elizabeth Hodgson was a self-educated botanist and geologist who researched the geology and botany of the Furness area, now part of Cumbria.

Hodgson, the second daughter of Captain James Hodgson of the Royal Navy, lived in Ulverston, Cumbria. She investigated the movement of granite fragments from the fells throughout the area and worked out the direction of the flow by looking at the rocks and glacial striae. She corresponded with Adam Sedgwick and other geologists at the British Museum and published papers in the *Geologist* and the *Geological Magazine* between 1864 and 1870; her paper on glacial drift appeared in the *North Lonsdale Magazine* in 1866. In 1867 her theories on the weathering of the carboniferous limestone in the Furness area, now part of Cumbria, were published in the *Geological Magazine.*

One of her sisters did the illustrations for Hodgson's papers.

Hodgson was also a competent botanist and had an extensive collection of mosses from the Furness area. She published "Flora of Lake Lancashire" in the *Journal of Botany* (1874).

Bibliography: Alic, M., *Hypatia's Heritage: A History of Women in Science from Antiquity to the Late Nineteenth Century*, London: Women's Press, 1986; Creese, M. R. S., *Ladies in the Laboratory? American and British Women in Science, 1800–1900: A Survey of Their Contributions to Research*, Lanham, Maryland: Scarecrow Press, 1998; "Deaths," *Ulverston Mirror* (29 December 1877); "Deceased Botanical Worthies," *Gardeners' Chronicle* (9 February 1878): 178; Desmond, R., *Dictionary of British and Irish Botanists and Horticulturalists, Including Plant Collectors and Botanical Artists*, London: Taylor and Francis, 1977.

Hofmann, Elise
5 February 1889–14 March 1955
geologist, paleobotanist

Education: high school, Vienna; University of Vienna, graduated 1920.
Employment: teacher in middle school, Vienna; lecturer and professor, University of Vienna.

Elise Hofmann was well known for her studies of fossils in Austrian lignite.

At university Hofmann studied plant anatomy, which provided a good foundation for her later work. She published over 120 articles between 1922 and 1955; *Palaeohistologie der Pflanze* (Paleohistology of the plant) (1934) was her major publication and was presented as her professional thesis. She was appointed correspondent for the Austrian State Geological Institution in 1931 and for the Niederoestreichischen Landesmuseum in 1933. She was made a professor emeritus at Vienna University in 1950.

Bibliography: Kühn, O., "Elise Hofmann," *Mitteilungen der Geologischen Gesellschaft Wien* 49 (1956): 357–364; Rohrmoser, M., University Library, Vienna, personal communication to the author, June 2001.

Holden, Edith Blackwell
26 September 1871–16 March 1920
naturalist, artist

Education: at home; Birmingham School of Art; studied art at Craigmill, Scotland, 1891–1892.
Employment: freelance artist.
Married: Ernest Smith, a sculptor, in 1911.

Edith Holden's illustrations became internationally famous after the publication of *The Country Diary of an Edwardian Lady* in 1977.

Holden was born in Moseley, near Birmingham; the family moved several times thereafter. She was the fourth child in the family and was given the second name "Blackwell" after Elizabeth Blackwell, the famous doctor, who was a cousin of the Holdens. Her father was manager of a varnish manufacturing company; her mother, a governess, taught the children at home when they were young. At the age of thirteen Holden started attending the Birmingham School of Art three mornings a week. In 1890 Holden had one of her pictures exhibited at the Royal Birmingham Society of Artists' autumn exhibition.

Having decided to specialize in animal painting, Holden went to study with Joseph Denovan Adam at Craigmill near Stirling in 1891. Adam had a farm with a variety of animals for his students to paint, and there was plenty of wildlife nearby. Holden thoroughly enjoyed her year there.

Holden returned to the Birmingham School of Art and continued to concentrate on animal studies. In 1906 she taught art part time at a private school in Solihull, Warwickshire near Birmingham. Her naturalist's diary for 1906 that was reproduced and published as *The Country Diary of an Edwardian Lady*.

In 1907 Holden's illustrations were used on a calendar for *Animals' Friend* magazine, published by the National Council for Animal Welfare. She also created illustrations for postcards and books produced by the

Royal Society for the Prevention of Cruelty to Animals (RSPCA). She illustrated several books, including *Daily Bread* (1910) by Margaret Gatty and *Woodland Whisperings* (1911) by Margaret Rankin.

After their marriage, Holden and her husband moved to Chelsea, where Holden continued to do book illustrations. In 1917 her painting *Young Bears Playing* was exhibited at the Royal Academy (under her married name of Mrs. E. Smith). She drowned in the River Thames at Kew while attempting to gather buds from chestnut trees.

Although Holden did gain some recognition for her work during her lifetime, only since the publication of *The Country Diary of an Edwardian Lady* has she become well known. By 2000 the book had sold over 6 million copies around the world and had been used as the basis for a range of merchandise, other books, including Holden's notebook from 1905, published as *The Nature Notes of an Edwardian Lady* (1989), and a television series.

Bibliography: Hall, S., "Flowering Passions of a Lady Revealed: Victorian Record of Love and Loss Typed To Be a Bestseller," *Guardian* (16 August 1999): 18; Taylor, I., *The Edwardian Lady—The Story of Edith Holden.* London/Exeter: Michael Joseph/Webb & Bower, 1980.

Holford, Ingrid née Bianchi
10 January 1920–
meteorologist, writer, teacher

Education: Cheltenham Ladies' College; University College, London, B.S. in economics, 1941.

Employment: Central Statistical Office, London; Women's Auxiliary Air Force, officer/weather forecaster, Royal Air Force Training Command, 1942–1946; Outdoor Publicity, London, 1946–1948; freelance journalist, writer, broadcaster, weather forecaster, and teacher from 1948; standby forecaster, Southern Television, 1978–1981.

Married: Garth Holford, in 1948.

Ingrid Holford, an experienced meteorologist, uses her expertise in writing articles and books for the general public.

After Holford graduated from University College, London, in 1941 with a first-class degree, her first post was as a statistician. She found this relatively unchallenging, so she answered an advertisement for graduates in science to train as weather forecasters with the Women's Auxiliary Air Force (WAAF) on a direct entry commission. She had three months' theory training at the Air Ministry in Kingsway, followed by two six-week periods training at different airfields. After that her commission was confirmed as a forecaster for the Royal Air Force, though she was still under the orders of the civilian Meteorological Office, as were all her fellow forecasters. Holford did forecasting and briefed and lectured air crews as needed. During the war, weather details were secret for fourteen days after they were made, and there were few observations arriving from either the Continent or the Atlantic.

After being demobilized, Holford worked for Outdoor Publicity, the outdoor advertising department of the London Press Exchange. She married Garth Holford, a yachtsman, in 1948. While their children were young, she began writing articles about the weather for a wide range of publications. She knew it was important for people, especially those pursuing outdoor sports, to appreciate the perils of the weather. Books followed articles. She pub-

Ingrid Holford (Courtesy of Ingrid Holford)

lished *Interpreting the Weather* (1973), *The Yachtsman's Weather Guide* (1979), and *The Air Pilot's Weather Guide* (1988), concise accounts clearly illustrated. Her *British Weather Disasters* (1976) is a lively, well-researched, illustrated account of both nationwide and local freak weather conditions. *The Guinness Book of Weather Facts and Feats* (1977) is a compendium of facts for laypeople on the history of meteorology, meteorological equipment, weather types, and notable climatological records.

Holford gave talks on BBC Radio and was a standby forecaster for three years for Southern Television. When she and her husband moved to the New Forest in Hampshire in 1978, she began giving lectures and seminars to yachting instructors in the area, and wrote a booklet, *Looking at Weather*, to accompany them, publishing it herself in 1985.

She was a fellow of the Royal Meteorological Society for nearly fifty years, and for three of those a member of its council.

Bibliography: Holford, I., "Golden Jubilee of the Met Queens." *Weather* 46, 1 (1991): 30–31; Holford, I., personal communications to the author, December 1999–March 2000; Walker, M., education officer, the Royal Meteorological Society, personal communication to the author, December 1999.

Holst, Clara
4 June 1868–15 November 1935
linguist

Education: high school, Oslo, until 1889; University of Oslo, from 1889; University of Cambridge, 1892–1893; Sorbonne, 1893–1894; University of Oslo, Cand. Mag., 1895, 1896; University of Leipzig, 1897–1898; University of Copenhagen, 1898–1899; University of Oslo, 1899–1902; Ph.D., 1903; University of Berlin, 1902–1903.

Employment: research in Magdeburg and Westphalia, 1903; lecturer, University of Oslo, spring terms, 1904 and 1906; teacher, Åag og Foss Skole, Oslo, autumn 1904; Wellesley College, Massachusetts, 1906–1907; University of Kansas, 1907–1908.

Clara Holst was the first Norwegian woman to graduate in philology (1895, 1896) and the first to defend a doctoral dissertation (1903).

Holst was born in Oslo, the seventh child out of nine, seven of whom survived. Her father was a physician; her mother came from Mecklenburg, Germany. Holst's grandfather Fredrik Holst was a professor of medicine who in 1817 was the first candidate in modern Norway to defend his doctoral dissertation. Clara Holst was the only girl in the family to go to university.

Holst graduated from high school with the highest possible honors. She went to Oslo University, then the only Norwegian university, which had admitted women since 1882. Her tutor was Professor Johan Storm, a well-known linguist. Holst went to Cambridge University for two terms in 1892 and moved on to the Sorbonne. While there she joined the International Phonetic Association.

When she came back to Oslo in 1894, Holst took examinations in English, French, Norwegian, and German and obtained her master's degree. To collect material for her doctorate she studied first at Leipzig and then Berlin. In Leipzig she was not allowed to take part in discussions, and in Berlin she was not even allowed to go to lectures and seminars; she could only read in the departmental library, in spite of requests from her research supervisor in Norway. She moved to the University of Copenhagen and studied Old Danish. Here she was an active member of various discussion groups.

From autumn 1899 Holst worked on her dissertation in Oslo before she traveled to Berlin. For the first time, she received financial help so that she could research the modern Low German dialects of northern Germany. This she did in 1903. Holst defended her thesis on 10 December 1903 and graduated two days later. Her dissertation, on Middle Low German loanwords in Danish in the fourteenth and fifteenth centuries, helped to increase what was known about Middle Low German.

Holst wanted to work at the University of Oslo, but no one was willing to offer her a post. Instead, she taught briefly at a high school in Oslo before leaving for the United

States, where she taught for a year at Wellesley College (at the time a women's college), followed by a year at Kansas University. It seems she had heavy teaching loads and taught a variety of courses. She published her last research paper in 1907. In 1908, at the age of forty, she returned to Norway and disappeared completely from academic life, though at the time she was probably the most up-to-date linguistic scholar in the country. One of the lecture halls on the new university campus in Kristiansand is named after her.

Bibliography: Aschehoug og Gyldendal's Stora Norske Leksikon, vol. 7, Oslo: Kunnskapsforleget, 1998; Jahr, E. H., Agder University College, Kristiansand, personal communication to the author, September 1999 and August 2001; Jahr, E. H. "Clara Holst (1868–1935): Norwegian Historical Linguist and Woman Pioneer," *Bulletin Henry Sweet Society* 32 (1999): 5–12.

Huggins, Lady Margaret Lindsay née Murray
1848–24 March 1915
astrophysicist

Education: at home and at school in Brighton.

Married: Sir William Huggins on 8 September 1875.

Lady Margaret Huggins was a pioneer in astrophysics. She worked with her husband at their own observatory in their home at Tulse Hill in London.

Huggins was brought up in Monkstown, Dublin, where her father was a solicitor. Her grandfather first interested her in astronomy. She had her own telescope and did experiments in physics and chemistry, learned basic photography, made observations of sunspots, and drew constellations. With a spectroscope she had made herself, she was able to observe the main Fraunhofer lines in the solar spectrum.

In 1873 Huggins read an article about astronomical spectroscopy written by the president of the British Association for the Advancement of Science that mentioned the work of William Huggins. The Royal Society was so impressed with his observations that it agreed to lend him two telescopes for his observatory at Tulse Hill in London. He traveled to Dublin to look at the telescopes before they were sent to him from the Dublin firm of Thomas and Howard Grubb. The latter, knowing of Margaret's interest in astronomy, introduced her to William Huggins; they were married in 1875, when William was fifty-one and Margaret twenty-seven.

Margaret Huggins assisted her husband in his work at Tulse Hill with almost complete dedication for over thirty years. The couple pioneered the use of the dry gelatin photographic plate for astronomy. Their first joint published paper, in 1889, was on the photographic spectra observed from Uranus and Saturn. They also investigated the spectra of nebulae and Wolf-Rayet stars and coauthored the *Atlas of Representative Stellar Spectra* (1899); Margaret Huggins prepared the photographic enlargements for the book.

Later they switched to laboratory spectroscopy, looking at the spectra of calcium and magnesium and investigating ways to examine radiation spectroscopically. Margaret Huggins edited *The Scientific Papers of William Huggins* (1909). He was awarded a knighthood in 1897 and the Order of Merit (OM) in 1902; she was made an honorary member of the Royal Astronomical Society in 1903 and was a founding member of the British Astronomical Association.

Her husband died of heart failure during an operation on 12 May 1910. Thereafter Margaret moved to a flat in Chelsea, where she continued to sort out the Tulse Hill papers and material to use for a biography of her husband. She was awarded a government pension of £100 a year in 1910 in honor of her service to science, in collaboration with her husband. She gave many of her scientific and artistic treasures to Wellesley Women's College in Massachusetts, as she had met Sarah Whiting, who was director of the observatory there from 1900 to 1916.

Bibliography: Bruck, M. T., "An Astronomical Love Affair," in *Stars, Shells, and Bluebells*, Dublin: Women in Technology and Science, 1997; Creese, M. R. S., *Ladies in the Laboratory? American and British Women in*

Science, 1800–1900: A Survey of Their Contributions to Research, Lanham, Maryland: Scarecrow Press, 1998; Crone, J. S., *A Concise Dictionary of Irish Biography*, Dublin: Talbot, 1928; Glass, I. S., *Victorian Telescope Makers: The Lives and Letters of Thomas and Howard Grubb*, Bristol: Institute of Physics Publishing, 1997; McKenna-Lawlor, S., *Whatever Shines Should Be Observed: Quicquid Nited Notandum*, Blackrock, Dublin: Samton, 1998.

Humphrey, Edith Ellen
September 1875–1977?
chemist

Education: North London Collegiate School; Bedford College, London, 1893–1897; University of Zurich, 1897–1901, Ph.D.
Employment: chemical laboratory assistant, Zurich University; chief chemist, Arthur Sanderson and Sons, London (wallpaper manufacturers).

Edith Humphrey carried out important work on crystals as part of her doctorate and later worked as assistant to professor Alfred Werner.

After graduating with honors in physical chemistry from Bedford College, London, Humphrey went to the University of Zurich to work toward her doctorate. Her supervisor was Alfred Werner, and her research was on cobalt salt crystals. Werner had been investigating the way in which two crystals with the same chemical makeup could polarize light in opposite directions. It appears that the crystals Humphrey prepared could have substantiated Werner's theory that the molecular arrangements in the crystals were mirror images of each other. But her crystals were simply stored away until they were rediscovered in the 1980s, after her death. In 1911 the theory was found to be valid when an American student prepared a set of crystals for Werner. In 1913 Werner was awarded the Nobel Prize for this work.

Humphrey obtained a double distinction for her doctorate, returned to England and set up a research laboratory for Arthur

Sanderson and Sons, where she was their chief chemist.

In 1975, when she was 100 years old, she considered herself to be the world's oldest living scientist. She died at the age of 102.

Bibliography: Bentley, L., *Educating Women: A Pictoral History of Bedford College*, Ham, Surrey: Alma Press, 1991; Bernal, I., "Edith Humphrey," *Chemical Intelligencer* (5 January 1999): 28–31; Dyer, L., archives assistant, Royal Holloway and Bedford College, University of London, personal communication to the author, January 2000; "Engines of Our Ingenuity, No. 1181: Edith Humphrey," Available at http://www.uh.edu/engines/epi1181.htm.

Humphries, Carmel Frances
3 June 1909–7 March 1986
freshwater biologist

Education: Ursuline Convent, Waterford; Loreto College, St. Stephen's Green, Dublin; University College, Dublin, 1929–1933; B.S., 1932; M.S. and higher diploma in education, 1933; Ph.D., 1938; D.Sc., 1952; research, Freshwater Biological Association laboratory, Windermere, 1934–1936, and at the Hydrobiologische Anstalt, Plön/Holstein, 1936–1938.
Employment: University College, Galway: assistantship in zoology, 1938–1939; senior demonstrator, 1939–1941; Queen's University, Belfast, 1941–1942; University College, Dublin: assistant lecturer, 1942–1947; lecturer, 1947–1957; lecturer, 1948–1956; professor, 1956–1979.

Carmel Humphries did important research on chironomids, nonbiting midges.

Humphries studied botany and zoology as an undergraduate. In 1933 she was awarded her M.S., the higher diploma in education, and a National University of Ireland Traveling Studentship in Zoology that enabled her to do research at the laboratories of the Freshwater Biological Association on Windermere, published in the *Journal of Animal Ecology*, vol. 5 (1936): 29–52. She then studied at Plön, Germany, where Professor

August Thienemann was her supervisor. Both her Ph.D. and D.Sc. degrees were awarded on the basis of her published work.

Humphries was involved in designing and selecting the equipment for the marine field station for University College, Dublin (with funding from the National University of Ireland Crawford-Hayes bequest). In 1948 the field station at Dun Laoghaire closed and was moved to Coliemore Harbour, Dalkey. Humphries started research on the Irish chironomidae and set up a Limnology Unit within the Department of Zoology.

She was elected a member of the Royal Irish Academy of Science in 1950 and of the Royal Dublin Society. She was the Irish representative for the International Limnological Association.

Bibliography: Librarian, University College, Dublin, "Report of the President, University College, Dublin," presented at the Governing Body meeting on 18 December 1979; Librarian, University College, Dublin, "Report of the President, University College, Dublin," presented at the Governing Body meeting on 16 December 1986; *Who's Who in the Republic of Ireland,* London: Geoffrey Chapman, 1973.

Hutchison, Isobel Wylie
30 May 1899–20 February 1982
botanist

Education: Rothesay House School, Edinburgh; Studley Horticultural College for Women.

Isobel Hutchison traveled alone in Greenland, Alaska, and the Aleutian Islands collecting plants.

Hutchison's first expedition was in 1927, to collect plants on the east coast of Greenland and in south Greenland for five months. Before she left Greenland, she climbed Kilertinguit (6,250 ft.) with two guides. On the summit she left a Union Jack in a bottle in memory of Edward Whymper, who had climbed the mountain in 1873.

From September 1928 to the following September, she lived in an Inuit village on her own. She traveled around Alaska on a coastal steamer in 1934; the journey back to Canada was a 120-mile cross-country trek using a dog sledge. She published an account of this trip in *North to the Rime-Ringed Sun* (1934). In 1936 she collected plants from the Aleutian Islands. The plants she collected are at the British Museum (Natural History) and at Kew.

Hutchison was honorary editor of the *Scottish Geographical Magazine* for many years. A fellow of the Royal Scottish Geographical Society, she served as the society's vice-president and was awarded its Mungo Park medal. She received an honorary doctorate from St. Andrews University for her contributions to horticulture. She wrote several books, including *Stepping Stones from Alaska to Asia* (1937; reprinted in 1943 as *The Aleutian Islands*). She also published articles in a number of journals, including the *National Geographic,* and four volumes of poetry. The Isobel Wylie Hutchison collection is held in the archives of the Royal Scottish Geographical Society in Glasgow.

Bibliography: Desmond, R., *Dictionary of British and Irish Botanists and Horticulturalists, Including Plant Collectors and Botanical Artists,* London: Taylor and Francis, 1977; Goring, R., ed., *Chambers Scottish Biographical Dictionary,* Edinburgh: Chambers, 1992; Hoyle, G., *Flowers in the Snow: The Life of Isobel Wylie Hutchison, 1889–1982,* Lincoln: University of Nebraska Press; Hutchison, I. W., "Greenland's Flowery Valleys," *Journal of the Royal Horticultural Society* 57 (1932): 21–31; "Miss Isobel W. Hutchison," *Scottish Geographical Magazine* 99 (1983): 54; Munro, D. M., director, Royal Scottish Geographical Society, Glasgow; personal communication to the author, January 2000; *Who Was Who, 1981,* London: Adam and Charles Black, 1981.

I

Inglis, Elsie Maud
16 August 1864–26 November 1917
doctor

Education: Edinburgh School for Girls (later Charlotte Square Institution); school in Paris, 1882–1883; Edinburgh School of Medicine for Women; Glasgow Royal Infirmary, 1891; Licentiate of the Royal College of Physicians and Surgeons (Edinburgh); LFPS, (Glasgow) 1892; MB, CM, (Edinburgh) 1899; midwifery, Rotunda Hospital, Dublin.

Employment: founder, Medical College for Women, Edinburgh, 1889; house surgeon/teacher, New Hospital for Women, London; surgeon, Edinburgh; private practice, 1895–1915; founder, nursing home, Edinburgh, 1902; founder, Scottish Women's Hospitals for Foreign Service, 1914.

Elsie Inglis established a medical school and later a nursing home for women and children in Edinburgh. During World War I she set up medical units to provide care and treatment on the front lines in Serbia and Russia.

Inglis was born at Naini Tal, India, a hill station in the Himalayas. Her father worked for the East India Company, and the family lived in India until he retired in 1878 then moved to Tasmania for two years before returning to Edinburgh. Inglis was a lively member of her school and was joint editor of the school magazine, *Edina.*

After her year in Paris, Inglis studied at the Edinburgh School of Medicine for women, founded and run by Sophia Jex-

Blake. Inglis established the Medical College for Women, Edinburgh, in 1889 with financial support from her father and some of his friends. In 1909 this merged with the Royal College of Physicians and Surgeons in Edinburgh. She also studied at Glasgow Royal Infirmary, and once she had qualified as a doctor, she was a teacher and house surgeon at Elizabeth Garrett Anderson's New Hospital for Women in London.

In 1902 she returned to Edinburgh and set up a seven-bed nursing home for women and children staffed by women. It was extended in 1904 to provide midwifery facilities and in 1910 merged with Sophia Jex-Blake's hospital in Bruntsfield.

Inglis worked in private practice with Dr. Jessie MacGregor. She recognized that poverty and bad housing were major causes of ill health, and she attempted to alleviate the situation of individual patients whenever she could by waiving her own fees. She always went away in September on holiday. The first two weeks she spent entirely alone. She used to book to a station, and then cycle round in the area till she found suitable lodgings that would provide her with a hot bath. The second fortnight she would ask friends to join her.

In 1906 Inglis founded the Scottish Federation of Women's Suffrage Societies and acted as the organization's honorary secretary until 1914. At the start of World War I, she and her colleagues in the federation decided to set up a women's medical unit and, despite opposition from the War Office, sent this unit to France. By the end of the war, the new organization, the Scottish Women's Hospitals for Foreign Service, had raised

£200,000 for hospitals in Serbia. By 1915 they had established a 200-bed auxiliary hospital at Royaumont Abbey. In April of the same year Inglis went to Serbia with a women's medical unit. She, her staff, and their patients were captured by advancing Austrian forces and held at the Czar Lazar Hospital, where the doctors and nurses continued their care of the wounded.

On their release, Inglis returned to Britain, though she was not in the best of health. In 1916 she took a women's medical unit to Russia, a mission financed by the London Committee of the Scottish Women's Hospitals. The work was physically demanding and included transporting the wounded and burying the dead. Inglis's health suffered, though she refused to return to Britain until the fighting had eased in the area. In October 1917 her unit set sail for Newcastle upon Tyne. She was very ill when she arrived, and Dr. Ethel Williams attended her twice, but she died on 26 November, the day after the ship had arrived in Britain. Her contribution to the war effort was recognized in the full military honors she was given at her funeral. Crowds lined the streets outside St. Giles Cathedral and Handel's "Hallelujah" chorus was sung as her cortege left the cathedral. She was buried in Edinburgh's Dean Cemetery.

Inglis was awarded Serbia's highest honor, the Order of the White Eagle; the citation stated that "Scotland made her a doctor but Serbia made her a Saint." Secretary of State for Foreign Affairs Arthur Balfour described her "enthusiasm, strength of purpose and kindliness," saying she had "earned an everlasting place of honour" in the history of World War I. Dr. Mary Scharlieb unveiled a memorial to Inglis in St. Giles Cathedral in 1922. In 1925 the Elsie Inglis Maternity Hospital was opened in Edinburgh (it closed in 1988).

Bibliography: Balfour, Frances, *Dr. Elsie Inglis,* London: Hodder and Stoughton, 1918; *Dictionary of National Biography, 1912–1921,* Oxford: Oxford University Press, 1927; "Elsie Inglis." *Sunday Herald,* 19 December 1999.

Irvine, Jean Kennedy
c. 1877–3 March 1962
pharmacist

Education: pharmaceutical apprenticeship, Hawick, Scotland (qualified, 1900).

Employment: pharmacist, Glasgow Hospital, 1900–1904; assistant pharmacist, then chief pharmacist, Glasgow Apothecaries Company; pharmacist with John McMillan, Glasgow; helped to manage husband's two pharmacies, Glasgow, 1904–1914; retail pharmacist, 1914–1916; superintendent, South-Eastern Pricing Bureau, 1916–1946.

Married: Peter Irvine, pharmacist.

Jean Irvine was the first woman to be president of the Royal Pharmaceutical Society, an office she held from 1947 to 1948.

Irvine was born in Hawick, Scotland, and undertook her pharmaceutical training there. She held a number of pharmacist posts in Glasgow before helping her husband to manage his two pharmacies. He joined the army during World War I, and Irvine moved to London to be nearer to him. In 1916 she became superintendent of the South-Eastern Pricing Bureau, the body responsible for overseeing prescription pricing in the region; she remained in charge for over thirty years. She was made a Member of the Order of the British Empire (MBE) in 1928 for her services to the Insurance Committee.

Irvine was the first woman president of the Insurance Officers' Association for England and Wales in 1932, and of the staff side of the Whitley Council for the National Health Insurance administrative, technical, and clerical services. She was a member of the Royal Pharmaceutical Society's council from 1937 to 1952.

Bibliography: "Jean Kennedy Irvine MBE," *Pharmaceutical Journal* (10 March 1962): 203–204; Jones, L., assistant archivist, Museum of the Royal Pharmaceutical Society, personal communication to the author, July 2001.

Isaacs, Susan Sutherland née Fairhurst
24 May 1885–12 October 1948
primary school teacher, child psychologist

Education: council school; Bolton Secondary School, from 1897; University of Manchester, nursery teaching course; B.A. in philosophy, 1912; D.Sc., 1931; University of Cambridge, 1912–1913; M.A., 1913.

Employment: teacher in private school, Bolton; lecturer in infant school teaching, Darlington Training College, 1913–1914; lecturer in logic, University of Manchester, 1914–1915; tutor for tutorial classes in psychology, University of London, 1916–1933; principal, Malting House School, Cambridge, 1924–1927; head of Child Development Unit, University of London, Institute of Education, 1933–1943.

Married: W. B. Brierley, plant pathologist, in 1914 (marriage dissolved); Nathan Isaacs, psychologist, in 1922.

Susan Isaacs was a leading child psychologist. She believed strongly in observing children at work and play and in accurately recording their activities and conversations.

Isaacs was born at Bromley Cross, near Bolton, Lancashire, the seventh surviving child in the family. Her father was a journalist and editor of the *Bolton Journal and Guardian*. Her mother died when Isaacs was quite young, and her father later married the nurse who had looked after her mother.

Isaacs left school at fourteen and was apprenticed to a photographer; she spent a year in Morocco as a governess. After teaching in a private school, she realized she wanted to learn more herself and won a grant to take a two-year course at Manchester University for nongraduates to qualify as nursery school teachers. She did well but decided to study further. With the help of her brother, she learned the Greek and German necessary at that time for entrance to a university course. She was admitted to the University of Manchester and graduated with a first-class degree in philosophy. Using her father's legacy to repay her teacher training grant so that she was not committed to teaching, she studied for a year at the psychological laboratory at the University of Cambridge and wrote up her research for a master's.

Isaacs lectured in infant school education at Darlington and after marrying moved to Manchester and lectured in logic at the university then went on to tutor small groups in psychology at the University of London. Her second marriage, in 1922 to Nathan Isaacs, a psychologist ten years her junior, was successful, and he helped her to formulate her ideas.

In 1924 she became principal of Malting House School in Cambridge. The school started with ten boys from two to four years old; they came from professional families and were of above-average intelligence. Isaacs described the setup of the school in *Intellectual Growth in Young Children* (1930), which she dedicated "to my child companions." The children had a stimulating environment and were encouraged to ask questions. Isaacs, her colleagues, and the children's parents recorded in as much detail as they could how the children responded to each other, their teachers, and the learning materials. By the time Isaacs left Malting House, there were twenty children, aged two to eight, some of whom were boarders, and there were more staff. She wrote numerous articles about Malting House. Her *Social Development in Young Children: A Study of Beginnings* (1933), "dedicated to Joan Riviere who has taught me to understand my own childhood," also used information gathered there.

Under the pseudonym "Ursula Wise," Isaacs answered letters from parents for *Nursery World* from 1929 to 1936. Among her books are *Introduction to Psychology* (1921) and *The Nursery Years* (1929).

Her philosophy concerning the education of nursery school and infant children (five to seven years old) had a great influence on the way education for this age group developed, particularly when she was head of the Child Development Unit at the University of London's Institute of Education. While there she was allowed only a part-time post and was paid £300 a year, with £100 for secretarial help; she was not even given a telephone in her office. She had several other commitments, including as psychologist to the London Clinic of Psychoanalysis, assistant editor of the *British Journal of Psychology* (1921–1948), chair of the Education Section of the British Psychological Society (1923–1939), and member of the training committee of the Institute of Psychoanalysis (1945–1946).

At the start of World War II, she and many other psychologists moved to Cambridge, and in September 1939 more than 30,000 children were evacuated there. By January 1940 over 85 percent of the mothers with young children and 43 percent of the older children were back in London. Isaacs thought it was important to look at why the evacuation had not succeeded, so with the cooperation of Sibyl Brown and Robert Thonless, she edited *The Cambridge Evacuation Survey: A Wartime Study in Social Welfare and Education* (1941).

She was made a Commander of the Order of the British Empire (CBE) in 1948 and died of cancer later the same year. A complex in Bolton is named the Susan Isaacs Nursery School in her memory.

Bibliography: Aldrich, R., and P. Gordon, *Directory of British Educationalists,* London: Woburn Press, 1989; Gardner, D. E. M., *Susan Isaacs,* London: Methuen Educational, 1969; Smith, Lydia A. H., *To Understand and Help: The Life and Work of Susan Isaacs (1885–1948),* Cranbury, NJ: Associated Universities Press, 1985; *Who Was Who, 1941–1950,* London: Adam and Charles Black, 1952.

J

Jahoda, Marie
26 January 1907–28 April 2001
social psychologist

Education: University of Vienna, D. Phil.

Employment: professor of social psychology, New York University, 1949–1958; research fellow and professor of psychology, Brunel University, 1958–1965; professor of social psychology, University of Sussex, 1965–1973; senior research consultant, Science Policy Research Unit, University of Sussex, 1971–1983; professor emeritus, University of Sussex, 1983–2001.

Married: Paul F. Lazarsfeld, 1927; Austen Albu, 1958 (he died in 1994).

Marie Jahoda taught and carried out research on a wide range of themes within the area of social psychology. She was founding professor of the Social Psychology Department of the University of Sussex.

Jahoda was born in Vienna and went to the University of Vienna. She wrote her first paper in 1932 in Vienna and published *Die Arbeitslosen von Marienthal* (The Unemployed of Marienthal; a joint study with Paul Lazarsfeld and Hans Zeisel) in 1933. As an antifascist, she was imprisoned by the Austrian government from 1936 to 1937. French President Leon Blum intervened on her behalf, but she had to leave Austria, and went to England. There, she did research on unemployment and ran the secret radio station Radio Rotes Wien at the Ministry of Information. After the war ended, she became a researcher with the American Jewish Committee at Columbia University, and founded and directed the Research Center on Human Relations in New York. In 1949 she was appointed professor of social psychology at New York University. During her time there, she published *Research Methods in Human Relations* (1953) and *Current Concepts of Modern Mental Health* (1958). In 1958 she moved back to England when she was appointed as professor of psychology at Brunel University in Uxbridge, Middlesex.

When social psychology was introduced into the curriculum of the University of Sussex in 1965, Jahoda was appointed as professor. The university awarded her an honorary doctoral degree upon her retirement in 1973. She was also senior research consultant to the Science Policy Research Unit at Sussex from 1971 to 1983 and published *Freud and the Dilemmas of Psychology* (1977) and *Employment and Unemployment* (1982).

Her career was characterized by a wide range of research interests, including race relations, subsistence farming, and nursing as a profession. She was a recognized expert in several fields and was consulted by various bodies, including the government Home Office, which deals with crime and punishment, and the Social Science Research Council. She was awarded honorary doctorates from the Universities of Leicester (1973), Stirling (1988), Bremen (1984), Vienna (1998), and Linz (1998). She was made a Commander of the Order of the British Empire (CBE) in 1974.

Bibliography: Briggs, Asa, address given during presentation of Marie Jahoda's honorary D. Litt, *University of Sussex Fourteenth*

Annual Report, 1972–1973, Brighton: University of Sussex, 1973; Freeman, C., and H. Rush, "Marie Jahoda, Social Psychologist," *The Guardian* (2 May 2001): 18; Jahoda, Marie, address given upon receipt honorary D. Litt., *University of Sussex Fourteenth Annual Report, 1972–1973,* Brighton: University of Sussex, 1973; *Who's Who, 2000,* London: Adam and Charles Black, 2000.

Janovskaja, Sof'ja Aleksandrovna née Neimark
31 January 1896–24 October 1966
mathematician

Education: Higher School for Women, Odessa, from 1915; Moscow State University, from 1923; Ph.D., 1935.
Employment: Red Army; editor of *Kommunist* newspaper during Russian Revolution (1917); Moscow State University: professor from 1931, head of Department of Mathematical Logic from 1959.
Married: Mr. Janovskaja.

In 1959 *Sof'ja Janovskaja* became the first head of the Moscow State University's Department of Mathematical Logic. She made an important contribution to mathematical logic in the USSR.

Janovskaja was born in Pruzhany, Poland (now Kobrin, Belarus), though she moved to Odessa with her family at an early age and was educated there. During the Russian Revolution she joined the Red Army and worked as editor of the *Kommunist* newspaper. In 1923 she began taking courses at Moscow State University, eventually gaining her doctorate in 1935 even though she had already been appointed professor at the university in 1931.

Janovskaja specialized in mathematics and logic and the history of mathematics. Among her published material were works on Zeno's paradoxes, Egyptian mathematics, Descartes's geometry, and Rolle's views on calculus. Her contribution to mathematical logic was recognized in 1959 when she became head of the department. She was awarded the Order of Lenin in 1951.

Bibliography: Website: http://www-groups.dcs.st-and.ac.uk/~history/Mathematicians/Bari.html.

Jefferys, Margot née Davies
1 November 1916–3 March 1999
medical sociologist

Education: Berkhamsted School for Girls; London School of Economics, 1935–1938; B.A. with honors, 1938.
Employment: manager, Communist Party bookshop, Coventry, 1940–1944; part-time teacher, Workers' Educational Association, London; research assistant, Bedford College, London, 1949–1953; postgraduate lecturer, London School of Hygiene and Tropical Medicine, 1953–1965; director, Social Research Unit, Bedford College, London, from 1965; visiting professor, Centre for Medical Law and Ethics, King's College, London, from 1992.
Married: James Jefferys, in 1941.

Margot Jefferys was a pioneer in medical sociology.

Jefferys was born in Madras, India, the daughter of the principal of the law college there. When she was seven years old, she and her family returned to Britain. She originally planned to train as a physical education teacher but decided to study history at the London School of Economics. There she met her future husband, James Jefferys, who was a research student. After she had graduated with first-class honors James Jefferys was offered a scholarship at Harvard, and she accompanied him to the United States. The couple returned to Britain at the start of World War II. James Jefferys went to work as a laborer in a factory in Coventry; Margot ran the Communist Party bookshop in Coventry until 1944, when they decided to go back to London.

Jefferys taught part time for the Workers' Educational Association and from 1949 was a research assistant at Bedford College, London. Her move into the new field of medical sociology came in 1953, when she became a postgraduate lecturer at the London School of Hygiene and Tropical Medicine. Through her teaching and research work, she was a key figure in the development of the field during the following decades. She was director of the Social Research Unit at Bedford College from 1965, and London University awarded her a personal chair three years later. A new master's degree in "sociology with special reference to the sociology of medicine" was set up at Bedford College in 1969.

Jefferys was consultant to the Economic and Social Research Council on its Ageing Initiative from 1982 to 1987; in this role she was the editor of a collection of essays on ageing written by various experts, *Growing Old in the Twentieth Century* (1989).

She was honored by the Royal College of Physicians in 1984 when she was made a fellow of the faculty of public health medicine and by the Royal College of General Practitioners in 1988 when she became an honorary fellow. She was visiting professor at the Centre for Medical Law and Ethics at King's College, London, from 1992 to 1997.

Bibliography: Saville, John, "Professor Margot Jefferys: Diagnosing Society," *Guardian* (17 March 1999).

Jeffrey, Carol
31 October 1898–6 November 1998
psychotherapist, psychoanalyst

Education: at home, taught by her mother; school, 1913–1916; University of London; B.A., 1919; postgraduate teaching diploma, 1920; postgraduate diploma in individual psychology, 1945.

Employment: teacher of music and English, 1920–1925; private tutor, 1925–1944; Child Guidance Service, Kent, 1945–1952; staff member, Open Way Association, Psychotherapy Clinic, from 1952.

Married: Tom Jeffrey, in 1925. He died in 1985.

Carol Jeffrey, a founding member of the Open Way Association, an alternative psychotherapy group, had a gift for discovering the reasons for the suffering of the children and adults she treated.

Jeffrey was born and brought up in rural Worcestershire. She went to school when she was fifteen and managed to pass her school examinations. She then studied at the University of London. She would have liked to have been a doctor but her family could not afford to support her while she trained.

Jeffrey taught music and English until she married in 1925; at that time women teachers had to leave their jobs when they married. She decided to teach her own three children at home for the first part of their education and took on several private pupils with special needs, either physical or emotional. She was on an adult education panel of lecturers in child development and from 1944 to 1945 studied for a postgraduate diploma in individual psychology. This qualified her for child guidance work, which was just being established in Britain.

In 1945 Jeffrey joined the Child Guidance Service team in Kent. There were three clinics and only two staff, and she found that there were too many regulations that adversely affected the way she worked. Dr. Graham Howe was also becoming disillusioned with the way the Child Guidance Service was developing. In 1952 he collected together several people who were working in this field and looking for a different way to help their patients; Jeffrey was among them. Howe founded the Open Way Charitable Trust. Jeffrey became a member of the staff of the Open Way Psychotherapy Clinic and worked there full time until she was of retirement age. She also built up a large private practice and continued with this until she was well into her nineties. She did psychological research with the Open Way Association and was its secretary for many years and copresident with Dr. Tom Farewell.

From 1947 Jeffrey began being analyzed by Dr. Michael Fordham, a close colleague of C. G. Jung and translator of Jung's books. Her analysis continued at intervals for twenty years, and she felt it was immensely helpful and was aware of the influence Jung had on her development as a therapist. She had corresponded with him, and he had interpreted some of her peacock drawings, as illustrated in *That Why Child.*

Jeffrey believed that child rescue is the basic principle of all therapy. In her semiautobiographical book *That Why Child* (1996), she demonstrated how many children have suffered needlessly through lack of imaginative understanding by the adults responsible for them.

Bibliography: Barlas, C., "Carol Jeffrey: Radical Therapy," *Guardian* (25 November 1998).

Jekyll, Gertrude
29 November 1843–8 December 1932
horticulturalist, writer

Education: at home; Kensington School of Art, 1861–1863.
Employment: self-employed designer and writer.

Gertrude Jekyll was an eminent garden designer.

Jekyll was born in London, the fifth of seven children, and was taught at home by her parents. Her mother had been a pupil of Felix Mendelssohn, and her father was an expert on classical Greek art. Jekyll was given C. A. Johns's *Flowers of the Field* (1853) and became interested in wildflowers. When she was a student at the Kensington School of Art, she learned "color beauty" from the artist Hercules Brabazon and was influenced by the writings of John Ruskin and William Morris.

After leaving Kensington she traveled in Greece, Italy, and Algeria with her friend Mary Newton and made numerous drawings of plants. Newton died in 1866, and during that year Jekyll spent a considerable time studying paintings in the Louvre in Paris. In early 1868 she traveled in Italy and was particularly interested in the carving and gilding she saw there.

In April 1868 her family moved to Wargrave Hill, Berkshire, and Jekyll was in charge of the renovations to the house. In 1870 she designed some silk embroidered panels for the duke of Westminster. She also gave advice on the interior decoration at Girton College, Cambridge. When her fa-

ther died in 1876, the family moved back to West Surrey.

In 1891 she visited an eye specialist and was told she had progressive myopia and would have to give up close work; from then on she concentrated on garden design. She met Edwin Lutyens, a young and enthusiastic architect who lived nearby, and together they drove around the country lanes in a dogcart, stopping at intervals to sketch and photograph plants and architectural features. In 1897 Lutyens designed Jekyll's home at Munstead Wood, near Godalming, Surrey, and she designed the gardens.

Jekyll planned over 300 gardens, some of them in Europe and America. A hundred of these gardens were to accompany buildings designed by Lutyens. The gardens she designed at Hestercombe in Somerset, Lindisfarne Castle in Northumberland, Upton Grey in Hampshire, and Folly Farm in Berkshire have been restored and as far as possible kept to the original design. Many of her drawings are in the Reef Point Gardens Collection at the University of California, Berkeley.

Jekyll was chief gardening adviser for *Country Life* and wrote for many gardening magazines. She also wrote books about gardening, such as *Wood and Garden* (1899), *Home and Garden* (1900) and *Colour in the Flower Garden* (1908). Her writing had a considerable influence on gardeners throughout the world, and her example inspired the establishment of horticultural training schools for women in the 1920s and 1930s.

In 1916 Jekyll was invited to be vice-president of the Women's Farm and Garden Union, which later became the Women's Farm and Garden Association (WFGA). Folly Farm, designed by Gertrude Jekyll, is one of the gardens where trainees who are members of the WFGA can garden for fifteen hours a week, under the Women Returners to Amenity Gardening Scheme (WRAGS) launched in 1992. Jekyll was awarded the Victoria Medal of Honour by the Royal Horticultural Society in 1897 and the Veitch Gold Medal in 1922.

Bibliography: Desmond, R., *Dictionary of British and Irish Botanists and Horticultural-*

ists, Including Plant Collectors and Botanical Artists, London: Taylor and Francis, 1977; King, P., *Women Rule the Plot,* London: Gerald Duckworth & Co., 1999; Massingham, B., *Gertrude Jekyll,* Aylesbury: Shire Publications, 1975; Nicholls, C. S., ed., *Dictionary of National Biography: Missing Persons,* Oxford: Oxford University Press, 1993; Penn, H., *An Englishwoman's Garden,* London: BBC Books, 1993.

Jenkin, Penelope M.
1902–1994
zoologist

Education: Newnham College, Cambridge, 1921–1925, 1927–1931; M.S., 1948; University of Glasgow, 1925–1927 (postgraduate); Freshwater Biological Association, Windermere, 1931–1932; Marine Biological Association laboratory, Plymouth, 1932–1933; D.Sc. (Bristol).

Employment: University of Birmingham, teaching scholarship, 1927–1929; University of Bristol, lecturer in zoology, 1934–1962.

Penelope Jenkin was the first person to carry out independent research at the laboratory of the Freshwater Biological Association.

After her undergraduate studies at Cambridge, Jenkin went to the University of Glasgow. During vacations she worked at the marine biological station at Millport. She used a diatom culture to measure photosynthesis rates in Loch Awe. She was the first person to measure daily photosynthetic rates using one species of algae. In 1929 she measured photosynthesis in Lakes Nakuru and Naivasha in Kenya as a member of the Percy Sladen expedition. Starting from the algal samples she collected, she did important work on the role of the lesser flamingo in the food web of Lake Nakuru.

In 1931 Jenkin arrived at the laboratory of the Freshwater Biological Association (FBA) in England's Lake District to conduct research toward a Ph.D. When she presented her thesis it was inadequate for the degree and she withdrew from the Register of Research Students in 1936. In 1948 she asked the Board of Research Studies to award her a master's degree on the basis of some of her published papers. The statute allowing women to obtain degrees from the University of Cambridge came into force in 1948. Jenkin was probably the first woman to be approved for a postgraduate degree by the Board of Research Studies.

After her time at the FBA, Jenkin worked at Plymouth researching oxygen production by a marine diatom, publishing her results in the *Journal of the Marine Biological Association* in 1937. From 1934 she was a lecturer in zoology at the University of Bristol. She changed her field of research and published *Animal Hormones: A Comparative Survey:* part 1, *Kinetic and Metabolic Hormones* (1962), and part 2, *Control of Growth and Metamorphosis* (1970). She did a considerable amount of research for both of these volumes, completing the second after she had retired from Bristol University.

On an interesting note, her father, B. M. Jenkins, was an engineer and he devised a corer and surface mud sampler. This equipment was used by Winifred Pennington when she was doing research at Ferry House, Windermere, the new FBA research laboratory. Upon Penelope Jenkins's death, she bequeathed £7,000 to the FBA.

Bibliography: Lund, J. W. G., and E. B. Monaghan, "Dr. P. M. Jenkin (1902–1994) and the Earliest Days of the FBA's Laboratory at Wray Castle," *Freshwater Forum* 13 (2000): 2–15.

Jérémine, Elisabeth
née Tschernaieff
28 October 1879—10 March 1964
geologist

Education: St. Petersburg (Women's University); University of Lausanne, Ph.D., 1911.

Employment: assistant in Petrography Department, St. Petersburg University; Geology Department, Sorbonne, Paris; Institute of Applied Geology, Nancy.

Married: Mr. Jérémine.

Elisabeth Jérémine was an outstanding geologist.

Jérémine was born in Russia. She graduated from the University of St. Petersburg and was then assistant to the professor of petrography, F. J. Loewinson-Lessing, who believed fervently in higher education for women. He ensured that Jérémine was able to travel abroad both for her research and to international congresses. At one of these conferences, she met Professor Maurice Lugeon, who invited her to study for her doctorate at the University of Lausanne. Her research was published in 1911. She returned to Russia and took part in a geological expedition to the Kola Peninsula.

After the October 1917 revolution, Jérémine fled from Russia, using a false name. She was able to gain employment at the Sorbonne in Paris. She kept her Russian nationality, unlike many of the other Russian emigrants, and was always pleased to welcome fellow Russians. She worked for over forty years on the rock collection at the Sorbonne Museum. Besides studying the geology of France, she studied the museum's collections from abroad. She was also an expert on meteorites. Between 1905 and 1964 she published over 200 papers. In 1959, the French Académie des Sciences awarded her the Jérôme Ponti Foundation Prize.

Bibliography: Orcel, Jean, "Elisabeth Jérémine (1879–1964)," *Bulletin de la Société géologique de France* 7 (1965): 608–618.

Jex-Blake, Sophia
21 January 1840–7 January 1912
doctor

Education: boarding school, Brighton; Queen's College, London, from 1858; medical studies in Boston and New York, 1866–1868; University of Edinburgh, 1869–1873.

Employment: mathematics tutor, Queen's College, London, 1859–1861; founder, London School of Medicine for Women, 1874; physician, Edinburgh, 1878–1899; founder, Dispensary for Women and Children, Edinburgh, 1878; founder, Cottage Hospital, Edinburgh, 1885; dean of the Edinburgh School of Medicine for Women, 1886–1899.

Sophia Jex-Blake was a prominent campaigner for the rights of women to qualify and practice as doctors in Britain. She challenged the views of the medical establishment and in the course of her career set up two medical schools for women, one in London and one in Edinburgh.

Jex-Blake was born in Hastings, Sussex, the daughter of Thomas Jex-Blake, proctor of Doctor's Commons. She went to Queen's College for Women, London, and also taught mathematics there. She traveled in Europe and America, and it was in the United States that she began her medical training, albeit informally, with Dr. Lucy Sewall in Boston. She studied on a more formal basis during 1868 with Dr. Elizabeth Blackwell in New York but returned to Britain the same year when her father died.

Jex-Blake found it impossible to continue her training at the University of London and applied to the University of Edinburgh, where she was accepted on her second application, together with several other women. Separate classes were arranged for their teaching, and they experienced an increasing level of hostility from some staff and students. One of the women students won the Hope Scholarship but was then denied the award; it was given to a male student instead. The Royal Infirmary then refused the women permission to pursue their training there. On one occasion a large group of male students and others formed a blockade at Surgeon's Hall so that the women could not enter, and the situation deteriorated into a riot.

Despite some public sympathy for the women's cause, the university court judged that circumstances made it impossible for the women to graduate, though they could be awarded "certificates of proficiency." Jex-Blake and her fellow women students took legal action against the university that was initially successful but was reversed on appeal in 1873.

Jex-Blake left Edinburgh and decided to

set up her own medical school in London: the London School of Medicine for Women opened in October 1874. Jex-Blake continued to lobby for the qualification of women as the issue was debated in Parliament, and she presented much material in support of the case, including a draft bill. At a personal level, her own attempts to qualify were thwarted once more when in 1876 all the examiners resigned from the College of Surgeons' license in midwifery examinations that she was due to take. In the same year, however, the Russell Gurney Enabling Act finally gave medical bodies the power to examine women. In 1877 Jex-Blake was the first woman to take advantage of the change in the law when she qualified as a practitioner through the Irish College of Physicians (Queen's University, Belfast), having already obtained her M.D. from Berne, Switzerland.

Jex-Blake returned to Edinburgh in 1878 and practiced medicine there until her retirement twenty-one years later. She continued to take a pioneering approach, opening a dispensary for women and children in 1885 and the Cottage Hospital. The following year she founded the Edinburgh School of Medicine for Women, which received sixteen applications for places during its first month. As a physician, she used her own home for treating women and children. She also continued to fight for the rights of women to qualify as doctors; the battle was eventually won in Scotland in 1889, when the Universities (Scotland) Act was passed. The University of Edinburgh finally allowed women to graduate in medicine in 1894.

Jex-Blake published a number of books, including *Medical Women* (1872) and *Care of Infants* (1884). On her retirement in 1899, she returned to live in Sussex, at Mark Cross, and was buried in the churchyard at Rotherfield.

Bibliography: *Dictionary of National Biography, 1912–1921*, Oxford: Oxford University Press, 1927; Ogilvie, M. B., *Women in Science: Antiquity through the Nineteenth Century*, New York: MIT Press, 1986; Roberts, S., *Sophia Jex-Blake: A Woman Pioneer in Nineteenth Century Medical Reform*, London: Routledge, 1993; Smith, C. J., *Historic South Edinburgh*, vol. 3, Edinburgh: John Donald Publishing, 1986; *Who Was Who, 1897–1915*, London: Adam and Charles Black, 1920.

Johnson, Amy
1 July 1903–5 January 1941
aviator

Education: University of Sheffield, 1922–1925; B.A., 1925; secretarial training at Kingston-upon-Hull.

Employment: secretarial work in London, 1927–1929; freelance aviator and writer; pilot, Solent Air Ferry, June 1939; Air Transport Auxiliary, 1939–1941.

Married: Jim A. Mollinson, on 29 July 1932 (divorced in 1938).

In 1930 *Amy Johnson* became the first woman to fly solo from London to Australia, a flight that took her seventeen days.

Johnson was brought up in Kingston-upon-Hull, where her father was a fish merchant. She started at the University of Sheffield as a B.A. honors student, but as she failed part of her first-year examination in French, she was demoted to a B.A. general degree and took her final examinations in French, Latin, and economics. Because she did not want to teach, she returned home and took a secretarial course, working locally until moving to London in 1927.

Johnson had her first flight in 1926 when a team of joyriders came to Hull. She began taking flying lessons at the London Aeroplane Club and made her first solo flight on 9 June 1929. She was awarded her pilot's A license that July. She trained as a ground engineer and in December 1929 was the first woman to be awarded a ground engineer's C license by the Air Ministry. As she was spending so much time learning about planes and flying, her work as a secretary suffered; her father then decided to give her an allowance so she no longer had to keep a paying job.

The next challenge Johnson set herself was a solo flight to Australia. Her initial efforts to achieve funding were unsuccessful, so she wrote letters to several businessmen to ask for donations; in the end Lord Wake-

Amy Johnson (Bettmann/Corbis)

lent Air Ferry. She joined the Air Transport Auxiliary (ATA) as a ferry pilot in 1939 and that same year published her autobiography, *Sky Roads of the World.* Her last flight was from Blackpool airport; she crashed in the Thames Estuary on Sunday 5 January 1941, some distance from her destination.

She was made a Commander of the Order of the British Empire (CBE) in 1930. She was an associate of the Royal Aeronautical Society and president of the Women's Engineering Society from 1935 to 1937. She was awarded the Egyptian Gold Medal for Valour in 1930 and the President's Gold Medal from the Society of Engineers in 1931.

Bibliography: Boase, W., *The Sky's the Limit: Women Pioneers in Aviation,* London: Osprey, 1979; Smith, C. B., *Amy Johnson,* London: Collins, 1967; Aspden, L., curator of the special collections and archives, University of Sheffield, MS 195, personal communication to the author, January 2000; *Who Was Who, 1941–1950,* London: Adam and Charles Black.

field paid all her expenses, apart from £500 from her family. She bought a secondhand Gypsy Moth, naming it *Jason.* She left Croydon Aerodrome on 5 May 1930 and after several accidents and mishaps arrived in Darwin, northern Australia, on 24 May, to tremendous publicity. The *Daily Mail* arranged a six-week tour in Australia for her. She came home by sea, flying from Port Said to London. The *Daily Mail* gave her £10,000 for the flight, which was supposed to fund a tour when she was back in Britain. Her health broke down after a week, but she was allowed to keep the money, which meant she could dedicate herself to flying.

Johnson flew to Japan and in 1931 broke the flight time record for a light plane. With her husband she tried to break the world long-distance record in June 1933. Their De Havilland Dragon, *Seafarer,* crashed in Connecticut on the way to New York.

She was divorced from her husband in 1938 and moved to the Cotswolds, concentrating on gliding. In June 1939 she was given paid employment as a pilot for the So-

Joliot-Curie, Irène née Curie
12 September 1897–17 March 1956
physicist

Education: taught at home—physics by her mother, Marie Curie; mathematics by Dr. Paul Langevin; and chemistry by Dr. J. P. Perrin; College of Sevigne, Paris; Sorbonne, Paris, 1914–1916, Ph.D., 1925.

Employment: instructor in radiology, 1916; assistant and researcher, Curie Institute, University of Paris 1918–1937; professor, Sorbonne, 1937–1947; director of the Radium Institute, 1947–1956; member of the French Atomic Energy Commission, 1946–1951.

Married: Frédéric Joliot, on 29 October 1926.

Irène Joliot-Curie, the elder daughter of Marie and Pierre Curie, made important contributions to research in nuclear physics.

After graduating from the Sorbonne, Joliot-Curie helped her mother as a mobile radiologist in World War I, then became her mother's assistant at the Radium Institute in Paris. In 1921 she began her own research into the measurement of radioactivity and the atomic weight of chlorine; she published her findings the same year. In 1925 she submitted her doctoral thesis, which was about the alpha rays of polonium, an element Marie Curie had discovered in 1898. Joliot-Curie's future husband, Frédéric Joliot, worked at the Radium Institute from 1924. They married in 1926, both taking the name "Joliot-Curie." They worked as a team, specializing in nuclear physics, and began to publish together in 1928.

During the 1920s, a number of disputes took place between various European scientists about the merits of different measurement techniques used in artificial disintegration experiments. The development of electrical counting methods helped to resolve these disputes, and polonium was found to be particularly useful in studying these processes. The Joliot-Curies had considerable experience in the preparation of polonium.

In 1928 they attended a conference at the Cavendish Laboratory in Cambridge at which leading researchers in the field of radioactivity met to discuss current research. The Joliot-Curies decided to investigate artificial disintegration, with the aim of resolving matters that were still being debated. They returned to Paris and made full use of the facilities there to accumulate large quantities of polonium. During the early 1930s, there was more controversy, this time about the nature of cosmic rays and their relationship to gamma radiation. On 18 January 1932 the Joliot-Curies presented a paper to the Académie des Sciences in which they described their findings on penetrating radiation.

Shortly after this, they obtained funding and permission to carry out a study at the Jungfraujoch mountain research station in Switzerland, an ideal location to study cosmic rays. In February 1932, however, James Chadwick at the Cavendish Laboratory announced a new hypothesis concerning the neutron in a letter to *Nature*. The Joliot-Curies, together with others working in this field, quickly began to undertake research into these particles. In April they traveled to Switzerland as planned and took the opportunity to investigate whether cosmic rays

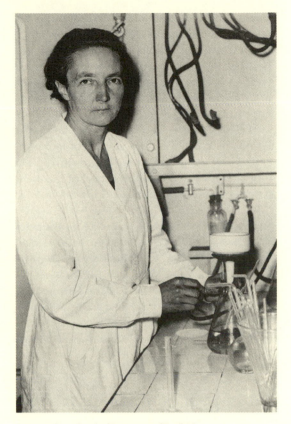

Irène Joliot-Curie (Bettmann/Corbis)

were actually made up of neutrons. Their results did not support this idea, and on their return to Paris they resumed their work on nuclear physics.

Between 1932 and 1934 they jointly published a number of important papers on the effect of alpha particles on various elements. This led to their discovery of artificial radiation, in 1934, for which they received the Nobel Prize for chemistry in 1935. They created the first artificial radioactive element, phosphorus 30, which has a half-life of 2.5 minutes.

In 1936 Irène Joliot-Curie was made undersecretary of state for scientific research in the French government. She continued with her scientific work, studying artificial radioelements in great detail. After spending part of World War II in Switzerland with her children, she returned to France. In 1946 she and her husband were appointed as scientific commissioners of the newly established French atomic energy project. Irène Joliot-

Curie held this post until 1951, though her husband was dismissed in 1950 as a result of his Communist activities. She served on a number of committees during this time, as well as continuing to research and publish in the field of radioactivity. She was a member of the World Peace Council.

She was made an officer of the Legion of Honor in 1939. She died in 1956 of leukemia caused by exposure to radiation during her work. Frédéric Joliot-Curie died of the same disease two years later.

Bibliography: Chadwick, J., "Mme Irène Joliot-Curie," *Nature* 177 (26 May 1956): 964–966; Hughes, J., "The French Connection: The Joliot-Curies and Nuclear Research in Paris, 1925–1933," *History and Technology* 13 (1997): 325–343; Opfell, O. S., *The Lady Laureates: Women Who Have Won the Nobel Prize,* Metuchen, New Jersey: Scarecrow Press, 1978.

Joshua, Joan Olive
11 July 1912–21 February 1993
veterinary surgeon

Education: St. Michael's Convent, Finchley, London; Royal Veterinary College, London, 1933–1938.

Employment: house surgeon at Beaumont Hospital, 1938–1939; veterinary practice, Finchley, 1939–1962; reader, Department of Clinical Studies, University of Liverpool, 1962–1993.

Joan Joshua was the first woman fellow of the Royal College of Veterinary Surgeons (1950), awarded for her study on canine leptospirosis. With Margaret Bentley, she founded the Society of Women Veterinary Surgeons in 1941; Joshua was its first president.

Joshua's father died when she was eleven, and so her mother had to work through the postwar depression. Joshua was not able to go to veterinary college until she was twenty-one, as there were few student grants, but once there she worked hard and was awarded two Centenary Medals by her college as the best overall student in her fourth and final years.

After a year as a house surgeon, she set up her own practice at her mother's home in Finchley. She wrote numerous clinical publications, and through her membership on several committees, especially in the war years, she campaigned successfully for the establishment of the Animal Health Trust, the removal of unqualified practitioners, and the education of veterinary surgeons only in universities, including the new schools at Bristol and Cambridge. She was a councillor of the National Veterinary Medical Association (British Veterinary Association) from 1941 to 1953. She was the first woman to join the council of the Royal College of Veterinary Surgeons (RCVS) in 1953, staying on the council until 1963. She was the only woman member of the British Veterinary Codex Committee from 1950 to 1965. Among other awards she was the first woman to receive the Francis Hogg Prize (RCVS) in 1959 and the Victory Medal of the Central Veterinary Society in 1976–1977.

In 1962 she was appointed to a readership at the Department of Clinical Studies at Liverpool University; she taught there until retirement. She found this a vast change from running her own practice, as she was not used to cooperating with others, but she was well liked by both students and colleagues.

In 1968 she established the Society for Women Veterinary Surgeons Trust, which aimed to promote the education of women in veterinary science. After retirement she worked for her local People's Dispensary for Sick Animals (PDSA) clinic and was adviser to the Mutual Defence Society. She bred prize-winning chows and was vice-president of the National Chow Club and president of the Chinese Chow Club for ten years. She was a show judge for over fifty years.

Bibliography: Duncan, D., and L. Arnall, "Miss J. O. Joshua," *Veterinary Record* (March 27, 1993): 330; Grundy, A. M., "Miss J. O. Joshua," *Veterinary Record* (March 13, 1993): 280–281; Joshua, J. O., personal commucation to the author, *Veterinary Record* 54, 21 (1942): 212; "Miss J. O. Joshua," *Veterinary Record* (March 6, 1993): 253–254; "Women in the Veterinary Profession," *Veterinary Record* 57, 51 (1945): 674.

K

Kann, Edith
19 April 1907–7 October 1987
freshwater biologist

Education: University of Vienna, Ph.D., 1933.

Employment: Institute of Hydrobiology, Plon, Austria; grammar school teacher; independent researcher.

Edith Kann was a leading authority on cyanophytes (blue-green algae) and one of the founding members of the International Association of Cyanophyte Research, set up in 1961.

Kann was born in Vienna. For her undergraduate degree, she specialized in algae and hydrobiology. The subject of her doctoral dissertation was the littoral vegetation of the Lunzer Untersee.

While she held a post at the Institute of Hydrobiology in Plon, she studied the lakes in the Holstein region and lectured at the university on the taxonomy and ecology of littoral algae. After she left the institute, she worked as a grammar school teacher but continued with her research on littoral periphytic algae and the ecology and classification of cyanophyte genera from alpine aquatic habitats. Kann's most important work was probably her monograph on algae from some mountain streams in Austria. The alga *Homoeothrix kannae* was named after her to celebrate her eightieth birthday. She published over thirty papers as sole author and several coauthored ones.

Bibliography: Anagnostidis, K., J. Komárek, B. Hickel, and D. Mollenhauer, "In Memoriam: Edith Kann (1907–1987)," *Archiv für Hydrobiologie,* suppl. 92 (1991): 559–561; Hickel, B. and D. Mollenhauer, "In Memoriam: Edith Kann (1907–1987)," *Algological Studies* 64 (1991): 559–561; Kann, E., "Systematik und Okolgie der Algen osterreichischer Bergbache," *Archiv für Hydrobiologie,* suppl. 53 (1978): 405–643.

Kennard, Olga née Weisz
23 March 1924–
crystallographer

Education: Prince Henry VIII Grammar School; Cambridge University, M.A., 1948; Sc.D., 1971.

Employment: research assistant, Cavendish Laboratory, University of Cambridge, 1944–1948; Medical Research Council (MRC) Scientific Staff, Vision Research Unit, London, 1948–1951; MRC National Institute for Medical Research, London, 1951–1961; University Chemical Laboratory (to set up Crystallography Unit); MRC special appointment, 1974–1989; scientific director, Cambridge Crystallographic Data Centre (CCDC), 1965–1997; visiting professor, University of London, 1988–1990.

Married: David William Kennard, in 1948 (marriage dissolved in 1961); Sir Arnold Burgen, president Academia Europaea, in 1993.

Olga Kennard has worked in crystallography for some fifty years, studying the structure of organic and biologically active molecules. She has shown how chemical

Olga Kennard (Julia Hedgecoe)

properties and biological activity can be correlated with crystal structure and developed several innovations in X-ray crystallography.

Since the 1940s X-ray crystallography has made an enormous contribution to many areas of science, including physics, chemistry, material science, and biology. Indeed molecular biology is based on the discovery, using this technique, of the structure of the genetic material DNA and of protein structures. The Cambridge Crystallographic Data Centre (CCDC), one of the most important scientific databases, was founded by Kennard in 1965 when she was a member of the Medical Research Council (MRC) external staff at the University Chemical Laboratory in Cambridge. The CCDC began the systematic compilation of bibliographic and numerical information on organic crystal structures at a time when such compilations were very unusual.

The CCDC was supported initially by the Office for Scientific and Technical Information (OSTI) and later by various research councils. At first the CCDC issued the information collected in the form of printed publications that helped scientists keep pace with a rapidly developing subject. With improvements in technology and the use of computers, the number of papers published in this field increased from three in 1935 to 530 in 1969 and to well over 10,000 by 2000. Printed publications became impractical, and the CCDC concentrated on creating a computerized database where information could be searched for and analyzed using software developed by the CCDC. Today the Cambridge Structural Database stores experimental data for over 200,000 crystal structures and has become an important tool for various fields, including drug development. Kennard has described its function in "From Data to Knowledge—Use of the Cambridge Structural Database for Studying Molecular Interactions" (*Journal of Supramolecular Chemistry* 1 [1993]: 227–295).

Parallel with the development of the database, Kennard and her colleagues were active in determining the structure, by X-ray crystallography, of a wide variety of increasingly complex molecules. Many of these were of biological importance. One of the highlights was the analysis, in 1970, of the structure of adenosine 5-triphosphate (ATP), with only four crystals available for experiments. The structure was one of the first to be solved by direct mathematical methods (*Nature* 225 [1970]: 333–336). Other compounds analyzed included natural products, especially those with antibiotic functions, various drugs, complex organic molecules, and eventually synthetic fragments of the genetic material DNA. They analyzed the first fragment of double helical DNA at atomic resolution (*Nature* 273 [1978]: 687–688), the first fragment with mismatched base pairs (*Nature* 315 [1985]: 604–606), as well as DNA fragments complexed with anticancer drugs. Together with Robin Taylor, Kennard studied hydrogen-bond geometry in organic crystals and showed the existence of the C-H . . . X hydrogen bond (*Accounts of Chemical Research* 17 [1984]: 320–326).

Kennard was awarded the Structural Chemistry Prize of the Chemical Society in

1980. She was elected to fellowship in the Royal Society in June 1987 and is one of the forty women fellows in a membership of around 1,000. She was appointed an Officer of the Order of the British Empire (OBE) in 1988.

Bibliography: Debrett's People of Today 2001, London: Debrett's Peerage, 2001; Kennard, O., personal communication to the author, 2000; *Royal Society News* (March 1987): ii; *Who's Who, 2000,* London: Adam and Charles Black, 2001.

Kingsley, Mary Henrietta
13 October 1862–3 June 1900
ethnologist, sociologist, traveler

Education: at home.
Employment: freelance explorer, writer, and collector.

Mary Kingsley explored West Africa, often on her own, and collected numerous biological specimens.

Kingsley was born in London, the daughter of George Kingsley, a scholar and writer. Her uncle was Charles Kingsley, author of *Westward Ho!* and *The Water Babies.*

Because her mother was ill most of the time, Kingsley had to do the housework. The family moved to Cambridge to be nearer to her brother, and Kingsley yearned to study. In 1892 her parents died within six weeks of each other; quite unexpectedly, Kingsley was free to do whatever she liked.

She decided to travel in West Africa, so in August 1893 she sailed for Nigeria on the *Lagos.* She always dressed in feminine clothes and took drums of spirits with her so that she could preserve and send back any interesting specimens of animals she found. She learned all she could on board ship from anyone who would volunteer information.

Kingsley traveled around West Africa making sketches and recording notes about local customs. She was in favor of the traders, thinking they were doing the right things; she was not happy with the way the missionaries condemned the customs of the

Mary Henrietta Kingsley (Hulton-Getty/Archive Photos)

West Africans, which she believed should be preserved. In late December 1894 she sailed to Free Town in Sierra Leone to explore the area.

When she returned to England, she lectured to help raise money for her next trip. In May 1895 she explored Gabon and French Congo and collected fish for Dr. Alfred Gunther at the British Museum. He named two new species of fish she collected after her: *Ctenopoma kingsleyae* and *Mormyrus kingsleyae.*

Kingsley wrote several books—*Travels in West Africa* (1897), *West African Studies* (1899), and *The Story of West Africa* (1900). She lectured both to the general public and to chambers of commerce whose members wanted to trade in West Africa.

In March 1900 she went out on a troopship to the Palace Hospital in Simonstown, South Africa, as both a special correspondent and a volunteer nurse to look after the Boer prisoners of war, who were dying of enteric fever. Kingsley caught the disease herself, and died of heart failure following an operation. She was buried at sea, as she had wished, with a military and naval funeral, lowered from a torpedo boat off Cape

Point. She was greatly mourned, as she had packed so much into her few years of freedom. The African Trade Section of the Liverpool Chamber of Commerce held a special meeting to commend her courage, ability, honesty, and perseverance.

Bibliography: Dictionary of National Biography, supplement, vol. III, Oxford: Oxford University Press, 1901; Frank, K., *A Voyager Out: The Life of Mary Kingsley,* Boston: Houghton Mifflin, 1986; Gwynn, S., *The Life of Mary Kingsley,* London: Macmillan, 1932; Longford, E., *Eminent Victorian Women,* London: Weidenfeld and Nicholson, 1981; "Mary Kingsley," Obituary, *Times* (6 June 1900): 8D; "Mary Kingsley," *Times* (7 June 1900): 9E.

Kipling, Charlotte
née Harrison
7 June 1919–9 August 1992
statistician, fish biologist

Education: Liverpool College, Huyton; St. Leonards School, St. Andrews; Newnham College, Cambridge, 1937–1940; M.A., 1948; University College, London, 1946–1947.
Employment: cipher officer, Women's Royal Navy Service, 1940–1946; statistician and biologist, Freshwater Biological Association, 1947–1983.

Charlotte Kipling was a statistician and fish biologist at the Ferry House, Windermere, the headquarters of the Freshwater Biological Association (FBA).

The daughter of a ship broker, Kipling was educated in Liverpool and Scotland and read economics at Newnham College, Cambridge. She was a cypher officer during World War II, then took a statistics course at University College, London. She was appointed as part-time statistician at Ferry House in 1947. She carried out calculations for the scientific staff of the Freshwater Biological Association (FBA) and advised them on the presentation and interpretation of their results. She became interested in fish

biology and published thirty-two papers on the subject. She looked at the analysis of long-term data and produced a series of papers (many written in collaboration with Winifred Frost) summarizing changes in the char, pike, and perch populations in Windermere from 1941 to 1982. She also investigated the history of the fisheries of Windermere.

In the early 1960s Kipling introduced computers to the FBA. She was a fellow of the Statistical Society and a member of the Institute of Biology.

Bibliography: Le Cren, David, "Obituary: Charlotte Kipling, 1919–1992," *Freshwater Forum* 2, 3 (1992): 166–168; Le Cren, David, "The Windermere Perch and Pike Project: An Historical Review," *Freshwater Forum* 15 (2001): 3–34; *Newnham College Register, 1924–1950,* vol. 2, Cambridge: Newnham College, 1981.

Kirkaldy, Jane Willis
c. 1869–19 June 1932
zoologist

Education: Wimbledon High School; Somerville College, Oxford, 1887–1891; B.S. with honors, 1891; M.A., 1920.
Employment: assistant mistress, Wimbledon High School; science lecturer and visiting teacher, London; private tutor, Castle Howard, Yorkshire; tutor, Association for the Education of Women, Oxford, 1894–1930; tutor and lecturer for the Oxford Women's Societies.

Jane Kirkaldy was a tutor in natural science at Somerville College, Oxford, for thirty-six years. She graduated with first-class honors in natural sciences (animal morphology), one of the first two women to achieve this. She spent a short time as a private tutor at Castle Howard in Yorkshire. In 1894 she returned to Oxford when the Association for the Education of Women offered her the post of tutor to the women students in the School of Natural Sciences. She was also tutor and lecturer to the Oxford Women's Societies. She was made an honorary fellow of

Somerville College in 1929 and was on the council of St. Hugh's College.

She was known as a lively individual with a strong character who enjoyed discussing all aspects of science. A committed Christian, she was also keen on religious debate. She studied Darwin's theories and accepted his ideas on evolution, though this did present some difficulties for her religious faith and her relationship with her strictly Presbyterian family. In her laboratory work she was extremely thorough and expected every one of her students to have the same dedication to scientific research that she had.

With E. Pollard, she translated J. E. V. Boas's *Textbook of Zoology* (1896); she coauthored *An Introduction to the Study of Biology* (1909) with I. M. Drummond. She bequeathed funds to Oxford University for the Jane Willis Kirkaldy prize, which was established in 1936. Somerville College named a prize for natural science in her honor.

Bibliography: Adams, P., archivist, Somerville College, Oxford, personal communication to the author, November 1999; "Jane Willis Kirkaldy," *ASM Supplement to the Somerville College Report* (1931–1932): 10–12; *Somerville College Register,* Oxford: Somerville College, 1971.

Klein, Melanie *née* Reizes
30 March 1882–22 September 1960
psychoanalyst

Education: high school, Vienna.
Employment: freelance psychoanalyst.
Married: Arthur Stephan Klein, a chemical engineer.

Melanie Klein pioneered the use of psychoanalysis in understanding young children.

Klein was born in Vienna, the youngest of four. While still in high school in Vienna, she decided that she wanted to be a doctor. She studied hard, but partly because she was engaged when she was seventeen, did not go on to university. When she was twenty-one she married. The couple had three children, and they lived in Budapest during World War I. Here she read through the work of Sigmund Freud and became interested in psychoanalysis. Sando Ferenczi analyzed her and realized that she had a gift for analyzing children. She began to help him in the clinics he held for disturbed children.

In 1919 she read her first paper on psychoanalysis, "The Development of a Child," to the members of the Hungarian Psycho-Analytical Society. As a result she was accepted as a full member.

Karl Abraham, who had also analyzed her, suggested that she should move to Berlin. So in 1921 she started to practice with the Berlin Psychoanalytical Society. At that time very little was known about the psychological development of very young children. Klein developed a technique of talking with the child in a room containing a variety of simple toys and interpreting the child's reaction to them. She felt it was better for the child's anger to be directed against the analyst rather than offer assurance. After each session she wrote up detailed notes.

In 1925 she was invited by Ernest Jones to give six lectures on child development to the British Psychoanalytical Society. She settled in London in 1926 with her youngest son and was given British nationality in 1934. She published *The Psycho-analysis of Children* in 1932. From 1938 onward several Viennese psychoanalysts came to Britain. Many of them disagreed with Klein's methods, which remained separate from the Freudian method of analysis.

Klein was a hard worker and published several books about her work. She was responsible for changing many of the ideas about the way children should be cared for in their early years. She stressed how early emotional deprivation can cause lasting harm. Besides her work with children, she helped both manic-depressives and schizophrenics, showing for some how the problems had originated in early childhood. Her archives are held at the Wellcome Institute in London.

Bibliography: *Dictionary of National Biography, 1951–1960,* Oxford: Oxford University Press, 1971; Grosskurth, G., *Melanie Klein,*

London: Hodder and Stoughton, 1986; Klein, Melanie, *The Writings of Melanie Klein*, 4 vols., New York: The Free Press, 1975; Mitchell, J., ed., *The Selected Melanie Klein*, Harmondsworth, Middlesex: Penguin, 1986; "Mrs. Melanie Klein," obituary, *Times* (23 September 1960): 20; Rosenfield, H. A., "Klein, Melanie," in *International Encyclopaedia of the Social Sciences*, edited by D. L. Sills, New York: Cromwell, Collier, and Macmillan, 1968.

British Ferns," giving full descriptions for the forty-five British species, excluding the water ferns, in *Transactions of the Botanical Society of Edinburgh*. She bequeathed her collection of books and papers on fossil botany to the Botanical Garden in Edinburgh.

Bibliography: Gault, R., archivist, Botanical Society of Scotland, personal communication to the author, March 2000; Mathew, M. V., *The History of the Royal Botanic Garden Library*, Edinburgh: Her Majesty's Stationery Office, 1987.

Knox, Elizabeth May
née Henderson
26 March 1899–14 December 1963
paleobotanist, palynologist

Education: St. George's School for Girls, Edinburgh; University of Edinburgh; M.A., 1922; B.S., 1923; D.Sc., 1949.
Married: Mr. Knox, a geologist for the Geological Survey of Scotland.

Elizabeth Knox published a series of papers on spores found in various coal deposits.

Knox was born in Edinburgh, the third daughter of Andrew Henderson, a biscuit manufacturer well known in the Edinburgh business community. Her husband, a geologist employed by the Geological Survey of Scotland, surveyed the Scottish coalfields. Knox decided to carry out her own research using his coal samples: she hoped that by comparing the abundance of different types of spores in the coal, she would be able to identify fragments of coal seams fractured by faulting. In spite of her careful work, her project was only partially successful, but she increased the knowledge about spores and palynology considerably. Her research was published between 1938 and 1959 in *Transactions of the Botanical Society of Edinburgh*, *Transactions of the Institute of Mining Engineers*, and *Transactions of the Edinburgh Geological Society*.

From 1949 to 1950 she was president of the Botanical Society of Edinburgh. Her presidential address was "Microspores and Their Significance in Biological Problems." She published "Spore Morphology in

Kovalevskaya, Sonya
(Sofya) Vasilyevna
née Korvin-Krukovsky
15 January 1850–10 February 1891
mathematician

Education: tutors and governesses at home; informally at St. Petersburg; courses at University of Heidelberg, Germany, 1869–1871; pupil of Karl Weierstrass, Berlin, 1871–1874; Ph.D. 1874 (awarded by University of Göttingen).
Employment: University of Stockholm, lecturer, 1883–1884; temporary professor from 1884; full professor, 1889–1891.
Married: Vladimir Kovalevski, a paleontologist, in 1868.

In 1874 *Sonya Kovalevskaya* was the first woman to obtain a doctorate in mathematics. It was awarded on the basis of her published papers, and she did not have to defend her thesis.

Kovalevskaya was born in Moscow, the middle daughter of an artillery general. The family had a country estate at Palabino, and Kovalevskaya spent her early years there. She was educated by tutors and governesses and encouraged in her intellectual interests by two of her uncles and a neighbor, one Professor Tyrtov. At the age of eleven, she began to take an interest in some old lecture notes that had been used temporarily to cover the walls of the nursery. These contained information and formulas on differential and integral analysis, and

Kovalevskaya gradually absorbed the details, recalling them years later when she studied calculus. Tyrtov recognized her aptitude for mathematics and suggested she receive formal instruction. Eventually it was agreed that she would take lessons in St. Petersburg while on visits to the city with her mother. These included tutorials at the naval school where Tyrtov himself taught and lectures by, among others, Dmitry Mendeleyev, the chemist. She applied to study at the Russian Mathematical School but was not allowed to do so.

Kovalevskaya decided to continue her education abroad. With the help of her older sister, she made a plan to marry someone who also wished to study in another country, a type of arrangement often made at that time. Her wish was realized, and despite some disapproval from her family she married Vladimir Kovalevski in 1868, the couple leaving for Germany in 1869. Kovalevskaya studied mathematics and Kovalevski geology, both at the University of Heidelberg. Kovalevskaya found she could attend lectures only on an informal basis, as women were not able to register formally as students at the university. Kovalevskaya and her husband experienced difficulties in their domestic arrangements, and he eventually left to study in Munich.

After making a very favorable impression academically at Heidelberg, Kovalevskaya, too, moved on. In 1871 she went to Berlin and began to work with Karl Weierstrass. Here again she was unable to enter the university, so Weierstrass offered her private tuition. She produced three important pieces of work, dealing with partial differential equations (published in *Crelle's Journal* in 1875), Abelian integrals, and Saturn's rings, and these earned her a doctorate from the University of Göttingen. Her living conditions in Berlin were poor, as was her relationship with her husband, who at one point joined her and then decided to move out and live with a friend.

Despite her doctorate and support from Weierstrass, Kovalevskaya was unable to obtain an academic position. She returned to Russia and gave up her mathematical research for a number of years. She was rec-

onciled with her family and her husband, and in 1878 gave birth to a daughter. By 1880 she had begun to work on mathematics once more. Her personal life, however, continued to be unsettled. In 1883 her husband committed suicide after getting into debt and being disgraced.

With Weierstrass's help, Kovalevskaya was finally able to obtain a teaching post, at the University of Stockholm. Although there was controversy over her appointment, she was made a professor and took up a chair in 1889. During this period she consolidated her reputation as a mathematician, edited the journal *Acta Mathematica*, and became involved in organizing international conferences. She wrote her memoirs and coauthored a play, *The Struggle for Happiness.*

In 1888 she was awarded the Prix Bordin of the French Academy of Sciences for work on the rotation of a solid body about a fixed point. The prize money she received was 5,000 instead of the usual 3,000 francs, ostensibly in recognition of the high standard of the research, though her precarious financial circumstances may also have been a factor. At this time she was involved in a troubled relationship with Maxim Kovalevski (no relation to her husband), a Russian historian who wanted her to give up her academic post and move with him to Paris. Again she took up literary pursuits, producing a number of autobiographical novels. Her mathematical work did continue, and her last published paper concerned Brun's theorem on a property of the potential function of a homogeneous body. In 1889 she was elected a corresponding member of the Russian Academy of Sciences.

In January 1891, returning to Stockholm by train after spending Christmas with Maxim Kovalevski in France, Kovalevskaya caught a chill that eventually became pneumonia, of which she died.

Bibliography: Barrow-Green, J., "Sonia Kovalevskaya," *Woman's Hour*, BBC Radio 4, 5 November 1999; Millar, D., et al., *The Cambridge Dictionary of Scientists*, Cambridge: Cambridge University Press, 1996; Ogilvie, M. B., *Women in Science: Antiquity through the Nineteenth Century*, New York: MIT Press,

1986; Website: http://www.groups.dcs.st-and.ac.uk/~history/Mathematicians/Kovalevskaya.html.

Kuroda, Chika
24 March 1884–8 November 1968
chemist

Education: Saga Normal School (women's section), 1901; Women's Higher Normal School (science), Rika, Japan, 1902–1906; Women's Higher Normal School, Kenkyuka, 1907–1909; Tohoku Imperial University, 1913–1916; B.S., 1916; Oxford University, 1921–1923.

Employment: primary school teacher, 1901–1902; teacher, Fukui Normal School, 1906–1907; assistant professor, Tohoku Imperial University, 1916–1918; professor, Tokyo Joshi Koto Shihan Gakko, 1918–1921; researcher, RIKEN (Institute of Physical and Chemical Research), Majima Laboratory, 1924–1949; Ochanomizu Women's University: professor, 1949–1952; honorary professor from 1952; part-time lecturer, 1952–1963.

Chika Kuroda carried out important research into natural pigments. In 1916 she was the first woman to be awarded a bachelor of science degree in Japan.

Kuroda was born in Japan in what is now Matsubara, Saga city. She was an assistant professor at the Tokyo Joshi Koto Shihan Gakko and was then admitted as a student in the Chemistry Department at the Tohoku Imperial University, the first woman to gain a place. She began her research on natural pigments there under Professor Majima Toshiyuki. When she graduated in 1916, she was appointed assistant professor at the university. In 1918 she took up a post as professor at the Tokyo Joshi Koto Shihan Gakko. In the same year she presented a paper on the pigment from *Lithospermum erythrorhizon* to the Chemical Society of Japan, the first woman to give a talk to the society.

In 1921, as a Ministry of Education overseas student, Kuroda studied at Oxford University under Professor W. H. Perkin. She returned to Japan in 1923. Japan suffered a major earthquake at this time, and Kuroda was unable to pursue research at Tokyo Joshi Koto Shihan Gakko. The following year she joined the Institute of Physical and Chemical Research (RIKEN) at Majima Laboratory, and in 1929 her thesis on the structure of the pigment of the safflower, *Carthammus tinctorius*, earned her a doctorate; she was only the second woman in Japan to attain the degree. She continued to research pigments from various natural sources, including the skins of eggplant and black soybean.

She received the first Majima Prize from the Chemical Society of Japan in 1936 and over the next few years concentrated her research on naphtoquinone compounds and their derivatives. This included work on the pigment found in the spines of sea urchins, an area in which she worked with others until 1964. She was appointed professor at the Ochanomizu Women's University in 1949, at which time she began to study onion skin pigment. This work eventually contributed to the development of a drug for the treatment of high blood pressure, Keruchin C. Following her retirement in 1952, she was made honorary professor and continued to lecture part time at the university. After a period of illness, she died in 1968 in Fukuoka, aged eighty-four.

She was awarded a Medal with Purple Ribbon in 1959 and the Order of the Precious Crown, Butterfly, in 1965 and was posthumously made a Third Grade Junior of the Court Rank.

Bibliography: Yamauchi, Mizue, British Embassy, Tokyo, personal communication to the author, May 2000.

L

Laby, Jean
1915–
atmospheric physicist

Education: University of Melbourne, Australia; B.S., 1939; M.Sc., 1951; Ph.D., 1959.
Employment: Physics Department, University of Melbourne: demonstrator, senior demonstrator, from mid-1940s; lecturer, from 1959; senior lecturer, Royal Australian Air Force Academy, Point Cook, 1961–1982.

Jean Laby carried out research in a number of areas, including cosmic rays, wind, and the composition of the stratosphere.

Laby was born in Melbourne, Australia, the daughter of Thomas Howell Laby, who was professor of natural philosophy at the University of Melbourne for almost thirty years. After graduating, she worked in the Physics Department for many years. In 1961 she was appointed to the post of senior lecturer at the Royal Australian Air Force Academy at Point Cook. As well as teaching, she carried out research. During the 1970s she collaborated with scientists from the University of Wyoming as part of the Climate Impact Assessment Program, which involved measuring atmospheric aerosols, ozone, and water vapor in the stratosphere.

Bibliography: Allen, N., "The Exception to the Rule: The Career of an Australian Woman Physicist," *Australian and New Zealand Physicist* 30, 12 (1993): 305–309; Website: http://www.asap.unimelb.edu.au/bsparcs/biogs/P002419b.htm.

Lathbury, Kathleen
née Culhane
14 January 1900–1993
biochemist

Education: Hastings and St. Leonards Ladies' College; Royal Holloway College, University of London, 1918–1922; B.S., 1922.
Employment: teacher and private tutor in London; industrial chemist, Neocellon, Wandsworth; chemical adviser, London Hospital Diabetic Clinic; research chemist, British Drug Houses (BDH); physiology department and statistician, Royal Ordnance Factory, Hereford and later Bridgend.
Married: Major G. P. Lathbury, in July 1933.

Kathleen Lathbury was well known for developing analytical techniques in food chemistry and medicine.

After graduating in chemistry from Royal Holloway College, Lathbury could not find a post in industry. Because both her parents had died, she needed a paying job. Initially she worked as a teacher in a school and then as a private tutor. She had joined the Institute of Chemistry and through this association met Dr. Marrack, who was responsible for the diabetic clinic at the London Hospital. She worked there in her free time, unpaid, and often did emergency sugar determinations.

Lathbury was offered a paid job at the woman's rate of £120 a year at Neocellon of Wandsworth, a company that made lacquers and enamels. She did well in this post, but Marrack asked her to return to the diabetic clinic, this time paid at £265 a year. She did all the insulin testing and was general chemical adviser.

Also through Marrack, Lathbury was given a post at British Drug Houses (BDH). She was responsible for overseeing the manufacture of insulin and running tests to make sure it was effective.

In 1928 she visited the United States and Canada on a travel grant from the Messel Travel Fund. The trip was organized by the Society of Chemical Industry, and the group visited similar societies. In the same year she also joined the League of Nations Health Organization Committee to look at the physiological assay of crystalline insulin. She became involved with the estimation of hormones and wrote the section on hormones in *Allen's Commercial Organic Analysis* (1933). She then turned to the determination of vitamin A and published research on this.

Lathbury married in 1933 and was allowed to keep her job but resigned from BDH in 1936. She was made a fellow of the Institute of Chemistry in 1935.

When World War II began, she was appointed to the Royal Ordnance Factory, initially at Hereford and later at Bridgend; she ended up as shop manager of a statistical quality control department. On the basis of this work, she was made a fellow of the Royal Statistical Society in 1943.

When the war ended she and her family settled at Grayshott in Hampshire. She did no more chemistry but instead became a successful botanical artist. She was a member of the Haslemere and Farnham Art Society and exhibited her paintings in Paris and at the Salon des Nations.

Bibliography: Bramley, J. V. (Lathbury's son-in-law), personal communication to the author, October 1999; Bramley, R., "Kathleen Culhane Lathbury," *Chemistry in Britain* 24, 5 (1991): 428–431; Dyer, L., archives assistant, Royal Holloway/Bedford College, University of London, personal communication to the author, January 2000; Horrocks, S. M., "A Promising Pioneer Profession? Women in Industrial Chemistry in Inter-war Britain," *British Journal for the History of Science* 33(118) (2000): 351–367.

Laverick, Elizabeth
25 November 1925–
engineer

Education: Dr. Challoner's Grammar School, Amersham, Buckinghamshire; University of Durham, B.S. with honors, 1946; Ph.D., 1950.

Employment: technical assistant, Radio Research Station, Ditton Park, Slough, 1942–1943; GEC Stanmore (Marconi Defence Systems), 1950–1953; Elliott Brothers, section leader, then head of the Radar Research Laboratory, 1954–1968; Marconi general manager, 1968–1971; deputy secretary, Institute of Electrical Engineers (IEE), 1971–1985.

Elizabeth Laverick was the first woman to be awarded a Ph.D. in a scientific subject at the University of Durham and the first woman to reach top management level in a British defense firm. She was the first woman deputy secretary of the Institute of Electrical Engineers (IEE) and its eighth female fellow.

Laverick did very well in mathematics at school and would have liked to have gone straight to university when she was sixteen. As Durham University would not admit her until she was seventeen, she spent a year working at the radio research station at Ditton Park, Slough, Berkshire. For the most part, she analyzed and plotted the results of measurements of the ionosphere, but one day a week she worked in the laboratory—the first time a woman had ever been admitted.

When she started studying physics at Durham, she was the only woman among twenty men in her class. After she completed her B.S., she did research on audio frequency dielectric measurements and was awarded her Ph.D. in 1950. She started working at GEC at Stanmore, Middlesex, on the design of microwave antennae.

When she moved to Elliott Brothers, she worked on microwave instruments at 4-millimeter wavelengths and devised a system to detect intruders using an off-the-shelf seismic sensor. This device was used at a British military base in Myanmar and at a prison in Wales. Later she was in charge of Elliotts' Radar Research Laboratory, and her team worked on ways of monitoring aircraft landings. The system was used at Heathrow Airport in the 1960s. Marconi took over Elliotts in 1968, and Laverick as technical director continued with the work she had been doing at Elliotts on infantry and airborne radar systems.

In 1971 she decided to leave practical engineering, as she had become more interested in the management of projects, and she accepted the post of deputy secretary at the IEE. She worked particularly hard on issues of career development and set up programs for the members to ensure they were familiar with the latest developments. She was responsible for the qualifications department, schools liaison, and technical regulations.

Laverick is a member of the Women's Engineering Society and was their president from 1967 to 1969 and honorary secretary from 1991 to 1995. She was editor of the *Journal of the Women's Engineering Society* from 1983 to 1990. She was made an Officer of the Order of the British Empire (OBE) in 1993 and is a fellow of the Institute of Physics.

Bibliography: Geppert, L., "Trials and Triumphs: Women Engineers in Europe," *IEEE Spectrum* (August 1997): 44–55; Laverick, E., "ICWES One to Nine," *Journal of the Women's Engineering Society* (1991): 1–5; Laverick, E., personal communications to the author, February 1998, May 2000; Zorpette, G., "Elizabeth Laverick," *IEEE Spectrum* (May 1992).

Lavoisier, Marie Anne Pierrette née Paulze
1758–1836
artist, chemist, translator

Education: convent until 1771.
Married: Antoine Laurent Lavoisier, chemist, 1771 (he died in 1794); Sir Benjamin Thompson, physicist, 1805.

Marie Anne Pierrette Lavoisier (Bettmann/Corbis)

Marie Lavoisier married the chemist Antoine Lavoisier in 1771 and worked with him as his assistant.

Lavoisier's father was a lawyer and financier and a member of the Ferme Générale, a group that collected taxes for the government.

Antoine Lavoisier was a member of the Academy of Sciences, and the Lavoisiers' home provided a meeting place for scientists. Marie Lavoisier used to help her husband with his experiments and often recorded the results. She was taught by the artist Jacques-Louis David and did the illustrations for her husband's books, such as *Traité élémentaire de chimie* (Elementary treatise on chemistry) (1789).

In 1775 Antoine Lavoisier was appointed scientific director at the Royal Gunpowder Administration, and the Lavoisiers moved to the Paris Arsenal, where he was able to have a well-equipped laboratory. Marie Lavoisier translated several scientific books into French, such as Richard Kirwan's *Essay on Phlogiston, and the Constitution of Acids* (1787).

In the turmoil of the French Revolution, Antoine Lavoisier was executed on 8 May 1794. Marie Lavoisier was arrested but later released. She edited her husband's memoirs and paid for them to be privately printed. As life in Paris settled down, she was able to set up her salon again as a venue for scientists. In 1805 she married Sir Benjamin Thompson, Count Rumford, a physicist who often visited her salon. The marriage was not a success, and the couple separated in 1809.

Bibliography: Gillispie, C. C., ed., *Dictionary of Scientific Biography*, vol. 8, New York: Charles Scribner's Sons, 1975; Ogilvie, M. B., *Women in Science: Antiquity through the Nineteenth Century*, New York: MIT Press, 1986.

Lawrie, Jean Eileen née Grant
7 June 1914–
doctor

Education: private; Walthamstow Hall, Sevenoaks, 1928–1932; London School of Medicine for Women (Royal Free Hospital), 1932–1938; M.B., B.S. 1938.

Employment: general practitioner, 1940–1946; Peckham Pioneer Health Clinic, 1943–1947; clinical assistant, Elizabeth Garrett Anderson Hospital, 1947–1978; school doctor, Godolphin and Latymer School, Hammersmith, 1949–1974; general physician to the royal women and children, Brunei, 1978–1982.

Married: Reginald Seymour Lawrie, in April 1941.

As president of the Medical Women's Federation in 1997 and honorary secretary for the preceding thirteen years, *Jean Lawrie* successfully campaigned for improvements in career training for women doctors. She was the first woman fellow of the Medical Society of London.

Lawrie was born in southern Rhodesia. She trained at the London School of Medicine for Women and worked in general practice in London. She married in 1941 and had four children. Lawrie also worked at the Peckham Pioneer Health Clinic and was a founding member of the Women's National Cancer Control Campaign. After the war she was a clinical assistant to Dame Josephine Barnes at the Elizabeth Garrett Hospital for thirty-one years.

Although not a feminist, Lawrie realized that the establishment of the National Health Service had redefined career training and appointments to specialties and general practice in a rigid way that made progress more difficult for women (and some men) with domestic responsibilities than for most men at a similar stage in their careers.

In 1965 Lawrie and Dr. Molly Newhouse conducted a survey of women doctors registered with the General Medical Council (GMC). The results were published in the *British Medical Journal* the following year (2 February 1966, 409–412). Contrary to the views of many, the survey showed that more than 80 percent of an 80-percent respondent rate were employed, although some considered themselves underemployed. Many women with domestic responsibilities found it difficult to undertake the required full-time specialist training. Lawrie campaigned for the establishment of flexible training with some success. The retainer scheme was set up by the Department of Health and Social Security (DHSS).

Negotiations to relieve temporarily unemployed but duly qualified doctors of the fee for the General Medical Register were unsuccessful. Because registered names did not always identify the sex of the registrant, Lawrie persuaded the GMC to identify women with a "w" ("f" being reserved for foreign registrants).

Lawrie was a member of the Medical Women's International Association (from 1952), a member and council member of the Women's National Commission (1968–1974), a founding member of the Association for the Study of Medical Education, a member of the British Medical Association (BMA) Council (1968–1978), a member of the BMA Board of Science and Social Services Committee, and BMA representative for the EEC Standing Committee of Doctors.

In 1978 she and her husband went to Brunei, where she was general physician to the royal women and children while her husband was general physician to His Highness, the Sultan of Brunei and director of postgraduate medical studies for the government of Brunei.

Lawrie is a fellow of the British Medical Association. She was made a Commander of the Order of the British Empire (CBE) in recognition of her work with the Medical Women's Federation.

Bibliography: Lawrie, Jean, personal communicaton to the author; *The Medical Directory 1998*, vol. 1, London: F. T. Healthcare, 1998; "Women in Medicine," *Woman's Hour*, BBC Radio 4, 14 September 1998.

Le Sueur, Frances Adams née Ross
6 August 1919–17 May 1995
botanist, ornithologist

Education: Carlisle and County High School for Girls; University of Manchester.
Employment: Jersey College for Girls: teacher from 1948, later head of Mathematics Department.
Married: Dick Le Sueur, in 1952.

Frances Le Sueur was an important botanist and conservationist on the Channel Island of Jersey.

Le Sueur was born in Carlisle, Cumbria, and won a scholarship to attend high school there. She studied mathematics at Manchester University and from 1948 taught at the Jersey College for Girls. She joined the local natural history society, the Société Jersiaise, and became a key member of the ornithology section. She was the British Trust for Ornithology's Channel Island representative for a number of years and in 1973 wrote a paper on Cetti's warblers for *Bird Study*.

Her interest in botany developed as a result of her birdwatching activities, and she began to study the plants of Jersey. She met T. W. Attenborough, a senior pharmacist whose knowledge of Jersey's flora was in-

valuable. Le Sueur recorded many of the details he passed on to her. The botany section of the Société Jersiaise had not been active since before World War II, and Le Sueur decided to reestablish it in 1953. She joined the Botanical Society of the British Isles (BSBI) in 1955. She and some colleagues started to collect information for the *Atlas of British Flora* (1962); a record number of plants were listed for Jersey in the book. In 1976 Le Sueur published her first book, *A Natural History of Jersey*.

She began a long and detailed study of the herbarium of Frère Louis-Arsène, a Jesuit priest who had compiled a herbarium of species from Jersey between 1922 and 1952. The Société Jersiaise had been given the herbarium by the monastery at Morbihan to which the priest had retired. He had not been a conservationist, as he had often collected more than one specimen, for exchange, and thus may have been responsible for the demise of some plant species in Jersey. Le Sueur sorted the specimens and checked the dates and provenances where possible, publishing the results in 1982 in *Watsonia* (14: 167–176). In 1982 she became recorder for Jersey for the BSBI.

Following on from the work she had done for the *Atlas of British Flora*, Le Sueur had set up a local mapping scheme, through which she was able to record information for her *Flora of Jersey* (1985), a comprehensive record of Jersey's flora, including eighteen paintings by Pandora Sellars commissioned especially for the book. Le Sueur helped local and visiting naturalists and showed them the plants of Jersey. She gave talks to groups and taught botany at a continuing education college. She visited a number of different countries in order to study plants, making two trips to Tibet. Closer to home, she contributed to plant lists for Alderney, Sark, and Herm, three other Channel Islands.

In the late 1960s Le Sueur became increasingly concerned about the conservation of Jersey's countryside; she campaigned for many years in the local media on a number of issues. The States of Jersey Nature Conservation Advisory Body was established in response to the lobbying of Le Sueur and two other naturalists, and this provided information and guidance to Jersey's planning authorities.

Le Sueur was made an honorary member of the Société Jersiaise for her contribution to natural history in Jersey. A study center in the St. Ouen's Bay Conservation Area was named in her honor.

Bibliography: Long, M. L., "Frances Le Sueur," *Watsonia* 21 (4) (1995): 412–413; Marren, P., "County Floras," *British Wildlife* (August 1999): 373–380.

Mary Douglas Leakey (Bettmann/Corbis)

Leakey, Mary Douglas née Nicol
6 February 1913–
paleoanthropologist

Education: privately; University College, London.
Married: Louis Seymour Bazett Leakey, paleoanthropologist, on 24 December 1936.

Mary Leakey was director of excavations at the Olduvai Gorge in Tanzania.

Leakey was born in England, though she spent much of her childhood abroad. Her father was an artist, and the family traveled throughout Europe so that he could paint during the summer. When she was eleven, she stayed at Les Eyzies in southern France and visited the caves; this sparked off her interest in paleolithic archaeology. She studied anthropology and geology at University College, London. In 1934 she led an investigation into the Clactonian culture in Essex. She reported the discoveries in her first published paper, coauthored with Kenneth Oakley, in *Proceedings of the Prehistoric Society* (1937).

Leakey had met the paleoanthropologist Louis Leakey in Cambridge, and he asked her to do some drawings for him. He divorced his first wife and later married Mary. She traveled to Africa to work with him during the summer; in the winter they returned to Britain. Louis Leakey wrote up some of his work and obtained funding to enable him to continue with his excavations

in Africa and to study the Kikuyu people. The Leakeys worked hard, often in difficult conditions.

In 1948 they found the first *Proconsul* skull on Rusinga Island on Lake Nyanza. There was great excitement when they brought it to Britain, and it was put on display in the Natural History Museum. It was later returned to Kenya when a museum of anthropology was built there.

The Leakeys investigated rock art at Kondoa-Irangi in the summer of 1951. They looked at 186 sites and traced over 1,600 figures, some of which are published in Mary Leakey's book *Africa's Vanishing Art* (1983). During the 1950s they began working at the Olduvai Gorge in northern Tanzania. In July 1959 the Leakeys carried out general survey work in the gorge. While her husband was recovering from influenza, Mary Leakey continued to excavate on site FLKI. She found two premolar teeth and a fragment of temporal bone that belonged to a large hominid, *Australopithecus boisei* (named *Zinjanthropus boisei* at the time); they were estimated to be 1.75 million years old. Mary's discovery was reported in *Nature* in September 1959.

When her husband died in 1972, Mary Leakey carried on with the excavations in Tanzania and in 1975 made another significant discovery: parts of a 3.75 million-year-old skull belonging to a *Homo* species in Laetoli, Tanzania. This was in an area of aolian tuff that was some 2.4 million years old, from a nearby volcano. She and her team also found 18,400 individual prints of different animals preserved in the tuff of the site, including those of a bipedal fossil hominid.

Leakey received honorary doctorates from several universities, including Witwatersrand in 1968, Yale in 1976, Oxford in 1981, and Cambridge in 1982. She was elected as a foreign member of the Royal Swedish Academy of Sciences in 1978 and a foreign associate of the American National Academy of Science in 1987. She was awarded the Linnaeus Gold Medal of the Royal Swedish Academy in 1978, the Gold Medal of the U.S. Society of Women Geographers, and, with her late husband, the Hubbard Medal of the National Geographic Society.

Bibliography: Daintith, J., S. Mitchell, E. Toothill, and D. Gjertsen, eds., *Biographical Encyclopaedia of Scientists*, second edition, Bristol: Institute of Physics Publishing, 1994; Leakey, L. S. B., *Olduvai Gorge, 1951–1961*, Cambridge: Cambridge University Press, 1965; Leakey, L. S. B., and V. Morris-Goodall, *Unveiling Man's Origins: Ten Decades of Thought about Human Evolution*, London: Methuen, 1969; Leakey, M., *Disclosing the Past: An Autobiography*, London: Weidenfeld and Nicolson, 1984; *Who's Who*, 1997, London: Adam and Charles Black, 1997.

Lebour, Marie Victoire
20 August 1877–2 October 1971
marine biologist

Education: Armstrong College (University of Durham), Newcastle upon Tyne, training in art and later science; A.Sc., 1903; B.S., 1904; M.Sc., 1907; D.Sc., 1917.

Employment: Department of Zoology, University of Leeds, junior demonstrator, 1906–1908; demonstrator, 1908–1909; assistant lecturer and demonstrator, 1909–1915; marine biologist, Marine Biological Association (MBA), Plymouth, 1915–1946.

Marie Lebour was well known for her studies on the larval stages of decapods.

Lebour was born in Woodburn, Northumberland. Her father was a lecturer and then professor of geology at Armstrong College, Newcastle upon Tyne. She studied zoology and was a demonstrator while doing research for her M.Sc. In 1906 she moved to Leeds University, which had a marine biological station at Robin Hood's Bay.

Lebour's first published paper was on land and freshwater mollusks in Northumberland (*Naturalist* 518 [1900]: 65–68). While at Durham and Leeds, she specialized in trematodes, parasites in a variety of animals. Her several papers on this subject enabled her to obtain her D.Sc.

Lebour joined the staff of the Plymouth marine laboratory of the Marine Biological Association (MBA) in 1915, while four staff members were on war service and one had gone to Antarctica with Ernest Shackleton. She was given a permanent position in 1917.

Lebour started off by studying the stages in the development of the planktonic shrimp, *Calanus finmarchius,* and then moved on to studying the planktonic larvae of the decapods (crabs), publishing altogether over forty papers on them. She followed the development of thirty-three of the thirty-seven known species in the area and drew or photographed each stage. (These larvae are difficult to rear beyond the first stage, as they are highly sensitive to temperature change and have precise food needs. Most larvae are grown in plunger jars originally invented by E. T. Browne, director at Plymouth.) She also collected plankton samples throughout the year from various points in the area. Most of her work was published in the *Journal of the Marine Biological Association* and the *Proceedings of the Zoological Society of London.*

When Lebour's father died in 1931, her mother and sisters came to live with her. Her mother soon became ill and could not be left alone, so Lebour's work commitment was reduced by two-thirds. In 1937 her mother died, and Lebour was able to travel abroad.

In 1938 Lebour was one of the scientists who went on the Royal Society ship *Culver* to Bermuda. Walter Garstang and Robert Gurney, both known for their studies on marine plankton, were also on the cruise. Lebour collected numerous samples of plankton and other specimens, which she subsequently wrote about, and did watercolors of the fish she saw. She returned to Britain in 1939.

Although Lebour retired in 1946, she continued with her research for some years. For her eightieth birthday, Professor Lily Newton wrote to a large number of biologists who knew Lebour asking for a maximum £1 gift, their signature, and a drawing or sketch of their own work. The end result was a magnificent leather-bound volume of drawings and photographs from her colleagues, including Mary Parke and Vera Fretter. The book was presented at a special MBA tea on 5 April 1957, with a cake shaped and decorated like a diatom. When she died she bequeathed the album to the MBA.

Her archives are held at the MBA in Plymouth. The Marie Lebour Library is one of the MBA's special collections and consists of her published papers, reprints sent to her by other scientists, and her personal library. In 2000 her developmental series of decapod larvae was transferred from Plymouth to the Natural History Museum in London.

Bibliography: Marie Lebour commemorative album (PLE1 60, letters PBR 20, papers MD4.23), Royal Society research ship, Culver to Bermuda, U.M. 169, all available at the MBA Library in Plymouth; Russell, F. S., "Dr. Marie Lebour," *Journal of the Marine Biological Association UK* 52 (1972): 777–788.

Lee, Alma Theodora
née Melvaine
12 April 1912–20 October 1990
botanist

Education: Ascham School, Sydney; University of Sydney, B.S. with honors, 1936; M.Sc., 1940.

Employment: honorary curator, National Herbarium of New South Wales, Sydney; Plant Introduction Section, Commonwealth Scientific and Industrial Research Organisation (CSIR), Canberra; National Herbarium, botanist, 1938–1949; returned part time from 1960s to 1982.

Married: David Lee, entomologist, in 1941.

Alma Lee was a pioneer taxonomist in New South Wales and helped to raise the standard of systematic botany in Australia.

Lee's father was a gold prospector and dredge operator in Tingha, New South Wales. When Lee won a scholarship to Ascham School in Sydney, the family moved to Sydney so that she could take up her place. She later won another scholarship, to study botany at the University of Sydney, where she particularly enjoyed the ecological expeditions. For her M.Sc., she studied soil algae and worked as a part-time curator of the cryptograms at the National Herbarium in Sydney. She returned to work there as a full staff member after a year at the Commonwealth Scientific and Industrial Research Organisation (CSIR) in Canberra.

At the herbarium most of Lee's work was concerned with identification, but she also began investigating the taxonomy of the legumes. Her revision of *Swainsona* was published in 1948. She also revised work on *Typha*.

Lee left full-time work in 1949 to bring up her family, returning in the 1960s on a part-time basis. In particular, she studied the Fabaceae, *Lupinus* (with J. S. Gladstones), and *Hovea* (with Joy Thompson). Lee was an honorary research associate at the National Herbarium from 1982 to 1986.

Bibliography: Briggs, B., "Alma Theodora Lee (1912–1990)," *Telopea* 4, 2 (1991): 141–143; Russell, J., archives assistant, University of Sydney, personal communication to the author, 28 May 2001.

Lehmann, Inge
13 May 1888–21 February 1993
seismologist

Education: Faelleskole, Copenhagen; University of Copenhagen, 1907–1910; Newnham College, Cambridge, 1910–1911; University of Copenhagen, 1918–1920; B.S., 1920; Ph.D., 1928.

Employment: actuary's office until 1918; assistant to the professor in actuarial science, 1923–1925; assistant to the director of Gradmaalingen, 1925–1928; chief of

Seismological Department, Royal Danish Geodetic Institute, 1928–1953.

In 1936 *Inge Lehmann* discovered the earth's inner core; the inner-core boundary is named the Lehmann discontinuity in recognition of her discovery.

Lehmann lived in Copenhagen for most of her life. Her father was a psychology professor at Copenhagen University. She was educated at an enlightened coeducational school run by Hannah Adler, an aunt of Niels Bohr. At Copenhagen University Lehmann studied mathematics, physics, chemistry, and astronomy. After she passed her examinations she went to Newnham College, Cambridge, for a year.

She had hoped to take the mathematical tripos, but she overworked herself while preparing for the entrance examination and had to return to Copenhagen in December 1911. It took her a long time to recover, but she was able to find employment in an actuary's office, where she became skilled at computations. In 1918 she returned to full-time study. After graduating she learned the theory of observations while employed as an assistant to the professor of actuarial science.

Professor N. E. Norland, the director of Gradmaalingen, an institute at the university in Copenhagen, employed her as his assistant from 1925. It was his aim to set up seismographic stations in Copenhagen and at Ivitut and Scoresbysund in Greenland. With three male assistants, Lehmann helped set up the stations while she taught herself seismology. For three months in 1927 she was sent to learn more about the subject from leading experts elsewhere in Europe.

She passed her geodesy examination in 1928 with a thesis on seismography, obtaining a master of science degree. She was appointed head of the Seismological Department at the Royal Danish Geodetic Institute; it was her job to ensure that the three seismographic stations were operating correctly. The one at Scoresbysund in Greenland was a major problem as it was so isolated, visited by just one boat a year.

Denmark has only very minor earthquakes—Lehmann remembered one from when she was fifteen—but seismic waves from around the world were recorded on the Danish equipment. Lehmann interpreted the waves and published the results in the stations' bulletins.

Lehmann had the ability to clear out extraneous data from her mind and see relationships that others had missed. After studying the seismic waves taken at several places after the earthquake on 16 June 1929 in New Zealand, she realized that there must be a distinct inner core in which the velocity of the seismic waves is greater than in the outer core. She made this discovery public in her 1936 paper "P′"—probably the shortest title for any scientific paper. In 1936 she was a founding member of the Danish Geophysical Society and its chair in 1941 and 1944. She was the first president of the European Seismological Federation in 1950.

In seismology, international cooperation is essential, and Lehmann attended numerous meetings, starting in Prague in 1927, including the meetings of the International Union of Geodesy and Geophysics. Readings of seismograms for the major earthquakes were sent to the International Seismological Summary (ISS) based in Kew, London. Lehmann was concerned that these readings were not strictly comparable because of variations in the accuracy of measurements from each station. She decided to investigate small local earthquakes and explosions and was able to show how the readings could be standardized from each station. Seismology became more important as it became necessary to monitor secret underground nuclear explosions. In the United States, increased funding for a progam called VELA UNIFORM led to improved seismographs.

In the 1960s the ISS was closed and the International Seismographical Centre in Edinburgh was set up instead; Lehmann was involved with the changeover. Also around this time, as part of the Worldwide Standardized Seismographic Network (WWSSN), 200 new recorders were installed, one of which was at Copenhagen. Her analyses of seismic waves were based on the results from the WWSSN from this time.

When Lehmann retired, she studied and

worked abroad, visiting the Lamont Geological Observatory at Columbia University several times. Over her career she was given many honors, including honorary fellow of the Royal Society of Edinburgh (1959), foreign member of the Royal Society of London (1969), the Tagea Brandt Award (1938 and 1967), the Bowie Medal from the American Geophysical Union (1971), and honorary doctorates from the University of Columbia (1964) and Copenhagen University (1968).

Bibliography: Bolt, B. A., "50 Years of Study on the Inner Core," *EOS (Transactions of the American Geophysical Union)* 68, 10 (1987): 73, 80–81; Bolt, B. A., "Inge Lehmann, 13 May 1888–21 February 1993," *Biographical Memoirs of Fellows of the Royal Society London* 43 (1997): 287–301; Lehmann, I., "P'." *Publications du Bureau Central Séismologique International Traveau Série Scientifiques* 14 (1936): 87–115; Lehmann, I., "Seismology in the Days of Old," *EOS (Transactions of the American Geophysical Union)* 68, 3 (1987): 33–35.

Lemon, Margaretta Louisa née Smith
22 November 1860–8 July 1953
ornithologist, conservationist

Employment: voluntary honorary secretary of the Society for the Protection of Birds, 1893–1904; honorary secretary of the Publications and Watchers Committees of the Royal Society for the Protection of Birds, from 1904; Voluntary Aid Detachment commandant in charge, Redhill War Hospital, 1914–1918.
Married: Frank E. Lemon, in 1892.

Margaretta Lemon was one of the founding members of the Royal Society for the Protection of Birds (RSPB).

The impetus for the setting up of a society to protect birds came from a group of women in Croydon, Surrey, who in February 1889 pledged not to wear the feathers of any birds not killed for food, except ostriches. They called themselves the Fur, Fin

and Feather Group. In 1891 they joined with the Society for the Protection of Birds (SPB), a group in Manchester with similar aims. The SPB received its royal charter in 1904 and continued to fight for the preservation of birds. The Importation of Plumage (Prohibition) Act was passed in April 1922. Lemon regularly visited the RSPB's Watchers, traveling throughout Britain to do so. Watchers were paid a small "reward" by the RSPB for guarding the breeding grounds of rare species during the breeding season. Without Lemon's determination the RSPB would not have developed into such a successful society.

Bibliography: Dawson, I., librarian, Royal Society for the Protection of Birds, personal communication to the author, July 2001; "Margaretta Louisa Lemon (1860–1953)," *Bird Notes* 25, 8 (1953): 293–294.

Lepaute, Nicole-Reine Etable de la Brière
1723–1788
astronomer

Education: at home.
Employment: freelance astronomer and mathematician.
Married: Jean André Lepaute, in 1748.

Nicole-Reine Lepaute was an important astronomer in her native France, contributing a number of sets of calculations for astronomical phenomena.

Lepaute was born in the Luxembourg Palace, Paris, the daughter of an attendant of the queen of Spain, Elisabeth d'Orléans. She was a lively child, both intellectually and socially. She gained much of her education through books and lectures. She married in 1748, her husband later becoming France's royal clockmaker; through his work she became interested in astronomy and mathematics.

In 1757 Lepaute, together with the astronomer Joseph Jérôme Lalande, was asked by the astronomer Alexis Claude Clairaut to assist in working out when exactly during 1759 Halley's comet would appear. It took her six months to do the complex calculations, which were a key part of the work. In 1762 she produced a map showing the times and percentages of the next eclipse of the sun across Europe. She assisted Lalande when he was editor of the Academy of Sciences' astronomical almanac (1760–1776). She also worked on a table listing the daily positions of stars.

With Lalande and her husband, she studied pendulums, producing a table of calculations showing the number of oscillations per second made by pendulums of different lengths. This was published in the book *Traité d'horlogerie* (Treatise on Clockmaking) (1775), attributed to her husband. Many of her calculations were published in books written by other astronomers. Her astronomical work was curtailed because of her deteriorating eyesight and her husband's ill health.

Bibliography: Ogilvie, M. B., *Women in Science: Antiquity through the Nineteenth Century,* New York: MIT Press, 1986.

Leslie, May Sybil
14 August 1887–3 July 1937
chemist

Education: University of Leeds, 1905–1909; B.S., 1908; M.Sc., 1909; research, Institut Curie, Paris, 1909–1911; research, Victoria University, Manchester, 1911–1912; University of Leeds, D.Sc., 1918.

Employment: teacher, Municipal High School for Girls, West Hartlepool, 1912–1914; assistant lecturer and demonstrator in chemistry, University College, Bangor, 1914–1915; HM Factory in Litherland, Liverpool, research chemist, then in charge of the laboratory, 1915–1918; research chemist, HM Factory, Penrhyndeudraeth, North Wales, 1918–1920; University of Leeds: demonstrator, then assistant lecturer, Chemistry Department, 1920–1924; assistant, then lecturer, Physical Chemistry Department, 1924–1929; research, Chemistry Department, 1933–1937; subwarden of a hall of residence, 1935–1937.

Married: Alfred Hamilton Burr, lecturer in chemistry at the Royal Technical College, Salford, in 1923.

May Sybil Leslie was an outstanding researcher in chemistry, achieving fame through her research in World War I on the chemical reactions involved in producing nitric acid and the optimum conditions for its manufacture. Nitric acid was vital for the munitions industry. She was in charge of her laboratory, a rare responsibility for women at the time.

Leslie was given a county major scholarship to study chemistry at Leeds, and she graduated with first-class honors. During the next year she worked with H. M. Dawson on the reactions of iodine and acetone. They published their research jointly in 1909 in *Transactions of the Chemistry Society*. When she was awarded an 1851 Exhibition Scholarship, she opted to work in the Institut Curie in Paris, run by Marie Curie. During the two years she spent there, Leslie worked with large quantities of thorium ores, calculating the molecular weight of the emanation from thorium and studying decomposition products of thorium. In 1911 and 1912 she published three papers on her findings in the journal of the French Academy of Sciences.

Though Curie was in charge, Leslie had little contact with her, as André Debierne took care of the day-to-day organization. Leslie worked in the laboratory with the Norwegian Ellen Gleditsch. The precautions against the harmful effects of radioactivity were slight, and it is quite likely that Leslie's overexposure at this time affected her health in the long term. Because her scholarship was for three years, she returned to Britain to work for a year in Ernest Rutherford's physical laboratory, studying the emanations from thorium and actinium.

She left full-time research for two years' teaching but was able to fit in some part-time research collaborating with Dawson from Leeds. After a year of teaching at University College, Bangor, she was taken on to do research at Her Majesty's Factory in Litherland, Liverpool, in 1915. She was promoted to be in charge of the research laboratory, and the research she did on nitric acid earned her a D.Sc. from Leeds University. She wrote the first two parts (*The Alkaline Earth Metals* and *Beryllium and Its Congeners*) of the three-volume *A Textbook of Inorganic Chemistry* (1925), edited by J. Newton Friend, under her married name (Burr).

Leslie had married Alfred Hamilton Burr in 1923, when she was a lecturer at Leeds. He was then a lecturer in Salford but was promoted to head of the Chemistry Department at Coatbridge in 1931. Leslie resigned her post at Leeds in 1929, but when her husband died, in 1933, she moved back to Leeds. Here she continued with her research, completing one of her late husband's research projects on wool dyes and working with Dawson. She was highly thought of at the university and was a subwarden of one of the women's residences.

In 1918 she was elected an associate of the Institute of Chemistry and was a fellow of the Chemical Society from 1920.

Bibliography: Rayner-Canham, G., and M. Rayner-Canham, "A Chemist of Some Repute," *Chemistry in Britain* (March 1993): 206–208.

Rita Levi-Montalcini (Reuters/ANSA/Archive Photos)

Levi-Montalcini, Rita
22 April 1909–
neurophysiologist

Education: Turin University, medicine and surgery from 1930–1936.

Employment: research assistant to G. Levi, Turin, in neurobiology, assistant to Luria and Dulbeco, Turin University; Washington University, St. Louis, Missouri: associate professor, 1951–1958; professor, 1958–1977; director, Neurobiological Research Unit, Higher Institute of Health, Rome, 1960–1977; director, Cellular Biology Laboratory, National Council of Scientific Research, Rome, 1969–1979.

Married: G. Levi, professor.

In 1986 **Rita Levi-Montalcini** was awarded the Nobel Prize for medicine jointly with S. Cohen for her work on nerve growth factor. She was the first woman to be admitted to the Pontificia delle Scienze.

Initially her Italian Jewish family opposed her going to Turin University to study medicine, but Levi-Montalcini persevered. After graduation she assisted Dr. Guiseppe Levi, one of her instructors, with his research into the neuroembryology of the chick. The research had a very limited budget and was done mostly in her own home (when Mussolini was in power, she could not work at the university). She was able to get eggs as she needed them for her family: when she had finished with her observations, they ate the eggs, as there was a food shortage.

Levi-Montalcini spent part of the war in Florence, attending to the medical needs of refugees. In 1947 she went to the United States and worked at Washington University in St. Louis with Dr. Viktor Hamburger. She showed that the embryonic nerve system produces more nerve cells than needed; the number produced was related to the volume of tissue. From this she went on in 1952 to discover nerve growth factor (NGF) and subsequently the related epidermal growth factor (EGF). She showed that mouse saliva was a good source of NGF. She returned to Italy in 1960 to direct the neurobiological research unit at the Higher Institute of Health in Rome, simultaneously retaining her tenure at Washington University until 1977. Thereafter she worked only in Italy, as director of the Cellular Biology Laboratory at the National Council of Scientific Research in Rome.

Levi-Montalcini published numerous scientific papers and her book, *Il Messaggio nervoso* (Transmission of Nerve Impulses), was published in 1975. She was elected foreign member of the Académie des Sciences on 17 April 1989, in the molecular and cell biology section. Among her many honors, she was made Commander of the Italian Republic in 1986 and is a member of the American Academy of Science.

Bibliography: Holloway, M., "Profile: Rita Levi-Montalcini: Finding the Good in the Bad," *Scientific American* (January 1993): 15–16; Millar, D., et al., *The Cambridge Dictionary of Scientists*, Cambridge: Cambridge University Press, 1996; *Who's Who in Italy, 1987*; Yount, L., *Twentieth-Century Women Scientists*, New York: Facts on File, 1986.

Leyel, Hilda Winifred Ivy née Wauton
6 December 1880–15 April 1957
herbalist

Education: studied medicine.
Employment: shop proprietor from 1927.
Married: Carl Frederick Leyel, in 1900. He died in 1925.

Hilda Leyel did much to revive the popularity of herbalism in the twentieth century and founded the Society of Herbalists.

Leyel was born in London. Her father taught French at Uppingham School, Rutland, from 1881. While the family lived at Uppingham, she became enthusiastic about herbs and flowers. After leaving school she studied medicine; in 1900 she married a theatrical manager. During this time she socialized with a number of influential people. She was involved in raising money for hos-

pitals and ex-servicemen but in 1922 was prosecuted for running a questionable fundraising scheme known as "The Golden Ballot," which raised £300,000. Her influential friends came to her aid, and she was eventually acquitted.

Despite a lack of botanical knowledge, Leyel began to study herbalists, particularly Nicholas Culpeper. In 1926 she published *The Magic of Herbs*. Her aim was to present information on the use of herbs for a variety of purposes. In 1927 she opened a shop, Culpeper House, at 10 Baker Street, London. This and similar shops were designed to appeal to women in particular and were very successful. She founded the Society of Herbalists to promote the study of herbs, especially their healing properties. She had an extensive personal library available for use by society members. She wrote several more books of her own as well, including *Herbal Delights* (1937) and *Green Medicine* (1952). She also edited the two volumes of *A Modern Herbal* by M. Grieve in 1931.

In 1941 her profession was threatened by proposed legislation relating to medicines, but her influential friends again helped her, having the bill altered so that members of the Society of Herbalists could legally be treated with herbs.

Leyel believed that herbs could have both physical and mental effects and that this was more beneficial than the action of drugs, which though quicker could be superficial. She campaigned for a number of causes, including those relating to pure food, pure water, and the use of artificial fertilizers.

Bibliography: *Dictionary of National Biography, 1951–1960*, Oxford: Oxford University Press, 1971; "Hilda Leyel," *Times* (18 April 1957): 14A; Jacobs, J., "History of Culpeper House," available online at http://gen.culpeper.com.

Lindsay, Lilian née Murray
24 July 1871–31 January 1960
dental surgeon

Education: Camden School for Girls; North London Collegiate School, 1886–1889; Edinburgh Dental Hospital and School, 1892–1895.

Employment: self-employed dentist, London, 1895–1905, and with her husband in Edinburgh, 1905–1919.

Married: Robert Lindsay, dental surgeon, in 1905.

Lilian Lindsay was the first British woman to be licensed as a dentist.

Lindsay was born in London, the third child in a family of eleven. Her father died when she was fourteen. She was educated at the Camden School for Girls.

In 1886 she won a scholarship to the North London Collegiate School, where Miss Buss, a forceful person, was the headmistress. Miss Buss wanted Lindsay to be a teacher for people with hearing and speech disabilities, and when she refused, Miss Buss told her she would prevent her from doing anything else, so Lilian said that she could not be prevented from becoming a dentist. Miss Buss would not renew Lindsay's scholarship, so she left school in 1889.

Via a family friend who was a dentist, Lindsay was apprenticed to a dental practitioner. She passed the preliminary examination and registered as a dental student. In 1892 she applied to the National Dental Hospital in London. The dean would not even interview her inside the building but met her in the street. So she went instead to the Edinburgh Dental Hospital and School. At that time the English Royal College of Surgeons would not admit women, but the Scottish Royal College did.

In Edinburgh she was the only woman student. On her first day she met her future husband, Robert Lindsay, a tutorial dental surgeon at the time. After qualifying with honors in 1895, Lilian Lindsay practiced on her own in London and at a branch practice in the country. Both she and her future husband had debts to repay for their training and were responsible for other members of their families, so they did not marry until 1905. Lindsay was in a joint practice with her husband in Edinburgh until 1919, when he was appointed dental secretary to the British Dental Association, meaning a move to London.

Lilian Lindsay published over fifty papers about dentistry but rarely included lists of references. She was particularly interested in British dental history; she wrote *A Short History of Dentistry* in 1933. She also prepared translations, such as that of Fauchard's *Le Chirugien dentiste* (The Dental Surgeon) in 1946, and wrote letters, notes, and annotations for the *British Dental Journal.*

In 1894 she was awarded the Watson Medal for dental surgery and pathology and the medal for materia medica and therapeutics. She was the first woman president of both the British Society for the Study of Orthodontics and the British Dental Association. She founded the British Dental Association Library in 1962, and the Society for the History of Dentistry was later created in her honor.

Bibliography: Cohen, E. M., and R. A. Cohen, "The Autobiography of Dr. Lilian Lindsay," *British Dental Journal* 171 (1991): 325–328; Cohen, R. A., "Lilian Lindsay, 1871–1960," *British Dental Journal* 131 (1971): 121–122; Hunter, J., "Women in Dentistry: Past and Present," *The Probe* (November 1995): 3.

Lloyd, Dorothy Jordan
1 May 1889–21 November 1946
biochemist

Education: King Edward VI High School, Birmingham, until 1907; Newnham College, Cambridge, 1908–1914; natural science tripos, 1912; M.A., 1925; B.S. (London), 1910; D.Sc. (London), 1916.

Employment: researcher, Medical Research Council, 1915–1920; British Leather Manufacturers' Research Association, researcher, 1920–1927; director, 1927–1946.

Dorothy Jordan Lloyd was an influential biochemist whose work on the science of leather manufacture brought her international recognition.

Lloyd was born in Birmingham, one of four children. Her father was a surgeon who later became professor of surgery at the University of Birmingham. After taking her natural science tripos, she stayed at Newnham College, Cambridge, as a Bathurst Student, becoming a fellow of the college in 1914. Her research at Newnham was initially on the regeneration of muscle and problems associated with osmosis. During World War I she received a grant from the Medical Research Council, under the direction of Sir Frederick Gowland Hopkins, to investigate bacteriological culture media and the causes of ropiness in bread.

After the war she worked for the British Leather Manufacturers' Research Association, applying her skills in chemical research to the leather manufacturing business. Many of the techniques she used became accepted practice across the industry. She took over from Sir R. H. Pickard as director of the association in 1927, a position she held until her death. Under her leadership the activities and influence of the association increased significantly. Lloyd was the only woman at that time to head such an organization, and she worked hard through some difficult times, including, in 1940, an air raid that destroyed the new laboratories.

Lloyd was on the International Society of Leather Trades' Chemists' executive committee. The Tanners' Council of America awarded her their Fraser Muir Moffat medal in 1939. She was a member of the Council of the Royal Institute of Chemistry in 1936 and vice-president from 1943 to 1946. She published over 100 articles in scientific journals and several textbooks, including *The Chemistry of the Proteins and Its Economic Applications* (1926). She was involved in the planning stages of *Progress in Leather Science, 1920–1945,* published in three volumes between 1946 and 1948. She died at Great Bookham, in Surrey, in 1946.

Bibliography: Candler, W. I., *King Edward High School for Girls,* Part I 1883–1925, Birmingham, 1971; *Dictionary of National Biography, 1941–1950,* Oxford: Oxford University Press, 1959; "Dorothy Jordan Lloyd DSc (Lond.) F.I.C.," *Newnham College Roll Letter* (January 1947): 54–55; *Newnham College Register, 1871–1923,* vol. 1, Cambridge: Newnham College, 1963; York, K., archivist.,The Schools of King Edward in Birmingham, personal communication with the author, December 1999.

Longfield, Cynthia
16 August 1896–27 June 1991
entomologist, explorer

Education: at home.
Employment: wartime service, 1914–1918; entomologist (Odonata specialist), British Museum (Natural History), 1927–1957.

Cynthia Longfield was a leading expert on dragonflies and damselflies, the order of insects known as the Odonata. She traveled thousands of miles collecting insects, plants, and archaeological artifacts.

Longfield came from a financially secure Anglo-Irish family. Her father, Mountifort Longfield, and his family had lived at Castle Mary in County Cork for some time. Her mother, Alice Mason, the daughter of a professional scientist, had grown up near Oxford. Longfield was the youngest of three daughters. Part of the year the family lived in Ireland and the rest of the time in London.

Longfield was due to come out as a debutante into London society when World War I intervened. Having learned how to drive in Ireland, she joined the Royal Army Service Corps as a driver. Later, when there were enough male drivers, she was sent to work in an airplane factory. She learned carpentry and had to work long hours.

In the summer of 1920, the family home at Castle Mary was burned down by Irish rebels, so the family stayed in London. Park House was built later in the grounds of Castle Mary.

In December 1921 Longfield went on a three-month voyage with her parents to South America on the *S.S. Almanzora.* She had already started collecting insects and was also very interested in bird life; she decided that she would pursue her interests in natural history.

In 1923 she saw an advertisement for an assistant to join a group of scientists on the *St. George* on an expedition to the Pacific Islands. Evelyn Cheesman was the only woman on the expedition, and another woman was needed. Longfield's parents agreed to let her go, and after much preparation the expedition left on 9 April 1924 with Longfield as an amateur entomologist.

Cheesman collected mosquitoes; Longfield's responsibility was to collect beetles and butterflies as Cyril Collinette's assistant. This was the start of a lifelong working partnership with Collinette.

The voyage was full of exciting incidents. Among other places, they went to the Galápagos, Tahiti, Panama, and the Marquesas, always collecting. Cheesman left the expedition at Tahiti and stayed there on her own for another year. After the ship was damaged in a storm and was going to take some time to repair, Longfield decided to leave the ship at Balboa and arrived home on 29 June 1925. The expedition had amassed a vast collection of insects, archaeological artifacts, and plants.

Longfield had learned a great deal about insects on the expedition. She joined the Entomological Society of London in 1925 and the Royal Geographical Society later the same year. She worked in the Natural History Museum sorting out and identifying the insects she had collected and was given the Odonata as her specialty. She always encouraged anyone interested in dragonflies and enjoyed meeting young enthusiasts. She had a private income and financed her trips abroad from a family trust. Although she was only a volunteer at the Natural History Museum, she worked virtually full time—but had the freedom to go on collecting expeditions.

Cyril Collinette went off on a six-month collecting trip to West Africa in 1926, and he missed Longfield's company. She joined him on his next expedition to Brazil, Gwen Dorrien-Smith coming along as both a watercolor artist and a chaperone. They traveled over 4,000 miles in Brazil and came back with thirty-eight species of dragonflies, three of them new records.

In 1929 Longfield published her first research paper, "The Odonata of the State of Mato Grosso, Brazil." Her next expedition was to Southeast Asia, with Lettice Rimington-Wilson as her traveling companion. They visited an amazing number of countries, collecting wherever possible.

In 1932 she was elected as the first woman president of the London Natural History Society (she served as vice-president in 1934–1936 and 1944–1946). In 1932 she was also elected as the first woman member of the Council of the Entomological Society. Collinette married Celie Gloor in 1932, but he kept up his friendship with Longfield, as they had many shared interests.

Longfield's next expedition was with Ruth Blezzard to Canada, where her sister's brother-in-law was governor-general. After staying in Ottawa for a short time, Longfield and her friend went camping in the Canadian Rockies and explored British Columbia, even going trail riding on their own. In 1934 she went off alone to explore Africa, visiting Kenya, Uganda, the Congo, Southern Rhodesia (now Zimbabwe), and Northern Rhodesia (now Zambia), countries that were then part of the British Empire. Her last major trip was to South Africa in 1937.

Meanwhile she had been working hard on the production of a popular book on dragonflies. *Dragonflies of the British Isles* came out in 1937. It had keys to use for identification and illustrations of most of the species described.

With the outbreak of World War II, she joined the Auxiliary Fire Service. Her prompt action saved the Natural History Museum from harm in April 1941.

When her mother died in 1945, Longfield bought a flat in Kensington and lived there until she retired from the Natural History Museum in 1957, after thirty years of service. (She had been made an honorary associate in 1948.) She went to live at Park House in the grounds of Castle Mary but continued to work on her dragonfly collection and had thirty-four publications to her credit between 1929 and 1964. *Dragonflies* (1960) was an immensely popular volume in the Collins New Naturalist series. She wrote three chapters and provided the species distribution maps. In 1983 the British Dragonfly Society was founded; Longfield was made its first honorary fellow. The library of the Freshwater Biological Association at The Ferry House, Windermere, has reprints of most of her published papers.

Bibliography: Corbet, P. S., C. Longfield, and N. W. Moore, *Dragonflies*, New Naturalist Series, London: Collins, 1960; "Cynthia Longfield" obituary, *Times* (7 July 1991); Hayter-Hames, J., "Cynthia Longfield: In Search of Gossamer Wings," *Guardian* (6 July 1991); Hayter-Hames, J., *Madam Dragonfly*, Edinburgh: Pentland Press, 1991; Longfield, C., *The Dragonflies of the British Isles*, Wayside and Woodland Series. London: Warne, 1937; Power, M., "Madame Dragonfly—A Scientific Odyssey," in *Stars, Shells, and Bluebells*, edited by M. Mulvihill and P. Deevy, Dublin: Women in Technology and Science Series, 1998.

Longstaff, Mary Jane
née Donald
c. 1855–19 January 1935
paleontologist

Education: private school, London; Carlisle School of Art.
Married: George Blundell Longstaff, entomologist, in 1906. He died in 1921.

Mary Longstaff was an amateur paleontologist who specialized in Paleozoic Gastropoda. She was awarded the Murchison Fund of the Geological Society of London in 1898, only the second woman to be honored in this way by the society.

Longstaff was born in Carlisle, Cumbria, the eldest of four children. After education at school in London and art school in Carlisle, she began her research. Her early interest was in mollusks, and in 1881 her first paper, "Notes on the Land and Freshwater Shells of Cumberland," was read at the annual meeting of the Cumberland Association for the Advancement of Literature and Science at Carlisle. She was encouraged by the editor of the association's transactions, J. G. Goodchild, to focus on the fossil shells of the area. She published some twenty papers on Paleozoic Gastropoda, mainly in the *Quarterly Journal of the Geological Society of London*. From 1885 to 1933 she traveled in Britain and abroad, visiting museums to examine specimens. Although she had no formal scientific training, her published work was regarded as thorough and

accurate, and she illustrated her own papers. As well as her work on Gastropoda, she published a number of papers on mollusks and bred *Cochlitoma*, large South African land snails.

In 1893 Longstaff was invited to the World's Fair Congress in Chicago as a representative of women geologists, though she was not able to attend. She was elected a fellow of the Geological Society of London in 1919. Her nephew donated her collection of recent shells to the British Museum (Natural History) after she died.

Bibliography: Cox, L. R., *Proceedings of the Geological Society of London* 91, part 3 (1935): xcvii–xcviii.

Lonsdale, Kathleen
née Yardley
28 January 1903–1 April 1971
crystallographer

Education: Downshall Elementary School, Seven Kings, Essex, 1908–1914; Ilford County High School for Girls, 1914–1919; Bedford College, London, 1919–1922; B.S. with honors, 1922; University College, London, 1922–1923; Royal Institution, London, 1923–1927, D.Sc.
Employment: part-time demonstrator, Physics Department, University of Leeds, 1927–1929; Royal Institution, London: research assistant, 1931–1944; Dewar Fellow, 1944–1946; University College, London: reader in crystallography, 1946–1949; professor of chemistry and head of Department of Crystallography, 1949–1968.
Married: Thomas Jackson Lonsdale, a physicist, in 1927.

In 1945 *Kathleen Lonsdale* was one of the first two women (the other was Marjory Stephenson) to be elected as a fellow of the Royal Society. She was the first woman to be president of the British Association for the Advancement of Science, in 1968.

Lonsdale was born in Newbridge, southern Ireland, the youngest of ten children.

Kathleen Lonsdale (Hulton-Getty/Archive Photos)

Her father, a postmaster, read widely. Her mother came from London and because of "the Troubles" in Ireland, brought the family to England in 1908. They lived at Seven Kings, Essex.

Lonsdale did well at school and at sixteen was accepted by Bedford College for Women to study mathematics. After her first year she switched from mathematics to physics. She had the highest marks in the B.S. honors examination in 1922. One of the examiners, William Bragg, a crystallographer, asked her to join him at University College, London, with a grant of £180 a year. He had a large number of research students, including several from abroad. In 1923 he moved to the Royal Institution; Lonsdale joined him. The first crystal Lonsdale measured was succinic acid.

After her marriage, she moved to Leeds. Her enlightened husband said he had not married "to get a free housekeeper," and to a certain extent they shared domestic chores. Their three children were born in 1929, 1931, and 1934.

At Leeds Lonsdale had an Amy Lady Tate scholarship from Bedford College from 1927 to 1929 and was a part-time demonstrator in physics; she continued her research in crystallography, the Royal Society giving her an equipment grant of £150. She worked out the crystal structure of hexamethylbenzene and investigated the structure of hexachlorbenzene using Fourier analysis, the first time this had been tried for an organic compound.

In 1929 her husband accepted a post at the Road Research Laboratory, so the family moved to London. William Bragg was able to find a grant of £300 a year for Lonsdale, allowing her to pay a housekeeper while she worked at the Royal Institution from 1931 to 1946.

She did a wide variety of research within the general field of crystallography; for example, she used space group theory in relation to analyzing the structure of crystals. She was responsible for the revision of the *International Tables for X-ray Crystallography* in 1946. The International Union of Crystallography (IUC) was founded in 1948, and Lonsdale was the first chairperson of the new commission on tables. She was vice-president of the IUC in 1960–1966 and president in 1966.

She did experiments on diamagnetic anisotropy using a large electromagnet and calculated the orientation of resorcinol molecules in a benzene crystal. She became interested in the thermal movement of atoms in crystals. She tried divergent-beam X-ray photography and studied synthetic diamonds. A new type of diamond made synthetically in 1965 was named lonsdaleite in her honor.

In 1962 the chief medical officer of the Salvation Army asked Lonsdale's help in analyzing his collection of bladder stones and gallstones. She obtained a grant from the Medical Research Council, which financed a crystallographer, a technician, and a Guinier camera. Her team analyzed over 3,000 stones; Lonsdale wrote about these in "Human Stones" in *Scientific American* (29 [1968]).

As a member of the Society of Friends, Lonsdale was convinced that war was evil. At the beginning of World War II in 1939, although exempt from war duties because of her children, she had to register for employment and civil defense duties. She felt that as a conscientious objector she could not register. In 1943 she had to go to court and pay a £2 fine. She refused to pay, and the magistrates had to fulfill their duty: they sent her to Holloway Prison for a month amid considerable publicity.

Although she was a small, frail person, in prison Lonsdale was made to scrub and clean the prison officers' quarters. When she collapsed under the strain of carrying heavy loads, she was given lighter chores. She was, however, allowed to have scientific papers and instruments to work on in her cell in the evenings, and she did around seven hours of scientific work a day. She talked with prisoners, and when she was released felt she could talk to anyone. In 1949 she was appointed a member of the Board of Visitors at Aylesbury Prison for Women and Borstal Institution for Girls, and in 1961 she was deputy chair of the board of visitors at Bullwood Hall Borstal Institution for Girls.

Lonsdale worked immensely hard in the cause of pacifism, writing *Is Peace Possible?* (1957) in six weeks when she was particularly depressed about the world's problems. In 1951 she was one of a delegation of Friends who visited the USSR, and she edited the report on this visit, *Quakers Visit Russia* (1952). On 22 May 1953 at Friends House, London, she gave the Swarthmoor lecture: "Removing the Causes of War." She was a member of the Atomic Scientists' Association and became their vice-president.

At University College, London, Lonsdale set up an intensive short course in crystallography for undergraduates and an M.Sc. intercollegiate course with Professor J. D. Bernal at Birkbeck College, London. This attracted many students from overseas. Lonsdale campaigned with quiet determination to encourage more girls to take up science, helping to start the Young Scientists' Section (now BAYS) of the British Association for the Advancement of Science. She almost always accepted invitations to speak at schools.

Lonsdale was appointed Dame Commander of the Order of the British Empire (DBE) in 1956. She was awarded honorary D.Sc. degrees from the universities of Wales (1960), Leicester (1962), Manchester (1962), Lancaster (1967), Kent (1968), Oxford (1969), and Bath (1969) and honorary LL.D.s from Leeds (1967) and Dundee (1968). She received the Davy Medal from the Royal Society in 1957. In the last twenty-five years of her life, she traveled and lectured in Japan (1954), China (1955), and Czechoslovakia (1969), among other countries. In 1947 she had six months in the United States as special research fellow of the U.S. Health Service, during which time she traveled throughout the United States giving lectures.

In 1965, after her husband retired, they moved to Bexhill-on-Sea, Sussex. Lonsdale was still professor of chemistry and had a five-hour commute each day, but she felt it was worth it. In December 1970 she was admitted to a hospital; she died of cancer on 1 April 1971.

Bibliography: "Dame Kathleen Lonsdale, 1903–1971," *Shell Times* 69 (1989); *Dictionary of National Biography, 1971–1980*, Oxford: Oxford University Press, 1986; Hodgkin, D. M. C., "Kathleen Lonsdale, 28 January 1903–1 April 1971," *Biographical Memoirs of Fellows of the Royal Society* 21 (1975) 447–484; Lonsdale, K., "Women in Science: Reminiscences and Reflections," *Impact of Science on Society* 20 (1) (1970): 45–59; Roberts, F. C., comp., *Obituaries from the Times, 1971–1975*, London: Newspaper Archives Developments, 1978; *Who Was Who, 1971–1980*, London: Adam and Charles Black, 1981.

Lowe-McConnell, Rosemary Helen née Lowe
24 June 1921–
biologist, ichthyologist

Education: Howell's School, Denbigh, 1934–1939; University of Liverpool, 1939–1942; B.S., M.Sc., D.Sc.
Employment: scientific officer, Freshwater Biological Association (FBA), Windermere, Cumbria, 1942–1945; researcher,

United Kingdom Colonial Development and Welfare Fund, Malawi, 1945–1947; research officer, British Overseas Research Service, East African Fisheries Research Organisation, 1948–1953; scientist, Guyana Department of Agriculture and Fisheries, 1957–1962; associate, Fish Section, British Museum (Natural History), 1962–1967.

Married: Richard McConnell, on 31 December 1953. From 1957 to 1962 he was director of the Geological Survey in British Guyana, South America.

Rosemary Lowe-McConnell was a pioneer in tropical fish ecology.

Lowe-McConnell was born in Liverpool. After graduating from Liverpool University, she worked at the Freshwater Biological Association (FBA) at Wray Castle in Windermere, studying the migration of silver eels.

After World War II she went to Malawi to survey tilapias and fishery in the southern part of Lake Nyasa (now Lake Malawi). (The survey was begun by Ethelwynn Trewavas and Kate Ricardo in 1938.) Lowe-McConnell had an old diesel in-board engine boat, the *Pelican,* and with the help of local fishermen she surveyed the area, distinguishing five species of tilapias, each of which had a distinct breeding season and place. She collected information about other economically important species of fish as well. Some of her research on tilapias was published in *Proceedings of the Zoological Society of London* (1953).

At Jinja, Uganda, Lowe-McConnell investigated the tilapias in East African lakes and found four new species in Lake Jipe and the Pangani River in Kenya. She described the physiological changes from growth to reproduction of tilapias in ponds. For a short time, she was acting director of the East African Fisheries Research Organisation and wrote several papers about her work.

When she married, she had to retire from the civil service. She continued to work, but as an honorary fisheries officer and was only given her expenses. From 1954 to 1956 she and her husband lived in Botswana, where she collected fishes from the Okavango delta. In 1957 they moved to British Guyana, South America, as Richard Mc-

Connell was director of the Geological Survey there. The Guyana Department of Agriculture and Fisheries gave her a laboratory, transport, flights to the interior, and accommodation on the research ship. The only scientist on the *Cape St. Mary,* she surveyed the freshwater fishes in the Rupununi District with the help of local fishermen. This was the first survey to be done of the Guyana shelf between the West Indies and Brazil. She described some of her work in Guyana in *Land of Water: Explorations in the Natural History of Guyana, South America* (2000).

When Lowe-McConnell returned to Britain in 1962, she was based at the British Museum, where she studied the fishes she had sent there. She wrote several books, including *Ecological Studies in Tropical Fish Communities* (1987).

In 1968 Lowe-McConnell was the ichthyologist on the Royal Society of London/ Royal Geographical Society Xavantina-Cachimbo Expedition to northeastern Mato Grosso in Brazil. The expedition was planned because a new road, part of the Amazon highway system, was expected to go through the area. The researchers often had to set gill nets in areas where there were piranhas and electric eels.

As Lowe-McConnell did not have a full-time post, she was able to get involved in a wide variety of activities, such as the World Symposium on Warm-Water Fish Culture (1966) and the International Biological Programme (1964–1974); she took part in a United Nations Development Project (UNDP) mission to Ghana, planning an artificial lake on the River Volta. In September 1974 she went to the First International Congress of Ecology in The Hague and was coeditor, with W. H. van Dobben, of the report of the plenary sessions, published as *Unifying Concepts in Ecology* (1975).

Lowe-McConnell's greatest contribution to ecology is seen by some to be her ability to pull her knowledge together on a wide range of themes, such as evolution, predation pressure, and population dynamics. She is fascinated by the ways in which behavior and ecology contribute to evolution and concerned about maintaining biodiversity. She has run courses on fish and ecology at

Makerere University in Uganda and Salford University and more generalized courses on ecology at Sussex University. She has been a Ph.D. supervisor for the Open University.

She was vice-president of the Linnean Society of London in 1967 and was elected a fellow in the same year. She was the first editor of the *Biological Journal of the Linnean Society*, an original member of the Association for Tropical Biology, and is an honorary member of the Freshwater Biological Association.

Bibliography: Bruton, M. N., "The Life and Work of Rosemary Lowe-McConnell: Pioneer in Tropical Fish Ecology," *Environmental Biology of Fishes* 41 (1994): 67–80; Lowe-McConnell, R., personal communications to the author, September and October 2000; Worthington, E. B., and R. H. Lowe-McConnell, "African Lakes Reviewed: Creation and Destruction of Biodiversity," *Environmental Conservation* 21, 31 (1994): 99–213.

Lyon, Mary Frances
15 May 1925–
geneticist

Education: King Edward VI High School for Girls, Birmingham, 1936–1939; Woking Grammar School for Girls, 1939–1943; Girton College, Cambridge, 1943–1946; B.A., 1946; postgraduate study in genetics, University of Cambridge, 1946–1950; Ph.D., 1950; Sc.D., 1968.

Employment: Medical Research Council (MRC), scientific staff, Institute of Animal Genetics, Edinburgh, 1950–1955; MRC Radiobiology Unit, Harwell, 1955–1990, head of Genetics Division, 1962–1987; deputy director, 1982–1990.

Mary Lyon is known for her work in genetics, especially in relation to X-chromosome inactivation. She was elected a fellow of the Royal Society in 1973 and was awarded the society's Gold Medal in 1984.

Lyon was born in Norwich. Her father was an inspector of taxes; the family had to move as his work demanded. Her mother was a teacher.

Mary Frances Lyon (Godfrey Argent Studio)

Lyon went to primary schools in Bradford and Norwich. When she was ten, the family moved to Birmingham. Her interest in biology first developed in 1935 when she won a set of four books on wildflowers, birds, and trees as the prize for an essay competition to mark the silver jubilee of King George V. At the King Edward VI School, her biology teacher was a very clear and precise thinker, and Lyon became interested in the analytical aspects of biology. The family's next move was to Woking at the beginning of World War II. Here Lyon did not have the chance to study biology in the sixth form; instead, she had to do physics, chemistry, and mathematics.

At Girton College Lyon was able to study the subjects of her choice—zoology, physiology, organic chemistry, and biochemistry, with zoology as her main subject. At this time there were particularly interesting advances in experimental biology, and Lyon was influenced by the writing of C. H. Waddington, head of the Institute of Animal

Genetics at Edinburgh. Genetics as such was not yet taught at Cambridge, but Lyon attended a course of lectures on genetics, given by R. A. Fisher, which explored the subject from a mathematical standpoint. Undergraduates had the opportunity to help count the various mutants that appeared in his linkage experiments with mice, and they counted flower types in his genetics garden. For her doctorate, Lyon studied the genetics of a balance defect she had noticed in mice that had the mutant gene pallid and published her results in *Journal of Genetics* 51 (1953): 638–650. She used mice from Fisher's mouse colony.

In 1950 she moved to the Institute of Animal Genetics in Edinburgh and did research into the genetic effects of atomic radiation in mice, with a grant from the Medical Research Council (MRC). In 1955 Lyon's team, led by T. C. Carter, was moved to the MRC Radiobiology Unit at Harwell, Oxfordshire, which had more room for expansion. Lyon worked there until she retired, except for 1970–1971, when she held a Clothworkers' Visiting Research Fellowship at Girton College and worked with Richard Gardner.

While at Harwell, Lyon looked into many aspects of mouse genetics. Her most important work was the discovery of the phenomenon of X-chromosome inactivation in mammals, published in *Nature* 190 (1961): 372–373. This was known as the Lyon hypothesis, as she was the first to describe it, sometimes known as the principle of X-chromosome inactivation. She suggested that one of the two X chromosomes in each cell of female mammals becomes inactive early in development (in humans this is thought to occur the sixteenth day after conception). This means that the dose of X-linked genes in XX females and XY males is equal. Previously, small pieces of chromatin called Barr bodies were found in "resting" cells. With the Lyon hypothesis, it was realized that the number of Barr bodies reflected the number of X chromosomes above one found in a sex cell. Thus an individual with Klinefelter's syndrome, whose cells all have XXY sex chromosomes, would have one Barr body representing the condensed, inactivated X chromosome, whereas a normal XY male would not have any Barr bodies. Lyon's hypothesis accounted for the patchy color of tortoiseshell cats, as it appears that the orange color is X-linked, and the coat is a mosaic of cells with either the maternal or paternal X chromosome active.

Further testing confirmed her hypothesis, and it has led to a large amount of research related to this—not least of which is the search for the switch that makes one chromosome inactive.

Lyon has taken on many responsibilities related to her work. She was editor of *Mouse Newsletter* (now *Mouse Genome*) from 1956 to 1970 and chair of Mouse News Letter Ltd. She joined the Committee for Standardised Genetic Nomenclature for Mice in 1958 and was chair from 1975 to 1990. She was on the editorial board of *Genetical Research Cambridge* from 1968 and on the editorial board of other journals. She was honorary treasurer of the Genetical Society for several years and also its vice-president.

Lyon contributed several chapters to *Genetic Variants and Strains of the Laboratory Mouse*, first published in 1981 and edited by Margaret Green. Lyon edited the second edition (1989) with Tony Searle and the third, two-volume edition (1996) with Sohaila Rustan and S. D. M. Brown.

Lyon was made a foreign honorary member of the American Academy of Arts and Science in 1980 and a foreign associate of the U.S. National Academy of Sciences in 1979. She was given the prize for Genetics, San Remo, Italy (1985); the Gairdner Foundation Award (1985); the Allan Award from the American Society for Human Genetics (1986); and the Wolf Prize for Medicine from the Wolf Foundation (1996).

Bibliography: Cattanach, B., J. Peters, and T. Searle, "Mary Lyon: An Appreciation," *Genetical Research Cambridge* 56 (1990): 83–89; *Girton College Register 1869–1946*, vol. 1, Cambridge: Girton College, 1948; Lyon, M. F., "Some Milestones in the History of X-chromosome Inactivation," *Annual Review of Genetics* 26 (1992): 17–28; Lyon, M. F., personal communications to the author, 2000; Passarge, E., *Color Atlas of Genetics*, New

York: Thieme Medical Publishers, 1995; *Who's Who, 1999,* London: Adam and Charles Black, 1999; York, K., archivist, The Schools of King Edward the Sixth in Birmingham, personal communication to the author, December 1999.

M

MacGillavry, Carolina Henriette
22 January 1904–9 May 1993
crystallographer

Education: Barlaeus Gymnasium, Amsterdam; Gemeente Universiteit, Amsterdam, Ph.D., 1937.

Employment: research assistant; Laboratory for General and Inorganic Chemistry, Amsterdam: assistant to Professor A. Smits, 1932–1934; research, 1934–1941; conservator of the Crystal Laboratory, Amsterdam, 1941-1942; Gemeente Universiteit, Amsterdam: lecturer, 1946–1950; professor, 1950–1972.

Carolina MacGillavry, a crystallographer, in 1950 became the first woman to be elected to the Dutch Academy of Sciences (Koninklijke Nederlandse Akademie van Wetenschappen, KNAW).

MacGillavry was born in Amsterdam, the second child of Donald MacGillavry, a neurosurgeon. She studied chemistry at the Gemeente University in Amsterdam and then obtained a post as a research assistant. In 1932 she took a course in physical chemistry, which included work on crystals. From 1932 to 1934 she worked as a research assistant to Professor A. Smits at the Laboratory for General and Inorganic Chemistry in Amsterdam. In the years before World War II, she published several articles, many of them jointly written with her friend and colleague Jo Bijvoet.

During the war, despite practical and financial difficulties, she continued with her research, producing some twenty papers for publication. The laboratory was forced to close in 1942 with the German occupation of the Netherlands. In the same year, MacGillavry began to act as coeditor of the *Nederlandsch Tijdschrift voor Natuurkunde* (Dutch journal for natural science), and continued in this post until 1959. From 1948 to 1966 she was also coeditor of the *International Tables for X-ray Crystallography.*

In 1946 MacGillavry obtained a post as lecturer in chemical crystallography at Gemeente University in Amsterdam. She traveled to the United States in 1949 to work with Ray Pepinsky at the Alabama Polytechnic Institute. She carried out a great deal of important work on the Harker-Kasper equations. Because of her thoroughness in checking her work before sending it in for publication, however, she did not receive full recognition for her research, in contrast to her colleague Jerome Karle, who was awarded the Nobel Prize for his work in this area.

MacGillavry was made an emeritus professor in 1972.

Bibliography: Bruinvels-Bakker, M., and A. De Knecht-Van Eekelen, "Carolina H. MacGillavry: eerste vrouw in de Koninklijke Nederlanse Akademie van Wetenschappen," *Gewina* 20 (1997): 309–331.

Maclean, Ida née Smedley
14 June 1877–2 March 1944
biochemist

Education: King Edward VI High School, Birmingham, 1886–1896; Newnham College, Cambridge, 1896–1899; Central Technical College, London, postgraduate research, 1901–1903; Davy-Faraday Research Laboratory, Royal Institution, 1903–1905; D.Sc. (London), 1905.

Employment: demonstrator in chemistry, Newnham College, Cambridge, 1903–1906; assistant lecturer and demonstrator in chemistry, Victoria College (Manchester University), 1906–1910; research fellowship, Lister Institute for Preventive Medicine, 1910–1914; Admiralty and Gas Warfare Department, 1914–1918; Department of Scientific and Industrial Research, 1918–1932; staff member, 1932– 1943.

Married: Dr. Hugh Maclean, later professor of Medicine at the University of London and St. Thomas's Hospital, on 28 March 1913.

Ida Maclean was the first woman to be appointed to the staff of the Chemistry Department at Manchester University.

Maclean was born in Birmingham and was taught at home until she was nine, when she went to the King Edward VI High School in Birmingham. She was a talented pianist but decided to concentrate on her scientific studies. She held a Gilchrist Scholarship at Newnham College and obtained first-class honors in chemistry and physiology.

After a break from studying, she held a Bathurst Research Scholarship at the Central Technical College in London. She continued with her research at the Royal Institution, concurrently holding a post as demonstrator in chemistry at Newnham College. Her next appointment was at Victoria College (now Manchester University) as assistant lecturer, and she was a demonstrator in the chemistry laboratories for women students. As well as teaching, she did research into the optical properties of organic compounds.

Funded by a Beit Research Fellowship, she returned to London in 1901 and worked at the Lister Institute for Preventive Medicine. She was based there for the rest of her working life. In 1915 she was awarded the Ellen Richards Prize by the American Association of University Women in recognition of her outstanding research as a woman scientist. During World War I she worked at the Admiralty on the large-scale production of acetone from starch by fermentation and at the Gas Warfare Section.

Maclean was particularly interested in fat synthesis from carbonates and the biochemical functions of fatty acids in animals. She published around thirty papers in the *Biochemical Journal* between 1920 and 1941. She wrote a monograph, *The Metabolism of Fat* (1943) and with her husband coauthored the second edition of *The Lipins* (1927).

Maclean worked hard to improve the status of university women. In 1907 she was one of the founders of the British Federation of University Women and was its president from 1929 to 1935. She was determined that women be allowed to join the London Chemical Society, a goal achieved in 1920, when she became the first woman to be formally admitted. She was a member of the Cambridge University Women's Appointments Board from 1941 to 1944.

Bibliography: Creese, M. R. S., *Ladies in the Laboratory? American and British Women in Science, 1800–1900: A Survey of Their Contributions to Research*, Lanham, Maryland: Scarecrow Press, 1998; *Newnham College Register, 1871–1923*, vol. 1, Cambridge: Newnham College, 1963; Nicholls, C. S., ed., *Dictionary of National Biography: Missing Persons*, Oxford: Oxford University Press, 1993; Nockles, P., archivist, John Rylands Library, University of Manchester, personal communication to the author, 1999.

MacLeod, Anna Macgillivray
15 May 1917–
botanist

Education: Edinburgh Ladies' College; Edinburgh University; B.Sc. with honors, 1939; Ph.D., 1951; D.Sc.

Employment: Heriot-Watt College (later University), Edinburgh: lecturer, 1945–1971; professor of brewing, 1971–1977.

In 1970 *Anna MacLeod* became the first woman president of the Institute of Brewing and the first woman professor of brewing.

MacLeod was born in Kirkhill, Inverness-shire, where her father was a minister. She studied botany at the University of Edinburgh and was awarded a first-class honors degree. As an undergraduate, she had started a survey of the plant ecology of the island of Barra. Delayed because of the war, her research was finally published in 1948 in the *Transactions of the Botanical Society of Edinburgh* (vol. 35).

While working at Heriot-Watt College, MacLeod combined teaching and research on plant ecology as applied in brewing methods. She realized the importance of understanding the functions of the various tissues of grain, which led to the ability to control the quality of malt more efficiently. She investigated the various sugars involved in brewing, such as the fructosans, noticing that in barley the leaves and internodes accumulate sucrose and fructosans rather than starch, and fructosans are still present in the grain. MacLeod did research on the lipases in the aleurone layer and looked at some of the enzymes associated with aerobic respiration. She pioneered work with gibberellic acid (GA), which regulates growth in plants, and found that adding GA to steep liquor speeds the transformation of barley grain to malt.

For twelve years, MacLeod was the editor of the *Journal of the Institute of Brewing*. She was awarded the Horace Brown Medal in 1976 in recognition of her scientific work and services to the malting, brewing, and distilling industries.

She was president of the Botanical Society of Edinburgh from 1960 to 1962. Her 1961 presidential address, "On Barley," was published in the *Transactions of the Botanical Society of Edinburgh* (vol. 39). She was elected a fellow of the Royal Society of Edinburgh and was a council member from 1981 to 1983 and secretary from 1983 to 1985. A fellow of the Institute of Brewing, she was awarded an honorary D.Sc. by Heriot-Watt University.

Bibliography: Gault, R., archivist, Botanical Society of Scotland, Edinburgh, personal communication to the author, 21 March 2000; Palmer, G., "Professor Anna Macgillivray MacLeod: Happy Eightieth Birthday," *Ferment* 10, 2 (1997): 73–74.

McMillan, Margaret
July 1860–27 March 1931
educator, pioneer in child health

Education: at home; Inverness High School, 1870–1874; Inverness Academy, 1874–1876; studied music, Frankfurt am Main; studied in Switzerland, 1881–1883; drama training, 1889.

Employment: governess, Edinburgh, 1879; London 1883–1889; companion to Lady Meux, 1889–1892.

Margaret McMillan campaigned to improve the health of children in Britain.

McMillan began her career as a governess in London. She joined the Fabian Society in 1892 and in 1893 played an active part in the Bradford Independent Labour Party. She felt that the government should be responsible for the health of schoolchildren. From 1894 she was a member of the Bradford School Board and in this capacity took part in the government's first medical inspection of schoolchildren.

Her *Education through the Imagination* (1904) had considerable influence on the organization of nursery schools; the preface for the second edition (1923), written by J. L. Paton, called it "a book of the dawning light." McMillan opened the first school clinic in Bow in 1908. Two years later she founded a health center at Deptford, followed by a camp school for needy children. She also set up a garden nursery for children living in poverty in 1913.

In 1923 McMillan was elected the first president of the Nursery Schools Association (later named the British Association for Early Childhood Education). In 1930 she founded the Rachael McMillan Training College for nursery nurses and teachers in memory of her sister. McMillan was made a Commander of the Order of the British Empire (CBE) in 1917 and a Companion of Honour (CH) in 1930.

Bibliography: Bradburn, E., *Margaret McMillan: Framework and Expansion of Nursery Education*, Redhill, Surrey: Denholm House Press, 1976; Crawford, A., et al., eds., *The Europa Biographical Dictionary of British*

Women: Over a Thousand Notable Women from Britain's Past, London: Europa Publications, 1983; Mansbridge, A., *Margaret McMillan: Prophet and Pioneer,* London: Dent, 1932.

Macphail, Katherine Stewart
1888–1974
doctor

Education: Glasgow University Medical School, M.B., 1911.

Employment: doctor, Scottish Women's Hospital Unit, Salonika; founder and doctor, Anglo-Yugoslav Children's Hospital, 1919–1933; doctor, Belgrade Hospital, 1945–1947.

Katherine Macphail worked as a doctor during both world wars, mainly in Yugoslavia.

Macphail, the daughter of a physician, graduated from Glasgow University Medical School in 1911; she was awarded a number of prizes during her studies and is listed in the university's roll of honor.

During World War I Macphail went to Salonika with the Scottish Women's Hospital Unit. She worked at the headquarters of the Serbian army in its military medical unit. In 1917 she worked behind enemy lines for civilians in Macedonia; the following year she went to Belgrade. She founded the Anglo-Yugoslav Children's Hospital there in 1919, at which she worked until 1933. She also organized a surgical tuberculosis hospital for children, Sremska Kamenitsa, at Kamenica on the Danube. The Yugoslavian government honored Macphail with many decorations. In 1932 she was awarded the Russian Red Cross Insignia for her work among White Russian refugees and children. She was interned by the Italians for two years, from 1941 to 1943; on her release she returned briefly to Scotland.

In 1944 Macphail was in charge of the Save the Children Fund medical relief unit, and she spent the last two years of her working life practicing at Belgrade Hospital. She subsequently retired to Scotland.

Bibliography: Bennett, S., assistant archivist, Archives and Business Centre, University of Glasgow, personal communication to the author, 4 February 2000; Goring, R., ed., *Chambers Scottish Biographical Dictionary,* Edinburgh: Chambers, 1992; Wilson, F. M., *In the Margins of Chaos: Reflections of Relief Work in and between Three Wars,* London: John Murray, 1944.

MacRobert, Lady Rachael
née Workman
c. 1883–1 September 1954
geologist

Education: Cheltenham Ladies College; Royal Holloway College, 1901–1907, B.Sc.; University of Edinburgh, Royal College of Science and School of Mines; Christiana Mineralogisk Institutet, Oslo.

Married: Sir Alexander MacRobert, director of the Cawnpore Woollen Mills Company and founder of the British India Corporation, in 1911. He died in 1922.

Rachael MacRobert was one of the first eight women to be elected as fellows of the Geological Society of London in 1919.

MacRobert was born in Worcester, Massachusetts, the daughter of Dr. William Hunter Workman, the Himalayan explorer. She studied geology and political economy at the University of Edinburgh and went to the Royal College of Science and School of Mines. Later she did a postgraduate course in petrology and mineralogy in Oslo.

After her marriage, MacRobert moved to India with her husband, founder of the British India Corporation. She carried out research in the Kolar goldfields. Her first published paper was on calcite as a primary constituent of igneous rocks in 1911. In 1914 she wrote a paper on the rocks of the Eildon Hills in Roxburghshire. She also investigated the iron-producing area of Sweden.

When her husband died in 1922, MacRobert became a director of the British India Corporation. She returned to Britain to look after her husband's estates in Scotland, including his herds of pedigree cattle. She became a justice of the peace in Aberdeen and was a director of the Scottish Chamber of Agriculture. She was also president of the British Friesian Cattle Society and vice-president of the Royal Northern Agricultural Society.

All three of her sons died in aircraft tragedies, one in an accident in 1938 and two on active service in 1941. MacRobert used her considerable resources to help the Royal Air Force (RAF), donating £25,000 to the RAF to buy a Stirling bomber, "MacRobert's Reply," in August 1941. The following year she gave £20,000 to buy four "MacRobert's Fighters" to help Russia's war efforts. She allowed the RAF to use her country home as an RAF hospital and rest center. In 1945 she founded the MacRobert Reply Association, which helped various youth organizations in Scotland.

Bibliography: Badham, S., archivist, Royal Holloway/Bedford College, University of London, personal communication to the author, January 2000; Roberts, F. C., comp., "Lady McRobert," *Obituaries from the Times,* 1951–1960, Reading: Newspaper Archives Developments, 1979; Smith, W. C. "Lady Rachael MacRobert," *Proceedings of the Geological Society of London* 1529 (1955): 46.

Malleson, Joan Graeme
née Billson
3 June 1900–14 May 1956
doctor

Education: Bedales School; Charing Cross Hospital, Member, Royal College of Surgeons; Licentiate, Royal College of Physicians, 1925; M.B.; B.S., 1926.

Employment: medical officer, Holborn Borough Council; clinical assistant, West End Hospital for Nervous Diseases; medical officer, clinic for sexual difficulties, North Kensington Women's Welfare Centre; medical officer, contraceptive clinic, Obstetrics Department, University College Hospital; writer and broadcaster.

Married: Miles Malleson, actor and dramatist, in the 1920s.

Joan Malleson, an important figure in the development of family planning in Britain, was on the executive committee of the Family Planning Association and had an international reputation as an authority in her field.

Malleson went to Charing Cross Hospital in London to train and qualified there as a doctor in 1925, undertaking further training in the following year.

Her eventual choice of an area of specialization was greatly influenced by her experiences in her early posts for Holborn Borough Council and in the West End Hospital for Nervous Diseases. She encountered so many patients with sexual problems that she was able to gain an in-depth understanding of the subject. Her approach was based on her belief that education and information could do much to alleviate such difficulties. She had also met the psychologist and writer Havelock Ellis, whose ideas and research methods shaped her own work. Her enthusiasm for the promotion of family planning was balanced by her tactful approach to what was a sensitive issue.

Malleson continued her career at the North Kensington Women's Welfare Centre and at University College Hospital. She was a member of the Eugenics Society and the executive committee of the Family Planning Association. She published several books, including *The Principles of Contraception—A Handbook for GPs* (1935) and *Problems of Fertility in General Practice* (with J. Stallworthy, 1953). Because of the controversial nature of the subject area, she sometimes used the pseudonym "Medica."

In 1956 Malleson went to New Zealand for four months on a professional exchange scheme. On the journey back to Britain, she decided to spend a day in Fiji, and it was there that she died suddenly of a coronary thrombosis.

Bibliography: Roberts, F. C., comp., "Dr. Joan Malleson," *Obituaries from the Times,* 1951–1960. Reading: Newspaper Archives Developments, 1979.

Mann, Ida Caroline (Mrs. Gye)
6 February 1893–18 November 1983
ophthalmologist

Education: Wycombe House, West Hampstead, 1900–1909; Clarke's Business College; Regent Street Polytechnic (evenings); London School of Medicine for Women (Royal Free Hospital), from 1914; St. Mary's Hospital, Paddington, Member, Royal College of Physicians, Licentiate, Royal College of Physicians.

Employment: Post Office Savings Bank; research student, Institute of Pathology, St. Mary's Hospital, Paddington, and the Imperial College of Science and Technology, 1920–1922; ophthalmic surgeon, Elizabeth Garrett Anderson Hospital, 1922–1925; assistant surgeon and pathologist, Central London Ophthalmic Hospital, 1925–1927; surgeon, Royal London Ophthalmic Hospital (Moorfields), 1927–1949; ophthalmic surgeon, Royal Free Hospital, 1928–1939; Margaret Ogilvie Reader, University of Oxford, 1941–1946; professor of ophthalmology, University of Oxford, 1942–1949; war service as head of ophthalmic research team for the Ministry of Supply, 1940–1945; consultant ophthalmologist to the Western Australia Public Health Department, 1951–1976.

Married: Professor William Ewart Gye, director of the Imperial Cancer Research Laboratories at Mill Hill, in 1944.

Ida Mann was the first woman consultant at Moorfields Eye Hospital, London; the first professor of ophthalmology in Britain; and the first woman professor at Oxford University.

Mann was brought up in West Hampstead, where her father worked for the investigation branch of the post office. When she left school at sixteen, she went to Clarke's Business College, where she excelled in everything except shorthand. Her first job was in the Post Office Savings Bank. One Saturday Mann and fellow employees of the post office were invited to visit the London Hospital at Whitechapel, for which they had collected funds. The hospital enthralled her, and she decided to study medicine. At that time the only medical school open to women was the London School of Medicine for Women. She took evening classes at Regent Street Polytechnic in order to matriculate and was among the top eight students for that year.

Mann started her studies at medical school in October 1914. She was offered some voluntary work in the X-ray department at Fulham Military Hospital but was soon asked to help in the military surgery department, even doing small operations. She worked enthusiastically throughout her training and always seemed to have a sideline, such as serving as a demonstrator, writing a text book, or teaching privately.

For her clinical training, she went to St. Mary's Hospital, Paddington. In her spare time she helped Professor E. S. Frazer with his embryological studies, sectioning and mounting some of his collection of human embryos while he wrote a textbook.

In 1920 Mann served as a part-time ophthalmic house surgeon at St. Mary's. While there she wrote *The Development of the Human Eye* (1928), which she initially presented as a thesis for her D.Sc. from London University in 1924; on the strength of this she was admitted as a fellow of the Royal College of Surgeons.

Mann was clearly exceptional, and she was fortunate in being awarded a succession of research scholarships. She joined the Anatomical Society and often lectured to the members. Between 1921 and 1927 she published nineteen scientific papers. After gaining her diploma of ophthalmic medicine and surgery at Moorfields, she worked there as senior clinical assistant and lectured on the embryology of the eye to students in Oxford and London.

Mann's first staff appointment was to the Elizabeth Garrett Hospital for Women in 1922. As was common at the time, she did not get paid for her work there. Like many doctors, she volunteered with the poor in the mornings and in the afternoons saw private patients, eventually fulfilling her dream of a Harley Street practice.

In 1925 she was appointed to the Central London Eye Hospital, a stepping-stone until she was given a full appointment at

Moorfields in 1927. She continued her research and was awarded the Nettleship Gold Medal and the Doyne Memorial Medal, both prestigious awards in her field.

Mann's next line of research was on vertebrate eyes. She had earlier traveled to Zurich to find out about a device called the slit lamp, which enabled an ophthalmologist to see inside the eye; she was the first to introduce the lamp to England. Taking her slit lamp to the London Zoo, she examined the eyes of a wide range of animals and exhibited photographs and drawings of the iris pattern of *Sphenodon* at a Zoological Society meeting in 1932.

Mann visited friends in India and Egypt, always looking at the local eye hospitals. In 1939 she traveled to Australia to the first annual general meeting of the Ophthalmic Society of Australia. She had a short holiday in Scotland and returned to find Moorfields Hospital had been closed and requisitioned as a first-aid station. Mann worked indefatigably to relocate to another hospital and found one in a convent. She also managed to keep Moorfields partly open.

In 1940 she embarked on research to show that ascorbic acid could not help with mustard gas burns, as had been suggested. She was given space at the Imperial Cancer Research Fund's laboratories at Mill Hill. The Ministry of Supply asked Mann to lead a research team dealing with the effects of gases on the eye. She was joined by Antoinette Pirie, a biochemist.

In 1941 Sir Hugh Cairns invited her to work in Oxford, and she was appointed the Margaret Ogilvie Reader in ophthalmology. She held a fellowship at St. Hugh's College, Oxford, from 1942 onward and was allowed to resign from her post at the Royal Free Hospital. Pirie came to Oxford and worked with Mann; they coauthored *The Science of Seeing* (1946), Mann writing the first half mainly about how the eye functions and Pirie discussing types of blindness, what welfare was available, and the best place to go for an eye test.

In 1944 Mann married Professor William Gye, with whom she had worked at the Imperial Cancer Research Laboratories for some time. Gye had a severe heart condition

and resigned his position soon after their marriage. Mann by then was professor of ophthalmology at Oxford and worked hard appealing for funds to build up the department. Her husband, however, became more ill and so in 1949 the couple moved to Australia, settling near Perth.

Once there Mann and her husband took a year off from academic work. Mann resigned her position at Moorfields. She reluctantly returned to London in July 1950 to give a paper at the English Speaking Ophthalmic Congress; after this she resigned her post in Oxford and was based in Australia for the rest of her life. Her husband did manage to restart some of his research but was never in good health; he died in 1952. Mann was in shock for some time but eventually was able to build up the private practice she had started before her husband died.

Mann served as consultant ophthalmologist to the Western Australia Public Health Department. She was very interested in the eye problems of the Aborigines and traveled throughout Australia testing their sight and checking for trachoma. She wrote about this experience in *The Cockney and the Crocodile* (1962).

Mann's public roles included membership on the World Health Organization's Expert Committee on Trachoma, on the board of advisers to the Asia-Pacific Academy of Ophthalmology, and a member of the International Ophthalmology Congress. She was made a Commander of the Order of the British Empire (CBE) in 1954 and a Dame Commander of the Order of the British Empire (DBE) in 1980.

Ida Mann wrote a very long autobiography, which was abridged for publication by Elizabeth Imlay Buckley. Mann's original manusript is at the Battye Library of Western Australian History in Perth.

Bibliography: Buckley, E. I., and D. U. Potter, eds., *Ida and the Eye, a Woman in British Ophthalmology*, Turnbridge Wells: Parapress, 1998; "Dame Ida Caroline Mann," Obituary. Institute of Ophthalmology, 1983; Imlay, Elizabeth (Mrs. Buckley), personal communication to the author, 2 November 1997; Mann, I., "Memories of the Oxford Eye Hospital and the Beginnings of the Nuffield Laboratory of Ophthalmology," *Experimental Eye Research* 31, 5 (1980): xiv; *Who's Who, 1983,* London: Adam and Charles Black, 1983.

Manton, Irene
17 April 1904–31 May 1988
botanist

Education: Froebel Educational Institute, London, 1906–1917; St. Paul's Girls' School, London, 1917–1921; Girton College, Cambridge, 1923–1926; M.A., 1926; Ph.D., 1930; Sc.D., 1940; University of Stockholm, 1926–1927.

Employment: University of Manchester: assistant lecturer, 1928–1930; lecturer, 1930–1946; professor of botany, University of Leeds, 1946–1948.

Professor *Irene Manton* was the president of the Linnean Society, London, the first woman to hold this office.

Manton was born in London, where her father was a dental surgeon. She and her sister, Sidnie, went to school at the Froebel Educational Institute in London, and it was there they both first became interested in natural history. Manton often explored the Natural History Museum on weekends. Both went on to St. Paul's Girls' School, where Manton became particularly keen on biology. The drawings in her sixth-form exercise book, held at the University of Leeds Archives, are both beautiful and accurate.

Manton won a Clothworkers Scholarship to Girton College, where she specialized in botany. For some time, she had been determined to study chromosomes but was not sure where to start her research. Dr. Kathleen Blackburn, a leading cytologist, and Dr. Hamshaw Thomas, a paleobotanist, suggested that Manton study under the direction of Professor Otto Rosenberg in Stockholm; she was awarded an Ethel Sargant Scholarship to do so. Her initial research idea turned out to be impractical, so instead she studied the chromosome structure of the Cruciferae family, which includes plants such as wallflowers. Altogether she looked at 250 species from this family. She returned to Cambridge from 1927–1929 to continue her research, funded by a Yarrow Scholarship, and presented her thesis in 1930. She published her results in 1932 in the *Annals of Botany.*

Professor Heslop Harrison, her external examiner, showed Manton that although she had said watercress had thirty-two chromosomes, she had drawn forty-eight. Concerned about this difference, she collected more watercress and this time found sixty-four chromosomes. In fact she had discovered a new species, confirming this by measuring the number of chromosomes. She developed an improved method of counting chromosomes: rather than taking sections of preserved material, Manton developed the squash technique, whereby root tips, after gentle heating to macerate the tissues, can be put on a slide, stained with acetocarmine, and gently squashed with the coverslip. This method displays the chromosomes, which can then be drawn or photographed. Manton also worked on the development of ferns and published her only book, *Problems of Cytology and Evolution in the Pteridophyta,* in 1950.

Her first lectureship began at Manchester University in late 1928; she was promoted to a full lectureship two years later. Under the direction of W. H. Lang, professor of cryptogramic botany, she studied fern development, especially the royal fern, *Osmunda regalis.* Lang emphasized the importance of both photography and using fresh material when possible, and Manton adopted these principles throughout her work.

When the professor of botany at Leeds, J. H. Priestley, died, Meirion Thomas, a plant physiologist, was offered the post. He turned it down; Manton was the next choice, and she was so thrilled at the offer that she accepted before visiting the Botany Department to check the areas of interest. When she did eventually get there, she realized that she had made a mistake, as the research done at that time was almost entirely on "higher" plants rather than "lower" plants such as ferns. She tried to return to Manchester but in the end accepted the situation and brought her housekeeper Edith with her.

During her time at Leeds, she worked immensely long hours with tremendous energy and expected the same dedication from her staff. She had to arrange for an enlarged Botany Department, more staff, and changes in the teaching program while at the same time continuing with her own research. She published a large number of papers from 1930 to 1986.

In 1950 an electron microscope was purchased for the department, and Manton used it for her work on ferns; her first paper on the results of this research was published in *Nature* that year. When another electron microscope was later purchased, it was designated solely for her use. She cooperated with Mary Parke at the Marine Laboratory, Plymouth, in studying marine flagellates. She discovered the thylakoid structure of chloroplasts and other details of cell ultrastructure. When she retired, the Botany Department at Leeds gave her a room for her research but would not allow her access to the electron microscope, which was reserved for staff use. Manton traveled to Lancaster to use that university's electron microscope instead, as she knew Kenneth Oates, a professor there whom she had helped earlier in his career. Manton was Honorary Research Fellow in Electron Microscopy at Lancaster from 1971 to 1988.

Manton was keen on art and had a wide collection of original works. She had stipulated in her will that the collection should go to the institution where it was being exhibited at the time of her death. When she died, much of her collection was on display at Lancaster University, as she had lent it to Lancaster University for the opening of the Peter Scott Gallery. After much discussion and debate, Leeds University gave the remainder of the collection to Lancaster so that it could stay intact.

Manton was given the Trail Award and Medal of the Linnean Society in 1954. She was elected a fellow of the Royal Society in 1961, following in the footsteps of her sister, Sidnie (and making the Mantons the only sisters to have been made fellows). When the planet Venus was mapped in 1993, it was decided to name its craters after women; one is called the Manton Crater after Sidnie and Irene Manton. She was awarded five honorary doctorates, from the Universities of McGill, Oslo, Durham, Lancaster, and Leeds. She was given honorary membership in several learned societies, such as the Botanical Society of Edinburgh, and honorary fellowships from the Linnean Society; the Royal Microscopical Society; Girton College, Cambridge; and the Department of Biology at Lancaster University.

Manton left a bequest of almost £250,000 to the Linnean Society of London. The Irene Manton Prize for a Ph.D. in botany was set up in 1990, the prize being not only a cash award but also a work of art.

Bibliography: Gavagan, M., director, Peter Scott Gallery, Lancaster University, personal communication to the author, August, 2001; "The Irene Manton Prize," *Linnean Newsletter and Proceedings of the Linnean Society, London* 12, 3 (1996): 12–13; Leedale, G. F., "Emeritus Professor Irene Manton FRS," *University of Leeds Review* 31 (1988/1989): 275–277; Leedale, G. F., "Professor Irene Manton," *Independent* (13 June 1988); "The Manton Crater," *CAM* (Cambridge University News) (1993): 35; Nockles, P., archivist, John Rylands Library, University of Manchester, personal communication to the author, 2000; Preston, R. D., "Irene Manton," *Biographical Memoirs of Fellows of the Royal Society* 35 (1990): 249–261; "Professor Irene Manton," *Times* (3 June 1988); Shipway, M., archivist, University of Leeds, personal communication to the author, 31 March 1998; Walker, T. G., "Irene Manton (1904–1988)," *Watsonia* 17 (1988): 379–381; *Who Was Who, 1981–1990*, London: Adam and Charles Black, 1991.

Manton, Sidnie Milana (Mrs. Harding)
4 May 1902–2 January 1979
zoologist

Education: Froebel Educational Institute, London; St. Paul's Girls' School, London; Girton College, Cambridge, 1922–1925 and 1926–1928; Imperial College, London, 1925–1926; Ph.D., 1928; Sc.D., 1934.

Employment: demonstrator in comparative anatomy, University of Cambridge, 1927; Girton College, Cambridge, staff fellow, 1928–1935 and 1942–1945; director of studies, 1935–1942; research fellow, 1945–1948; King's College, London: visiting lecturer in zoology, 1943–1946; reader in zoology, 1949–1960.

Married: Dr. John Philip Harding, later keeper of zoology at the British Museum (Natural History), in 1937.

Sidnie Manton was a zoologist who worked out how the arthropods had evolved and analyzed their movement.

Manton was born in London, the elder daughter of George Manton, a dentist; Irene Manton was her younger sister. Manton became interested in natural history while at school. She excelled in zoology at the University of Cambridge, and held an Alfred Yarrow Scholarship at Imperial College, London, where she started her postgraduate studies on arthropods. In 1927 she became university demonstrator in comparative anatomy at the University of Cambridge and continued with her research. In 1928 she studied freshwater crustaceans in Tanzania and in 1929 traveled with an expedition to the Great Barrier Reef in Australia. Here she recorded information on corals, and her work included a series of drawings.

Manton held a series of posts at Girton College, Cambridge, between 1928 and 1948, and did research on the embryology, functional morphology, and evolution of arthropods. In 1933 she was president of the Cambridge Natural History Society. She was particularly interested in the Onychophora and was able to throw new light on the features of this group of unusual creatures, of which *Peripatus* is the best-known example. In 1931, with J. T. Saunders, she published *A Manual of Practical Vertebrate Morphology.*

From 1949 she was reader in zoology at King's College, London. Her research interests had shifted to crustacean feeding mechanisms. In 1950 she began to publish her findings on arthropod locomotion, including work on how many-legged arthropods such as centipedes and millipedes coordi-

nate their movements. She continued to publish these studies at intervals for over twenty years. *The Arthropoda: Habits, Functional Morphology and Evolution* (1977) brought together many strands of her research over the previous decades.

After she retired from King's College, she became an honorary fellow at Queen Mary College, London. She was also an honorary associate at the British Museum (Natural History). She was elected a fellow of the Royal Society in 1948. When her sister, Irene, was later elected to a fellowship as well, they became the only sisters to have both achieved this. Manton received the Linnean Society's gold medal for zoology in 1963 and the Zoological Society's Frink Medal in 1977. She was awarded an honorary doctorate by the University of Lund, Sweden. A keen breeder of cats, she published *Colourpoint, Himalayan and Longhair Cats* (1971), and in 1973 she founded the Colourpoint Society of Great Britain.

Bibliography: "Dr. Sidnie Manton," *Times* (4 January 1979): 12F; *Dictionary of National Biography, 1971–1980;* Oxford: Oxford University Press, 1986; Fryer, G., "Sidnie Milana Manton," *Biographical Memoirs of Fellows of the Royal Society* 26 (1980): 327–356.

Manzolini, Anna née Morandi
1716–1774
anatomist

Employment: University of Bologna, Italy: lecturer, professor of anatomy, 1760–1774.

Married: Giovanni Manzolini, professor of anatomy, in the mid-1730s.

Anna Manzolini was renowned throughout Europe as an expert on anatomy and a skilled wax modeler.

Manzolini first became interested in anatomy through the work of her husband, a professor of anatomy at the University of Bologna. Despite an aversion to dead specimens, Manzolini began making wax anatomical models. She continued this work while bringing up her six children, all born in a five-year period.

When Giovanni Manzolini was unable to hold classes because of illness, the university authorities agreed to let Anna Manzolini take over his lecturing duties. She was eventually given the post of professor of anatomy in 1760, when her husband died. In recognition of her skill as a wax modeler, she also had the title *modellatrice*. Her expertise in this area, combined with her teaching ability, brought her to the attention of the European rulers of the time. The Emperor Joseph II of Austria purchased several of her wax models, and Catherine II asked her to lecture in Russia. During this visit she was elected to the Russian Royal Scientific Society.

Such was her skill that her models were used as the basis for many subsequent models and were shown widely around Europe. In the course of her dissection work, she discovered the termination of the oblique muscle of the eye. Busts of her were placed in the University of Bologna's museum and in the Pantheon in Rome.

Bibliography: Ogilvie, M. B., *Women in Science: Antiquity through the Nineteenth Century,* New York: MIT Press, 1986.

Marcet, Jane née Haldimand
1769–28 June 1858
writer on chemistry, economics, and other subjects

Education: at home.
Married: Dr. Alexander Marcet, on 4 December 1799.

Jane Marcet wrote almost thirty books on topics ranging from chemistry to religion.

Marcet's father, Anthony Francis Haldimand, was a Swiss merchant and banker. He had an English wife, and they lived in London. Marcet was educated at home with her brothers and learned chemistry, biology, history, and Latin, plus art, music, dancing, and riding. Her mother died when Marcet was fifteen, and from then on Marcet was responsible for managing the household. Because her father usually entertained guests two or three times each week, she met many interesting people.

She broke off an engagement to a cousin in the navy; at the age of thirty, and potentially well-off, she was open to alternative offers of marriage. She wed Alexander Marcet, a physician in London, after a month's engagement. They lived in Russell Square and had four children.

Like her husband, Marcet was very interested in chemistry. Although she went to Humphrey Davy's lectures at the Royal Institution, she could not quite follow all the experiments. Certain that there must be a great many women with even less information than she had, she wrote *Conversations in Chemistry, Intended More Especially for the Female Sex*, published anonymously in 1806. Between 1806 and 1853 there were sixteen editions of the book in English and three in French. For each new edition, Marcet updated information where she could. When Michael Faraday was working as a bookseller's apprentice, he read one of the early editions; later, when he was a famous scientist, Marcet wrote to him for permission to include his latest work on electricity in her next edition.

Marcet wrote *Conversations on Political Economy* (1819), again anonymously. Her *Conversations on Natural Philosophy* (1819) explained basic science to young children. She also wrote books on astronomy, botany, mineralogy, and physics.

Marcet became so depressed after her husband died in 1822 that she stopped writing for two years. As she recovered she researched information for a religious book, *Conversations on the Evidences of Christianity* (1826), in which she sought to explain whether or not the Gospels were inspired by God; she felt that if they were, this would prove that Jesus Christ was divine. After writing this book, Marcet was able to get back to her other writing. Her books were both popular and influential, especially as introductions to the various subjects.

Bibliography: Bahar, S., "Jane Marcet and the Limits to Public Science," *British Journal for the History of Science* 34 (2001): 29–49; *Dictionary of National Biography, 1899,* vol. 36, Oxford: Oxford University Press, 1899; Ogilvie, M. B., *Women in Science: Antiquity through the Nineteenth Century*, New York: MIT Press, 1986; Polkinghorn, B., and D. L. Thomson, *Adam Smith's Daughters: Eight Prominent Women Economists from the Eighteenth Century to the Present*, Cheltenham, UK: Edward Elgar, 1998.

Markham, Beryl
née Clutterbuck
26 October 1902–3 August 1986
aviator and horse trainer

Education: European School, Nairobi; Miss Seccombe's School, Nairobi.

Employment: horse trainer, Soyambu Farm, Kenya, 1921–1924; freelance commercial pilot, Kenya, from 1933; horse trainer, Kenya, from 1950.

Married: Jock Purves, on 15 October 1919 (divorced); Mansfield Markham, in 1927 (divorced in 1942); Raoul Schumacher, in 1942 (divorced in 1960).

Beryl Markham was the first woman to fly across the Atlantic from east to west and the first person to fly alone in that direction nonstop. She did this on 4 September 1936, in a Vega Gull, with no radio.

Markham's family left England for Kenya in 1906. Her father, Captain Charles Clutterbuck, bought a farm and built a timber and flour mill; her mother returned to England later the same year with her son and later divorced her husband. Beryl Markham stayed in Kenya with her father, becoming an expert horsewoman and hunting in the Rongai Valley. When she was sixteen Captain Jock Purves, a Scottish international rugby player, paid her school fees on the condition that she marry him later. She was expelled from the school after a short time and was married on 15 October 1919.

The marriage broke up after six months. There was a severe drought in 1919, so Markham's father had to sell the farm. He went to Peru, but Markham stayed in Kenya, training horses and living at Soysambu, a farm owned by the third Baron Delamere, from 1921 to 1924. She was the first woman in Africa to be given a racehorse trainer's license, in 1920.

Beryl Markham (Bettmann/Corbis)

In 1927 she married Mansfield Markham, the son of a wealthy colliery owner but carried on an affair with Henry, Duke of Gloucester, when he visited Kenya. She returned with him to England as his mistress, taking up lodging in a suite at the Grosvenor Hotel. While there, she had a son, Gervase, in 1929. The timing was such, however, that Henry could not have been the baby's father; the boy was brought up by Markham's mother and Markham rarely saw him. She cited Henry as corespondent when she sought a divorce. In order to reduce the scandal, Queen Mary ordered Henry to give Markham a settlement of £15,000, which provided an annuity of £500 for her lifetime.

While in England, Markham learned to fly. Once she returned to Kenya, she gained a commercial pilot's license in 1933 and worked freelance as a pilot. She pioneered the observation of elephants and other wild animals from the air and piloted mail for East African Airways.

In 1936 she took off from Abingdon, near Oxford, in bad weather, and twenty-one hours and twenty-five minutes later landed in a bog in Nova Scotia, 100 yards from the ocean and out of fuel. Her east-west transatlantic flight was hailed in the United States as a great triumph.

She moved to the United States in 1939 and three years later married Raoul Schumacher, a ghostwriter. In 1942 she published *West with the Night*, a lyrical account of her life in Africa, ending with her flight across the Atlantic. The book received widespread acclaim at the time and was reprinted shortly before Markham's death.

Markham returned to Kenya alone in 1950 and trained horses there and in South Africa and Rhodesia. She won Kenya's top trainer award five times and the Kenya Derby six times. The Jockey Club of Kenya gave her a bungalow near the race course.

She died in 1986 of pneumonia, which developed after she broke her hip. A service of thanksgiving was held in London on 5 September 1986, the fiftieth anniversary of her transatlantic flight.

Bibliography: "Beryl Markham," obituary, *Times* (5 August 1986): 12G; *Dictionary of National Biography, 1986–1990*, Oxford: Oxford University Press, 1996; "Thanksgiving Service," *Times* (5 September 1986): 18A.

Marshall, Sheina Macalister
20 April 1896–7 April 1977
marine biologist

Education: at home, by governess; Rothesay Academy; St. Margaret's School, Polmont; University of Glasgow, 1914–1922; B.Sc. with distinction, 1919; D.Sc., 1934.
Employment: researcher, Scottish Marine Biological Association Laboratory, 1922–1977.

Sheina Marshall was a marine biologist who studied planktonic marine crustaceans. She was particularly known for her work with A. P. Orr on the feeding mechanisms and habits of the copepod *Calanus*, an important food of the herring.

Marshall was born in Rothesay on the island of Bute, off the west coast of Scotland,

the second of three daughters. Her father, a general practitioner, founded the Buteshire Natural History Society, and Marshall showed a keen interest in science during her childhood.

Marshall began her studies at the University of Glasgow in 1914. After completing her first year, she decided to take a year off to work in her uncle's small factory in Balloch, Scotland, at which radium was used to produce luminous clock faces and instrument dials for the military. She then returned to the University of Glasgow, studying physiology, zoology, and botany, and graduated in 1919. She continued to study at the university for three years under a Carnegie Fellowship.

In 1922 she joined the staff of the Scottish Marine Biological Association (SMBA) at their Millport Laboratory on a small island off the west coast of Scotland. At Millport she began work on what was to be her major research interest, the feeding mechanism and habits of copepods, especially *Calanus* spp. In 1924 she published "The Food of *Calanus finmarchicus* during 1923" (*Journal of the Marine Biological Association UK* (12: 473–479), and over the next fifty years she wrote or cowrote numerous papers in the same field.

In 1924 Andrew Picken Orr was appointed as a biochemical assistant at Millport and began surveying the physical conditions of the sea in the area. He and Marshall soon started to work together, and over the years they developed a very productive working relationship. During the mid-1920s they did a detailed study of the conditions in one part of Loch Striven in order to identify the physical and chemical conditions that could account for differences in the numbers and types of organisms they had observed in various areas. This was an important survey in that it was the first to make use of a wide range of methods of analysis. Marshall and Orr were also the first to experiment with cultured diatoms (a type of algae) suspended in the sea. They used blackened and clear bottles to investigate the effects of light at different depths.

In 1927 Marshall and Orr took eighteen months' leave of absence to join the Great Barrier Reef expedition organized by C. M.

Yonge. They were based on the Low Isles of the Queensland Coast, where they investigated the physical and chemical conditions in the tropical seawater and studied microplankton. They compared these findings with what was known about conditions in temperate waters. Marshall also studied other types of microorganisms, and she and Orr analyzed sediments from the reef. Marshall investigated the oxygen production of coral planulae (the planktonic larvae), the first time this had been done.

When she came back to Millport, Marshall resumed her work on copepods. With Orr and A. G. Nicholls, she surveyed the seasonal characteristics of the *Calanus* population in Loch Striven. In 1934 and 1935 the three scientists also looked at the development of herring and spent a considerable time tracking the larvae north, from the sea off the Isle of Arran to Loch Fyne.

During World War II, Marshall carried out research for the government on the production of agar gel from seaweed. Marshall undertook chemical testing to identify the best seaweed for agar production, as well as survey work to find which areas of the coast could be used for seaweed harvesting. She organized volunteers to gather the seaweed and devised an efficient method of transporting it.

In 1942 Marshall, together with Orr, began working with scientists from the University of Edinburgh on the effects of commercial fertilizers on plankton, fish, and plant and animal organisms on the bed of Loch Craiglin, part of Loch Sween in Inverness. The numbers and characteristics of the various species were recorded after nitrogen and phosphorus fertilizers had been added. With Orr, F. Gross, J. E. G. Raymond, Marshall published the first results of the experiment in 1944 in *Nature (London)* (153: 483–485).

After the war Marshall and Orr continued to investigate the biology of *Calanus*. With J. P. Harding they studied its egg production and feeding under different conditions and investigated the role of phosphorus in the diet, showing that *Calanus* required phosphorus for egg production. In 1955 Marshall and Orr published *The Biology of a Marine Copepod.* After Orr's death in 1962, Marshall contin-

ued to publish papers based on their research together. A children's book the two scientists had cowritten, *Seashores,* appeared in 1965. The following year a collection of papers by various scientists, *Some Contemporary Studies in Marine Science* (ed. H. Barnes), was published in honor of Marshall and Orr. Marshall subsequently prepared for publication the Buckland Lectures Orr had delivered in 1957; they appeared as *The Fertile Sea* in 1969.

In 1965 Marshall began to work with E. D. S. Corner from the Marine Biological Association laboratory in Plymouth. They investigated nitrogen excretion by *Calanus* under different conditions, work that in turn led to a study of phosphorus assimilation, an area in which Marshall already had a great deal of experience. In 1970–1971 Marshall was in La Jolla, California. She had planned to study the feeding mechanism in copepods using holographic techniques, but because of technical problems, together with the death of the leader of the research team, she was unable to do so; instead she spent her time in California preparing a comprehensive account of the respiration and feeding of zooplankton. This was published in 1973.

On her return to Britain, Marshall resumed her work with Corner on *Calanus*. They investigated the hypothesis that these organisms must become carnivorous during the winter months, since sources of plant material would be insufficient to sustain them. The study was completed in 1973; the resulting paper, published in 1974, was Marshall's last scientific publication.

The Royal Society of Edinburgh elected her a fellow in 1949 and awarded her the Neill Prize in 1971. She was elected a fellow of the Royal Society in 1963 and made an officer of the Order of the British Empire (OBE) in 1966. In recognition of her research achievements and continuing contribution to marine biology, the Scottish Marine Biological Association made her its first honorary fellow. The university of Uppsala, Sweden, awarded her an honorary degree on its 500th anniversary.

Bibliography: Russell, F., "Sheina Macalister Marshall," *Biographical Memoirs of Fellows of the Royal Society* 24 (1978): 369–389.

Mary, Countess of Rosse
née Field
21 July 1813–1885
photographer

Education: at home.

Married: William Parsons, an astronomer and later third earl of Rosse, on 14 July 1836.

Mary, Countess of Rosse, was the first person to be awarded the Silver Medal from the Photographic Society of Ireland, in 1859, for the best paper negative. She was one of the first women to join the Dublin Photographic Society, in 1856.

Mary, Countess of Rosse was born at Heaton Hall, near Bradford. After her marriage to William Parsons, an astronomer, she moved to Birr Castle, in County Offaly, Ireland. They set up a darkroom at the castle in June 1842 (the earliest known darkroom in the world), and the countess of Rosse became seriously interested in photography over the next decade. Meanwhile, she financed the designing and building of a huge telescope, known as "the Leviathan of Parsonstown," organized by her husband. The final mirror was 6 feet in diameter, and the telescope tube was 57 feet long. From 1845, when the telescope was first used, until 1917, it was the largest reflecting telescope in the world. With it her husband discovered the Whirlpool Nebula in 1845 and by 1850 had seen the spiral structure of some fourteen galaxies. The countess took many photographs of the telescope, which were exhibited at the first show of the Photographic Society in 1854, at the request of famous photographer William Fox Talbot.

During the same period that William and Mary were practicing their astronomy and photography, Ireland suffered the great potato famine. To provide work for many of the unemployed men living in the area, the countess decided to redesign the demesne at Birr Castle. She designed the buildings herself and made scale models using visiting cards. She paid for the employment of 500 men on the project. The peat forge that had been used for the telescope was used to make the keep gate.

In 1870 Mary, Countess of Rosse moved to London, as both her husband and her great friend Mary Ward had died. Of her eleven children, only four lived to adulthood; her son Charles was the inventor of the steam turbine engine. In the church at Heaton, there is a memorial window to her, designed by C. E. Kemp. Her photographs of her husband's telescope were instrumental when the seventh Earl of Rosse, under the auspices of the Birr Scientific Heritage Foundation, rebuilt the telescope tube and its motion system in 1997. Staff at the Optical Sciences Laboratory at University College in London restored the telescope to full working order in 1999, and some of the astronomers attending the 2000 International Astronomy Congress flew from Manchester to Dublin to see it.

Bibliography: Barry, S., "Photographs from the Birr Darkroom," in *Stars, Shells, and Bluebells,* edited by M. Mulvihill and P. Deevy, Dublin: Women in Technology and Science (WITS), 1998; Brooks, David, Optical Science Laboratory, University College, London, personal communication to the author, 2000; Davison, D. H., *Impressions of an Irish Countess: The Photography of Mary, Countess of Rosse, 1813–1885,* Dublin: Birr Scientific Heritage Foundation, 1989; Glass, I. S., *Victorian Telescope Makers: The Lives and Letters of Thomas and Howard Grubb,* Bristol: Institute of Physics Publishing, 1997; McKenna-Lawlor, S., *Whatever Shines Should Be Observed: Quicquid Nited Notandum,* Blackrock, Dublin: Samton, 1998; Parsons, C., comp., *The Scientific Papers of William Parsons, Third Earl of Rosse, 1800–1867,* London: Percy Lund, Humphries and Co., 1926.

Massy, Annie Letitia
1867–16 April 1931
marine biologist

Education: self-educated.

Employment: biologist, Fisheries Division, Department of Agriculture and Technical Instruction, Dublin, 1901–1931.

Annie Massy was an international expert on mollusks, with a particular interest in cephalopods (squids).

Massy collected shells from an early age, first publishing her results in the *Irish Naturalist* in June 1899. She was a member of the Conchological Society of Great Britain and Ireland. In 1907 her first paper on cephalopods was published in the *Annals and Magazine of Natural History* (where she was referred to as "Mr. A. L. Massy," as she only gave her initials). A cephalopod, *Cirroteuthis (Cirroteuthopsis) massyae* Grimpe was named after her. The type specimen is in the Natural History Museum in Dublin.

Though she collected specimens only locally, while she was working in the Fisheries Division she identified cephalopods and other mollusks sent in from several expeditions, such as those of the fisheries cruiser *Helga* (1901–1907), the British Antarctic expedition, with the *Terra Nova* (1910), and the SS *Pieter Faure* (1923), around South African coasts. Several museums, such as the Indian Museum and the Natal Museum, sent specimens for her to describe and identify. The results of a survey of the Irish trawling grounds enabled her to publish accounts of the cephalopods, pteropoda, heteropoda, and holothurians found in Irish coastal waters.

Massy was also a keen amateur ornithologist. In 1885 she was the first to record redstarts nesting in Ireland, at Powerscourt Deer Park. In 1904 she became one of the initial members of the Irish Society for the Protection of Birds (ISPB, now the Irish Wildbird Conservancy) and published notes of her observations of local birds. She became the society's secretary in 1926. She worked hard for bird protection, especially to ensure the passage of the Wild Birds Protection Act in 1930.

She died before retirement, aged sixty-four, with a reputation as a careful, critical, and hardworking zoologist.

Bibliography: Byrne, A., "Bringing a Shy Biologist out of Her Shell," in *Stars, Shells and Bluebells*, edited by M. Mulvihill and P. Deevy, Dublin: Women in Science and Technology (WITS), 1997; "Miss Anne L. Massy," *Nature* (11 July 1931): 59.

May, Valerie
c. 1915–
phycologist

Education: University of Sydney; B.Sc., 1936; M.Sc., 1939.

Employment: research work, Commonwealth Scientific Industrial Research Organisation (CSIRO) Fisheries Division, Cronulla, from 1940; Herbarium of New South Wales: part-time volunteer work, honorary custodian of cryptograms (later renamed honorary phycologist), 1960–1986.

Married: Ern Jones, later a senior staff member of the Faculty of Dentistry, University of Sydney, in 1940.

Valerie May did research on the algae of Australia and studied environmental influences on algal populations.

May originally intended to focus on chemistry at the University of Sydney but decided to change her main subject after taking botany as an extra course. She won all the botany prizes and graduated in 1936 with first-class honors. Her chief area of interest was algae, and although it appeared that employment opportunities would be limited in this field, May was determined to make it her career. Despite the minimal level of specialist guidance at the university at that time, she continued her studies and was awarded an M.Sc. The papers she published during this period were important in that they collated data from a range of previously published literature, making the information more accessible to others interested in the subject.

May continued her phycological research with various scholarships, although she found she was expected to work on other projects, according to the priorities of the department at any one time. On her marriage to Ern Jones in 1940, she was told that her scholarship would not be renewed, so she took a post with CSIRO. World War II had led to a need for supplies of agar for use in medicines and foods, and May worked long hours collecting and cataloguing specimens of seaweed. After the war the industry declined, though May was able to publish a number of papers relating to her work on algae during this time.

She turned her attention to a large collection of algae that had been bequeathed to Australia by A.H.S. Lucas. She arranged for it to be moved from the CSIRO offices in Canberra to the National Herbarium of New South Wales, where it could be accessed more easily by researchers. May herself had used the resources of the National Herbarium of New South Wales during her studies and while working for CSIRO. She had worked there voluntarily while bringing up her four children, and in 1960 she was made honorary custodian of cryptograms, a post that offered no job security and little financial benefit; she held it until 1986. The post had originally been intended to offer limited resources to an individual botanist, though May devoted much time and energy to the role, above and beyond the job's requirements. The initial focus was marine algae, particularly the Rhodophyta (red seaweeds), but her later research concerned freshwater environments. Valerie undertook an investigation into the deaths of farm stock caused by the Cyanobacteria (blue-green algae) in the water. This work formed the basis of a series of published papers and a number of contributions to international conferences.

Throughout her career, May worked with many scientists from other disciplines, such as veterinarians, ecologists, and statisticians. She became a recognized expert in the area of toxic algae and water quality and was consulted by a variety of individuals and organizations on a wide range of topics relating to algae. Her later work focused on environmental influences affecting algae, including the effects of dams and outflows.

May authored and coauthored a large number of articles published in journals mainly in Australia. She was made an honorary research associate of the Royal Botanic Gardens, Sydney, in 1987.

Bibliography: King, R. J., and B. G. Briggs, "Valerie May—Fifty Years of Phycology," *Telopea* 3, 2 (1988): 273–279.

Mee, Margaret Ursula
née Brown
May 1909–30 November 1988
botanical artist, conservationist

Education: art school, Watford; St. Martin's School of Art, 1945–1947; Camberwell School of Art, London, 1947–1950.
Employment: draftswoman in aircraft factory; art teacher, St. Paul's School, São Paulo, Brazil, from 1952; São Paulo Botanical Institute, from 1960–1968.
Married: Greville Mee, a commercial artist.

Margaret Mee, a botanical artist noted for her work on the plants of the Amazon, became involved in the conservation of the rainforests.

Mee was born in Chesham, Buckinghamshire. In her twenties she was a trades unionist and represented the Union of Sign, Glass, and Ticket Writers at the trades union congress in Norwich in 1937. After working as a draftswoman in an aircraft factory in World War II, she studied art at St. Martin's School of Art and at Camberwell, where she was taught by Victor Pasmore. At Camberwell she met Greville Mee, her future husband, who became a commercial artist.

In 1952 the couple traveled to São Paulo to look after Mee's sister. Margaret Mee taught art, while Greville Mee set up a studio. They both became interested in the Brazilian flora, and Margaret Mee in particular applied her artistic skills to recording coastal rainforest species.

Her first journey to Amazonia was in 1956, and in 1958 her work was exhibited at the Botanical Institute in São Paulo and in Rio de Janeiro. In 1960 her rainforest paintings were shown in London, and she received the Royal Horticultural Society's Grenfell Medal. From 1960 to 1965 Margaret made a number of journeys to the northeast of Brazil, where she recorded examples of bromeliads for Dr. Lyman B. Smith, an expert on these plants. Three new species of bromeliads were named after her. In 1967 she became the first woman explorer to climb the south side of Brazil's highest peak, the Pico de Nebline. In the same year there was an exhibition of her work at the Tryon Gallery in London. Thirty-two of her paintings were published in *Flowers of the Brazilian Forests* (1968), an expensive folio edition of 400 copies.

In 1971–1972 Mee made two journeys to an area south of the main part of the Amazon, funded by a Guggenheim Fellowship. She discovered several new species, some of which (*Aechmea meeana* and *Aechmea polyantha*) are known to the outside world only through her records of them. She decided never to sell any of her original first paintings of individual species, insisting that these be preserved as records. Initially she painted solitary plants, using gouache, but later she filled in the background plants as well. She included all the plants' distinguishing features, so that their identification is indisputable.

In 1980 there was an exhibition of her paintings of the flowers of the Amazon at the Natural History Museum. Mee made fifteen major journeys to the Amazon, many on her own, often in dangerous conditions. Over the years she became increasingly concerned about the disappearance of Brazil's rainforest habitats because of both the flora and the people that lived there. On her last visit to the Amazon, during which she was accompanied by well-known explorer Tony Morrison, she recorded the Amazon moonflower, *Selenicereus wittii*, in bloom, an event that occurs on just one night once a year. She had seen the plant on previous journeys but had never before been able to paint it.

She died in a road accident in England. Her diaries, published as *Margaret Mee: In Search of the Flowers of the Amazon Forests* (1988), came out shortly before her death, edited by Tony Morrison. Mee had been made a Member of the Order of the British Empire (MBE) in 1975 and was elected a fellow of the Linnean Society in 1986. As well as allowing for the preservation of her collection at the Royal Botanic Gardens, Kew, the Margaret Mee Amazon Trust, established shortly before her death, provides funding for young botanists from Brazil to study in Britain, especially in relation to Amazonia.

A service to celebrate her life was held at St. Anne's church in Kew on 16 January 1989. In 1997 an exhibition of eighty-five of her paintings was held at the Houston, Texas, Museum of Natural Science. She was awarded the Brazilian decoration of the Order of the Southern Cross for her paintings and her work with the Ameridian peoples of the Amazon.

Bibliography: Archivist, Library at Kew Gardens, personal communication to the author, August 1999; Buckman, D., *Dictionary of Artists in Britain since 1945*, Bristol: Art Dictionaries, 1988; "Margaret Mee," *Times* (3 December 1988): 12F; Massingberd, H., ed., *Daily Telegraph Book of Obituaries: A Celebration of Eccentric Lives*, London: Macmillan, 1995; Mee, M., "Plant Hunting," *Times* (20 November 1988): 98A; Morrison, T., "Margaret Mee," *Independent* (12 December 1988); Stiff, R., "Return to the Amazon" [exhibition program], London: Her Majesty's Stationery Office, 1996.

Meitner, Lise
7 November 1878–27 October 1968
nuclear physicist

Education: private tuition, 1899–1901; University of Vienna, 1901–1905; Ph.D., 1905; University of Berlin, 1907–1912.

Employment: Kaiser-Wilhelm Institut für Chemie, Berlin; research, 1912–1918; head of Physics Department, 1918–1938; University of Berlin: assistant to Max Planck, 1912–1915; teacher, from 1922; extraordinary professor, from 1926; X-ray nurse, Austrian Army, 1916–1918; research, Nobel Institute for Experimental Physics, Stockholm, 1938–1947; research, Swedish Atomic Energy Committee, Royal Institute for Technology, Stockholm, from 1947; research, Royal Academy for Engineering Sciences, Stockholm, until 1960.

Lise Meitner, known as the "German Madame Curie," carried out pioneering research in nuclear fission. In 1926 she was the first woman to become a professor of physics in Germany.

Meitner was born in Vienna, Austria, the third of eight children. Her father was a

Lise Meitner (Corbis)

Hahn, a young chemist who was working on the chemistry of radioactivity. He was looking for a physicist to work with him, and Meitner was looking for a laboratory in which to carry out experiments related to her studies with Planck. They decided to work together. Because she was a woman, however, Meitner was not allowed to work at the Chemical Institute, where Hahn was based, so the two found an old carpenter's workshop that could be equipped for her experiments. In 1909 the rules governing women's education were changed, and Meitner was able to carry out experiments at the Chemical Institute itself.

Meitner and Hahn continued to work together until World War I, Hahn's area of interest being the discovery of new elements and Meitner's concerned the analysis of their different radiations. Although their research was important, resulting in a number of published papers, they were working in a new area and consequently had to base their research and its conclusions on inaccurate assumptions.

Meitner began working as an assistant to Max Planck in 1912, and in the same year she joined the new Kaiser-Wilhelm Institut für Chemie. During World War I she worked as a volunteer X-ray nurse in an Austro-Hungarian hospital; Hahn did active military service. The two were sometimes able to meet in Berlin during periods of leave, and they continued their research sporadically throughout the war. In 1918 they announced their discovery of protactinium, the precursor of actinium. In the same year Meitner became head of the Physics Department at the Kaiser-Wilhelm Institut, and she continued to work on protactinium until the postwar situation in Germany had stabilized.

In 1922 she was made a docent (teacher/ lecturer) at the University of Berlin; her inaugural lecture was on cosmic physics, which the press reported as "cosmetic physics." In the same year she was also able to start her own research on the relationships between beta and gamma rays. Throughout the 1920s there were rapid developments in nuclear physics, with scientists regularly announcing new theories and

lawyer, her mother a pianist. The family was of Jewish origin, though the children were brought up as Protestants. Meitner studied French so that she would be able to work as a teacher in girls' finishing schools, but her true interest was physics.

After two years of private tuition, she took the entrance exam for the University of Vienna and was admitted in 1901. Female students were something of a novelty, and though some of the other students were hostile, Meitner received much support from her tutors. Her doctoral dissertation in 1905 dealt with heat conduction in nonhomogeneous materials. After completing her studies, she remained in Vienna and began to take an interest in radioactivity. She wrote to Marie Curie to ask if she could work in her laboratory but was refused. Meitner planned to work in theoretical physics, and her father agreed to give her some financial support to enable her to study with Max Planck at the University of Berlin. In 1907 she traveled to Berlin, where she met Otto findings. Meitner both tested these new theories and put forward her own. She was keen to make use of new instruments, such as Wilson's cloud chamber and the Geiger-Müller counter. The developments in nuclear physics continued apace through the 1930s; the neutron was discovered in 1932, the positron in 1933, and artificial radioactivity in 1934, and Meitner and her colleagues produced numerous papers in order to keep up with events.

In 1934 she began working with Hahn on Enrico Fermi's findings that elements bombarded with neutrons in most cases formed a heavier isotope of the element. Fermi's experiments with uranium had given different results, though the substances produced were still assumed to be heavier isotopes. Ida Noddack had put forward the theory that the unusual results were due to the splitting of the uranium atom, but her work was dismissed or ignored. Over the next few years, Meitner and Hahn carried out their own experiments, struggling to explain the production of lighter elements following the bombardment of uranium.

Meanwhile, with the rise to power of Hitler, Meitner had to be cautious because of her Jewish origins. By 1938 she was in an especially vulnerable position, since the German occupation of Austria rendered her Austrian nationality effectively worthless and the German government had banned all university teachers from leaving Germany. She secretly left for the Netherlands and after a short stay there was able to join the physicist Niels Bohr and his wife in Denmark. Although there were good research facilities there, she decided to take up a post at the new Nobel Institute for Physics in Stockholm, where the first cyclotron (a machine for splitting atoms) on mainland Europe was being built.

Meitner continued to follow developments in nuclear physics. Hahn and his colleague Fritz Strassmann were still experimenting with uranium in Germany and kept Meitner informed of their results. Her nephew, Otto Frisch, was a physicist working in Copenhagen, and she invited him to spend Christmas with her in Sweden in 1938. They discussed Hahn and Strassmann's findings and formulated the theory of nuclear fission to explain the division of the uranium nucleus and the resultant massive release of energy. They published the theory in *Nature* (143 [1939]: 239).

Meitner continued to analyze the products of uranium bombardment, and her work eventually led others to the discovery of plutonium, used in the first atomic bomb. She turned down an invitation to work on the development of the bomb and hoped against hope that the project would not succeed. After the war she worked on the unsymmetrical nature of the products of nuclear fission in uranium. This was her last contribution to developments in nuclear fission.

She spent time as a visiting professor at the Catholic University, Washington, D.C., in 1946 and retired from the Nobel Institute the following year. She continued to work in Stockholm, first at the Royal Institute for Technology, under the auspices of the Swedish Atomic Energy Committee, and later at the Royal Academy for Engineering Sciences, where an experimental nuclear reactor was being constructed. She remained at the academy until 1960, carrying out research, supervising the research of others, and discussing physics problems. She retired to England to be near relatives, including her nephew Otto Frisch, and was active for several years, traveling to visit friends and delivering and attending lectures. She died in a nursing home in Cambridge, only days before her ninetieth birthday.

Meitner was awarded honorary doctorates from the University of Stockholm and several institutions in the United States. She was a member of the science academies of a number of European cities and elected a foreign member of the Royal Society in 1955. She received the Leibnitz Medal (Berlin Academy of Sciences, 1924), the Planck Medal (1949, German Physical Society, joint award with Hahn), and the Enrico Fermi Prize (1965, U.S. Atomic Energy Commission, joint award with Hahn and Strassmann). Although Hahn won a Nobel prize in 1944 for his work on nuclear fission, Meitner's vital contribution was not recognized at the time. Element 109 is named meitnerium in her memory. Some of Lise Meitner's letters are at the Churchill Archives Centre in Cambridge.

Bibliography: Frisch, O. R., "Lise Meitner," *Biographical Memoirs of Fellows of the Royal Society* 16 (1970): 405–420; Kerner, C., *Lise, Atomphysikerin: Der Lebensgeschichte der Lise Meitner,* Basel: Beltz Verlag, 1986; Lemmerich, J., comp. *Lise Meitner—Max von Laue: Briefwechsel, 1938–1948,* Berlin: EPS Verlag, 1998; "Professor Dr Lise Meitner," *Times* (28 October 1968): Ramsey, K. L., "Women of the Manhattan Project," available at www:manhattanproject/a-s.clayton.edu; Rayner-Canham, M. F., *Women in Chemistry,* Washington, D.C.: American Chemical Society, 1998; Sime, R. L., *Lise Meitner: A Life in Physics,* Berkeley: University of California Press, 1996.

Mellanby, Helen
7 June 1911–
zoologist

Education: University College, London; B.Sc. with honors, 1931; Ph.D., 1937; Medical School, University of Sheffield, 1939–1949; M.B., Ch.B., 1944; M.D., 1949.

Employment: honorary research assistant, University of Sheffield, Department of Zoology, Faculty of Medicine, 1937–1938; associate worker, Sorby Research Institute, Sheffield, 1939–1940; clinical assistant, Sheffield Children's Hospital; Medical Research Council (MRC), Mill Hill, London, 1940–1953; Postgraduate Medical School, University of London, 1953–.

Married: Dr. Kenneth Mellanby.

Helen Mellanby wrote *Animal Life in Fresh Water: A Guide to British Fresh-water Invertebrates* (1938), just as ecology was beginning to be part of most biology courses.

Mellanby did postgraduate work in zoology at University College, London, and studied reproduction in the tsetse fly. Her *Animal Life in Fresh Water,* for which she did most of the illustrations herself, was a great help to students in identifying freshwater invertebrates.

She moved to Sheffield with her husband and helped on a part-time or honorary basis in the Zoology Department before enrolling at the Medical School in Sheffield and qualifying in medicine.

While Mellanby was employed at the MRC at Mill Hill most of the time, she was based in the Nutrition Building. She worked on the development of the enamel of teeth, the effects of maternal vitamin deficiency, and the relationships between dental caries and nutrition. During the 1947 influenza outbreak, she worked in the Bacteriology and Virology Department, conducting some of the trials of the influenza vaccine.

Bibliography: Aspden, L., curator of special collections and archives, University of Sheffield, personal communication to the author, January 2000; Davison, C., operational manager, Student Services, School of Medicine, University of Sheffield, personal communication to the author, August 2000; Mojonier, L., Document Management Services, Medical Research Council, Public Record Office, Kew, London, personal communication to the author, 2000.

Mellanby, Lady May
née Tweedy
1 May 1882–5 March 1978
dental researcher

Education: Hampstead High School; Bromley High School; Girton College, Cambridge, 1902–1906, Sc.D.

Employment: research scholar and lecturer, Bedford College, University of London, 1906–1914; lecturer in physiology, Chelsea and Battersea Polytechnics, 1914–1918; dental research for Medical Research Council, from 1918.

Married: Sir Edward Mellanby, a lecturer in physiology at Kings College for Women, in 1914. He died in 1955.

Lady May Mellanby did considerable research on the structure of teeth and dental caries.

Mellanby was born in London, where her father was a shipowner and businessman who was developing the oil industry in Russia, where the family spent some time. After studying at Girton College, she was did research and lectured at Bedford College. During World War I she continued lecturing at Chelsea and Battersea Polytechnics, and in 1918 she began carrying out dental research for the Medical Research Council (MRC). In their report for 1918, she and her husband were the first to announce that the calcification of the dental enamel needed a fat-soluble vitamin. She was an honorary lecturer in the Department of Dentistry at Sheffield University in 1921 while her husband was a professor of pharmacology there.

Between 1929 and 1934 she published *Diet and the Teeth: An Experimental Study* as part of the Medical Research Council Special Report series (numbers 140, 153, and 191). As a result of this work, a practical dietetic trial was set up in 1926, using children in institutions in Birmingham, some of whom were given a vitamin D supplement and a control group who were not. The results were published in 1936. Mellanby did research in Germany between 1934 and 1938 on the relationship between the quality of bread and the amount of dental caries.

She lectured on dental research around the world, including addresses to scientific meetings in France, South Africa, the United States, Hungary, and Germany. She published papers in the *British Medical Journal, The Lancet,* the *British Dental Journal,* and several foreign journals.

As well as doing research, she served on a number of committees, including the Dental Disease Committee of the Medical Research Council and the Empire Marketing Board Research Grants Committee. When her husband became secretary of the Medical Research Council, Mellanby supported him in his administrative role so that he could continue with his own scientific research. She also helped him with his research and was said to be ideally equipped to halve his troubles and double his joys.

Lady May Mellanby was awarded honorary doctorates from the Universities of Sheffield (1933) and Liverpool (1934). In 1935–1936 she and her husband were Charles Mickle Fellows at the University of Toronto. She was made an honorary fellow of Girton College in 1958 and an honorary member of the International Association for Dental Research. In 1975 she was given the association's Science Award.

Bibliography: Bishop, A., "Obituaries of Past Fellows," *Girton Newsletter* (1978): 31; *Girton College Register 1869–1946,* vol. 1, Cambridge: Girton College, 1948; Marsh, N., *The History of Queen Elizabeth College,* London: King's College, 1986; Mojonier, L., Document Management Services, Medical Research Council, Public Record Office, Kew, London, personal communication to the author, 2000; Thomson, L., *Half a Century of Medical Research,* vol. 2; *Who Was Who, 1971–1980,* London: Adam and Charles Black, 1981.

Merian, Maria Sibylla
1647–1717
entomologist, natural history artist, writer

Education: apprenticed to Jacob Marell and Abraham Mignon.
Married: Johann Graff in 1665 (divorced in 1692).

Maria Merian was one of the first naturalists to investigate and illustrate the life cycles of European butterflies and some of those in Surinam, in tropical South America.

Merian was born in Frankfurt-am-Main. Her father was an artist and engraver. He died when she was three, and at age thirteen Merian was apprenticed informally to Jacob Marell, her stepfather, a member of the painters' guild. His apprentice, Abraham Mignon, also taught her. Merian specialized in studies of insects. Most of her drawings were engraved on copperplates and the prints hand colored.

When she married, she moved to Nuremberg and sold silks, satins, and linens handpainted with flower designs. Merian developed a type of watercolor for fabrics that could be washed. She had several women apprentices and assistants to help with the printing and coloring.

The first book she published (under her married name) was *Der Raupen wunderbare Verwandlung und sonderbare Blumen Nahrung* (The wonderful metamorphosis of caterpillars and the plants they eat) (1683). The book had fifty copperplates, each illustrating the life cycle of a named butterfly. *Neues Blumenbuch* (New book of flowers) (1680) used a new printing technique she had developed that enabled her to produce two prints each time, both of which were softer than a color plate. (A facsimile edition was published in 1999 using the copy in the state library of Saxony in Dresden. Volume 1 has thirty-six color plates, and volume 2 has comments in English and German, with a contribution by Thomas Buerger.)

In 1682 Merian and her daughters returned to Frankfurt to look after her widowed mother. She left her husband a few years later and reverted to her maiden name. She and her daughters moved to the experimental religious community of the Labadists in west Friesland, where they stayed for a decade. After the community broke up in 1688, Merian returned to Frankfurt, then moved to Amsterdam when her mother died in 1691.

In the Netherlands Merian continued to trade in fabrics and paints as she had done before, but she was also asked to illustrate several books on natural history, such as G. E. Rumphius, *D'Amboinsche Rariteitkamer* (The Ambonese Curiosity Cabinet, 1705).

In 1699 Merian and her daughter Dorothea traveled to the Dutch colony of Surinam; they spent two years collecting, studying, and drawing plants and animals, especially insects. She would have liked to stay longer but was badly affected by malaria and so returned to Amsterdam.

She sold specimens to refund her costs and worked on the illustrations and text for *Metamorphosis insectorum Surinamensiam* (1705), a beautiful book but expensive to produce; Merian sold subscriptions in advance.

Merian had six plants, nine butterflies, and two beetles named after her.

Bibliography: Brough, C., librarian, Royal Botanic Gardens, Kew, personal communication to the author, June 2001; Kaden, V., *Victoria and Albert Museum: The Illustration of Plants and Gardens, 1500–1850*, London: Her Majesty's Stationery Office, 1982; Rucker, E., and W. T. Stearn, *Maria Sibylla Merian in Surinam*, London: Pion, 1982; Schiebinger, L., *The Mind Has No Sex?* Cambridge: Harvard University Press, 1991; Wettengl, K., ed., *Maria Sibylla Merian, 1647–1717; Kuensterlehrin und Naturforscherin*, Ostfilder-Ruit: Gerd Hatje, 1997.

Millis, Nancy Fannie
10 April 1922–
microbiologist

Education: business college, Melbourne; University of Melbourne, agricultural science; MAg.Sc., 1946; M.Sc., 1948; University of Bristol, Ph.D., 1952.

Employment: bookkeeper, custom agent's office, Melbourne; Commonwealth Scientific Industrial Research Organisation (CSIRO) Forest Products Division, part time; Microbiology Department, University of Melbourne: lecturer, from 1952; reader, from 1968; professor of microbiology, 1982–1987.

Nancy Millis was one of the first two women to be elected a fellow of the Australian Academy of Technological Sciences and Engineering.

After leaving school Millis could not afford to go on to university, so she took a bookkeeping course and found a job. But she decided she would study to matriculate and go to university, so she worked part time in the Forest Products Division of CSIRO. She eventually studied agricultural science at the University of Melbourne.

In 1946 Millis went to New Guinea to work but had to return home because of her health. When she had recovered, she applied for a Boots Scholarship and went to the University of Bristol to study for her Ph.D. in fermentation.

On coming back to Australia, she worked in the Department of Microbiology at the University of Melbourne. In 1954–1955 she took a leave to study at the Biochemistry Department of the University of Wisconsin. During 1963 she worked on aspects of fermentation at the Institute of Applied Microbiology at the University of Tokyo. While there she coauthored the groundbreaking *Biochemical Engineering* (1965) with an American, Arthur Humphrey, and Shuichi Aiba, the head of the department.

Millis became interested in environmental problems, especially water treatment and pollution control. She was a member of the food technology group of the Australian Academy of Sciences. In 1980 she visited China to advise on food production and food processing. She was president of the Australian Society for Microbiology from 1978 to 1980.

She is well known to the Australian public through her work on the genetic engineering advisory committee and her appearances on television and radio. She was made a Member of the Order of the British Empire (MBE) in 1977, awarded an honorary doctorate by the University of Melbourne in 1988 for her outstanding academic record, and made a Companion of the Order of Australia in 1990.

Bibliography: Allen, N., "Test Tubes and White Jackets: The Careers of Two Australian Women Scientists" [Nancy Millis and Beryl Nashar], *Journal of Australian Studies* 52 (1997): 126–137; *Who's Who in Australasia and the Far East*, second edition, Cambridge: Melrose Press, 1991.

Milner, Marion
1 February 1900–29 May 1998
psychoanalyst, author

Education: B.Sc. psychology and physiology, London University; holder of a Laura Spelman Rockefeller Memorial Fellowship, United States, 1927–1929; trained as psychoanalyst, 1940.

Employment: investigator, National Institute of Industrial Psychology; research funded by the Girls' Public Day School Trust on "problem" pupils, 1935–1938; psychoanalytic counselor.

Married: Dennis Milner, inventor and writer. He died in 1954.

Marion Milner initially worked as a psychologist but trained as a psychoanalyst in 1940 and from then on worked in this field. Her first book, *A Life of One's Own* (1934), published under the pseudonym "Joanna Field," was concerned with her own self-analysis, an unusual start.

Milner initially worked as an industrial psychologist. In 1934 the headmistresses of the twenty-five schools belonging to the Girls' Public Day School Trust (GPDST) asked her to conduct a study at the schools. The GPDST schools had been set up in 1872 and by 1934 had a total of over 9,000 pupils. Because the schools were considered centers of excellence, with rigorous admission standards, it was surprising that the administrators thought the students and teachers needed scrutinizing; some teachers clearly felt uneasy about it as well. Initially Milner was asked to see why some girls with high potential were nonachievers and troublemakers. The headmistresses had overly ambitious plans for Milner, but she was able to negotiate with them so that her research would be both manageable and worthwhile. She began the project in January 1935, and it was extended from one year to three. The results were published in 1938 as *The Human Problem in Schools*. Milner discovered the imposition of inappropriate adult standards where teachers and parents had perceived mental laziness or disobedience. She came up with several imaginative and practical suggestions to help "difficult" students. This book deserves to be better known, as the observations remain relevant, particularly in relation to gifted children.

Milner then trained as a psychoanalyst, becoming highly respected in the field. She was interested in art, especially the significance of doodling in communicating ideas. She felt that the imagination thrives when the artist is in a state of creative surrender and risks the void.

Milner believed that Western culture overvalues the "male" qualities, which involve taking action, and undervalues the "female" qualities, which are concerned with receptiveness and being, and she helped men who found it hard to cope with the "feminine" traits in their personalities. Her final book, based on her son's drawings, was *Bothered by Alligators,* in which she considered how children communicate with adults through symbols and drawings. She also wrote *On Not Being Able to Paint* (1950), *The Hands of the Living God* (1969), *An Experiment in Leisure* (1980), *The Suppressed Madness of Sane Men* (1987), and *Eternity's Sunrise* (1987).

Bibliography: Karpf, A., "Marion Milner: Journey to the Centre of the Mind," *Guardian* (3 June 1998): 21.

Montagu, Lady Mary Wortley née Pierrepont
1689–1792
advocate of inoculation

Education: self-educated at home.
Married: Edward Wortley Montagu, in 1712.

Lady Mary Montagu was a pioneer in the field of smallpox inoculation, her work contributing much to the acceptance of the practice in Britain, Europe, and North America.

Montagu was the daughter of the Duke of Kingston and the granddaughter of the diarist Sir John Evelyn. Her mother died while Montagu was a child, and her father appears to have had little interest in his children. Montagu decided to educate herself in her father's library and soon became known for her scholarly pursuits, which she recognized were not considered appropriate for women at that time.

In 1712 she eloped with Edward Wortley Montagu in order to avoid an arranged marriage. In 1717 the couple traveled to Constantinople, where Edward Montagu was the British ambassador. In Turkey Mary Montagu first came across variolation, a practice that appeared to give protection against smallpox. The procedure involved introducing pus from a mild case of the disease into the vein of a patient by means of a scratch with a needle. Montagu observed that those treated suffered a fever around a

Lady Mary Wortley Montagu (Hulton-Deutsch Collection/Corbis)

week afterward, though none died and all seemed to recover completely.

She was so convinced of the safety and efficacy of the procedure that she had her own children treated. When she returned to England, she set up a series of experiments involving condemned prisoners and orphans. Caroline, Princess of Wales, took an interest, and with the success of Montagu's experiments had two of her daughters inoculated. The royal seal of approval did much to bring about the rapid spread of the practice. The Anglican Church and most doctors were against it, so Montagu anonymously published a "Plain Account of the Inoculating of the Small-Pox by a Turkey Merchant" in response to this opposition. It was found that the inoculation did in fact cause death in perhaps 3 percent of patients, a small number compared to the 20 or 30 percent who died after contracting the disease. Smallpox prior to inoculation killed 45,000 people a year in Britain.

In 1736, when she was forty-seven, Montagu fell in love with twenty-four-year-old Francesco Algarotti, a popular science writer. Although her feelings were not reciprocated, she decided to leave her husband three years later and travel to Italy to be with Algarotti, who by then was at the court of Frederick the Great in Berlin. Montagu chose to establish herself in Venice, finding the Italians much more accepting of women of learning than were the British.

It was undoubtedly the case that Montagu's connections with the rich and famous enabled her to put her ideas so successfully into practice. But these ideas were based on practical observations and (albeit limited) empirical experiments, and as such they were an important contribution to science and medicine.

Bibliography: Alic, M., *Hypatia's Heritage: A History of Women in Science from Antiquity to the Late Nineteenth Century,* London: Women's Press, 1986; Bozman, E. F., ed., *Everyman's Encyclopaedia,* vol. 8, fourth edition, London: Dent, 1958; Grundy, I., *Lady Mary Wortley Montagu: Comet of the Enlightenment,* Oxford: Oxford University Press, 1999.

Montessori, Maria
31 August 1870–6 May 1952
educator, psychologist

Education: Regia Scuola Technica Michelangelo Buonarroti, 1883–1886; Regio Istituto Tecnico Leonardo da Vinci, 1886–1890; University of Rome, 1890–1892 (physics, mathematics, and natural sciences); medical school, 1890–1896; M.D., 1896; courses in pedagogy and research, Clinica Psichiatrica, Rome, 1897–1898; University of Rome, educational philosophy, experimental psychology, and anthropology, 1900.

Employment: San Giovanni Hospital, University of Rome, from 1896; lecturer in hygiene and anthropology, Regio Istituto Superiore di Magistero Femminile, Rome, 1899–1901; external lecturer, 1911–1916; director, Scuola Magistrale Ortophrenica, Rome, 1900–1901; lecturer in anthropology, University of Rome, 1904–1908; Istituto di Beni Stabili (Children's House), 1907–1911; Montessori training courses given in Europe and United States, from 1913; director of the Montessori Association, from 1916; government inspector of nursery and elementary schools in Italy using the Montessori method, from 1922.

Maria Montessori was a pioneer in early childhood education.

Montessori was born in Chiaravalle, Ancona. Her family moved to Rome in 1875 when her father, an accountant, was transferred there. Although her parents suggested she become a teacher, Montessori originally intended to be an engineer, attending a boys' technical school when she was thirteen. She then decided against engineering and chose instead to be a doctor.

Initially refused entry to the medical school in Rome because she was a woman, she enrolled at the University of Rome; she took courses in physics, mathematics, and natural science, gaining the *diploma di licenza* that allowed her to enter medical school. She persevered and was admitted, though not without the imposition of certain conditions: she was not allowed into lectures until all the men were seated, and she had to do her anatomical dissections in the evenings alone, when no male students were present.

In June 1894 Montessori won the Rolli Prize and a scholarship; with this and the money she earned from private tuition she was able to support herself. In 1895 she took a position as hospital assistant and practiced pediatrics at the children's hospital. She attended the psychiatric clinic to collect material for her thesis and worked at the children's outpatient and emergency service. She successfully defended her thesis on 10 July 1896 and published a scientific paper about the use of crystals of Leyden in bronchial asthma in the same year. She was the first Italian woman to qualify as a doctor.

Her first job, at the Psychiatric Clinic at Rome University, involved visiting children in mental asylums. Upset by the appalling conditions in these institutions and certain that the children could be educated, she looked into the work of Jean Itard and

Maria Montessori (Hulton-Getty/Archive Photos)

Edouard Seguin, then leaders in the field of educating the mentally handicapped.

From 1899 to 1901 she was a lecturer at the teacher training college in Rome. In 1900 she became codirector with Dr. Guiseppe Montesano at the Scuola Ortophrenica. The two became romantically involved, and Montessori had a son, Mario, by Montesano. She did not bring up her son but only visited him at intervals; it was not until 1913, when he was fifteen, that he even realized she was his mother. From then on he traveled with her and helped her in numerous ways.

At the Ortophrenica School Montessori observed the children in the school, from 8 a.m. to 7 p.m. In the evenings she wrote up her observations and planned the next day's activities. She introduced very basic equipment, such as a frame with laces for learning to tie shoes and a set of blocks for learning shapes, so the children could learn simple tasks, including reading and writing. The

students amazed officials and educators with their performance on the state examinations. Montessori realized that not only were the standards for the state examinations set too low, but if these children could develop using her methods then surely there must be hundreds of normal children not reaching their potential in Italian schools.

Montessori returned to university to study anthropology, psychology, and philosophy. In 1904 she was appointed as a lecturer in anthropology, and in 1907 she was asked to supervise a *casa dei bambini* (children's home) in the new Beni Stabili housing in the slums of San Lorenzo. About thirty children, aged three to seven years, were cared for in a center while their parents were at work. Montessori hired an assistant to attend to the children but provided learning materials similar to those she had used with the retarded children, adapting them as the children progressed. As she watched the children develop and quickly become literate, she gave numerous talks about her observations, and the project received considerable publicity. In 1907 a second house was opened in San Lorenzo, a third in Milan, and in 1908 one for the children of wealthy parents in Rome. By 1909 all of Italian Switzerland was using her methods in their orphanages and children's homes.

Her first book about the Montessori method of teaching was published in 1908. From 1913 she gave lectures around the world. Professor William Kilpatrick, then the leading educator in the United States, traveled to Italy to see her school. As a result he published *The Montessori System Examined* (1914), which attacked her methods. He was such an influential educator that it was forty years until Montessori schools regained credibility in the United States.

In 1922 Montessori was made government inspector of the Italian schools that used the Montessori method. With the development of fascism in Italy, however, her methods became less popular, and she moved first to Barcelona and then to Amsterdam, where she was based for the rest of her life. She lived in India from 1939 to 1944, where her son was interned in a camp.

There was such a public outcry in Britain that he was released as a seventieth birthday present for Montessori. The viceroy of India sent her a telegram to let her know. It was the first time that Mario was publicly recognized as her son.

Montessori continued to give courses and write. She believed strongly that teaching should be geared to each individual child, and her equipment was designed for each child to work through stages in his or her development. Perhaps one problem was that the equipment was too structured. With greater emphasis on free development of young children, her methods fell out of favor. Even so, there are still many Montessori-based schools throughout the world. She died on 6 May 1952 in her home at 161 Koninginneweg in Amsterdam. Her study is kept untouched as a memorial to her, and the house serves as headquarters of the Association Montessori Internationale, which she founded in 1929.

Montessori was nominated for the Nobel Peace Prize in 1949, 1950, and 1951. She was given many honors, including the Order of Orange-Nassau in the Netherlands (1950) and honorary doctorates from the Universities of Durham (1923) and Amsterdam (1950).

Bibliography: Devine, Patricia, "Montessori, Maria," in *Thinkers of the Twentieth Century,* edited by Roland Turner, second edition, London: St. James Press, 1987; Kramer, R., *Maria Montessori,* Oxford: Basil Blackwell, 1978; Lilliard, P. P., *Montessori: A Modern Approach,* New York: Schocken, 1972; Lilliard, P. P., *Montessori Today: A Comprehensive Approach to Education from Birth to Adulthood,* New York: Schocken, 1996; Montessori, M., *The Absorbent Mind,* translated by Claude A. Claremont, New York: Holt, Rinehart, 1967; Montessori, M., *Dr. Montessori's Own Handbook,* New York: Stokes, 1914; Montessori, M., *The Montessori Method: Scientific Pedagogy as Applied to Child Education in the Children's Houses,* translated by A. E. George, revised edition, London: Heinemann, 1909; Standing, E. M., *Maria Montessori,* New York: Mentor-Omega, 1957.

Muir, Isabella Helen Mary
20 August 1920–
biochemist

Education: Downe House, Newbury; Somerville College, Oxford; M.A., 1944; D.Phil., 1947; D.Sc., 1973.

Employment: research fellow, Sir William Dunn School of Pathology, University of Oxford, 1947–1948; member of scientific staff, Biochemical Division, National Institute for Medical Research, London, 1948–1954; St. Mary's Hospital, London: Empire Rheumatism Council Fellow, 1954–1958; Pearl Research Fellow, 1959–1966; Kennedy Institute of Rheumatology, London: head of Biochemistry Division, 1966–1986; director, 1977–1990; honorary professor, Charing Cross and Westminster Medical School, 1979–1995.

Helen Muir was an influential biochemist whose work on osteoarthritis was of particular importance.

Muir spent her childhood in India, and it was here that she became fascinated with the natural world. She read chemistry at Oxford, then began a career in biochemical research.

During the 1950s Muir investigated the chemical composition of joints and ligaments. She discovered the protoglycan molecule, which prevents tissue from being compressed by acting as a shock absorber. It had previously been thought that osteoarthritis in athletes developed through too much physical activity. Muir showed that an injury could trigger the disease. Her findings have enabled work to be carried out on how the progress of the disease can be slowed down.

As a result of this research, Muir was offered a post at the Kennedy Institute of Rheumatology in London. After heading the Biochemistry Division, she was appointed director of the institute in 1977, a post she held until 1990. Under her direction the institute developed an international reputation for teaching and research.

Her work was published in various journals, including the *Biochemical Journal* and *Nature.* She was on the editorial board of the

Biochemical Journal, Annals of the Rheumatic Diseases, Connective Tissue Research, and the *Journal of Orthopaedic Research.*

Muir was elected a fellow of the Royal Society in 1977, a Commander of the Order of the British Empire (CBE) in 1981, a foreign member of the Royal Swedish Academy of Sciences in 1989, and an honorary member of both the American Society of Biological Chemists (1982) and the European Society of Arthrology (1988). She was the first woman to serve on the council of the Medical Research Council (1973–1977). She was awarded honorary doctorates from the Universities of Edinburgh (1982), Strathclyde (1983), and Brunel (1990). In March 1996 she opened the Wellcome Centre for Cell Matrix Research in Manchester.

Bibliography: Debrett's People of Today, London: Debrett's Peerage Ltd., 1998; "Sex and the Scientist—Our Brilliant Careers," Postproduction filmscript, ZKK Productions. Aired 19 August 1996 on Channel 4; *Who's Who, 2000,* London: Adam and Charles Black, 2000.

Muir-Wood, Helen Marguerite
February 1895–16 January 1968
paleontologist

Education: Bedford College, University of London, B.Sc., 1918; University College, London, 1918–1919; D.Sc., 1934.
Employment: British Museum (Natural History): part-time curator, 1919; assistant, 1920–1955; deputy keeper, 1955–1965.

Helen Muir-Wood was a specialist in brachiopods, a phylum of marine invertebrates. In 1955 she became the first woman to be deputy keeper of paleontology at the British Museum.

Muir-Wood was born in London. After graduating she did research at University College, London, on the brachiopods found in Middle and Upper Paleozoic rocks. She began working at the British Museum in 1919 and the following year was put in charge of the brachiopod collections.

She published over fifty articles on the Brachiopoda, including those found in India, Iraq, Iran, and Palestine. In 1930 she was awarded the Lyell Fund of the Geological Society. During the 1930s she carried out pioneering work on a classification system for Mesozoic species and genera.

After three years working with the Admiralty in Bath during World War II, Muir-Wood continued her research at the British Museum (Natural History). During the 1950s she collaborated with Dr. G. A. Cooper of the Smithsonian Institution in Washington, D.C.; they coauthored *Morphology, Classification and Life Habits of the Productoidea (Brachiopoda)* (1960). She was subsequently invited to contribute to and oversee the Brachiopoda section of *A Treatise on Invertebrate Palaeontology* (Teichert, 1960).

She was awarded the Lyell Medal of the Geological Society in 1958.

Bibliography: Owen, E. F., "Dr. H. M. Muir-Wood," *Nature* 217 (30 March 1968): 1294–1295.

Murray, Alice Rosemary
28 July 1913–
chemist, educator

Education: Downe House school, near Newbury; Lady Margaret Hall, Oxford; B.Sc. in chemistry, 1934; D.Phil., 1939.
Employment: assistant lecturer, Royal Holloway College, University of London, 1938–1941; scientific civil servant, Naval Signal School, Portsmouth, 1941; lecturer in chemistry, University of Sheffield, 1941–1942; Women's Royal Navy Service (WRNS), 1942–1946; Girton College, Cambridge: lecturer, 1946–1954; fellow, 1949; tutor, 1951; demonstrator in chemistry, University of Cambridge, 1947–1952; head of New Hall, Cambridge, as tutor in charge, 1954–1964, and as president, 1964–1981; vice-chancellor, University of Cambridge, 1975–1977.

In 1975 *Rosemary Murray* became the first woman to be vice-chancellor of the University of Cambridge; she was the first president of New Hall, Cambridge.

Murray was the daughter of an admiral and the granddaughter of William A. Spooner, warden of New College Oxford (and for whom the spoonerism is named). She read chemistry at Lady Margaret Hall, Oxford, and for her doctorate did research in organic chemistry, on various aspects of isomerism. After completing her D.Phil. in 1939 she was an assistant lecturer in chemistry at Royal Holloway College. During World War II, after a short spell as a scientific civil servant, she returned to chemistry as a lecturer at the University of Sheffield and did research in organic chemistry as a member of a team working for the Ministry of Supply. In 1942 she joined the Women's Royal Navy Service (WRNS), undertaking a variety of roles and rising to the rank of chief officer.

In 1946 Murray was lecturer in chemistry at Girton College Cambridge, becoming a fellow of the college and tutor in 1949 and demonstrator in organic chemistry at the university. She continued to teach in college and university for over twenty years, as well as carrying out research. Because of her academic background as a chemist, combined with her wartime experience, she was appointed head (tutor in charge) of the newly established foundation for women, New Hall. In the early days New Hall had only two senior members, the tutor in charge and a lecturer in English. Between them, they had to cover all aspects of a college—administration, academics, fund-raising, and buildings. In 1964 the title of tutor was changed to president, and in 1972 New Hall became a college of the university with a royal charter and new buildings. Murray described her experiences in *New Hall, 1954–1972: The Making of a College*, published in 1980.

While at New Hall Murray became increasingly involved in university administration through her work on numerous university committees. In 1975 she became vice-chancellor of the university for two years, the normal term of office at that time. She was a member of governing bodies of schools, on the Council of the Girls' Public Day School Trust (GPDST), chair of the Keswick Hall College of Education and of the Cambridge Institute of Education, and a member of the Lockwood Committee for Higher Education in Northern Ireland. She was also the only female member of the Armed Forces Pay Review Body (1972–1984), a liveryman of the Goldsmith's Company (1978), a director of the Midland Bank (1978–1984), a justice of the peace for the city of Cambridge (1953–1983), and deputy lieutenant for Cambridgeshire (1982–).

She received honorary degrees from universities in Britain and the United States and was made a Dame Commander of the Order of the British Empire (DBE) in 1977.

Bibliography: Murray, R., personal communications to the author, May and June 2000; Walton, C. D., "In Retrospect: Dame Rosemary Murray," in *Against the Tide*, Bloomington, IN: Phi Delta Kappa Educational Foundation, 1996; *Who's Who, 1998,* London: Adam and Charles Black, 1998.

Murray, Margaret Alice D.
13 July 1863–13 November 1963
archaeologist

Education: private education in England and Germany; nurse training at Calcutta General Hospital, India, 1883–1886; Department of Egyptology, University College, London, 1894–1895.

Employment: sister in charge, Calcutta General Hospital, 1883; Department of Egyptology, University College, London: junior lecturer, 1899; assistant lecturer, 1909; lecturer, 1921; senior lecturer and fellow, 1922; assistant professor, 1924–1935; extension lectures at Oxford and London, 1910 and 1911; cataloguer of Egyptian antiquities in the Ashmolean Museum, Oxford, the Manchester University Museum, the National Museum of Ireland, and the Royal Scottish Museum.

Margaret Murray was the first woman to work full time in Egyptology.

Murray was born in Calcutta. Her father was the managing partner of a Manchester firm of merchants; his family had lived in Calcutta for some time. Her mother, a

Northumbrian, had come to India as a missionary and social worker. After spending her early childhood in India, Murray was educated in England and France.

Murray decided to train as a nurse and in 1883 was the first "lady probationer" at the Calcutta General Hospital. At seventeen, during an epidemic, she was acting ward sister and the only white woman in such a position. She alternated between England and India until 1886, when she finally left India.

Prevented from training as a nurse in England because she was "too small" in stature, Murray decided to study Egyptology at University College, where Flinders Petrie was in charge. She quickly learned how to decipher Egyptian hieroglyphics and in 1899 started teaching elementary hieroglyphics at University College, initially on a part-time basis. She also catalogued Egyptian antiquities in several major collections, such as the one at Manchester University Museum. After her mother died, she moved near University College, becoming more involved in teaching Egyptology. In 1902 she helped Flinders Petrie in his excavation at Abydos but did relatively little other fieldwork until she retired, as she was occupied with both teaching and administrative duties at University College.

During her lifetime Murray published over eighty books and articles on ancient Egypt, among them *The Splendour That Was Egypt* (1949) and *Egyptian Temples* (1931). She was also interested in witchcraft and folklore and published *The Witch-Cult in Western Europe* in 1921. She was a fellow of the Royal Anthropological Institute from 1926 and president of the Folklore Society from 1953 to 1955. Her autobiography, *My First Hundred Years*, appeared in 1963.

Bibliography: Dictionary of National Biography, 1961–70. Oxford: Oxford University Press, 1981; Dyhouse, C., *No Distinction of Sex: Women in British Universities, 1870–1939*, London: University College London Press, 1995; Roberts, F. C., comp., "Dr. Margaret Murray," *Obituaries from the Times, 1961–1970*. Reading: Newspaper Archive Development, 1975.

N

Nashar, Beryl née Scott
9 July 1923–
geologist

Education: Newcastle Girls' High School; University of Sydney; diploma in education; B.Sc. with honors, 1947; Department of Minerology and Petrology, University of Cambridge, 1949–1950; University of Tasmania, Ph.D.

Employment: research associate, University of Tasmania, until 1952; Newcastle University College, University of New South Wales: lecturer in geology, 1955–1960; senior lecturer, 1960–1963; professor of geology, 1963–1980; dean, Faculty of Science, 1969–1970.

Married: Mr. Ali, a philosopher from Cambridge, on 13 July 1952.

Beryl Nashar was the first woman dean of science in any Australian university. She was the first woman in Australia to win a Rotary Foundation Fellowship and was the first Australian to be awarded a Ph.D. in geology from an Australian university.

Beryl Nashar was born in Newcastle, New South Wales, and was top of her year's state matriculation examination. She gained a first-class degree in geology at the University of Sydney and was awarded the University Medal.

She then trained as a teacher, working in a classroom for only a day, as she was offered both a position in the Geology Department at the University of Tasmania and a Rotary Foundation Fellowship to Cambridge University. She accepted the latter but came back to Australia and completed her Ph.D. studies at the University of Tasmania. After she graduated, Professor S. W. Carey arranged a research position for her with a private company in Tasmania until 1952, when she went to Cairo for three years.

After securing a well-paid job in Tasmania, Nashar traveled to Cairo to marry her fiancé, a philosopher. She later returned to Australia, taking a post at Newcastle University College, University of New South Wales, as she wanted her son to be born there. Her husband did not follow as she had expected, and the couple decided to pursue their respective careers, making Nashar in effect a single parent. She met her husband when work commitments allowed her to travel abroad. Although she retired early so that she could be with him, he died before they could be together.

Nashar wrote four books, including *The Geology of the Hunter Valley* (1964), and around thirty research papers. She was made an Officer of the Order of the British Empire (OBE) in 1972.

Bibliography: Allen, N., "Test Tubes and White Jackets: The Careers of Two Australian Women Scientists" [Nancy Millis and Beryl Nashar], *Journal of Australian Scientists* 52 (1997): 126–137; Mancini, R., archivist, University of Sydney, personal communication to the author, February 2000; *Who's Who in Australasia and the Far East,* second edition, Cambridge: Melrose Press, 1991; *Who's Who in Australia,* thirty-fourth edition, Melbourne: Information Australia Group, 1998.

Needham, Dorothy Mary
née Moyle
22 September 1896–22 December 1987
biochemist

Education: Claremont College, Stockport; St. Hilary's School, Alderley Edge, Cheshire; Girton College, Cambridge, 1915–1919; M.A., 1923; Ph.D., 1926; Sc.D., 1945.

Employment: research and teaching, Biochemical Laboratory, University of Cambridge, 1920–1940 and 1946–1963; research worker, Ministry of Supply, 1940–1943; chemical adviser and acting director, Sino-British Science Co-operation Office, Chongqing, China 1944–1945.

Married: Joseph Needham, a specialist in the history of Chinese science and technology, in 1924.

Dorothy Needham carried out important research on the biochemistry of muscle.

Needham was born in London. After reading chemistry at Girton College, Cambridge, in 1920 she began research at the Biochemical Laboratory at the University of Cambridge. For the first four years, she worked under F. G. Hopkins, concentrating on the aerobic synthesis of the muscle fuel glycogen for the Food Investigation Board of the Department of Scientific and Industrial Research. Joseph Needham was also working in the laboratory, and the two occasionally collaborated on research projects. From 1925 to 1928 she held a Beit Memorial Fellowship that allowed her to begin research on carbohydrate metabolism in muscle and the role of adenosine triphosphate (ATP) in muscle contraction. Although still based at the University of Cambridge, from 1928 to 1940 she did some teaching and research abroad, including in Belgium, France, Germany, and the United States.

During World War II she worked with the chemical defense research group that provided information to the Ministry of Supply, investigating the effects of chemical weapons, mainly mustard gas, on the metabolism of skin and bone marrow. In 1944 Needham traveled to China, where she became chemical adviser and acting director of the Sino-British Science Co-operation Office in Chongqing, where her husband was scientific counselor at the British embassy.

After the war Needham returned to Cambridge and started research on enzyme biochemistry for the Medical Research Council (MRC). Because the MRC would not fund long-term research by individuals, however, Needham's financial support ran out in 1952. She was able to obtain further funding from the University's Broodbank Fund, but in 1955 she was once more without a grant. Although she had been elected a fellow of the Royal Society in 1948, the society declined to support her, apparently because the president believed that married women did not need a salary. Needham was eventually given a grant by the Agricultural Research Council, enabling her to work mainly on the proteins of smooth muscle in the uterus.

When she retired in 1963, Needham concentrated on writing *Machina carnis: The Biochemistry of Muscular Contraction in Its Historical Development* (1971). In the preface she states that she "wanted to visualise in a single perspective the path of man's knowledge about the function of muscles, progressing so slowly for many centuries, but then during the last seventy years reaching speedily towards the goal in a rush of great discoveries." With over 2,000 references, the book is an important starting point for anyone working in this area. Needham also coauthored (with M. Teich) *Sourcebook in the History of Biochemistry, 1740 to 1940,* although she died before its completion.

Needham was a fellow of Lucy Cavendish College (foundation fellow, 1965; emeritus fellow, 1966), Girton College (1976), and Gonville and Caius College (the college's first woman fellow, 1979), all of these at the University of Cambridge. When she was elected to fellowship of the Royal Society in 1948, she and her husband (elected in 1941) became the first married couple to be fellows since Queen Victoria and Prince Albert. Her archives are held at Girton College, Cambridge.

Bibliography: "Catalogues of the Papers and Correspondence of Dorothy Needham, FRS

(1896–1987)," available at the National Cataloguing Unit for the Archives of Contemporary Scientists Website: www.bath.ac.uk/Centres/NCUACS/cambio/dneedham.htm; "Needham, Dorothy (Mary Moyle)," *The Penguin Biographical Dictionary of Women,* available at: http://w2.xrefer. com/entry/173103; *Who Was Who, 1981–1990,* London: Adam and Charles Black, 1991.

Bibliography: Brough, C., librarian, Royal Botanic Gardens, Kew, personal communication to the author, June 2001; *Curtis Botanical Magazine—Dedications, Portraits, and Biographical Notes 1827–1927* (1931): 115–116; Nicholls, C. S., ed., *Dictonary of National Missing Persons,* Oxford: Oxford University Press, 1993.

Nevill, Lady Dorothy Fanny née Walpole
1 April 1826–24 March 1913
horticulturist

Married: Reginald Nevill, in 1847.

Lady Dorothy Nevill built up a collection of rare plants that at one time was regarded as the best in existence. Her specialties were orchids and tropical plants such as the pitcher plant, *Nepenthes.*

Nevill was born in Berkeley Square, London. Her father was the third earl of Orford of Wolterton, in Norfolk, and the family was descended from the brother of Sir Robert Walpole. Nevill spent most of her early years in Norfolk, though she made two grand tours of Europe with her family and was particularly impressed by Rome and Munich. After her marriage, she lived at Dangstein, Reginald Nevill's estate near Midhurst in Sussex. The couple also kept a house in London, and Nevill enjoyed the social life of the city, mixing with many of the leading scientists, artists, writers, and politicians of the day. Through a mutual interest in orchids, she became friendly with Joseph Chamberlain. She also developed a close friendship with Benjamin Disraeli, a friend of her brother, and was involved in the establishment of Primrose Day in his honor—the primrose being her favorite flower.

At Dangstein Nevill was able to indulge her love of plants, building up an impressive collection of rare specimens. When the estate was dismantled in 1976, the collection was dispersed. Nevill continued to pursue her interest in plants into her old age through regular attendance at Royal Horticultural Society meetings.

Newbigin, Marion Isobel
1869–20 July 1934
biologist, geographer, writer

Education: Edinburgh Association for the University Education of Women; University College, Aberystwyth; School of Medicine for Women, Edinburgh; B.Sc., (London) 1893; D.Sc., (London) 1898.

Employment: lecturer, School of Medicine for Women, Edinburgh; editor, *Scottish Geographical Magazine,* 1902–1934.

Marion Newbigin was the editor of the *Scottish Geographical Magazine* for thirty-two years.

Newbigin was born in Alnwick, Northumberland, one of eight children, of which the five daughters were ardent feminists. Her father, James Lesslie Newbigin, was a pharmacist. After studying at the Edinburgh Association for the University Education of Women, she went to University College, Aberystwyth, returning to Edinburgh to study at the School of Medicine for Women. She later lectured in biology and zoology at the school and did research into the coloration of plants, crustaceans, and fish at the Royal College of Physicians. In 1898 she published a monograph, *Colour in Nature—A Study in Biology.* Research work carried out at the Marine Biological Station in Millport and her observations of marine life on the Northumbrian coast formed the basis of her next book, *Life by the Sea Shore—An Introduction to Natural History* (1901), which contained many illustrations by her sister Florence.

Newbigin took up the post as editor of the *Scottish Geographical Magazine* in 1902, a time when geography was not fully developed. Her contribution to the discipline over the next three decades was important, particularly in terms of the breadth of her work. She published seventeen books during her lifetime, several of which became key texts in the field. *An Introduction to Physical Geography* (1912) showed her interest in the educational aspects of geography; she was an examiner for several different examination boards. Her other books included *Animal Geography* (1913), *Ordnance Survey Maps* (1913), *Geographical Aspects of Balkan Problems* (1915), *Commercial Geography* (1923), and *Southern Europe* (1932). She died before the publication of *Plant and Animal Geography* (1936), based on a series of lectures given to students at Bedford College, London, and again illustrated by her sister. Revised by H. J. Fleure, it was a popular textbook.

Newbigin was president of the Geographical Section of the British Association for the Advancement of Science in 1922 and a member of the Royal Scottish Geographical Society.

Bibliography: Creese, M. R. S., *Ladies in the Laboratory? American and British Women in Science, 1800–1900: A Survey of Their Contributions to Research*, Lanham, Maryland: Scarecrow Press, 1998; "Marion I. Newbigin," *Geography* 19 (1934): 220; "Marion Newbigin (Dr)," *Times* (21 July 1934): 17B; Nicholls, C. S., ed., *Dictionary of National Biography: Missing Persons*, Oxford: Oxford University Press, 1993; Steel, R. W., ed., *British Geography, 1918–1945*, Cambridge: Cambridge University Press, 1987; *Who Was Who, 1929–1940*, London: Adam and Charles Black, 1947.

Newton, Lily née Batten
26 January 1893–25 March 1981
botanist, educator

Education: Colston Girls' School, Bristol; University of Bristol; B.Sc., 1917; M.Sc., 1918; Ph.D., 1922; D.Sc., 1950.

Employment: lecturer, Bristol University, 1919–1920; lecturer, Birkbeck College, University of London, 1920–1923; researcher, Imperial College, University of London, 1923–1925; research worker, John Innes Horticultural Institute, 1927–

1928; University College of Wales, Aberystwyth: lecturer, 1928–1930; professor of botany, 1930–1958.

Married: Dr. W. C. F. Newton, a cytologist at the John Innes Horticultural Institute, in 1925. He died in 1927.

Lily Newton was a leading authority on seaweeds; her *Handbook of British Seaweeds* was published in 1931.

Newton had been married only two years when her husband died. She was able to work at the John Innes Institute for the first year after his death, completing a handbook and preparing his research for publication with coauthors from the institute. She was then appointed to the University College of Wales in Aberystwyth as a lecturer and then professor of botany. During World War II she helped with the scientific research needed to ensure that seaweeds were successfully harvested. (Agar, which can be made from seaweed, is used as the substrate, with added nutrients, on which to culture bacteria; it is also used in many foods, such as ice cream.)

Newton was concerned about the pollution caused by heavy metals in lakes and rivers. With other workers she was involved in a study of the River Rheidol in mid-Wales, which had been polluted by lead and zinc from mining. In the 1920s, when the study began, there were almost no living organisms in the river; by the time the study was completed, in the 1960s, the river had recovered and become a favorable environment for salmon ("Pollution Problems of the R. Rheidol," *Transactions of the Botanical Society of Edinburgh* 38 [1959]: 141f).

Newton was vice-principal of the University College of Wales from 1951 to 1952 and acting principal from 1952 to 1953. She was president of the Botany Section at the annual meeting of the British Association for the Advancement of Science in 1949 and president of the British Phycological Society in 1955 and 1956.

She was responsible for organizing the collection of memorabilia and funds for Marie Lebour's eightieth birthday presentation in August 1957. Her contribution to the album for Lebour was a display of the red seaweed *Lapathum marinum sanguineum*.

Newton published over twenty papers and reports, some of them coauthored. In 1973 she was awarded an honorary LL.D. from the University of Wales.

Bibliography: Jones, G., "Lily Newton (née Batten) (1893–1981)," *British Phycological Journal* 17 (1982): 1–4; "Professor Lily Newton," *Times* (2 April 1981).

Nicholas, Charlotte
fl. 1914
inventor

On 15 July 1915 *Charlotte Nicholas* of Cardiff was granted patent no. 22625 for the minesweeping apparatus she developed.

Nicholas's minesweeping equipment resembled a railroad cow-catcher. The apparatus consisted of a set of rails into which a net was laced, arranged below the waterline at or before the bow of a vessel. It could also be affixed to any firm structure. Nicholas also claimed to have developed the idea of using tanks in World War I some weeks before Winston Churchill did. A fellow of the Institute of Inventors, she also took out patent no. 22552 on 17 February 1915 for "disintegrators."

Bibliography: Letters from Charlotte Nicholas to Agnes E. Conway, honorary secretary of Women's Work sub-committee, Library of the Imperial War Museum, Emp. 66/15–18; details of her inventions Emp. 66/4; portrait Emp. 66/5.

Nightingale, Florence
12 May 1820–13 August 1910
nursing pioneer, social statistician

Education: at home, by her father and governess; nurse training, Kaiserswerth Institution for Deaconesses, Düsseldorf, Germany, 1851.
Employment: superintendent, Hospital for Invalid Gentlewomen, London, 1853–1854; nurse superintendent, Scutari Barrack Hospital, Crimea, 1854–1856; campaigner on various issues, from 1856.

Florence Nightingale became internationally famous for her pioneering work in nursing in hospitals in the Crimea. Her experiences led her to campaign for more general improvements in living conditions, particularly in sanitation, and in this she made important use of statistics to support her arguments. In 1907 she became the first woman to receive the Order of Merit.

Nightingale was born in (and named after) the Italian city of Florence. She was the younger daughter of a wealthy country gentleman with homes in Derbyshire and Hampshire. She and her sister were taught history, philosophy, Greek, Latin, German, French, and Italian by their father and music and drawing by a governess. At the age of seventeen, Nightingale felt she had been called to serve God, though she had little opportunity at that time to fulfill this calling. She also found her life somewhat unchallenging intellectually and studied different subjects on her own, including mathematics.

During the early 1840s Nightingale started to visit the sick and infirm in the villages near the family's two homes. By 1844 the idea of working in hospitals became clear in her mind, though her family did not approve. Returning to Britain from a tour of Egypt with friends in 1850, she visited the Kaiserswerth Institute for Deaconesses near Düsseldorf in Germany, where women were trained as nurses. She was impressed by their dedication and the following year attended the institute herself, her family grudgingly allowing her to do so (but keeping her stay at the institute a secret). When she came back to Britain, she visited a number of hospitals and in 1853 spent time in various hospitals in Paris.

In August 1853 she was appointed superintendent of the Hospital for Invalid Gentlewomen in London, an unpaid position. Fourteen months later she volunteered to help in the war in the Crimea, which had begun in March 1854. She was asked by Secretary of State for War Sidney Herbert to organize a team of nurses. In November 1854 she and her thirty-eight nurses arrived at the Barrack Hospital at Scutari. Conditions there were extremely bad; the poor sanitation and lack of proper supplies made treat-

Florence Nightingale (Hulton-Getty/Archive Photos)

woman, Nightingale would not have been expected to serve on the commission, though she acted as an adviser and was involved with the selection of its members. One member, Dr. William Farr, a leader in the developing science of statistics, helped Nightingale interpret her figures and was impressed with her diagrammatic representations of the information. Her *Notes on Matters Affecting the Health, Efficiency and Hospital Administration of the British Army* (1858) contained many diagrams that were reproduced by Farr in the royal commission's report. One type, the polar-area diagram, in which wedges of a circle are proportionate in area to the figures they represent (a kind of pie chart), was in fact invented by Nightingale. She was elected a member of the Statistical Society in 1858.

Nightingale's campaign led to major improvements in the living conditions of soldiers and reorganization of aspects of the army medical system, including changes in the gathering of statistics. In the late 1850s she launched a similar campaign on behalf of soldiers serving in India. She collated data on sickness and mortality rates, as well as background information on sanitary conditions and medical facilities. A royal commission was set up and reported its results in 1863. Ten years later, after living conditions of soldiers in India had improved, Nightingale reported that the mortality rate had fallen from sixty-nine to eighteen per 1,000.

After her return from the Crimea, Nightingale lived a reclusive existence, ostensibly because she had been weakened by a fever. But she was able to work energetically, though in the main out of the public eye, for causes to which she was committed. In 1860 she founded the Nightingale Training School for Nurses with £50,000 raised in recognition of her contribution to the war in the Crimea. She published *Notes on Hospitals* (1859) and *Notes on Nursing* (1860).

In 1860 her proposals for uniform hospital statistics were discussed at the International Congress of Statistics in London. Major London hospitals began to apply her system in order to produce standardized statistics on patient numbers and outcomes. There were problems with the forms used

ing the wounded very difficult. Nightingale quickly realized that many men were dying from diseases contracted once they reached the hospital, and improvements in cleanliness became one of her main priorities.

During her time in the Crimea, Nightingale kept records on the numbers of soldiers treated and the mortality rate among patients. Upon her return to Britain in the summer of 1856, she began to analyze her data and was able to demonstrate that improvements made at Scutari had resulted in a definite fall in the mortality rate. Death rates were higher for soldiers in Britain, however, than for the troops as a whole in the Crimea. Her statistics also showed that the mortality rate of soldiers in England was almost twice that of civilians. In September 1856 she met Queen Victoria and Prince Albert at Balmoral and was able to persuade them that a Royal Commission on the Health of the Army was necessary; Secretary of State for War Lord Panmure was similarly convinced.

In May 1857 the War Office approved the establishment of the commission. As a and the disease classification devised by Farr, however, and the system was not widely accepted. Despite its practical difficulties, her vision of the organization and administration of health care was ahead of its time: she wrote that her universal hospital statistics would "enable us to ascertain the relative mortality of different hospitals, as well as of different diseases and injuries at the same and at different ages." She also recognized the importance of finance in health care and stated that proper hospital records "would show subscribers how their money was being spent, what amount of good was really being done with it and whether the money was not doing mischief rather than good" (from *Clinical Governance*, 179).

Nightingale contributed much to the Nightingale Training School for Nurses and to developments in other aspects of nurse training and practice. In 1867, following an outbreak of puerperal sepsis (childbirth fever) in the training school for midwives at King's College Hospital, London, she began an investigation into mortality rates in childbirth. She discovered that no standard data were kept, so she collected them herself. Her analysis of the statistics showed that mortality rates were much higher in hospitals than for home deliveries because of the higher levels of infection. With Dr. John Sutherland's help, she wrote *Introductory Notes on Lying-in Institutions* (1871).

Nightingale also kept up her interest in India, widening her scope from the living conditions of soldiers there to every aspect of Indian society. She wrote on issues such as famine and irrigation and was widely considered an expert on the country. In 1890 she contributed a paper on village sanitation in India to the Eighth International Congress on Hygiene and Demography held in Budapest.

She was given the "freedom" of the City of London in 1908, an honor like the "key to the city" in the United States, only the second woman to be honored in this way. She received awards from various countries, including the badge of honor of the Norwegian Red Cross, the gold medal of Secours aux Blessés Militaires from France, and the order of the Cross of Merit from Germany,

these last two in recognition of the practical advice on the organization of medical services that she gave to both sides in the Franco-Prussian War in 1870–1871.

Nightingale's health declined gradually, and she died at the age of ninety at her home in London.

Bibliography: Baly, M., *Florence Nightingale and the Nursing Legacy*, London: Croom Helm, 1987; Beavan, C., "Florence Nightingale: Iron Maiden," in BBC2 Series *Reputations*, aired 17 July 2001; Cohen, I. B., "Florence Nightingale," *Scientific American* (March 1984): 98–107; *Dictionary of National Biography*, supplement, vol. III, Oxford: Oxford University Press, 1912; Goldie, S. M., ed., *Florence Nightingale: Letters from the Crimea, 1854–1856*, Manchester: Manchester University Press, 1997; Ingram, D., Department of Health Informatics, Royal Free and University College Medical School, London, personal communication to the author, May 1999; Patterson, D., D. Ingram, and D. Kalra, "Information Data Quality and Clinical Governance," in *Clinical Governance: Making It Happen*, edited by M. Lugon and J. Secker-Walker, London: Royal Society of Medicine, 1999; Pollard, E. F., *Florence Nightingale: The Wounded Soldier's Friend*, London: Partridge, 1891; Vicinius, M., "Tactful Organising and Executive Power: Biographies of Florence Nightingale for Girls," in M. Shortland and R. Yeo, eds., *Telling Lives in Science: Essays in Scientific Biography*, Cambridge: Cambridge University Press, 1996; Woodham-Smith, C., *Florence Nightingale*, London: Constable, 1950.

Nihell, Elizabeth
1723–post 1772
midwife

Education: Hôtel-Dieu, Paris, late 1740s.
Employment: midwife, London, from early 1750s.
Married: Edward Nihell, a surgeon.

Elizabeth Nihell was a practicing midwife whose opposition to male midwives sparked a public debate.

Nihell was born in London but undertook her midwifery training in Paris. As she was not French, she came up against resistance when she applied to the Hôtel-Dieu to be an apprentice, though she was eventually admitted thanks to help from the Duke of Orleans.

She returned to London in the 1750s after she had completed her training. Her husband was a surgeon, and the couple had at least one child. In 1760 she published *A Treatise on the Art of Midwifery*, in which she attacked the growing trend of employing male midwives, and at higher rates of pay than women. She described their lack of sensitivity and their overuse of instruments during childbirth. Her criticism of Dr. William Smellie, who trained male surgeons in midwifery, brought about a vigorous debate in the form of a series of articles. Tobias Smollett defended Smellie, who had been his teacher, and derided Nihell's views. It was even suggested that not she herself but her husband had written the book.

She continued to practice as a midwife and to stick to her strong opinions. In 1771 an updated version of her book was translated into French and published. Her name appeared in a register of midwives practicing in London in 1772.

Bibliography: Klukoff, P. J., "Smollett's Defence of Dr. Smellie in *The Critical Review*," *Medical History* 14 (1970): 31–41; Nicholls, C. S., ed., *Dictionary of National Biography: Missing Persons,* Oxford: Oxford University Press, 1993.

Noach, Ilse née Hellman
28 September 1908–3 December 1998
psychoanalyst

Education: Roman Catholic Boys' School, Vienna; two-year course in treatment of juvenile delinquency; psychology courses, Sorbonne, Paris, 1931; University of Vienna, 1935–1937; Institute of Psycho-Analysis, London, 1942–1945.

Employment: work in home for young offenders, Paris, 1931–1932; child assessment center, Paris, 1933–1935; lecturer in psychology, University of Vienna, 1935–

1937; Parents' Association Institute, London, 1937–1939; work with child evacuees, Home Office, 1939–1941; Anna Freud's war nurseries, 1941–1945; psychoanalyst, Hampstead Clinic, 1945–1992; training of analysts, Institute of Psycho-Analysis, London, 1952–1978.

Married: Arnold Noach, a Dutch art historian. He died in 1976.

Ilse Noach was an expert on child development and a well-known psychoanalyst.

Noach was born in Vienna. The ethologist Konrad Lorenz and art historian Ernst Gombrich went to the same school and were friends of hers. After taking a two-year course on the treatment of juvenile delinquents, the first year theory and the second devoted to practical work, she was offered the chance to work at a home near Paris at which young offenders were cared for in small, family-like groups. While she was there, she took evening classes in psychology at the Sorbonne. She spent the next two years working in a child assessment center, at the end of which the French had trained their own social workers, and she returned to Vienna.

Noach studied at the Department of Child Development at the University of Vienna, which was led by Professor Charlotte Bühler, who had started on a detailed child observation study. Noach joined in the project, observing children from birth to six years. Anna Freud was working in Vienna at that time, but Bühler forbade Noach to go to her lectures or seminars.

In 1937 Bühler asked Noach to travel to London to help her study children with learning disabilities. When World War II began, Noach was sent to the Isle of Man, as she was considered an enemy alien. Because of the shortage of psychiatrists, however, she was soon released and asked to work for the Home Office, a government department. She worked with children evacuated from London, many of whom suffered psychological problems because of separation from their homes and families. Noach's own family suffered terribly during the war; her mother and brother died in concentration camps.

In 1941 Anna Freud asked Noach to work

at her war nurseries, which also cared for children who had undergone family disruption. Noach remained there until the end of the war. She kept in touch with the children from the nurseries for many years, and wrote about her work in *From War Babies to Grandmothers: Forty-eight Years in Psychoanalysis* (1990).

As well as carrying out research into the development of the children in the nurseries, Noach studied psychoanalysis. Her fees for her psychoanalytical training came indirectly from Susan Isaacs, a noted child development expert. She answered letters to the editor of *Nursery World* under the pseudonym "Ursula." Isaacs paid Noach a weekly fee to answer some of the letters. Noach became a leading member of the British Psycho-Analytical Society.

After the war Noach took a post at the Hampstead Clinic, established by Anna Freud and Dorothy Burlingham. She was head of the Adolescent Study Group for some years and published several papers on the development and treatment of adolescents. She built up her own practice and trained psychoanalysts herself. One area in which she was very interested was the simultaneous analysis of mothers and children: one analyst for the mother and one for the child, with a coordinator who had the case notes from both analysts and explored the connections between mother and child.

Bibliography: "Ilse Noach," obituary, *Times* (18 December 1998): 25A; Peers, B. C., letter to the editor, *Times* (30 December 1998): 17F; Yorke, C., "The Analytic Grandmother," *Guardian* (16 December 1998).

Noble, Mary
23 February 1911–
plant pathologist, expert on Beatrix Potter

Education: Edinburgh Ladies' College; University of Edinburgh; B.Sc., 1933; Ph.D., 1935.
Employment: Department of Agriculture and Fisheries for Scotland, East Craigs, 1935–1971.

Mary Noble has done important work in plant pathology; her research on wart disease in potatoes resulted in its control and elimination from Scotland.

Noble's father was a pharmacist in Leith. She became interested in natural history when she was young. For her doctorate, she studied the heterothallism of the clover pathogen, *Typhula trifolii;* her research was published in the *Annals of Botany* (1937). She also investigated how diseases were transmitted from one crop to the next by pathogens in the seed of clover, publishing this research in 1948 in *Transactions of the British Mycological Society.*

Noble surveyed the flax fields in west Scotland for disease that could affect the quality of the linen produced from the flax, which was still used for covering aircraft wings during World War II. Later she was involved with the Danish government's Institute of Seed Pathology for Developing Countries. Noble traveled worldwide giving courses and seminars on seed pathology. With I. Tempe and P. Neergaard, she published *An Annotated List of Seed-borne Diseases* (1958).

In 1970 Noble was researching the history of mycology in Scotland and was particularly interested in Charles McIntosh, the Perthshire naturalist (1839–1922). His niece gave her a bundle of papers that had not been looked at for fifty years. To her amazement, among the collection she found twelve letters from Beatrix Potter and three from her father, Rupert Potter, to McIntosh. Beatrix Potter's letters were about fungi, lichens, and mosses; as did her diary entries, they showed that she was a serious student of mycology. Noble has become an expert on Potter and has helped to ensure that Potter's skills as a mycologist are more widely known. Noble coauthored, with E. Jay and A. S. Hobbs, *A Victorian Naturalist* (1992). She advised the Armitt Museum in Ambleside about the collection of Potter's drawings and paintings now housed there.

Noble was awarded the Imperial Service Order, and the Benefactors' Medal of the British Mycological Society. She is a fellow of the Royal Society of Edinburgh, the Botanical Society of Scotland, and the Institute of Biology.

Bibliography: Battrick, E., *Beatrix Potter: The Unknown Years,* Ambleside: Armitt Library and Museum Centre, 1999; Gault, R., archivist, Botanical Society of Scotland, personal communication to the author, March 2000; Mathew, M. V., *The History of the Royal Botanic Garden Library,* Edinburgh: Her Majesty's Stationery Office, 1987.

Noddack, Ida Eva née Tacke
1896–1979
chemist

Education: Technical University, Berlin; diploma, 1919; doctorate, 1921.

Employment: chemist, Allgemeine Elektrische Gesellschaft (AEG), Berlin, 1921–1923; chemist, Siemens and Halske, Berlin, 1924–1925; chemist, Physikalisch-Technische Reichsanstalt, Berlin, 1925–1935; research associate, Department of Physical Chemistry, University of Freiburg, Germany, 1935–1941; University of Strasbourg, 1947–1955; Institute for Geochemical Research, Bamberg, Germany, 1956–1968.

Married: Walter Karl Noddack, a chemist, in 1926.

Ida Noddack, with her husband (and O. Berg), discovered the element rhenium in 1925. In 1934 she was the first to propose the concept of nuclear fission, though her ideas were largely dismissed at that time.

Noddack was born near Cologne, Germany, and educated at the Technical University in Berlin, where she won a prize for chemistry and metallurgy in 1919. After obtaining her doctorate, she worked as a commercial chemist. In 1925 she took up a post at the Physical Chemistry Testing Laboratory in Berlin. Here she met Walter Noddack, and they worked together on the search for "element 75" with O. Berg. Their discovery of the element, in the mineral columbite, was published in a paper entitled "Die Ekamangan" (*Naturwissenschaften* 13 [1925]: 567). They named the element rhenium, after the River Rhine. In the same paper they reported the discovery of "element 43," though this claim was disputed; the element (technetium) was eventually conclusively identified by C. Perrier and E. Segre in 1937.

In 1925 Noddack became the first woman to deliver a major address to the Society of German Chemists. She continued her work at the Testing Laboratory and in 1934 published another key paper, "Über das Element 93" (About element 93) (*Zeitschrift für Angewandte Chemie* 47: 653). Commenting on Enrico Fermi's observations on the bombardment of uranium by neutrons, Noddack put forward the theory of nuclear fission to explain his results. Her suggestion was not taken seriously, though it was proved true five years later through the work of Lise Meitner.

In 1935 Noddack became a research associate at the Institute of Physical Chemistry at the University of Freiburg. After World War II she went to work at the University of Strasbourg, returning to Germany in 1956 to take up a post at the Institute for Geochemical Research in Bamberg.

For the discovery of rhenium, Noddack was awarded the Justus Leibig Medal of the German Chemical Society in 1931. She also received the Swedish Chemical Society's Scheele Medal in 1934. In 1966 the University of Hamburg awarded her an honorary doctorate, and in the same year she was given the High Service Cross of the German Federal Republic. She was an honorary member of the Spanish Society of Physics and Chemistry.

Bibliography: Gillispie, C. C., ed., *Dictionary of Scientific Biography,* vol. 9, New York: Charles Scribner's Sons, 1981; "Ida Tacke Noddack," Biography available online at www.physics.ucla.edu/~cwp/Phase2/Noddack,_Ida_Tacke_@844157201.html; Millar, D., et al., *The Cambridge Dictionary of Scientists,* Cambridge: Cambridge University Press, 1996; Rayner-Canham, M., and G. Rayner-Canham, *Women in Chemistry: Their Changing Roles from Alchemical Times to the Mid-Twentieth Century,* Washington, D.C.: American Chemical Society, 1998.

North, Marianne
24 October 1830–3 August 1890
botanical artist

Marianne North spent thirteen years traveling around the world, creating oil paintings of the plants she saw. She arranged for a gallery to be constructed at the Royal Botanical Gardens, Kew, and here 848 of her paintings have been displayed since 1882.

North was the daughter of a member of Parliament, and her family traveled often. In the winter they lived at Hastings, moved to London in springtime, and spent the summers at Rougham in Norfolk and Gawthorpe in Lancashire. In 1847 the family went to Heidelberg for eight months and then traveled around Europe for two years. North was interested in music and had a fine singing voice. She worked hard at her musical training, but just when she might have embarked on a singing career her voice changed.

When her mother died in 1855, North and her sisters continued to live with their father, who besides being a member of Parliament was very keen on horticulture. At Hastings he had three greenhouses, and North used to help him with the plants. In 1867 she had her first lessons in oil painting from Robert Dowling, an Australian artist. She was so thrilled with the brilliance and textural possibilities of oil painting that from then on this was her medium.

Following the death of her father in 1869, North was initially at a loss as to what to do. In 1871 she went to the United States to stay with friends. This was the start of her painting expeditions. She was fortunate in having adequate funds for travel as well as letters of introduction to people in high places; she rarely had to find her own accommodations. Besides painting, North kept a detailed diary describing both the plants she painted and all the events of her travels. She used whatever means of transport was available and preferred to travel alone.

After North America she went to Jamaica and on to Brazil, thrilled with the tropical vegetation and the richness of its color. On her return to Britain, she learned the art of copper etching. In 1875 North went to the Canary Islands and, after a brief return to England, went on to Japan via San Francisco and California. Finding Japan cold and damp, she went on to Singapore and then Sarawak, where she stayed with Rajah Charles Brooke and his wife. She moved on to Java and Sri Lanka, where she met the photographer Julia Margaret Cameron, who had a house there.

On returning to England in February 1877, she held an exhibition of her paintings at the British Museum in Kensington. By September she was off again, this time to India, painting as she traveled. She painted on prepared cardboard and was said to put the colors onto the board directly from the tubes rather than mixing them first. She did the rough outline of a painting outside, finishing it later.

In March 1879 she was back in England and held another exhibition in Conduit Street. In August 1879 she wrote to the director of Kew Gardens to ask if he would accept her paintings for display, offering to finance a building for them. He agreed, and Sir James Fergusson designed the building. North chose a site well away from the main gate.

North's next trip was to Australia and New Zealand. She stayed with Ellis Rowan at Albany, Western Australia, and taught Rowan how to use oil paints. Tasmania and New Zealand were too cold for North's taste, so she traveled home via Honolulu. On a later trip to South Africa, she was particularly thrilled with the proteas. Although she suffered tiredness and deafness as she grew older, she continued to travel, visiting the Seychelles and Chile so that she could paint the monkey puzzle tree, Araucaria araucana, and puya, Puya alpestris, in their natural habitat.

Back in England, North prepared for the opening of the gallery on 7 June 1882. North arranged the pictures according to country and decorated the woodwork. As refreshments were not allowed in the gallery, she painted tea plants over one arch and coffee plants over another. The gallery was well received and everyone realized what an amazing achievement it was for one person. Sir Joseph Hooker made clear how much the paintings would be valued as a historical record, for so many of the plants were likely to disappear with the clearance of forested areas. The gallery was renovated in 1933 and again in 1981.

In 1886 North moved to Mount House in Alderley, in the Cotswolds. With many gifts of plants, she made a wonderful garden.

She suffered from increasing deafness and was found to have liver disease; she died when she was fifty-nine and was buried in the parish churchyard.

Bibliography: Ponsonby, L., *Marianne North at Kew Gardens*, Exeter: Webb and Bower, 1990.

O

Ormerod, Eleanor Anne
11 May 1828–19 July 1901
entomologist

Education: at home.

Employment: assistant estate manager, Sedbury Park, Gloucestershire, until 1873; lecturer in economic entomology, Royal Agricultural College, Cirencester, 1881–1884; honorary consulting entomologist, Royal Agricultural Society of England, 1882–1889; assistant to Charles Whitehead (preparation of government reports), 1884–1890;.

Eleanor Ormerod was consulting entomologist to the Royal Agricultural Society of England from 1882 to 1892. She specialized in economic entomology. In 1878 she was the first woman to be elected a fellow of the Meteorological Society.

Ormerod was born in Gloucestershire, the youngest of ten children. She was educated at home by her mother, though she learned Latin and modern languages on her own and was instructed in painting by William Hunt. Ormerod was also interested in botany and helped her brother sort out his botanical specimens.

In 1852 she bought James Stephens's *Manual of British Beetles* (1839) and taught herself about insects by dissecting specimens and referring to his text. In 1868 she replied to a request for help from the Royal Horticultural Society (RHS). The committee had decided to establish a collection of insects important in British horticulture and agriculture. Ormerod and helpers on the family estate gathered specimens for the

RHS. The society awarded her its Silver Flora Medal in 1870 for her collection. She received further medals in 1872 for a collection of plaster models and other representations of plants and reptiles that she exhibited at the International Polytechnic Exhibition in Moscow.

Following the death of her father, Ormerod moved to Torquay with her sister. They lived there for three years then moved to Isleworth in London to be near Kew Gardens. The director of Kew at that time was Sir Joseph Hooker, and he and his wife were friends of the Ormerod sisters.

Ormerod took a keen interest in meteorology while at Isleworth, and she began to keep meteorological records. She continued with her entomological work, in 1877 publishing *Notes for Observations of Injurious Insects,* a pamphlet that she funded herself. It appeared at a time when there were calls in several quarters for the appointment of a government entomologist in Britain, as had been done in France and the United States. Ormerod produced twenty-four *Annual Reports of Observations of Injurious Insects* from 1877 to 1900. In 1881 she gave a lecture at the Royal Agricultural College in Cirencester in which she drew a clear distinction between traditional entomology and the applied entomology she practiced. She continued to give lectures at the Royal Agricultural College until 1884 and at the South Kensington Museum. Her lectures at the museum were published in 1884 as *A Guide to the Methods of Insect Life.*

After a report she had written on the turnip fly was published, Ormerod became honorary consulting entomologist to the

Eleanor Anne Ormerod (Hulton-Getty/Archive Photos)

Royal Agricultural Society of England (RASE) in 1882. On her first day in office, she had an accident at Waterloo Station that left her permanently lame.

From 1884 onward she helped Charles Whitehead prepare government reports on injurious insects. With the establishment of the Board of Agriculture, Whitehead was officially appointed as an adviser. Ormerod continued to help, though she eventually resigned in 1890. She cited pressure of work as a reason, though she also felt her status as a professional scientist had not been fully recognized, since the government seemed happy to take advantage of her unpaid expertise.

The lack of professional recognition also contributed to her resignation from her honorary post at the RASE in 1892. She felt that her skills and knowledge were not fully appreciated because of the unpaid nature of her position. Her successor, Cecil Warburton, appointed in 1893, received an annual salary of £200.

Ormerod was committed to the promotion of economic entomology as an educational subject. As well as lecturing, she helped William Fream write *Elements of Agriculture* (1892). As a result of her influence, the RASE and the Royal Agricultural College introduced agricultural entomology as voluntary and compulsory subjects, respectively, in their examinations. She was an examiner for the University of Edinburgh. In 1889 the university set up a chair in economic entomology, but Ormerod was not in a position to put herself forward for consideration because she was a woman.

In 1884 she began research on the ox-warble fly, *Hypoderma bovis*, and published her results in her annual report to the RASE (*Journal of the Royal Agricultural Society of England*, 3rd series, 1 [1890]: 181–184). By the end of the 1880s, she had become interested in the use of Paris green as an insecticide, particularly against the possible threat of the Colorado potato beetle. The long-term toxic effects of Paris green, a copper acetoarsenite, were not recognized at the time. In 1892 Ormerod wrote in a letter to James Fletcher, dominion entomologist of Canada, that her epitaph should be "She introduced Paris-green into England."

In 1897 she took up another cause: the extermination of the house sparrow. As a result of changes in land use in Britain, these birds were seen in increasing numbers, particularly around farmland near settlements, and were thought to be a direct threat to grain crops. W. G. Tegetmeier published his book *The House Sparrow (The Avian Rat)* in 1899, with an appendix written by Ormerod. Her view that the birds should be eliminated from Britain brought her into opposition with conservationists such as Edith Carrington.

In 1900 Ormerod was the first woman to receive an honorary LL.D. from the University of Edinburgh. She made several gifts to the university, including some paintings of insects by her sister Georgiana. The university also received a bequest of £5,000 from her estate.

She died of liver cancer at St. Albans in 1901. Her life formed the basis of Virginia Woolf's 1924 short story "Miss Ormerod."

Bibliography: Chevalier, J., "Eleanor Ormerod," on *Woman's Hour*, BBC Radio 4, 19 July 2001; *Dictionary of National Biography*, Oxford: Oxford University Press, 1912; McDiarmid Clark, J. F., "Eleanor Ormerod (1828–1901) as an Economic Entomologist: Pioneer of Purity Even More Than of Paris Green," *British Journal of the History of Science* 25 (1992): 431–452; Ogilvie, M. B., *Women in Science: Antiquity through the Nineteenth Century.* New York: MIT Press, 1986.

P

Parke, Mary
23 March 1908–17 July 1989
marine biologist

Education: Notre Dame Convent School, Everton Valley, Liverpool; University of Liverpool, 1926–1929; B.Sc. with honors in botany, 1929; Ph.D., 1932; D.Sc., 1950.

Employment: phycologist, Marine Biological Station, Port Erin, Isle of Man, 1930–1940; research on algae for the Development Commission and the Ministry of Supply, 1941–1946; senior phycologist, Marine Biological Association, Plymouth, 1947–1973.

Mary Parke contributed much to the study of marine algae, but her pioneering work on culturing algae in the laboratory may be considered her most enduring contribution. She found that the flagellate *Isochrysis galbana* was ideal for feeding oyster larvae; cultures of this species are used for fish farming and in research laboratories throughout the world.

Parke was a promising pianist but decided to study botany at Liverpool University. She was awarded an Isaac Roberts Research Scholarship in biology in 1929, allowing her to undertake research on marine algae at the Port Erin Marine Laboratory on the Isle of Man, owned by Liverpool University. She was coauthor with Dr. Mary Knight of *Manx Algae* (1931).

In 1930 Parke was appointed as phycologist (seaweed specialist) at Port Erin; her doctoral thesis, "The Mesogloiaceae and Associated Families," was accepted in 1932. Besides working on seaweeds, she investigated the food of oyster larvae and started working on algal cultures, moving to Plymouth Marine laboratory in 1940 to learn from marine biologists involved in this work.

From 1941 to 1946 she was enlisted by the government to study the distribution of marine algae on the coasts of Britain. Algae were a valuable source of agar, used for culturing bacteria and in food such as ice cream. When she was released from this work, Parke was appointed as phycologist at the Marine Research Laboratory at Plymouth and stayed there until she retired. A meticulous worker, she set high standards for her colleagues. She returned to research on algal cultures, and the Plymouth Culture Collection was set up under her direction. Most researchers at that time who needed the correct food for feeding marine animals such as crab larvae or filter feeders such as mussels contacted Parke for guidance on the most suitable algae and its subculture. In 1953 she published *A Preliminary Checklist of British Marine Algae,* a useful guide for other workers when making their own checklists.

Parke drew beautiful and accurate drawings of algae using the light microscope. In the 1950s Professor Irene Manton at Leeds University started using the electron microscope for her research and collaborated with Parke on investigating algal structure. The electron microscope photographs linked to Parke's drawings and observations set new standards.

Parke published numerous research papers, most of them in the *Journal of the Marine Biological Association, UK.* She was a founding member of the British Phycological Society and a member of the International Phycological Society. She was a fellow of the Royal Society (elected 1972), the Institute of Biology, and the Linnean Society. She was a corresponding member of the Royal Botanical Society of the Netherlands (1970) and the Norwegian Academy of Science and Letters (1971). In 1986 she was awarded an honorary doctor of science degree from Liverpool University. Because she was not well enough to go to Liverpool, a party from the university flew to Plymouth for an awards ceremony at the Marine Laboratory. The Mary Parke Fund gives financial aid to young scientists who want to do research on algae at the Plymouth Laboratory.

Bibliography: Allen, A., archivist, University of Liverpool, personal communication to the author, July 2001; Archives, Marine Biological Association, Plymouth, Letters, notes, reports, photographs, drawings, and videotape (1942–1986), accessed by author March 1999; Boalch, G. T., "*In memoriam* Mary Parke (1908–1989)," *Phycologica* 29, 4 (1990): 541–542; Green, J. C., "Mary Parke, FRS, 1908–1989," *British Phycological Journal* 25 (1990): 212–216; Green, J. C., "The Plymouth Culture Connection of Algae," *Marine Biological Association News* 22 (1999): 4; *Who Was Who, 1981–1990*, London: Adam and Charles Black, 1991.

Partridge, Margaret Mary
8 April 1891–
electrical engineer, contractor

Education: Bedford College, London, 1911–1914; B.Sc. with honors in mathematics.
Employment: self-employed electrical engineer.

An electrical engineer, *Margaret Partridge* encourage other women to enter the field.

Partridge graduated in 1914 from Bedford College, where she was the Arnott and Jane Benson Scholar.

She lectured on behalf of the newly formed Electrical Association for Women (EAW) and worked with Caroline Haslett to produce the journal *Electrical Age for Women*,

which first came out in June 1926.

By 1921 Partridge had wired four English villages for electricity. In 1927 Partridge and Haslett set up Electrical Enterprise Inc., a company that aimed to provide electricity for rural communities. They wanted rural households to enjoy the benefits of electricity and believed women should be encouraged to work in the industry. Partridge took on both men and women as apprentices.

Bibliography: Dyer, L., Archives assistant, Royal Holloway/Bedford College, University of London, personal communication to the author, January 2000; Bentley, L., *Educating Women: A Pictorial History of Bedford College, University of London, 1849–1985*, Surrey, England: Alma Publishers, 1991; Pursell, C., "Domesticating Modernity: The Electrical Association for Women, 1924–1986," *British Journal for the History of Science* 32 (1999): 47–67.

Patten, Marguerite
4 November 1915–
home economist, cookery writer

Employment: demonstrator, Eastern Electricity Board; actor; home economist, Frigidaire, 1938–1939; senior food adviser: Ministry of Food, 1942–1943; Ministry of Food Advice Bureau, Harrods, London, 1943–1947; Harrods Food Advice Bureau and Home Service Bureau, 1947–1951; freelance presenter and writer, from 1951.
Married: Bob Patten. He died in 1997.

Marguerite Patten became a household name in Britain through her broadcasts on cooking and particularly through her writing on food.

Patten was the eldest of three children. Her father died when she was twelve, and her mother returned to her job as a teacher in order to support her family. After leaving school, Patten took a cookery course. She started her working life as a demonstrator in the fuel industry, which gave her experience in cooking for an audience. One of her early ambitions was to go on stage, and she

Marguerite Patten (Hulton-Getty/Archive Photos)

decided to leave her job and join a professional theater company. After a short period as an actor, during which she used the stage name Marguerite Eve, she returned to the profession for which she became famous.

Patten was employed as senior food adviser by the Ministry of Food during World War II, demonstrating how families could keep healthy on the somewhat meager rations. She was in charge of an advice bureau the Ministry of Food set up in Harrods department store in central London. In 1944 she was one of the speakers on the BBC's *Kitchen Front* broadcasts, and she has given talks on *Woman's Hour* from its inception in 1946 to the present. She was also the regular cooking expert on the BBC's first television magazine program, *Designed for Women,* from its beginning in 1947 until it ended in 1960.

After the war Harrods continued to run a food advice bureau and a home service bureau. Patten managed a team of home economists who demonstrated both cooking and how to use the various appliances on sale. In 1947 electrical appliances were only just beginning to be widely used, and an electric washing machine was still a luxury.

Patten left Harrods in 1951 and from then on worked as a freelance presenter and cookery writer. For the BBC's *Cookery Club* from 1956 to 1961, Patten's role was to test recipes sent in by viewers and then select the most interesting ones to make on televi-

sion. She also demonstrated recipes all over Britain, in town halls and theaters, even in the London Palladium. Later she gave talks on cruise ships; she was also a visiting lecturer in various colleges.

Patten wrote cookbooks for use in schools and at home. In the 1990s she published eleven books, including *The Victory Cookbook* (1995), which described dishes used to celebrate VE and VJ days during World War II; her autobiography, *What's Cooking* (1999), which includes some of her favorite recipes; and *Marguerite Patten's Century of British Cooking* (1999), which gives recipes and historical details from each decade of the twentieth century (and inspired a BBC Radio 4 series of the same name). In 2000 she published *Spam—the Cookbook,* in which she provides the story of this brand of processed meat as well as recipes. She has written more than 165 cookbooks; over 17 million copies of her books have been sold, together with 500 million of her cookery cards.

Patten is a member of the Royal Society of Medicine's Forum on Food and of the Guild of Food Writers, and she was president of the Microwave Association. She makes regular cassette recordings on cookery for blind people for the charity Soundaround. Her most recent book, coauthored with Jeannette Ewin, is *Eat to Beat Arthritis: Say Goodbye to Pain the Natural Way—Over 60 Recipes and a Treatment Plan to Transform Your Life* (2001).

She was made an Officer of the Order of the British Empire (OBE) in 1991, awarded a lifetime achievement award by the Guild of Food Writers in 1995, and honored by the Trustees of the Andre Simon Memorial Fund in 1996. She has also received lifetime achievement awards from the BBC in 1998 and Waterford Wedgwood in 1999.

Bibliography: Patten, M., *Desert Island Discs,* London: BBC Radio 4, programs aired 21 January 2001 and 26 January 2001; Patten, M., *Marguerite Patten's Century of British Cooking,* London: Grub Street, 1999; Patten, M., personal communications to the author, March and November 2000.

Payne-Scott, Ruby Violet
28 May 1912–25 May 1981
radiophysicist

Education: University of Sydney; B.Sc., 1933; M.Sc., 1936; diploma of education, 1938.

Employment: research fellow, Cancer Research Committee, University of Sydney, 1932–1935; engineer, AWA Ltd., 1939–1941; research, Commonwealth Scientific Industrial Research Organisation (CSIRO), Radiophysics Division, 1941–1951; teacher, Danebrook Church of England School, Sydney, 1963–1975.

Married: Mr. Hall.

Ruby Payne-Scott was Australia's first woman radioastronomer.

Payne-Scott was born in Grafton, New South Wales, and educated at the University of Sydney. While still an undergraduate, she investigated the relative intensity of the spectral lines in indium and gallium, and her results were published in *Nature* (131 [1933]: 365–366). She held a Cancer Research Committee Fellowship at the University of Sydney and investigated the use of photographic film for measuring gamma radiation as well as the effects of a magnetic field on tissue cultures; again, the results, coauthored by W. H. Love, appeared in *Nature* (137 [1936]: 277). After working as an engineer at AWA Ltd., she moved to the Radiophysics Division at CSIRO. She published several more papers, including one in the *British Journal of Radiology* (10 [1937]: 850–870) and one in *Wireless Engineer* (19 [1942]: 290–302). She was based at home from 1951 to 1963 and then taught science and mathematics until retirement.

Bibliography: Website: www.asap.unimelb.edu.au/bsparcs/physics/P001778p.htm.

Peirce, Mary Sophie Catherine Teresa
10 November 1896–May 1939
aviator

Education: St. Margaret's Hall, Dublin; Agricultural Science, University College, Dublin, 1920–1921; postgraduate studies, University of Aberdeen, 1921–?.

Employment: dispatch rider in Women's Auxiliary Air Force in France and Belgium, 1915–1918; demonstrator in zoology, University of Aberdeen, 1921–?; pilot with KLM, 1929–1933; instructor at Kildonan Aerodrome, Dublin.

Married: Major William Davies Elliott-Lynn, in 1919 (he died in 1927); Sir James Heath, on 12 October 1927 (divorced in 1932); George Anthony Reginald Williams, an aviator, in 1932 (divorced in 1936).

Sophie Peirce was a pioneer in aviation. In 1926 she became the first woman to gain a B aviator's license and the first woman to loop-the-loop and make a parachute jump from 15,000 feet.

Peirce had initially intended to study medicine. Instead she became a dispatch rider in France and Belgium during World War I, working with the Royal Flying Corps. When the war ended, she returned to Ireland and met Major William Elliott-Lynn, who was on holiday there; they married. Elliott-Lynn funded Peirce through her first year at University while he went to Kenya to attend to 1,000 acres of land given in lieu of some of his army pay.

She gave up studying in Dublin and moved to Aberdeen University. While there Peirce became keen on athletics, winning numerous prizes and campaigning for a women's athletic organization. With the help of Major Manchart, the Women's Amateur Athletic Association (WAAA) was founded in 1922 with Peirce as vice-president. By 1925 there were 500 clubs with over 25,000 women members, ranging from factory workers to university students. Peirce moved to Kenya in October 1923 to live with her husband and work on their coffee farm. The poems she wrote about Africa,

East African Nights and Other Verses (1925), helped raise funds for the WAAA.

Peirce returned to England in 1924. She wrote *Athletics for Women and Girls—How to Be an Athlete and Why* (1925), the first book of its kind. The profits from its sale went to the WAAA and the Playing Fields Association. The preface of the book was read on BBC radio by Mrs. Elliot Lynn on 9 April 1925. In it Peirce described the development of women's participation in international athletic events and gave her ideas on physical activities for girls and women. The key piece of advice she gave was "Don't overdo things." In 1926, representing the International Athletics Federation, she explained to the International Olympic Council in Prague why women should be allowed to compete in Olympic track and field events. Three events in the 1928 Olympic Games were subsequently opened to women.

On her flight back from Prague, Peirce sat next to a Royal Air Force pilot who said he could arrange flying lessons for her. She learned to fly at the London Aeroplane Club and by 1925 had gained her pilot's A license.

Women were excluded from employment as pilots by the International Commission for Air Navigation (ICAN). Peirce campaigned for this ban to be lifted. During 1926 she worked hard for her B license, which she gained by the middle of the year, having demonstrated her competence in day and night flying, engine fitting and rigging, navigation, and meteorology. In May 1926 she flew newspapers to Paris during the British general strike, proof that women were quite capable of being commercial pilots. At the next ICAN meeting, the ban was lifted.

Peirce worked actively in aviation, breaking a height record at 19,000 feet on 8 October 1927. One of her dreams was to fly from South Africa to London. She left Pretoria on 25 February 1928 in her *Avian* and arrived in Croydon, London, on 17 May. She had numerous stops on the way and spent days staying with friends before moving on. She was even overcome by sunstroke six hours after leaving Bulawayo, Zimbabwe, and had a blackout and crash-landed; she was rescued by some Matabele women but was unconscious for four hours.

After the success of the flight, Peirce worked as a pilot for KLM and traveled extensively in the United States. She had a severe flying accident in 1932 when her plane suddenly lost height and she crashed into the roof of a factory in Cleveland, Ohio, watched by thousands at the flying exhibition. She was unconscious for three weeks. Though she recovered, she lost her confidence and her public status. She returned to Ireland in 1933.

With her third husband she toured Ireland giving air shows. She was the first woman instructor at Kildonan Aerodrome, near Dublin, and bought the aerodrome in 1936, running it as Dublin Air Ferries. When the business and her marriage failed, Peirce went to England. She fell down the steps of a tram in 1939 and died from shock caused by her numerous injuries.

Bibliography: Boase, W., *The Sky's the Limit: Women Pioneers in Aviation,* London: Osprey, 1979; Elliott-Lynn, S. C., "Athletics for Women," program aired 9 April 1925 on BBC station 2LO; Heath, Lady, and S. W. Murray, *Women and Flying,* London: John Long, 1929; Scanlan, M., "The Flying Irish Woman," in *Stars, Shells and Bluebells,* edited by M. Mulvihill and P. Deevy, Dublin: Women in Technology and Science (WTIS), 1997.

Pennington, Winifred Anne
8 October 1915–
freshwater biologist

Education: Barrow-in-Furness Grammar School, 1927–1935; Reading University; B.Sc., 1938; Ph.D., 1941.

Employment: research student, Freshwater Biological Association (FBA), Windermere, 1940–1945; University of Leicester: lecturer, 1947; special lecturer, 1961; honorary professor, 1980; principal scientific officer, NERC Quaternary Research Unit, 1965; Freshwater Biological Association, 1956–1967.

Married: Dr. Thomas Gaskell Tutin, in 1942.

Winifred Pennington pioneered the examination of cores of bottom deposits from lakes.

After leaving Barrow-in-Furness Grammar School, Pennington studied at Reading University. During her first summer vacation in 1936, she worked in the laboratories of the Freshwater Biological Association (FBA), which at that time were located at Wray Castle, near Ambleside. Here she started her investigations into algae.

She stayed on at Reading for her postgraduate work, obtaining her Ph.D. Her thesis was based on her investigation of some problems of the ecology of freshwater algae, especially in relation to the process of sedimentation. Pennington was fascinated by paleobotany. B. M. Jenkin, the technician at Wray Castle, had developed an efficient corer to take samples of Lake District sediments, and Pennington was able to analyze the samples for the remains of plants. She was based at the Freshwater Biological Association from 1940 to 1945. Thomas Tutin, then a lecturer at Leicester University, came to Wray House at intervals to collect information for his work in plant ecology. He and Pennington were married in 1942. Pennington spent time at the Department of Botany at the University of Cambridge with Professor Harry Godwin, learning about pollen analysis.

From 1945 she was mostly based in Leicester, bringing up her family. She was on the staff of the Botany Department at Leicester University, eventually becoming honorary reader in botany then honorary professor from 1980.

Beginning in 1955 she was able to become more involved again with the Freshwater Biological Association, which had moved to The Ferry House, on the shores of Windermere. She started to work again on the postglacial deposits in the Lake District. Mr. Mackereth, the FBA's chemist, devised an improved pneumatic corer that could be used by two people from a rowboat, and this helped in collecting samples. Pennington used the prototype for twenty years.

After the National Environmental Research Council was set up in 1965, the FBA gave her a position as principal scientific officer in charge of the Quaternary Research Unit. Pollen analyses were done in Leicester and chemical analyses at Ferry House.

Besides numerous publications in scientific journals, Pennington wrote *The History of British Vegetation* (1969). W. H. Pearsall of Leeds University had made notes for a book in the New Naturalist series, but he died before he had started the final draft. Pennington took over and finished the book with the help of specialists; *The Lake District, a Landscape History* was published in 1973.

Pennington was elected a fellow of the Royal Society in 1978. In 1974 she was elected as a foreign member of the Royal Danish Academy.

Bibliography: Haworth, E. Y., and J. W. G. Lund, *Lake Sediments and Environmental History: Studies in Palaeolimnology and Palaeoecology in Honour of Winifred Tutin*, Leicester: Leicester University Press, 1984; *Who's Who, 1997*, London: Adam and Charles Black, 1997.

Perey, Marguerite
19 October 1909–13 May 1975
nuclear chemist

Education: licence, doctorat des sciences, 1946.
Employment: researcher (various posts, initially junior laboratory assistant), Radium Institute, Paris, 1929–1949; nuclear research center, Strasbourg: head of research; administrator; professor, from 1949; director, from 1958.

Marguerite Perey carried out important research work in nuclear chemistry and discovered the radioactive element francium in 1939. She was the first woman to be elected to the French Academy of Sciences, an honor she achieved in 1962.

Perey was born in Villemomble, Seine, in France, and originally planned to study medicine. Her father's death meant that she was unable to fulfill this ambition, and she took up a post as junior laboratory assistant, working with Marie Curie at the Radium Institute in Paris. She disliked the working conditions to such an extent that she soon decided to give her three months' notice and leave, but she changed her plans and stayed for twenty years. In 1939 she discovered the element actinium K, later named francium. This element is so rare that a cubic kilometer of the earth's crust contains only an estimated 15 grams of it.

Having built up her professional reputation as a nuclear scientist, Perey was persuaded to reinforce this academically, and she took her degree in 1946. She was awarded her *licence* and *doctorat des sciences* in the same year, a remarkable feat. From 1949 she held a chair at the nuclear research center in Strasbourg. She also served there as head of research and administrator and was director from 1958.

Perey received many honors, including the Légion d'honneur, the Grand Prix Scientifique de la Ville de Paris (1960), Lauréate de l'Académie des Sciences (1950 and 1960), and the Lavoisier Silver Medal of the Chemistry Society of France (1964). During the last fifteen years of her life, she suffered from radiation-caused illness; she died in 1975.

Bibliography: Demeulenaere-Douyère, C., archivist, Académie des Sciences, Paris, personal communication to the author, January 1999; Millar, D., et al., *The Cambridge Dictionary of Scientists,* Cambridge: Cambridge University Press, 1996; Roberts, F. C., comp., *Obituaries from the Times, 1971–1975,* Reading: Newspaper Archives Developments, 1978.

Perry, Frances Mary
née Everett
19 February 1907–11 October 1993
horticulturalist

Education: Swanley Horticultural College for Ladies (now Wye College), qualified 1925.

Employment: Perry's Nursery, 1927–; horticultural adviser to Middlesex County Council, 1943; chief educational adviser for agriculture and horticulture, Middlesex County Council, 1951–1953; principal of Norwood Hall College of Horticulture and Agricultural Education, 1953–1967.

Married: Gerald Perry, fern specialist, in 1930; he died in 1964; Robert Hay, in 1977; he died in 1989.

In 1968 *Frances Perry* became the first woman member of the Royal Horticultural Society's council, and in 1978 she was elected as one of the Royal Horticultural Society's vice-presidents.

Perry's interest in flowers began in her childhood. She used to ask for help in identifying wildflowers from E. A. Bowles, a neighbor who was vice-chairman of the Royal Horticultural Society council. Her mother took her to the Chelsea Flower Show when she was ten, and a decade later she was one of the first women exhibitors.

After training at Swanley, Perry was employed by Amos Perry, a well-known perennial plant nurseryman. She married Gerald Perry, Amos's son, and had two children. She continued with her horticultural work after she married. Her books included *Water Gardening* (1938), *Herbaceous Borders* (1949), and *The Collins Guide to Border Plants* (1957). She was the gardening correspondent of the *Observer* for twenty-six years, following on from Vita Sackville-West. Perry contributed to the *Royal Commission on Allotments* (1960), an investigation of small plots of land often council-owned and traditionally rented by individuals for growing produce. She also appeared in some early television programs on gardening.

When she retired from Norwood Hall, Perry traveled extensively. She visited over seventy countries, lecturing on horticulture and studying gardens and wild plants. She was made a Member of the Order of the British Empire (MBE) in 1962 and was awarded the Veitch Memorial Medal in 1964 and the Victoria Medal of Honor in 1971, both of these from the Royal Horticultural Society.

Bibliography: "Frances Perry, MBE," *Independent* (15 October 1993); Hewitt, B., *The Crocus King: E. A. Bowles of Myddleton House,* Ware, Herts, UK: The Rockingham Press, 1997; Whitsey, F., "Frances Perry, a Memoir," *The Garden* (January 1994): 10–11.

Petrie, Hilda Mary Isobel
née Urlin
1871–1957
archaeologist

Education: at home.

Married: Sir Flinders Petrie, professor of Egyptology at University College, London, on 26 November 1897. He died in 1942.

Hilda Petrie worked with her husband when he was excavating in Egypt and helped him prepare his findings for publication. When he died in 1942, she became director of the British School of Archaeology in Egypt until 1947, when she returned to England.

Petrie was the youngest daughter of Denny Urlin, a Dublin lawyer. The family moved to Sussex in 1875. In the winter the family lived in their London house, in Kensington. Petrie was interested in Gothic architecture, wildlife, and church antiquities. She went to lectures at King's College for Women and became skilled at drawing.

Henry Holiday, the Pre-Raphaelite painter, was a friend of her parents. Petrie was a model for him, and he painted her as Aspasia. When he discovered how good she was at copying, he asked her to make some drawings for him. In 1896, at his request, she visited Flinders Petrie's exhibition of his discoveries in Thebes and sketched some of the exhibits for Holiday.

Flinders Petrie was entranced by her and asked her to draw some scarabs for him, lent her books about Egypt, and gave her lecture tickets. When she said she had always longed to go to Egypt, Flinders decided to propose. They married on the morning of 26 November 1897, leaving the family behind to celebrate while they traveled to Africa.

Hilda Petrie enjoyed camping with her husband, especially as he had his own cook, freeing her from domestic chores. She helped him by drawing some of the small objects found during their excavations, explored the local area with him, and copied hieroglyph inscriptions as needed.

When they returned to England early the following year, Hilda Petrie was on hand to help her husband with his excavation report. For forty years, she was responsible for the financial side of the Egyptian Research Account. She became a competent lecturer and often spoke about her husband's work to various groups in order to raise funds.

In 1905 Flinders Petrie decided to separate his work from the Egypt Exploration Fund (EEF) and form the British School of Archaeology in Egypt. Funding was to come from the EEF. He was the director and Hilda Petrie served as joint secretary with Dr. Walker. She worked hard to raise funds for the EEF.

In 1907 Petrie had her first child, John. Though she did leave him in England for a few weeks to join her husband in Egypt, she soon returned to England, as she found she was pregnant again. She supported her husband in his work and ensured his books reached publication. When he died in Jerusalem in 1942, after spending twenty-one months in hospital, Hilda Petrie stayed on to sort out his books. After she returned to England, she continued with her work in archaeology; her book *Seven Memphite Tomb Chapels* was published in 1952.

Almost 1,500 of the Petries' books, photographs, and pamphlets formed the nucleus of the library of the National Museum of Antiquities in Khartoum. The British School of Archaeology was finally dissolved in 1954. The remaining funds were held by University College, London, to be used for traveling scholarships in memory of Flinders Petrie.

Hilda Petrie had a stroke in 1957 and died in the same year at University College Hospital.

Bibliography: Drower, M. S., *Flinders Petrie: A Life in Archaeology*, London: Victor Gollancz, 1985.

Philbin, Eva Maria née Ryder
4 January 1914–
organic chemist

Education: National University of Ireland, B.Sc., M.Sc., Ph.D., D.Sc.

Employment: chief chemist, Cold Chon Ltd., Galway, 1939–1943; chief chemist, Hygeia Ltd., Galway, 1940–1943; University College, Dublin: staff, from 1945; professor of organic chemistry, 1962; head of Department of Chemistry, 1963.

Married: John Madden Philbin, a company secretary, in 1943.

Eva Philbin became head of the Chemistry Department at University College, Dublin, in 1963. She has published some ninety papers on flavanoids.

Philbin was born in Ballina, County Mayo. In 1939 she began her career as a chemist in industry and worked for two commercial companies as chief chemist. She joined the staff of University College, Dublin, in 1945 and was made professor of organic chemistry in 1963.

She is a member of the Council of the Royal Irish Academy and the Natural Science Council and a fellow of the Royal Institute of Chemistry and the Institute of Chemistry of Ireland. Philbin has also taken a keen interest in the welfare of people with learning disabilities, serving as chair of the Consultative Council on Mental Handicap and as honorary treasurer of the National Association for the Mentally Handicapped of Ireland.

Bibliography: Who's Who, What's What, and Where in Ireland, Dublin: Geoffrey Chapman, 1973.

Pickford, Lillian Mary
14 August 1902–
physiologist

Education: Wycombe Abbey School; Bedford College, University College, London; B.Sc., 1924; B.Sc. in physiology, 1925; M.Sc., 1926; Member of the Royal College of Surgeons, Licentiate of the Royal College of Physicians, 1933.

Lillian Mary Pickford (Godfrey Argent Studio)

Employment: house physician and casualty officer, Stafford General Infirmary, 1935; Department of Physiology, University of Edinburgh: lecturer, 1939–1942; reader, 1952–1966; professor, 1966–1972; University of Nottingham, special professor of endocrinology, 1973–1983.

Mary Pickford, a leading physiologist, specialized in hormones. She was elected a fellow of the Royal Society in 1966.

Pickford studied physiology at Bedford College and then at University College, London, obtaining her M.Sc. in physiology in 1926. She trained as a doctor and spent a year working in a hospital before returning to research. After holding a Junior Beit Memorial Research Fellowship from 1936 to 1939, she went to the University of Edinburgh, where she was initially a lecturer in physiology and is now an emeritus professor. Her research has been published in many journals and as a book, *The Central Role of Hormones* (1969).

She has been a fellow of University College, London, since 1968 and was awarded an honorary D.Sc. by Heriot-Watt University in Edinburgh, in 1991.

Bibliography: Who's Who, 2000, London: Adam and Charles Black, 2000.

Pirie, Antoinette (Tony)
née Patey
4 October 1905–11 October 1991
ophthalmologist

Education: Wycombe Abbey School, Newnham College, Cambridge, 1924–1930; natural science tripos, part 1, 1927; part 2, biochemistry, 1928; M.A., 1947; Ph.D., 1933; research in biochemistry, Cambridge, 1928–1930.

Employment: Imperial Cancer Research Fund, Mill Hill Laboratories; research on war gases; research assistant, Oxford Nuffield Laboratory of Ophthalmology, 1942–1947; Margaret Ogilvie Reader in Ophthalmology, Oxford, 1947–1973; professorial fellowship, Somerville College, Oxford, 1947–.

Married: Norman Wingate Pirie, university demonstrator in the Biochemistry Laboratory, Cambridge, on 11 March 1931.

Dr. Antoinette Pirie was able to combine her interest in biochemistry with a career in ophthalmology; she was committed to the prevention of blinding eye disease.

Pirie gained a first-class degree from Cambridge and researched vitamins for her doctorate in the Biochemistry Department of Cambridge University. She then studied tumor viruses at the Imperial Cancer Laboratories. When war broke out she worked with Ida Mann on the way the eyes respond to various gases used in chemical warfare. From 1942 the two were a dynamic research team in Oxford at the Nuffield Laboratory, looking at problems of eye development and metabolism. In 1946 they published *The Science of Seeing* to help in understanding how the eye functions and what can go wrong with it.

From 1947 Pirie was in charge of the lab, and she attracted a team of researchers to Oxford, mostly to investigate the changes in cataracts. With Ruth van Heyningen, she published *The Biochemistry of the Eye* (1956). In 1962 she invited scientists from all over the world to Oxford for the symposium "Lens Metabolism in Relation to Cataract," and as a result of this symposium the International Society for Eye Research was founded. She chaired the committee from 1968 to 1972. In 1968 she was the first woman to receive the Proctor Award.

In 1971, when she was due to retire from Oxford University, the director of the Royal Commonwealth Society for the Blind (now Sightsavers International) asked her to be the consultant for a new project in Tamil Nadu, southern India. The aim of the program was to help prevent nutritional blindness (xerophthalmia), which strikes more than 250,000 children a year in Asia. In India Pirie taught mothers how to use the local dark green leaves and yellow fruits, which were rich in vitamin A, to help prevent their children from going blind. She showed the women how to set up kitchen gardens in their villages to grow vegetables. Her experimental work showed that retinoic acid applied to the eye could prevent blindness. In 1990 Pirie was given an award by the International Association for the Prevention of Blindness for her services to xerophthalmia.

Pirie, a person of strong convictions, was an active member in the Campaign for Nuclear Disarmament (CND). She spoke at rallies about the dangers of radioactivity and edited *Fall-Out* (1958).

Bibliography: Bloemendal, H., et al., Special issue dedicated to Antoinette Pirie and Ruth van Heyningen, *Experimental Eye Research* 31, 5 (1980): i–xiv; Darnborough, A., *Under a Drumstick Tree: A History of the Nutritional Rehabilitation Centre at Madurai*, Haywards Heath, Sussex: Royal Commonwealth Society for the Blind, 1985; "Dr. Antoinette Pirie," *Times* (21 October 1991); Hallendorf, M., chief executive, Royal College of Ophthalmologists, personal communication to the author, July 2001; McLaren, D., and C. Driver, "Dr. Antoinette Pirie: Beacon for Science and Peace," *Guardian* (25 October 1991); *Newnham College Register, 1924–1950*, vol. 2, Cambridge: Newnham College, 1981; Wilson, John, autobiographical notes and retrospect, notes on the Development of the Royal Commonwealth Society for the Blind: 1950–1983, transcribed from tape 11 of John Wilson's diaries, archives. Sightsavers International.

Pitt-Rivers, Rosalind Venetia née Henley
4 March 1907–14 January 1990
physiologist

Education: at home; Notting Hill High School, Girls' Public Day School Trust, 1920–1924; Bedford College, University of London; B.Sc. with honors, 1930; M.Sc., 1931; Department of Pathological Chemistry, University College Hospital Medical School, Ph.D., 1939.

Employment: National Institute for Medical Research (part of the Medical Research Council), 1942–1972, head of the Chemical Division, 1969–1972 (retirement).

Married: Captain George Henry Lane-Fox Pitt-Rivers, in 1931 (divorced 1937).

Rosalind Pitt-Rivers discovered the thyroid hormone triiodothyronine.

Pitt-Rivers came from an aristocratic family and was initially educated at home by a French governess. Her father, a brigadier general, was often away. Pitt-Rivers was given a chemistry set when she was twelve and used to conduct experiments when she stayed with her mother's parents.

She went to Bedford College London and obtained a first-class honors degree. For her M.Sc., she studied the reactions of substituted ammonium aryloxides and cinchona alkaloids.

In 1931 she married her mother's cousin. Their son, Anthony, was born in 1932. She moved to the Pitt-Rivers estate in Dorset, returning to research in 1937, after her divorce. She joined Sir Charles Harington in the Department of Pathology at University College Medical School in London as a research student, investigating methyl glu-

cosaminides and their hydrolysis by snail enzymes.

Once she had finished her doctorate, Pitt-Rivers did research on the biosynthesis of the thyroid hormone L-thyroxine and iodinated peptides at Harington's laboratory. When Harington moved to the National Institute for Medical Research (NIMR), part of the Medical Research Council, sited in Hampstead, Pitt-Rivers moved with him as a member of NIMR's staff. She worked there until she retired in 1972, concentrating on thyroid hormones. She published two important papers, one on the preparation of thyroxine from iodated casein and the other about a new way of synthesizing thyronine, before the outbreak of war interrupted her work.

Pitt-Rivers was sent to the South-east Blood Transfusion Unit, then to the Maudsley Hospital, back to University College to work on artificial iodoproteins, and finally seconded to the Twenty-first Army Group to go to Belgium. She and Dr. Charles Dent and Dame Janet Vaughan had to carry out a nutritional study of force-marched prisoners of war, spending three weeks at the Bergen-Belsen concentration camp after it had been liberated. Pitt-Rivers was so shocked by the condition of the inmates that she became a heavy smoker, a habit that affected her health adversely with increasing age.

After the war she returned to NIMR, which had moved to Mill Hill. Harington was the new director, but as he had to spend so much time on administration, Pitt-Rivers soon found she was working virtually independently. Radioactive isotopes were then available, as was paper chromatography, and this was a great help in further research on thyroxine.

In 1950 Dr. Jack Gross, a Canadian, came to work with Pitt-Rivers at NIMR. He had used radioactive iodine to research how the thyroid hormone was formed and secreted. NIMR was then a world leader in the technique of paper chromatography, and agar electrophoretic analysis was being developed as well. Gross and Pitt-Rivers worked on an unknown substance in human plasma related to thyroxine. In 1951 they published "The Identification of 3:3':5-L-Triiodothyronine in Human Plasma" in *The Lancet*, the most important paper in Pitt-Rivers's career. Two later papers showed that T_3 had substantial biological activity and in humans could reverse the effects of myxedema, severe hypothyroidism. Later more details of the structure were published. Olga Kennard's X-ray diffraction analyses of the different forms of the two thyroid hormones T_3 and T_4 confirmed that the unknown substance was the same as synthetic L-T_3. At the same time the Roche group in Paris were also working on T_3, but Pitt-Rivers's group won the race.

After the discovery of T_3, Pitt-Rivers received many honors, the greatest of which was becoming a fellow of the Royal Society in 1954, only two years after she had identified triiodothyronine. The MRC benefited from the royalties resulting after T_3 was patented, as it is used to diagnose and cure thyroid disorders.

From the late 1950s until her retirement, Pitt-Rivers worked on triiodothyronine and its derivatives, the structure of thyroglobulin and its formation in the thyroid gland, and the preparation and used of immunological reagents. After she retired she transferred to the Department of Pharmacology at University College and worked there from 1975 until she was seventy-eight, when, in poor health, she moved to Dorset to be near her family.

Pitt-Rivers thoroughly enjoyed her career as a scientist. She preferred to break down a problem into its component parts and work through each one. She usually had only three or four coworkers. Besides the theoretical aspects of her work, she was keenly interested in medical problems related to the thyroid gland and attended many medical gatherings. She was made an honorary fellow of the Royal Society of Medicine in 1983 and of the Royal College of Physicians in 1986.

Bibliography: Pitt-Rivers, R., ed., *Advances in Thyroid Research,* London: Pergamon Press, 1961; Pitt-Rivers, R., "Some Biological Reactions of Iodine," in K. Fellinger and R. Hofer, eds., *Further Advances in Thyroid Research,* vol. 1, Wien: der Wiener Medizinischen Akademie, 1971; Tata, J. R., "Rosalind Venetia Pitt-Rivers, 4 March 1907–14 January 1990," *Biographical Memoirs of Fellows of the Royal Society* 39 (1993): 325–348; *Who Was Who, 1981–1990,* London: Adam and Charles Black, 1991.

Platt of Writtle, Baroness
née Beryl Catherine Myatt
18 April 1923–
aeronautical engineer

Education: Tower House School, Leigh-on-Sea; Westcliff High School for Girls; Slough High School for Girls; Girton College, Cambridge, 1941–1943; mechanical sciences tripos, 1943; M.A., 1948.
Employment: technical assistant in Experimental Flight Test Department, Hawker Aircraft, Langley, 1943–1946; Project and Development Department, British European Airways Corporation, 1946–1949.
Married: Stewart Sydney Platt, in 1949.

Baroness Platt of Writtle was made a life peer in 1981. She was chair of the Equal Opportunities Commission from 1983 to 1988 and is a member of the House of Lords Select Committee for Science and Technology.

Because Platt's family moved around the country, she went to three different secondary schools, her last being in Slough. She won a place at Girton College, Cambridge, to read mathematics in 1941, the third year of the war. The government, aware of the gaps in certain areas, wrote to prospective students suggesting they study a subject other than mathematics; Platt chose aeronautics from the list. She did a two-year honors course in mechanical sciences. In her first year she went to lectures on a broad variety of subjects covering all aspects of engineering but also including management, psychology, and timber and surveying. In her second year she took more specialized courses in engineering, such as aeronautics. When she completed her tripos examinations in 1943, she was one of five women among 250 men.

Her first job was at Hawker Aircraft's Experimental Flight Test Department. She was involved in practical, top secret projects on fighters and through her hard work won the respect of her male colleagues.

After the war she joined the research and development department at British European Airways. At that time passengers had to be weighed before takeoff to ensure the correct weight distribution for safe operation of the aircraft. Platt taught herself statistics, and she and a senior engineer plotted a host of passenger weights from the records, eventually deciding there was no need for having passengers weighed before boarding larger aircraft (which would have been an impossibility with today's passenger numbers). She studied engine failure over mountains and on takeoff to ensure the safe operation of aircraft on one engine, however seldom it might happen.

When she married in 1949, she had to give up her job, as was customary. She became involved in a wide variety of mainly voluntary commitments, initially based near her home while she was bringing up her family. She was a member of Chelmsford Rural District Council from 1958 to 1974 and Essex County Council from 1965 to 1985, becoming alderman from 1969 to 1974, vice-chair from 1980 to 1983, and chair of the Education Committee from 1971 to 1980. She helped set up an Education-Industry Committee to bring about more understanding between scientists and teachers and tried to encourage girls to get involved in science and engineering. She enjoyed her work as a nonexecutive director of British Gas from 1988 to 1994 and was especially pleased to meet their women's groups and encourage equal opportunities.

After being made a life peer, Platt was in great demand to serve in various roles with organizations concerned with engineering and science. She was the only woman on the Engineering Council, established in the early 1980s, and in 1984 she helped set up the Women into Science and Engineering (WISE) campaign. Though there is still a long way to go, about 15 percent of engineering undergraduates in Britain are women, compared to 7 percent in 1984.

She was president of the Association of Science Education in 1988 and on the committee of Committee on the Public Understanding of Science (COPUS), which was formed to increase public awareness and understanding of science.

Platt was made a freeman of the City of London and a liveryman of the Worshipful Company of Engineers in 1988. She has been awarded honorary degrees by several universities, including the Open University in 1985, Cambridge University in 1988, Loughborough University in 1993, and Middlesex University (of which she was the first chancellor) in 1993.

Bibliography: Baroness Platt of Writtle, personal communications to the author, February–April 2000; Baroness Platt of Writtle, "Are Opportunities for Girls' Education Equal Now?" Constance Maynard Lecture, Suffolk County Council, 1989; Baroness Platt of Writtle, "Women in Science and Engineering," Dame Caroline Haslett Memorial Lecture, Royal Society of Arts, Manufacturers and Commerce, 25 November 1984; Baroness Platt of Writtle, "Women in Technology," Edith Leggett Lecture, University of Surrey, 13 June 1984; *Debrett's People of Today, 1998*, London: Debrett's Peerage Ltd., 1998; *Dod's Parliamentary Publishing Companion 2001*, London: Vacher Dod, 2001; *Girton College Register 1869–1946*, vol. 1, Cambridge: Girton College, 1948; *Who's Who, 1999*, London: Adam and Charles Black, 1999.

Pockels, Agnes
14 February 1862–1935
chemist

Education: Brunswick Municipal School for Girls, Germany; subsequently self-taught.

Agnes Pockels was a self-taught, amateur chemist who carried out research on the properties of water surfaces. The term "Pockels point" is still in use to describe a point in the contraction of surface molecules subjected to a horizontal force.

Pockels was born in Venice, the daughter of a Royal Austrian Army officer stationed there. Pockels and her parents alike suffered bouts of ill health, and her father was discharged from the army for medical reasons, after which the family moved to Brunswick in Lower Saxony. At school Pockels was interested in science, though she was initially unable to pursue a higher education because she was a woman. Even when this situation changed, her parents asked her not to enter university; Pockels instead educated herself, reading books belonging to her brother, who was then a student at the University of Göttingen.

She decided to concentrate on more practical aspects of chemistry and did research based on normal household activities, namely, washing up in the kitchen. With no special facilities she was able to collect a significant amount of information on the properties of water surfaces. She worked alone, and her findings were not communicated to the wider scientific community until 1891. In 1890 Pockels had subscribed to the science abstract journal *Naturwissenschaftliche Rundschau,* and in it she read about the discoveries made by Lord Rayleigh, a British physicist who had published three papers on the subject of oil films on water. Pockels wrote to Rayleigh to tell him about her own experiments and the equipment she had devised, such as a trough for studying the water surface and a beam balance for measuring surface tension. Lady Rayleigh translated her letter, and Lord Rayleigh replied, asking for further information. He then submitted Pockels's research to *Nature;* her first paper was published in 1891 (43: 437–439).

She published a second paper in the following year (*Nature* 46 [1892]: 418–419). In it she reported that water-insoluble layers could be added to the surface of water if the substance concerned was dissolved in benzene, which evaporated. This method of measuring the thickness of the insoluble monolayer was still in use a century later. Though still an amateur chemist, Pockels continued to publish her findings, and eventually began to be invited to professional gatherings in Germany.

Because of the ill health that had long affected her family, Pockels spent increasing amounts of time as a caregiver, and after 1902 she did less research. She found it more and more difficult to keep abreast of developments, particularly with the upheavals caused by World War I. Her eyesight and general health worsened, and in her later years she lived quietly in Brunswick, her scientific expertise eventually reduced to a mere rumor among her fellow citizens.

Pockels did, however, receive the German Colloid Society's Laura Leonard Prize in 1931. This was a joint award given for "qualitative investigations of the properties of surface layers and surface films." In 1932 the Carolina-Wilhelmina University of Brunswick awarded her an honorary doctorate.

Bibliography: Grinstein, L. S., ed., *Women in Chemistry and Physics: A Bibliographic Sourcebook,* Westport, CT: Greenwood, 1993; Rayner-Canham, M. F., *Women in Chemistry,* Washington, DC: American Chemical Society, 1998.

Porter, Annie
(Mrs. H. B. Fantham)
20 February 1880–9 May 1963
parasitologist

Education: University College, London; B.Sc. with honors in botany, 1902–1905; zoology research, 1906–1910; D.Sc., zoology, 1910.

Employment: assistant in helminthology, Quick Laboratory, University of Cambridge; head of the Department of Parasitology, South African Institute for Medical Research, Johannesburg, 1917–1933; senior lecturer in parasitology, University of Witwatersrand, Johannesburg, 1921–1933; examiner in parasitology at the Universities of South Africa and Witwatersrand; research associate, Department of Zoology, McGill University, Montreal, 1933–1937.

Married: Dr. Harold Benjamin Fantham, on 24 November 1915. He died in 1937.

Annie Porter, a leading parasitologist, published numerous papers on a wide variety of parasites, many coauthored with her husband, Professor H. B. Fantham.

Porter, the elder daughter of Samuel Porter, was born in Sussex. The family moved to Brighton soon after she was born, and she was educated there. She studied botany at University College, London, specializing in mycology, and took up parasitology for her postgraduate work. She was awarded her D.Sc. in 1910 for six papers on parasites found in sheep, mice, and water bugs. She worked as an assistant helminthologist in the Quick Laboratory in Cambridge and held a Beit Memorial Research Fellowship in 1914–1916.

H. B. Fantham, whom she married in 1915, was an assistant to the Quick Professor of Biology. Porter and Fantham coauthored *Some Minute Animal Parasites* (1914), which has fifty-six drawings of parasites, most of them by Porter. (She retained her maiden name for all her scientific publications.)

Fantham was appointed professor of zoology at the University of Witwatersrand in Johannesburg in 1917 and stayed there until 1933. This was Porter's most active time, as she held several posts concurrently and continued with her research. She was said to have run the department for her husband. He belonged to the Eugenics Society and was known to have racist views. Porter took an active part in the scientific life of South Africa. In 1922 she was president of the zoology section of the South African Association for the Advancement of Science and in 1924 president of the South African Geographical Society. She was a fellow of the Royal Society of South Africa and vice-president and a council member; in 1927 she was a South Africa Medalist.

In 1933 her husband took up the position of Strathcona Professor of Zoology and chairman of the department at McGill University, Montreal. Porter became a research associate in the department. She investigated various aspects of parasitology, including the endoparasites of humans such as those causing amebic dysentery, and proved that the disease was endemic in Montreal.

Fantham died in October 1937, and Porter returned to Britain soon after this. She was a fellow of the Zoological Society of London, and Sir Julian Huxley, then secretary to the society, asked her to be honorary parasitiologist at Regent's Park. She held this position until shortly before she died. She wrote an annual report on the parasites she had found in many of the animals, published in the *Proceedings of the Zoological Society of London.* During her time in London she became interested in the education of children with cerebral palsy and once a year she arranged for some animals from the zoo to be taken to visit the children at their school. During the war she used her knowledge of fungi to collect edible specimens for staff members and propagated the spores in suitable areas in Regent's Park.

She was elected a fellow of the Linnean Society in 1911. When she died, of bronchopneumonia and diverticulitis, she left substantial bequests for research to Christ's College, Cambridge; University College, London; the University of Witswatersrand; the Zoological Society of London; and McGill University.

Bibliography: Ashhill, C., archivist, Senate House Library, University of London, personal communication to the author, June 1999; Farrar, M., archivist, Cambridge University Library, personal communication to the author, August 1999; Hanrahan, S. A., professor of zoology, University of Witwatersrand, personal communication to the author, May 1999; Hill, W. C. Osman, "Dr. Annie Porter," *Nature* (5 October 1963): 20–21; Martin, G. T., keeper of the Muniment Room, Chart's College, Cambridge, personal communication to the author, March 1999; Murray, B. K., *WITS: The Early Years: A History of the University of the Witwatersrand, Johannesburg and Its Precursors 1896–1939,* Johannesburg: Witwatersrand University Press, 1982; Pelletier, J., archivist, McGill University, personal communication to the author, March 1999; Porter, Annie, letter to the Royal Society Library, 15 March 1914 (Letter No. 14197, accessed by the author in 1999); Shacklock, J., supervisor, Records Office, University College London, personal communication to the author, April 1999; *Who Was Who, 1961–1970,* London: Adam and Charles Black, 1972; Zoological Society of London Library, Regent's Park, visit by the author April 1999.

Porter, Helen Kemp
née Archbold
10 November 1899–3 December 1987
plant physiologist

Education: Clifton High School for Girls, Bristol, 1906–1917; Bedford College, London, 1917–1921; B.Sc. with honors, 1921; D.Sc., 1932; Imperial College, London, 1921–1922.

Employment: Low Temperature Research Station, Cambridge, 1922–1931; Research Institute for Plant Physiology, Imperial College, London, 1931–1939; visiting lecturer in biochemistry, Swanley Horticultural College, Rothamsted, 1939–1947; Coris' Laboratory, St. Louis, Missouri, 1947–1948; Bangor University, 1949 (six months); Imperial College Nuffield Foundation grant, 1953–1957, reader in enzymology and principal scientific officer at the Research Institute of Plant Physiology; professor of plant physiology, 1959–1964 (retirement).

Married: Dr. William George Porter, in 1937; Professor Arthur St. George Huggett, in 1962.

Helen Porter was one of the first scientists in Britain to use radioactive tracers to study the stages of processes such as photosynthesis in plants. In 1959 she became the first woman professor at Imperial College, London.

Porter was the younger of two daughters. Her father taught in Aysgarth Preparatory School at Bedale in Yorkshire; her mother had trained as a singer. When World War I began, Porter and her sister were boarders at Clifton High School for Girls in Bristol. Porter was head of the boarding house in her final year and played in the school teams.

In 1917 she went to Bedford College and studied chemistry, physics, and pure and applied mathematics. She graduated with a double honors degree in chemistry and physics. She was given a London County Council place to study at Imperial College, London. Her research on barbiturate derivatives was directed by Dr. Martha Whiteley.

In 1922 Porter was asked to join the team at a low-temperature research station set up in Cambridge by the Department of Scientific and Industrial Research to investigate why apples imported in the refrigerated holds of ships often went brown. Porter went to evening classes at Birkbeck College to learn biology. She became particularly interested in carbohydrate metabolism. With the economic depression, funding for the research stopped in 1931, even though a reason for the browning of apples had not yet been found.

Porter was transferred to the Plant Physiology team at Imperial College, directed by Professor V. H. Blackburn. She and her colleagues worked on barley and investigated the pathway by which starch came to be stored in the barley grain. During the war Imperial College was needed for defense purposes, so Porter was sent to Rothamsted. In 1947 she spent a year at the Coris' Laboratory in St. Louis, Missouri.

When Porter returned to Imperial College, she worked on starch metabolism and had six months at Bangor University. In 1953 the Nuffield Foundation gave her a large grant so that she could set up her own research unit at Imperial College. She pioneered the techniques of chromatography and the use of radioactive tracers and published a series of papers on tobacco metabolism.

She was elected a fellow of the Royal Society in 1956. The following year she was both reader in enzymology in the Botany Department at Imperial College and principal scientific officer at the Research Unit of Plant Physiology, also at Imperial College. She was on the Committee of the Biochemical Society from 1962 and chair from 1965. She set up small groups within the society and altered the format of the *Biochemical Journal*. She published thirty-nine research papers during her working life, several coauthored.

An excellent administrator, she became the second secretary and then secretary at the Agricultural Research Council after she retired from Imperial College. Both her husbands died after only a few years of marriage; she had no children of her own but had two stepdaughters from her second marriage.

When she died she left a substantial legacy to the Royal Society with no stipulations as to its use.

Bibliography: Northcote, D. H., "Helen Kemp Porter, 10 November 1899–7 December 1987," *Biographical Memoirs of Fellows of the Royal Society* 37 (1991): 400–409; *Who Was Who, 1981–1990,* London: Adam and Charles Black, 1991.

Porter, Mary (Polly) Winearls
26 July 1886–25 November 1980
crystallographer

Education: Oxford; Munich University; Bryn Mawr College, Pennsylvania; Heidelberg; Somerville College, Oxford; B.Sc., 1918; D.Sc., 1932.
Employment: cataloguer, University Museum, Oxford, 1905–1907; research in crystallography, London, 1910–1911; cataloguer, National Museum, Washington, D.C., 1911–1912; cataloguer, Bryn Mawr College, Pennsylvania; 1913–1914; research in crystallography, Heidelberg, 1914–1915; research in crystallography, University Museum, Oxford, 1916–1959.

Mary Porter carried out important research in crystallography, her findings appearing in a wide range of publications.

Porter was the daughter of a *Times* correspondent and received little in the way of a stable education, as the family traveled extensively. Her mother became ill when Porter was fifteen, necessitating a stay in Rome, where Porter collected fragments from classical sites. Her brothers recognized her potential and suggested she should be given proper schooling, but their parents disagreed.

The family returned to Britain, and Porter began to visit the University Museum in Oxford to look at the Corsi Collection of antique Italian marbles. The Waynflete Professor of Mineralogy, Sir Henry Miers, noted her interest and gave her the task of identifying exhibits and translating the catalogue from Italian. He wanted her to go to university; again, her parents were against this.

Following a series of research and cataloguing posts, however, Porter eventually earned her B.Sc. from Oxford in 1918. She was appointed to the Mary Carlisle Fellowship at Somerville College, Oxford, in 1919, despite her lack of formal educational credentials.

She continued with her research until 1959, and her contribution to the subject was acknowledged in the tribute paid to her in a lecture by Dorothy Hodgkin to mark 100 years of crystallography at Somerville. Porter contributed much to the college in other ways, including taking part in fundraising. She was a member of the College Council from 1937 to 1947 and was made an honorary research fellow in 1948.

She published her first book, *What Rome Was Built With,* in 1907, drawing on her early interest in the city. She was joint editor of all three parts of *The Barker Index of Crystals* (1951, 1956, and 1963) and contributed to many journals, including *Mineralogical Magazine, American Mineralogist, Proceedings of the Royal Society, Nature,* and *Acta Crystallographica.* She was a member of council for the Mineralogical Society of Great Britain from 1918 to 1921 and from 1929 to 1932 and a fellow of the Mineralogical Society of America between 1921 and 1927.

Bibliography: Adams, P., archivist, Somerville College, personal communication to the author, July 2001; De Villiers, Anne, "Mary Winearls Porter, 1886–1980," *Somerville College Report and Supplement* (1980): 32–33; *Somerville College Register 1879–1971,* Oxford: Somerville College.

Potter, Helen Beatrix
28 July 1866–22 December 1943
botanical artist, author, mycologist

Education: at home, by governesses.
Married: William Heelis, on 14 October 1913.

Beatrix Potter was a biorecorder: she drew or painted what she saw. Better known for her children's books, she was one of the first to suggest that lichens were in fact a fungus and an alga growing and living symbiotically, in mutual interdependence. She also recorded the growth of fungal spores.

Potter was born in London. Her father was a qualified barrister, though he never practiced; both her parents had substantial incomes from the Lancashire cotton industry. The family had holidays in Perthshire, Scotland, from 1870 onward. While staying at Dalguise House, Dunkeld, in 1871, they met Charles McIntosh, the local postman, who was a keen amateur naturalist. It was not until 1892, however, that Potter consulted him about her own work. In 1888 she started to paint watercolors of fungi, though she had painted since she was eight. When McIntosh looked at her paintings and drawings, he was able to identify the fungi and noticed that some of them were rare species. He agreed to send Potter specimens of fungi when she returned to London, and she sent him copies of her watercolor illustrations. Potter continued to correspond with McIntosh, asking his advice on her technique. He suggested that she include separate paintings of different sections of the fungi in order to produce a clearer representation of each plants' features.

In 1896, when they returned to the Lake District, Potter began to formulate her theory on how fungi reproduce, and she carried out her own experiments. She put forward the idea that the fungi spores form threads underground from which new fungi develop. This, together with her theories on lichen, was later found to be correct.

Her uncle, Sir Henry Roscoe, a noted chemist and vice-chancellor of London University, arranged for Potter to visit the Royal Botanic Gardens at Kew, and to meet the director, William Thiselton-Dyer. But most of the staff at Kew were less than helpful, and Thiselton-Dyer refused to take her seriously. Supported by her uncle, and by William Massee, who worked at Kew, Potter decided that the Linnean Society of London should know about her research. Her paper "On the Germination of the Spores of Agaricineae" was due to be read at a meeting of the society in April 1897. Massee was to read it, since Potter, as a woman, was not allowed to attend. It is not known whether the reading took place, although Potter was told after the meeting that the members felt further work was required—in other words, the paper would not be published in the society's journal.

Following this setback, Potter's enthusiasm for research on fungi gradually diminished; her last painting of fungi is dated 1899, though fifty-nine of her depictions were later used in W. P. K. Findlay's *Wayside and Woodland Fungi* (1947). She turned her attention to writing stories about animals, using her skills as an artist in her illustrations for the books that made her famous around the world. The tales had started as letters to Noel Moore, the young son of one of her former governesses, and derived in part from her fondness for her pet rabbit, Tommy, and Benjamin H. Bouncer, her Belgian hare. *The Tale of Peter Rabbit* was published privately in 1901; this and her twenty-three other books were then published by Frederick Warne from 1902 onward.

When she was thirty-nine, Potter became engaged to Norman Warne, her publisher's son, but he died a few months after their engagement was announced. In 1913 she married William Heelis, a solicitor from Ambleside, and thereafter concentrated on farming. She bred Herdwick sheep and in 1943 was president-elect of the Herdwick Association.

With the proceeds from the sale of *Mrs. Tiggywinkle* and *Squirrel Nutkin*, she bought Hill Top Farm at Near Sawrey in the Lake District in 1905. This, together with farms in Troutbeck, Langdale, Eskdale, Wray, and Sawrey and more than 4,000 acres of land in the Lake District, she bequeathed to the National Trust. The Armitt Museum in Ambleside has 300 of her paintings of fungi, lichens, and mosses. Other paintings by Potter are in Perth City Museum and the Victoria and Albert Museum in London.

Bibliography: Bassom, E., R. Knox, and I. Whalley, "Beatrix Potter and Mrs. Heelis," *Beatrix Potter Studies* 4 (1991); Battrick, E., *Beatrix Potter—The Unknown Years.* Ambleside, Cumbria: Armitt Library and Museum Centre, 1999; Desmond, R., *Dictionary of British and Irish Botanists and Horticultural-*

ists, Including Plant Collectors and Botanical Artists, London: Taylor and Francis, 1977; *Dictionary of National Biography, 1941–50,* Oxford: Oxford University Press, 1959; Jay, Eileen, Mary Noble, and Anne Stevenson Hobbs, *A Victorian Naturalist,* London: Frederick Warne, 1992; Lane, M., *The Tale of Beatrix Potter,* London: Frederick Warne, 1946; Pearsall, W. H., and W. Pennington, *The Lake District,* New Naturalist Series, London: Collins, 1973; Taylor, J., *Beatrix Potter—Artist, Storyteller, and Countrywoman,* London: Frederick Warne, 1986; Taylor, J., *That Naughty Rabbit—Beatrix Potter and Peter Rabbit.* London: Frederick Warne, 1987; Taylor, J., ed., *Beatrix Potter's Letters,* London: Frederick Warne, 1989; Watling, R., "Before Her Time: Beatrix Potter's Contribution to Mycology," Lecture given at Charlotte Mason College, Ambleside, 3 September 1999.

R

Raisin, Catherine Alice
24 April 1855–12 July 1945
geologist

Education: North London Collegiate School; University College, London, 1873–1877 and 1879–1884; B.Sc. with honors, 1884; D.Sc., 1898.

Employment: Bedford College, University of London: demonstrator, 1886–1890; head, Geology Department, 1890–1920; head, Botany Department, 1891–1908; resident vice-principal, 1898–1901; head, Geography Department, 1916–1920.

Catherine Raisin was the first woman to be an academic head of any geology department in Britain and the first woman to lead an academic department at Bedford College, University of London.

Raisin was born in London and studied at University College, London, from 1873 to 1877, returning in 1879 after the rules had been changed to allow women to obtain degrees. She studied geology and zoology, the latter subject taught by T. H. Huxley. Following her graduation, she worked on a voluntary basis as a research assistant to Professor T. G. Bonney, under whom she had studied geology. In 1886 she became demonstrator in botany at Bedford College for Women, a post she held until 1890 when she became head of the Geology Department; she was also head of the Botany Department from 1891.

In 1898 she obtained her D.Sc. from the University of London, only the second woman geologist to achieve this. Between 1887 and 1905 she published twenty-four papers, mainly in the *Quarterly Journal of the Geological Society* and the *Geological Magazine.* She was best known for her work on serpentine rocks, some of it in collaboration with Bonney; she also had a reputation as an expert microscopist.

She established the Somerville Club, a discussion group for women, in 1880, and was its honorary secretary and later its chairperson. In 1893 she received the Lyell Fund from the London Geological Society, the first woman to be honored in this way. Bonney had to accept the award on her behalf, since the society did not allow women to attend its meetings at that time. It was not until the rules were changed in 1919 that she became a fellow of the society. She was elected a fellow of the Linnaean Society in 1906.

Bibliography: Bentley, L., *Educating Women: A Pictorial History of Bedford College, University of London, 1849–1985,* Surrey, England: Alma Publishers, 1991; E. L. G., "Dr. Catherine Raisin," *Proceedings of the Geological Society of London* 102, 2 (1946): xliv–xlv; Nicholls, C. S., ed., *Dictionary of National Biography: Missing Persons,* Oxford: Oxford University Press, 1993; Tuke, M. J., *A History of Bedford College for Women, 1849–1937,* Oxford: Oxford University Press, 1939.

Ratcliffe, Edna Jane
2 June 1917–3 December 1999
naturalist, writer

Employment: home economics teacher; work in an old people's home; wildlife campaigner and writer.
Married: Teddy Ratcliffe, in 1940.

Jane Ratcliffe was an influential campaigner whose work influenced legal developments in wildlife protection.

Ratcliffe was born in Dewsbury, West Yorkshire, and showed an early interest in caring for animals. Initially she taught home economics but later decided to concentrate on the protection of wildlife.

As well as looking after all kinds of injured animals and, where possible, returning them to the wild, Ratcliffe took up the cause of badgers, particularly with regard to the practice of badger baiting. Following the adoption of her resolution on badger protection by the national conference of the Women's Institute in 1970, she directed her efforts to changing the law. Lord Arran's private member's bill became the 1973 Badgers Act, Ratcliffe assisting him in getting the legislation passed. It was the first time that Parliament had given protection to wild land animals. Ratcliffe also took a practical interest in the badger population, recording their declining numbers, rescuing individual badgers, and moving threatened sets. She wrote an account of this work in *Through the Badger Gate* (1974).

She published her second book, *Fly High, Run Free*, in 1979, and her last, *Wildlife in My Garden*, in 1986. Ratcliffe also wrote a wide range of articles for magazines, covering many aspects of wildlife protection and conservation. A paper she delivered to the Institute of Highway Engineers dealt with motorway underpasses for badgers and hedgehogs. She gave lectures in Britain and overseas, and some of her writings were translated into Japanese, German, and Italian.

She and her husband retired to the Lake District in 1980; Ratcliffe gave several lectures at Brockhole, the Lake District Visitor Centre, during the 1980s.

Bibliography: Barkham, Patrick, "Jane Ratcliffe," *Guardian* (4 January 2000).

Rayner, Mabel Mary Cheveley
c. 1894–17 December 1948
botanist

Education: University College, London; University College, Reading; B.Sc. with honors in botany, 1908; D.Sc., 1915.
Employment: head of Botany Department, University College, Reading; research, Forestry Commission.
Married: William Neilson Jones, in 1912.

Mabel Rayner was an authority on mycotrophy in plants.

In 1910 Rayner started research on the ecology of common heather, *Calluna vulgaris*, on the Wiltshire and Berkshire Downs. In particular, she was interested in mycorrhiza, the relationship between the plant and a particular fungus. It was also in this year that she began her scientific collaboration with Dr. William Neilson Jones. Her paper "Obligate Symbiosis in *Calluna vulgaris*" earned her a D.Sc. from London University. In 1927 she published the monograph *Mycorrhiza*, a *New Phytologist* reprint.

Following a discussion in 1926 at the Oxford meeting of the British Association for the Advancement of Science, she became interested in mycorrhiza in relation to conifers on Wareham Heath, Dorset. The Forestry Commission gave her a research nursery and an assistant, allowing her to carry out valuable work on the cultivation of the conifers. In 1944 her findings were published, with other material by herself and her husband, as *Problems in Tree Nutrition*. Facilities were also set up at Bedford College, where her husband was the professor of botany, to enable her to carry out further research on the conifers.

She wrote three books, *Trees and Toadstools* (1915), *Practical Plant Physiology* (1911), with F. Keebel, and *A Text Book of Plant Biology* (1920), with her husband. She traveled widely in her work and studied mycorrhizal associations in a range of other plant species. Though not in good health, she continued to work, visiting her experimental plots only a few hours before she died.

Bibliography: Desmond, R., *Dictionary of British and Irish Botanists and Horticulturalists, Including Plant Collectors and Botanical Artists,* London: Taylor and Francis, 1977; Garrett, S. D., "Dr. M. C. Rayner," *Nature* 163, 4138 (1949): 275–276; Tuke, M. J., *A History of Bedford College for Women, 1849–1937,* Oxford: Oxford University Press, 1939; *Who Was Who, 1941–51,* London: Adam and Charles Black, 1952.

Florence Gwendolen Rees (Godfrey Argent Studio)

Rees, Florence Gwendolen
3 July 1906–4 October 1994
zoologist

Education: Intermediate School for Girls, Aberdare, 1918–1924; University College, Cardiff, 1924–1930; B.Sc. with honors in zoology, 1928; Ph.D., 1930.

Employment: University College of Wales, Aberystwyth: assistant lecturer in zoology, 1930–1937; lecturer, 1937–1946; senior lecturer, 1946–1966; reader 1966–1971; professor, 1971–1974.

In 1971 Professor **Gwendolen Rees** became the first Welsh woman to be elected as a fellow of the Royal Society. She was one of the first parasitologists to look for the larval stages of parasites in invertebrates and vertebrates and was particularly interested in the helminths, parasitic worms of fish.

Rees was born in Aberdare and won three scholarships, which enabled her to go to University College, Cardiff, where she studied chemistry, biology, and zoology, obtaining an honors degree in zoology. For her doctorate, which she completed in eighteen months, she studied the trematode parasites in four species of snails; these parasites cause liver fluke in sheep. She looked at over 5,000 snails from eighty-six locations in Glamorgan and Monmouthshire, collected on a hundred separate days. She was skilled at drawing, as can be seen from the many detailed illustrations in her research papers. By the time she was eighty, she had published sixty-eight papers.

In 1930 she was appointed to the staff of the University College of Wales at Aberystwyth and during her time there, she was responsible for supervising 215 honors students and twenty-five postgraduate students. She was on the editorial board of *Parasitology* from 1960 to 1970 and chair of the board from 1970 to 1981. She was vice-president (1970–1972) and president (1972–1974) of the British Society for Parasitology. She became a professor emeritus of the University of Wales after her retirement.

Always elegant and well dressed, Rees was featured in *Vogue* in 1975 in an article about Britain's most influential and interesting women at that time.

Bibliography: Jones, Arlene, "Professor Gwendolen Rees," *Independent* (20 October 1994): 16; "Professor Gwendolen Rees," *Times* (28 October 1994): 23; Williams, Harford, "Gwendolen Rees FRS—Fifty-six Years (1930 to Date) in Research," *Parasitology* 92 (1986): 483–498.

Resvoll, Thekla Susanne Ragnhild
22 May 1871–14 June 1948
botanist

Education: University of Christiana (Oslo), 1892–1899; University of Copenhagen, 1899–1900; Universities of Zurich and Munich, 1903–1904; Ph.D., 1917.
Employment: assistant professor at botanical laboratory, University of Christiana, 1902–1936; sabbatical year at the Botanical Garden in Buitenzog (Bogor), Java, 1923–1924.
Married: Mr. Holmsen in 1895.

Thekla Resvoll was an authority on the mountain flora of Norway.

Until she was seven, Resvoll lived in the Vågå valley in the mountains of southern Norway. She always enjoyed the mountains and their flowers and later created a mountain garden at the Kungsvall railway station at 885 m.

She took the entrance examination for the University of Christiana (Oslo) in 1892 and graduated seven years later, with botany as her main subject. She was appointed as a lecturer at the university from 1902 until she retired in 1936.

On study leave, Resvoll went to Munich and Zurich in 1903–1904. In Munich she met Marie Stopes, who was also studying there. They became firm friends and used to walk in the mountains together, both in the Alps and later in Norway. Stopes enjoyed the fresh air so much that when she visited Resvoll she insisted on sleeping in the garden. Visits to the high Alps convinced Resvoll that she wanted to study mountain flowers, hence the subject for her thesis: the adaptations of mountain plants to short and cold summers. Although Stopes offered to have Resvoll's thesis translated into English, for reasons that are not clear Resvoll did not accept.

An independent person, Resvoll was involved in the women's liberation movement. She helped to provide information for women about contraception and insisted, in spite of opposition from her employers, on keeping her maiden name after marriage. She had a son in 1905.

She published several research papers about the mountain flora, mostly in Norwegian journals. She was also well known by the general public for her many articles about wildflowers. She was an excellent and enthusiastic teacher. Resvoll was elected a member of the Norwegian Academy of Sciences in 1923.

Bibliography: Heggen, L., National Library, Oslo, personal communication to the author, June 2001; Hoeg, O. A., [Obituary for Thekla Resvoll], *Blyttia* 6 (1948): 3–7; Henriksen, P., ed., *Aschehoug og Gyldendals Stove Norsk Leksikon*, vol. 12, Oslo: H. Aschehoug & Co. (W. Nygaard), 1998; Nordhagen, R., *Det Norske Videnskaps Akademi Arbok*, (1949): 29–37; *Norsk biografisk leksikon*, vol. XI, Oslo: H. Aschehoug & Co. (W. Nygaard), 1998; Eeg-Henriksen, V., University of Oslo, personal communication to the author, September 1999.

Richards, Audrey Isabel
8 July 1899–29 June 1984
anthropologist

Education: Downe House School, Newbury; Newnham College, Cambridge, 1918–1921; London School of Economics, 1928–1930; Ph.D., 1931.
Employment: teacher, Downe House School, 1921–1922; assistant to Gilbert Murray, Oxford, 1922; volunteer relief work, Friends Ambulance Family Welfare Settlement, Frankfurt, 1923–1924; secretary to Labour Department, League of Nations Union, London, 1924–1928; lecturer in anthropology, Bedford College, London, 1928–1930; fieldwork in Northern Rhodesia (now Zambia), 1930–1931, 1933–1934; London School of Economics: lecturer, 1933–1937; special lecturer in colonial studies, 1944–1945; reader, 1946–1950; senior lecturer, University of Witwatersrand, Johannesburg, 1937–1940; temporary principal, Colonial Office, London, 1940–1944; director, East African Institute of Social Research, Makerere University, Uganda, 1950–1956; Newnham College, Cambridge: fellow, 1956–

1961, vice-principal, 1958–1959; Smuts Readership in Commonwealth Studies; University of Cambridge, 1961–1966; director, African Studies Centre, University of Cambridge, 1956.

Audrey Richards was one of the first women to do ethnographical and anthropological applied research in Africa.

Richards was born in London into an intellectual family, the second of four daughters. Her father was a legal member of the Indian Vice-regal Council from 1904 to 1909, and during this time the family lived in Delhi and Simla. From 1911 he was Chichele Professor of International Law at Oxford University and fellow of All Souls. Richards studied natural sciences at Cambridge, as her parents would allow her to go to university only if she studied science. After Cambridge, she taught at Downe House School and was then an assistant to the classical scholar Gilbert Murray.

After eighteen months as a volunteer with the Friends Ambulance Unit in Frankfurt, Richards worked for the League of Nations Union in London. She decided to study at the London School of Economics, and her work was influenced from then on by the anthropologist Bronislaw Malinowski. Her Ph.D. dissertation was entitled "Hunger and Work in a Savage Tribe: A Functional Study of Nutrition among the Southern Bantu." It was published a year after her first expedition, from 1930–1931, to study the Bemba people in Northern Rhodesia. The Bemba relied on shifting agriculture, with millet as the staple of their diet. At that time 48–60 percent of the able-bodied males from the Bemba villages had emigrated to work in the copper mines in the south.

Richards learned the Bemba language and used to camp in a village for a few weeks to find out about their customs and their food. On her return to England, she enlisted the help of Elsie Widdowson and Robert McCance, who advised her on the best way to study the diet of the Bemba people. When she went back to Rhodesia in 1933, with funding from the Rockefeller Foundation, she weighed the food eaten during the main meals of the day in selected families in four of the villages and sent back samples of the food, which Widdowson analyzed. Richards published the results of her studies as *Land, Labour and Diet in Northern Rhodesia: An Economic Study of the Bemba Tribe* (1939).

In 1935 the International African Institute set up a Diet Committee, with Richards as its chairperson. She was also on the Nutrition Committee (1937) created by the Colonial Economic Advisory Group to look at food problems in all British colonial territories.

Richards lectured for three years in the University of Witwatersrand. When she returned to Britain in 1940, she became a temporary principal at the Colonial Office in London. After the end of World War II, she returned to the London School of Economics to lecture in colonial studies before going to Makerere College in Uganda to serve as director of the East African Institute of Social Research. While there she wrote up observations she had made in 1931 of the Bemba female initiation ceremony, "a long succession of ritual acts—miming, singing, dancing and handling sacred emblems." She published her account as *Chisungu* (1956).

In 1957 she held a senior Leverhulme Fellowship that allowed her to go back to the Bemba community to see if there had been any changes since she had last visited in 1934. After she returned to Britain, she became a fellow of Newnham College, director of studies, and vice-principal. She was the first director of the African Studies Centre at the University of Cambridge and held the Smuts Readership in Commonwealth Studies for her last five years before retirement.

Richards believed strongly in applied research in social anthropology rather than the more theoretical aspects. Yet in some ways she seemed entrenched in the ideas of colonial administration rather than the independence of African countries and reluctant to accept the developing trends in social anthropology. Nevertheless, her descriptions of the Bemba and other communities will remain valuable in the history of Africa.

Richards was made a Commander of the Order of the British Empire (CBE) in 1955 for her work in Uganda. She was the first woman anthropologist to be elected to the British Academy for the Advancement of Science and was the first woman president of the Royal Anthropological Institute (1959–1960).

Bibliography: Dictionary of National Biography, 1981–1985, Oxford: Oxford University Press, 1990; Kuper, A., "Audrey Richards, 1899–1984," in *Cambridge Women: Twelve Portraits,* Cambridge: Cambridge University Press, 1996; O'Hanlon, M., secretary, Royal Anthropological Institute, personal communication to the author, February 2000; Strathern, M., "Audrey Richards," *Royal Anthropological Institute News* 64 (October 1984).

Richter, Emma née Hüther
4 March 1888–15 November 1956
paleontologist

Married: Rudolf Richter.

Emma Richter was an eminent paleontologist and published numerous papers, most in collaboration with her husband, Rudolf Richter.

The Richters were experts on trilobites. They were based at the University of Frankfurt and associated with the Senckenberg Museum in Frankfurt. In 1928 Rudolf Richter founded the Senckenberg research station for marine geology at Wilhelmshaven. The entire fossil collection was stored in salt mines and other safe places before the start of World War II.

Emma Richter was made an honorary member of the Palaeontological Society of America in 1934 and was awarded an honorary doctorate by the University of Tübingen in 1949.

Bibliography: Schmidt, H., "Emma Richter," *Natur und Volk* 86, 12 (1956): 428–429; Teichert, C., "From Karpinsky to Schindewolf—Memories of Some Great Palaeontologists," *Journal of Palaeontology* 50, 1 (1976): 3–4.

Rickett, Mary Ellen
4 March 1861–20 March 1925
mathematician, educator

Education: by private tutor; school in Brighton; Priory School, Dover; Bedford College, London, 1878–1881; B.A., 1881; Newnham College, Cambridge, 1881–1886.
Employment: Newnham College, Cambridge: mathematics lecturer, 1886–1908; vice-principal of Old Hall, 1889–1908.

Mary Ellen Rickett lectured in mathematics at Newnham College, Cambridge, for over twenty years and for most of that time also served as vice-principal of Old Hall, part of the college.

Rickett initially took a degree in French and German at Bedford College (University of London) and became the first woman to be awarded the university's Gold Medal. At Newnham College, Cambridge, she took classics and mathematics, excelling in her studies once again and becoming the first Wrangler of the college (the highest honor for students of mathematics at Cambridge). Following graduation in 1886, she became a mathematics lecturer at the college, a post she held until her retirement in 1908. She was known as an energetic teacher with a clear and precise approach who could adapt her teaching to suit individual students according to their intellectual strengths.

Bibliography: A.-H., L., E. Home, and M. Dallas Edwards, "Mary Ellen Rickett," *Newnham College Roll Letter* (1926): 87–97; *Newnham College Register, 1871–1923,* vol. 1, second edition, Cambridge: Newnham College, 1963; Tuke, M. J., *A History of Bedford College for Women, 1849–1937,* Oxford: Oxford University Press, 1939.

Robb, Mary Anne née Boulton
1829–1912
plant collector, botanist

Married: Captain John Robb, in 1856. He died in 1858.

Mary Robb collected plants over many years and introduced into Britain the species of spurge since named *Euphorbia robbiae* Turrill.

Robb was brought up in Oxfordshire, the granddaughter of the noted Birmingham engineer, coinmaker, and manufacturer Matthew Boulton. Her father, Matthew Robinson Boulton, purchased the Tew Park estate, at Great Tew, Oxfordshire, and moved out of Birmingham. Robb was the youngest of six children, and her mother died in the year of Robb's birth. The grounds at Tew Park inspired her love of plants and trees at an early age. She married in 1856, but her husband died two years later, and she brought up their two sons on her own.

Robb bought a house with 150 acres at Liphook, in Hampshire, at some point before 1890 and began cultivating a garden there. She successfully discouraged trespassers by erecting notices that read "Beware of the Lycopodium"—*Lycopodium* being a species of club moss. In 1890 she donated plants and seeds from her garden to the Royal Botanic Gardens, Kew, and contacted Kew again in February 1891 while she was on the Greek island of Ithaca. She asked for an introduction to any botanist in Greece to enable her to study the species she observed. She was put in touch with Theodor von Heldreich, a German who had been director of the Athens Botanical Garden since 1851. He was able to arrange excursions for Robb and teach her about the native trees and flowers of Greece.

On her return to England in the spring of 1891, Robb introduced a hardy perennial evergreen spurge, which was given its official name, *Euphorbia robbiae*, in 1953. It is said that she discovered the plant in Turkey, transporting it back to England in a hatbox, hence its colloquial name, Mrs. Robb's bonnet. Since the plant has not yet been found again in the wild, however, the exact location of her discovery is not known. She established the plant at Liphook and shared it with friends, among them E. A. Bowles, whose garden at Myddleton House, Bulls Cross, in Enfield produced most of the initial stock of this species.

After Robb's death in 1912, one of her sons tried to maintain the garden at Liphook, though it fell into disrepair during World War I. In 1929 the estate was sold and broken up.

Bibliography: Stearn, W. T., "Mrs Robb and 'Mrs. Robb's bonnet' (*Euphorbia robbiae*)," *Journal of the Royal Horticultural Society* 98 (1973): 306–310.

Roberts, Mary
18 March 1788–13 January 1864
natural history writer

Mary Roberts wrote about natural history, especially the countryside around her.

Roberts was the granddaughter of Reverend Thomas Lawson (1630–1691), known as the father of Lakeland Biology. She lived at Painswick, in Gloucestershire, until her father died, when she and her mother moved to London.

She wrote fifteen books, most about natural history. *The Conchologist's Companion* (1824 and 1834), a mixture of fact and myth, is perhaps the most widely known but she also wrote *Annals of My Village, Being a Calendar of Nature for Every Month in the Year* (1831).

Bibliography: Desmond, R., *Dictionary of British and Irish Botanists and Horticulturalists, Including Plant Collectors and Botanical Artists*, London: Taylor and Francis, 1977; *Dictionary of National Biography*, vol. 16, Oxford: Oxford University Press, 1896.

Robertson, Dorothea
June 1892–August 1952
occupational therapist, teacher

Education: Elgin Academy; Newnham College, Cambridge, 1912–1915.

Employment: welfare worker in Nat. Filling Factory, Gretna Green, 1916; munitions factory, Sheffield, 1917–1918; Guy's Motor Works, 1920–1923; J. and P. Coats, Paisley, 1923–1925; occupational therapist, Glasgow Royal Mental Hospital, Gartnavel 1922–1929; trainee and teacher of people with mental handicaps at Kirkintilloch, Glasgow, 1929–1935; warden for women students, Jordanhill Training College, 1935–1952.

Dorothea Robertson was the first person to be employed as an uncertified occupational therapy instructor in Britain. The first occupational therapy department in Britain was set up at the Glasgow Royal Asylum, Gartnavel, by Professor David Henderson in 1922. Essentially, Robertson learned by trial and error on the job.

Bibliography: Henderson, D. K., "Occupational Therapy," Journal of Mental Science 71 (1925): 59–66; Newnham College Register, 1871–1923, vol. 1, Cambridge: Newnham College, 1963.

Robertson, Muriel
8 April 1883–14 June 1973
protozoologist

Education: at home by governesses; Glasgow University; M.A., 1905; postgraduate research, 1905–1910; D.Sc., 1922.

Employment: assistant, then full staff member, Lister Institute of Preventive Medicine, 1909–1911; protozoologist, Colonial Office, Protectorate of Uganda, 1911–1914; protozoologist, Lister Institute, 1914–1961.

Muriel Robertson's greatest contribution to protozoology was her research on the disease of sleeping sickness.

Robertson was born in Glasgow. Her father was an engineer. She started to train as a doctor but decided to concentrate on zoology instead. In 1905 she published her first paper, on the development of the protozoan Pseudospora volvocis.

After graduating, Robertson became a Carnegie Research Scholar, then held a Carnegie Research Fellowship at Glasgow University. From 1907 to 1908 she went to Ceylon (now Sri Lanka) to study the blood parasites of reptiles, especially trypanosomes. She was assistant to Professor E. A. Minchin at the Lister Institute of Preventive Medicine in London for three years, and from 1910 was a full staff member.

In 1911 she was appointed as a protozoologist by the Colonial Office and was a member of the Royal Society's commission to investigate sleeping sickness in Uganda. At that time there was no cure for the disease, and around 200,000 Africans had died from it in Uganda alone by the turn of the century. Sleeping sickness is caused by the protozoan parasite Trypanosoma brucei, transmitted to humans via the bite of the tsetse fly, Glossina palpalis. Robertson worked out the sequence of development of the trypanosome and discovered the pathway by which the trypanosomes migrated to the salivary glands of the tsetse fly. As she did her research, she traveled throughout Uganda, often by bicycle, always taking along her embroidery and a rifle.

She returned to the Lister Institute in 1914, and continued to be based there until 1961, twelve years after her statutory retirement. During World War I she did important work on tetanus, a frequent cause of death among soldiers at the time, and helped make an antitoxin used by the army. During World War II she worked in Cambridge on the bacteria that causes gas gangrene. With Dr. W. P. Kerr she worked on the immunopathology of trichomoniasis in cattle.

Robertson was always ready to help other researchers. She had at hand an old aquarium so that she always had a source of protozoa to show young enthusiasts who visited her. She published thirty papers on protozoology, fourteen on bacteriology, and nineteen on immunology. She was a founding member (1945) of the Society for General Microbiology. She was elected a fellow of the Royal Society in 1947 and awarded an honorary LL.D. by the University of Glasgow in 1948.

Bibliography: Bishop, A., and A. Miles. "Muriel Robertson, 1883–1973," *Biographical Memoirs of Fellows of the Royal Society* 20 (1974): 317–347; Roberts, F. C., comp., "Dr. Muriel Robertson," *Obituaries from the Times, 1971–1975,* London: Newspaper Archives Developments, 1978; *Who Was Who, 1971–1980,* London: Adam and Charles Black, 1981.

Ross-Craig, Stella
1906–
botanical artist

Education: Art School, Thanet Chelsea Polytechnic, London.
Employment: botanical artist at the Royal Botanical Gardens, Kew.
Married: J. R. Sealy.

Stella Ross-Craig, an outstanding botanical artist, creates drawings that are both artistic and scientifically accurate.

Ross-Craig is best known for her *Drawings of British Plants,* published in thirty-one parts between 1948 and 1974. The 1,286 full-page black-and-white plates, all of a uniformly high quality, are organized by family and provide a standard set of illustrations of all the thoroughly established flowering plants growing wild in the British Isles. Each plant or part thereof is depicted in its natural size; detailed analyses of the flowers and fruits clearly explain their structure.

Ross-Craig did botanical illustrations for many other publications as well, such as the *Botanical Magazine,* and over 3,000 of her drawings are held in the Kew collection. She was a fellow of the Linnean Society from 1948 to 1974.

Bibliography: Blunt, W., and W. T. Stearn, *The Art of Botanical Illustration,* London: Antique Collectors' Club, Royal Botanic Gardens, Kew, 1994; Buckman, D., *Dictionary of*

Artists in Britain since 1945, Bristol: Art Dictionaries, 1988.

Rosser, Celia Elizabeth
née Prince
1930–
botanical artist

Education: Royal Melbourne Institute of Technology, fashion illustration, 1945–1947.
Employment: Melbourne advertising agency; Science Faculty artist, Monash University, 1970–1974; university botanical artist, 1974–.

Celia Rosser is one of Australia's finest botanical artists.

After a career in fashion illustration and advertising, Rosser moved to rural Victoria and began drawing the native plants for *Wild Flowers of Victoria* (1967), which includes fifty-one of her illustrations. Starting in 1974, she aimed to paint all the Australian species of *Banksia.* Each illustration takes two months from collection to completion. In 1977 she received the Jill Smythies Award for botanical illustration from the Linnean Society of London. The first volume of *The Banksias* was published in 1981, the second in 1988, and the third in 2000, each with twenty-four plates. Monash University awarded her an honorary M.Sc. in 1981 and an honorary Ph.D. in 1999.

Bibliography: Blunt, W., and W. T. Stearn, *The Art of Botanical Illustration,* London: Antique Collectors' Club, Royal Botanic Gardens, Kew, 1994.

Rothschild, The Honourable
Miriam Louisa
5 August 1908–
entomologist, campaigner
for nature conservation

Education: at home.
Employment: freelance biologist; researcher, Department of Agriculture, Washington,

Miriam Louisa Rothschild (Christopher Cormack/ Corbis)

D.C.; cipher operator, Bletchley Park, 1940–1944; visiting professor of biology, Royal Free Hospital, London.
Married: Captain George Lane, in 1943.

Miriam Rothschild is a world authority on bird fleas and is widely recognized for her support for nature conservation.

Rothschild was brought up in the family home and farm at Ashton Wold, Northamptonshire. Her mother had been the Hungarian ladies' lawn tennis champion. Her father, Charles Rothschild, was a keen botanist and entomologist and an expert on fleas. In 1901 he had discovered the flea *Xenopsylla cheopis* Rothschild in Egypt; this species was later shown to be responsible for transmitting bubonic plague.

Rothschild was taught at home and learned a great deal about natural history from her father. When she was seventeen, she went to evening classes in zoology at Chelsea Polytechnic. In 1931 the class went to the marine biological laboratory at Plymouth, where Rothschild discovered a larval trematode that even Dr. Marie Lebour, an expert on trematodes, could not identify. The trematode turned out to be a new species, and this discovery so thrilled Rothschild that she spent the next seven years doing research on trimatodes. Most of this time she spent at Plymouth, but she was also able to occupy the London University table at the marine laboratory in Naples.

In 1940 a night of carpet bombing by German planes damaged the laboratory in Plymouth, and all of Rothschild's jars of specimens, notebooks, and other records and equipment were destroyed. Aware of how much she was restricted by the demands of her research, Rothschild left Plymouth almost immediately and started on a new type of life.

Her home had been taken over as a military hospital, and on one of her leaves home from her war work as a cipher operator, she met her future husband, Captain George Lane, a Polish refugee who served in the British army. They married in 1943 and had six children.

After the war Rothschild brought up the children and in the evenings continued her research in zoology, initially on fleas. She classified her father's collection of fleas, which he had given to the British Museum (Natural History), creating the six-volume *Catalogue of the Rothschild Collection of Fleas,* (1953–1983). She collaborated with Theresa Clay on *Fleas, Flukes, and Cuckoos* (1952) for the New Naturalist series, writing most of her chapters initially from memory when she was stuck in Calais for a week in 1947. She also wrote the text for a collection of beautiful micrographs by Y. Schlein and S. Ito, *A Colour Atlas of Insect Tissues via the Flea* (1986).

She suggested that myxomatosis (a severe viral disease) in rabbits was transmitted by fleas and theorized as well that the reproductive cycle of the rabbit flea was dependent on the reproductive cycle of its host, which was later proved to be true. It was found that the fleas respond to the hormones produced by the female rabbit, and as soon as the doe gives birth the rabbit fleas move to the young, mate, and lay their eggs.

Rothschild studied butterflies as well, and found that the monarch butterfly sequesters pyrazines from its food plants, which helps to protect the butterfly from predation. She demonstrated this work at the Royal Society Conversazione in 1989.

Rothschild's father had founded the Society for the Promotion of Nature Reserves in 1912, as he was concerned about the disappearance of so many natural habitats. Miriam Rothschild followed in his footsteps and in 1947 founded the International Union for the Protection of Nature.

Rothschild also was concerned about preserving wildflowers, particularly after she moved back permanently to the family home of Ashton Wold in 1970. She has wonderful arrays of wildflowers, their planting carefully planned. Besides collecting the seeds and creating a seed bank, she has spent time studying the genetics of the flowers in order to get the strongest varieties. Rothschild has done a great deal to publicize the need for conservation, and her advice has been followed for many wildflower projects. In 1990 she was awarded the Victoria Medal of Honour by the Royal Horticultural Society for her work.

She was honored with the Defence Medal (1940–1945) and made a Dame Commander of the Order of the British Empire (DBE) in 1999 and a Commander of the Order of the British Empire (CBE) in 1982; she became a fellow of the Royal Society in 1985. She was awarded honorary doctorates from the universities of Oxford (1968), Gothenburg (1983), Hull (1984), Northwestern University (1986), Leicester (1987), Open University (1989), Essex (1998), and Cambridge (1999). Rothschild is a patron of the British Dragonfly Society, had a dragonfly sanctuary set up in 1989 at Ashtonwold, and is an honorary fellow of St. Hugh's College, Oxford. She was awarded a medal from the International Society of Chemical Ecology in 1989, and the Mendel Award from the Czech Science Academy in 1993.

Bibliography: Dodds, R. A., "How a Dream Came True: Ten Years of Dragonflies and the Public at Ashton Water," *Dragonfly News* 39 (spring 2001): 19; Keen, M., "Alice in Tigerland," *Standard* (19 May 1983); Kendall, E., "A Room of My Own: Miriam Rothschild," *Observer Magazine* (12 August 1984): 28–29; Marren, P., *The New Naturalists,* London: HarperCollins, 1995; "Miriam Rothschild: Self-taught Naturalist and Biologist," *Shell Times* 72 (1990); Penn, H., *An Englishwoman's Garden,* London: BBC Books, 1993; Rothschild, M., "A Liberating Aerial Bombardment," *Scientist* 1, 18 (1987): 17; Salmon, M. A., *The Aurelian Legacy: British Butterflies and Their Collectors,* Colchester, Essex: Harley Books, 2000; *Who's Who, 2000,* London: Adams and Charles Black, 2000.

Rowan, Marian Ellis née Ryan
30 July 1848–4 October 1922
botanical artist

Married: Frederic Charles Rowan, of the New Zealand Armed Constabulary, on 23 October 1873. He died in 1892.

Ellis Rowan explored Australia and New Guinea and illustrated many of the plants and animals she found, exhibiting her paintings throughout the world.

Rowan was born in Melbourne and went to school in Brighton. She did not have any formal training in art, but her family encouraged her in her painting of wildflowers.

In 1873 she married Frederic Rowan, a British army officer who had joined the New Zealand forces in 1866. After their marriage they went to Taranaki in New Zealand, where her husband was a subinspector in the armed constabulary. In 1877, two years after their only child, Eric, was born, they moved to Victoria. Frederic Rowan first promoted a system of light railways, then managed two electrical companies, and in 1886 he was appointed consul-general for Denmark. He died of pneumonia in 1892.

In 1880 Ellis Rowan met Marianne North, who stayed with Rowan and tutored her in oil painting. As a result Rowan decided to travel the world, painting and exhibiting her work. From 1873 to 1893 she did just that, winning ten gold medals, fifteen silver ones, and four bronze. She exhibited at the London International Exhibition at Crystal Palace in 1884; at Melbourne's 1888 Centennial International Exhibition she was awarded the highest honors.

In spring 1895 Rowan went to London and took her paintings to Windsor Castle. Queen Victoria chose three of them and had them made into a screen. The following April Rowan held an exhibition in London of a hundred paintings of Australian wildflowers. She sold many of these and received commissions to paint murals in drawing rooms. Her son died in 1897 of chronic Bright's disease in a jail in Zimbabwe, where he was being held for forgery. Rowan did not allow herself to be deterred from her work by this tragedy.

After traveling throughout Europe and meeting several dignitaries, she went to the United States, where she held further exhibitions and met Alice Lounsberry, an American botanist. Rowan illustrated three of Lounsberry's books: *A Guide to the Wild Flowers* (1899), *A Guide to the Trees* (1900), and *Southern Wild Flowers and Trees* (1901).

Rowan returned to Australia from 1905 to 1906 and painted numerous species of wildflowers. She wrote *Flower Hunter in Queensland and New Zealand* (1898), an account of her travels. She visited Papua and New Guinea twice, in 1916 and 1917, the first visit to paint flowers and the second to search for and paint endangered birds of paradise, of which she painted forty-five. Her flower paintings from this trip were used by the Royal Worcester Porcelain Company. The original hundred paintings are at Kew; each has a vivid flower within a rose-purple edging. She lived in primitive conditions on these trips and returned to Australia badly affected by malaria and exhaustion. But in March 1920 she put together an exhibition of over 1,000 of her paintings at the Fine Arts Gallery in Sydney. In 1923 more than 900 of her paintings were bought for Australia by the federal government; they are held at the National Library of Australia, Canberra. Further public collections of her works are in Sydney, Adelaide, and Brisbane.

Bibliography: Hazzard, M., *Australia's Brilliant Daughter Ellis Rowan: Artist, Naturalist, Explorer, 1848–1922,* Victoria: Greenhouse Publications, 1984; Hazzard, M., "Rowan, Marian Ellis," in *Australian Dictionary of Biography* (1891–1939), edited by J. Ritchie, Melbourne: Melbourne University Press, 1988; "Lady Casey's Aunt [Ellis Rowan]," *Eastern Daily Press* (19 June 1962); McKay, J., comp., *Brilliant Careers: Women Collectors and Illustrators in Queensland,* Brisbane: Queensland Museum, 1997; Shaw, J., "Artist Who Caught Beauty of Jungle," *Times* (19 April 1995): 7.

Rozhanskaya, Mariam née Mikhaylovna
28 July 1928–
historian of mathematics and mechanics

Education: school, Moscow; Moscow State University (history), 1945–; Rostov-on-Don University (mathematics and mechanics), 1951–1952; Moscow University, 1952–1958; Ph.D., 1968; D.Sc., 1987.

Employment: teacher, Military School of the Supreme Soviet, Moscow, 1958–1959; Academy of Sciences of the USSR, Moscow: researcher, Institute of Ethnography; researcher, then senior fellow, Institute for the History of Science and Technology, from 1967.

Married: Professor Vladimir Nikolaevich Rozhanskiy, physicist at the Crystallography Institute, Russian Academy of Sciences.

Mariam Rozhanskaya is internationally known as a historian of mathematics.

Rozhanskaya was born in Shigry, near Kursk, Russia, but shortly thereafter moved to Moscow with her mother. During World War II she spent three years as an evacuee in Middle Volga but returned to Moscow and completed her schooling in 1945. She decided to study history, encouraged by Professor S. P. Tolstov, a noted archaeologist and ethnographist at Moscow University. After she graduated, however, she was unable to become a history teacher as she was not a member of the Communist Party, nor, because of a number of circumstances, was she able to continue her studies.

In 1951, while visiting her husband's parents, Rozhanskaya decided to attend the Correspondence Department of the Faculty of Mathematics and Mechanics at the University of Rostov-on-Don. She continued her mathematical studies the following year on her return to Moscow, graduating in 1958. After teaching higher mathematics for almost two years, she was offered a post at the Institute of Ethnography of the Academy of Sciences of the USSR by the director, her former professor, S. P. Tolstov. He was planning a scientific biography of the ancient astronomer and mathematician al-Biruni and felt that Rozhanskaya's knowledge of Arabic, together with her background in mathematics and history, would enable her to contribute to this work.

With B. A. Rosenfeld and P. G. Bulgakov, she produced an annotated translation of al-Biruni's astronomical encyclopaedia, *Canon of Mas'ud* (published in 1973 and 1976); she also published papers analyzing al-Biruni's work. In 1967 she joined the Institute for the History of Science and Technology at the Academy of Sciences of the USSR and later became a senior fellow of the Department of History of Mechanics and Physics there. With Rosenfeld and Z. K. Sokolovskaya, she coauthored a biography of al-Biruni that appeared in 1973.

Al-Biruni's work formed the basis of Rozhanskaya's Ph.D. thesis; her D.Sc. thesis dealt with aspects of mechanics in the Middle Ages. She contributed chapters to several books on the history of science and mathematics and published numerous articles. Her annotated translation of *The Book of the Balance of Wisdom* by the noted medieval Muslim scholar al-Khazani was published in 1983.

Rozhanskaya was elected a corresponding member of the Académie Internationale d'Histoire des Sciences in 1991 and a full member in 1997.

Bibliography: Demidov, S. S., I. O. Luther, and V. S. Kirsanov, "Mariam Mikhaylovna Rozhanskaya on the 70th Anniversary of Her Birth," *Archives internationales d'histoire des sciences* 48, 141 (1998): 374–378.

Rule, Margaret Helen
née Martin
27 September 1928–
archaeologist

Education: University of London.
Employment: director of excavations, Chichester Civic Society, 1961–1979; honorary curator, Fishbourne Roman Palace and Museum, 1968–1979; Mary Rose Trust: archaeological director, 1979–1982; research director, 1983–1994; consultant, from 1994.
Married: Arthur Walter Rule, in 1949.

Dr. Margaret Rule was responsible for organizing the raising of the *Mary Rose*, Henry VIII's flagship, in 1982. The ship is now on permanent display at Portsmouth.

The *Mary Rose* project commenced in 1965, and Rule became its archaeological director in 1979. She did not learn to dive until she was well into her forties. Following the raising of the ship, she published numerous articles and several books about the project, including *The Mary Rose: The Excavation and Raising of Henry VIII's Flagship* (1982). She has also published *Life at Sea: Tudors and Stuarts* (1994).

She was made a Commander of the Order of the British Empire (CBE) in 1983 in recognition of her work. In 1982 she was made an honorary fellow of Portsmouth Polytechnic and was awarded an honorary doctor of letters from Liverpool University in 1984. The Stoke-on-Trent Association of Engineers awarded her the Reginald Mitchell Medal in 1983. In 2001 she was chair of the Council for Nautical Archaeology and a member of the government advisory committee that deals with historic shipwrecks.

Bibliography: Gale, G. D., "The Mary Rose," *Omega* (January 2000): 8–9; "What Sunk the Mary Rose?" program aired 21 August 2000 on BBC Channel 4; *Who's Who, 1998*, London: Adam and Charles Black, 1998.

Russell, Annie Scott Dill
1868–1947
astronomer

Education: Victoria College, Belfast; Girton College, Cambridge, 1886–1889.
Employment: Ladies' College, Jersey, 1889–1891; "computer," Royal Observatory, Greenwich, 1891–1895 and 1915–1920; editor, British Astronomical Association journal, 1894–1896 and 1917–1930.
Married: Edward Walter Maunder, first as-

sistant for photographic and spectroscopic observations, Royal Observatory, in 1895.

Annie Russell made a significant contribution to astronomy, her particular interests being the sun and sunspots. She held a paid job at the Royal Observatory, unusual for a woman at that time, and was an important figure in the British Astronomical Association.

Russell was born in Strabane, County Tyrone, Northern Ireland, the daughter of a clergyman. At Girton College she achieved the Senior Optime in the Mathematical Tripos, the highest award possible for female mathematics students at that time. From 1891 she worked at the Royal Observatory, Greenwich, as a "lady computer" for £4 a month (rising to £8). The work involved recording data from daily sunspot photographs and led to her meeting her future husband.

In 1892 Russell tried to be elected to fellowship of the Royal Astronomical Society with two other women astronomers, Alice Everett and Elizabeth Brown. None of the women was admitted, falling short of the number of votes required. Women were admitted beginning in 1915, and Russell was elected in 1916. She joined the British Astronomical Association (founded by her husband in 1890) and from 1894 to 1896 and again from 1917 to 1930 served as the editor of its journal. More than once she was invited to be the association's president, an honor she always refused as she felt her voice would not carry in a large room.

Russell produced several significant pieces of work. She had a Pfeiffer Research Student Fellowship from Girton College to carry out a photographic survey of the Milky Way, and she observed a number of solar eclipses, including those in Norway (1896), India (1898), Algiers (1900), Mauritius (1901), and Labrador (1905). She put forward theories on the interaction between sunspots and the earth, and she was interested in historical astronomical recordings. She and her husband collaborated on many projects, including a book, *The Heavens and Their Story* (1908), her husband remarking in the preface that the work was "almost wholly that of his wife."

Bibliography: Creese, M. R. S., *Ladies in the Laboratory? American and British Women in Science, 1800–1900: A Survey of Their Contributions to Research,* Lanham, Maryland: Scarecrow Press, 1998 Daintith, J., et al., eds., *Biographical Encyclopaedia of Scientists,* second edition, Bristol: Institute of Physics Publishing, 1994; Ogilvie, M. B., "Obligatory Amateurs: Annie Maunder (1868–1947) and British Women Astronomers at the Dawn of Professional Astronomy," *British Journal for the History of Science* 33 (2000): 67–84; Ogilvie, M. B., *Women in Science: Antiquity through the Nineteenth Century,* New York: MIT Press, 1986.

Russell, Dorothy Stuart
27 June 1895–19 October 1983
pathologist

Education: Perse High School for Girls, Cambridge; Girton College, Cambridge, 1915–1919; London Hospital Medical College, 1919–1922; M.D., 1930; B.A., f 1942 (Cantab); Sc.D., 1943 (Cantab); Member, Royal College of Physicians, 1943 (London).

Employment: junior medical posts, 1922; Bernhard Baron Institute of Pathology: pathology assistant, 1922–1923; assistant to Professor Turnbull, 1923–1939; Rockefeller Traveling Fellow, 1928–1929; scientific staff, Medical Research Council, 1933–1946; neuropathologist, Radcliffe Infirmary, Oxford, 1940–1944; neuropathologist, London Hospital, 1944–1946; director, Bernhard Baron Institute of Pathology, London Hospital, and professor of morbid anatomy, University of London, 1946–1960.

Dorothy Russell was the first woman head of a department of pathology in Great Britain.

Russell was born in Sydney, Australia; her father was a bank clerk. Following his death when she was three years old and the death of her mother two years later, Russell and her sister were sent to England to live with their aunt near Cambridge. After excelling in all subjects at school, Russell studied at Girton College, Cambridge. She took the natural science tripos, winning honors in zoology. She stayed at Girton for a further year on a Gilchrist Studentship, carrying out research in medical entomology.

She went on to the London Hospital Medical College in 1919, qualifying in 1922. Inspired by Henry Turnbull, professor of morbid anatomy, she decided to specialize in pathology and became a pathology assistant in the Institute of Pathology (Bernhard Baron Institute), where Turnbull was director. She spent three years as Junior Beit Research Fellow in Turnbull's department, researching Bright's disease (published as *A Classification of Bright's Disease*, Medical Research Council Special Report No. 142, 1929). It was during this period that she met Hugh Cairns, a neurosurgeon who had spent some time in the United States. He persuaded Russell to specialize in neuropathology. Between 1928 and 1930 she was in the United States and Canada on a Rockefeller Fellowship and worked with Wilder Penfield on the staining of nerve tissues using metallic impregnation. While she was away, Cairns found funds for a technician and new equipment for her at the Bernhard Baron Institute, which would allow her to concentrate on neuropathology on her return to England. He and Russell worked together on a number of projects in the following years.

In 1933 she joined the external staff of the Medical Research Council (MRC). She continued her work at the Bernhard Baron Institute and began her work on neuro-oncology. Working with J. O. W. Bland, she grew tumor cells in tissue culture, the first time this had been done. She did research on pituitary disease, jointly publishing papers with A. C. Crooke.

By 1939 Cairns had established a new clinical medical school at the Radcliffe Infirmary in Oxford and a specialist military head injuries unit based at St. Hugh's College. Russell accepted his invitation to be the neuropathologist for the military unit, and the day before war was declared she

moved to Oxford. During World War II, her work at St. Hugh's provided valuable information on the treatment of head injuries. Her findings on fatal motorcycle accidents, for example, brought about a change in military regulations so that helmets became compulsory for army motorcyclists. While in Oxford she also did civilian neuropathology work at the Radcliffe Infirmary.

In late 1944 Russell decided to return to the Bernhard Baron Institute, where Turnbull was still in charge. She began to take over his teaching duties and post mortem demonstrations. In 1946, when Turnbull retired, she was appointed his successor as professor of morbid anatomy and director of the Bernhard Baron Institute. The teaching and administrative duties of her new role limited her time for research, though she was still able to work on a number of important studies. In 1949 the MRC published her *Observations on the Pathology of Hydrocephalus*, which she had been working on since her time in Oxford. She published articles on a range of topics, including organic mercury poisoning, the division of the pituitary stalk, and aspects of Friederich's ataxia, an inherited degenerative disease of the muscles.

In 1959, with Lucien Rubenstein, she published *Pathology of Tumours of the Nervous System*, which for thirty years was the standard textbook in neuro-oncology. After her retirement, she worked on further editions of this book and attended meetings of the British Neuropathological Society.

Throughout her career, Russell encouraged colleagues and students. Although she suffered from epilepsy, she did not publicize this fact during her lifetime but requested that it be made known after her death, to inspire other epileptics. The British Neuropathological Society established a biannual memorial lecture in her honor, with Lucien Rubenstein giving the inaugural lecture on 9 July 1986.

In 1934 Russell was awarded the John Hunter Medal and triennial prize of the Royal College of Surgeons. She was awarded honorary degrees from McGill and Glasgow Universities and was a fellow of the Royal College of Pathologists.

Bibliography: "Dorothy Stuart Russell," *The Lancet* (29 October 1983): 1039; Geddes, J. F., "A Portrait of 'The Lady': A Life of Dorothy Russell," *Journal of the Royal Society of Medicine* 90 (1997): 455–461; *Girton College Register 1869–1946*, vol. 1, Cambridge: Girton College, 1948; Smith, J. F., "Dorothy Russell," *Bulletin of the Royal College of Pathologists* 59 (June 1987): 1–2.

Ruttner-Kolisko, Agnes
née Kolisko
14 July 1911–22 November 1991
freshwater biologist

Education: primary and secondary schools in Gmunden, Austria; Vienna University, natural history and zoology, 1929; Ph.D., 1936; teacher training, 1937.
Employment: biology teacher, 1937–1939; science assistant, Lunz Biological Station, 1939–1945; Vienna Water Authority, 1945; docent, Vienna University; research assistant, Lunz Biological Station; deputy director, Lunz Biological Station, 1972–1976.
Married: Dr. W. A. Ruttner, geologist, in 1938.

Agnes Ruttner-Kolisko was the first to apply genetic concepts to rotifers, planktonic spinning microscopic organisms. She published many papers about their behavior and taxonomy.

Ruttner-Kolisko was the first deputy director of the Biological Station at Lünz, a department of the Institute of Limnology, of the Austrian Academy of Sciences. She successfully maintained cultures of algae in her laboratory for many years, a difficult feat as the cultures tend to become diseased.

Winning numerous travel awards to study diatoms, Ruttner-Kolisko went to Swedish Lapland, salt deserts in Persia, and the English Lake District. She had sixty-seven publications to her credit, almost half of them written after she retired.

She and her husband had five children.

Bibliography: Bretschko, G., "The Biological Station Lunz (Austria)," *Freshwater Biological Association Newsletter* 6 (1998): 1–2; Schmid-Araya, J. M., C. E. King, and H. J. Dumont, "Agnes Ruttner-Kolisko," obituary, *Hydrobiologia* 255/256 (1991): xv–xviii, xxi–xxii, xix.

Ryman, Brenda Edith
6 December 1922–20 November 1983
biochemist

Education: Colston Girls School, Bristol; Girton College, Cambridge; B.A.; M.A., 1943; Birmingham University, Ph.D.
Employment: Royal Free Hospital Medical School, Biochemistry Department, assistant lecturer, 1948–1951; lecturer, 1952–1961; senior lecturer, 1961–1969; reader, 1970–1972; professor of biochemistry, 1972–1983, Charing Cross Hospital Medical School, University of London; mistress of Girton College, Cambridge, 1976–1983.
Married: Dr. Harry Barkley, in 1948. He died in 1978.

Professor *Brenda Ryman* was the first married mistress of Girton College, Cambridge.

After graduating from Cambridge, Ryman went on to do research in biochemistry at Birmingham University. She was awarded the Gamble Prize by Girton College for the originality of her research. She worked initially at the Royal Free Hospital Medical School, becoming reader in biochemistry in 1970. From 1972 she was professor of biochemistry at Charing Cross Hospital Medical School. She was particularly interested in the healing powers of liposomes. In this productive time of her life, she published over ninety papers.

Ryman was appointed mistress of Girton College in 1976, at the time the college was deciding to admit male students. She had experienced this situation at the Royal Free Hospital, so she was able to ensure that the transition to a mixed student population went smoothly. Because she saw how easily Girton students could become isolated (Girton is 3 miles from the center of Cambridge), she made sure she invited a wide range of people to Girton to talk with the members of the college.

Her husband died suddenly when Ryman had been mistress for only two years, but she continued to work tremendously hard in both her posts until cancer forced her to give them up. She was a great inspiration to the students. She was awarded a D.Sc. by Cambridge University posthumously.

Bibliography: Jondorf, G., "Brenda Edith Ryman," *Girton College Newsletter* (1984): 29–30; *Who Was Who, 1981–1990,* London: Adam and Charles Black, 1991.

S

Sackville-West, Victoria May (Vita; Lady Nicholson)
9 March 1892–2 June 1962
horticultural journalist

Education: at home; Mrs. Woolf's School, London.
Married: Sir Harold Nicholson, a diplomat, in 1913.

The writer *Vita Sackville-West* is perhaps best remembered for transforming the gardens of Sissinghurst Castle in Kent.

Sackville-West, the daughter of the third Baron Sackville, was born at Knole, Sevenoaks, in Kent, one of the largest houses in England, with 365 rooms, fifty-two staircases, and seven courtyards. The house had been in her family since 1586, and her vivacious mother enjoyed entertaining there.

Sackville-West wrote her first novel in 1906, when she was fourteen; the following year she won a poetry competition in the *Onlooker*. Her first published novel was *Chatterton* in 1909.

She came out as a debutante in 1910 and met Harold Nicholson at a party. Later that summer she had pneumonia and then spent six months near Monte Carlo to recover. Nicholson frequently visited, and Sackville-West and he were secretly engaged. They were married on 1 October 1913 in the private chapel at Knole and spent their honeymoon in Italy and Egypt. Nicholson was a diplomat and was initially based in Turkey but was recalled to London in June 1914 because of the threat of war. The couple

Victoria May (Vita) Sackville-West (Illustrated London News/Archive Photos)

owned a house in London and bought another near Knole in 1915. Here they spent their summers, taking up year-round residence there in 1925.

Sackville-West had two sons, Benedict, born in 1914, and Nigel, born in 1917, the year her *Poems of West and East* were published. Though she wrote novels, such as

The Edwardians (1930) and *All Passion Spent* (1931), she most enjoyed writing poetry. Her two long epic poems, *The Land* (1927) and *The Garden* (1946), were divided into four sections by the seasons, and each gives accurate descriptions of farming and horticulture. Sackville-West won the Hawthornden Prize in 1927 for *The Land* and the Heinemann Prize for *The Garden* in 1947.

In 1930 Sackville-West and her husband bought Sissinghurst Castle, and she set about turning the garden into a series of "rooms," each with a particular theme. The White Garden is the best known. Sackville-West became an expert on roses, and had many old French roses and ramblers. Her work influenced subsequent garden design. She was awarded the Veitch Memorial Medal in 1955 by the Royal Horticultural Society. She was the gardening correspondent for the *Observer* and wrote many books about gardening, such as *The Garden* (1946) and *Even More for Your Garden* (1958). Her last novel, *No Signposts in the Sea*, was published in 1961. She had a hemorrhage in January 1962 and in March was diagnosed with abdominal cancer. She died the following June.

She was made a Companion of Honour in December 1947 and awarded a D.Litt. by the University of Durham in 1950. Sissinghurst Castle now belongs to the National Trust.

Bibliography: Cross, R., and A. Ravenscroft-Hulme, *Vita Sackville-West: A Bibliography,* Winchester: St. Paul's Bibliographies, 1999; Penn, H., *An Englishwoman's Garden,* London: BBC Books, 1993; "A People Place: Sissinghurst Castle Garden," *National Trust Magazine Complimentary Gardens Supplement* (2001); Stevens, M., *V. Sackville-West: A Critical Biography,* London: Michael Joseph, 1973; *Who Was Who, 1961–1970,* London: Adam and Charles Black, 1972.

Salmons, Josephine Edna
1904–?
anthropologist

Education: University of Witwatersrand, 1922–1925; B.Sc. with honors, 1925.

Josephine Salmons discovered a hominid skull that facilitated a theory of the geographical origins of humankind.

In November 1924, Josephine Salmons, a student demonstrator of anatomy at the University of Witwatersrand, brought Professor Raymond Dart a hominid skull partially embedded in limestone. Mr. Izod, one of the directors of the Northern Lime Works, had taken the skull as a souvenir from the limecliff at Buxton, west of Tuangs, north of Kimberley, in Bechuanaland in southern Africa. Salmons was astute enough to recognize the importance of the skull, which was that of an *Australopithecus africanus.*

It was his interpretation of the skull, with the suggestion that Africa rather than Asia had been the cradle of humankind, that made Dart's reputation. He published his findings in 1925 in an article entitled "*Australopithecus africanus:* The Man-Ape of South Africa" (*Nature* 115, 2884: 195–199). He described how Salmons had brought the skull to him and expressed his indebtedness to her, "without whose aid the discovery would not have been made." In general, however, Salmon is given little credit for the part she played in bringing the skull to his attention.

Bibliography: Coetzee, M., Records Manager, University of Witwatersrand, personal communication to the author, November 1999; Daintith, J., et al., eds., *Biographical Encyclopaedia of Scientists,* second edition, Bristol: Institute of Physics Publishing, 1994; Tobias, P. V., "Raymond Arthur Dart (1893–1988)," *Nature* 337 (1989): 211.

Sampson, Kathleen
23 November 1892–21 February 1980
mycologist, plant pathologist

Education: Royal Holloway College, University of London; B.Sc., 1914; M.Sc., 1917.

Employment: assistant lecturer in agricultural botany, University of Leeds, 1915–1917; Board of Agriculture, seed testing service, 1917–1919; senior lecturer in agricultural botany, University College of Wales, Aberystwyth, 1919–1945.

Kathleen Sampson pioneered research into the diseases of herbage crops and cereals, based on her work at the Welsh Plant Breeding Station at Aberystwyth.

Sampson was brought up in Chesterfield, Derbyshire, where her father was a pharmacist. He was intrigued by natural history and shared his interest with his younger daughter.

Sampson studied at Royal Holloway College, at the University of London. She was awarded the London University Gilchrist Scholarship for Women in 1913 and the Driver Scholarship for Botany and the Driver essay prize in 1914. Her postgraduate studies at Royal Holloway College were guided by Professor Margaret Benson, a specialist in fossil ferns. For her M.Sc. thesis, Sampson investigated the fern *Phylloglossum,* publishing her results in the *Annals of Botany* in 1916.

Sampson belonged to the British Mycological Society for sixty years and was president of the society in 1938. She was an assistant lecturer at Leeds and investigated common scab of potato, then worked with Professor George Stapledon on a wartime project to test seeds for farmers.

When the war ended, she joined Stapledon at Aberystwyth and was a lecturer there until her early retirement in 1945. While at Aberystwyth, she not only organized the teaching in the Department of Agricultural Botany but also was involved in setting up the Welsh Plant Breeding Station. She investigated the various diseases and was particularly interested in the smuts; she published numerous papers on her research. She and Dr. J. H. Western coauthored *Diseases of British Grasses and Herbage Legumes* (1941).

On her retirement she moved to a property near Aylesbury, Buckinghamshire, where she set up a beautiful garden and bird sanctuary. She left most of her estate to the Royal Society for the Protection of Birds.

Bibliography: G. C. A. [G. C. Ainsworth] and J. H. W. [J. H. Western], "Kathleen Sampson, B.Sc., M.Sc. (1892–1980)," *Transactions of the British Mycological Society* 75, 3 (1980): 353–354.

Sandars, Nancy Katharine
29 June 1914–
archaeologist

Education: at home; Wychwood School for Girls, Oxford; Institute of Archaeology, University of London; diploma, 1949; British School at Athens, 1954–1955; St. Hugh's College, Oxford; B.Litt., 1957; 1958–1961.

Nancy Sandars is well known through her books such as *Prehistoric Art in Europe* (1968).

After obtaining her diploma in archaeology, Sandars traveled extensively, conducting archaeological research in Europe from 1949 to 1969 and exploring the Middle East in 1957, 1958, 1962, and 1966. She took part in conferences in Prague, Sofia, and at McGill University in Montreal. While studying at St. Hugh's College, she had an Elizabeth Wordsworth scholarship.

Among her books was *The Sea Peoples: Warriors of the Ancient Mediterranean, 1250–1150 BC* (1978) In 1984 she was made a fellow of the Society of Archaeologists.

Bibliography: Who's Who, 1998, London: Adam and Charles Black, 1998.

Sanger, Ruth Ann
6 June 1918–
hematologist

Education: Abbotsleigh, Sydney; University of Sydney, B.Sc., 1939; University of London, Ph.D., 1948.
Employment: member of scientific staff, Red Cross Blood Transfusion Service, Sydney, 1940–1946; Medical Research Council (MRC), Blood Group Unit, 1946–1973; director, MRC Blood Group Unit, 1973–1983.
Married: Dr. Robert Russell Race, in 1956; he died in 1984.

Dr. Ruth Sanger has done outstanding work in hematology and was director of the Medical Research Council Blood Group Unit for ten years.

Ruth Ann Sanger (Godfrey Argent Studio)

Sanger's father was the headmaster of Armadale School, New South Wales. Sanger went to school in Sydney and graduated from the University of Sydney just before the start of World War II. She worked at the Red Cross Blood Transfusion Unit during the war.

In 1946 she went to England to study for her doctorate on human blood groups (there were no facilities for postgraduate studies in Sydney) while working at the Blood Group Unit of the Medical Research Council (MRC). While continuing with her research at MRC, she collaborated with Dr. Robert Race, who was at the Lister Institute, to write *Blood Groups in Man* (1950), an immensely readable and interesting text that was widely translated. Sanger was elected a fellow of the Royal Society in 1972.

She has received many awards for her research in hematology, including an honorary M.D. from Helsinki University in 1990 and the Oliver Memorial Award for Blood Transfusion, British Red Cross. She is an honorary member of the International Soci-

ety of Blood Transfusion and of hematology societies in Mexico, Germany, Norway, and Canada.

Bibliography: Sanger, R. A., personal communication to the author, April 1999; *Who's Who, 1999*, London: Adam and Charles Black, 1999.

Sansome, Eva née Richardson
9 September 1906–
mycologist

Education: Girls' Secondary School, Bishop Auckland; Armstrong College, Newcastle upon Tyne (Durham University), 1924–1927; B.Sc. with honors, 1927; diploma in the theory and practice of teaching, 1928; M.Sc., 1941; Manchester University, D.Sc.
Employment: lecturer in horticulture, Department of Botany, University of Manchester; Department of Botany, University of Ghana, lecturer, from 1960, senior lecturer; reader, Department of Botany, Ahmadu Bello University, Zaria, Nigeria.
Married: Dr. Frederick Whalley Sansome, lecturer in botany, University of Manchester.

Eva Sansome did research in mycology and genetics and taught in West Africa.

Sansome took her diploma in the theory and practice of teaching before moving to the University of Manchester to do research in genetics there. She became a fellow of the Linnean Society in 1928. She published papers in *Nature* in 1937 and 1938.

While at the University of Ghana, she investigated meiosis in the oogonium and antheridium of *Pythium debaryanum*, the mold that causes damping-off of seedlings. Using a light microscope and simple staining techniques, she showed that meiosis occurs just before the gametes are formed, indicating that the vegetative phase, that is, the hyphae, is diploid. This was contrary to ideas held at the time, but Sansome was proved correct. Her results were published in the *Transactions of the British Mycological Society* in 1963.

Bibliography: Barkham, V., librarian, British Mycological Society, personal communication to the author, August 1998; Dane, G., Registrar's Office, University of Newcastle upon Tyne, personal communication to the author, March 1999; Odamtten, G. T., head of Botany Department, University of Ghana, personal communication to the author, November 2000.

Sargant, Ethel
28 October 1863–16 January 1918
botanist

Education: North London Collegiate School for Girls; Girton College, Cambridge, 1881–1885.
Employment: research, Jodrell Laboratory, Kew Gardens, London, 1892–1893; independent research at home, from 1893.

Ethel Sargant was noted for her work on plant anatomy, particularly the anatomy of seedlings.

Sargant was born in London, one of six children of a barrister. She studied natural science at Girton College and in 1892–1893 worked under D. H. Scott at the Jodrell Laboratory, Kew Gardens, gaining a useful grounding in laboratory techniques. In 1893 she began to carry out research in a laboratory in the grounds of her mother's house. She continued this at the Old Rectory, Girton, Cambridge, when she moved there in 1912. Botany students from the university periodically visited her laboratory, and Sargant acted as their research adviser.

Sargant's research initially focused on cytology. In 1896 and 1897 she had papers published in the *Annals of Botany* describing her work on showing the existence of the synaptic phase in living cells. However, the high-power microscope she needed for such research was straining her eyes, so she decided instead to concentrate on plant anatomy. Between 1903 and 1908 she published three important papers on the relationship between monocotyledons and dicotyledons, "A Theory of the Origin of Monocotyledons Founded on the Structure of Their Seedlings," "The Evolution of Monocotyledons," and "The Reconstruction of a Race of Primitive Angiosperms." Altogether she published more than twenty papers, many in the *Annals of Botany*.

As well as carrying out this research, Sargant looked after her invalid sister and elderly mother. She chose to concentrate on research rather than teaching, though in 1907 she did give a course at the University of London on the ancestry of the angiosperms.

In 1900 she wrote "Women and Original Research" for the Frances Mary Buss School's *Jubilee Magazine.* In the article she explored the practical aspects of pursuing independent scientific research, particularly for women. She highlighted the limitations of education for girls and society's expectations of them once they had completed their schooling and described the problems of earning a living while carrying out research. Sargant's article also celebrated those women whose dedication enabled them to pursue scientific research despite the difficulties involved.

In 1904 Sargant was elected to fellowship of the Linnean Society and from 1906 to 1910 served on the society's council, the first woman to do so. She was the first woman to be president of a section of the British Association for the Advancement of Science, presiding over the botany section in 1913. In the same year she was elected as an honorary fellow of Girton College.

Sargant was president of the Federation of University Women in 1918. From 1914 to 1918 she produced the register of university women "qualified" to do war work during World War I.

Bibliography: *Girton College Register, 1869–1946,* vol. 1, Cambridge: Girton College, 1948; Nicholls, C. S., ed., *Dictionary of National Biography: Missing Persons,* Oxford: Oxford University Press, 1993; Scott, Mrs. D. H., "Miss Ethel Sargant FLS," *Annals of Botany* (1918): i–v; *Who Was Who, 1916–1928,* London: Adam and Charles Black, 1967.

Saunders, Cicely Mary Strode
22 June 1918–
doctor, specialist in terminal care

Education: Southlands, Seaford, 1928–1932; Roedean School, 1932–1926; St. Anne's College, Oxford, 1937–1939 and 1944–1945; diploma in public and social administration, 1945; B.A., 1945 (war degree); Nightingale School of Nursing, 1940–1944, State Registered Nurse; Institute of Almoners 1945–1946; St. Thomas's Hospital Medical School, 1951–1957. M.A. 1960.

Employment: assistant almoner, Northcote Trust, St. Thomas's Hospital, 1947–1951; research, St. Mary's Hospital, Paddington, 1958–1960; director, St. Christopher's Hospice, 1967–.

Married: Professor Marian Bohusz-Szyszko, in 1980.

Cicely Saunders was the first person to found a modern hospice. Her ideas revolutionized the theory and practice of pain control.

Saunders was the eldest in her family. She was sent to boarding school when she was ten, first to Southlands in Seaford, and then to Roedean. An immensely shy person, she had a gift for understanding the loneliness of others.

She did not win immediate entry to Oxbridge, but she persevered with her studies after leaving school and went to St. Anne's College in Oxford, then the Society for Home Students, reading politics, philosophy, and economics. With the outbreak of war, Saunders felt restless and in December 1939 left her studies to train as a nurse. It took almost a year before she could start training; she joined the Nightingale School of Nursing in November 1940.

She did well in her nursing training and was well liked, but she had suffered from back pain for years and near the end of her training had to stop, as the pain was overwhelming. Nevertheless, she became a State Registered Nurse.

She taught at St. Thomas's Hospital for six months then returned to St. Anne's College, where she finished her degree and simultaneously studied for a diploma in public and social administration in order to become a medical social worker (an almoner). She completed her training at the Institute of Almoners and was appointed as almoner for the Northcote Trust, a charity that specialized in helping cancer patients.

In 1945 Saunders had converted to Christianity, and from then on her faith affected every corner of her life. On a ward at St. Thomas's Hospital she met David Tasma, a Polish Jew, and though they both knew his death was imminent, they became attached to each other. Desolate after his death in February 1947, she began thinking about the care of the terminally ill and decided this was her vocation.

Saunders worked voluntarily at St. Luke's, a hospice founded in 1893, and discovered that unlike other hospitals, where patients received painkillers only after hours of agony, the patients at St. Luke's were given drugs at regular intervals to allow them to be more in control of their lives.

When Saunders was thirty-three, the consultant at St. Luke's told her she should read medicine because, he said, "It's the doctors who desert the dying." Her father had unexpectedly given her some money so she could concentrate entirely on her studies; she trained at St. Thomas's Medical School and qualified in 1957. After qualifying, she was given a research scholarship at St. Mary's Hospital, Paddington, to work on painkilling drugs. She specialized in pain in the terminally ill. Three days a week she went to St. Joseph's Hospice in Hackney, where she was allowed to put patients on regular doses of painkillers; she made detailed notes about 1,000 cancer patients.

The public was gradually becoming aware of how poorly terminally ill people were cared for. So in June 1959 Saunders decided it was time for her to act. After a private two-week retreat at St. Mary's Convent, Wantage, she outlined in "The Need" and "The Scheme" her plans for a 100-bed hospice, to cost about £200,000. Saunders continued her work at St. Joseph's but contacted influential friends and set about raising money. The St. Christopher's Association was registered in 1961, and the St. Christopher's Hospice opened in 1967 in

Sydenham, southeast London. The St. Christopher's Association aims to promote research into the care and treatment of the dying, to encourage the teaching and training of doctors and nurses, and to provide care not only in the hospice but also in patients' homes. St. Christopher's aims to be a community, with relatives, friends, and even pets permitted almost unrestricted visiting. Patients are also free to go home for special events.

In December 1963 Saunders was drawn to and quickly bought the painting *Christ Calming the Waters* by Polish artist Marian Bohusz-Szyszko, which she saw in the window of an art gallery. Saunders wrote to him and told him the painting was to be hung in the hospice chapel. This was the start of a long friendship; eventually the two married in 1980, when Saunders was sixty-two. They had fifteen years of truly happy married life. He died in 1995.

Meanwhile the work of St. Christopher's was becoming known throughout the world, and the modern hospice movement spread throughout Britain and elsewhere. Saunders wrote about the work in books such as *Care of the Dying* (1960) and in numerous journals, and she wrote the section on terminal care in the *Oxford Textbook of Medicine* (1983) edited by D. J. Weatherall, J. G. G. Ledingham, and D. A. Warrell.

Saunders was made a Dame Commander of the Order of the British Empire (DBE) in 1980 and given the Templeton Foundation Prize for Progress in Religion in 1981. She has been awarded honorary doctorates by many universities, including Yale (1969), Columbia (1979), Glasgow (1990), and Durham (1995). In 2001 she received a $1 million award from a charity foundation for her life's work.

Bibliography: "Dame Cicely Saunders," interview on *Woman's Hour*, BBC Radio 4, 17 August 2001; Du Boulay, S., *Cicely Saunders: The Founder of the Modern Hospice Movement*, London: Hodder and Stoughton, 1984; *Who's Who, 1997*, London: Adam and Charles Black, 1997.

Saunders, Edith Rebecca
14 October 1865–6 June 1945
botanist

Education: Handsworth Ladies' College, Birmingham; Newnham College, Cambridge, 1884–1889.

Employment: Newnham College, Cambridge: demonstrator in natural sciences, 1888–1889; director of studies in natural sciences, 1889–1925.

Edith Saunders played a leading role in the teaching of botany as a science during the first quarter of the twentieth century. She was director of studies in natural sciences at Newnham College, Cambridge, for thirty-six years.

Saunders was born in Brighton, the daughter of a hotel keeper. After completing her undergraduate studies in botany at Newnham College, she became a demonstrator in the Botany Department. She was director of studies in natural sciences at Newnham, and for over twenty years taught practical work in the natural sciences to women students.

Saunders did a considerable amount of detailed research in plant genetics and floral morphology. She worked with William Bateson, who was doing pioneer work on inheritance in plants and animals. She conducted most of her genetics experiments using the garden stock, *Matthiola incana*, summarizing the work in her two-volume *Floral Morphology* (1938–1939). She was one of the first women to become a fellow of the Linnean Society, in 1905; she was a member of the society's council from 1910 to 1915 and vice-president from 1912 to 1913. In 1906 she was awarded the Banksian Medal of the Royal Horticultural Society. She joined the British Association for the Advancement of Science in 1903 and was president of the botany section in 1920; she headed the Genetical Society in 1936.

When World War II broke out, Saunders left her research to work for the YWCA, the Women's Voluntary Service (WVS), and Addenbrooke's Hospital library. She died as a result of a cycling accident.

Bibliography: Godwin, H., A. R. Clapham, M. R. Gilson, and E. M. C., "Edith Rebecca Saunders, F. L. S.," *Newnham College Roll* (January 1946): 38–41; Nicholls, C. S., ed., *Dictionary of National Biography: Missing Persons*, Oxford: Oxford University Press, 1993.

Sayer, Ettie
28 August 1875–7 July 1923
doctor

Education: Rossell School, Paignton, Devon; University College, London, Royal Free Hospital, Queen Charlotte's Hospital, M.B., B.S., London University, 1899.

Employment: house surgeon, Tunbridge Eye and Ear Hospital, 1899; physician, Cowley Mission to Mohammedan and Kaffer Women; assistant medical officer, London County Council (Education Department); honorary medical officer to the Society for Distressed Gentlefolks; consulting physician to the National Society for the Welfare of the Feeble-minded.

Ettie Sayer began her career as a doctor, in 1899, taking on various posts over her life.

She was physician to the Cowley Mission to Mohammedan and Kaffer Women and in 1901 was the medical officer for plague to the Cape Colonial government.

During the Boer War Sayer visited concentration camps and the lepers on Robben Island off South Africa. Employed by the London County Council (LCC), she gave lectures on first aid to LCC staff and others. Sayer was medical officer to the International Safety Emigration Society and wrote several books, including a textbook for nurses on medical electricity and light.

She was a fellow of the Royal Society of Medicine and belonged to the British Association for the Advancement of Science.

Bibliography: North, V., archivist, Royal Free Hospital Archives Centre, personal communication to the author, July 2001; *Who Was Who, 1916–1928*, vol. 2, London: Adam and Charles Black, 1967.

Scharlieb, Mary Ann Dacomb née Bird
16 June 1844–21 November 1930
doctor

Education: boarding schools at Manchester, New Brighton, and St. John's Wood; Madras Medical College, licentiate of medicine, surgery, and midwifery, 1878; Royal Free Hospital (London School of Medicine for Women); M.B. and B.S., 1882; M.D., 1896; master of surgery, 1897.

Employment: nursing assistant, lying-in hospital, Madras; lecturer and examiner in obstetrics and gynecology, Madras Medical College, from 1883; medical superintendent, Royal Victoria Hospital for Caste and Gosha Women, Madras, until 1887; joint lecturer on medical jurisprudence, London School of Medicine for Women; physician, New Hospital for Women (later Elizabeth Garrett Anderson Hospital); gynecologist, 1892–1902, Royal Free Hospital; gynecological surgeon, 1902–1908, Royal Free Hospital.

Married: William Mason Scharlieb, in December 1865. He died on 9 January 1891.

Mary Scharlieb was the first woman in England to be appointed to a medical position on the staff of a general hospital, becoming gynecologist at the Royal Free Hospital in London.

Scharlieb was born in London, her mother dying ten days after giving birth. Her father worked in Manchester, and Scharlieb was governess to her three half sisters from her father's second marriage. At the age of twenty, she met her future husband, and after their marriage in December 1865, they traveled to India, where William Scharlieb intended to practice as a barrister.

After the birth of her second child, Scharlieb helped local women in childbirth, their plight having come to her notice while helping her husband with his legal writing. For a year, she worked at the lying-in hospital in Madras, and she decided that she wanted to train as a doctor in London. She did not want to leave her husband, and her father had financial difficulties, so he and his family traveled to India to stay with Scharlieb and her family. They lived at Ootacamund and looked after Scharlieb's children while she was studying at the Madras Medical College. She returned to London because of ill health and was determined to complete her medical studies there. She was encouraged by, among others, Florence Nightingale and Elizabeth Garrett Anderson.

In 1881 Scharlieb took first-class honors in forensic chemistry and materia medica and for her subsequent M.B. examination was awarded a gold medal and a scholarship in obstetric medicine, as well as honors in medicine and forensic medicine. She did a postgraduate course in operative midwifery at the Frauenklinik (women's clinic) in Vienna. On her return to London, she was asked to visit Queen Victoria in order to describe the plight of Indian women who for religious and cultural reasons were unable to obtain assistance from male doctors.

In 1883 Scharlieb became a lecturer at the Madras Medical College. She founded the Royal Victoria Hospital for Caste and Gosha Women in Madras in 1884–1886, building up her own large medical practice during this period as well. But her health suffered, and in 1887 she again returned to London. She lectured in medical jurisprudence at the School of Medicine for Women and was a physician at the New Hospital for Women (since renamed the Elizabeth Garrett Anderson Hospital). She was able to study for her M.D., which she was awarded in 1888, the first woman to earn the degree from the University of London. The quality of her surgical work and the relationships she had with other staff dispelled much of the criticisms against her.

She became a gynecological surgeon in 1902, an appointment that was renewed annually, although Scharlieb had reached the official retiring age in 1905. After retirement at the end of 1908, she served as consulting gynecological surgeon and remained an influential figure at the hospital in terms of both surgery and the training of new women doctors. While employed at the hospital, she ran her own consulting practice, which involved performing major surgery.

She also did a great deal of private coaching and wrote numerous articles.

In 1889 she campaigned with Elizabeth Garrett Anderson to obtain funds for the New Hospital for Women in London. Her side of the appeal was the usefulness of the hospital to train women doctors for India.

She played an active role in the Association of Registered Medical Women (later the Federation of Medical Women), became involved in the Obstetric Society when it began to admit women, and was also a member of the obstetric section of the Royal Society of Medicine. She was a member of the Royal Commission on Venereal Diseases, which published its report in 1916. She was active as a justice of the peace from 1920, having a particular interest in the Children's Court. She was made a Commander of the Order of the British Empire (CBE) in 1917 and a Dame Commander of the Order of the British Empire (DBE) in 1926.

Of her three children, two became doctors. One of them, a son, assisted her in her medical practice, often acting as anesthetist while she operated.

She published a number of books on popular aspects of medicine, including *The Welfare of the Expectant Mother* (1919); *Reminiscences*, her autobiography (1924); and *The Psychology of Children* (1927).

Bibliography: "Dame Mary Scharlieb, DBE, MD, MS Lond.," *The Lancet* (29 November 1930): 1211–1212; *Dictionary of National Biography, 1922–30*, Oxford: Oxford University Press, 1937; *Who Was Who, 1929–1940*, London: Adam and Charles Black, 1947.

Schuster, Norah Henriette
14 July 1892–14 March 1991
pathologist

Education: Withington Girls' School, Manchester; Bedales School; Newnham College, Cambridge, 1912–1915; University of Manchester School of Medicine; M.B.; Ch.B., 1918.
Employment: assistant pathologist, St. George's Hospital, London; assistant

pathologist, Infants' Hospital, London; pathologist, Royal Chest Hospital, London, 1927–1954; Pinewood Hospital, Wokingham, 1954–1959.

Married: Marriott Fawchner Nicholls, on 2 July 1925.

Norah Schuster was the first woman to take the preclinical science course at the University of Cambridge and the first woman president of the Association of Clinical Pathologists (1950).

Schuster took the natural science tripos at Newnham College, achieving a first. In 1916, while studying medicine at the University of Manchester, she worked as an unpaid assistant at the Pathology Department of Manchester Royal Infirmary, which was experiencing acute staff shortages because of World War I. She became interested in pathology and worked under the supervision of Professor H. R. Dean.

After qualifying, she held a number of junior posts before becoming a pathologist at the Royal Chest Hospital. During her career she wrote several research papers, including an early survey of lung tumors (1929); she always prefaced her papers with a historical introduction, as she was fascinated by the history of medicine. Her father, Arthur Schuster, was professor of physics at Manchester, and was involved in the introduction of X-ray technology into clinical practice. Schuster wrote an entertaining account of his work and in 1983 presented the Royal College of Pathologists with her own memoirs describing her work as a hospital pathologist. She also donated several books of historical importance to the Library of the Royal College and was made an honorary fellow in 1981.

Bibliography: *Newnham College Register, 1871–1923*, vol. 1, Cambridge: Newnham College, 1963; Rinsler, M. G., "Norah Henriette Schuster," *Newnham College Roll* (1991): 107–109; Rinsler, M. G., "Norah Henriette Schuster, 1892–1991: Honorary Fellow," *Bulletin of the Royal College of Pathologists*, 1991.

Schütte-Lihotsky, Margarete
née Lihotsky
23 January 1897–18 January 2000
architect

Education: Imperial and Royal Arts and Crafts School, Vienna, 1915–1919; Kunstgewerbeschule (high school for applied arts), Vienna.

Employment: architect, public housing scheme, Vienna, 1922–1926; architect, structural engineering department, Frankfurt, 1926–1930; architect, Soviet Union, 1930–1937; freelance architect in various countries.

Married: Wilhelm Schütte, an architect, in 1927.

Margarete Schütte-Lihotsky was Austria's first woman architect, and the work she produced reflected her concern for the way people actually lived.

Schütte-Lihotsky was born in Vienna and in 1915 became one of Austria's first woman architecture students. She later commented that at the time "no one could possibly imagine anyone allowing a woman to build a house—not even me." As a student she won several prizes. One such award led to a meeting with the renowned architect Adolf Loos, an influential figure in the Vienna housing movement set up to tackle the housing shortage that existed in Austria as a consequence of World War I. In 1922 Schütte-Lihotsky began to work with Loos on the first public housing scheme in Austria for disabled servicemen. Her work came to the attention of the German architect Ernst May, and he asked her to come to Frankfurt in January 1926 to join the structural engineering department. Here, she concentrated on the way users of facilities, particularly women, actually lived and worked. She designed laundries and kindergartens and subsequently what became known as the Frankfurt kitchen, which was based on ergonomic principles. She tested the kitchen by timing herself carrying out certain tasks in it. The kitchen was fitted into 10,000 apartments. To explain the underlying purpose of her designs, Schütte-

Lihotsky wrote the article "How Can We Make Housework Easier by Building Appropriate Apartments?"

In 1930 she went to the Soviet Union with seventeen other architects, including her husband and Ernst May. For seven years, she worked on designs for everyday facilities such as nurseries, traveling around the country in her work.

Schütte-Lihotsky had decided not have any children because both her parents had died of tuberculosis, and at that time it was thought there might be a family tendency to the disease. When it was clear that she was not at risk, she and her husband tried to start a family but were not able to have children.

She traveled to Japan in 1934 and also visited China. At the end of 1940 she began a journey back to Vienna, as her work permit had expired. On the way she visited Paris, Berlin, and Istanbul, working in Istanbul for a period. Soon after returning to Vienna, she was arrested as a Communist by the Nazis and given a death sentence, which was commuted to a fifteen-year term in prison. She actually served just over four years in prison in Bavaria, then returned to Austria in January 1947. Her autobiographical *Erinnerungen aus den Widerstand 1939–1945* (Memories of the resistance, 1985) describe her time in prison. Her political opinions forced her to continue her career abroad, mainly in the Soviet Union. In 1963 she traveled to Cuba, where she worked for three months.

Her reputation in Austria was restored only in 1980, when she was awarded the Architekturpreis der Stadt Wien (the Vienna city prize for architecture). She initially turned down the Austrian Honorary Medal for Science and Art in 1988, since it was to be presented by the controversial, conservative president Kurt Waldheim, though several years later she accepted the award. An exhibition of her life and work was presented by the Museum of Applied Arts in 1993. In the 1990s the Swedish company IKEA honored her for her influence on furniture design. The last project she advised on was a housing estate in Vienna that was designed by women for women. The authorities decided to name the estate after her, and announced their decision on her 100th birthday.

Bibliography: Connolly, K., "Margarete Schütte-Lihotsky," *Guardian* (31 January 2000): 20.

Scudder, Ida Sophia
1870–24 May 1960
medical missionary, teacher

Education: seminary, Northfield, Massachusetts; Women's Medical College of Pennsylvania, 1895–1897; Cornell University Medical School, 1897–1899; M.D., 1899.

Employment: medical missionary, Vellore; director, Mary Taber Schell Memorial Hospital, Vellore (later Christian Medical College Hospital), from 1902; principal, Christian Medical College, from 1914.

Ida Scudder founded the first hospital for women in southern India and the first medical school for women in southern India, both in Vellore.

Scudder was born in Ranipet, Madras, into an American family with a long missionary tradition. Her father, a missionary doctor in India, ran a dispensary in Vellore. One night when Scudder was a teenager, her father received three separate calls for emergency medical help. Scudder went with her father to respond to each one, but none of the families would allow a male doctor to see the woman patient. All three women died. After this incident, Scudder knew that she wanted to become a doctor to help women in India. She went to the United States to train, earning an M.D. from Cornell University in 1899.

Once back in Vellore, Scudder helped her father with his work. When he died, Scudder decided to set up her own dispensary. At first women were reluctant to come, but soon she had a steady stream of patients. In her first two years she treated over 5,000 patients.

The Mary Taber Schell Memorial Hospital for women opened in Vellore in 1902, with Scudder as its director. During that first year over 12,000 patients were treated; Scudder carried out twenty-one major operations that year and more than 400 minor ones. Bubonic plague broke out in 1903, so many people were afraid to go to the hospital, but once the plague had subsided, they returned.

In September 1909, so that she could get to outlying villages, Scudder was given a Peugeot—the first car seen in Vellore. Scudder was aware of the need not only to treat but to train women in medicine. On 27 May 1914 the Union Medical College for women was opened, with funding from the South India Missionary Association.

Scudder traveled in the United States to raise more funds, and the medical school was opened officially with full accredited status on 12 August 1918 by the governor of Madras. The first medical students graduated in 1922.

In 1922 Scudder bought 8 acres of land outside Vellore at Hilltop; her holiday/retirement home was built there in 1924. In the same year her faithful companion, the evangelist Annie Hancock, died of cholera. Scudder's mother, who had stayed with Scudder in India, died the following year.

Mahatma Gandhi visited the Union Missionary Medical School in 1927, and new hospital buildings were completed in 1928. Scudder's niece, Ida Belle Scudder, who had also trained as a doctor, came to Vellore in the 1930s and gradually took over Scudder's responsibilities.

The Friends of Vellore was founded in 1938 as a worldwide prayer fellowship; it is also concerned with publicity and fundraising. The Vellore Christian Medical College, which developed from Scudder's work, was founded in 1942 and became coeducational in 1947. The hospital is said to be the largest teaching hospital in Asia. Besides the usual medical and related staff, many people from abroad work there either voluntarily or on charity-funded contracts.

Scudder was awarded the Kaisar-i-Hind medal (gold medal, first class) in 1920 for her services to India since 1900. In April 1959 she was given an Award of Distinction from the Medical College at Cornell University for her contribution to medical education, public health, and international understanding.

Bibliography: Parry, M., ed., *Chambers Biographical Dictionary of Women,* Edinburgh: W. and G. Chambers, 1996; Uglow, J. S., ed., *The Macmillan Dictionary of Women's Biography,* London: Macmillan, 1989; Wilson, D. C., *Dr. Ida: Passing on the Torch of Life,* Vellore: Christian Medial College Board (USA) Inc., 1959.

Sexton, Alice (Elsie) Wilkins née Wing
27 April 1868–18 February 1959
zoologist, artist

Education: Truro School of Art, Cornwall.
Employment: director's research assistant and zoologist, Marine Laboratory, Plymouth, 1924–1948.
Married: Louis E. Sexton.

Alice (known as Elsie) *Sexton,* an outstanding marine artist, was based at the laboratory of the Marine Biological Association in Plymouth from 1900.

Soon after her family moved from Truro to Plymouth in 1885, Sexton married a dentist with an interest in microphotography. He joined the Marine Biological Association (MBA) in 1900 and through his friendship with the director, Dr. J. E. Allen, Sexton was asked to illustrate polychaete worms and other invertebrates for Allen's publications. Her first illustrations were published in 1902.

In 1906 Allen went on a collecting cruise in the MBA vessel SS *Huxley* in the Bay of Biscay. On his return Sexton was given the amphipods (shrimps) to identify. She had never been trained as a zoologist, but she worked meticulously on the thirty-five different species collected, writing to zoologists worldwide for examples of type specimens. Her first publications on these were in the *Proceedings of the Zoological Society* (1908 and 1909).

Sexton decided to study the life history of a species of shrimp that could easily be kept under laboratory conditions. She settled on *Gammarus* and in 1912 set about rearing specimens of *G. chevreuxi* found locally.

From the progeny of one of these pairs, a shrimp with red instead of black eyes appeared, the first type of a Mendelian recessive for this species. In these early days of genetics research, the breeding of *G. chevreuxi* with different recessive characteristics was of considerable interest. Sexton published studies on its life history in 1924. She continued the genetic work until 1936 and published over thirty research papers between 1908 and 1951. In Plymouth she cultivated a garden filled with plants sent to her from friends abroad. She was a fellow of the Linnean Society for forty-three years.

Bibliography: Gordon, I., "Mrs. Elsie Wilkins Sexton, F.L.S.," *Proceedings of the Linnean Society of London,* 171st session, 1958–1959, pt. 1 (June 1960): 134–135; Russell, F. S., "Mrs. E. W. Sexton," *Nature* (21 March 1959): 790; Spooner, G. M., "Mrs. E. W. Sexton, F.L.S. (1868–1959)," *Journal of the Marine Biological Association* 39 (1960): 1–4.

Shakespear, Ethel Mary
Reader née Wood
17 July 1871–17 January 1946
geologist, public servant

Education: Bedford High School; Newnham College, Cambridge, 1881–1885; Mason College, Birmingham, 1896.
Employment: assistant to Professor C. Lapworth, Mason College, Birmingham, 1896–1906; work on behalf of disabled servicemen, from 1915; member of Special Grants Committee of Ministry of Pensions, 1917–1926.
Married: Gilbert Arden Shakespear, lecturer in physics, in 1906.

Ethel Shakespear was a noted geologist. After carrying out welfare work during World War I, she devoted her energies to public service, particularly in Birmingham.

Shakespear was born in Biddenham, Bedfordshire, the daughter of a clergyman, and began her education at Bedford High School. At one time she considered pursuing a career as a pianist but then decided to study geology. In 1895, while still a student at Newnham College, she jointly published (with her friend and colleague Gertrude L. Elles) her first paper in *Geological Magazine,* on a group of rocks in the Lake District. Following her graduation, she was awarded a Bathurst Studentship, which continued in 1896 for her work with Professor C. Lapworth at Mason College, Birmingham. She held the post of research assistant to Lapworth until her marriage in 1906.

Shakespear published three important geological works. The first was "The Lower Ludlow Formation and Its Graptolite Fauna" in the *Quarterly Journal of the Geological Society* in 1900, which she followed in 1906 with "The Tarannon Series of Tarannon" in the same journal. A much larger work, representing years of meticulous research, was the *Monograph of British Graptolites,* written jointly with G. L. Elles.

During World War I Shakespear began her long career in public service. In 1915 she carried out welfare work on behalf of disabled servicemen. She was involved in the setting up of the Association of War Pensions Committees in London and in 1917 was part of the Special Grants Committee of the Ministry of Pensions. She continued this latter work until 1926, by which time she had also become a member of the Birmingham and Sutton Coldfield War Pensions Committee and honorary secretary of the Birmingham Citizens Society. She was made a Member of the Order of the British Empire (MBE) in 1918 and a Dame Commander of the Order of the British Empire (DBE) in 1920. In 1922 she became a justice of the peace in Birmingham and was the first woman in the city to be elected to the Licensing Committee.

Shakespear was also active in a number of women's groups: she was president of the Birmingham branch of the National Council of Women (1929–1932), the Midland branch of the Women's Electrical Association (1932–1935), and the Birmingham and Midland branch of the Federation of University Women. She took an interest in the welfare of children in Birmingham's pioneering fostering scheme and offered help and support to women and girls who were in reduced circumstances.

In 1929 she and her husband moved to an old house near Bromsgrove and began to farm the land, though Shakespear continued many of her public roles in Birmingham. During World War II she worked extremely hard to keep the farm going despite reduced staff numbers. The relentless work brought fatigue, and she died in 1946 after becoming ill.

She was elected to fellowship of the Geological Society soon after women were admitted and was awarded the society's Murchison Medal in 1920. On this latter occasion, the society's president expressed the hope that Shakespear would resume her geological research once her public duties had reduced; this was not to be.

Bibliography: Elles, G. L., "Dame Ethel Shakespear, J.P., D.Sc. Birmingham," *Newnham College Roll Letter* (January 1947): 47–49; Elles, G. L., "Dame Ethel Mary Reader Shakespear (née Wood), D.B.E., D.Sc.," *Proceedings of the Geological Society of London* 102 (1946): 37–38; *Newnham College Register, 1871–1923,* vol. 1, Cambridge: Newnham College, 1963; Sarjeant, W. A. S., *Geologists and the History of Geology: An International Bibliography from the Origins to 1978,* vol. 3, London: Macmillan, 1980; *Who Was Who, 1941–1950,* London: Adams and Charles Black, 1952.

Shilling, Beatrice (Tilly)
8 March 1909–18 November 1990
aeroengineer

Education: Manchester University.
Employment: electrician, 1920s; scientific officer, Royal Aircraft Establishment, Farnborough, 1933–1969.
Married: George Naylor.

Beatrice Shilling worked for many years as an aeroengineer at Farnborough, carrying out important work on aircraft engines and associated safety problems.

Shilling was born in Waterlooville, Hampshire, the daughter of a butcher. As a child she liked to play with building sets, and when she was sixteen she dismantled and rebuilt her own motorbike. She took a degree in engineering at Manchester University after working as an electrician. After graduating, she began her long career at the Royal Air Establishment at Farnborough, starting off as a scientific officer. During World War II she investigated a dangerous defect in the design of the Rolls-Royce Merlin engine, solving the problem with a small piece of metal that was used throughout Fighter Command until redesigned carburetors could be fitted. She was in charge of investigations after the war, looking into problems such as wet runways and their effect on braking. She also worked on supersonic aircraft and rocket propulsion.

Shilling had a great interest in motorcycle racing, an interest shared with her husband, George Naylor. She achieved a Gold Star at the Brooklands circuit in the 1930s for lapping the track at over 100 mph on a motorbike she had modified herself.

Shilling was made an Officer of the Order of the British Empire (OBE) in 1948 and awarded an honorary D.Sc. from the University of Surrey in 1969.

Bibliography: The Baroness Platt, "Women in Technology," Edith Leggatt Lecture, University of Surrey, 13 June 1984; Massingberd, H., ed., *The Daily Telegraph Book of Obituaries: A Celebration of Eccentric Lives.* London: Macmillan, 1995.

Shorten, Monica Ruth
1923–1993
zoologist

Employment: Bureau of Animal Population, Oxford, 1943–1953; Ministry of Agriculture, Fisheries, and Food, from 1954; Game Conservancy.
Married: A. D. Vizoso.

Monica Shorten, an authority on the gray squirrel, wrote *Squirrels* (1954) in the Collins New Naturalist series.

After graduating Shorten worked under Charles Elton at the Bureau of Animal Population, initially on the ecology of rats and mice. In 1943 Elton asked her to check the distribution of the gray squirrel. This developed into a ten-year research project. She studied the behavior of wild and captive squirrels, made several films about squirrels, and lectured in the United States and Britain on squirrels.

Starting in 1954, Shorten did research for the Ministry of Agriculture, Fisheries, and Food (MAFF) on squirrels and toxic chemicals and coauthored *The World of the Grey Squirrel* (1973) with F. Barkalow. She also worked for the Game Conservancy studying the woodcock. Family commitments and ill health due to diabetes later curtailed her research.

Bibliography: Marren, P., *The New Naturalists,* London: HarperCollins, 1995; Shorten, M., "The Distribution of the Grey Squirrel (*Sciurus carolinensis* Gmelin) and the British Red Squirrel (*S. vulgaris leucourus* Kerr) in Lincolnshire," *Transactions of the Lincolnshire Naturalists' Union* (1946): 108–114; Shorten, M., *Squirrels,* New Naturalist Series, London: Collins, 1954; Shorten, M., "A Survey of the Distribution of the American Grey Squirrel *Sciurus carolinensis* and the British Red Squirrel *S. vulgaris leucourus* in England and Wales in 1944–5," *Journal of Animal Ecology* 15, 1 (1946): 82–92.

Singer, Eleanor
12 November 1903–10 September 1999
doctor

Education: University College London, M.Sc., 1929; qualified as a doctor, 1941.

Employment: teaching, University of California at Berkeley; research under J. C. Drummond, London; head of medical unit of postwar relief in Balkans, Save the Children Fund, until 1948; assistant medical officer of health, from 1948; family planning doctor (first in Colchester, then in Sheffield and Derbyshire), 1948–1983.

Married: Sidney Fink, full-time organizer for Communist Party of Great Britain (he died in 1943); Michael Barratt Brown, economist, in 1948.

Eleanor Singer was an important figure in

family-planning medicine, working for many years in a clinic for young people.

Singer was born in Hampstead, London, in 1903, the granddaughter of a rabbi. Her mother's sisters were active in the suffragette movement, and her father was to become chairman of the London Stock Exchange. After she obtained her M.Sc., she taught at Berkeley, returning to London to do research on vitamins. In the 1930s the writer and scholar Yvonne Kappe influenced her decision to join the Communist Party of Great Britain as a response to the growth of fascism. She decided to follow a career in medicine, qualifying as a doctor in 1941. Her first husband, Sidney Fink, a key figure in the Communist Party of Great Britain, was killed in 1943 in an air raid.

Singer began working for the Save the Children Fund in the Balkans as head of a medical unit for relief work. She went to Sarajevo at the end of the war to help women and children in Yugoslavian villages devastated by the fighting. She was decorated by Marshall Tito for her efforts to relieve suffering.

In 1948 she returned to England and married Michael Barratt Brown, an economist. They started a family when they settled in Colchester, where Singer began her work as assistant medical officer for health and as a family-planning doctor. These two jobs continued for many years. When the family moved in the early 1960s, Singer worked as schools medical officer for north Derbyshire and carried out a study on goiter in the area.

She was an important figure in the establishment of the Young People's Consultation Centres, which offered advice on contraception, a controversial issue at the time. She worked at one clinic in Sheffield until she retired at the age of eighty.

Bibliography: McCrindle, J., "Eleanor Singer," *Guardian* (13 September 1999).

Slávíkova, Ludmila
née Kaplanova
23 February 1890–18 February 1943
geologist

Education: Charles University, Prague, Ph.D. 1914.

Employment: teacher, Minerva Girls' High School, Prague; assistant to Professor F. Slávík, Mineralogy Department, Charles University; head, Department of Mineralogy and Petrology, National Museum, Prague, 1921–1939.

Married: Frantisek Slávík, professor of mineralogy, in 1917.

Ludmila Slávíkova was a geologist. Born in Prague, she studied mathematics and physics at Charles University. For her doctorate, she researched the crystals in Bohemian pyrargyrite. She and her husband wrote a monograph about the Ordovician iron ores of Bohemia, and she wrote several papers, including some about the history of the mineral collections in the National Museum in Prague.

In 1943 she and her husband were arrested by the Nazis and taken to the concentration camp at Oswiecim. She died fourteen days after her arrival there.

Bibliography: Burdova, P., and H. Turkova, National Museum, Prague, personal communications to the author, January and February 2000; Spencer, L. J., "Biographical Notices of Mineralogists Recently Deceased," *Mineralogical Magazine* 28, 199 (1947): 219.

Smith, Annie Lorrain
1854–1937
botanist

Employment: assistant in the Botany Department, British Museum (Natural History), 1902–1934.

Annie Lorrain Smith was president of the British Mycological Society in 1907 and 1917.

She was born in Dunfriesshire, Scotland, and studied in Germany and France. She was a governess for a short time and then studied botany with D. H. Scott at South Kensington.

She was assistant at the British Museum (Natural History) to W. C. Carruthers. She helped him with early work on seed testing and arranged the exhibits of microfungi and lichens at the museum. She wrote a second volume of *A Monograph of the Lichens Found in Britain* (1911), which had been begun by J. M. Crombie (1894). She wrote the first volume, published in 1918. Her monograph, *A Handbook of the British Lichens* (1921), took the form of a key, to aid with identification. *Lichens* was a textbook for students and perhaps her best known work. She was made an Officer of the Order of the British Empire (OBE) in 1934.

Bibliography: Barkham, V., librarian, British Mycological Society, personal communication to the author, July 2001; Gage, A. T., and W. T. Stearn, *A Bicentenary History of the Linnean Society of London,* London: Academic Press, 1988.

Snelling, Lilian
8 June 1879–12 October 1972
botanical artist

Education: Royal Botanic Garden, Edinburgh.

Employment: freelance botanical artist, based at the Royal Botanical Gardens, Kew.

Lilian Snelling was considered one of the greatest botanical artists of her time.

Snelling was taught botanical art at the Royal Botanic Garden, Edinburgh, by Sir Isaac Bayley Balfour; Frank Morley Fletcher instructed her in lithography.

Snelling was the main artist for *Curtis's Botanical Magazine* from 1922 to 1952. Copies of her original folio-sized drawings were reduced and lithographed. She colored them by hand as a guide before the final color printing. Her paintings were both detailed and accurate and immensely beautiful. She was awarded the Victoria Medal by the Royal Horticultural Society in 1955.

Her masterpiece was considered to be drawings of lilies she did in 1933–1940 for Grove and Cotton's *Supplement to Elwes' Monograph of the Genus Lilium*. Other remarkable collections were her illustrations for Stoker's *Book of Lilies* (1943) and Sir Frederick Stern's *Study of the Genus Paeonia* (1946). She lithographed many of the paintings that Stella Ross-Craig did for *Curtis's Botanical Magazine*.

Bibliography: Blunt, W., and W. T. Stearn, *The Art of Botanical Illustration*, London: Antique Collectors' Club, Royal Botanic Gardens, Kew, 1994; Desmond, R., *Dictionary of British and Irish Botanists and Horticulturalists, Including Plant Collectors and Botanical Artists*, London: Taylor and Francis, 1977; The Earl of Morton, "Miss Lilian Snelling, V.M.H.," *Journal of the Royal Horticultural Society* 98 (1973): 139; LeLievre, A., "Benevolent Bounty Hunter," *Country Life* (19 May 1988): 156–159.

Sohonie, Kamala née Bhagwat
18 July 1911–?
biochemist

Education: Bombay University, B.Sc., 1933; Indian Institute of Science, Bangalore; Institute of Biochemistry, University of Cambridge, from 1937; Ph.D., 1939.
Employment: founder, Biochemistry Department, Lady Hardinge Medical College, Delhi; assistant director, Nutritional Research Laboratory, Coonoor; Institute of Science, Mumbai, from 1942: professor, 1949–1969; director, 1965–1969.
Married: Madhav Sohonie in 1947.

Kamala Sohonie was the first Indian woman to obtain a scientific Ph.D. and the first to head a scientific research institute.

Sohonie graduated from the University of Bombay with a first-class degree in chemistry and physics. Despite her academic achievements as an undergraduate, she was denied a place at the Indian Institute of Science in Bangalore established and headed by the Nobel Prize–winning physicist C. V. Raman because she was a woman. She traveled to Bangalore to challenge this decision in person and was finally admitted to the institute as its first woman student. Although she was not classed as a regular student, she completed the course with distinction. Thereafter a small number of women students were admitted to the institute each year.

Sohonie gained a place at Cambridge University in 1937 and worked under another Nobel Prize winner, Frederick Gowland Hopkins, isolating and purifying the aldehyde oxidase of potato. She returned to India to become assistant director of the Nutritional Research Laboratory in Coonoor.

In 1942 she joined the Institute of Science in Mumbai, establishing the Biochemistry Department and becoming director of the institute. She trained numerous students; her research focused on three main areas: the trypsin inhibitors and hemaglutinins of Indian legumes, the biochemistry of palm juice, and the nutritive qualities of paddy flour.

Bibliography: Eapen, S., secretary, Indian Women's Scientists Association, personal communication to the author, August 2001; Rethnaraji, T. S. G., "Woman Who Overcame 'Raman Effect,'" *Indian Express* (8 July 1997); "Kamala Sohonie," in D. Richter, ed., *Women Scientists: The Road to Liberation*, London: Macmillan, 1982.

Somerville, Mary Grieg
née Fairfax
26 December 1780–29 November 1872
scientific writer

Education: at home; Miss Primrose's School, Musselburgh, 1790–1791.
Employment: freelance writer.
Married: Captain Samuel Grieg, in 1804 (he died in 1807); Dr. William Somerville, in 1812.

Mary Somerville, known as the "queen of science" in her time, wrote clearly and concisely on various scientific topics, inviting a lay audience into the magic of science and encouraging them to persevere in understanding its complexities and the excite-

Mary Grieg Somerville (Kean Collection/Archive Photos)

ment of new discoveries.

Somerville was born at Jedburgh, in the Scottish borders. She spent her childhood near Edinburgh and was able to roam the countryside. Her father sent her to boarding school when she was ten, but she did so badly that she was not enrolled again. The family spent winters in Edinburgh, where Somerville learned some Latin, Greek, and French and had lessons in dancing, music, painting, and cooking.

She encountered algebra in a ladies' magazine and tried to find out more. Her painting teacher having suggested Euclid's *Elements of Geometry* to help with perspective, Somerville started studying geometry and then algebra. Because her parents were not keen on her studying, she had to get up before breakfast to read secretly in her bedroom. Eventually she was allowed to take lessons from the village teacher, who helped her with astronomy and interested her in geography.

When she married Captain Samuel Grieg, she moved to London. They had two boys, Woronzow, who survived, and David, who died as a child. When her husband died in 1807, Somerville returned to her parents' home in Scotland and started in earnest on her mathematical studies.

Her second husband, Dr. William Somerville, was appointed as an inspector for the Army Medical Board in 1816 in London. Dr. Somerville, a fellow of the Royal Society, knew most of the scientists of the day and invited them to their home. In 1817 the Somervilles traveled to France and wintered in Italy, meeting many scientists on their trip.

In 1824 Dr. Somerville was appointed as physician at the Chelsea Hospital. Somerville missed the scientific life of central London but still took an active part when she could. She tried out some simple experiments at home, drawing up the results of one experiment, to magnetize a sewing needle, for the Royal Society's journal in 1826. Apart from Caroline Herschel's observations, it was the first paper by a woman the Royal Society had published under the woman's own name (although it included a commentary by Somerville's husband).

In 1827 Henry Lord Brougham wrote to Dr. Somerville to ask if his wife would translate the Marquis de la Place's *Traité de mécanique céleste* (Treatise on celestial mechanics). The project took her four years, for not only did she translate the book but also explained the methods and added diagrams. It turned out to be too long for Brougham to publish but the publisher, John Murray, brought it out in 1831. It was an instant success, widely used as a textbook, and went through ten editions, the last in 1877. In recognition of the work, the Royal Society had a bust of Somerville made and placed in its building.

Somerville published *On the Connexion of the Physical Sciences* in 1834. It, too, went through several editions and was translated into German, French, and Italian. She was given a civil pension of £200 a year, a great help as her family worked through a financial crisis. She and Caroline Herschel were the first women to be made honorary members of the Royal Astronomical Society in 1835. The Royal Academy of Dublin and the Bristol Philosophical Institution gave Somerville honorary membership in their societies.

Somerville's *Physical Geography* (1848), the first English textbook on the topic, was similarly successful and brought her the Victoria Gold Medal of the Royal Geographical Society. Her fourth book, *On Molecular and Microscopic Science* (1869), was not as successful in terms of sales. Her publisher felt that the science in the book was old-fashioned and accepted it for publication only because of Somerville's status and previous success.

Beginning in 1833, Somerville and her family spent most of their time in Italy, and in order to check on facts and theories, Somerville kept up correspondences with a great many leading scientists. There are over 10,000 pieces in the Somerville Collection, held in the Bodleian Library, and at Somerville College, Oxford.

Bibliography: Alexander, D. E., and R. W. Fairbridge, eds., *Encyclopaedia of Environmental Science*, London: Kluwer Academic Publishers, 1999; Creese, M. R. S., *Ladies in the Laboratory? American and British Women in Science, 1800–1900: A Survey of Their Contributions to Research*, Lanham, Maryland: Scarecrow Press, 1998; Patterson, E. C., "Mary Somerville," *British Journal for the History of Science* 4, 10 (1969): 311–339; Patterson, E. C., *Mary Somerville and the Cultivation of Science, 1815–1840*, Boston: Martinus Nijhoff Publishers [an imprint of Kluwer Academic Publishers], 1983; Williams, T. I., ed., *A Biographical Dictionary of Scientists*, London: Adam and Charles Black, 1982.

Hertha Sponer carried out important research in quantum mechanics and its application to molecular and atomic physics.

After obtaining her Ph.D. in 1920, Sponer began her career at the Physics Institute in Göttingen and was made of professor of physics in 1932. During her time at Göttingen, she published a number of articles, including "Free Paths of Slow Electrons in Mercury and Cadmium" (*Zeitschrift für Physik,* 1923) and "Nitrogen Absorption Bands" (*Zeitschrift für Physik,* 1927). She wrote two books about molecular spectra, *Molekulspektren I* and *II* (1935 and 1936). Following Hitler's rise to power, she was dismissed from her professorship because she was a woman.

After serving as visiting professor at the University of Oslo, Sponer was appointed professor at Duke University, the president of the university ignoring advice against the appointment of a woman in the physics department. Sponer continued to research and publish in molecular physics. With M. Bruch-Willstater, she produced important material on the lattice energy of carbon dioxide. She was made a Guggenheim Fellow in 1952–1953 and was a fellow of the New York Academy of Sciences, the Optical Society of America, and the American Physical Society.

Bibliography: "Hertha Sponer, 1895–1968," available at: www.physics.ucla.edu/~cwp/ Phase2/Sponer,_Hertha@838834963.html.

Sponer, Hertha
1895–1968
physicist

Education: University of Göttingen, Germany, Ph.D., 1920.
Employment: assistant, Physics Institute, Göttingen, 1921–1925; University of Göttingen: teaching and research, 1925–1932; professor of physics, 1932–1934; visiting professor, University of Oslo, 1934–1936; professor, Duke University, Durham, North Carolina, 1936–1966.
Married: James Franck, a physicist, in 1946.

Spooner, Mary Florence (Molly) née Mare
10 July 1914–27 August 1997
marine biologist

Education: King Edward VI High School for Girls, Birmingham; Newnham College, Cambridge, 1933–1938; M.A., Ph.D., 1941.
Employment: researcher, Scottish Marine Biological Association Laboratory, Millport, 1942–1945; part-time teacher at schools in Plymouth, 1955–1958; researcher, Marine Biological Association Laboratory, Plymouth, 1967–1976.

Married: Malcolm Spooner, zoologist at the Marine Biological Association Laboratory, on 14 May 1943.

Molly Spooner, a marine biologist, was an expert on oil spills.

Spooner was born in Birmingham. She won a scholarship to Newnham College, Cambridge, where she read zoology and won prizes for her work. She took part in the 1936 Easter class of the Marine Biological Association (MBA) at their laboratory in Plymouth. After her graduation in 1938, she had a Bathurst Research Studentship and the following year a Maitland Balfour Research Studentship, allowing her to spend two years at the MBA in Plymouth. For her doctorate, she did research into the role of microorganisms and organic detritus in the food chains of a marine benthic community (published in the *Journal of the Marine Biological Association* 25 [1942]: 517–554).

She married in 1943, but until 1945 she lived away from her husband while she carried out research on the antifouling of ships at the Millport Marine Laboratory near Glasgow. Her husband, Malcolm, worked as a code-breaker in Bedfordshire, near Milton Keynes. In 1945 they both returned to Plymouth. They had two children, and in 1948 the family moved to Crapstone, on the edge of Dartmoor, where Spooner helped her husband with the studies in which he was involved in his spare time, including a long-term survey of dwarf oak trees in Wistman's Wood. The couple also undertook a significant amount of recording work for the *Atlas of the Devon Flora* (1984).

During the 1950s she taught part time in various schools in Plymouth. In 1967 she made an unexpected return to her career as a marine biologist, following the grounding of the oil tanker *Torrey Canyon* on rocks to the west of the Scilly Isles. The staff of the MBA in Plymouth, including Spooner's husband, were deployed to study the effects of the oil spill. Spooner joined them and was soon immersed in research once more, contributing to a book on the disaster, *Torrey Canyon Pollution and Marine Life* (1970). Dispersants had been used on the oil spill, and Spooner was one of the first to recognize

that these could cause more damage than the oil itself. Her reputation as an expert spread from Britain to the rest of the world, and she carried out research and gave advice on oil spills in a number of different countries. In 1973 she was appointed the Department of the Environment's adviser on oil pollution precautions and procedures.

Spooner retired from active research in 1976 and was made a Member of the Order of the British Empire (MBE) in 1977 for her work on marine oil pollution. She was a founding member of the Devon Wildlife Trust and was its vice-president in 1987 and a council member from 1987 to 1995. She raised funds for the trust by painting and selling watercolors of places in the West Country. She was also involved in the establishment of a visitor center at the voluntary marine nature reserve at Wembury in Devon.

Spooner made a bequest to the MBA to fund bursaries, each valued at £800–£1,000, for eight to ten weeks' work experience in marine biology.

Bibliography: "Dr. Molly Spooner," *MBS Annual Report* (1997): 16; "Mrs. M. F. Spooner," *Tavistock Times* (11 September 1997): 33; "Molly Leaves Impressive Legacy of Conservation," *Western Morning News* (5 September 1997); *Newnham College Register, 1924–1950,* vol. 2, Cambridge: Newnham College, 1981; Whitfield, M., and G. T. Boalch, "Oil in a Day's Work," *Guardian* (13 September 1997); Wilson, W., "Molly Spooner Bursaries," *MBA News* 24 (2000): 7.

Staveley, Dulcie
1898–1995
radiologist

Education: Royal Free School of Medicine, M.D., 1922; University College Hospital, diploma in medical radiology and electrotherapy (DMRE), 1923.

Employment: radiologist, University College Hospital, 1924–1926; clinical assistant in radiology, later senior radiologist, Royal Free Hospital, 1926–1958; radiologist in private practice, Portland Place,

London; major, Royal Army Medical Corps (RAMC), 1939–1944.

Dulcie Staveley was the first woman radiologist to be employed at the Royal Free Hospital.

During her medical training, Staveley was sent to the Endell Street (Covent Garden) hospital run by Flora Murray and Margaret Garrett Anderson. By chance Staveley went to the X-ray department and was taught how to use the machines. Staveley enjoyed this initial fortnight in radiology and later took her diploma in medical radiology and electrotherapy at University College Hospital.

When a post came up for a clinical assistant to the radiologist at the Royal Free Hospital, Staveley applied for the post and was appointed, eventually becoming senior radiologist. She and the other hospital staff were not paid until the National Health Service started in 1948, so to support herself she set up a private practice equipped with the essential X-ray equipment. As time progressed the equipment improved; there was more protection from radiation, and portable X-ray machines came into use.

When World War II began in 1939, the Royal Free Hospital was evacuated out of London, and Staveley was based at a former workhouse, Oster House at St. Albans, which was equipped with X-ray equipment taken from a children's hospital that had closed. Staveley joined the Royal Army Medical Corps as a major and worked in army hospitals in Belgium and Germany. She returned to the Royal Free Hospital when the war ended.

She retired to Alford, Lincolnshire, where she became a lively member of the community and chair of the local council. A residential street in Alford is named after her.

Bibliography: Thomas, A. M. T., Bromley Hospital, unpublished account of Dulcie Staveley's work (1987), supplied to the author October 2000.

Stephansen, Mary Ann Elizabeth
10 March 1872–23 February 1961
mathematician

Education: Bergen Katedralskole, 1887–1891; Eidgenössische Polytechnikum Zurich, graduated, 1896; University of Zurich, doctorate, 1902; University of Göttingen, 1902–1903 (winter semester).
Employment: teacher, Bergen, 1896–1898; teacher, Oslo, 1904–1906; Norwegian College of Agriculture, Ås; assistant, 1906–1921; docent in mathematics, 1921–1937.

Elizabeth Stephansen was the first Norwegian woman to obtain a doctorate, which she received in 1902 from the University of Zurich.

Stephansen was born in Bergen, the eldest of seven children. Her father had a textile shop then started his own firm, A.S. Stephansen A/S, known as the Janusfabrikken.

In 1887 Stephansen was one of three girls at the Bergen Katedralskole, where she took part in the science program, obtaining her diploma in 1891.

Although women had been admitted to the university in Norway since 1887, if she had stayed there it would have taken her six years to graduate. Instead, Stephansen took an entrance examination to get into the polytechnic in Zurich and was the only Norwegian who passed. She studied mathematics at the school on a grant from Queen Josefine's endowment and graduated in 1896.

Stephansen returned to Bergen to teach. Women had just been permitted to teach in secondary schools in Norway, but they were not allowed permanent contracts until 1906, so Stephansen served as a substitute and part-time teacher at her old school in Bergen, then in 1898, won a year's contract at the Bergen Tekniske Skole. She did four hours of teaching a week and was paid at the same rate as a man. She was also working on a doctoral thesis on partial differential equations, which she submitted to the University of Zurich. The quality of her work was high enough for her to be awarded her doctorate without an oral examination. It was published in 1902 in *Archiv for Mathematik og Naturvidenskab,* band 24, no. 4.

Stephansen was awarded a Norwegian travel grant and studied at the University of Göttingen during the winter semester of 1902–1903, attending several courses there. Once back in Norway, she returned to teaching, this time at Olaf Berg's Pigeskole (school for girls) in Oslo. She applied for but did not receive a university stipend and so continued to do research on her own, publishing two more papers.

In 1906 she was appointed to the staff of the Landbrukshoiskole (Agricultural College of Norway) at Ås. She worked there until she retired in 1937. Initially she taught physics and mathematics then was appointed as docent in mathematics from 1921. She had the nickname "Trasa" because her male predecessor was called "Trasen," referring to the function of the trace in geometry. She always took her work to class in her knitting basket, along with her knitting and lived in the student residences the entire time she worked in Ås. While there she was also responsible for processing all the meteorological results and writing these up for the college's annual report.

After retirement she moved to Espeland to live with one of her sisters. During World War II, at great personal risk, she helped the Norwegians in the German prisoner of war camp at Espeland, as she spoke fluent German. She was awarded the King's Medal of Service for her efforts.

Bibliography: Hag, K., and P. Lindqvist, "Elizabeth Stephansen—A Pioneer," *Skrifter det Kongelige Norske Videnskabers Selskab* 2 (1997): 1–23; Heggen, Liv, librarian, National Library in Oslo, personal communication to the author, June 2001.

Stephenson, Marjory
24 January 1885–12 December 1948
microbiologist

Education: by governess; Berkhampstead High School for Girls, 1897–1903; Newn-

Marjory Stephenson (Godfrey Argent Studio)

ham College, Cambridge, 1903–1906; Gloucester County Training College for Domestic Science, Gloucester; M.A. 1924, Sc.D. Cantab, 1936.

Employment: teacher, Gloucester County Training College for Domestic Science; teacher, King's College for Household Science, London; research assistant and lecturer in the biochemistry of nutrition, University College, London, 1911–1914; war work, British Red Cross (in France and then Salonika); Biochemical Laboratory, University of Cambridge, 1919–1948; lecturer, 1943–1947; reader in chemical microbiology, 1947–1948; director of Medical Research Council (MRC) unit for chemical microbiology, 1945–1948.

Marjory Stephenson was a noted microbiologist. With Kathleen Lonsdale, she was one of the first two women to be elected to fellowship of the Royal Society.

Stephenson was born in Burwell, Cambridge, the youngest of four children. Her father was a farming landowner who became involved in educational causes and who was committed to the use of new scientific techniques in agriculture. Stephenson was educated at home by a governess until the age of twelve, when she went to Berkhampstead High School for Girls. At Newnham College, Cambridge, she read zoology, chemistry, and physiology for the natural sciences tripos. After finishing at Newnham, she had hoped to train in medicine but was prevented from doing so because of her financial situation. Instead she studied and subsequently taught domestic science at the Gloucester County Training College for Domestic Science. She also taught at King's College for Household Science, London.

In 1911 she obtained a part-time post at University College, London, working with Professor R. A. Plimmer. In the same year her first paper was published, "On the Nature of Animal Lactase" (*Biochemical Journal* 6: 250).

During World War I Stephenson worked for the British Red Cross in France and Salonika. She was superintendent of a convalescence home for nurses and was also involved in patient diets. She was made an associate of the Royal Red Cross and in 1918 was made a Member of the Order of the British Empire (MBE) for her war work.

Before the war she had held a Beit Memorial Fellowship, and in 1919 she was able to take this up once more, working under Sir Frederick Gowland Hopkins at the University of Cambridge's Biochemical Laboratory. When her fellowship expired, she obtained annual Medical Research Council grants. In 1929 she became a permanent member of the Medical Research Council's external staff.

By 1922 she had started research on bacterial metabolism. Her first research student was Margaret Whetham (later Anderson), with whom she cowrote several articles. Her work with Professor Juda Hirsch Quastel on "strict" anaerobes was also important.

Stephenson's use and development of the "washed cells" technique at this time was a significant contribution to microbiology. The technique enabled bacteria to be studied in much more detail and in a more controlled environment than had been possible before. Stephenson found the method useful in her research on the enzyme systems of bacterial cells. In 1928 she was the first person to separate an enzyme from a bacterium (lactic dehydrogenase from *Eschericia coli*).

In 1930 Stephenson's book *Bacterial Metabolism* was published. It was widely used as a textbook for university students. In 1930 she and Dr. L. H. Strickland began to investigate the transfer of hydrogen and identified an enzyme that was a key part of the process, hydrogenase. They published a series of papers in the *Biochemical Journal*.

Stephenson worked with several other scientists. With John Yudkin she studied the adaptive enzyme galactozymase (in the yeast *Saccharomyces cerevisiae*), and with Ernest Gale she investigated enzyme adaptation. During the 1930s she was involved in the Cambridge Scientists' Anti-War Group, which included Stephenson's colleague Dorothy Needham among its members.

During World War II she worked with R. Davies on acetone-butyl alcohol fermentation. The main importance of their research was a method of preparing active cell suspensions. In 1941 she organized a meeting at which a number of scientists discussed pathogenic anaerobes, leading to a renewed interest in this area of research. She was secretary of the Chemical Microbiology Committee of the Medical Research Council and was also involved with the Toxin Committee, which looked at the development of protective mechanisms against the toxins produced by bacteria, such as those causing gas gangrene.

In March 1945 Stephenson became one of the first women to be elected a fellow of the Royal Society after much debate within the society. Stephenson traveled to the country to avoid the expected attention from the media, but the event was not even reported in *Nature*.

After the war Stephenson continued with her research. She investigated the enzymes responsible for the production of acetyl choline in sauerkraut and the nucleic acids of bacteria and their breakdown by enzymes within the cells. She was still active in this research when she became ill with cancer. Her final paper, written with Ernest Gale, was "Metabolic Processes in Microorganisms," published in the *British Medical Bulletin* 5 (1948): 1196.

In 1944 she was involved in the establishment of the Society for General Microbiology and was its president in 1947.

Bibliography: Anderson, M., "Marjory Stephenson, M.B.E., F.R.S., Sc.D.," *Newnham College Roll Letter* (January 1949): 54–57; *Dictionary of National Biography, 1941–1950*, Oxford: Oxford University Press, 1959; Mason, J., "Marjory Stephenson," in E. Shils and C. Blacker, eds., *Cambridge Women: Twelve Portraits.* Cambridge: Cambridge University Press, 1996; Robertson, M., "Marjory Stephenson, 1885–1948," *Obituary Notices of Fellows of the Royal Society 1948–1949*, vol. 6 (1949): 563–577; Stephenson, M., preface to *Bacterial Metabolism*, London: Longmans Green, 1930.

Alice Mary Stewart (Julia Hedgecoe)

Stewart, Alice Mary née Naish
4 October 1906–
epidemiologist

Education: Sheffield Girls' High School (GPDST), until 1920; St. Leonard's School, St. Andrews, 1920–1923; Girton College Cambridge, 1925–1929; Royal Free Hospital, London, 1929–1932.

Employment: Royal Free Hospital, house physician, 1932–1933; locum in Tyldesley, Manchester, 1933–1934; London School of Hygiene and Tropical Medicine, from 1934; registrar, Royal Free Hospital, 1935–1938 (part time); consultant, Elizabeth Garrett Anderson Hospital, 1939–1941; Nuffield Department of Clinical Medicine, Oxford, 1941–1945; Institute of Social Medicine, Oxford, 1945–1950; reader, 1950–1974; emeritus professor, Department of Public Health and Epidemiology, University of Birmingham, from 1974.

Married: Ludovick Stewart, on 17 June 1933 (divorced in 1953).

Alice Stewart was the head of a small research team that first found evidence of a cancer risk at low levels of radiation. This project showed that children who had been X-rayed before birth were twice as likely to develop any form of cancer as children who were not X-rayed.

Stewart was born in Sheffield. Her parents were doctors who specialized in pediatrics. Her mother started the first infant welfare clinic in Sheffield in 1907 and during World War I lectured at the Sheffield Medical School.

Stewart first went to Sheffield Girls' High School, then was sent to boarding school at St. Andrews. She went to Girton College to read medicine, one of only four women in her year. In her fourth year she specialized in comparative anatomy, moving on to the Royal Free Hospital for her resident year.

After her marriage, she moved with her husband to Manchester, where he had a teaching post at the Manchester Grammar School; she worked as a locum. In 1934 her husband's new job took the couple to London, and Stewart began work at the London School of Hygiene and Tropical Medicine. She was appointed to the post of registrar at the Royal Free Hospital in 1935. After passing the examinations leading to membership of the Royal College of Physicians, she obtained a post as consultant at the Elizabeth Garrett Anderson Hospital in September 1939. Her husband was sent to Bletchley Park, Buckinghamshire, to work as a decoder for the duration of the war. The women staff at her hospital were sent to Oster House in St. Albans to avoid the bombing.

In 1941 Stewart went to the Radcliffe Infirmary in Oxford as a temporary replacement. Professor Leslie Witts asked her to be a senior assistant at the Nuffield Hospital in Oxford. The Medical Research Council (MRC) wanted her to look at the risks to factory workers of developing jaundice or aplastic anemia if they filled shells with TNT, as this had been a problem in World War I. She decided the best way forward was to use volunteers. Sixty-two undergraduates were chosen from those who volunteered. They had initial blood counts and screening tests. They worked for four weeks in the factory and were retested at regular intervals. Most of them showed some reaction to the TNT by increasing the rate of red cell formation. But there were no signs of lasting damage to the source of these cells, namely, red marrow. Six months after the students had left the factory, no adverse effects could be detected. The results were published in the *British Journal of Industrial Medicine* 2 (1945): 76–82.

Her next investigation was looking at the effect on workers of carbon tetrachloride, then used to impregnate the clothes of service personnel as protection against gas. The effects of carbon tetrachloride were similar to those of chloroform, and because of the wartime blackout the workers were in a poorly ventilated area. They did not have any liver or kidney damage, however. At Professor Witts's suggestion, she spoke about this work to the Association of Physicians and in 1946 was the first woman to be elected to the association. The same year she was elected as a fellow of the Royal College of Physicians. After the war the MRC council asked Stewart to study pneumoconiosis among coal miners in Wales.

After the war, her husband decided to follow a career in music rather than teach French. He moved to Cambridge and lived with his mother. Unable to find a job in Cambridge so that she could join him, Stewart stayed in Oxford. They were divorced in 1953.

In 1943 Dr. John Ryle was appointed as chair of the new Institute of Social Medicine in Oxford. Stewart was his first assistant. Her initial assignment was to discover why there were so many cases of active tuberculosis among workers in the shoe industry in Northamptonshire. She realized that when workers with tuberculosis felt better, they returned to work, even though they were still infective. This accounted for the spread of tuberculosis in the factories. By checking the Civilian Medical Board lists, she confirmed that the less fit had been sent into factory work rather than active service.

After Ryle died in 1950, Stewart continued his work. Her department was demoted to the Social Medicine Unit, and she was appointed as reader rather than professor, but she did have security of tenure until retirement. With no specific teaching or research duties, she was able to decide what to study. She hired David Hewitt as statistician and Josefine Webb, who had worked for the MRC.

She and her coworkers decided to find out why there was an increase in the number of cases of leukemia. In 1951 the disease was affecting not only people over fifty, as was expected, but also children between the ages of two and four, who developed lymphatic rather than myeloid leukemia. Stewart's team devised a questionnaire to ask mothers about their pregnancies—for example, the illnesses they had had, their social class, whether they had had a pelvic X-ray, and so on. This was the start of the Oxford Survey of Childhood Cancer. Case control pairs were set up, matching each child who had died from cancer with a living child of the same age, sex, and from the same area. Because Alice was a doctor, she was allowed to access the birth notifications and compile lists for each region of England and Wales.

When the team started analyzing the data, they were struck by the fact that if the mother had had a pelvic X-ray during pregnancy, the chances of the child's developing cancer were twice as high as those of children born to mothers who had not been X-rayed. Stewart's first paper, in *Lancet* 1 (1956), caused a great stir—initially of congratulations. Obstetricians were reluctant to give up X-raying women, however, and the government was promoting the use of nuclear power. Stewart and her team persevered with their analysis of the data, publishing fuller results in the *British Medical Journal* in 1958. In their summary they stated that "foetal irradiation does not account for the recent increase in childhood malignancies, but the finding of a case excess for this event does underline the need to use the minimum doses for essential medical X-ray examinations and treatments" (1508).

Stewart hoped that the pelvic X-raying of pregnant women would stop immediately in the light of her evidence, but it took many years before this happened. Due to the opposition to her ideas in Britain, Stewart could not obtain funding to continue, but she did obtain financial help from the United States, and so the Oxford Survey of Childhood Cancer continued until 1980. The survey remains an invaluable source of information.

After David Hewitt moved on, George Kneale took over as Stewart's statistician. With Stewart's ability to think laterally and his skill in seeing trends, they made a formidable pair. They realized that since the use of antibiotics had become universal, many children who would have died of pneumonia and other diseases survived. The lower death rate from these diseases contributed to the higher numbers of recognized leukemia cases: previously one would not have known whether children were developing leukemia because they died before the leukemia reached its peak.

In 1974 Stewart was asked to go to the United States to work with Dr. Thomas Mancuso on data he had been collecting from workers at Hanford, a large nuclear weapons complex. She and Kneale showed that people over fifty were more sensitive to radiation than those between twenty and forty. At Hanford, besides lung cancer, the workers were also developing pancreatic cancer and cancers of the blood-forming tissue.

When the U.S. government became aware of the trend in the results, they ordered Mancuso to turn over his files. He would not, and he lost his job. Stewart and Kneale, however, returned to Britain with copies of much of the data and published some of their findings (*Health Physics* 33 [1977]: 369–385). It was clear that the safe level of radiation for workers was set too high. The government could see that the families of workers who died or became ill could successfully sue for negligence if Stewart's results became known. When she was criticized for basing her deductions on too small a sample, she asked for the files on all U.S. nuclear industry workers. It was twenty years before the files were released to her.

With Kneale providing the statistical interpretation, Stewart gave evidence in the inquiries into the safety of the nuclear plants at Windscale (now Sellafield) in 1977, Sizewell from 1982 to 1985, and Dounreay in 1986. She has been a witness in numerous cases of compensation and has lectured all over the world. Stewart never flinched from the truth, and her work on the dangers of radiation is finally becoming accepted.

Stewart also studied sudden infant death syndrome (SIDS), which increased in spite of antibiotics. It is more common in winter than in summer and usually affects infants between one and six months old. Stewart believes that some SIDS victims may have had myeloid leukemia. Healthy children gradually develop their own immune systems after having relied on their mothers', but victims of myeloid leukemia gradually lose immune competence and are more likely to succumb to disease. Such leukemia sufferers have a defect in their hemoglobin. Infants who died of SIDS often have an above average ratio of fetal to adult hemoglobin. Stewart thinks that as these children have both proportionately less adult hemoglobin and a defective immune system, they are more likely to die of SIDS, and she has proposed routine testing of levels of fetal hemoglobin in infants at one and four weeks of age in order to provide evidence of the connection between SIDs and high fetal hemoglobin levels.

Stewart was presented with the Right

Livelihood Award in 1986 "for vision and work forming an essential contribution to making life more whole, healing our planet and uplifting humanity." In 1991 she was awarded the Ramazzini Prize, the leading Italian honor for epidemiology. She was given an honorary doctorate by the University of Bristol in 1997. Stewart was a founding member of the Society for Social Medicine and the International Epidemiological Association.

Bibliography: Barber, C. R., ed., *Half a Century of Social Medicine: An Annotated Bibliography of the Work of Alice Stewart*, Billingshurst, W. Sussex: Piers Press, 1987; Cassel, C. K., *Profiles in Responsibility: Alice Stewart*, available at www.family reunion.org./health/cassel/astewart.html, accessed 1999; Greene, G., *The Woman Who Knew Too Much: Alice Stewart and the Secrets of Radiation*, Ann Arbor: University of Michigan Press, 1999; Mott, M. G., "Honorary Degrees: Professor A. M. Stewart," *Bristol University Newsletter* 27 (31 July 1997): 3; Stewart, A. M., interview on *Woman's Hour*, BBC Radio 4, 14 September 1998; Stewart, A. M., personal communication to the author, October 2000; ZKK Productions, "Sex and the Scientist: Our Brilliant Careers," program aired on BBC Channel 4 on 19 August 1996.

Stewart, Olga Margaret née Mounsey
1 July 1920–6 August 1998
botanist, botanical artist

Education: schools in Edinburgh and Kent; Art College, Edinburgh (architecture), 1938–1939; Dalhousie University, Halifax (engineering), 1939–1940.
Employment: draftswoman, Naval Dockyard, National Research Council of Canada, Halifax, Nova Scotia, 1940–1943; Royal Navy, Edinburgh, 1943–1945.
Married: Frank Stewart, a lawyer, on 28 November 1946.

Olga Stewart, a field botanist, was renowned in her native Scotland and beyond. She was a prolific artist, recording botanical information in paintings and drawings.

Stewart was born in Edinburgh. She was a draftswoman in Halifax, Canada, and she returned to Edinburgh in 1943 to do research for the Royal Navy. In her twenties she began recording her botanical observations in paintings, and over time she produced a large number of accurate representations of plants. She joined the Wild Flower Society in 1947, becoming a branch secretary. In her diary she recorded over 3,400 plants during her thirty-three-year membership in the society. She joined the Botanical Society of the British Isles in 1965, becoming a vice-county recorder ten years later for Kirkcudbrightshire in Scotland. She published her *Check List of the Plants in Kirkcudbrightshire* in 1990.

Stewart contributed to many books and journals and left a valuable legacy for botanists in the form of over 3,000 paintings of flowers. She did the majority of the drawings for Mary McCallum Webster's *Flora of Moray, Nairn and East Inverness* (1978).

Bibliography: Ellis, R. G., honorary secretary, Botanical Society of the British Isles, personal communication to the author, July 2001; Jermy, A. C., "Olga Margaret Stewart (1920–1998)," *Watsonia* 22(4) (1999): 445–447; White, A., "Olga Margaret Stewart," *Wild Flower Magazine* (Spring 1999): 38–39.

Stjernstedt, Rosemary
11 June 1912–31 October 1998
architect

Education: in Birmingham.
Employment: architect, town and country planning officer, Stockholm, Sweden, in the 1930s (for six years); London County Council: architect, then senior grade one architect, in 1950; Lambeth Council, 1964; Ministry of Housing and Local Government.
Married: Mr. Stjernstedt, a Swedish lawyer, during the 1930s.

Rosemary Stjernstedt was an important figure in the design of public housing in Britain. She was the first woman architect to gain the senior grade one status in a county council housing division, in 1950.

Stjernstedt was born in Birmingham and educated there. During the 1930s she moved to Sweden and worked in the town and country planning office in Stockholm for six years. The skills and experience she gained in Sweden contributed much to her later architectural work in Britain. When she returned to England, she worked for the London County Council and on the formation of its new housing division and in 1950 attained senior grade one status. She worked on the Alton East estate at Roehampton, a key development for the council. In 1964 the London County Council ceased to exist, and Stjernstedt moved to a post at Lambeth Council, where she was in charge of the large Central Hill housing development. Later she worked for the Ministry of Housing and Local Government; she moved to Wales when she retired.

Stjernstedt was clear-thinking and determined, combining a dedication to architecture with a concern for members of her team. Many younger architects with whom she worked became very successful, and her influence was recognized in the 1984 Royal Institute of British Architects exhibition on women architects.

Bibliography: Rowntree, D., "Homes Fit for Londoners," *Guardian* (13 November 1998).

Stones, Margaret
28 August 1920–
botanical artist

Education: Swinburne and National Gallery Art Schools, Melbourne, Australia; University of Melbourne.

Employment: nursing, Australia, during World War II; freelance botanical artist, from 1951 at the Herbarium, Royal Botanical Gardens, Kew.

Margaret Stones is an botanical artist of international repute. She has produced illustrations of plants from all over the world, and her work has been widely published, collected, and exhibited.

Stones was born in Colac, Australia. She initially studied fine art at the Swinburne and National Gallery Art Schools in Melbourne. While working as a nurse in Australia in World War II, she became ill with tuberculosis. During the year that she spent in hospital recovering from the illness, she began to draw plants, and it was then that she decided to follow a career as a botanical artist. She studied botany for a year at the University of Melbourne and moved to Britain in 1951. Although she had no job and no connections, she went to Kew Gardens in order to continue her work and soon established herself in her chosen field.

Kew provided Stones with a valuable resource in terms of its plant collections, library, and botanists. Her work has been commissioned by the Royal Botanic Gardens (Kew) and the Royal Horticultural Society, among many others. One of her main patrons has been Lord Talbot of Malahide, who invited her to produce illustrations for *The Endemic Flora of Tasmania*, a work of several volumes, the first of which was published in 1967. Stones found that it was more practical to have plant specimens flown from Tasmania to Kew for her work on the book rather than for her to travel to Tasmania. As artist in residence at Louisiana State University, she was commissioned to produce 200 watercolor drawings of the flora of Louisiana. She made annual visits to the United States until the illustrations were complete. An exhibition of her paintings entitled "Naturally Louisiana" was held at the Louisiana State Museum in 1985.

Stones is the principal illustrator for *Curtis Botanical Magazine*, and her work has been widely published. Her illustrations have been exhibited worldwide, from her native Australia to the United States and Europe. Produced mainly in watercolor, her illustrations are often very detailed. Stones works only from living specimens and often goes to great lengths to capture the essence of a plant in its natural surroundings. Her work combines an aesthetic quality with the accuracy required for the identification of botanical specimens.

Bibliography: Archivist, Royal Botanic Gardens, Kew, London, personal communication to the author, August 1999; Calder, J., and M. Calder, "Beauty in Truth," *Art and Australia* 43, 3 (1997): 413; "Colours of Nature—The Work of Margaret Stones," *Colour Review* (October 1968): 3–5; "Tasmanian Wildflowers in a Kew Garden," *Sydney Morning Herald* (13 June 1968); *Who's Who in Australia 1971*, Melbourne: Herald and Weekly Times, 1971.

Stopes, Marie Charlotte Carmichael
15 October 1880–2 October 1958
paleobotanist, writer, advocate of birth control

Education: St. George's School, Edinburgh; North London Collegiate School; University College, London; B.Sc. with honors, 1902; D.Sc., 1905; University of Munich, Ph.D., 1903–1904.

Employment: lecturer in botany, University of Manchester, from 1904; lecturer in paleobotany, University College, London; freelance writer and campaigner for birth control, 1918–1958; owner and manager, Alexander Moring Ltd., Publishers, during 1940s and 1950s.

Married: Dr. Reginald Ruggles Gates, in 1911 (marriage annulled in 1916); Humphrey R. Verdon Roe, in 1918.

Marie Stopes was well known for her research in paleobotany. In 1905 she became the youngest person in England to be awarded a D.Sc. (on the basis of published papers). She was the first woman appointed to teach science at the University of Manchester.

Stopes was born in Edinburgh. Her father was an architect and had a large collection of fossils and stone tools. Her mother was an expert on Shakespeare and was the first woman to take the Edinburgh University certificate in literature.

Stopes's chemistry teacher suggested that she study science at University College, then regarded as the best college in London. She did the first-year botany course there and in the evenings studied zoology at Birkbeck College. She graduated after two years

Marie Charlotte Carmichael Stopes (Bettmann/Corbis)

with a double first honors degree in botany and geology, and she was a gold medalist.

Stopes did a year's research at University College before going on to the University of Munich to study for her doctorate, conducting research on the structure of the ovules and their fertilization in cycads. The rules at the university had to be altered when she arrived because she was the first woman to study there. She made great friends with the Norwegian botanist Thekla Resvoll, and they used to go walking in the mountains together. Stopes became so proficient in German that she was able to defend her thesis in the language.

On returning to England, Stopes wrote up her research and was awarded a D.Sc., which enhanced her reputation as a scientist. She was appointed lecturer at the University of Manchester, where she started a humor magazine, *The Sportophyte,* and gave adult education lectures in addition to doing her university lecturing and research. Her stay in Manchester was cut short by a case of neuraglia, which disappeared when she returned to London.

Stopes won a grant from the Royal Society to study angiosperm fossils in Japan. Stopes stayed at the Hokkaido Institute and traveled around Japan as an honored guest. There were no women scientists in Japan then, and the people in the more remote parts of the country had never seen a white woman, so she sometimes drew large crowds. She taught herself Japanese and soon grew impatient with public transport and began cycling everywhere. She gave a lively account of her travels in *A Journal from Japan: A Daily Record of Life as Seen by a Scientist* (1910).

On the basis of her published research from Japan, she was made a fellow of University College, London, in 1910. She compiled *A Cretaceous Flora of the World* for the Geological Department of the British Museum. An article in the *Daily News* in 1913 showed clearly the esteem she had in the eyes of the British public.

In 1911, at the annual meeting of the American Association of Science in St. Louis, she met Dr. Ruggles Gates, a Canadian. They were married in Montreal that summer, and Gates returned to London with Stopes. It was not a happy arrangement. Part of the problem was that Gates had no proper employment, while Stopes was lecturing at University College and had to earn enough for them both to live on. He became increasingly violent and dispirited. Stopes was convinced something was missing from their relationship but was ignorant about sexual matters. With her research training and determination to solve queries, she went to the British Library and read all the books they had on sex and divorce. She realized that their marriage could be annulled because it had not been consummated; she won her divorce in 1916.

Stopes resolved to enlighten other British women ("primarily of our educated classes") about sexual matters and in 1918 wrote *Married Love: A New Contribution to the Solution of Sex Difficulties*, which went through three editions that year. The book was dedicated to young husbands and all those who betrothed in love. Her starting point was that the menstrual cycle was not understood; she explained it as well as the importance of the "receptive times." Stopes suggested that readers write her about their experiences and was amazed at the number of letters she received from both men and women. She had taken a revolutionary step in bringing the subject of sex out into the open.

Stopes met her second husband, Humphrey Roe, at a lunch arranged by a mutual friend. He was interested in birth control, knew of Stopes's work, and had funds available to set up the first birth control clinic in Britain. Their marriage was on the whole happy, though they did separate later (mainly because Roe's ill health strained the relationship). Their first child died in childbirth, but Buffkins, a son, was born in 1924.

In 1918 Stopes published *Wise Parenthood*, which advocated practical methods of birth control. It was "dedicated to all who wish to see our race grow in strength and beauty" (now, of course, known to be a racist sentiment). Many church officials were opposed to her ideas, but Stopes believed she had had a vision from God and delivered *A New Gospel, a Revelation of God Uniting Physiology and the Religion of Man* (1920) to the Anglican bishops in session at Lambeth Palace, where it was not well received.

In 1921 she founded the Society for Constructive Birth Control and Racial Progress (CBC) and opened the Mother's Clinic for Constructive Birth Control in north London amid considerable opposition. But Stopes persevered, and other clinics opened. From 1931 birth control was allowed on health grounds. She set up a library for members of the CBC so that they could borrow books, and she was responsible for the journal *Birth Control News*. Always concerned with the scientific aspects of birth control as well, Stopes gave the lecture "Some Points in the Technique of Contraception" at the British Association for the Advancement of Science annual meeting in 1934. Marie Stopes International, founded in 1976, continues to work in twenty-six countries to ensure that children come by choice, not chance.

Besides her work in paleontology and birth control, Stopes wrote numerous poems, several plays, and some books for children, such as *A Road to Fairyland* (1926).

Bibliography: Allen, M., "Chapters and Verses: Treasures of the British Library—The Marie Stopes Story," BBC Radio 4, January 2000; archivist, John Rylands Library, University of Manchester, personal communication to the author, November 1998; Aylmer, M., *Marie Stopes: Her Work and Play,* London: Peter Davies, 1933; "The Bunkum of Birth Control: A Perilous Propaganda. The Mischief of Marie Stopes—Hands off Our Women," *John Bull* (8 April 1922): 10–11; Eaton, P., and M. Warnick, *Marie Stopes: A Preliminary Checklist of Her Writings Together with Some Biographical Notes,* London: Croom Helm, 1977; Hall, R., *Marie Stopes,* London: Andre Deutsch, 1977; Kohler, M. S., ed., *Marie Stopes and Birth Control,* Dorking: C. C. Kohler, 1989; Peel, R. A., *Marie Stopes, Eugenics and the English Birth Control Movement,* London: Galton Institute, 1997; "Tragedies of the Flowers," *Daily News* (19 July 1913): 10; *Who Was Who, 1951–1960,* London: Adam and Charles Black, 1967.

T

Tammes, Jantine (Tine)
1871–1947
geneticist

Education: Middlebare Meisjesschool, from 1883; private education; University of Groningen, from 1890, teacher's certificates, 1892 and 1897.

Employment: teaching at Middlebare Meisjesschool, until 1897; Botany Department, University of Groningen: assistant to Professor J. W. Moll, 1897–1899; supervisor of botany practical classes, 1912–1917; professor of variability and heredity, University of Groningen, 1919–1937.

Tine Tammes was the second Dutch woman to be made a university professor.

After Tammes had worked for Professor J. W. Moll in the Botany Department at the University of Groningen for a few months, he arranged for her to visit Hugo de Vries, a leading geneticist, in Amsterdam, which inspired her to start her own genetic research. She chose to investigate the characteristics of cultivated flax, *Linum usitatissimum*, publishing this research in 1907 and receiving a prize of 500 guilders for it.

Tammes used flax for experiments on the inheritance of characters, crossing common flax with an Egyptian variety, then *L. crepitans* with Egyptian flax, and finally *L. angustifolium* with both Egyptian and common flax. She recorded eight characters, such as flower color, and proved conclusively that the heredity of continuous characters could be explained by the multifactor hypothesis, which states that certain traits are a result of collective action of several genes. Her results appeared in German, in 1911 in a Dutch journal, and reprinted in *Genetica* in 1941. Because her findings were published in little-known journals the importance of her work was not widely acclaimed. She was a rather shy person and tended not to go to international gatherings.

After influential academics such as the Swedish professor Herman Nilsson-Ehle advocated on her behalf, Tammes was appointed as the first female professor at the University of Groningen in 1919, (although at a lower salary than other professors). She was professor of variability and heredity until 1937.

Bibliography: Stamhuis, I. M., "A Female Contribution to Early Genetics: Tine Tammes and Mendel's Laws for Continuous Characters," *Journal of the History of Biology* 28 (1995): 495–531.

Taylor, Janet
1804–
nautical teacher, writer

Education: at her father's grammar school.
Employment: founder of nautical academy, 1830s.
Married: Mr. Taylor.

Janet Taylor established a nautical academy at which merchant navy officers could learn navigation techniques.

Taylor was a clergyman's daughter, and went to her father's free grammar school for boys, where he taught the principles of navigation. In the 1830s she set up a nautical academy and instructed merchant navy officers in a range of subjects relating to navigation, including astronomy, algebra, and geometry. She wrote *Lunar Tables for Calculating Distances* (third edition c. 1840) and a pilot book for the Brazilian coast. She also adjusted compasses in iron merchant ships. She gained international renown and was awarded gold medals by both the king of Holland and the king of Prussia. Janet Taylor had five children.

Bibliography: The Baroness Platt of Writtle, "Women into Science and Engineering," *Journal of the Royal Society of Arts* (1984): 269f.

Taylor, Mary
15 July 1898–26 May 1984
radio researcher, mathematician

Education: Pomona St. Elementary School, Sheffield; Sheffield High School (GPDST); Girton College, Cambridge; B.Sc., 1920; M.A., 1924; University of Göttingen, Germany, Ph.D., 1926.

Employment: assistant lecturer in mathematics, Girton College, 1922–1924; scientific officer, Radio Research Station, Slough, 1929–1934; abstractor and translator, *Wireless Engineer*, 1930–1940; mathematics teacher, Worcester Grammar School for Girls, and Lawnside, Malvern.

Married: (Ernest) Clive Slow, in 1934.

Mary Taylor was the first woman to take up the study of radio as a profession.

Taylor was born in Sheffield; both her parents were teachers. She gained a Clothworkers' Scholarship that enabled her to study at Girton College, Cambridge. Following her graduation in mathematics and natural sciences, she continued at Girton under a series of research studentships and also taught at the college. During this time she began her work on radio, under Edward Appleton.

Taylor studied at the Mathematics Institute at the University of Göttingen in Germany and was awarded a Ph.D. there in 1926. For her thesis, which she wrote in German, she studied aspects of electromagnetic waves. Under a Yarrow Research Fellowship, she continued her work at Göttingen with Professor Richard Courant, returning to England in 1929.

She worked as a scientific officer at the Radio Research Station in Slough, Berkshire, which was a part of the Department of Scientific and Industrial Research and the National Physics Laboratory. She specialized in the magneto-ionic theory of radio wave propagation along with differential equations and their application in physics and radio.

When she married in 1934, she had to leave her post because of civil service rules. She carried out translation and abstracting of papers relating to radio for *Wireless Engineer*. She moved with her husband to Malvern when he took up a post at the Air Defence Research and Development Establishment. They had two daughters. Later Taylor taught mathematics in two local schools.

She had scientific papers published in the *Proceedings of the Physics Society* and was a member of the London Mathematics Society and the Cambridge Philosophical Society.

Bibliography: *Girton College Register 1869–1946*, Cambridge: Girton College, 1948; Jeffreys, B., "Dr. Mary Taylor (Mrs. Slow)," *Girton College Newsletter* (1984): 31–32.

Tonolli, Livia née Pirocchi
15 September 1909–15 December 1985
freshwater biologist

Education: University of Milan, natural sciences, 1932.

Employment: lecturer, Institute of Zoology, University of Milan; Institute of Hydrobiology, Pallanza, Italy: assistant professor, from 1939; deputy director, then director, 1967–1978; commissioner, then chair of the Scientific Committee, until 1985; lecturer, University of Milan, 1968–1972.

Married: Vittorio Tonolli, who became director of the Pallanza Institute.

Livia Tonolli was a world expert in hydrology.

Initially Tonolli was a lecturer at the University of Milan. In 1939 she was appointed assistant professor at the Institute of Hydrobiology in Pallanza, taking over from Edgardo Baldi as deputy director when he left for military service. She met Vittorio Tonolli there, and later they married. They formed a good team and worked on microevolution, population genetics, and planktonic ecology. When her husband died in 1967, Tonolli was appointed as director of the Pallanza Institute in his place.

Tonolli's enthusiasm for ecology led to her involvement in the International Biology Programme and the Italian Commission for the Conservation of Nature and Natural Resources. She belonged to many scientific organizations, such as the International Association for Ecology, the British Ecological Society, and the Italian Society of Ecology. She was a founding member and president (1976–1978) of the Italian Association for Oceanography and Limnology.

Tonolli was responsible for editing *Memorie,* the journal from the Pallanza Institute, and she was on the editorial boards of several research journals, including *Hydrobiologie.* She published over eighty articles between 1938 and 1983.

She set up two foundations—the International Vittorio Tonolli Memorial Fund, to promote freshwater research in developing countries and the Vittorio Tonolli Foundation for Cardiological Culture. She received many honors, including the Silver Medal for Merit in Culture, Science, and Art in 1974 from the president of Italy; the E. Naumann–A. Thieneman medal in 1983 from the Societas Internationalis Limnologiae; and the Gold Medal of the Italian Ecological Society.

Bibliography: de Bernardi, R., "Livia Tonolli 15-9-1909–15-12-1985," *Memorie dell' Instituto Italiano di Idrobiologia* 43 (1985): 11–18.

Trewavas, Ethelwynn
5 November 1900–16 August 1992
freshwater biologist, ichthyologist

Education: West Cornwall College, Penzance, 1917; University College, Reading, 1917–1921, B.Sc. Hon. 1921; King's College for Women (now Queen Elizabeth College, University of London) 1926–1928, 1925; D.Sc. 1934. Lond.

Employment: science teacher at Camborne Country School for Girls, 1923–1924; Miss Meade's School, 1924; Penzanze County School for Girls, 1925; West Kensington Central School for Girls, 1925; King's College of Household and Social Science, 1925–1928; British Museum (Natural History): research assistant to Tate Regan (director) 1928–1935; assistant keeper of freshwater fish, provisional, 1935–1937; permanent keeper, 1937–1946; principal scientific officer, 1946–1958; deputy keeper, zoology, 1958–1961.

Ethelwynn Trewavas was one of the world's leading experts on freshwater fishes. She was the first (and so far the only) woman to be deputy keeper of zoology at the British Museum (Natural History).

Trewavas was born in Penzance, Cornwall. After graduating from University College, Reading, she returned to Cornwall and taught at several schools there. Then, after teaching for a year at a girls' school in London, she taught at King's College and was awarded a Gilchrist Research Scholarship at King's College for Women. She researched the anatomy of frogs for her doctorate. While she was employed at the British Museum, she studied deep-sea fishes, then cichlid fishes from Lakes Malawi and Tanganyika. She was responsible for compiling the fish section of the Zoological Record.

Once "retired," she continued with her research and went on several fish-searching expeditions in Africa. She wrote over 100 scientific contributions and two books, one on tilapine cichlid fishes (1983) and the other (with David Eccles) on Malawian cichlid fishes. She was awarded the Gold Medal of the Linnean Society of London in 1968 and made an honorary fellow in 1991. Stirling University awarded her an honorary doctorate in 1986. More than a dozen species of fish have been named after her.

Bibliography: Lowe-McConnell, R., "Ethelwynn Trewavas, 1900–1992," *Freshwater Forum* 4, 1 (1994): 5–7; West, V., archivist, Natural History Museum, London, personal communication to the author, July 2001.

Turner, Emma Louisa
1866–13 August 1940
ornithologist, photographer

Education: private schools.
Employment: warden for the National Trust on Scolt Head, Norfolk, 1924–1925.

Emma Turner was a pioneer of bird photography.

In 1911 Turner photographed the first young bitterns known to have hatched in Norfolk since the species returned to the county. She was awarded the Gold Medal of the Royal Photographic Society. She was one of the first ten women to be elected as fellows of the Linnean Society and the first honorary lady member of the British Ornithologists' Union. She spent much of her time living in a houseboat so that she could study marsh birds. She published *The Home Life of Some Marsh Birds* (1907) and *Broadland Birds* (1925).

In December 1923 the secretary of the Norfolk and Norwich Naturalists' Society announced in the monthly meeting that he could not find a Watcher to observe and record bird species for the Scolt Head bird reserve, a remote spit of land on the Norfolk coast. Turner volunteered. She was the first Watcher on Scolt Head, an area popular with birdwatchers during the autumn and spring migrations and also because of the large colonies of common terns and other birds. During her seven months on the 1,200 acres of the reserve, Turner was said to be "the loneliest woman in England," but in fact she had a steady stream of visits from journalists and local people. She usually had an assistant to help her record data, and the society sent someone out daily with letters and supplies, and if the flag was flying from Turner's hut, he knew she was all right. She had two adult terriers and three puppies whom she trained to flush out birds so that she could count them.

Her time on Scolt Head was a great joy to her, and she worked hard recording data.

Turner had a lively sense of humor, as is clear in her books. She published *Bird Watching on Scolt Head* in 1928.

She was an honorary member of the British Federation of University Women.

Bibliography: A. H. W., "Miss Emma Louise Turner," *Ibis* 5(1) (January 1941): 188–189; B. B. R., "Miss E. L. Turner," *British Birds* 34, 4 (1940): 85; Dawson, I., librarian, Royal Society for the Protection of Birds (RSPB), personal communication to the author, July 2001; Gage, A. T., and W. T. Stearn, *A Bicentenary History of the Linnean Society of London*, London: Academic Press, 1988; *Who Was Who, 1929–1940*, London: Adam and Charles Black, 1947.

Turner, Helen Alma Newton
15 May 1910–26 November 1995
geneticist

Education: University of Sydney; B.Arch. with honors, 1930; D.Sc., 1970.
Employment: Commonwealth Scientific and Industrial Research Organisation (CSIRO): clerical officer, 1931–1934; statistician, 1934–1936; technical officer, 1936–1938; consulting statistician, 1939–1941; statistician, Department of Home Security, Canberra, 1942; statistician, Department of Manpower, Sydney, 1943–1944; consultant statistician, Division of Animal Health and Production, CSIRO, 1945–1956; senior principal research scientist, Division of Animal Genetics, CSIRO, 1956–1976.

Helen Turner led a research team working on selective sheep breeding. The team's results led to improvements in merino fleece. She was one of the pioneers of population genetics in Australia.

Turner was born in Sydney, Australia, the eldest of three children. She decided to take a degree in architecture since she was particularly interested in mathematics.

She started work as a secretary in an architect's office, but when the firm closed down after a few months, she obtained a clerical post with the state government. In

1931 she was appointed as secretary to Dr. Clunies Ross, the first chair of the Commonwealth Scientific and Industrial Research Organisation (CSIRO). While in this position, she became interested in statistics and took statistics courses at the University of Sydney. She was promoted to statistician and then technical officer. Ross arranged for her to have a year's paid leave in 1938 in Britain. She studied in Cambridge, directed by Sir Ronald Fisher, and visited laboratories in the United States concerned with sheep production. In 1940, with Isobel Bennett, she formed the University Women's Land Army, which was so successful that later it amalgamated with the Women's Australian National Services.

She took time out from CSIRO for war service. After the war she returned to CSIRO and dealt with data from large-scale sheep-breeding experiments. She had another year of paid study leave in 1954 and looked at sheep-breeding programs in Europe and the United States. In 1956 she was put in charge of CSIRO's new Division of Animal Genetics. She had a team of eight scientists investigating the inheritance of different characteristics and the correlations among them. With S. S. Y. Young, she coauthored a textbook on genetics, *Quantitative Genetics and Sheep Breeding* (1969); she published over 100 research papers as well. Turner also worked with sheep breeders in developing countries.

She was awarded a D.Sc. by Sydney University in 1970 and an honorary doctorate by Macquarie University in 1991. In 1973 she became one of the two women who were foundation fellows of the Australian Academy of Technological Science and was the first woman to be awarded the Farrer Memorial Medal for services to agriculture. She was made an Officer of the Order of the British Empire (OBE) in 1977 and of the Order of Australia in 1987.

Bibliography: Allen, N., "Australian Women in Science: Two Unorthodox Careers," *Women's Studies International Forum* 15, 5/6 (1992): 551–562; Mancini, R., archivist, University of Sydney, personal communication to the author, February 2000; *Who's Who in Australasia and the Far East,* second edition, Cambridge: Melrose Press, 1991.

Turner-Warwick, Margaret née Moore
19 November 1924–
immunologist, thoracic doctor

Education: Maynard School, Exeter; St. Paul's Girls' School, London; Lady Margaret Hall, Oxford; B.A., 1946; University College Hospital Medical School, London, 1947–1950; M.D. (Oxon), 1956, Ph.D. (London), 1961.

Employment: junior doctor posts, University College and Brompton Hospitals, 1950–1957; senior registrar and chief medical assistant, Brompton Hospital, 1957–1960; consultant in general medicine, Elizabeth Garrett Anderson Hospital, 1960–1967; senior lecturer, Institute of Diseases of the Chest (Brompton Hospital), 1963–1972; Cardiothoracic Institute, London: professor of medicine, director of Department of Thoracic Medicine, 1972–1987; dean, 1984–1987.

Married: Richard Trevor Turner-Warwick, a surgeon, in 1950.

From 1989 to 1992 *Margaret Turner-Warwick* was the first woman to serve as president of the Royal College of Physicians, the only woman appointed in the 471 years since the college was founded.

After graduating from Oxford University, Turner-Warwick did her medical training at University College Hospital in London, then began her work as a doctor in a series of house physician, registrar, and subsequently more senior posts. She became interested in thoracic medicine when her work was focused on tuberculosis. She was also involved in research into the use of corticosteroids in the treatment of asthma. She was appointed to the post of consultant physician at the Elizabeth Garrett Anderson Hospital and then to a senior lecturer post at Brompton Hospital.

Turner-Warwick had a particular interest in immunology, and her pioneering work with Deborah Doniach and Jack Pepys resulted in the publication of her textbook *Immunology of the Lung* (1978). In 1972 she became chair of medicine at the Cardiothoracic Institute, an appointment she held until 1987; the institute's international reputation grew under her leadership. From 1992 to 1995 she chaired the Royal Devon and Exeter Health Care Trust.

Her personal reputation is illustrated by the list of visiting professorships and lectureships she has held at universities all over the world, and by the numerous committees, boards, and councils on which she has served. She has been awarded honorary doctorates by several universities, including New York, Exeter, Cambridge, and Leicester. She is an honorary fellow of several colleges, including Girton College, Cambridge, and Green College, Oxford, and has been on the editorial boards of several medical journals. She was made a Dame Commander of the Order of the British Empire (DBE) in 1991.

Bibliography: Citron, K. M., "Professor Margaret Turner-Warwick," *Postgraduate Medical Journal* 64, supplement 4 (1988): 4–7; *Who's Who, 1999,* London: Adam and Charles Black, 1999.

U

Uvarov, Olga Nikolaevna
9 July 1910–29 August, 2001
veterinary surgeon

Education: Royal College of Veterinary Surgeons; Member of the Royal College of Veterinary Surgeons, 1934; Fellow of the Royal College of Veterinary Surgeons, 1973.

Employment: assistant in general mixed practice, 1934–1943; own small animals practice, 1944–1953; clinical research, Glaxo laboratories, 1953–1967; head of Veterinary Advisory Group, Glaxo, 1967–1970.

Olga Uvarov was the first woman president of the Royal College of Veterinary Surgeons in 1976–1977.

After qualifying as a veterinary surgeon, Uvarov worked as an assistant in general practice before setting up her own practice in 1944. Between 1945 and 1968 she held a license to practice and work at a greyhound stadium.

She was an active member of the Society of Women Veterinary Surgeons (founded by Joan Joshua), its secretary in 1946, and president from 1947 to 1949. From 1951 to 1952 she was president of the Central Veterinary Society, which awarded her its Victory Gold Medal in 1965.

In 1953 she moved to Glaxo Industries, becoming a veterinary adviser to Glaxo's United Kingdom establishments. She developed products for veterinary use, trained a new force of representatives, and advised on appropriate packing and publicity. While she was testing Cerates (a type of penicillin) used for treating mastitis in cattle, she had to be present for the morning milking at 5 and the same day had to check the samples at the Greenford Laboratory near Ealing, London.

In the early 1960s, when Glaxo's Medical Department was using cortisone to make substances to treat skin problems, Uvarov did clinical trials on using cortisone for animals. She did small-scale tests at Glaxo first, then as these were successful extended the tests to field conditions. By 1963, under her direction, Glaxo had developed a range of betamethasone eye and skin ointments, ear and eye drops, tablets, and injections.

She tried out griseofulvin to cure an attack of ringworm affecting a large cattery of Persian cats. She and her colleague developed a way of periodically filming the progress of the trial on individual cats, the first time this had been done. All the cats recovered, and the kittens born during the trial were free of the disease.

When the 1968 Medicines Bill was passed, companies had to provide depositions on the quality, efficacy, and safety of all medicinal products used on humans and animals alike. Glaxo had its own farm, which helped in providing information for the trials, and with the help of Glaxo staff tests acceptable to the licensing authority were validated.

Uvarov became interested in the legal aspects of this act and did a course in legal studies. After retirement she was able to work on several government committees that dealt with product information.

She was president of the Association of Veterinary Teachers and Research Workers (1967–1968), the comparative medicine section of the Royal Society of Medicine

(1967–1968), and the Laboratory Animals Science Association (1984–1986). Before becoming the first woman president of the Royal College of Veterinary Surgeons (RCVS) in 1976, she was the first woman junior vice-president of the RCVS. She later served as senior vice-president.

After Uvarov retired from Glaxo, she was involved with the British Veterinary Association's Technical Information Service (1970–1976), then became an adviser for the information service (1976–1978); she later became vice-president of the Universities Federation of Animal Welfare (1986–1992).

Besides her numerous research papers, she was a frequent contributor to the *Veterinary Record* and contributed to the *Veterinary Annual* and *The International Encyclopaedia of Veterinary Medicine* in 1966.

She was made a Commander of the Order of the British Empire (CBE) in 1978 and a Dame Commander of the Order of the British Empire (DBE) in 1983. Guelph University in Ontario awarded her an honorary D.Sc. in 1976. She was named a fellow of the Royal College of Veterinary Surgeons in 1973 and an honorary fellow of the Institute of Biology in 1983.

Bibliography: Boden, E., "Dame Olga Uvarov," *The Independent Friday Review* (7 September 2001): 6; "Dame Olga Uvarov," *Times* (18 September 2001): 21; Greening, P., librarian, Royal College of Veterinary Surgeons, personal communication to the author, July 2001; "Retired Staff in Honours," *Glaxo Group News* 185 (1983): 1; Turner, C., *Gold on the Green,* London: Glaxo Pharmaceuticals Limited, 1985; "Veterinary College Honours Miss Uvarov," *Glaxo Group News* 100 (1975): 1; *Who's Who, 1999,* London: Adam and Charles Black, 1999.

V

Vachell, Eleanor
1879–6 December 1948
botanist

Education: Manse school, Malvern Wells; St. John's School, until 1896.

Eleanor Vachell was the first woman president of the Cardiff Naturalists' Society. She bequeathed her extensive collection of plants to the National Museum of Wales.

Vachell was born in Cardiff. Her father, Dr. C. T. Vachell, was a keen botanist and encouraged his daughter to take up the study of plants. She began to record her botanical discoveries at the age of twelve, and it was around this time that she and her father set up a herbarium. They collected specimens together until his death in 1914. Both became recording secretaries for the Cardiff Naturalists' Society's *Flora of Glamorgan* (published in parts from 1906 to 1909). The society did not initially admit women to its biological and geological section; Vachell was its first female member when the rules were changed in 1903 and served as its president in 1932–1933.

Vachell looked after the herbarium of the National Museum of Wales while the keeper fought in World War I. She continued her involvement with the museum, in later years serving on a number of its committees. At one time she was the only woman member of its council and court of governors.

After the war Vachell was able to expand the collection she had started with her father. She added the majority of specimens between 1919 and 1940, traveling widely to do so. She hoped to see every native British species of plant; by the time she died, she had observed all but thirteen of the 1,800 species.

In addition to having a personal enthusiasm for botany, she was eager to inform the public about the varieties of plants that existed in her native Wales. From 1921 until just before her death, she wrote a weekly column on wildflowers for "Wales Day by Day" in the *Western Mail.* Her "List of Glamorgan Flowering Plants" was published in the *Botanical Society and Exchange Report* for 1933, and in 1936 "Glamorgan Flowering Plants and Ferns" appeared in the first volume of the *Glamorgan County History.* When Welsh regional radio broadcasting began, she gave a series of forty talks on wildflowers.

Vachell's work was notable for several discoveries as well as the volume of her collection. In the early 1930s, a microspecies she had found was named in her honor (*Taraxacum vachellii*), and around the same time she observed the rare *Arum italicum neglectum* (Italian lords-and-ladies) in the Dinas Powis area. Near Port Talbot she made another discovery that was confirmed as a new hybrid of *Limosella* (mudwort).

She bequeathed her collection of wildflowers to the National Museum of Wales, along with funding for display cabinets. She also left money to pay for a new flora of Glamorgan.

Vachell was a member of the Wild Flower Society and was elected a fellow of the Linnean Society in 1917.

Bibliography: *Catalogue of the C. T. and E. Vachell Herbarium,* National Museum and

Gallery of Wales, Cardiff; "Miss Eleanor Vachell," *Western Mail and South Wales News* (7 December 1948); "Miss Eleanor Vachell," *Wild Flower Magazine* 407 (Autumn 1986): 45.

Van Heyningen, Ruth Eleanor
née Treverton
16 October 1917–
ophthalmologist

Education: Cheltenham Ladies College, 1930–1936; Newnham College, Cambridge, 1937–1940; Biochemistry Department, University of Cambridge, 1940–1943; M.A., (Cantab) 1944; D.Phil. (Oxon), 1951; D.Sc., (Oxon) 1972.

Employment: research assistant, Lister Institute, London, 1943–1948; researcher, Department of Anatomy, University of Oxford, 1948–1952; Nuffield Laboratory of Ophthalmology: research assistant, 1952–1969; senior research officer, 1969–1977.

Married: Dr. William Edward van Heyningen, reader in bacterial chemistry in the Department of Pathology and master of St. Cross College at the University of Oxford, on 24 June 1940.

Ruth van Heyningen did landmark research on the biochemical processes involved in the formation of cataracts.

Van Heyningen was born in Newport, Monmouthshire; her father was a shipowner. She was an exhibitioner at Newnham College, where she read biochemistry and held a Benn Levy Studentship at the Biochemistry Laboratory. She had a contract with the Ministry of Supply to investigate the effect of poison gases on enzyme systems; she worked under the direction of Dr. Malcolm Dixon.

At the Lister Institute in London, Van Heyningen did research on substances in blood groups. The Medical Research Council (MRC) funded her research on adaptation to hot climates. She presented her doctoral thesis on this subject to the Department of Human Anatomy in Oxford.

Van Heyningen moved into the biochemical side of ophthalmology in 1952 when she was appointed as research assistant for Antoinette Pirie, the Margaret Ogilvie Reader in Ophthalmology at the Nuffield Laboratory of Ophthalmology. Van Heyningen and Pirie had previously worked together. In 1956 they coauthored *Biochemistry of the Eye,* a thorough summary of what was known up to that time, with particularly interesting information on the ocular effects of nutritional disease.

In her research Van Heyningen concentrated on the biochemical processes that result in cataract formation. Cataracts in themselves are not life-threatening in humans, but they are associated with the ageing process. In the developed world, most cataracts can now be dealt with, thus improving the well-being of the elderly population.

Cataracts normally develop when a person has diabetes or because of slow physical and chemical changes involved in ageing that affect the lens proteins. Van Heyningen first investigated sugar cataracts, mainly using the reactions in calf lenses. She also studied xylose, galactose, and alloxan diabetic cataracts in rats.

With Pirie she investigated the way naphthalene is changed chemically and enzymatically. She analyzed the enzymes that break down protein (proteases) in the eye and looked at the proteases in normal and cataractous lenses in humans aged fifty-five to sixty-two. Van Heyningen also investigated the way some cataracts are induced by light. She identified the fluorescent compound that sensitizes some of the chemicals in lens proteins to light and alters light absorption by lens proteins.

Van Heyningen served on several committees, including the International Committee for Eye Research founded by Pirie, which established the International Society for Eye Research. She addressed meetings and conferences worldwide and published numerous articles in journals such as *Experimental Eye Research.*

She received grants from various bodies, including the Royal National Institute for the Blind. In 1970 she was given an unsolicited grant of $10,000 from the Pak-Khan Trust for research on senile cataracts. She received the Proctor Award in 1976.

Bibliography: Bloemendal, H., et al., eds., Special issue dedicated to Antoinette Pirie and Ruth van Heyningen, *Experimental Eye Research* 31, 5 (1980): i–xiv; Hallendorf, M., chief executive, Royal College of Ophthalmologists, personal communication to the author, July 2001; *Newnham College Register, 1924–1950,* vol. 2, second edition, Cambridge: Newnham College, 1981.

Vansittart, Henrietta née Lowe
1840–8 February 1883
engineer

Married: William Vansittart, in 1855.

Henrietta Vansittart was said to be the first woman engineer in Britain.

Vansittart was born in London. Her father was a smokejack maker and machinist. In 1855 she married William Vansittart in the British embassy in Paris. As the couple had no children, Vansittart was able to help her impoverished but inventive father, who had spent some time on whaling ships and as an apprentice to a master mechanic before setting up his own business. Vansittart went with him on the HMS *Bullfinch* in 1858 for the trials of the screw propeller he had invented.

The following year she began a secret affair with Edward Bulmer-Lytton, later the first earl of Lytton. Their friendship lasted until 1871.

During the last few years of his life, her father was involved in disputes regarding his inventions, and he used up all his financial resources in pursuing the case through the courts. Following his death in 1866, Vansittart decided to carry on his work in order to gain proper recognition for him. In 1868 she obtained patent number 2,877 for the Lowe-Vansittart propeller, which was used in Admiralty trials on the HMS *Druid.* The propeller won a first-class diploma at the 1871 Kensington Exhibition and was fitted to many ships, including the *Scandinavian* and the *Lusitania.*

In 1876 Vansittart made a speech at the anniversary dinner of the London Association of Foremen Engineers and Draughts-

men. This was the first time she had given a public address, and she spoke on the role of women in society as their husband's helpmates. In the same year she presented a paper to the association, "The Screw Propeller of 1838 and Its Subsequent Improvements." This occasion was described several years later in her obituary in the association's journal as the only time "that a lady ever wrote and read a scientific paper, illustrated by drawings and diagrams made by herself, before the members of a scientific institution."

Vansittart continued to develop and promote the propeller. In September 1882 she went to the Tynemouth Exhibition. She was required to pay £600 to renew her patent but failed to do so. The day after payment was due, the police found her wandering around, and the magistrates ordered her to be kept in the county lunatic asylum near Newcastle. A few months later she died there of acute mania and anthrax.

Bibliography: Nicholls, C. S., ed., *Dictionary of National Biography: Missing Persons,* Oxford: Oxford University Press, 1993; O'Mahoney, B. M. E., "Henrietta Vansittart—Britain's First Woman Engineer?" *The Woman Engineer* 13, 4 (1983): 1–2, 10.

Vaughan, Janet Maria
18 October 1899–9 January 1993
pathologist, administrator, radiobiologist

Education: at home with governesses; North Foreland Lodge; Somerville College, Oxford, January 1919; B.Sc. with honors, 1922; Bachelor of Medicine, Bachelor of Surgery, 1924; D.M.; University College Hospital, 1922–1924.

Employment: assistant clinical pathologist, University College Hospital, 1927–1929; Boston City Hospital (Rockefeller Travelling Fellowship), 1929–1930; Bernard Baron Institute of Pathology, London Hospital (Beit Memorial Fellowship, 1931–1934; Leverhulme Research Scholarship, 1934–1935); Royal Postgraduate Medical School, Hammersmith Hospital, assistant in clinical pathology, 1935–1939;

North West London Blood Supply Depot, Slough, 1939–1945; principal of Somerville College, Oxford, 1945–1967; Medical Research Council Unit for Research on Bone-seeking Isotopes, Churchill Hospital, Oxford, 1947–1967.

Married: David Gourlay, founder of the Wayfarers' Travel Association, in 1930.

Janet Vaughan is probably best known for her influence on science as principal of Somerville College, Oxford. Prior to this she had done important research in pathology and hematology; while at Somerville she worked in radiobiology.

Vaughan was born in Clifton, Bristol. Her father was then an assistant master at Clifton College. He was successively headmaster at Giggleswick (1904), Wellington (1910), and Rugby (1921). Her mother, Margaret Symonds, was an author and a friend of Virginia Woolf.

After leaving North Foreland College, Vaughan decided to study medicine and was determined to enter Somerville College. She was successful on her third attempt. She did well there and was awarded a Goldsmith Entrance Scholarship to do her medical training at University College Hospital (UCH). She found the social conditions around Camden Town appalling and resolved to work to abolish poverty. Vaughan had temporary posts until she was appointed as an assistant in clinical pathology at UCH in 1927.

At UCH Cecil Price-Jones taught her hematology and stressed the importance of applying statistical techniques to biological problems. Vaughan experimented with treatments for pernicious anemia, continuing this work for a year at Boston Memorial Hospital with George Minoti. She wrote up the findings for her doctoral thesis. Although she was asked to stay on for another year, she returned home to marry David Gourlay in 1930.

Gourlay had founded the Wayfarers' Travel Association with a friend. They specialized in educational tours for schoolchildren, a novel idea at the time. Vaughan and Gourlay lived above the office in Gordon Square and had two children, Mary and

Janet Maria Vaughan (Godfrey Argent Studio)

Priscilla. The family had numerous friends and went for many walking holidays abroad.

After a short spell in a nonteaching hospital, Vaughan did research at the Bernard Baron Institute of Pathology at the London Hospital, where she worked on blood and bone diseases with Donald Hunter and H. M. Turnbull. Dorothy Russell was there at the same time, and apart from their immediate coworkers, they were ignored by the male medical staff. At her next post, at the Royal Postgraduate Medical School (PGMS) in Hammersmith, however, Vaughan was treated as an equal.

At PGMS Vaughan taught hematology, did research, and was in charge of the hematological and blood transfusion services at Hammersmith Hospital. Vaughan was a pioneer in integrating her observations of patients with her pathological research. She investigated celiac disease, a chronic nutritional disorder, theorizing it was caused when certain essential nutrients were not absorbed from the intestine. In 1934 she wrote *The Anaemias*.

During World War II Vaughan was the medical officer in charge at the Slough Blood Supply Department (Walls Ice Cream vans were used for cold storage and delivering blood). In that period she did important research on collecting, preserving, and overseeing supplies of blood.

With Rosalind Pitt-Rivers and Charles Dent, she was sent to Europe by the Medical Research Council after the war to see if protein preparations would aid the starving. They visited the concentration camp at Bergen-Belsen and found that giving small amounts of food orally was the best way to help the victims recover.

Vaughan was a trustee of the Nuffield Foundation from 1943 to 1967, a member of the Royal Commission on Equal Pay (1944), and a member of the Goodenough Committee (1942) that examined the organization of postwar medical training.

In 1945 she became principal of Somerville College, Oxford. At that time Dorothy Hodgkin was the only scientific fellow. Vaughan worked hard to change the position of women in Oxford and to make science more important there.

She considered it essential to continue with her own research. From 1947 to 1967 she investigated the effect of the major radionuclides on the skeleton, mainly using rabbits in her experiments. She was in charge of the Medical Research Council Unit for Research on Bone-seeking Isotopes, which was based in a hut in the grounds of the Churchill Hospital, Oxford. Hoping to minimize the potential damage from radioactivity to her younger colleagues, she gave all the injections of radioactive solutions to the animals herself

After she retired, she wrote *The Physiology of Bone* (1971) and *The Effects of Irradiation on the Skeleton* (1973). She was a member of the International Commission on Radiological Protection from 1968 to 1972.

Vaughan was made an Officer of the Order of the British Empire (OBE) in 1944 and a Dame Commander of the Order of the British Empire (DBE) in 1957, and she was elected a fellow of the Royal Society in 1979. She was given six honorary degrees, from the Universities of Wales in 1964, Oxford in 1967, London in 1968, Leeds in 1970, Bristol in 1971, and Liverpool in 1973.

Bibliography: Dacie, J., "Dame Janet Vaughan DBE FRS DM FRCP," *British Medical Journal* 36 (1993): 326; Owen, M., "Dame Janet Maria Vaughan, D.B.E.," *Biographical Memoirs of Fellows of the Royal Society* 41 (1995): 483–497.

Vickery, Joyce Winifred
1908–1979
botanist

Education: University of Sydney, 1927–1936; B.Sc., 1931; M.Sc., 1933; D.Sc., 1959.

Employment: demonstrator, Botany Department, University of Sydney; National Herbarium, Department of Agriculture, Sydney: assistant botanist, 1936–1964; senior botanist, 1964–1971; honorary research fellow, 1973–1979.

In 1936 *Joyce Vickery* became the first woman ever appointed as a scientific professional officer in the public service in Australia.

Vickery was particularly keen on fieldwork in botany and organized many excursions for her students. While she was involved in postgraduate studies, she published her research on insectivorous plants, was president of the university Biological Society, and was elected to the Royal Society of New South Wales (as her father had been).

On gaining her M.Sc. (at a time when it was not possible to obtain a Ph.D. in Australia), Vickery was appointed as assistant botanist to the National Herbarium. She was the first woman in such a post and had to fight to ensure that she received the salary her qualifications merited.

After a year in this post, she had leave of absence to work at the Royal Botanical Gardens at Kew. She was paid for only three months and had to fund herself for the rest of the year. She was bonded to the National Herbarium for the next three years.

During World War II Vickery set up a branch depot of the National Emergency Services Ambulance Drivers and taught both first aid and motor mechanics.

She revised the taxonomy of the genus *Poa* (meadow grass) and the Poaceae family, publishing her results as part of the new *Flora of New South Wales* (part 1 in 1961 and part 2 in 1975).

Vickery was made a Member of the Order of the British Empire (MBE) for her work in botany and awarded the Clarke Medal from the Royal Society of New South Wales. In her lifetime she endowed the Joyce Vickery Fund, a research fund now administered by the Linnean Society of New South Wales.

She left a generous bequest to this fund, which gives small annual grants for research projects, usually in ecology.

Bibliography: Mancini, R., archivist, University of Sydney, personal communication to the author, February 2000.; Lee, A., "Joyce Winifred Vickery 1980–1979," *Telopea* 2, 1 (1980): 1–7; Martin, H. A., secretary, Linnean Society of New South Wales, personal communication to the author, June 2000.

W

Wakefield, Priscilla née Bell
31 January 1751–12 September 1832
natural history writer, philanthropist

Married: Edward Wakefield, on 3 January 1751.

Priscilla Wakefield, well known in her day as an author of children's books, also wrote about botany and natural history.

Wakefield published *An Introduction to Botany, in a Series of Familiar Letters* in 1796. In 1816 she published *An Introduction to the Natural History and Classification of Insects in a Series of Letters.*

She was a member of the Society of Friends. She founded "frugality," or savings, banks, one of the first of which opened in Tottenham, London, in 1798. She also formed a charity for expectant mothers in Tottenham.

Bibliography: Desmond, R., *Dictionary of British and Irish Botanists and Horticulturalists, Including Plant Collectors and Botanical Artists,* London: Taylor and Francis, 1977; *Dictionary of National Biography,* vol. 20, Oxford: Oxford University Press, 1899; Gates, B. T., *Kindred Nature: Victorian and Edwardian Women Embrace the Living World,* Chicago: University of Chicago Press, 1998.

Ward, Mary née King
27 April 1827–31 August 1869
astronomer, microscopist, writer

Education: at home.

Married: Captain Henry William Crosbie Ward, in December 1854.

Mary Ward was the first woman to publish books about the microscope.

Ward was born in Ballylin, Ireland, and as a child spent a great deal of time collecting botanical and zoological specimens on the grounds of the family's home. Her cousin William, the third earl of Rosse, was an astronomer and constructed a huge telescope known at the "Leviathan of Personstown" at his home at Birr Castle. Ward was a frequent visitor to the castle, and at the official launch of the telescope, in March 1845, met some leading scientists. Sir James South was so impressed by her that he suggested to her parents that she needed a better microscope. The microscope they ordered for her arrived in parts, and she struggled—but succeeded—in putting it together correctly.

From 1855 Ward began to write about her observations. She published *A Windfall for the Microscope* (1856) and *Entomology in Sport, and Entomology in Earnest* (1857), coauthored with her sister, Lady Jane Mahon. Ward wanted to promote the pleasures of scientific observation and to make the subject as accessible as possible to the general public, particularly young people. *A World of Wonders Revealed by the Microscope* (1858) was intended as a book for young students; Ward did the colored illustrations herself. Her books *Microscope Teachings* (1864) and *Telescope Teachings* (1859), both with illustrations by Ward, were very popular. *The Microscope* ran to a third edition (1869), as did *The Telescope* (also 1869). Ward contributed articles to journals such as the *Intellectual Observer.*

She was killed in what was said to have been the first fatal "car" accident in Ireland: She was thrown out of the steam-powered road carriage in which she was traveling and died instantly. The vehicle had been designed by her cousin, the earl of Rosse, who had taught her so much about astronomy.

Bibliography: Kavanagh, I., "Mistress of the Microscope," in M. Mulvihill and P. Deevy, eds., *Stars, Shells, and Bluebells*, Dublin: Women in Technology and Science, 1997; McKenna-Lawlor, S., *Whatever Shines Should Be Observed: Quicquid Nited Notandum*, Dublin: Samton, 1998.

Warington, Katherine
5 September 1897–3 July 1993
botanist

Education: Royal Holloway College, University of London, B.Sc. with honors; Ph.D. University of Lund, Sweden.
Employment: Rothamsted Experimental Station, Harpenden, 1921–1957.

Katherine Warington was the first person to show that boron, as boric acid, was essential for the healthy growth of broad beans.

Warington was born in Harpenden, Hertfordshire, and lived there for ninety years. Her father worked at Rothamsted Experimental Station. Warington studied botany at Royal Holloway College and later attended the University of Lund in Sweden. She started her research at Rothamsted in 1921, working with Dr. Winifred Brenchley.

Her initial research focused on the importance of boron for plant nutrition. This required meticulous care, as she had to maintain a boron-free solution as a control. Her first experiments were with broad beans, but she repeated the tests with other plants. Her doctorate, awarded on the basis of this work, was published in 1923 in the *Annals of Botany* as "The Effect of Boric Acid and Borax on the Broad Bean and Certain Other Plants." Warington also investigated the importance of other trace elements, such as manganese and molybdenum.

In collaboration with Brenchley, she worked on the field survey of weeds ongoing since 1921 on two of Rothamsted's classic sites: Broadbalk, which had grown wheat continuously since 1843, and Park Grass, started in 1856 to look at the manuring of permanent grassland for hay. She collected soil samples and checked the germination dates of any weed species, showing that for most species there was an optimum germination time. She published numerous papers on her work, most in the *Annals of Botany*.

Bibliography: "Happy Birthday, Katherine Warington," *Micronutrient News* 8, 1 (1987): 3; Thurston, J. M., "Katherine Warington," *Independent* (9 August 1993): 14.

Watson, Janet Vida
1 September 1923–29 March 1985
geologist

Education: South Hampstead High School (GPDST); University of Reading; B.Sc. with honors, 1943; Imperial College, London; B.Sc. with honors, 1947; Ph.D., 1949.
Employment: researcher, research institute, from 1943; teacher, girls' school, until 1945; senior studentship, Royal Commission for the Exhibition of 1851, 1949–1952; Imperial College, research and teaching, 1952–1974; personal chair, 1974–1983.
Married: John Sutton, a geologist, in 1949.

Janet Watson made valuable contributions to geological research, particularly in areas of Scotland. She was the first woman president of the Geological Society of London (1982–1984).

Watson was born in Hampstead, London. Her father, David Meredith Seares Watson, was a vertebrate paleontologist of international repute and a fellow of the Royal Society. Her mother, Katharine Margarite Watson, had been involved in embryological research prior to her marriage. Watson took a general science degree at the University of Reading, graduating with first-class honors. After working in a research institute and as a schoolteacher, she decided to concentrate

Janet Vida Watson (Godfrey Argent Studio)

on geology, and went to Imperial College. For her Ph.D., she worked on the Lewisian gneisses in Sutherlandshire, Scotland, the oldest rocks in the British Isles. Her research involved collaboration with a fellow student, John Sutton. Their results, which showed that the gneiss was made up of two separate rock types, were presented to the Geological Society of London in 1951. The work was acknowledged as an important development, and their findings were eventually confirmed by radiometric dating techniques.

Watson married Sutton in 1949, and she had a studentship so she could continue her research on the Lewisian gneisses. From 1952 she was a research assistant to Professor H. H. Read, her Ph.D. supervisor. Since 1948 her husband had had a lecturing post at Imperial College, and he and Watson were able to continue their joint research. They investigated various aspects of the geology of the Scottish Highlands, publishing their findings in numerous articles. Their work on the Banffshire coast was of particu-

lar note. During the 1950s they also carried out research and produced articles on the geology of the Channel Islands and on Tanganyika. Ward and Sutton received a joint award from the Lyell Fund of the Geological Society of London in 1954 for their work in the Scottish Highlands.

In 1964 Sutton became head of the Geology Department at Imperial College, which allowed him less time for research. Watson continued her work in Scotland, moving her attention to the Outer Hebrides. A number of research students carried out work there under her supervision, and the group's findings were published jointly. Watson's active research in the Outer Hebrides spanned some thirteen years (1965–1978) and included work on the production of a series of geological maps of the islands (eventually published in 1984) as a joint venture between Imperial College and the British Geological Survey. She was awarded the Lyell Medal of the Geological Society of London in 1973, which her father had been awarded in 1935.

During the 1970s she organized a meeting on women in geology, one of the first of its kind in the UK. It attracted participants from the public, private, and academic sectors.

From 1974 to 1983 Ward held a personal chair in geology at Imperial College. In 1983 she became president of the Geological Society of London. Her presidential address dealt with aspects of orogenesis (the formation of mountains) in the Scottish Highlands, an aspect of geology in which she had been interested for many years. Ore genesis was another area in which she made a significant contribution: she herself felt that her 1973 article "Influence of Crustal Evolution on Ore Deposition" was one of her most important papers. She also wrote *Introduction to Geology* (vol. 1 in 1962; vol. 2 in 1976) and *Beginning Geology* (1966), both with H. H. Read.

She was also active in geochemistry, collaborating with the British Geological Survey in its analysis of Scottish geochemical information, making use of new computer technology. In 1978 her first paper on this theme (coauthored with J. Plant) was presented at a conference on theoretical and practical aspects of uranium geology and published in *Philosophical Transactions of the Royal Society of London.*

In 1965 she and her husband were joint recipients of the Geological Society of London's Bigsby Medal. Watson received the Clough Medal of the Edinburgh Geological Society in 1980. When she retired from her post at Imperial College in 1983, she became an emeritus professor. In the same year she was vice-president of the Royal Society, of which she had been elected a fellow in 1979. She held a number of other positions with learned societies, including vice-president of the Geologists' Association (1973–1977), member of the National Water Council (1973–1976), member of the International Geological Correlation Programme (IGCP) (1977–1982), chair of the Royal Society's National Committee for IGCP (1981–1985), and president of the Geological Society of London (1982–1984).

In 1985 she and her husband set up an initiative that enabled geological projects to be carried out in China, and this research continued after she died. Despite illness, she had kept working during her retirement. The day before her death, her last paper, "Lineaments in the Continental Lithosphere," coauthored with her husband, was read to the Royal Society.

Bibliography: *Dictionary of National Biography, 1981–1985.* Oxford: Oxford University Press, 1990; Fettes, D. J., and J. A. Plant, "Janet Watson," *Biographical Memoirs of the Fellows of the Royal Society* (1995): 500–514; "Janet Vida Watson," *Times* (3 April 1985): 16G; *Who Was Who, 1981–1990,* London: Adam and Charles Black, 1991.

Webster, Mary McCallum
31 December 1906–7 November 1985
botanist

Education: by governesses at home; boarding schools at West Heath and Ham Common; finishing school, Brussels.

Employment: domestic work; cook and sergeant, Army Training Service, Tenth Battalion, Gordon Highlanders, on Orkney and Shetland, during World War II; cook, Bournemouth Officers' cadet training unit; staff captain, Germany; freelance cook, various locations.

Mary McCallum Webster published the *Flora of Moray, Nairn and East Inverness* (1978), an outstanding achievement reflecting fifty years of studying plants.

Webster was born in Sussex to Scottish parents. Her grandmother, Louisa Wedgwood, was a noted botanist. She was taught by a total of nineteen governesses in a period of seven years, then went to boarding school. In 1915 she joined the Wild Flower Society. She was also an avid tennis player and at one time qualified for Wimbledon. During the 1950s she won the North of Scotland Ladies' Open Singles tennis title four years running.

After she went to finishing school in Brussels, Webster took up a succession of domestic posts without allowing them to interfere with her passions for tennis and botany. She joined the Botanical Society of the British Isles (BSBI) in 1936. During World War II she joined the Army Training Service and trained as an army cook at Aldershot, working on Orkney, Shetland, Bournemouth, and finally at Field Marshall Bernard Law Montgomery's headquarters in Germany. She continued her work as a cook after the end of the war, both on a freelance basis and in a number of different hotels. In order to pursue her botanical interests more fully, she decided to be a cook in the winter and devote the summers to the study of plants. During several successive summers, she walked 100 miles every week collecting information for the Scottish section of the *Atlas of the British Flora.* In 1954 she joined the Botanical Society of Edinburgh.

Webster went to Africa in 1958, going first to Natal to see her brother and then on a safari lasting seven months, to Tanganyika and northern Rhodesia (now Zimbabwe). During this trip she collected 5,000 specimens and presented them to Kew Gardens. She spent three winters working at Kew identifying these plants and worked at the herbarium in Cambridge for four winters.

Webster was a fellow of the Linnean Society from 1960 to 1974. She was on the council of the BSBI from 1960 to 1966 and on the meetings committee from 1960 to 1976. She was county recorder for a number of Scottish areas (vice-counties). She contributed details to the *Flora of West Sutherland,* her first published material.

While in her seventies, Webster was still leading BSBI and Wild Flower Society trips in Scotland, competing in tennis tournaments, and offering advice to young players. When she died, her collection of British plants was divided between the Botany Department of Aberdeen University, the Botany School at Cambridge, and the Royal Botanic Garden, Edinburgh.

Bibliography: Stewart, O. M., and P. D. Sell, "Mary McCallum Webster (1906–1985)" *Watsonia* 16(3) (1987): 356–358; "Miss Mary McCallum Webster (1906–1985)," *Wild Flower Magazine* 407 (Autumn 1986): 35, 47.

Welch, Ann Courtenay
1917–
pilot, aviation historian, writer

Employment: chief instructor, Surrey Gliding Club, 1938–1939; ferry pilot, Air Transport Auxiliary, during World War II; gliding instructor, 1944–1984; in charge of British instructor testing and standards, 1948–1968.
Married: Graham Douglas, in 1938; Lorne Welch, in 1953.

Ann Welch is an expert glider pilot who gained her airplane pilot's license in 1934, aged seventeen, and began gliding in 1937, founding the Surrey Gliding Club in 1938 and becoming its chief instructor. During World War II she joined the Air Transport Auxiliary, ferrying military airplanes in all weather without radio.

After the war Welch returned to teaching gliding from 1944 to 1984; she was in charge of instructor standards and testing for twenty of these years. She was also manager of the British gliding team in world championships from 1948 to 1968 and director in 1965, when the World Gliding Championships were held in England. She held the British women's goal distance record, of 528 km., from 1961 to 1998.

Welch has written many books on flying subjects, from meteorology to training manuals on gliding, microlight flying, and hang gliding and accidents. These include *New Soaring Pilot* (1968), *Pilot's Weather, a Flying Manual of Cloud Reading for Pilots* (1973), and *The Story of Gliding* (1980). She has also published two books of children's fiction. She contributes to airplane and gliding magazines, including the *Royal Aeronautical Society Journal* and *Aerospace.*

As British delegate to the Fédération Aeronautique Internationale (FAI), she founded the Microlight and the Hang Gliding Commission and was vice-president of the Gliding Commission. She was awarded the FAI Gold, Lilienthal, Bronze, and Pelajia Majewska Medals and the Royal Aero Club Gold and Silver Medals. She is chair of the Royal Aeronautical Society Light Aviation Group.

Bibliography: Walker, M., education officer, Royal Meterological Society, personal communication to the author, December 1999; Welch, A., personal communications to the author, December 1999, March 2000, and June 2000.

Welch, Barbara née Gullick
c. 1904–April 1986
botanist, geologist

Education: B.Sc. in geology.
Employment: assistant curator (archaeology), Salisbury and South Wiltshire Museum; assistant secretary, Botanical Society of the British Isles, from 1953; volunteer work, Botany Department, British Museum (Natural History).
Married: Dr. F. B. A. Welch, a geologist, in February 1939.

Barbara Welch was an enthusiastic botanist, contributing botanical records to a number of county floras and other books on plants.

Welch was born in Cheltenham, Gloucestershire, the daughter of two nursery proprietors. After graduation, she was an assistant curator at the Salisbury and South Wiltshire Museum. She joined the Wild Flower Society in 1921 and won several local prizes for diary recordings of plants over the next few years. She joined the Botanical Society of the British Isles (BSBI) in 1928. Her first coauthored botanical paper, "Notes on the Flora of the Salisbury District," was published in 1932 in the *Wiltshire Archaeological and Natural History Magazine.* She subsequently produced articles, both jointly and alone, for several publications. She presented the Salisbury and South Wiltshire Museum with a series of drawings in 1936.

When she married, Welch moved to Richmond in Surrey. During World War II she was engaged in war work, although she remained involved in the activities of the Wiltshire Archaeological and Natural History Society. She studied plants and recorded their distribution in Middlesex, providing material for the flora of that county by D. H. Kent.

In 1953 the BSBI appointed her as assistant secretary. She did volunteer work at the British Museum, assisting with the collections held at the British herbarium. Over several years she contributed information for J. D. Grose's *Flora of Wiltshire* (1957). She was invited to become honorary secretary and recorder to the Surrey Flora Committee in 1957.

Welch provided information for the *Flora of Monmouthshire* by A. E. Wade (1970) and the *Flora of Essex* by S. T. Jermyn (1974). She and her husband retired to Cheltenham in 1963, and her last botanical paper was published in 1964.

Bibliography: Kent, D. H., "Barbara Welch (c. 1904–1986)," *Watsonia* 15 (July 1987): 461–463.

White, Margaret
c. 1888–1977
meteorologist

Education: University of Manchester; B.Sc. with honors, 1909; postgraduate studies, University of Manchester, M.Sc. 1910, D.Sc. 1919.

Employment: lecturer in charge of Howard Estate Observatory, 1910–1911; lecturer, University of Manchester, 1911–1916; head of research team, Manchester Corporation, 1916–1922.

Married: Mr. Fishenden.

Margaret White carried out research in meteorology.

White was awarded a university graduate scholarship in 1909 and the Beyer Fellowship in 1910. Her work was published in a number of journals, including the *Quarterly Journal of the Royal Meteorological Society.* She gave papers on meteorology at annual meetings of the British Association for the Advancement of Science in Dublin in 1907 and in Dundee in 1911.

In 1916 she was appointed the head of a research team with the Air Pollution Advisory Board of Manchester Corporation.

Bibliography: Rayner-Canham, M. F., and G. W. Rayner-Canham, "Pioneer Women in Nuclear Science," *American Journal of Physics* 58, no. 11 (1990) 1036–1043; Winterburn, E., "Rutherford at Manchester, 1907–1919," M.Sc. thesis, Centre for the History of Science, Technology, and Medicine, Manchester University, 1998.

Widdowson, Elsie May
21 October 1906–14 June 2000
nutritionist

Education: Sydenham High School; Imperial College, London; B.Sc. with honors; Ph.D.; D.Sc., 1948; King's College of Household and Social Science, 1933–1934.

Employment: researcher, Courtauld Institute of Biochemistry, Middlesex Hospital, 1931–1933; King's College Hospital, London, 1933–1938; Department of Experimental Medicine, Cambridge University, 1938–1966; Dunn Nutrition Laboratory, Cambridge (Medical Research Council); divisional head, Infant Nutrition Research Division, 1966–1972; Department of Investigative Medicine, Cambridge

Elsie May Widdowson (Godfrey Argent Studio)

University (at Addenbrooke's Hospital), 1972–1988 (postretirement position).

Elsie Widdowson was a pioneer in the scientific analysis of food, in nutrition, and in demonstrating the effect of diet on development before and after birth.

Widdowson was born in Dulwich, London, and studied chemistry at Imperial College, London. She passed her B.Sc. with honors examinations after two years but had to stay at the college for a further two years before her degree was awarded. During this time she worked on the breakdown of proteins and the separation of the different carbohydrates in apples. This was the subject of her Ph.D. thesis. Initially she was a member of a team led by Helen Porter to investigate the browning of apples when stored.

In 1933 Widdowson studied for a diploma in dietetics at King's College and met Robert McCance, who was studying the loss of nutrients from food during cooking.

Widdowson challenged his results for carbohydrates, and from this developed a lifelong partnership in research on nutrition. They produced food composition tables with values before and after cooking. Their joint publication *The Composition of Foods* came out in 1940 and went through several editions. They investigated the separate effects on humans of deficiencies in water and salt, studies that were useful in the World War II campaigns in North Africa.

Widdowson and McCance (and a few others in their research group) tried a minimal diet for six months, with calcium supplements, and then went to the Lake District to test their endurance. They showed that survival was possible on this "starvation" diet. In 1946 Sir Edward Mellanby, secretary of the Medical Research Council, asked Widdowson to assess the effects of different breads. She spent three years studying how five types of bread affected the growth of children in an orphanage in Duisberg, Germany.

Widdowson then looked at the way the composition of the body changed during fetal development and at times of fast growth after birth. She showed how the type of diet can permanently affect physiology at these stages. She became involved with all aspects of infant feeding and was particularly interested in variation in the fat content of artificial and natural milk, traveling to Labrador to study the fat composition of baby seals when she was nearly eighty.

Widdowson edited *Studies in Perinatal Physiology* (1980) and contributed a summary of the first fifty years of research in this field to the book. In 1993 the British Nutrition Foundation published a book to commemorate her joint work with McCance.

In December 1999 she attended the inauguration of the Elsie Widdowson Laboratory in Cambridge, set up to be the Medical Research Council's center for human nutrition research. She was elected a fellow of the Royal Society in 1976, made a Commander of the Order of the British Empire (CBE) in 1979 and a Companion of Honour in 1993, and awarded honorary doctorates by Manchester (1974) and Salford (1995) Universities. Widdowson was given several prizes for her work in nutrition by organizations in

Britain and abroad. She was president of the Nutrition Society (1977–1980), the Neonatal Society (1978–1981), and the British Nutrition Foundation (1986–1996).

Bibliography: "Elsie Widdowson: Nutritionist Who Helped to Formulate Britain's Wartime Rations," *Times* (27 June 2000): 21; Tucker, A., et al., "Elsie Widdowson," *Guardian* (22 June 2000): 22; *Who's Who, 2000,* London: Adam and Charles Black, 2000.

Wiggins, Philippa Marion
16 July 1925–
chemist

Education: Rangiruru School, Christchurch, New Zealand, 1939–1943; Canterbury College, University of New Zealand, 1944–1947; M.Sc., 1947; Royal Institution, London, 1949–1951; King's College, London, 1951–1952; Ph.D., 1952.

Employment: Department of Chemistry, Canterbury College (later University of Canterbury), New Zealand: junior lecturer, 1947–1948, part-time research assistant, 1960–1961; research scientist, Department of Physiology, University of Otago Medical School, New Zealand, 1962–1966; University of Auckland, Department of Cell Biology, 1967–1968; research associate, School of Medicine, 1968–1969; senior research fellow, 1970–1973; Medical Research Council Career Fellow, 1973–1990; cofounder, BioStore New Zealand, 1994; research scientist, Genesis Research and Development Corporation, from 1997.

Philippa Wiggins has worked on various aspects of the physical chemistry of water in gels and cells. She has developed a theory of enzyme activity in which transient changes in the properties of water connect the energy-donating reaction with the work performance of the enzyme.

Wiggins was educated at Christchurch, New Zealand, and graduated from the University of New Zealand with a first-class M.Sc. honors degree in chemistry.

In 1947 Wiggins was awarded a Royal Institution Scholarship as the best-qualified predoctoral student in the Commonwealth that year. With this funding, she did postgraduate research in the Davy-Faraday laboratory at the Royal Institution in London. Her doctoral research was on the rate of evaporation from different faces of rhombic sulfur; the results were published jointly with Sir E. K. Rideal in 1951 in *Proceedings of the Royal Society*. For her third year in Britain, she held a Monsanto Chemical Fellowship at King's College, London, and was able to complete her doctorate.

On her return to New Zealand, Wiggins worked with Dr. W. S. Metcalfe at Canterbury University on the measurement of the decay of fluorescence of anthracene derivatives. She moved to the University of Otago and was employed as a research scientist by the New Zealand Medical Research Council. Here she worked on the state of ions and water in surviving slices of rat kidney. When she moved to the University of Auckland, she continued this research using concentrated hemoglobin solutions. For the next twenty years, from 1970 to 1990, she developed and tested her theory of active transport.

Some of her ideas are summarized in "Role of Water in Some Biological Processes" (*Microbiological Reviews* 54 [1990]: 432–449). The unique properties of water as revealed by the latest studies on intracellular water may provide explanations for various structures and functions in living cells. For example, water is known to be important in maintaining the native structure of proteins and involved in the assembly of proteins into more complex structures. Wiggins found that gels and polyelectrolyte solutions had coexisting populations of water molecules that had different density, hydrogen-bond strength, viscosity, reactivity, and solvent properties. She believes that the conditions that lead to the abnormal populations of water molecules must exist in all cells and extracellular matrices and affect both physiological and biochemical processes. Experiments done by physicists have shown that pure liquid water has a mixture of high- and low-density microdomains. These interact with solutes and surfaces in some of the ways Wiggins had predicted.

Using the principles she had formulated, Wiggins designed solutions that induce a state of dormancy in cells and tissues so that they can be revived later and resume their metabolism. These solutions can be used for improving the storage of blood cells and hearts before transplantation. She holds six U.S. patents for the composition of the solutions and methods of preservation.

She and Dr. A. B. Ferguson founded Bio-Store New Zealand, a biotechnology company, in 1994. This work is now being carried out in Genesis Research and Development Corporation, another Biotechnology Company in Auckland.

She is a fellow of the Royal Society of New Zealand (1991) and of the New Zealand Institute of Chemistry (1972).

Bibliography: Martin, P., *Lives with Science: Profiles of Senior New Zealand Women in Science,* Wellington: Museum of New Zealand/Te Papa Tongarewa, 1993; Wiggins, P. M., personal communications to the author, February 2000, September 2000, and October 2000.

Wijnberg, Rosalie
1887–1973
gynecologist

Education: as a gynecologist with Professor Treub in Amsterdam.

Rosalie Wijnberg was the fourth woman to be accepted as a member of the Dutch Society of Surgery, though her acceptance was not unanimous, perhaps because she was a gynecologist.

In 1933 Wijnberg founded the Dutch Society of Women Doctors. Because she was Jewish, in World War II Wijnberg was transported to the concentration camp at Westerbrook. She was the only doctor in the camp and was ordered to sterilize any Jewish women who were in mixed marriages. Risking her own life, she refused to do this, and after a few days the order was canceled.

Bibliography: Mulder, M., and E. de Jong, "De eerste vrouwelijke chirurgen in Nederland," *Gewina* 20 (1997): 243–255.

Williams, Cicely Delphine
2 December 1893–13 July 1992
doctor, nutritionist

Education: Bath High School, 1906–1912; Somerville College, Oxford, 1917–1920; King's College Hospital, London, 1920–1923; Bachelor of Medicine, Bachelor of Surgery, 1923; doctor of medicine, 1935; Doctor of Tropical Medicine and Hygiene, 1929; Royal College of Physicians; Member of the Royal College of Physicians, 1933; Fellow of the Royal College of Physicians, 1949.

Employment: teacher, Montessori School, Jamaica, from 1913; physician, South London Hospital for Women and Children, Queen Elizabeth's Hospital for Children, and infant welfare centers in London, 1923–1927; medical officer, American Farm School, Salonika, Greece, 1927–1928; British Colonial Medical Service, Ghana, 1929–1936; pediatrician, College of Medicine, Singapore, 1936–1944; child health adviser, Federation of Malaya, Kuala Lumpur, 1944–1948; World Health Organization: head of Maternal and Child Health (MCH) section, Geneva, 1948–1949; head of MCH section, Southeast Asia, 1949–1951; visiting professor in MCH, University of Beirut, Lebanon, 1951–1953; University of London: senior lecturer in nutrition, 1953–1955; research on toxemia of pregnancy, 1955–1957.

Cicely Williams was the first woman physician in the British Colonial Service (1929), the first woman to be made a Commander of the Most Distinguished Order of St. Michael and St. George (1968), and the first woman to become an honorary fellow of the Royal Society of Medicine (1977). She was also the first Western doctor to describe the disease of kwashiorkor, a severe form of malnutrition in infants and children.

Williams was born and brought up at Kew Park, Bethel Town, Jamaica, where her father was director of education. She was the second of three daughters. In 1906 she was sent to school in Bath, where she stayed with her aunt Mary Farewell. After leaving Bath, she studied in Oxford and passed the entrance examination for Somerville College. She returned to Jamaica in 1913 and taught in a Montessori school until 1917, when she returned to Britain to train as a doctor. Although she did not enjoy the science course at Somerville, a preliminary to the medical training, once she was at King's College Hospital, London, she became more happily caught up and from then on was fully involved in medicine. When she qualified in 1923, there was still a distinct prejudice against women in private practice, so she worked in various hospitals in London, specializing in pediatrics.

Williams's next move was to Greece, where she worked for the Quakers as the medical officer on an American Farm School near Salonika. She was then accepted by the British Colonial Medical Service and worked in Ghana for the next seven years. She found that many of the children had a disease with the local name of "kwashiorkor," meaning "the disease the deposed baby gets when the next one is born," for the disease developed when a breast-fed baby was switched from milk to a mainly maize diet. Children with kwashiorkor develop reddish hair, stop putting on weight, become irritable, and develop dark patches on their skin. Of the sixty cases Williams saw, the children's ages ranged from nine weeks to five years and the mortality rate was 90 percent. She found the best treatment was condensed milk with cod-liver oil and malt. Initially she wrote up her findings in the Gold Coast Medical Report for 1931–1932, but she was not taken seriously until she published the articles "Kwashiorkor" in *The Lancet* in 1935 and "Child Health in the Gold Coast," also in *The Lancet*, in 1938.

Williams fought ceaselessly for improvements in nutrition and encouraged mothers to stay in hospital with their sick children, not only to keep the child happier but to allow the mother to learn about improving the nutrition of her family. She was often forthright in her opinions and was criticized for her simple, commonsense suggestions, but in the end her ideas were accepted.

From Ghana she moved on to Singapore in 1936. Her time there included internment by the Japanese for two and a half years at Changi jail and five months in Kampeitai in conditions of unbelievable hardship. These were described in *Dear Philip: A Diary of Captivity, Changi 1942–45* (1980) by Freddie Bloom, who was also interned.

After World War II Williams traveled all over Malaya in her role as adviser in child health to the Federation of Malaya. She had a short stay in Oxford before becoming the first head of Maternal and Child Health (MCH) with the World Health Organization (WHO) at its headquarters in Geneva. She did not take to Geneva but was able to move to the WHO office in New Delhi as first head of the MCH section in Southeast Asia. The countries under her remit included India, Burma, Ceylon, Thailand, Pakistan, and Afghanistan. She felt strongly that more money should be spent on training health workers to go into the villages rather than on mass inoculation and malaria eradication programs.

After retiring from WHO, Williams spent five years as visiting professor in MCH at the University of Beirut, working with students from all over the world and taking them into the villages to see what family life was really like. She continued to publish articles about her work and in February 1958 gave the Milroy Lecture to the Royal College of Physicians in London; her talk, "Social Medicine in Developing Countries," emphasized the need for improving maternal and child health, especially in the developing countries and was subsequently published in *The Lancet*.

When she returned to Britain, she became an adviser for the training programs run by the Family Planning Association from 1964 to 1967. She traveled to about seventy countries giving lectures and did surveys of child health concerned with malnutrition and its eradication in northern Burma, Italy, Yugoslavia, Tanzania, Cyprus, and Uganda. She was based at University College, London, and was a senior lecturer in nutrition for two years then conducted research on toxemia of pregnancy.

The University of the West Indies awarded her an honorary doctorate in 1969, as did the Universities of Maryland and Tulane in 1973 and Smith College, Massachusetts, in 1976. She was made an honorary fellow of Somerville College, Oxford (1977); King's College Hospital Medical School (1978); and Green College, Oxford (1985).

To mark her ninetieth birthday, a symposium was held at Somerville College, Oxford, with the twin themes "Kwashiorkor Revisited" and "The Organization of Family Health." The symposium was attended by experts in these fields, many of whom had worked with Williams.

Bibliography: Beinart, J., and R. King, "Cicely Williams: Memoirs of a Doctor," *Centre for Social History Newsletter* 3 (1986): 67; Bloom, F., *Dear Philip: A Diary of Captivity, Changi, 1942–45,* London: Bodley Head, 1980; Craddock, S., *Retired Except on Demand: The Life of Cicely Williams,* Oxford: Green College, 1983; Dally, A., *Cicely: The Story of a Doctor.* London: Gollancz, 1968; "Dr. Cicely Williams," *Medical Journal of Australia* 1 (1968): 364; Wellcome Trust, Contemporary Medical Archives Centre, London, Box no. PP/CDW/A1, visit by the author, February 2000; *Who Was Who, 1991–1995,* London: Adam and Charles Black, 1996.

Williams, Ethel May Nucella
8 July 1863–29 January 1948
doctor

Education: Norwich High School; Newnham College, Cambridge, 1882–1885; M.B., London 1891; London School of Medicine for Women; M.B.; M.D., 1895; Diploma in Public Health, 1899; Medical School, University of Vienna.

Employment: resident medical officer, Clapham Maternity Hospital (Battersea Bridge); medical officer, Blackfriars Dispensary for Women and Children; general practitioner, Newcastle upon Tyne, 1897–1924.

Ethel Williams was one of the first woman general practitioners in Newcastle upon Tyne.

Williams was born in Cromer, Norfolk, where her father was a country squire. She was the first school doctor for Gateshead High School, which later became the Central Newcastle Girls' High School, holding this position until she retired.

Williams was the first woman in Newcastle to have a driver's license and in 1906 the first woman in northern England to be seen driving a car. In 1907 she took part in the first suffragist procession in London and was involved with the North-East Society for Women's Suffrage. In 1917 she was secretary of the Newcastle Workers' and Soldiers' Council, which was formed to show support for the revolution in Russia. She worked for European refugees between the two wars. When World War II started, she moved back into Newcastle from her retirement home in the country so that she could help with casualties.

She was vice-chair and later president of the Federation of Medical Women and honorary secretary of the North-east Association of Medical Women. She cofounded the Northern Women's Hospital in Newcastle upon Tyne and helped set up residential care for the mentally ill in the Tyneside area of northeast England.

Williams was a member of Newcastle Education Committee, a justice of the peace, and a member of senate for the University of Durham. Ethel Williams Hall was founded in her memory as a hostel for women students of King's College, Newcastle (now the University of Newcastle), in 1950. Her portrait was presented to her in 1946 by the local branch of the National Council of Women.

Bibliography: "Bright Walls and Chintz Make College Hall Ideal," *Newcastle Weekly Chronicle* (18 November 1950); Carter, O., *History of Gateshead High School, 1876–1907, and Central Newcastle High School, 1895– 1955.* N.d.; Godfrey, D., "Dr. Ethel Had Will to Find a Way," *Newcastle Journal* (25 October 1996): 9; Landreth, A., "A Doctor Who Had to Kill Prejudice," *Newcastle Journal* (8 October 1946); *The Newcastle upon Tyne Official Blue*

Book, The City of Newcastle-upon-Tyne, 1920; *Newnham College Register, 1871–1923*, vol. 1, Cambridge: Newnham College, 1963; "Suffragette Doctor Dead," *Newcastle Journal* (31 January 1948): 1.

Willmott, Ellen
c. 1859–1934
horticulturist

Ellen Willmott was at one time the most renowned horticulturist in Britain, her fame due to the impressive garden she created at Warley Place, Essex.

Willmott was given an alpine garden by her mother for her twenty-first birthday; her enthusiasm for gardening was much influenced by her mother and her sister. Her 55-acre garden at Warley Place became famous in Britain and abroad. She also had a garden in France and one in Italy. She initially became well known as a daffodil grower, though her interests were much wider than this.

Willmott spent large amounts of money on her gardens, at one time employing 104 gardeners at Warley Place alone. She purchased a variety of costly equipment, including a wood-turning machine, a microscope, and a printing press on which to produce lists of seeds. She photographed her garden and its staff and developed her own film.

She invested not only money but also a great deal of time, effort, and study in her garden. She had a reputation for being able to cultivate difficult plants and studied the conditions required for growing seeds, recording her observations meticulously. She grew seeds brought from China and several plants from New Zealand. Her garden at one time contained over 100,000 plant varieties. In 1897 her contribution to horticulture was recognized when she and Gertrude Jekyll were jointly awarded the Royal Horticultural Society's Victoria Medal of Honour, becoming the first two women to receive this medal. She was elected the first woman fellow of the Linnean Society in 1904 and wrote *Warley Garden in Spring and Summer* (1909) and *The Genus Rosa* (1910).

Willmott once admitted to a friend that "my gardens come before anything in life for me and all my time is given up to working in one garden or another." So great was the amount of money she put into her gardens that by 1907 her personal fortune had dwindled substantially and she needed to borrow money. In 1913 she had to begin selling her possessions and was even threatened with bankruptcy. The garden fell into disrepair, and although with the help of family and friends she managed to keep her home, she had no money left at the time of her death in 1934.

Bibliography: Brough, C., librarian, Royal Botanic Gardens, Kew, personal communication to the author, June 2001; "Ellen Ann Wilmott," *Curtis's Botanical Magazine Dedications, Portraits, and Biographical Notes 1827–1927*; Hewitt, B., *The Crocus King: E. A. Bowles of Myddelton House*, Ware, Hert.: Rockingham Press, 1997; Librarian, Royal Horticultural Society, personal communication to the author, May 1998; Penn, H., *An Englishwoman's Garden*. London: BBC Books, 1993.

Wilman, Maria
29 April 1867–9 November 1957
botanist, geologist

Education: Good Hope Seminary, Cape Town; Newnham College, Cambridge, 1885–1888; natural science tripos, 1888; M.A., 1931.
Employment: assistant, South African Museum, Cape Town, and to the professor of geology at South African College, until 1908; director, Alex McGregor Memorial Museum, Kimberley, 1908–1946.

Maria Wilman is known for her work on the plants, archaeology, and tribes of southern Africa.

Wilman was the fifth in a family of nine girls. She was brought up in the Karoo and later went to school at the Good Hope Seminary in Cape Town. She was the second student from South Africa to attend Newnham College.

When she returned to South Africa, she became an assistant in the South African Museum. In 1908 she became the first director of the newly opened Alex McGregor Museum in Kimberley and set about building up the collections, including a geological collection and the Duggan-Cronin collection of photographs of Bushmen and Bantu life. Seven thousand plants were placed in the herbarium, five of which were named after her.

Wilman helped organize fieldwork in archaeology and anthropology in Griqualand West and other areas. She collected local plants for a reference collection and was responsible for making the famous rock garden in Kimberley. She collected and distributed grass seed for soil restoration. Two of these grasses, *Eragrostis lehmanniana* and *E. curvula*, she sent to Arizona to be planted as part of the effort to reclaim the land after the Dust Bowl. In 1933 she published *The Rock Engravings of Griqualand West and Bechuanaland*, a beautifully produced book with seventy black-and-white photographs of the rock carvings, details of their history, and a full list of references. The book was reprinted in 1968 and includes a short biography of Wilman.

In 1946 she published the *Preliminary Checklist of the Flowering Plants and Ferns of Griqualand West*. She was responsible for selecting authors and editing *The Bushmen Tribes of Southern Africa* (1942) and for eleven sections of *The Bantu Tribes of South Africa* (1928–1954).

She was a life member of the Royal Society of South Africa and was awarded an honorary LL.D. from Witwatersrand University in 1939.

Bibliography: H. M. L. B., "Maria Wilman 1867–1957," *Transactions of the Royal Society of South Africa* 35 (1957): viii–xiv; *Newnham College Register, 1871–1923*, vol. 1, Cambridge: Newnham College, 1963.

Wilson, Fiammetta née Worthington
1864–1920
astronomer

Education: at home, by governesses; schools in Lausanne, Switzerland, and Germany; studied music in Italy.

Employment: teacher, Guildhall School of Music, London; orchestra conductor.
Married: S. A. Wilson.

Fiammetta Wilson produced valuable material relating to her astronomical observations, publishing several papers on her work.

Wilson was born in Lowestoft, Norfolk, the daughter of a doctor who encouraged her to take an interest in science and nature. She showed early promise as a musician and taught at the Guildhall School of Music in London. In 1910 she attended lectures by Alfred Fowler, an astrophysicist, and decided to join the British Astronomical Association. From then on she was devoted to astronomy. She observed meteors (over 10,000 in a ten-year period), comets, and the aurora borealis, and in 1913 she discovered Westphal's Comet when it returned. With Grace Cook, she was acting director of the British Astronomical Society's meteor section in World War I. She was elected a fellow of the Royal Astronomical Society in 1916.

Wilson published several articles, including "The Meteoric Shower of January" in *Monthly Notices of the Royal Astronomical Society* in January 1918. She was invited to take up a one-year research position at Harvard College Observatory in 1920 but died before receiving the offer.

Bibliography: Ogilvie, M. B., *Women in Science: Antiquity through the Nineteenth Century*, New York: MIT Press, 1986.

Winch, Hope Constance Monica
1895–8 April 1944
pharmacist

Education: Casterton School, Kirkby Lonsdale, Cumbria; trained as a dispenser, Royal Victoria Infirmary, Newcastle, 1912–1913; Pharmaceutical Society School, London 1916–1917; qualified as chemist and druggist 1917; pharmaceutical chemist, 1918.
Employment: dispenser to surgeon, Wigan, 1913–1916; researcher (Redwood scholar),

Pharmaceutical Society, 1918–1920; lecturer, Rutherford Technical College, Newcastle, 1920; Sunderland Technical College: lecturer, 1921; head of Pharmacy Department, 1929 (officially 1930)–1944.

Hope Winch became head of the Pharmacy Department at Sunderland Technical College and played a key role in the development of pharmaceutical studies there.

Winch trained as a pharmacy dispenser at the Royal Victoria Infirmary in Newcastle upon Tyne. In 1913 she passed the Apothecaries Hall Assistant examination. She decided to undertake further training after spending three years as a dispenser to a surgeon in Wigan, Dr. C. R. Graham.

Winch studied at the Pharmaceutical Society School in Bloomsbury Square, London, qualifying as a chemist and druggist in 1917 and as a pharmaceutical chemist in 1918. During her time at the school she won a number of academic awards, including the Pereira Medal (1918), the Pharmaceutical Society's Silver Medal for botany, their Silver Medal for materia medica, and the Hewlett exhibition (1917). A Redwood Scholarship allowed her to remain at the Pharmaceutical Society research laboratories from 1918 to 1920, and in 1920 she was made an associate of the Royal Institute of Chemistry (Food and Drugs Division).

Winch lectured at Rutherford Technical College, Newcastle upon Tyne, though she was unhappy with the conditions there. In 1921 she transferred to Sunderland Technical College. Although part-time pharmacy courses had been held there since 1914, she was the first full-time lecturer in pharmacy at the college. That pharmacy was a relatively new subject and that its first full-time lecturer was a woman brought about rivalry with the college's other staff and students, who were mainly involved in shipbuilding and engineering studies.

But the department expanded, with several new laboratories. In 1926 a second full-time lecturer was appointed, followed a year later by another lecturer and several demonstrators. Winch was appointed head of the department in 1929, though the department was not officially established until 1930. As well as pharmacy, she lectured in botany, a particular interest of hers, and was involved in setting up the Botanical Society at the college. She served for twenty years as secretary of the Sunderland and District Branch of the Pharmaceutical Society and was elected as chair in 1944.

Winch traveled around Europe during vacations, often mountaineering. She spent many weekends in the Lake District rock climbing and fell walking. While climbing Scafell, the highest of the lake District peaks, she fell 150 feet and died at the age of forty-nine.

Bibliography: "Winch," *Pharmaceutical Journal* (15 April 1944): 161; Nixon, W., "Profile: Miss Hope Constance Monica Winch," information section, Hutton Library, University of Sunderland, 1984.

Wood, Audrey
19 August 1908–21 March 1998
midwife

Education: Westfield College, University of London; B.A. with honors, 1930; nurse training, St. Thomas's Hospital, London; midwifery training, Radcliffe Hospital, Oxford; midwives teaching diploma, 1941.

Employment: district nursing sister and night sister, Oxford, 1937–1941; assistant matron/midwifery tutor, Heathfield Maternity Home, Birmingham, from 1941; assistant matron/midwifery tutor, Royal Maternity Hospital, Belfast, until 1951; midwifery tutor, Royal College of Midwives, London, 1951–1952; general secretary, Royal College of Midwives, 1952–1970.

In 1952 *Audrey Wood* was the first graduate to become general secretary of the Royal College of Midwives.

Wood was born in Cambridge, one of four children, to a Quaker family. Her father became Birmingham University's first professor of theology. After leaving Westfield College, she trained as a nurse at St. Thomas's Hospital in London then went on to midwifery training in Oxford and qualification as a midwifery tutor in 1941. From 1937 to 1941 she also worked as a district nursing sister and night sister. In 1941 she was assistant matron and midwifery tutor at Heathfield Maternity Home in Birmingham; she took a similar position at the Royal Maternity Hospital in Belfast, where she became involved with the Royal College of Midwives (RCM), serving as secretary of the RCM Northern Ireland Council for seven years.

In 1951 Wood returned to London as tutor to the Midwifery Teacher's Course at the RCM, and a year later she was appointed general secretary, a position she held for the next eighteen years. During this time she was involved with important developments within the organization, including the establishment of the midwifery diploma course, the significant expansion of the RCM library, and the movement of the headquarters to new premises. Her influence was felt outside the organization as well. She campaigned to have a qualified midwife appointed to the position of midwifery officer by the Ministry of Health; she worked to promote greater cooperation between hospital and domiciliary maternity services, and between midwives and other health professionals; she was appointed to the World Health Organization's expert committee on maternity care in 1965; and she published a number of articles on the changing role of the midwife, including "The Development of the Midwifery Service in Great Britain" in the *International Journal of Nursing Studies* in 1963.

She retired in 1970 and was made an Officer of the Order of the British Empire (OBE) that same year. She later became a vice-president of the RCM. Throughout her life she remained a Quaker and was assistant secretary of the Society of Friends' Social Responsibility Council from 1971 to 1978.

Bibliography: "Audrey Wood (1908–88)," *RCM Midwives Journal* 1 (May 1988): 136; Librarian, Royal College of Midwives Trust, 1881–1981, personal communication to the author, August 1998; MacMillan, M., "Mothers on the Agenda," *Guardian* (6 April 1998); "Party for Miss Wood," *Midwives Chronicle and Nursing Notes* (September 1970): 287.

X

Xie, Xide (Hsieh Hsi-teh)
19 March 1921–
physicist

Education: Amoy (now Xiamen) University, B.Sc., 1946; teaching assistant, Shanghai University, 1946–1947; Physics Department, Smith College, Massachusetts, 1947–1949; M.A., 1949; Massachusetts Institute of Technology (MIT), 1949–1951; research assistant, MIT, 1950–1951; Ph.D., 1951; research staff, MIT, 1951–1952.

Employment: Fudan University: lecturer, Physics Department, 1952–1956; associate professor, 1956–1962; professor, from 1962; director, Institute of Modern Physics, 1978–1983; vice-president of university, 1978–1983; president of university, 1983–1988; adviser to university, 1988–1994; adjunct director, Shanghai Institute of Technical Physics, Chinese Academy of Sciences, 1958–1966; director, Center for American Studies, from 1985.

Married: Cao Tianquin, on 17 May 1952.

Professor *Xie Xide* is a leading researcher and teacher in semiconductor physics and surface physics in China.

Xie's major interest is in theoretical studies of the electronic states of semiconductor surfaces and interfaces. She has written more than ninety papers, four books, and contributed to several important reviews of her subject. (Papers that appeared between 1949 and 1965 were published using the older romanization of her name, Hsieh Hsi-teh.) Her books include *Semiconductor Physics* (1958), coauthored with K. Huang (in Chinese), and *Group Theory and Its Applications* (1986).

She has been a member of the Chinese Academy of Sciences since 1980 and was a member of its Presidium from 1981 to 1996. She has received twelve honorary doctorates from universities worldwide, including Smith College (1981), Leeds University (1985), Mt. Holyoke (1986), Toyo University (1987), and McMaster University (1993). She has chaired several international conferences, the last being the Twenty-first International Conference on Semiconductor Physics held in Beijing in 1993. In 1997 she received the Award for the Advancement of Science and Technology from the Ho Leung Ho Lee Foundation of Hong Kong.

Bibliography: *Who's Who in Australasia and the Far East*, second edition, Cambridge: Melrose Press, 1991; Xie Xide, personal communication to the author, May 1998.

Y

Yasui, Kono
16 February 1880–24 March 1971
biologist, cytologist

Education: Kagawaken Shihan Gakko (Kagawa Prefecture High School), until 1898; Joshi Koto Shihan Gakko Rikka (Women's High School, Science), 1898–1902; Joshi Koto Shihan Gakko Kenkyuka (Women's Higher Normal School, Graduate Course), 1905–1907; University of Chicago, 1914; Harvard University, 1915–1916.

Employment: teacher, Gifu Koto Jogakko (Gifu Women's School), 1902–1904; teacher, Kanda Kyoritsu Jogakko (Kanda Kyoritsu Women's School), 1904–1905; assistant professor, Joshi Koto Shihan Gakko, 1907–1914; researcher, University of Tokyo, 1916–1927; researcher, Tokyo Joshi Shihan Gakko, from 1916; research supervisor, Tokyo Imperial University, 1918–1939; professor, Tokyo Joshi Shihan Gakko, 1919–1949; professor, Ochanomizu Women's University, 1949–1952.

Kono Yasui was a renowned biologist and the first woman to receive a doctorate from a Japanese University.

Yasui was born in what is now Sanbonmatsu Ouchicho and following school and college became a teacher. She published a paper on the Weberian apparatus of carp. In 1905 she entered Joshi Koto Shihan Gakko Kenkyuka (Women's Higher Normal School, Graduate Course) and during her time there did research in botany, concentrating on cytology. In 1907 she was appointed to the post of assistant professor.

In 1914, under a Ministry of Education scheme for overseas study, Yasui traveled to Germany and then to the United States to do research in cytology at the University of Chicago. In 1915 she conducted research on coal at Harvard University, continuing this work at the University of Tokyo on her return to Japan the following year. Her doctoral thesis was entitled "The Structure of Lignite (Brown Coal) and Bituminous Coal in Japan." She also resumed her research in cytology and genetics at Tokyo Joshi Shihan Gakko and was made a professor there in 1919. As well as her own research, she supervised the work of others in the Faculty of Science at Tokyo Imperial University from 1918 to 1939.

In 1924 Yasui began investigating the genetics of corn, red poppies, and *Tradescantia*. In 1929 she founded *Cytologya* magazine, involving herself in all aspects of the journal's production and developing its international reputation. In 1945 she started a survey of plants affected by fallout from the atomic bombs.

In 1949 she became a professor at the Ochanomizu Women's University. On her retirement in 1952, this became an honorary post. In 1955 she was awarded a Medal with Purple Ribbon, and in 1965, the Order of the Precious Crown, Butterfly, and Third Grade, Junior of the Court Rank.

Bibliography: Lynch, Paul, first secretary of science and technology, British embassy, Tokyo, personal communication to the author containing information prepared by Mizue Yamauchi, May 2000.

Yoshioka, Yoyoi
née Washiyama
10 March 1871–22 May 1959
doctor

Education: Saiseigakusha (medical school), 1889–1892.

Employment: work in Washiyama Clinic, Kitogun, 1892–1895; founder, clinic, Tokyo, 1895–1900; founder, Tokyo Women's Medical School, 1900; founder, Tokyo Women's Medical College, 1912; founder, midwifery and nursing school, Tokyo, 1930; member of Social Education Survey, Ministry of Education, from 1933; inspector, Ministry of Health and Welfare and Ministry of Education, from 1939; head of Tokyo Women's Medical University, from 1951.

Married: Arata Yoshioka, in 1895.

Yayoi Yoshioka was a pioneer in the education and training of women doctors in Japan.

Yoshioka was born in Shizuoka Prefecture, the second daughter of an herbalist. She trained as a doctor, qualifying in 1892 and becoming legally registered in 1893. After working in a clinic in her hometown, she moved to Tokyo in 1895 and opened her own clinic. She married in the same year, and in 1900 she and her husband founded the Tokyo Women's Medical School, intended to provide opportunities for women to train as doctors. In 1912 the couple founded the Tokyo Women's Medical College, and they added a training school for midwives and nurses in 1930.

Yoshioka was chairperson of the Women's Medical Association of Japan in 1920 and a member of the Social Education Survey Committee for the Ministry of Education. From 1939 she carried out inspections of different types of facilities, including those concerned with mother and child protection and medical education. This involved travel to the United States and Europe. She was removed from her government posts in 1947 because of internal political problems; once the situation had stabilized, she returned to public life. In 1951 she played a key role in the establishment of the Tokyo Women's Medical University and became its head.

Yoshioka published a number of books, including *From Marriage to Childcare* (1919) and *Pregnancy and an Easy Delivery* (1946) (both in Japanese).

She received several honors, including the Gold and Silver Star of the Order of the Sacred Treasure, and she was decorated fifth grade, senior of the court rank. An asteroid was named after her on the anniversary of the founding of the Tokyo Women's Medical University.

Bibliography: Lynch, Paul, first secretary of science and technology, British embassy, Tokyo, personal communication to the author containing information prepared by Mizue Yamauchi, May 2000.

Young, Grace née Chisholm
15 March 1868–29 March 1944
mathematician

Education: privately; Girton College, Cambridge, 1889–1893; University of Göttingen, 1893–1895; Ph.D., 1895; Universities of Göttingen and Geneva, medical studies.

Employment: self-employed as a writer and researcher.

Married: Dr. William H. Young, tutor at Peterhouse College, Cambridge, in 1896. He died in 1942.

In 1895 *Grace Chisholm Young* became the first woman in Germany to be awarded a doctorate in any subject.

Young was born in Haslemere, Surrey, the youngest of four children. Her father was a senior civil servant. He and Young's mother supervised their daughter's private education. She passed the Cambridge senior examination when she was seventeen and wanted to study medicine, but her mother would not let her. Young instead studied mathematics and won the Sir Francis Goldsmid Scholarship at Girton College. The women's examination results were always listed separately from the men's at this time. Young obtained the equivalent of a first-class degree. In 1892, after the Cambridge examination, she and a friend went straight to Oxford and unofficially took the Oxford degree examinations. She had the highest marks of any of the mathematics students at Oxford. She completed the second part of the mathematical tripos in Cambridge and went to the University of Göttingen to study for her doctorate under the direction of Felix Klein. She defended her dissertation, "The Algebraic Groups of Spherical Trigonometry," and was awarded her doctorate magna cum laude in 1895.

Her thesis was printed, and she sent copies to various people, including William Henry Young, who had been her tutor for a term in Cambridge. He suggested that they cooperate on a book about astronomy. They never pursued this project, but they became friends, and in 1896 they married. They lived in Cambridge, eventually having six children. He continued with his tutoring while she went on with the research she had started in Göttingen.

After Klein's visit to Cambridge in 1897 to receive an honorary doctorate, the Youngs moved to Göttingen, where they attended advanced mathematical lectures. In 1908 the family moved to Switzerland.

Young obtained a medical degree, brought up her children, and wrote books and research papers. She also completed numerous papers started by her husband. He usually acknowledged her help in a footnote, but "joint" papers were generally published under his name. They wrote about 214 mathematical papers in this way, several in French, Italian, and German. Young and her husband also collaborated on *The First Book of Geometry* (1905), which was translated into German, Italian, Swedish, and Hungarian. The book intended to "present primary ideas about geometry, show in a graphic form the primary geometrical theorems, and the development of practical methods requiring no special apparatus or supervision or serious expenditure of trouble or money." It was illustrated with black-and-white photographs showing what a child could do. In 1906 the Youngs came out with the first textbook on set theory, *The Theory of Sets of Points*

(1906). They hoped to produce a second edition, but after their eldest son was killed in World War I they lost some of their creative energy.

Young wrote two stories for children, *Bimbo: A Little Real Story for Jill and Molly* (1905) and *Bimbo and the Frogs: Another Real Story* (1907). The first, published under the pseudonym "Auntie Will," was an attempt to help children understand where babies come from. The second described family expeditions in search of tadpoles and frogs, explaining what cells are and stressing the need to check facts in reference books.

In 1915 Young won the Gamble Prize for Mathematics at Girton College for her essay "On Infinite Derivatives," published (under her own name) in the *Quarterly Journal of Pure and Applied Mathematics*.

In 1940 she returned to Britain from Switzerland with two grandchildren who had been staying with her, leaving her husband behind. He was not able to join her because of the German occupation of France, and he died in 1942. Young died in 1944. She had been recommended for a fellowship of Girton College but died before the governors held their election meeting.

Bibliography: Perl, T., *Maths Equals: Biographies of Women Mathematicians and Related Activities*, Menlo Park, California: Addison-Wesley, 1978; Rothman, P., "Grace Chisholm Young and the Division of Laurels," *Notes and Records, Royal Society of London* 50, 1 (1996): 89–100; Website: agnesscott.edu/lriddle/women.young/htm; *Who Was Who, 1941–1950*, London: Adam and Charles Black, 1952.

Yuasa, Toshiko
11 December 1909–1 February 1980
nuclear physicist

Education: Tokyo Joshi Koto Shihan Gakko Rika (Women's Higher Normal School, Department of Science), 1927–1931; Tokyo Bunrika University, 1931–1934; Laboratoire de Chimie Nucléaire du Collège de France, Paris, 1940–1944; Ph.D., 1943.
Employment: vice-assistant, Physics Depart-

ment, Tokyo Bunrika University, 1934–1935; lecturer, Tokyo Women's Christian College, 1935–1937; assistant professor, Tokyo Joshi Koto Shihan Gakko, 1938–1940; researcher, Physics Institute, University of Berlin, 1944–1945; professor, Tokyo Joshi Koto Shihan Gakko, 1945–1946; researcher, RIKEN Nishina Laboratory, 1946–1949; lecturer, Institute for Chemical Research, University of Kyoto, 1948–1949; researcher, Laboratoire de Physique Nucléaire du Collège de France, Paris, 1949–1952; professor, Ochanomizu Women's University, 1952–1955; Centre National de la Recherche Scientifique (CNRS), researcher, 1952–1957; head of research, 1957–1974; honorary head of research, from 1975.

Yuasa was a prominent physicist, considered by many to be Japan's equivalent of Marie Curie.

Yuasa was born in Tokyo and studied at Tokyo Bunrika University, completing her course in 1934. She remained at the university as a part-time assistant in the Physics Department, beginning research on atoms and molecular spectroscopy. The following year she was a lecturer at Tokyo Women's Christian College, and in 1938 she became assistant professor at the Tokyo Joshi Koto Shihan Gakko (Tokyo Women's Higher Normal School). In 1940 she went to Paris, and did research with Professor F. Joliot-Curie at the Laboratoire de Chimie Nucléaire du Collège de France. Yuasa's doctoral thesis was entitled, "Research on ß-ray Continuous Spectra, Which Are Emitted from Artificial Radiation Nuclei."

In 1944 Yuasa began research at the University of Berlin's Physics Institute. In 1945 she developed a double-focus spectroscope for ß-ray spectrum measurement. She returned to Japan and in December 1945 became a professor at Tokyo Joshi Koto Shihan Gakko, though at the time nuclear research experiments were prohibited by the occupying U.S. forces. Yuasa worked at the RIKEN Nishina Laboratory from 1946 to 1949 and as a lecturer at Kyoto University for a year thereafter. In 1949 she returned to France to continue her research on nuclear spectroscopy at the Laboratoire de Physique Nucléaire du Collège de France as a researcher at the Centre National de la Recherche Scientifique (CNRS).

In March 1952 she became professor at the Tokyo Joshi Koto Shihan Gakko (by that time renamed Ochanomizu Women's University). She held this post until 1955 but during this period continued her involvement with CNRS. In 1957 she became head of research at CNRS. She was awarded a doctor of science degree from Kyoto University in 1962 for her thesis "Gamow-Teller Unchangeable Interaction Type on ß Decay of He_6." She continued her work at CNRS until 1974, when she retired. She was then made honorary head of research. She spent time in Japan attending conferences, and in 1978 proposed a Japanese-French collaboration on a nuclear research project.

In 1976 she was awarded the Medal with Purple Ribbon and was honored with the Order of the Sacred Treasure, Gold Rays with Neck Ribbon.

Bibliography: Lynch, Paul, first secretary of science and technology, British embassy, Tokyo, personal communication to the author containing information prepared by Mizue Yamauchi, May 2000.

Select Bibliography

Aldrich, R., and P. Gordon. *Directory of British Educationalists.* London: Woburn Press, 1989.

Alic, M. *Hypatia's Heritage: A History of Women in Science from Antiquity to the Late Nineteenth Century.* London: Women's Press, 1986.

Allen, D. E. *The Botanists: A History of the Botanical Society of the British Isles through a Hundred and Fifty Years.* London: St. Paul's Bibliographies, 1986.

——. *The Naturalist in Britain: A Social History.* Princeton, New Jersey: Princeton University Press, 1976.

Andrews, D., ed. *The Annual Obituary 1989.* London: St. James Press, 1990.

Barber, L. *The Heyday of Natural History, 1820–1870.* London: Jonathan Cape, 1980.

Bentley, L. *Educating Women: A Pictorial History of Bedford College, University of London, 1849–1985.* Surrey, England: Alma Publishers, 1991.

Blunt, W., and W. T. Stearn. *The Art of Botanical Illustration.* London: Antique Collectors' Club; Royal Botanic Gardens, Kew, 1994.

Bozman, E. F., ed. *Everyman's Encyclopaedia.* Fourth edition. London: Dent, 1958.

Brittain, V. *The Women of Oxford: A Fragment of History.* London: G. B. Harrap, 1960.

Cook, A. "Ladies in the Scientific Revolution." *Notes and Records of the Royal Society of London* 51, 1 (1997): 1–12.

Crawford, A., et al., eds. *The Europa Biographical Dictionary of British Women: Over a Thousand Notable Women from Britain's Past.* London: Europa Publications, 1983.

Creese, M.R.S. *Ladies in the Laboratory? American and British Women in Science, 1800–1900: A Survey of Their Contributions to Research.* Lanham, Maryland: Scarecrow Press, 1998.

Crone, J. S. *A Concise Dictionary of Irish Biography.* Dublin: Talbot, 1928.

Daintith, J., et al., eds. *Biographical Encyclopaedia of Scientists.* Second edition. 2 vols. Bristol: Institute of Physics Publishing, 1994.

——. *Chambers Biographical Encyclopaedia of Scientists.* Edinburgh: W. and G. Chambers, 1983.

Davis, N. Z. *Women on the Margins: Three Seventeenth Century Lives.* Cambridge, MA: Harvard University Press, 1995.

Desmond, R. *Dictionary of British and Irish Botanists and Horticulturalists, Including Plant Collectors and Botanical Artists.* London: Taylor and Francis, 1977.

Dictionary of National Biography. Oxford: Oxford University Press, 1885–.

Dictionnaire de Biographie Française. Paris: Libraire Le Touzey, 1965.

Dreyer, J. L. E., and H. H. Turner, eds. *History of the Royal Astronomical Society, 1820–1920.* London: Royal Astronomical Society, 1923.

Dyhouse, C. *No Distinction of Sex: Women in British Universities, 1870–1939.* London: University College London Press, 1995.

The Environmentalists: A Biographical Dictionary from the Seventeenth Century to the Present. New York: Facts on File, 1993.

Gage, A. T., and W. T. Stearn. *A Bicentenary History of the Linnean Society of London.* London: Academic Press, 1988.

Gillespie, C. C., ed. *Dictionary of Scientific Biog-raphy.* New York: Charles Scribner's Sons, 1975.

Girton College Register. Vols. 1 (1869–1946) and 2 (1944-1969). Cambridge: Girton College, 1948, 1991, respectively.

Goode, P., and M. Lancaster. *Oxford Companion to Gardens.* Oxford: Oxford University Press, 1986.

Goring, R., ed. *Chambers Scottish Biographical Dictionary.* Edinburgh: Chambers, 1992.

Grey-Turner, E., and F. M. Sutherland. *History of the British Medical Association.* Vol. 2. London: British Medical Association, 1982.

Grinstein, L. S., R. K. Rose, and M. H. Rafailovich, eds. *Women in Chemistry and*

Physics: A Bibliographic Source Book. Westport, Connecticut: Greenwood Press, 1993.

Guthrie, D. *A History of Medicine.* London: Nelson, 1945.

Haeger, K. *The Illustrated History of Surgery.* London: Harold Starke, 1989.

Harte, N., and J. North. *The World of UCL, 1828–1990.* Revised edition. London: University College, 1991.

Howard, A., and D. Heaton, eds. *The Times Lives Remembered: Obituaries from 1993.* Blewbury, England: Blewbury Press, 1993.

Howarth, O. J. R. *The British Association for the Advancement of Science: A Retrospect, 1831–1922.* London: British Association for the Advancement of Science, 1931.

Hutchinson Dictionary of Scientists. Oxford: Helicon, 1996.

Ireland, N. O. *Index to Scientists of the World, from Ancient to Modern Times.* Boston: F. W. Faxon, 1962.

Lambert, M., ed. *Who's Who in New Zealand.* Twelfth edition. Auckland, New Zealand: Octopus Publishing, 1991.

Legget, J. *Local Heroines: A Women's History Gazetteer to England, Scotland, and Wales.* London: Unwin Hyman, 1988.

Marren, P. *The New Naturalists.* London: HarperCollins, 1995.

Marsh, Neville N. *The History of Queen Elizabeth College: One Hundred Years of University Education in Kensington.* London: King's College, 1986.

Martin, P. *Lives with Science: Profiles of Senior New Zealand Women in Science.* Wellington: Museum of New Zealand/Te Papa Tongarewa, 1993.

Massingberd, H., ed. *The Daily Telegraph Book of Obituaries: A Celebration of Eccentric Lives.* London: Macmillan, 1995.

Mathew, M. V. *The History of the Royal Botanic Garden Library.* Edinburgh: HMSO, 1987.

McKay, J., comp. *Brilliant Careers: Women Collectors and Illustrators in Queensland.* Brisbane: Queensland Museum, 1997.

McKenna-Lawlor, S. *Whatever Shines Should Be Observed: Quicquid Nited Notandum.* Blackrock, Dublin: Samton, 1998.

The Medical Directory. London: F. T. Healthcare, various years.

Millar, D., et al. *The Cambridge Dictionary of Scientists.* Cambridge: Cambridge University Press, 1996.

Modern Scientists and Engineers. 3 vols. New York: McGraw-Hill, 1980.

Morrell, J. *Science at Oxford, 1914–1939: Transforming an Arts University.* Oxford: Clarendon Press, 1997.

Mozans, H. J. *Women in Science.* New York: D. Appleton, 1914.

Murray, P., and L. Murray. *A Dictionary of Art and Artists.* Fourth edition. Harmondsworth, England: Penguin, 1976.

Newnham College Register, Vols. 1 (1871–1923) (23) and 2 (1924–1950). Cambridge: Newnham College, 1963, 1981, respectively.

Nicholls, C. S., ed. *Dictionary of National Biography: Missing Persons.* Oxford: Oxford University Press, 1993.

Ogilvie, M. B. *Women in Science: Antiquity through the Nineteenth Century.* New York: MIT Press, 1986.

Opfell, O. S. *The Lady Laureates: Women Who Have Won the Nobel Prize.* Metuchen, New Jersey: Scarecrow Press, 1978.

Osen, L. M. *Women in Mathematics.* London: MIT Press, 1974.

Pannekoek, A. *A History of Astronomy.* London: George Allen and Unwin, 1961.

Peri, T. *Math's Equals: Biographies of Women Mathematicians and Related Activities.* Menlo Park, California: Addison-Wesley, 1978.

Porter, R., ed. *The Hutchison Dictionary of Scientific Biography.* Second edition. Oxford: Helicon, 1994.

Richter, D., ed. *Women Scientists: The Road to Liberation.* London: Macmillan, 1982.

Ritchie, J., ed. *Australian Dictionary of Biography.* Melbourne: Melbourne University Press, 1993.

Roberts, F. C., comp. *Obituaries from the Times, 1961–1970.* Reading: Newspaper Archives Developments, 1975.

Sarjeant, W. A. S. *Geologists and the History of Geology: An International Bibliography from the Origins to 1978.* 5 vols. London: Macmillan, 1980.

Schiebinger, L. *The Mind Has No Sex?* Cambridge, MA: Harvard University Press, 1991.

Shils, E., and C. Blacker, eds. *Cambridge Women: Twelve Portraits.* Cambridge: Cambridge University Press, 1996.

Stanley, A. *Mothers and Daughters of Invention: Notes for a Revised History of Technology.* Metuchen, New Jersey: Scarecrow Press, 1993.

Timbury, M. C. *The Golden Jubilee of the Public Health Laboratory Service, 1946–1996.* London: Public Health Laboratory Service, 1997.

Tuke, M. J. *A History of Bedford College for Women, 1849–1937.* Oxford: Oxford University Press, 1939.

Turner, R., ed. *Thinkers of the Twentieth Century.* Second edition. London: St. James Press, 1987.

Uglow, J. S., ed. *The Macmillan Dictionary of Women's Biography.* Third edition. London: Macmillan, 1998.

Who Was Who. London: Adam and Charles Black, various years.

Who's Who, an Annual Biographical Dictionary. London: Adam and Charles Black, various years.

Who's Who in Australasia and the Far East. Second edition. Cambridge: Melrose Press, 1991.

Who's Who in Australia. Melbourne: Herald and Weekly Times, 1971.

Williams, T. I., ed. *A Biographical Dictionary of Scientists.* Third edition. London: Adam and Charles Black, 1982.

Wintle, J. *Makers of Nineteenth Century Culture, 1800–1914.* London: Routledge and Kegan Paul, 1982.

"Women, Science, and the Royal Society." An exhibition to commemorate the fiftieth anniversary of the election of the first women to Fellowship of the Royal Society. 19 April 1995–22 September 1995.

Index

AAUW. *See* American Association of University Women

Abercrombie, Michael, 1

Abercrombie, Minnie Louie (Jane) née Johnson, 1–2

Aberdeen Royal Asylum, 106

Aborigines, 195

Abortion Act (1967), 21

Abraham, Karl, 161

Académie des Sciences, 32, 62, 78, 112, 152, 155, 163, 167, 175, 177, 242

Académie Internationale d'Histoire des Sciences, 269

Academy of Sciences of the USSR, 268–269

Academy of the Institute of Science (Bologna), 23

Acetone, 175, 190, 297

Acetylcholine, 50

Acrylics, 107

Acta Mathematica, 163

Actinium, 175, 243

Adam, Joseph Denovan, 137–138

Adam, Madge Gertrude, 2

Adams, Jacqueline Nancy Mary née Whittaker, 2

Adams, Mary Grace Agnes née Campin, 3

Adamson, George, 4

Adamson, Joy (Friedricke Victoria) née Gessner, 3–4

Adenosine triphosphate (ATP), 50, 158, 222

Adler, Hannah, 173

Admiralty Air Department, 61

Adolescent Study Group, 229

Adrenaline, 50

Advisory Committee on Oil Pollution of the Sea, 19

Aechmea meeana, 206

Aechmea polyantha, 206

AERE. *See* Atomic Energy Research Establishment

Aeronautical engineering, 248–249, 288

Aeronautics, 15–16, 107

Aerospace, 325

African Studies Centre, 261

Africa's Vanishing Art (Leakey), 170

Agar, 87, 130, 202, 204, 224, 237

Agnesi, Maria Gaetana, 4–5

Agricultural Research Council, 6, 222, 252

Agricultural Science—An Introduction for Australian Students and Farmers (Aitkin), 6

Agriculture, 5–6, 16, 43, 71–72, 116, 233–234

Agriculture, Board of, 234

Agriculture, Department of (Perth), 116

Aims and Techniques of Group Teaching (Abercrombie), 1

Air Defence Research and Development Establishment, 308

Air Ministry, 61, 138, 153

The Air Pilot's Weather Guide (Holford), 139

Air Transport Auxiliary (ATA), 154, 325

Air Warfare Analysis Section, 118

Aitkin, Yvonne, 5–6

Alabama Polytechnic Institute, 189

Alaska, 142

Albania, 89

Albert, Prince, 226

Alcock, Nora Lillian née Scott, 6–7

Alex McGregor museum, 333

Alford Field Club, 95

Algae, 10, 55, 57, 87, 98, 112, 157, 201, 204–205, 237–238, 242

Algarotti, Francesco, 214

Algebra, 292

"The Algebraic Groups of Spherical Trigonometry" (Young), 341

Alkaptonuria, 110

All Passion Spent (Sackville-West), 276

Allen's Commercial Organic Analysis, 166

Alpha particles, 155

Ambler superdraft process, 118

American Academy of Science, 171, 177

American Association of University Women (AAUW), 57, 70, 190

American Astronomical Society, 51

American Geophysical Union, 173

American Jewish Committee, 147

American National Committee for Mental Hygiene, 43

American Phycological Society, 55

American Physical Society, 293

American Society for Human Genetics, 186

American Women in Science, xvii

Amphicypellus, 54

The Anaemias (Vaughan), 318

Anaerobes, 297

Anatomical Society, 194

L'Anatomie des centres nerveux (Déjerine-Klumpke), 84

Anatomy, 32, 198–199

Anderson, Elizabeth Garrett. *See* Garrett Anderson, Elizabeth née Garrett

Anderson, Margaret Dampier née Whetham, 7, 297

Anderson, Margaret Garrett, 295

Anemia, 299

Anglo-Albanian Society, 89

Anglo-Irish War, 80

Anglo-Yugoslav Children's Hospital, 192

Animal Geography (Newbigin), 224

Animal Health Trust, 156

Animal Hormones: A Comparative Survey (Jenkin), 151

Animal Life in Fresh Water: A Guide to British Fresh-water Invertebrates (Mellanby), 209

Animal Population, Bureau of, 288

Animal, Vegetable, Mineral, 3

Animals' Friend, 137

Annals and Magazine of Natural History, 204

Annals of Botany, 43, 55, 196, 229, 277, 279, 322

Annals of My Village (Roberts), 263

Annals of the Rheumatics Diseases, 217

Anne, Princess, 106

Anning, Mary, 7–8

An Annotated List of Seed-borne Diseases (Noble, Tempe, and Neergaard), 59

Annual Reports of Observations of Injurious Insects (Ormerod), 233

Anthropology, 170–172, 260–262, 276

Antibiotic and Chemotherapy (Barber and Garrod), 19

Antibiotics, 18–19, 83, 300

Antiquaries Journal, 83

Antiquities, Department of (Israel), 110

Apicultural Abstracts, 74

Apiculture, 73–74

Apimondia, 74

Aplysia, 91

Apollo 12, 67

Apothecaries Hall examination, 334

Appleton, Edward, 308

Al Arab, 28

Die Arbeitslosen von Marienthal, 147

Arber, Agnes née Robertson, 8–9

Arber, E. A. N., 8

Arber, Muriel, 8

Archaeology, 9–10, 27–28, 83, 92, 110–111, 218–219, 244, 277

nautical archaeology, 269

The Archaeology of Beekeeping (Crane), 74

Architecture, 58, 284–285, 301–302

Archiv for Mathematik og Naturvidenskab, 296

Arctic Zoology (Pennant), 35

Armed Forces Pay Review Body, 218

Armitage, Ella Sophia née Bulley, 9–10

Armitt Museum, 254

Army Training Service, 324

Army Veterinary Corps, 80

Arnold, Lorna, 117

Arran, Lord, 258

Art, 209, 251, 286–287, 321

anatomical illustration, 32

animal illustrations, 39, 89, 137–138

insect illustrations, 210–211

medical illustrations, 130–131

photography, 10, 33, 54–55, 58, 126–127, 203, 310

symbols, 212–213

See also Botanical art

The Arthropoda: Habits, Functional Morphology, and Evolution (Manton), 198

Arthropods, 198

Artificial disintegration, 155

Arum italicum neglectum, 315

Ascidians, 40

Association for the Education of Women, 160

Association for the Study of Medical Education, 168

Association for Tropical Biology, 185

Association Montessori Internationale, 216

Association of Clinical Biochemists, 65

Association of Clinical Pathologists, 283

Association of Physicians, 300

Association of Registered Medical Women, 283

Association of Science Education, 249

Association of Veterinary Teachers and Research Workers, 313

Association of War Pensions Committees, 287

An Astronomical and Geographical Class Book for Schools (Bryan), 46

Astronomical Society of the Pacific, 67

Astronomical Union, 37

Astronomy, 2, 269–270, 321–322, 333

comets, 129, 175

galaxies, 50–51

lunar formations, 37–38

sidereal astronomy, 129–130

writers, 66–67

Astrophysics, 140–141

ATA. *See* Air Transport Auxiliary

Athens Botanical Garden, 263

Athletics, 86, 201, 240–241, 324

Athletics for Women and Girls—How to Be an Athlete and Why (Peirce), 241

Athlit Cave, Mount Carmel, 110–111

Atkins, Anna née Children, 10

Atkins, John Pelly, 10

Atlas of British Flora, 169, 324

Atlas of Representative Stellar Spectra (Huggins and Huggins), 140

Atmospheric physics, 165

Atomic energy. *See* Nuclear energy

Atomic Energy Research Establishment (AERE), 103

Atomic Scientists' Association, 183

ATS. *See* Auxiliary Territorial Service

Attenborough, David, 55

Attenborough, T. W., 169

Auerbach, Charlotte, 10–12

Aunt Judy's Magazine, 111

Australia, xvii, 5–6, 70–71
  aborigines, 195
  botany, 319–320
  Great Barrier Reef, 28–29, 133
  marine biology, 28–29, 133
  Queensland, 132–133

Australian Academy of Sciences, 133, 212

Australian Academy of Technological Sciences and Engineering, 211, 311

Australian Journal of Agriculture, 116

Australian Plant Pathology, 116

Australian Seashores (Dakin), 28

Australian Society for Microbiology, 212

Australopithecus africanus, 276

Australopithecus boisei, 170

Austria, 147, 284–285

Austrian State Geological Institution, 137

Auxiliary Fire Service, 180

Auxiliary Territorial Service (ATS), 121

Aviation, 15–16, 61, 153–154, 200, 240–241, 325

Avicultural Magazine, 19

Aylesbury Prison for Women, 183

Ayrton, Barbara, 13

Ayrton flapper fan, 13

Ayrton, Phoebe Sarah (Hertha) née Marks, 12–14

Ayrton, William, 12

Babbage, Charles, 52

Bacon, Gertrude, 15–16

Bacon, John Mackenzie, 15

Bacterial Metabolism (Stephenson), 297

Bacteriology, 60, 62–64, 82–83, 130–131, 264, 297

Baddeley, Florence, 31

Badgers, 258

Badgers Act, 1973, 258

Baghdad, 27–28

Bahn, Paul, 111

Baker, Ralph, 116

Balcombe Place, 84–85

Balderton Hospital, 102

Balfour, Arthur, 144

Balfour, (Elizabeth) Jean née Drew, 16–17

Balfour, Isaac Bayley, 290

Balfour Laboratory, 8, 30, 31

Balfour, Lady (Eve) Evelyn Barbara, 16

Ball, Anne Elizabeth, 17

Ballia callitricha, 17

Bally, Peter, 4

Baly, Monica E., 17–18

Bankfield Museum, Halifax, 89

Banksia, 265

The Banksias (Rosser), 265

The Bantu Tribes of South Africa, 333

Barber, Mary, 18–19

Barclay-Smith, Phyllis Ida, 19–20

Bari, Nina Karlovna, 20

Barkalow, F., 289

The Barker Index of Crystals, 233

Barnes, Alice Josephine (Mary Taylor; Dame Josephine Warren), 20–22, 168

Barnes, Penny, 21

Barr bodies, 186

Barra, Island of, 191

Barrack Hospital (Scutari), 225–226

Barry, James Miranda Steuart, 22

Barvel, P., 19

Basford, Kathleen, 22–23

Basseport, Madeleine, 32

Bassi, Laura Maria Catarina, 23–24

Batchelor Girls' Exhibition, 128

Bate, Dorothea Minola Alice, 24, 110–111

Bateson, William, 281

Battersea Polytechnic, 210

Battye Library of Western Australian History, 195

Baxendell, Joseph, 37

BBC. *See* British Broadcasting Corporation

BDH. *See* British Drug Houses

Beakes, G. W., 55

Beale, Dorothea, 24–25

Beare, Hudson, 47

Becker, Lydia Ernestine, 25–26

Becquerel, Henri, 76–77

The Bedfordshire Plant Atlas (Dony and Dony), 86

Bee Research Association (BRA), 73–74

Bee World, 74

Beers, Clifford, 43

Bees, 73–74

Bees and Beekeeping: Science, Practice, and World Resources (Crane), 74

Beeton, Isabella Mary née Mayson, 26–27

Beeton, Samuel, 26

Begg Collection, 79

Beginning Geology (Watson and Read), 323

Bégouen, Comte, 110
Belgrade Hospital, 190
Bell, Gertrude Margaret Lowthian, 27–28
Bemba people, 261
Benedetti (Benedictines), 23
Benedict XIV, 5, 23
Beni Stabili housing, 215
Bennett, Isobel Ada, 28–29, 311
Benson, Margaret, 277
Bentham, Ethel, 29
Bentley, Margaret, 156
Berg, O., 230, 296
Bergen Tekniske Skole, 295
Berlin Psychoanalytical Society, 161
Bernal, J. D., 101, 135, 183
Bernard Baron Institute of Pathology, 271, 318
BESO. *See* British Executives Services Overseas
Bidder, Anna McClean, 29–31
Bidder, George Parker, III, 30, 31
Bidder, Marion née Greenwood, 30, 31–32
Biheron, Marie-Catherine, 32
Bijvoet, Jo, 189
Bimbo: A Little Real Story for Jill and Molly
    (Young), 341
Bimbo and the Frogs: Another Real Story (Young),
    341
Biochemical Engineering (Millis, Humphrey, and
    Shuichi), 212
Biochemical Journal, 7, 190, 216–217, 252, 297
Biochemical Society, 252
Biochemistry, 60–61, 189–190, 216–217, 222–223,
    290–291
    insulin research, 165–166
    leather manufacture, 178–179
    liposomes, 272–273
The Biochemistry of the Eye (Pirie), 246
"Biogeographical Significance of Aneityum
    Island, New Hebrides" (Cheesman), 59
Biological Journal of the Linnean Society, 185
Biological Reviews, 11, 87
Biological Society (Australia), 319
Biological Standardisation (Burn), 49
Biological Station (Lünz), 272
Biology, 1–2, 223–224
    cytology, 97–98, 339
    freshwater biology, 92, 104–105, 141–142, 157,
        241–242, 272, 308–309
    microbiology, 211–212, 296–297
    molecular biology, 157
    World War II research, 202, 204
    See also Marine biology; Zoology
The Biology of a Marine Copepod (Marshall and
    Orr), 202
Bioluminescence, 94
Biomedical Sciences Section, 65
Biophysics, 100–101, 124–125
The Bird (Hess), 19

Bird, Isabella Lucy, 32–33
Bird Study, 169
Bird Watching on Scolt Head (Turner), 310
Birds. *See* Ornithology
Birds of the World (Barvel), 19
Birmingham Natural History Society (BNHS),
    54, 86
Birr Castle, 203
Birr Scientific Heritage Foundation, 203
Birth control, 84–85, 304–305
Birth Control News, 304
Bishop, Ann, 33–34
Bishop, John, 33
Bishop, Sally, 22
Blackburn, Kathleen Bever, 34–35, 196
Blackburn, V. H., 252
Blackburne, Anna, 35
Blackburnia, 35
Blackwell, Elizabeth, 36, 109, 137, 152
Blackwood, Margaret, 36–37
Blagg, Mary Adela, 37–38
Bland, J. O. W., 271
Bleeker, Caroline Emilie (Lili), 38
Blezzard, Ruth, 180
Blin-Stoyle, Roger, 103
Blood Groups in Man (Sanger and Race), 278
Bloom, Freddie, 330
Blum, Leon, 147
Blyth and Blyth, 98
BMA. *See* British Medical Association
BNHS. *See* Birmingham Natural History Society
BOA. *See* British Optical Association
Boas, J. E. V., 161
Bobath, Berta, 38–39
Bobath, Karel, 38
Bodichon, Barbara, 12
Bodleian Library, 292
Bodtker, Eivind, 113
Boer War, 159, 282
Bohr, Niels, 117, 173, 208
Bohusz-Szyszko, Marian, 281
Boltwood, Bertram, 113
Bomber Command, 118
Bonheur, Raymond, 39
Bonheur, Rosalie Marie, 39
Bonn Gymnasium, 48
Bonnevie, Kristine Elisabeth Heuch, 40–41
Bonneviella grandis, 40
Bonney, T. G., 257
Book Indexing (Anderson), 7
Book of Household Management (Beeton), 26
Book of Lilies (Stoker), 290
The Book of the Balance of Wisdom (trans.
    Rozhanskaya), 269
Booth, Evelyn Marie, 41
Born Free (Adamson), 4
Boron, 322

Borrowman, Agnes Thompson, 41–42, 47–48
Borstal Institution for Girls, 183
Boston Memorial Hospital, 318
Botanical art, 2, 3–4, 166, 231–232, 265, 301
    Australia, 267–268
    Brazil, 205–206
    Greece, 116–117
    Jersey, 169
    lilies, 290
    lithography, 290
    mycology, 253–255
Botanical Garden (Edinburgh), 162
Botanical Institute (Brazil), 205
Botanical Society of America, 9
Botanical Society of Edinburgh, 6, 87, 162, 191, 324
Botanical Society of London, 10
Botanical Society of Scotland, 229
Botanical Society of the British Isles (BSBI), 10, 54, 86, 112, 169, 301, 324, 326
Botany, 8–9, 41, 43–44, 69–70, 85–87, 95, 112–113, 142, 169–170, 258–259, 260, 301, 324–326
    Australia, 319–320
    brewing, 190–191
    collectors, 263, 315–316
    cytology, 34–35, 197
    education, 25–26, 133–134, 196–197, 281
    genetics, 22–23, 281
    marine botany, 2, 57–58, 98–99
    paleobotany, 70–71, 136–137, 162, 302–304
    palynology, 70, 162
    photography, 10, 196
    plant anatomy, 279
    plant nutrition, 322
    plant pathology, 6–7, 116, 229–230, 276–277
    plant physiology, 252–253
    South Africa, 332–333
    taxonomy, 172
    See also Botanical art; Horticulture; Mycology
Botany for Novices: A Short Outline of the Natural System of the Classification of Plants (Becker), 26
Botany: The Metamorphosis of Plants (Goethe), 9
Bothered by Alligators (Milner), 213
Boulton, Matthew, 263
Bowles, E. A., 243, 263
Boyle, Alice Helen Anne, 42–43
BRA. *See* Bee Research Association
Brabazon, Hercules, 150
Brachiopods, 217
Bragg, William, 182
Brazil, 180, 184, 205–206
Brenchley, Winifred Elsie, 43–44, 322
Breuil, Henri, 110
Brewing, 190–191
Bridgeman, Charlotte, 79
Bridges, 47

The Bridgewater Treatise (Buckland), 48
Brighton Polytechnic, 119
Bright's disease, 271
Bristol Philosophical Institution, 292
British Algae: Cyanotype Impressions (Atkins), 10
British and Foreign Bible Society, 53
British Army, 22, 131, 225–226
British Association for Early Childhood Education, 191
British Association for the Advancement of Science, 125, 258
    Biomedical Sciences Section, 65
    botany section, 9, 121, 224
    Geographical Section, 224
    members, 26, 261–262, 281, 282
    officers, 9, 126, 181, 279
    presentations, 13, 15–16, 26, 121, 304, 326
    Young Scientists' Section (BAYS), 183
British Astronomical Association, 16, 37, 67, 140, 270, 333
British Beekeepers' Association Research Committee, 74
British Broadcasting Corporation (BBC), 3, 55, 59–60, 139, 239, 241
British Coal Research Association, 100–101
British Colonial Medical Service, 330
British Colonial Service, 329
British Dental Association, 178
British Dental Journal, 178
British Dietetic Association, 65
British Dragonfly Society, 180, 267
British Drug Houses (BDH), 166
British Electrical Authority, 127
British European Airways, 248–249
British Executives Services Overseas (BESO), 74
British Federation of University Women, 190, 310
British Freshwater Fishes: Factors Affecting Their Distribution (Brown), 46
British Friesian Cattle Society, 192
British Gas, 249
British Geological Survey, 323
British India Corporation, 192
British Institute of Professional Photographers, 126, 127
British Journal of Industrial Medicine, 299
British Journal of Photography, 127
British Journal of Psychology, 146
British Journal of Radiology, 240
British Leather Manufacturers' Research Association, 179
British Medical Association (BMA), 20, 66, 169
British Medical Bulletin, 297
British Medical Journal, 82, 168, 300
British Museum, 7, 10, 111, 119, 137, 184, 217, 231, 303, 326

British Museum (Natural History), 196, 198, 266, 290, 309
   collections and donations, 99, 142, 172, 181, 266
   Crustacean Section, 115
   volunteers, 59, 64, 180
British Mycological Society, 229, 277
British Neuropathological Society, 271
British Nutrition Foundation, 61, 65–66, 328
British Optical Association (BOA), 88
British Ornithologists' Union, 19
British Pharmacological Society, 50
British Phycological Society, 87, 224, 237
British Physiological Society, 50
British Prosobranch Molluscs (Fretter), 103
British Psycho-Analytical Society, 161, 229
British Psychological Society, 146
British Red Cross, 278, 297
British Seaweeds (Gatty), 111
British Society for Parasitology, 34, 259
British Society for the Study of Orthodontics, 178
British Trust for Ornithology, 169
British Veterinary Association, 156, 314
British Veterinary Codex Committee, 156
British War Economy (Gowing and Hancock), 117
British Weather Disaster (Holford), 139
Broadland Birds (Turner), 310
Broch, Hjalmar, 40
Bromeliads, 205
Bromhall, Margaret Ann, 44
Brook Advisory Centre for Young People, 44
Brook, Lady Helen Grace Mary née Knewstub, 44–45
Brooke, Charles, 231
Brown, Dods, 106
Brown, Edith Mary, 45
Brown, Elizabeth, 270
Brown, Margaret Elizabeth (Mrs. Varley), 45–46, 105
Brown, Sibyl, 146
Browne, E. T., 171
Browning, Misses, 109
Bruch-Willstater, M., 293
Brunei, 169
Bryan House, 46
Bryan, Margaret, 46
BSBI. *See* Botanical Society of the British Isles
Bubonic plague, 266, 286
Buchanan, Dorothy (Mrs. Fleming), 47
Buchanan, Margaret Elizabeth, 42, 47–48
Buckland, Mary née Morland, 48
Buckland, William, 48
Buckley, Elizabeth Imlay, 195
Bühler, Charlotte, 228
Bülbring, Edith, 48–50
Bulgakov, P. G., 269

Bulletin de la Societe Chimique, 113
Bullfinch, HMS, 317
Burbidge, (Eleanor) Margaret née Peachey, 50–51
Burbidge, Geoffrey, 51
Burlingham, Dorothy T., 104, 229
Burn, J. H., 49
Burr, Alfred Hamilton, 176
Bush Nursing Association, 84
The Bushmen Tribes of Southern Africa, 333
Buss, Miss, 178
Buteshire Natural History Society, 201
Butterflies and Late Loves: The Further Travels and Adventures of a Victorian Lady (Fountaine), 99
BX Plastics, 107
Byrne, William, 80
Byron, Arthur, 69
Byron, Augusta (Ada), Countess of Lovelace, 51–52
Byron, Lord, 52

C. W. L. Huts, 110
Cable, Alice Mildred, 53
Cadbury, Dorothy Adlington, 54
Cairns, Hugh, 195, 271
Calanus finmarchius, 171
Calanus spp., 201–202
Calcutta General Hospital, 218
Callaghan, Jim, 19
Calluna vulgaris, 258
Cambridge Ancient History, 88, 111
Cambridge Crystallographic Data Center (CCDC), 158
The Cambridge Evacuation Survey: A Wartime Study in Social Welfare and Education (Brown, Thonless, and Isaacs), 146
Cambridge Institute of Education, 218
Cambridge Natural History, 89
Cambridge Natural History Society, 190
Cambridge Readings in the Literature of Science (Anderson and Whetham), 7
Cambridge Research Hospital, 97
Cambridge Scientists' Anti-War Group, 297
Cambridge Structural Database, 158
Cambridge University Women's Appointments Board, 190
Cambridge Voluntary Association for Mental Welfare, 31–32
Cambridge Women's Liberal Association, 31
Cameron, Julia Margaret, 231
Campaign for Nuclear Disarmament (CND), 246
Canning Town Mission Hospital, 42
Canon of Mas'ud (al-Biruni), 269
Canter-Lund, Hilda M. née Carter, 54–55
Cape Colony, 22

Carbon tetrachloride, 300
Carcinological Society of Japan, 115
Cardiff Naturalists' Society, 83, 315
Cardiothoracic Institute, 312
Care of Infants (Jex-Blake), 153
Care of the Dying (Saunders), 281
Carex microglochin, 16
Carey, S. W., 221
Carlisle, C. H., 135
Caroline Haslett Memorial Trust, 128
Caroline Walker Trust, 65
Carrington, Edith, 234
Carter, T. C., 186
Carthammus tinctorius, 164
Cartwright, Mary Lucy, 56–57, 136
Cassie Cooper, Una Vivienne née Dellow, 57–58
Casson, Elizabeth, 106
Casson, Hugh, 58
Casson, Lady Margaret née MacDonald, 58
Cassou de Saint-Mathurin, Suzanne, 111
Castle, Mary, 179
Castle Museum, 99
Catalogue of the Rothschild Collection of Fleas, 266
Cater, W. F., 99
Catherine the Great, 32
Catherine II, 199
Catholic Marriage Advisory Council (CMAC), 68
Cavendish Laboratory, 103, 155
Caves, 24, 110–111
CCDC. *See* Cambridge Crystallographic Data Center
Celiac disease, 318
Cell biology, 97–98
Cellular Biology Laboratory, 177
Central Health Services Council, 96
Central London Eye Hospital, 194
Central Midwives Board (CMB), 95–96
Central nervous system, 84
The Central Role of Hormones (Pickford), 245
Central Veterinary Society, 156, 313
Centre for Genetic Anthropology, 83
Centre for Medical Law and Ethics, 149
Centre National de la Recherche Scientifique (CNRS), 342
Cephalopods, 30, 203–204
Ceratium, 54
Chadwick, James, 117
Chamberlain, Joseph, 223
Channel Island, Jersey, 169
Charing Cross Hospital, 20, 193, 272
"Checklists of the Freshwater Diatoms of New England" (Cassie Cooper), 57
Cheesman, Lucy Evelyn, 58–60, 179–180
Chelsea Flower Show, 243
Chelsea Hospital, 292

Chelsea Polytechnic, 210, 266
Chemical Analyses of Igneous Rocks, Metamorphic Rocks, and Minerals (Guppy), 120
"Chemical Induction of Mutations" (Auerbach), 11
Chemical Institute, 207
Chemical Microbiology Committee, 297
Chemical pathology, 64–66
Chemical Pathology and the Sick Child (Clayton and Round), 65
Chemical Society, 158, 176
Chemical Society of Japan, 164
Chemical Society of Philadelphia, 105
Chemistry, 105, 141, 164, 199, 230, 245
    chemical pathology, 64–66
    educators, 217–218
    enzymes, 328–329
    industrial chemistry, 107–108
    nitric acid, 175–176
    nuclear chemistry, 242–243
    pharmaceutical chemistry, 41–42, 47–48
    water, 249–250, 328–329
    See also Biochemistry; Crystallography
The Chemistry of the Proteins and Its Related Economic Applications (Lloyd), 179
"The Chemistry of the Stars" (Clerke), 66
Chemistry Society of France, 243
Chick, Harriette, 60–61
Chick-Martin test, 60
Child Guidance Service, 149
"Child Health in the Gold Coast" (Williams), 330
Children
    education, 145, 212, 214–215
    health, 29, 65, 191, 299–300, 330
    psychology, 104, 144–146, 149–150, 161, 212, 228–229
Children, John George, 10
China, 222
China Inland Mission, 53
Chinese Academy of Sciences, 337
Chinese Chow Club, 156
Chironomids, 141–142
Chiropodists, 82
Chisungu (Richards), 261
Chitty, Letitia, 61
Chladni, Ernst F. F., 112
Chladni's figures, 112
Chlorine, 155
Chloroform, 300
Choquet-Bruhat, Yvonne, 62
Christ Calming the Waters (Bohusz-Szyszko), 281
Christie Cancer Hospital, 23
Chromosomes, 196
Chronica Botanica, 9
Churches' Council on Healing, 43
Churchill Hospital, 319

Chytrids, 54–55
Cipher operation, 71
Cirroteuthis massyae, 204
Civil engineering, 47, 61, 98
Civil Industry and Trade (Gower and
 Hargreaves), 117
Civil Service Department, 55
Civilian Medical Board, 300
Clactonian culture, 170
Cladium mariscus, 70
Cladophora balliana, 17
Clairaut, Alexis Claude, 88, 174
Clark, A. J., 11
Clarke, G. T., 9
Clarke, Patricia Hannah née Green, 62–64
A Classification of Bright's Disease (Russell), 271
Clay, Theresa Rachael, 64, 266
Claybury Asylum, 42
Clayton, Barbara Evelyn, 64–66
Clerke, Agnes Mary, 66–67
Clerke, Ellen Mary, 67
Climate Impact Assessment Program, 165
Clostridium oedomatiens, 63
Clubb, Elizabeth Mary Fitz-Simon née Thomas,
 67–69
Clubb, John, 68
Clutterbuck, Charles, 200
CMAC. *See* Catholic Marriage Advisory Council
CMB. *See* Central Midwives Board
CND. *See* Campaign for Nuclear Disarmament
Coal, 162
Coatbridge Chemistry Department, 176
Cobalt salt crystals, 141
Cochlitoma, 181
Cochran Boiler Company, 127
Cockburn, Claud, 69
Cockburn, Patricia Evangeline Ann née
 Arbuthnot, 69
The Cockney and the Crocodile (Mann), 195
Coelacanths, 72–73
Cohen, S., 176
Cole Library, 91
Collectors, 35, 92–93, 263, 315–316
Collett, Robert, 40
Collinette, Cyril, 180
The Collins Guide to Border Plants (Perry), 243
Collins New Naturalist series, 180
Colloquia Crustacea Mediterranea, 115
Colonial Economic Advisory Group, 261
Colonial Office, London, 261
A Colour Atlas of Insect Tissues via the Flea
 (Rothschild), 266
Colour in Nature—A Study in Biology (Newbigin),
 223
Colour in the Flower Garden (Jekyll), 150
Colourpoint, Himalayan, and Longhair Cats
 (Manton), 198

Colourpoint Society of Great Britain, 198
Comets, 130, 175, 333
Commercial Geography (Newbigin), 224
Committee for Standardised Genetic
 Nomenclature for Mice, 186
Committee of the Biochemical Society, 252
Committee on the Public Understanding of
 Science (COPUS), 126, 249
Committee on Women in Science, Engineering,
 and Technology, 17
Common Ground, 23
Commonwealth Reconstruction Training
 Scheme, 133
Commonwealth Scientific and Industrial
 Research Organisation (CSIRO), 172, 204,
 205, 211, 240, 311
Communist Party of Great Britain, 289
Compendious System of Astronomy (Bryan), 46
The Composition of Foods (Widdowson and
 McCance), 329
The Computer-mapped Flora of Warwickshire
 (Cadbury), 54
Computer programming, 51–52
Conchological Society of Great Britain and
 Ireland, 204
The Conchologist's Companion (Roberts), 263
Conchology, 69, 204, 263
The Concise Knowledge of Astronomy (Clerke,
 Gore, and Fowler), 66
"Conjugative Plasmids in Bacteria of the 'Pre-
 antibiotic' Era" (Datta and Hughes), 83
Connective tissue research, 217
Conservation, 16–17, 83, 205–206
 campaigners, 265–267
 flora, 116–117, 265–267
 wildlife, 3–4, 174
Consultative Council on Mental Handicap, 245
Consumers' Association, 3
Contemporary Scientific Archives Centre,
 117–118
*Conversations in Chemistry, Intended More
 Especially for the Female Sex* (Marcet), 199
Conversations on Chemistry (Bryan), 46
Conversations on Natural Philosophy (Marcet), 199
Conversations on Political Economy (Marcet), 199
Conversations on the Evidences of Christianity
 (Marcet), 199
Conway, Verona Margaret, 69–70
Conybeare, William, 48
Cookery Club, 239
Cookson, Isabel Clifton, 70–71
Cooper, Astley, 22
Cooper, G. A., 217
Copepods, 201–202
COPUS. *See* Committee on the Public
 Understanding of Science
Copy-editing: The Cambridge Handbook, 7

Coral planulae, 202
Corals, 115, 132
Coris's Laboratory, 252
Corner, E. D. S., 202
Corradi, Doris, 71
Corsi Collection, 253
Cosmic rays, 155
Cottage Hospital, 153
Council for Nautical Archaeology, 269
Council for the Representation of Women
  (League of Nations), 115
Council of the Entomological Society, 180
Council of the Royal Institute of Chemistry, 179
Council of the Royal Irish Academy, 245
Council of the Salmon and Trout Association,
  105
Councils of the Freshwater Biological
  Association, 46
The Country Diary of an Edwardian Lady
  (Holden), 137
Country Life, 150
Countryside Commission, 83
Countryside Commission for Scotland, 16
Courant, Richard, 308
Courtauld, Katherine, 71–72
Courtauld, Louisa Perina née Ogier, 72
Courtauld, Samuel, 72
Courtauld, Samuel, Jr., 72
Courtaulds, 107, 108
Courtelle, 107
Courtenay-Latimer, Marjorie Eileen Doris, 72–73
Cowan, S. T., 63
Coward, Katherine, 49
Cowley Mission, 282
Cox, Percy, 27, 28
Crabs (Malacostraca), 114, 171
Craib, W. G., 87
Crane, Eva née Widdowson, 73–74
Crawford, R. M. M., 16
A Cretaceous Flora of the World (Stopes), 304
Crete, 24
Crew, F. A. E., 11
Crick, Francis, 101
Crimea, 225–226
"The Crisis in Rhodesia" (Clerke), 67
Croasdale, Hannah, 98
Croydon Aerodrome, 154
Cruciferae, 196
Crustacean Society, 115
Crustaceans, 114, 190
Crypt analysts, 131
Crystallography, 100–101, 134–136, 141, 157–159,
  181–183, 189, 253
Crystals of Leyden, 214
CSIRO. *See* Commonwealth Scientific and
  Industrial Research Organisation
Ctenopoma kingsleyae, 159

Culpeper House, 177
Culpeper, Nicholas, 177
Culver (ship), 171
Cumberland Association for the Advancement
  of Literature and Science, 181
Cunliffe, Stella Vivian, 74–75
Curie, Bronya, 76
Curie, Eve, 77
Curie, Irène. *See* Joliot-Curie, Irène
Curie, Marya (Manya; Marie) née Sklodowska,
  75–79, 113, 154, 175, 207, 242
Curie, Pierre, 75–77, 154
Currie, Ethel Dobbie, 79
Curtis's Botanical Magazine, 290, 302
Cust, Aleen, 79–80
Cyanobacteria, 205
Cyanophytes, 157
Cyanotypes of British and Foreign Ferns (Atkins),
  10
Cyclotron, 208
Cytogenetics, 37
Cytology, 7, 34–35, 40, 97–98, 339
Cytologya, 339
Czar Lazar Hospital, 144
Czech Science Academy, 267

Daguerre, Louis, 10
Daily Bread (Gatty), 138
Daily Express, 69
Dakin, W. J., 28
Dal, Ingerid Blanca Juell, 81
Dale, Henry, 49
Dalton, Katharina Dorothea née Kuipers,
  82
Damselflies, 179
Dandy, J. E., 85
Danish Bacon Company, 74
Danish Geophysical Society, 173
Dapedius, 7
Dart, Raymond, 276
Darwin, Charles, 25, 26, 33, 161
Data Protection Committee, 75
Datta, Naomi née Goddard, 82–83
David, Jacques-Louise, 167
Davies, Margaret, 83
Davies, P. H., 116
Davies, R., 297
Davy, Humphrey, 199
Davy-Faraday laboratory, 328
Dawson, H. M., 175–176
De Vries, Hugo, 307
Dean, H. R., 284
Deane, Henry, 42
Dear Philip: A Diary of Captivity, Changi 1942–45
  (Bloom), 330
Debierne, André, 175
Decapods, 171

Déjerine-Klumpke, Augusta née Klumpke, 84
Dendroica fusca, 35
Denman, Gertrude Mary née Pearson, 84–85
Denmead, A. K., 133
Dent, Charles, 247, 319
Dent, Edith Vere née Annesley, 85–86
Dental Disease Committee, 210
Dental research, 209–210
Dental surgery, 177–178
Depression after Childbirth (Dalton), 82
The Desert and the Sown (Bell), 27
A Desert Journal: Letters from Central Asia (Cable, French, and French), 53
Design, 58
Designed for Women, 239
Deutsche Physiologische Gesellschaft, 50
"The Development of a Child" (Klein), 161
The Development of the Human Eye (Mann), 194
"The Development of the Midwifery Service in Great Britain" (Wood), 335
Devil's Tower Shelter (Gibraltar), 110
Devon Wildlife Trust, 294
Dewar, James, 67
DHSS. *See* Department of Health and Social Security
Diabetes, 165–166
Diatoms, 151, 201
Dictionary of Biology (Abercrombie and Abercrombie), 1
Diet and the Teeth: An Experimental Study (Mellanby), 210
Diet Committee (International African Institute), 261
Difference engine, 52
Dillard-Bleick, Margaret, 62
Diplomacy, 27–28
Disraeli, Benjamin, 223
Dixon, Anne, 10
DNA, 157
Dobell, Clifford, 34
Dokan Dam, 61
Domestic Economy in Theory and Practice (Bidder and Baddeley), 31
Domestic help, xviii, 12–13, 197, 244, 324
Dominion Observatory, 2
Doniach, Deborah, 312
Dony, Christina Mayne née Goodman, 86
Dony, John, 86
Dorman Long, 47
Dorrien-Smith, Gwen, 180
Dowling, Robert, 231
Downie, Dorothy G., 86–87
Dragonflies, 179–180
Dragonflies (Longfield), 180
Dragonflies of the British Isles (Longfield), 180
Drawings of British Plants (Ross-Craig), 265

Drew-Baker, Kathleen M. née Drew, 87
Drosophila, 11
Drower, Margaret S., 87
Drug research, 41–42, 47–48, 135–136, 164, 166, 214, 280, 313
Druid, HMS, 317
Drummond, I. M., 161
DSIR. *See* Scientific and Industrial Research, Department of
Du Châtelet-Lomont, Emilie Gabrielle née le Tonnelier de Breteuil, 88
Dublin Air Ferries, 241
Dublin Review, 67
Duggan-Cronin collection, 333
Dun Laoghaire, 142
Duncan, C., 79
Dunn, Barbara, 88
Dunscombe, Adaliza Amelia Clara Mary Elizabeth Emma Frances, 88–89
Dunscombe, Matthew William, 88
Durham, Mary Edith, 89
Dutch Academy of Sciences, 189
Dutch resistance, 38
Dutch Society of Surgery, 329
Dutch Society of Women Doctors, 329

Eales, Nellie B., 91–92, 103
The Early Norman Castles of the British Isles (Armitage), 9
Earth Sciences Library (University of Queensland), 133
Earth Sciences Society, 93
Earthquakes, 164, 173
East African Airways, 200
East African Fisheries Research Organisation, 46, 184
East African Nights and Other Verses (Peirce), 240–241
East India Company, 143
East London Museum, 72, 73
EAW. *See* Electrical Association for Women
Ecclesfield Church, 112
École Polytechnique, 112
École Supérieur de Physique, 76
Ecology, 184–185
Economic and Social Research Council, 149
Edinburgh Association for the University Education of Women, 223
Edinburgh Dental Hospital and School, 178
Edinburgh Geological Society, 324
Edinburgh Review, 66
Edinburgh School of Medicine for Women, 143, 153, 223
Edinburgh Soroptimists, 98
Education, xvii, 25, 34, 40, 46, 125–126, 138–139, 144–146, 191, 264
  botany, 224–225

childhood education, 214–215
  mathematics, 262
  nautical, 307–308
  rural life, 84–85
  South Africa, 96–97
Education through the Imagination (McMillan), 191
Education-Industry Committee, 249
The Edwardians (Sackville-West), 276
Edwards, Amelia Ann Blandford, 92
EEF. *See* Egypt Exploration Fund
Eelworms, 116
"The Effect of Boric Acid and Borax on the Broad Bean and Certain Other Plants" (Warington), 322
The Effects of Irradiation on the Skeleton (Vaughan), 319
The Ego and Mechanisms of Defence (Freud), 104
Egypt Exploration Fund (EEF), 244
Egyptian Research Account, 244
Egyptian Temples (Murray), 219
Egyptology, 87, 92, 218–219, 244
Ehrlich, Aline née Buchbinder, 92–93
Eildon Hills, Roxburghshire, 192
"Die Ekamangan" (Noddack, Noddack, and Berg), 230
The Electric Arc (Ayrton), 13
The Electrical Age for Women, 128
Electrical Association for Women (EAW), 127–128
Electrical engineering, 13, 127–129, 166–167
Electrical Handbook for Women (Haslett), 128
The Electrician, 13
Elements, 141, 230, 240
  actinium, 175, 243
  polonium, 76, 77, 155
  radium, 75–78, 113
  uranium, 208, 324
  See also Radiation
Elements of Agriculture (Fream and Ormerod), 234
Elements of Geometry (Euclid), 292
Elephas cypriotes, 24
Eliot, George, 12
Elizabeth Garrett Anderson Hospital, 21, 168, 194, 283, 299, 311
Elles, Gertrude L., 287
Elliott Brothers, 166–167
Elliott-Lynn, William, 240
Ellis, Havelock, 193
Elsie Inglis Memorial Maternity Hospital, 144
Elsie Widdowson Laboratory, 327
Elton, Charles, 288
Elwes, Simon, 38
Empire Marketing Board Research Grants Committee, 210
Employment and Unemployment (Jahoda), 147

Emperor Joseph II, 199
Encyclopaedia Britannica, 67
Endell Street (Covent Garden) Hospital, 294
The Endemic Flora of Tasmania (Stones), 302
Engineering, 317
  aeronautical engineering, 248–249, 288
  civil engineering, 47, 61, 98
  electrical engineering, 13, 127–129, 166–167
Engineering Council, 249
Engineering Our Future, 75
English Speaking Ophthalmic Congress, 195
An Englishwoman in America (Bird), 33
Englishwoman's Domestic Magazine, 26
Entomologist, 99
Entomology, 35, 58–60, 64, 179–181, 210–211, 265–267
  applied, 233–235
  lepidoptery, 99–100
  medical entomology, 271
Entomology in Sport, and Entomology in Earnest (Ward), 321
Environment, Department of, 75, 294
Enzymes, 62–64, 297, 328–329
Epidemiology, 213–214, 297–300
Epidermal growth factor (EGF), 176
Epilepsy, 271
Epping Forest and Essex Naturalists' Field Club, 95
Equal Opportunities Commission, 248
Equity in the Classroom (Murphy and Gipps), 125
Eragrostis curvula, E. lehmannia, 333
Erebus (ship), 100
Ergonomic principles, 284
Erinnerungen aus den Widerstand 1935–1945 (Schütte-Lihotsky), 285
Eschericia coli, 297
An Essay on Combustion (Fulhame), 105
Essential Electricity, a User's Guide (Haslett), 128
The Essentials of Chiropody for Students (Dalton), 82
Essentials of Family Planning (Barnes), 21
Esslemont, Mary, 106
Ethel Williams Hall, 331
Eugenics Society, 193, 251
Euphorbia robbiae, 263
European Commission, 116
European Movement, 116
European Parliament, 116
European Seismological Foundation, 173
European Society of Arthrology, 217
Eva Crane Library, 74
Even More for Your Garden (Sackville-West), 276
Everett, Alice, 270
Everyday Doings of Insects (Cheesman), 59
"The Evolution of Monocotyledons" (Sargant), 279
"Exhibits from the Caird Insect House," 57

Experimental Eye Research, 316
Experimental Flight Test Department (Hawker Aircraft), 248
Expert Committee on Trachoma, 195
Exploration, 32–32, 58–60, 69, 89, 99, 100, 179–181
Eyles, Joan Mary née Biggs, 93
Eyles Library, 93
Eyles, Victor, 93
Eymers, Johanna Geertruid (Truus), 93–94

Fabaceae, 172
Fabian Society, 191
Fabricus, Johann, 35
FAI. *See* Fédération Aeronautique Internationale
The Fairy Godmothers, and Other Tales (Gatty), 111
Fall-Out, 246
Family planning, 21, 44–45, 67–69, 84–85, 193, 289, 303–305
Family Planning Association, 85, 193, 330
Fantham, H. B., 250, 251
Faraday, Michael, 199
Farewell, Mary, 330
Farewell, Tom, 149
Farne Islands, Northumberland, 132
The Farne Islands: Their History and Wildlife (Hickling), 132
Farquharson, Marian Sarah Ogilvie née Ridley, 95
Farr, William, 226, 227
Farrer, Margaret Irene, 95–96
Fat synthesis, 190
Fawcett, Henry, 96
Fawcett, Millicent (née Garrett), 96
Fawcett, Philippa, 96–97
FBA. *See* Freshwater Biological Association
Fédération Aeronautique Internationale (FAI), 325
Federation of Medical Women, 283, 331
Federation of University Women, 40, 279, 287
Fell, Honor Bridget, 97–98
Female genital mutilation, 102
"Female Predominant Sex Ratios and Physiological Differentiation in Arctic Willows" (Balfour), 16
Ferenczi, Sando, 161
Fergusson, Mary (Molly) Isolen, 98
Ferme Générale, 167
Fermi, Enrico, 208
Ferns, 10, 95, 277
The Ferry House, Windermere, 105, 151, 160, 180, 242
Fertility—A Guide to Natural Family Planning (Clubb and Knight), 68
Fertility—Fertility Awareness and Natural Planning (Clubb and Knight), 68

Fertility File, 68
Field, Joanna. *See* Milner, Marion
Figures of Eight (Cockburn), 69
Findlay, W. P. K., 254
Fine Arts Gallery (Sydney), 268
Fink, Sidney, 289
Finniston Committee of Enquiry, 75
The First Book of Geometry (Young and Young), 341
First Congress of Polish Science, 123
First International Congress of Ecology, 184
Fish biology. *See* Ichthyology
Fisher, Ronald A., 186, 311
Fisheries Branch, Dublin, 105
Fleas, 64, 266
Fleas, Flukes, and Cuckoos (Clay and Rothschild), 64, 266
Fletcher, Frank Morley, 290
Fletcher, Walter, 97
Fleure, H. J., 83, 224
Flint, Elizabeth Alice, 98–99
Flora of County Carlow (Booth), 41
Flora of Essex (Jermyn), 326
Flora of Glamorgan, 315
Flora of Jersey (Le Sueur), 169
"Flora of Lake Lancashire" (Hodgson), 137
The Flora of Lincolnshire (Gibbons), 112
Flora of Monmouthshire (Wade), 326
Flora of Moray, Nairn, and East Inverness (Stewart), 301
Flora of New South Wales, 320
Flora of New Zealand, 99
Flora of Warwickshire, 54, 86
Flora of West Sutherland, 325
Flora of Wiltshire (Grose), 326
Floral Morphology (Saunders), 281
Flower Hunter in Queensland and New Zealand (Rowan), 268
Flowering Time, Climate, and Genotype (Aitkin), 6
Flowers of Fire (Clerke), 67
Flowers of the Brazilian Forests (Mee), 206
Flowers of the Field (Johns), 150
Fly High, Run Free (Ratcliffe), 258
Folklore Society, 219
Folly Farm, 150
Food Investigation Board, 222
"The Food of *Calanus finmarchicus* during 1923" (Marshall), 201
Fordham, Michael, 149
Forestry, 16–17
Forestry Commission, 258
Forster, John, 35
Fossil Fauna of the Wady el-Mughara Caves (Bate), 24
Fossils, 7–8, 24, 70–71, 72, 79, 115, 120, 277
Fountaine, Margaret Elizabeth, 99–100
Fourier analyses, 135

Fowler, Alfred, 66, 333
Franco-Prussian War, 227
Frankfurt kitchen, 284
Franklin, John, 100
Franklin, Lady Jane née Griffin, 100
Franklin, Rosalind Elsie, 100–101
Fraser, Roslin Margaret Ferguson, 101–102
Frauenklinik (Vienna), 283
Fraunhofer lines, 140
Frazer, E. S., 194
Fream, William, 234
"Free Paths of Slow Electrons in Mercury and
    Cadmium" (Sponer), 293
Freeman, Joan, 102–103
Freeman, Ralph, 47
French, Evangeline, 53
French, Francesca, 53
French Academy of Sciences. *See* Académie des
    Sciences
French Revolution, 168
*Freshwater Algae: Their Microscopic World
    Explored* (Canter-Lund and Lund), 55
Freshwater Biological Association (FBA), 54–55,
    141, 151, 160, 180, 184, 185, 242
Freshwater biology, 92, 104–105, 141–142, 157,
    184, 241–242, 272, 308–310. *See also* Marine
    biology
Fretter, Vera, 103–104, 172
Freud and the Dilemmas of Psychology (Jahoda),
    147
Freud, Anna, 104, 228, 229
Freud, Sigmund, 104, 161
Friedeman, Ulrich, 49
Friends Ambulance Unit, 261
Friends of Ludhiana, 45
Friends of the Royal Botanical Gardens, 134
Friends of Vellore, 286
The Fringe of the Sea (Bennett), 29
Frisch, Otto, 208
Fritsch, F., 55
Froebel Educational Institute, 196
"From Data to Knowledge—Use of the
    Cambridge Structural Database for
    Studying Molecular Interactions"
    (Kennard), 158
From Marriage to Child Care (Yoshioka), 340
*From War Babies to Grandmothers: Forty-Eight
    Years in Psychoanalysis* (Noach), 229
Frost, Winifred Evelyn, 46, 104–105, 160
Frugality (savings) banks, 321
Fryer, John, 6
Fuchs Transarctic expedition, 57
Fuchsias, 22–23
Fulham Military Hospital, 194
Fulhame, Elizabeth, 105
Fulton Clinic and Memorial Garden, 106
Fulton, Margaret Barr, 105–106

A Functional Anatomy of Invertebrates (Fretter),
    103
"The Functional Morphology of the
    Cephalopod Digestive System" (Bidder), 30
"Fundamental Principles for the Illumination of
    the Picture Gallery Together with Their
    Application to the Illumination of the
    Museum at The Hague" (Eymers), 94
Fungi. *See* Mycology
Fungi—An Introduction (Hawker), 129
Fungi: Ascomycetes, Ustilaginales, Uredinales
    (Gwynne-Vaughan), 121
Fur, Fin, and Feather Group, 174
Furness, Vera I., 107–108

Gale, Ernest, 297
Gallium, 240
Gambert, Earnest, 39
Game Conservancy, 289
Gammarus chevreuxi, 286–287
"Gamow-Teller Unchangeable Interaction Type
    on ß Decay of He$_6$" (Yuasa), 342
Gandhi, Mahatma, 286
The Garden (Sackville-West), 276
Gardening in East Africa (Adamson), 4
Gardner, Richard, 186
Garrett Anderson, Elizabeth née Garrett,
    109–110, 283
Garrett Anderson, Louise, 110
Garrod, Archibald, 110
Garrod, Dorothy Annie Elizabeth, 24, 110–111
Garstang, Walter, 171
Gas Warfare Section, 190
GASAT. *See* International Gender and Science
    and Technology Association
Gastropoda, 181
Gates, Ruggles, 304
Gatty, Margaret née Scott, 111–112, 138
Gauss, Carl Friedrich, 112
GCHQ. *See* Government Communications
    Headquarters
Genera of Shells (Lamarck), 10
General Medical Council (GMC), 65, 168
General Nursing Council, 102
*Genetic Variants and Strains of the Laboratory
    Mouse* (ed. Green), 186
Genetica, 307
Genetical Research Cambridge, 186
Genetical Society, 186, 281
Genetics, 83, 272, 278, 311
    botany, 22–23, 281
    cytogenetics, 36–37, 40, 339
    multifactor hypothesis, 307
    mutagenic effects, 10–12, 63
    recessive genes, 286–287
    sheep breeding, 310–311
    X-chromosome inactivation, 185–187

Genetics Institute, 40
The Genus Rosa (Willmott), 332
Geographical Aspects of Balkan Problems
    (Newbigin), 224
Geography, 32–33, 53, 69, 130, 223–224, 287–288,
    292
Geological Commission (Poland), 123
Geological Magazine, 24, 130, 136, 257, 287
Geological Map of 1815 (Smith), 93
Geological Museum, 93
Geological Society of Great Britain, 24, 93, 130,
    288
Geological Society of Australia, 133
Geological Society of Glasgow, 79
Geological Society of London, 79, 115, 133, 181,
    323, 324
    officers, 324
Geological Survey of Great Britain, 92, 120
Geological Survey of Scotland, 162
Geologist, 136
Geologists' Association, 324
Geology, 221, 257
    collections, 79, 92–93, 151–152, 333
    fossils, 24, 115–116
    iron ores, 289–290
    Lewisian gneisses, 323
    paleontology, 7–8, 24, 119, 132–133, 181, 217,
        262
    petrography, 151–152
    petrology, 123–124, 130, 132–133, 136–137,
        192–193, 289–290
    quaternary geology, 123–124
    South Africa, 332–333
The Geology of the Hunter Valley (Nashar), 221
George, T. Neville, 79
Geriatrics, 65
Germain, Sophie, 112
German Colloid Society, 250
"The Germination of *Goodyera repens* (L.) R.Br. in
    Fungal Extract" (Downie), 87
Ghana, 184, 330
Ghana Academy of Sciences, 136
Gibberellic acid (GA), 191
Gibbons, E. Joan, 112–113
Gibbons, Thomas, 112
Gibraltar, 110
Gill, David, 66
Gilmour, D. G., 15
Girl Guide Association, 113
Girl Technician Engineer Award, 128
Girls' Public Day School Trust (GPDST), 212,
    218
Gladstone, Mary, 72
Gladstones, J. S., 172
Glasgow Royal Asylum, 264
Glasgow Royal Hospital, 106
Glasgow Royal Infirmary, 143

Glasgow University Medical School, 190
Glaxo Industries, 313
Gleditsch, Ellen, 77, 113–114, 175
Gliding Commission, 325
Gloor, Celie, 180
Glossina palpalis, 264
Glycogen, 222
The Gobi Desert (Cable, French, and French), 53
Goddard, Russell, 132
Godwin, Harry, 70, 242
Goethe, Johann Wolfgang von, 8–9
Gold Coast Medical Report, 330
Goldsmiths' Company, 72
Gombrich, Ernst, 228
Goodchild, J. G., 181
Goodenough Committee, 319
Goodenough, William, 69
Gordon, Isabella, 114–115
Gordon, John, 115
Gordon, Maria Matlida née Ogilvie, 115–116
Gore, J. E., 66
Gosling, Raymond, 101
Goss, Olga May, 115–116
Goulandris, Angelos, 116–117
Goulandris Natural History Museum, 116
Goulandris, Niki née Kephalia, 116–117
Goulimis, C., 116
Gourlay, David, 318
Government Communications Headquarters
    (GCHQ), 71, 131
Gowing, Margaret Mary née Elliott, 117
Graded Bundles and Super Manifolds (Choquet-
    Bruhat), 62
Graham, Alaistair, 103
Graham, C. R., 334
The Graminae (Arber), 8
Grassé, Pierre P., 30
Great Barrier Reef, 28–29, 133, 198, 201–202
The Great Barrier Reef (Bennett), 29
Great Barrier Reef Committee, 29, 133
The Great Little Insect (Cheesman), 59
Greece, 116, 263
Green Man, 22, 23
The Green Man (Basford), 23
Green, Margaret, 186
Green Medicine (Leyel), 177
Greene, Raymond, 82
Greenford Laboratory, 313
Greenland, 142
Greenwich Observatory, 67
Gregory, J. W., 79
Greig, Dorothy Margaret née Hannah, 118–119
Greirson, Mary Anderson, 119
Grey Seals and the Farne Islands (Hickling), 132
Grieve, M., 177
Grigg, James, 117
Gromova, Vera Issacovna, 119

Grose, J. D., 326
Gross, F., 202
Gross, Jack, 247
Group Theory and Its Applications (Xie), 337
Groupe d'Etudes Carcinologiques, 115
Growing Old in the Twentieth Century (Jefferys), 149
"Growth Stages in Some Jurassic Ammonites" (Currie), 79
A Guide to the Methods of Insect Life (Ormerod), 233
A Guide to the Wild Flowers (Lounsberry), 268
Guild of Food Writers, 239
Guinness, 75
The Guinness Book of Weather Facts and Feats (Holford), 139
Gunther, Alfred, 159
Guppy, Eileen M., 119–120
Gurney, Robert, 171
Guyana, 184
Guy's Hospital, 22, 89
Gwynne-Vaughan, Helen Charlotte Isabella née Fraser, 120–121
Gye, William, 195
Gynecological Histology (Barnes), 21
Gynecology, 20–22, 36, 82, 282–283, 329

The Hague, 184
Hahn, Otto, 207–208
Halicka, Antonina née Jaroszewicz, 123–124
Hallam Moors, Sheffield, 70
Halley's comet, 175
Hamburger, Viktor, 176
Hammersmith Hospital, 19, 83, 318
Hampstead Child Therapy Course and Clinic, 104
Hampstead Wartime Nurseries, 104
Hancock, Annie, 286
Hancock, Keith, 117
Hancock Museum, 35, 132
Handbook of British Flora (Bentham and Hooker), 85
Handbook of British Seaweeds (Newton), 224
Hanford nuclear complex, 300
Hanson, Emmeline Jean, 124–125
Hardcastle, J. A., 37
Harding, J. P., 202
Harding, Jan née Ansell, 125–126
Hardy, G. H., 56
Hargreaves, E. L., 117
Harington, Charles, 247
Harker, Margaret Florence, 126–127
Harker Photography Centre, 127
Harker-Kasper equations, 189
Harland, S. C., 23
Harrison, Heslop, 35
Harrods, 239

Harvard College Observatory, 333
Harvard, Robert, 68
Harvey, R. D., 111
Harvey, W. H., 17
Haslemere and Farnham Art Society, 166
Haslett, Caroline, 127–129
Haughley Experiment, 16
Hauraki Gulf, 57
Hawker Aircraft, 248
Hawker, Lilian E., 129
Headmistress's Association, 25
Health, Department of, 65
Health and Social Security, Department of (DHSS), 168
Health Organization Committee (League of Nations), 166
Health Service, U. S., 183
Heathfield Maternity Home, 335
The Heavens and Their Story (Russell), 270
Heldrich, Theodor von, 263
Helga (ship), 204
Hellenic Radio, 116
Helminths, 259
Hematology, 277–278, 318
Henderson, David, 106, 264
Henderson, John, 72
Henry Peach Robinson (Harker), 127
Her Majesty's Factory, Liverpool, 175
Herbal Delights (Leyel), 177
Herbalism, 177
Herbals: Their Origin and Evolution—A Chapter in the History of Botany, 1470–1670 (Arber), 8
Herbert, Aubrey, 89
Herbert, Sidney, 225
Heron Island Marine Biological Station, 133
Herschel, Caroline Lucretia, 129–130, 292
Herschel, William, 129–130
The Herschels and Modern Astronomy (Clerke), 66
Heslop, Mary Kingdon, 130
Hesse, Fanny Angelina (Lina) née Eilshemius, 130–131
Hesse, Walther, 130
Hewitt, David, 300
Heyerdahl, Thor, 41
Heywood, Joan, 131
Hickling, Albert, 132
Hickling, Grace née Watt, 131–132
Hickson, S. J., 34
High Albania (Durham), 89
High Voltage Laboratory (MIT), 103
Higher Algebra (Bari), 20
Higher Institute of Health (Rome), 177
Hill, Dorothy, 132–133
Hindle, Edward, 19
Hindmarsh, Mary Maclean, 133–134
Hippopotamus minutus, 24
Hirohito, Emperor, 115

"The Hissing of the Electrical Arc" (Ayrton), 13
Historians, 17–18, 66–67, 92–93, 117–118,
    126–127
    mathematics, 148, 268–269
The History of British Vegetation (Pennington),
    242
History of Geology (Zittel), 115
History of Nursing Society, 17
Hjorts, Johan, 40
Ho Leung Ho Lee Foundation, 337
Hobbs, A. S., 229
Hodgkin, Dorothy Mary née Crowfoot, 134–136,
    253, 319
Hodgkin, Luke, 135
Hodgkin, Thomas Lionel, 135
Hodgson, Elizabeth, 136–137
Hodgson, James 136
Hofmann, Elise, 137
Hokkaido Institute, 304
Holden, Edith Blackwell, 137–138
Holford, Garth, 138
Holford, Ingrid née Bianchi, 138–139
Holiday, Henry, 244
Holst, Clara, 139–140
Holst, Fredrik, 139
Home and Garden (Jekyll), 150
Home economics, 26–27, 31, 85, 238–239
The Home Life of Marsh Birds (Turner), 310
Home Office, 75, 147, 228
Home Security, Department of (Canberra), 28
Homoeothrix kannae, 157
Honey: A Comprehensive Survey (Crane), 74
Hooker, Joseph, 231–232, 233
Hopkins, Frederick Gowland, 179, 222, 297
Hormones, 151, 166, 247–248
Horse Fair (Bonheur), 39
Horticulture, 6–7, 43, 142, 150–151, 223, 243, 332
    journalists, 275–276
Hospices, 280–281
Hospital for Invalid Gentlewomen, 225
Hospital for Sick Children, 65
House of Lords Select Committee for Science
    and Technology, 248
The House Sparrow: The Avian Rat (Tegetmeier),
    234
Hovea, 172
"How Can We Make Housework Easier by
    Building Appropriate Apartments?"
    (Schütte-Lihotsky), 285
Howe, Graham, 149
Hoyle, Fred, 51
Huang, K., 337
Huggins, Lady Margaret Lindsay née Murray,
    140–141
Huggins, William, 140
Hughes, Victoria, 83
Human Anatomy, Department of (Oxford), 316

Human Embryology Bill, 21
The Human Problem in Schools (Milner), 212
Humphrey, Arthur, 212
Humphrey, Edith Ellen, 141
Humphrey, John, 42
Humphries, Carmel Frances, 141–142
Hungarian Psycho-Analytical Society, 161
"Hunger and Work in a Savage Tribe: A
    Functional Study of Nutrition among the
    Southern Bantu" (Richards), 261
Hunt, William, 233
Hunter, Donald, 318
Hunterian Museum, 79
Hunterian Society, 21
Hutchison, Isobel Wylie, 142
Huxley, Hugh Esmoor, 124
Huxley, Julian, 3, 251
Huxley, T. H., 257
Hydrobiologie, 309
Hydrodynamics and Vector Field Theory (Greig and
    Wise), 118
Hydrogenase, 297
Hydroids, 40
Hydrology, 308–309
Hypoderma bovis, 234

IBRA. *See* International Bee Research
    Association
ICAN. *See* International Commission for Air
    Navigation
ICBP. *See* International Council for Bird
    Preservation
ICE. *See* Institution of Civil Engineers
Ichthyology, 45–46, 72–73, 160, 183–185, 309
Icthyosaurus, 7
"The Identification of 3:3':5-L-Triiodothyronine
    in Human Plasma" (Pitt-Rivers and Gross),
    247
IEE. *See* Institution of Electrical Engineers
IGCP. *See* International Geological Correlation
    Programme
IKEA, 285
Illustrations of the British Flora (Cadbury), 54
Immune system, 300
Immunology, 264, 311–312
Immunology of the Lung (Turner-Warwick), 312
Imperial Cancer Research Laboratories, 195,
    246
Imperial War Museum, 118
Importation of Plumage (Prohibition) Act, 174
In Search of the Flowers of the Amazon Forests
    (Mee), 206
*Independence and Deterrence: Britain and Atomic
    Energy 1945–1952* (Gowing and Arnold),
    117
Independent Labour Party, 191
Indexing, 7

India, 45, 218–219, 226, 227, 283, 285–286
  biochemists, 290–291
Indian Civil Service, 46
Indian Institute of Science, 291
Indium, 240
Industrial management, 107–108
Infectious Disease Unit (Virchow Hospital), 49
"Influence of Crustal Evolution in Ore
  Deposition" (Watson), 323
Influenza vaccine, 209
Inglis, Elsie Maud, 143–144
Ingold, C. T., 54
Inoculation, 213–214
Inorganic Plant Poisons and Stimulants
  (Brenchley), 43
Institute Curie, 175
Institute for Geochemical Research, 230
Institute for the History of Science and
  Technology, 269
Institute of Almoners, 280
Institute of Animal Genetics, 11, 186
Institute of Applied Microbiology, 212
Institute of Biology, 34, 46, 66, 160, 229
Institute of Brewing, 190–191
Institute of Chartered Foresters, 17
Institute of Chemistry, 165, 166, 175
Institute of Chemistry of Ireland, 245
Institute of Diseases of the Chest, 311
Institute of Ethnography, 268–269
Institute of Fisheries Management, 46
Institute of Highway Engineers, 258
Institute of Hydrobiology, 157, 309
Institute of Inventors, 225
Institute of Limnology, 272
Institute of Pathology (Bernhard Baron
  Institute), 271
Institute of Physical and Chemical Research
  (RIKEN), 164
Institute of Physical Chemistry, 230
Institute of Physics, 102, 167
Institute of Psychoanalysis, 146
Institute of Science (Mumbai), 291
Institute of Seed Pathology for Developing
  Countries, 229
Institute of Social Medicine, 300
Institution of Civil Engineers (ICE), 47, 61
Institution of Electrical Engineers (IEE), 12, 127,
  128, 166–167
Institutions de physique (du Châtelet-Lomont), 88
Insulin, 136, 166
Insurance Committee, 144
Insurance Officers' Association for England and
  Wales, 144
Integral Functions (Cartwright), 56
Intellectual Growth in Young Children (Isaacs), 145
Intellectual Observer, 321
International African Institute, 261

International Association for Dental Research,
  210
International Association for the Prevention of
  Blindness, 246
International Association of Academies, 37
International Association of Cyanophyte
  Research, 157
International Athletics Federation, 241
International Bee Research Association (IBRA),
  74
International Biology Programme, 184, 309
International Commission for Air Navigation
  (ICAN), 241
International Commission on Radiological
  Protection, 319
International Commission on the History of
  Geological Sciences, 124
International Committee for Eye Research, 316
International Conference on Atomic Masses and
  Fundamental Constants, 103
International Conference on Semiconductor
  Physics, 337
International Congress on Hygiene and
  Demography, 227
International Congress of Statistics, 226
International Council for Bird Preservation
  (ICBP), 19
International Electrical Congress, 13
International Epidemiological Association, 301
International Federation of Beekeepers'
  Associations, 74
International Federation of University Women,
  114
International Gender and Science and
  Technology Association (GASAT), 125
International Geological Correlation Programme
  (IGCP), 324
International History of Nursing Journal, 17
International Journal of Nursing Studies, 335
International Limnological Association, 142
International Lunar Committee, 37
International Museal Union, 124
International Phonetic Association, 139
International Phycological Congress, 57
International Phycological Society, 237–238
International Polytechnic Exhibition (Moscow),
  233
International Safety Emigration Society, 282
International Seismological Centre, 173
International Seismological Summary (ISS), 173
International Society for Eye Research, 246, 316
International Society of Blood Transfusion, 278
International Society of Chemical Ecology, 267
International Society of Leather Trades'
  Chemists, 179
International Tables for X-ray-Crystallography
  (Lonsdale, MacGillavry), 182, 189

International Union for the Protection of Nature, 266

International Union of Crystallography (IUC), 136, 182

International Union of Geodesy and Geophysics, 173

International Vittorio Tonolli Foundation for Cardiological Culture, 309

International Wildfowl Research Bureau, 19

International Wool Conference, 118

Interpreting the Weather (Holford), 139

An Introduction to Botany, in a Series of Familiar Letters (Wakefield), 321

Introduction to Geology (Watson and Read), 323

An Introduction to Physical Geography (Newbigin), 224

Introduction to Psychology (Isaacs), 145

An Introduction to the Natural History and Classification of Insects in a Series of Letters (Wakefield), 321

An Introduction to the Study of Biology (Kirkaldy and Drummond), 161

Introductory Notes on Lying-in Institutions (Nightingale and Sutherland), 227

Inventors, 225

Iodine, 175

Iodoproteins, 247

Iraq, 27, 28

Ireland, 16–17, 203, 204

Iris spuria, 113

Irish Central Veterinary Association, 80

Irish College of Physicians, 153

Irish Naturalist, 204

Irish Society for the Protection of Birds (ISPB), 204

Irish Wildbird Conservancy, 204

Irvine, Jean Kennedy, 144

Is Peace Possible? (Lonsdale), 183

Isaacs, Susan Sutherland née Fairhurst, 145–146, 229

Isobel Wylie Hutchison collection, 142

Isochrysis galbana, 237

Isotopes, 208

ISPB. *See* Irish Society for the Protection of Birds

ISS. *See* International Seismological Summary

Istituzoni analitiche ad uso della gioventi italiana (Agnesi), 5

Italian Association for Oceanography and Limnology, 309

Italian Commission for the Conservation of Nature and Natural Resources, 309

Itard, Jean, 214

Ito, S., 266

IUC. *See* International Union of Crystallography

Jahoda, Marie, 147–148

Jane Eyre (Brontë), 25

Janovskaja, Sof'ja Aleksandrovna née Neimark, 148

Japan, 115, 164, 240, 303, 330, 341–342

Jardin Royal des Herbes Médicinales, 32

Jason (plane), 154

Jauregg, Wagner, 104

Jaworski, G. H. M., 55

Jay, E., 229

Jefferys, James, 148

Jefferys, Margot née Davies, 148–149

Jeffrey, Carol, 149–150

Jekyll, Gertrude, 150–151, 332

Jelley, John, 103

Jenkin, B. M., 151, 242

Jenkin, Penelope M., 151

Jérémine, Elisabeth née Tschernaieff, 151–152

Jermyn, S. T., 326

Jersey, 169–170

Jewish women, 48–50, 206–209, 329

Jex-Blake, Sophia, 110, 143, 152–153

Jockey Club of Kenya, 201

Jodrell Laboratory, 279

John Innes Institute, 224

John Radcliffe Hospital, 68

Johns, C. A., 150

Johnson, Amy, 153–154

Johnstone, John, 105

Joliot, Frédéric, 155–156

Joliot-Curie, F., 342

Joliot-Curie, Irène née Curie, 76, 114, 154–156

Jones, Ernest, 161

Jones, Mabel, 42

Jones, Robert Armstrong, 42

Jones, William Neilson, 258

Joshi Koto Shihan Gakko Kenkyuka, 339, 342

Joshua, Joan Olive, 156, 313

A Journal from Japan: A Daily Record of Life as Seen by a Scientist (Stopes), 304

Journal of Animal Ecology, 141

Journal of Apicultural Research, 74

Journal of Botany, 137

Journal of Ecology, 70

Journal of Experimental Biology, 1

Journal of General Microbiology, 63

Journal of Orthopaedic Research, 217

Journal of Physiology, 31

Journal of the Fuchsia Society, 23

Journal of the Institute of Brewing, 191

Journal of the Marine Biological Association, 151, 171, 237, 294

Journal of the Textile Institute, 118

Journal of the Women's Engineering Society, 167

Journey with a Purpose (Cable, French, and French), 53

Joyce Vickery Fund, 320

Jubilee Magazine, 279

Jung, C. G., 149
Jungfraujoch research station, 155
"Jurassic and Eocene Echinoidea from
    Somaliland" (Currie), 79
Juvenile delinquents, 228

Kaiserswerth Institute for Deaconesses, 225
Kaiser-Wilhelm Institut für Biologie, 11
Kaiser-Wilhelm Institut für Chemie, 207
Kann, Elizabeth, 157
Kappe, Yvonne, 289
Karle, Jerome, 189
Kategorienlehre (Lask), 81
Keebel, F., 258
Kelly, Alison, 125
Kemp, C. E., 203
Kennard, Olga née Weisz, 157–159, 248
Kennedy Institute of Rheumatology, 216
Kent, D. H., 326
Kenya, 3–4, 151, 184, 200–201
Kerr, W. P., 264
Keruchin C, 158, 164
Key Centre for Science and Mathematics
    Education, 125
Kikuyu people, 170
Kildonan Aerodrome, 241
Kilpatrick, William, 215
King George III, 129
King's College Hospital, 227, 330
Kingsley, Charles, 159
Kingsley, Mary Henrietta, 159–160
Kipling, Charlotte née Harrison, 160
Kirkaldy, Jane Willis, 134, 160–161
"Kitchen Front," 239
Klarwill, Victor von, 4
Klein, Felix, 341
Klein, Melanie née Reizes, 161–162
Klinefelter's syndrome, 186
Klug, Aaron, 101
Klumpke, Anna, 39
Klumpke's paralysis, 84
Kneale, George, 300
Knight, B. C. J. G., 63
Knight, Jane, 68
Knight, Mary, 237
Knights Farm, 71–72
Knox, Elizabeth Mary née Henderson, 162
Koch, Robert, 130
Kola Peninsula, 152
Kommunist, 148
Kon-tiki, 41
Kovalevskaya, Sonya (Sofya) Vasilyevna née
    Korvin-Krukovsky, 162–164
Kovalevski, Vladimir, 163
Kuroda, Chika, 164
Kwashiorkor, 329–330
"Kwashiorkor" (Williams), 330

La Place, Marquis de, 292
Labadists, 211
Laboratoire Centrale des Services Chimiques de
    L'Etat, 101
Laboratoire de Chimie Nucléaire du Collège de
    France, 342
Laboratory Animals Science Association, 314
Laboratory for General and Inorganic
    Chemistry, 189
Laboratory technicians, 130–131
Laby, Jean, 165
Laby, Thomas Howell, 165
Lady Chichester Hospital for the Treatment of
    Early Nervous Disorders, 42–43
Lady computers, 270
Lady Margaret Hall, 21, 27, 50, 219
Lagrange, Joseph-Louis, 112
Lake District, 105, 151, 242
The Lake District, A Landscape History (Pearsall
    and Pennington), 242
Lake Malawi, 309
Lake Tanganyika, 309, 324
Lakeland Biology, 263
Lalande, Jopseh Jérôme, 174
Lambertini, Prospero, 23
Lamont Geological Observatory, 174
The Lancet, 300, 330
The Land (Sackville-West), 276
Land Army, 16
*Land, Labour, and Diet in Northern Rhodesia: An
    Economic Study of the Bemba Tribe* (Richards),
    261
Land management, 16–17
*Land of Water: Explorations in the Natural History
    of Guyana, South America* (McConnell),
    184
Landbrukshoiskole (Norway), 295
Landcare Research NZ Ltd., 58
Lane, George, 266
Lang, W. H., 196
Langevin, Paul, 78
Lathbury, Kathleen née Culhane, 165–166
Latimeria chalumnae, 73
Laverick, Elizabeth, 166–167
Lavoisier, Antoine, 167–168
Lavoisier, Marie Anne, 167–168
Lawrence, T. E., 27
Lawrie, Jean Eileen née Grant, 168–169
Lawson, Thomas, 263
Lazarsfeld, Paul, 147
LCC. *See* London County Council
Le Sueur, Frances Adams née Ross, 169–170
Le Tonnelier de Breteuil, Louis-Nicholas, 88
Lead paint, 65
League of Nations, 96, 115, 166
League of Nations Union, 261
Leakey, Louis S. B., 24, 170

Leakey, Mary Douglas née Nicol, 170–172
Learning disabilities, 102, 245
Leather manufacture, 178–179
Lebanon, 111
Lebour, Marie Victoire, 171–172, 224–225, 266
Lecturers, 15–16, 126–127
Lee, Alma Theodora née Melvaine, 172
Lefroy, Grace, 59
Lefroy, Maxwell, 59
Legendre, Adrien-Marie, 112
Legion of Honour, 39, 84, 156
Lehmann, Inge, 172–174
Lemon, Margaretta Louisa née Smith, 174
"Lens Metabolism in Relation to Cataract," 246
Lepaute, Nicole-Reine Etable de al Brière, 174–175
Lepidoptery, 99–100
Les Eyzies, 170
Leslie, May Sibyl, 77, 175–176
Leukemia, 300
Levi-Montalcini, Rita, 176–177
Leyel, Hilda Winifred Ivy née Wauton, 177
Life at Sea: Tudors and Stuarts (Rule), 269
Life by the Sea Shore—An Introduction to Natural History (Newbigin), 223
A Life of One's Own (Milner), 212
Life on Earth, 55
Lilly, Malcolm, 63–64
Limosella, 315
Lincolnshire Naturalist's Trust, 113
Lincolnshire Naturalist's Union, 113
Lindsay and Holland Rural Community Council, 113
Lindsay, Lilian née Murray, 177–178
Lindsay, Robert, 178
"Lineaments in the Continental Lithosphere" (Watson), 324
Linguistics, 81, 139–140
The Linked Ring (Harker), 127
Linnaeus, 35
Linnean Society, 254
  fellows, 6, 30, 43, 95, 99, 113, 115, 119, 121, 206, 251, 257, 258, 265, 279, 281, 315, 324
  officers, 185, 196
Linnean Society of New South Wales, 133, 134, 320
Linum usitatissimum, 307
The Lipins (Maclean and Maclean), 190
Liposomes, 272
"List of Glamorgan Flowering Plants" (Vachell), 315
List of the Vascular Plants of the British Isles (Dandy), 86
Lister Institute, 60, 190, 264, 278, 316
Listeria meningitis, 18

Lithospermum erythrorhizon, 164
Lithuania, 123
Lithuanian Geological Service, 123
Littlewood, J. E., 56
The Littoral Fauna of Great Britain: A Handbook for Collectors (Eales), 91
Liver fluke, 259
Liverpool Chamber of Commerce, 160
The Living Soil (Balfour), 16
Lloyd, Dorothy Jordan, 178–179
Loch Striven, 202
Lockwood Committee for Higher Education, 218
Loewinson-Lessing, F. J., 152
Loligo, 30
London Aeroplane Club, 153, 241
London Association of Foremen, Engineers, and Draughtsmen, 317
London Chemical Society, 190
London Clinic of Psychoanalysis, 146
London Committee of the Scottish Women's Hospitals, 144
London County Council (LCC), 96, 282, 302
London Hospital, 165–166, 194
London Mathematical Society, 56
London Natural History Society, 180
London School Board, 110
London School of Hygiene and Tropical Medicine, 148, 298
London School of Medicine for Women, 36, 110, 152–153, 168, 194, 283
London Zoo, 59, 195
Longfield, Cynthia, 59, 179–181
Longfield, Mountifort, 179
Longstaff, Mary Janes née Donald, 181
Lonsdale, Kathleen née Yardley, 181–183, 296
Looking at Weather (Holford), 139
Loos, Adolf, 284
Lorenz, Konrad, 228
Louis XIV, 88
Louis-Arsène, Frère, 169
Louisiana State Museum, 302
Lounsberry, Alice, 268
Love among the Butterflies: The Travels and Adventures of a Victorian Lady (Fountaine), 99
Love, W. H., 240
Lowe-McConnell, Rosemary Helen née Lowe, 183–185
"The Lower Ludlow Formation and Its Graptolite Fauna" (Shakespear), 287
Lower Paleolithic, 111
Lowe-Vansittart propeller, 317
Lowy, Jack, 124
L-thyroxine, 247–248
Lugeon, Maurice, 152

Lunacy and Mental Deficiency Acts, 29
Lunar Commission, 37
Lunar Tables for Calculating Distances (Taylor), 308
Lund, John, 55
Lupinus, 172
Lutyens, Edwin, 150
Luxembourg Gallery, 39
Lycopodium, 263
Lyon, Mary Frances, 185–187

Macedonia, 192
MacGillavry, Carolina, 189
MacGregor, Jessie, 143
Machina carnis: The Biochemistry of Muscular Contraction in Its Historical Development (Needham), 222
Maclean, Ida née Smedley, 189–190
MacLeod, Anna Macgillivray, 190–191
Macphail, Katherine Stewart, 192
Macquarie Island, 29
MacRobert, Lady Rachael née Workman, 192–193
MacRobert Reply Association, 193
"Madagascar Past and Present" (Clerke), 67
MAFF. *See* Ministry of Agriculture, Fisheries, and Food
The Magic of Herbs (Leyel), 177
Magnetic spectrometer, 103
Mahon, Lady Jane, 321
Malacological Society of London, 91, 103
Malaria, 33
Malaya, 330
Malinowski, Bronislaw, 261
Malleson, Joan Graeme née Billson, 193
Manchart, Major, 240
Manchester Royal Infirmary, 284
Manchester University Museum, 219
Mancuso, Thomas, 300
Mangold, Otto, 11
Manhattan Project, 117
The Manifold and the Eye (Arber), 9
Mann, Ida Caroline (Mrs. Gye), 194–196, 246
Manton, Irene, 196–197, 237
Manton, Sidnie Milana (Mrs. Harding), 34, 196–198
Manual of British Beetles (Stephens), 233
A Manual of Practical Vertebrate Morphology (Brown) (1949), 46
A Manual of Practical Vertebrate Morphology (Manton and Saunders) (1931), 198
Manuring of Grass Land for Hay (Brenchley), 43
Manx Algae (Parke and Knight), 237
Manzolini, Anna née Morandi, 198–199

Marcet, Jane née Haldimand, 199
Marell, Jacob, 210
Maret, R. R., 110
Margaret Mee Amazon Trust, 206
Margaret Ogilvie Reader in Ophthalmology, 316
Marguerite Patten's Century of British Cooking (Patten), 239
Marie Lebour Library, 172
Marie Stopes Clinic, 44
Marie Stopes International, 305
Marine Biological Association (MBA), 31, 91, 103, 171, 294
Marine Biological Station (Millport), 151, 223, 294
Marine biology, 91–92
    algae, 55, 57, 87, 98, 157, 201, 204–205, 237–238, 242
    Australia, 28–29, 133
    cephalopods, 30, 203–204
    conchology, 69, 204, 263
    corals, 115, 133
    crabs (Malacostraca), 115, 171
    diatoms, 151, 201
    ichthyology, 45–46, 72–73, 160, 183–185, 309
    mollusks, 29–31, 103, 171
    oil spills, 293–294
    plankton, 55, 57, 98, 171, 201–202
    seaweeds, 87, 112, 204, 224–225, 237
    See also Biology; Freshwater biology
Marine Laboratory, Plymouth, 30, 104, 172, 197, 202, 237, 266, 294
"Marine Phytoplankton in New Zealand Waters" (Cassie Cooper), 57
"Maritime Canals" (Clerke), 67
Markham, Beryl née Clutterbuck, 200–201
Markham, Mansfield, 200
Marooned in Du-Bu Cove (Cheesman), 59
Marrack, Dr., 165–166
Married Love: A New Contribution to the Solution of Sex Difficulties (Stopes), 304
Marshall, John, 68
Marshall, Sheina Macalister, 201–202
Martin, Charles, 60
Mary, Countess of Rosse née Field, 203
Mary Rose (ship), 269
The Mary Rose: *The Excavation and Raising of Henry VIII's Flagship* (Rule), 269
Mary Taber Schell Memorial Hospital, 285
Marylebone Court of Justices, 115
Mason, Alice, 179
Massachusetts Institute of Technology (MIT), 103, 124
Massee, William, 254
Massy, Annie Letitia, 203–204
Maternal and Child Health (MCH), 330
Mathematical Association, 56

Mathematics, 4–5, 20, 96–97, 112, 162–164, 182, 262, 308, 340–341
  applied, 118–119
  complex functions, 56–57
  computers, 51–52
  historians, 268–269
  mathematical physics, 62
  teachers, 262, 295–296
Mato Grosso, 180, 184
Matthiola incana, 281
Maudsley Hospital, 247
Maupertius, P. L. de, 88
May, Ernst, 285
May, Valerie, 204–205
MBA. *See* Marine Biological Association
McCance, Robert, 261, 327
McConnell, Richard, 184
MCH. *See* Maternal and Child Health
McIntosh, Charles, 229, 254
McMillan, Margaret, 191–192
McMullen, Ann, 128
Mechanics, 268–269
Media, 3, 55, 59–60, 139, 239, 241, 315, 317
Mediaeval Military Architecture in England (Clarke), 9
Medical Aid Foundation for Vietnam, 136
Medical College for Women, Edinburgh, 143
Medical illustrators, 130–131
Medical practitioners. *See* Physicians
Medical Register, 36
Medical Research Council (MRC), 12, 19, 65, 97, 124, 157, 182, 217, 247, 271
  biochemistry research, 222
  Blood Group Unit, 277–278
  Chemical Microbiology Committee, 297
  Dental Disease Committee, 210
  funding, 186, 297, 316
  nutrition, 209, 327
  Radiobiology Unit, 186
  Toxin Committee, 297
  Unit for Research on Bone-Seeking Isotopes, 319
  Unit of Mutagenesis Research, 12
Medical Society of London, 168
Medical sociology, 148–149
Medical Women (Jex-Blake), 153
Medical Women's Federation, 169
Medical Women's International Association, 168
Medicines Bill (1968), 313
Mee, Margaret Ursula née Brown, 205–206
Meiosis, 278
Meitner, Lise, 206–209
Meitnerium, 208
Mellanby, Edward, 327
Mellanby, Helen, 209
Mellanby, Lady May née Tweedy, 209–210

Meloney, Marie, 78
Memorie, 309
Menabrea, General, 52
Mendeleyev, Dmitri, 163
Mendelssohn, Felix, 150
The Menstrual Cycle (Dalton), 82
Merian, Maria Sibylla, 210–211
Il Messaggio nervoso (Levi-Montalcini), 177
"Metabolic Processes in Micro-organisms" (Stephenson and Gale), 297
The Metabolism of Fat (Maclean), 190
Metallurgy, 105, 230
Metamorphosis insectorum Surinamensiam (Merian), 211
Metcalfe, W. S., 328
"The Meteoric Shower of January" (Wilson), 333
Meteorological Office, 138
Meteorology, 138–139, 233, 326
Methyl glucosaminides, 247
Metropolitan Asylums Board, 29
Metropolitan Hospital (New York), 106
Metropolitan Museum of Art, 39
Microalgae: Microscopic Marvels (Cassie Cooper), 57
Microbiology, 211–212, 296–297
Microcycas calocoma, 87
Microlight and Hang Gliding Commission, 325
The Microscope (Ward), 321
Microscope Teachings (Ward), 321
Microscopy, 8, 33, 257, 321–322
Microwave Association, 239
Microwave instruments, 166–167
Middlesex Hospital, 17–18, 109
Midwife and Health Visitor, 96
Midwives, 95–96, 227–228, 334–335
Miers, Henry, 233
Military inventions, 225
Millis, Nancy Fannie, 211–212
Milner, Marion, 212–213
The Mind and the Eye (Arber), 9
Mineralogical Society of Great Britain, 253
Minesweeping equipment, 225
Ministry of Agriculture, 6
Ministry of Agriculture, Fisheries, and Food (MAFF), 289
Ministry of Defence, 118
Ministry of Education (Japan), 340
Ministry of Food, 239
Ministry of Food Supply and Trade (Lithuania), 123
Ministry of Health, 335
Ministry of Higher Education (Poland), 123
Ministry of Housing and Local Government, 302
Ministry of Information, 3, 147
Ministry of Pensions, 287
Ministry of Supply, 219, 222, 316

Minoti, George, 318
"Miss Ormerod" (Woolf), 234
Missionaries, 53, 285–286
MIT. *See* Massachusetts Institute of Technology
A Modern Herbal (Grieve), 177
Molekulspektren I and *II* (Sponer), 293
Mollusks, 103, 171, 181, 203–204
Molteno Institute, 34
The Monocotyledons (Arber), 8
Monograph of British Graptolites (Shakespear and Elles), 287
Montagu, Edward, 213
Montagu, Lady Mary Wortley née Pierpont, 213–214
Montesano, Guiseppe, 215
Montessori, Maria, 214–216
Montessori, Mario, 215–216
The Montessori System Examined (Kilpatrick), 215
Monthly Notices of the Royal Astronomical Society, 2, 333
Moore, Lucy B., 2
Moore, Noel, 254
Moorfields Hospital, 194–195
Mormyrus kingsleyae, 159
Morphology, Classification and Life Habits of the Productoidea (Muir-Wood and Cooper), 217
Morris, William, 150
Morrison, Tony, 206
Morse code, 71
Mortality rates, 226–227
Mosaics, 12
Mother's Clinic for Constructive Birth Control, 304
Mottes, 9
Mt. Albert Research Centre, 57
Mt. Stromlo Observatory, 2
Mount Carmel, 24
Mount Wellington, 100
Mouse News Letter Ltd., 186
Mouse Newsletter, 186
MRC. *See* Medical Research Council
Mrs. Tiggywinkle (Potter), 254
Muir, Isabella Helen Mary, 216–217
Muir-Wood, Helen Marguerite, 217
Muller, H. J., 11
Murray, Alice Rosemary, 217–218
Murray, Flora, 295
Murray, Margaret Alice D., 218–219
Muscle research, 49–50, 124, 222–223
Museum curators, 72–73, 93
Museum of Applied Arts, 285
Museum of Natural Science (Houston, Texas), 206
Museum of the Earth (Poland), 123
Musicians, 129, 130, 231, 333
Mustard gas, 10–12, 13

Mutation Research (Auerbach), 12
Mutual Defence Society, 156
My First Hundred Years (Murray), 219
My Work Is for a King (Brown), 45
Mycology, 54–55, 59, 121, 129, 251, 253–255, 276–277, 278–279, 290
Mycorrhiza, 258
Mycorrhiza (Rayner), 258
Myotragus, 24
Myxomatosis, 266

Naphthalene, 316
Napoleon, 112
Narrow Neck Reef (New Zealand), 57
Nashar, Beryl née Scott, 221
National Academy of Sciences, U. S., 12, 186
National Alliance of Women's Organisations, 102
National Association for the Mentally Handicapped of Ireland, 245
National Association of Women Pharmacists, 42
National Birth Control Council, 85
National Chow Club, 156
National Collection of Type Cultures, 63
National Council for Animal Welfare, 137
National Council for Mental Hygiene, 43
National Council of Nurses, 18
National Council of Scientific Research, Rome, 177
National Council of Women, 287, 331
National Dental Hospital, 178
National Emergency Services Ambulance Drivers, 319
National Environmental Research Council, 240
National Federation of Business and Professional Women, 6
National Federation of Women's Institutes (NFWI), 126
National Geographic Society, 171
National Health Insurance, 144
National Health Service (NHS), 18, 68, 96, 168, 295
National Health Society of London, 36
National Herbarium (Australia), 172, 319
National Herbarium of New South Wales, 205
National Institute for Medical Research (NIMR), 247
National Library of Australia, 268
National Museum, Dublin, 17
National Museum of Antiquities, 244
National Museum of Antiquities (Baghdad), 28
National Museum of Victoria, 71
National Museum of Wales, 83, 315
National Museum, Wellington, 2
National Physics Laboratory, 308
National Portrait Gallery, 118

National Society for Clean Air and Environmental Pollution, 65
National Society for Women's Suffrage, 26
National Trust, 132, 254
National Veterinary Congress, 80
National Veterinary Medical Association, 80, 156
National Water Council, 324
National Women Citizens Association, 115
Natural history, 132, 321
Natural History Museum, 206
Natural History Museum, Dublin, 204
Natural History Museum, Tring branch, 24
A Natural History of Jersey (Le Sueur), 169
Natural History of Man in Britain (Fleur), 83
Natural History Research, Department of, 123
Natural History Society of Northumbria, 132
The Natural Philosophy of Plant Form (Arber), 9
Natural Science Council, 245
Natural sciences, 35, 46, 48
Naturalists, 17, 35, 111–112, 137–138
Nature, 11, 59, 66, 73, 93, 101, 135, 155, 186, 197, 202, 208, 216, 240, 250, 270, 297
Nature Conservancy, 70
Nature Conservancy Council, 17
The Nature Notes of an Edwardian Lady (Holden), 138
Naylor, George, 288
Nazis, 11, 48, 49, 285, 289, 293, 329
Neanderthal humans, 110–111
Nederlandsch Tijdschrift voor Natuurkunde, 189
NED-OPTIFA, 38
"The Need for a National Statistical Council" (Cunliffe), 75
Needham, Dorothy Mary née Moyle, 222–223, 297
Needham, Joseph, 222
Neergaard, P., 59
Neilson, George, 9
Neimy, Khalil, 99
Nemytski, V. V., 20
Neocellon of Wandsworth, 165–166
Neonatal Society, 328
Nepenthes, 223
Nerve growth factor (NGF), 176
Netherlands, 189
NETI. *See* Neutral and Enemy Trade Index
Neues Blumenbuch (Merian), 211
Neuropathology, 271
Neurophysiology, 176–177
Neutral and Enemy Trade Index (NETI), 59
Neutrons, 155, 208
Nevill, Lady Dorothy Fanny née Walpole, 223
Nevill, Reginald, 223
New Biology, 1
A New Gospel, a Revelation of God Uniting Physiology and the Religion of Man (Stopes), 304

New Hall, Cambridge, 218, 219
New Hall, 1954–1972: The Making of a College (Murray), 218
New Hospital for Women, 2, 3, 110
A New Look at the Northern Ireland Countryside (Balfour), 16–17
New Naturalist series, 242
New Phytologist, 70
New Soaring Pilot (Welch), 325
New South Wales, 172
New Veterinary College, 79
New York Academy of Sciences, 293
New York Infirmary for Indigent Women and Children, 36
New Zealand, 2, 57–58, 98–99, 173, 267–268
New Zealand Association for the Advancement of Science, 29
New Zealand Limnological Society, 57, 99
New Zealand Marine Science Society, 57
New Zealand Medical Research Council, 328
New Zealand Oceanographic Institute (NZOI), 57
Newbigin, Florence, 223, 224
Newbigin, James Leslie, 223
Newbigin, Marion Isobel, 223–224
Newcastle Education Committee, 331
Newcastle Workers' and Soldiers' Council, 331
Newhouse, Molly, 168
Newton, Isaac, 23, 88
Newton, Lily née Batten, 172, 224–225
Newton, Mary, 150
NFWI. *See* National Federation of Women's Institutes
NHS. *See* National Health Service
Nicholas, Charlotte, 225
Nicholls, A. G., 202
Nicholson, Ben, 58
Nicholson, Harold, 275
Niederoestreichischen Landesmuseum, 137
Nightingale, Florence, 136, 225–227, 283
Nightingale Training School for Nurses, 226, 227, 280
Nihell, Elizabeth, 227–228
Nilsson-Ehle, Herman, 307
NIMR. *See* National Institute for Medical Research
Nitric acid, 175–176
"Nitrogen Absorption Bands" (Sponer), 293
No Signposts in the Sea (Sackville-West), 276
Noach, Ilse née Hellman, 228–229
Nobel Institute for Physics, 208
Nobel Peace Prize, 216
Nobel Prize, 38, 75–76, 77, 78, 134, 136, 141, 155, 176, 189, 208
Noble, Mary, 229–230
Noddack, Ida Eva née Tacke, 208, 230
Noddack, Walter Karl, 230

Nongovernmental Organization Forum, 125
Norfolk and Norwich Naturalists' Society, 310
Normality and Pathology in Childhood (Freud), 104
Norsk Tidsskrift for Sprogvitenskap, 81
North American Service, 3
North East Metropolitan Hospital Board, 96
North India Medical School for Christian Women, 45
North Kensington Women's Welfare Centre, 193
North Lonsdale Magazine, 136
North, Marianne, 231–232, 267–268
North Middlesex Hospital, 44
North of England Radium Institute, 44
North Sea Expedition, 40
North to the Rime-Ringed Sun (Hutchison), 142
Northcote Trust, 280
North-East Association of Medical Women, 331
North-East Society for Women's Suffrage, 331
Northern Women's Hospital, 331
Norway, 260, 295–296
Norwegian Academy for Language and Literature, 81
Norwegian Academy of Arts and Sciences, 40, 81, 113, 260
Norwegian Federation of University Women, 40
Norwegian General Scientific Research Committee, 81
"Note on Common Diseases Sometimes Seed-Borne" (Alcock), 6
Notes for Introductory Courses in Genetics (Auerbach), 12
Notes for Observations of Injurious Insects (Ormerod), 233
"Notes on the Land and Freshwater Shells of Cumberland" (Longstaff), 181
Notes on Hospitals (Nightingale), 226
Notes on Matters Affecting the Health, Efficiency, and Hospital Administration of the British Army (Nightingale), 226
Notes on Nursing (Nightingale), 226
"Notes on the Flora of the Salisbury District" (Welch), 326
NTF. *See* Nutrition Task Force
Nuclear chemistry, 242–243
Nuclear energy, 117, 155–156, 339, 341–342
Nuclear physics, 206–209, 341–342
Nuffield Foundation, 252, 319
Nuffield Hospital, 299
Nuffield Laboratory, 246, 316
Nursery World, 145, 229
The Nursery Years (Isaacs), 145
Nursing, 17–18, 68, 95–96, 219, 225–227, 280
    psychiatric nursing, 101–102
Nursing and Social Change (Baly), 18
Nutrition, 60–61, 65–66, 209, 261, 291, 316, 322, 326–327
Nutrition Committee, 261

Nutrition Society, 61, 328
Nutrition Task Force (NTF) for the Health of the Nation, 65–66
"Nutrition Tasks: Achievements and Challenges for the Future" (Clayton), 66
Nutritional Research Laboratory (Coonoor), 291
Nyasa, Lake (Lake Malawi), 184
NZOI. *See* New Zealand Oceanographic Institute

Oakley, Kenneth, 170
Oates, Ken, 197
"Obligate Symbiosis in *Calluna vulgaris*" (Rayner), 258
Observations on the Pathology of Hydrocephalus (Russell), 271
Observatory, 66, 67
Observer, 243, 276
Obstetric Society, 283
Occupational therapy, 105–106, 264
Odonata, 179–180
"The Odonata of the State of Mato Grosso, Brazil" (Longfield), 180
Odwara Carcinological Museum, 115
Office for Scientific and Technical Information (OSTI), 158
Oil industry, 19, 107–108, 293–294
Olav, King, 114
Old Rectory, Girton, 279
Olduvai Gorge, 170
Olympic Games, 241
"On Infinite Derivatives" (Young), 341
On Molecular and Microscopic Science (Somerville), 292
"On Some Supposed Differences in the Minds of Men and Women with Regard to Educational Necessities" (Becker), 26
On the Connexion of the Physical Sciences (Somerville), 292
"On the Germination of the Spores of Agaricineae" (Potter), 254
"On the Nature of Animal Lactase" (Stephenson), 297
Onychophora, 198
Open Way Association, 149
Open Way Charitable Trust, 149
Open Way Psychotherapy Clinic, 149
Ophthalmic Society of Australia, 195
Ophthalmology, 194–196, 246–247, 316–317
Optical Sciences Laboratory, 203
Optical Society of America, 293
Opticians, 88–89
Orchids, 87, 223
Ordnance Survey Maps (Newbigin), 224
Organic chemistry, 245
Orleans, Duke of, 228
Orleans, Elisabeth d', 174

Ormerod, Eleanor Anne, 233–235
Ormerod, Georgiana, 234
Ornithology, 19–20, 35, 132, 174, 204, 310
Ornstein, Leonard, 93
Orpen, Goddard, 9
Orr, Andrew Picken, 201–202
Osmunda regalis, 196
Osteoarthritis, 216–217
Oster House, 295, 299
OSTI. *See* Office for Scientific and Technical
    Information
Outdoor Publicity, 138
Outer Hebrides, 323
Oxford Medical Illustration, 68
Oxford Survey of Childhood Cancer, 300
Oxford Textbook of Medicine, 281
Oxford Women's Societies, 160

"P" (Lehmann), 173
Pak-Khan Trust, 316
Palace Hospital (South Africa), 159
Palaeohistologie der Pflanze (Hofmann), 137
Palaeontological Society of America, 262
Paleoanthropology, 170–171
Paleobotany, 70–71, 136–137, 162, 302–304
Paleontology, 24, 132, 217, 262
Paleozoic Gastropoda, 181
Pallanza Institute, 309
Pallas, Peter, 35
Palynology, 70, 162
Pandora (ship), 100
Panmure, Lord, 226
Paper Chase (Balfour), 16
Paper chromatography, 247
Parachutists, 240
Parasitology, 33–34, 251, 259
Parasitology, 259
Parasitology Group, 34
Parenteau-Carreau, Serena, 68
Paris Arsenal, 167
Paris green, 234
Parke, Mary, 172, 197, 237–238
Parsons, Charles, 128, 203
Parsons, Lady, 128
Parsons, William, 203
Partridge, Margaret, 128
Pasmore, Victor, 205
Pathology, 18–19, 270–272, 276–277, 283–284
Pathology of Tumours of the Nervous System
    (Russell and Rubenstein), 271
Paton, J. L., 191
Patten, Marguerite, 238–239
Payne-Scott, Ruby Violet, 240
PDSA. *See* People's Dispensary for Sick Animals
Pearsall, W. H., 70, 242
Peckham Pioneer Health Clinic, 168
Pegge, Christopher, 48

Peierls, Rudolf, 117
Peirce, Mary Sophie Catherine Teresa, 240–241
Pendulums, 175
Penfield, Wilder, 271
Penguin Dictionary of Biology, 1
Penicillin, 18–19, 135, 313
Pennant, Thomas, 35
Pennington, Winifred Anne, 151, 241–242
Peonies of Greece (Stearn and Davies), 116
People's Dispensary for Sick Animals (PDSA),
    156
The Peoples of Kenya (Adamson), 4
Pepinsky, Ray, 189
Pepys, Jack, 209, 312
Perey, Marguerite, 242–243
Peripatus, 198
Perrier, C., 230
Perry, Amos, 243
Perry, Frances Mary née Everett, 243
Perry, Gerald, 243
Perry, John, 13
Perth City Museum, 254
Pesticides, 234
Petrie, Flinders, 88, 219, 244
Petrie, Hilda Mary Isobel née Urlin, 244
Pharmaceutical chemistry, 41–42, 47–48
Pharmaceutical Codex, 42
Pharmaceutical Journal, 42
Pharmaceutical Society, 41–42, 47–48, 49
Pharmacology, 48–50
Pharmacy, 144, 333–334
Pharmocopedia, 42
Phenylketonuria (PKU), 65
Philanthropy, 321
Philbin, Eva Maria née Ryder, 245
*Philosophical Transactions of the Royal Society of
    London*, 136, 324
Photographic Intelligence Service, 111
Photographic Society of Ireland, 203
Photographing Architecture (Harker), 127
Photography, 10, 33, 54–55, 58, 126–127, 203, 310
Photokina World Fair, 127
Photosynthesis, 151
Phycologica Britannica (Harvey), 111
Phycology, 204–205
Phylloglossum, 277
"The Physical Chemistry of Solid Organic
    Colloids with Special Relation to Coal and
    Related Materials" (Franklin), 101
Physical Chemistry Testing Laboratory (Berlin),
    230
The Physical Education of Girls (Blackwell), 36
Physical Geography (Somerville), 293
Physical Society, 13
Physicians, 29, 84, 143–144, 152–153, 168–169,
    331, 340
    dental surgery, 177–178

family planning, 21, 67–69, 193, 289
gynecology, 20–22, 36, 82, 282–283, 329
India, 45, 282–283
medical missionaries, 285–286
ophthalmology, 194–196, 246–247, 316–317
pediatricians, 192
specialists in terminal care, 280–281
thoracic physicians, 311–312
Physics, 38, 62, 88, 93, 165, 240, 293, 337
astrophysics, 140–141
biophysics, 100–101, 124–125
educators, 23–24
electricity, 12–14
nuclear physics, 206–209, 341–342
See also Radiation
Physics Institute (Göttingen), 293
Physiology, 31–32, 48–50, 245–246
hormones, 247–248
neurophysiology, 176–177
plant physiology, 252–253
The Physiology of Bone (Vaughan), 319
Physiology of Fishes (ed. Brown), 46
Physiotherapy, 38–39
Phytophthora fragariae, 6
Pickard, R. H., 179
Pickford, Lillian Mary, 245–246
Pico de Nebline, 205
Pieter Faure (ship), 204
Piezoelectricity, 76–77
Pigments, 164
Pilot's Weather, a Flying Manual of Cloud Reading for Pilots (Welch), 325
Pinus radiata, 37
Pioneer Work in Opening the Medical Profession to Women (Blackwell), 36
Pirie, Antoinette (Tony) née Patey, 195, 246–247, 316
Pitchblende, 77
Pitt-Rivers Museum, 89
Pitt-Rivers, Rosalind Venetia née Henley, 247–248, 319
"Plain Account of the Inoculating of the Small-pox by a Turkey Merchant" (Montagu), 213
Planck, Max, 207
Plankton, 55, 57, 171, 202
Plant, J., 221
Plant and Animal Geography (Newbigin), 224
Plant pathology, 6–7, 116, 229–230, 276–277
Plant physiology, 252–253
Plasmodium gallinaceum, 34
Platt of Writtle, Baroness, née Beryl Catherine Myatt, 248–249
Playing Fields Association, 241
Plesiosaurus, 7
Ploughing the Nivernais (Bonheur), 39
Plutonium, 208
Plymouth Culture Collection, 235

Pneumatic corer, 242
Pneumoconiosis, 300
Poaceae, 320
Pockels, Agnes, 249–250
Pockels point, 249
A Pocket Guide to British Ferns (Farquharson), 95
Poems from the Divan of Hafiz (Bell), 27
Poems of West and East (Sackville-West), 275
Poison gases, 10–12, 13, 316
Poland, 123
Polish Academy of Sciences, 123–124
Polish National Culture Fund, 123
Pollard, E., 161
Pollution, 19, 65, 224, 293–294
Polonium, 75, 77, 155
Pontificia delle Scienze, 176
Pope, Elizabeth, 28
A Popular History of Astronomy (Clerke), 66
Port Erin Marine Laboratory, 237
Porter, Annie (Mrs. H. B. Fantham), 250–251
Porter, Helen Kemp née Archbold, 252–253, 327
Porter, Mary (Polly) Winearls, 253
Portmann, A. D., 30
Portsmouth Polytechnic, 269
Potamogeton x. cadburyae, 54
"Potential Impact of Climatic Warming on Arctic Vegetation" (Balfour), 16
Potter, Helen Beatrix, 229–230, 253–255
Potter, Rupert, 229
Practical Guidebook for Nursery Hygiene (Goss), 116
Practical Histology and Embryology (Eales), 91
Practical Plant Physiology (Rayner and Keebel), 258
Pregnancy and an Easy Delivery (Yoshioka), 340
Prehistoric Art in Europe (Sandars), 277
A Preliminary Checklist of British Marine Algae (Parke), 237
Preliminary Checklist of the Flowering Plants and Ferns of Griqualand West (Wilman), 333
"The Pre-Menstrual Syndrome" (Dalton and Greene), 82
The Pre-Menstrual Syndrome and Progesterone Therapy (Dalton), 82
Price-Jones, Cecil, 318
Priestley, J. H., 196
Primrose Day, 223
Princess Louise Hospital, 38
Princess Mary's Royal Air Force Nursing Service, 18
Principia mathematica (Newton), 88
The Principles of Contraception—A Handbook for GPs (Malleson), 193
Private Eye, 69
Problems in Astrophysics (Clerke), 66
Problems in Tree Nutrition (Rayner), 258

Problems of Cytology and Evolution in the Pteridophyta (Manton), 196
Problems of Fertility in General Practice (Malleson), 193
Proceedings of the Physics Society, 308
Proceedings of the Prehistoric Society, 170
Proceedings of the Royal Society, 7, 13, 135–136, 292, 328
Proceedings of the Royal Society of Edinburgh, 11
Proceedings of the Zoological Society of London, 1, 59, 171, 184, 251, 286
Proconsul, 170
Professions, xi–xvi, xvii–xviii
Progress in Leather Science, 179
Propositiones philosophicae (Agnesi), 4
Proteins, 179, 247, 330
Protoglycan molecule, 216
Protozoology, 33–34, 54–55, 264–265
Prudhoe Hospital, 102
Pseudomonas, 63
Pseudospora volvocis, 264
Psychiatric Clinic (University of Rome), 214
Psychiatric nursing, 101–102
Psychiatry, 42–43
Psychoanalysis, 104, 149–150, 161, 212–213, 228–229
The Psycho-analysis of Children (Klein), 161
Psychology, 214–215
    child psychology, 104, 144–146, 149–150, 161, 212, 228–229
    social psychology, 147–148
The Psychology of Children (Scharlieb), 283
Psychotherapy, 149–150
Pterosaur, 7
Public Health Laboratory, 83
Public Records Act, 1958, 117
Public service, 287–288, 321
Pugwash Conferences on Science and World Affairs, 136
Purves, Jock, 200
Pygmies, 69
Pyper, Cynthia, 68
Pythium debaryanum, 270

Quakers. *See* Society of Friends
Quakers Visit Russia (Lonsdale), 183
Quantitative Genetics and Sheep Breeding (Turner and Young), 311
Quarterly Journal of Microscopical Science, 30
Quarterly Journal of Pure and Applied Mathematics, 341
Quarterly Journal of the Geological Society of London, 181, 257, 287
Quarterly Journal of the Royal Meteorological Society, 326
Quasi-Stellar Objects (Burbidge and Burbidge), 51

Quastel, Juda Hirsch, 297
Quaternary geology, 123–124
Quaternary Research Unit, 240
Quick Laboratory, 251
Quinine, 34

Raat, Jan, 125
Race, Robert, 278
Radar Research Laboratory (Elliott Brothers), 167
Radcliffe Infirmary, 271, 299
Radiation, 75–79, 102–103, 113–114, 154–156, 175, 207–208, 246
    gamma radiation, 155, 240
    radiation poisoning, 77, 78, 156, 243, 300, 319
Radio operators, 88
Radio physics, 240
Radio research, 308
Radio Research Board, 56
Radio Research Station (Berkshire), 308
Radio Rotes Wien, 147
Radio Society of Great Britain (RSGB), 71, 88, 131
Radio Times, 55
Radiobiology, 317–319
Radiology, 294–295
Radiophysics Division (CSIRO), 240
Radiotherapy, 44
Radium, 75–78, 113
Le Radium, 77
Radium Institute, 77, 78, 154–155, 242
"Radium og de radioactive processor" (Gleditsch and Ramstedt), 113
RAF. *See* Royal Air Force
RAFARS. *See* Royal Air Force Amateur Radio Society
Rainbow (ship), 100
Raine, D. N., 65
Rainforests, 205–206
Raise the Roof campaign, 18
Raisin, Catherine Alice, 257
Raleigh, Lord, 250
Raman, C. V., 291
Rampton Hospital, 102
Ramsey, William, 27
Ramstedt, Eva, 113
Randall, John, 101
Rankin, Margaret, 138
Ratcliffe, Edna Jane, 258
Der Raupen wunderbare Verwandlung und sonderbare Blumen Nahrung (Merian), 211
Rawlins, Edith, 41
Raymond, J. E. G., 202
Rayner, Mabel Mary Cheveley, 258–259
RCM. *See* Royal College of Midwives
RCN. *See* Royal College of Nursing
RCVS. *See* Royal College of Veterinary Surgeons

Read, H. H., 323
"The Reconstruction of a Race of Primitive
    Angiosperms" (Sargant), 279
Red Army, 148
Red Cross Blood Transfusion Unit, 278
Reef Point Gardens Collection, 150
Rees, Florence Gwendolen, 259
Reformers and Rebels (Anderson), 7
Regent Street Polytechnic, 126–127
Regent's Park, 251
Reith, John (Baron), 3
Reminiscences (Scharlieb), 283
Remount Hospital for horses, 80
Research Center on Human Relations, 147
Research into the History of the German Language
    (Dal), 81
Research Methods in Human Relations (Jahoda), 147
"Research on ß-ray Continuous Spectra, Which
    Are Emitted from Artificial Radiation
    Nuclei" (Yuasa), 342
Research Studies, Board of, 151
Resvoll, Thekla Susanne Ragnhild, 260, 303
Retinoic acid, 246
"A Review of Worldwide Petroleum Resources"
    (Clerke), 67
Rhenium, 230
Rhizobium, 116
Rhizophydium planktonicum, 55
Rhodesia, 261, 324
Rhodophyceae, 87
Rhodophyta, 205
RHS. *See* Royal Horticultural Society
Ricardo, Kate, 184
Richards, Audrey Isabel, 260–262
Richter, Emma née Hüther, 262
Rickett, Mary Ellen, 262
RIKEN. *See* Institute of Physical and Chemical
    Research
RIKEN-Nishina Laboratory, 342
Rimington-Wilson, Lettice, 180
The Rising Tide (Balfour), 17
River Rheidol, 224
Riviere, Joan, 145
Road Research Laboratory, 182
A Road to Fairyland (Stopes), 305
Robb, Mary Anne née Boulton, 263
Roberts, Mary, 263
Robertson, Dorothea, 264
Robertson, Muriel, 264–265
Robinson, Henry Peach, 127
Robson, J. M., 11
Roche group, 248
*The Rock Engravings of Griqualand West and
    Bechuanaland* (Wilman), 333
Rock Wool (Guppy), 120
Rockefeller Foundation, 135, 136, 261
Roe, Humphrey, 304

"Role of Water in Some Biological Processes"
    (Wiggins), 328
Röntgen, Wilhelm Conrad, 76
Roscoe, Henry, 254
Rose, Arthur, 106
Rosenberg, Otto, 196
Rosenfeld, B. A., 269
Ross, Clunies, 311
Ross-Craig, Stella, 265, 290
Rosser, Celia Elizabeth née Prince, 265
Rothamsted Experimental Station, 43, 322
Rothschild, Charles, 266
Rothschild, The Honourable Miriam Louisa, 64,
    265–267
Rotoiti, Lake, 57
Rotorua, Lake, 57
Round, G. H., 9
Rowan, Frederic, 267
Rowan, Marian Ellis née Ryan, 267–268
Royal Academy, 89
Royal Academy for Engineering Sciences,
    Stockholm, 208
Royal Academy of Dublin, 292
Royal Aeronautical Association, 16, 154
Royal Aeronautical Society, 61
Royal Aeronautical Society Journal, 325
Royal Aeronautical Society Light Aviation
    Group, 325
Royal Agricultural Society of England, 233–234
Royal Air Force (RAF), 71, 131, 138–139, 193
Royal Air Force Amateur Radio Society
    (RAFARS), 131
Royal Aircraft Establishment, 107, 288
Royal Anthropological Institute, 89, 219, 262
Royal Army Medical Corps, 21, 295
Royal Army Service Corps, 179
Royal Astronomical Society, 37, 67, 130, 140, 270,
    292
Royal Australian Air Force Academy, 165
Royal Birmingham Society of Artists, 137
Royal Botanic Garden, Edinburgh, 290
Royal Botanic Gardens, Kew, 119, 134, 233, 254,
    263, 302, 319
  collections, 142, 206, 268, 324
  Jodrell Laboratory, 279
Royal Botanic Gardens, Sydney, 205
Royal Cancer Hospital, 134
Royal Central Asian Society, 53
Royal Chest Hospital, 284
Royal College of General Practitioners, 68, 82,
    149
Royal College of Midwives (RCM), 96, 334, 335
Royal College of Nursing (RCN), 17, 18, 101–102
Royal College of Pathologists, 65, 83, 271, 284
Royal College of Physicians and Surgeons, 21,
    143, 149, 194, 223, 248, 271, 299, 300, 311,
    330

Royal College of Practitioners, 82
Royal College of Psychiatrists, 42
Royal College of Science, 192
Royal College of Veterinary Surgeons (RCVS), 79–80, 313–314
Royal Commission on Allotments, 243
Royal Commission on Environmental Pollution, 65
Royal Commission on Equal Pay, 319
Royal Commission on the Health of the Army, 226
Royal Commission on Venereal Diseases, 283
Royal Commonwealth Society for the Blind, 246
Royal Cornhill Hospital, 106
Royal Danish Geodetic Institute, 173
Royal Devon and Exeter Health Care Trust, 312
Royal Entomological Society, 60, 99, 180
Royal Flying Corps, 240
Royal Free Hospital, 42, 82, 110, 195, 272, 282, 295, 298
Royal Geographical Society, 32, 69, 100, 180, 293
Royal Gunpowder Administration, 167
Royal Horticultural Society (RHS), 119, 150, 223, 233, 243, 267, 276, 281, 302
  medals, 4, 26, 332
Royal Infirmary, 152
Royal Institute for Technology, Stockholm, 208
Royal Institute of British Architects, 302
Royal Institute of Chemistry, 179, 245, 334
Royal Institution, 67, 127, 182, 190, 328
Royal Irish Academy of Science, 142
Royal Maternity Hospital, Belfast, 335
Royal Medico-Psychological Association, 42, 43
Royal Meteorological Society, 139
Royal Microscopical Society, 95
Royal National Institute for the Blind, 316
Royal Northern Agricultural Society, 193
Royal Observatory (Cape of Good Hope), 66
Royal Observatory, Greenwich, 51, 270
Royal Ordnance Factory, 166
Royal Pharmaceutical Society, 144
Royal Photographic Society, 55, 126–127, 310
Royal Photographic Society Journal, 127
Royal Red Cross, 297
Royal Scottish Geographical Society, 53, 142, 224
Royal Society, xviii, 8, 10, 12, 13, 31, 34, 50, 56, 62, 64, 83, 98, 117, 124, 129, 132, 140, 174, 208
  fellows, 136, 159, 181, 185, 197, 198, 217, 222, 240, 245, 252, 259, 265, 267, 295, 297, 319, 329
  foreign members, 208
  grants, 304
  medals, 183, 185
  officers, 324
Royal Society Conversazione, 266

Royal Society for the Prevention of Cruelty to Animals (RSPCA), 138
Royal Society for the Protection of Birds (RSPB), 19, 174
Royal Society National Committee for IGCP, 324
Royal Society of Arts, 17, 58, 126, 127
Royal Society of Edinburgh, 11, 12, 17, 79, 174, 191, 202, 229, 234
Royal Society of Hobart Town, 100
Royal Society of London/Royal Geographical Society Xavantina-Cachimbo Expedition, 184
Royal Society of Medicine, 82, 239, 248, 280, 282, 313–314, 329
Royal Society of Musicians, 82
Royal Society of New South Wales, 319, 320
Royal Society of South Africa, 251, 333
Royal Society of Victoria, 71
Royal Statistical Society (RSS), 74, 75, 166
Royal Sussex County Hospital, 43
Royal Swedish Academy of Sciences, 171, 217
Royal Victoria Hospital for Caste and Gosha Women, 283
Royal Victoria Infirmary, 334
Royal Worcester Porcelain Company, 268
Royal Zoological Society for Scotland, 17
Royaumont Abbey, 144
Rozhanskaya, Marian née Mikhaylovna, 268–269
RSGB. *See* Radio Society of Great Britain
RSPB. *See* Royal Society for the Protection of Birds
RSPCA. *See* Royal Society for the Prevention of Cruelty to Animals
RSS. *See* Royal Statistical Society
Rule, Margaret Helen née Martin, 269
Rumphius, 211
Rural life, 84–85
Rusinga Island, Lake Victoria, 24
Ruskin, John, 150
Russell, Annie Scott Dill, 269–270
Russell, Dorothy Stuart, 270–272, 318
Russell Gurney Enabling Act, 153
Russia, 20, 148, 152, 163, 199
Russian Academy of Sciences, 163
Russian Revolution, 148
Russian Royal Scientific Society, 199
Rutherford, Ernest, 113, 175
Ruttner-Kolisko, Agnes née Kolisko, 272
Ryle, John, 300
Ryman, Brenda Edith, 272–273

S. S. Almanzora (ship), 179
Saccharomyces cerevisiae, 297
Sackville-West, Victoria May (Vita), 243, 275–276
Safar Nameh: Persian Pictures—A Book of Travel (Bell), 27

St. Christopher's Association, 280–281
St. Christopher's Hospice, 280
St. Cuthbert's Cove, Farne Islands, 132
St. George (ship), 179
St. George's Expedition, 59
St. Giles Cathedral, 144
St. Luke's, 280
St. Mary's Hospital, 194, 280
St. Ouen's Bay Conservation Area, 170
St. Petersburg Academy of Sciences, 32
St. Thomas's Hospital, 18, 22, 280, 334
St. Thomas's Medical School, 280
Salisbury and South Wiltshire Museum, 325
Salmo trutta, 46
Salmons, Josephine Edna, 276
Samaritan Hospital, 21
*Sammlung kurzer Grammatiken germanischer
    Dialekte* (Dal), 81
Sampson, Kathleen, 276–277
Sandars, Nancy Katharine, 277
Sanger, Ruth Ann, 277–278
Sansome, Eva née Richardson, 278–279
SAOT. *See* Scottish Association of Occupational
    Therapists
Sargant, Ethel, 8, 275
Sars, G. O., 40
Saunders, Cicely Mary Strode, 280–281
Saunders, Edith Rebecca, 281
Save the Children Fund, 192, 289
Sayer, Ettie, 282
Scandinavian (ship), 215
Scharlieb, Mary Ann Dacomb née Bird, 144,
    282–283
Schlein, Y., 266
Schmidt, W., 107
School of Pharmacy for Women, 42, 47–48
Schumacher, Raoul, 201
Schuster, Arthur, 284
Schuster, Norah Henriette, 283–284
Schütte-Lihotsky, Margarete née Lihotsky,
    284–285
Schütte, Wilhelm, 284
Sciagrams, 58
Science education, 125–126
Science for Girls? (Kelly), 125
Science Museum Advisory Committee, 108
The Science of Genetics (Auerbach), 12
The Science of Seeing (Pirie and Mann), 195, 246
Science Policy Research Unit (University of
    Sussex), 147
"Science, You, and Everyday Life," 126
Scientific and Industrial Research, Department
    of (DSIR), 56, 57, 136, 222, 252, 308
The Scientific Papers of William Huggins
    (Huggins), 140
Scientific Research Expeditions Ltd., 59
Scolt Head, Norfolk, 310

Scoresbysund seismological station, 173
Scott, D. H., 279, 290
Scott, John, 6
Scottish Agriculture Development Council, 17
Scottish Association of Occupational Therapists
    (SAOT), 106
Scottish Chamber of Agriculture, 192
Scottish Federation of Women's Suffrage
    Societies, 143
Scottish Geographical Magazine, 142, 223–224
Scottish Marine Biological Association (SMBA),
    201, 202
Scottish Royal College of Surgeons, 178
Scottish Wildlife Trust, 17
Scottish Women's Hospital Unit, 192
Scottish Women's Hospitals for Foreign Service,
    143–144
"The Screw Propeller of 1838 and Its
    Subsequent Improvements" (Vansittart),
    317
Scripps Institute of Oceanography, 57
Scudder, Ida Belle, 286
Scudder, Ida Sophia, 285–286
Scuola Ortophrenica, 215
*The Sea Peoples: Warriors of the Ancient
    Mediterranean, 1250–1150 BC* (Sandars),
    277
Sea spiders (Pycnogonida), 114
Sea urchins, 115
Seafish Industry Authority (SIA), 17
Seashores (Marshall and Orr), 202
Seaweeds, 87, 112, 204, 224–225, 237
Secession movement, 127
Sedges, 70
Sedgwick, Adam, 136
Sedgwick Museum, 8, 132
Segre, E., 230
Seguin, Edouard, 215
Seismology, 172–174
*Selection and Academic Performance of Students in
    a University School of Architecture*
    (Abercrombie, Hunt, and Stringer), 1
Selenicereus wittii, 206
Sellars, Pandora, 169
Semiconductor Physics (Xie and Huang), 337
Serbia, 144
Seven Memphite Tomb Chapels (Petrie), 244
Sewall, Lucy, 152
Sex Disqualification (Removal) Act, 13, 80
Sexton, Alice (Elsie) Wilkins née Wing, 286–287
Shakespear, Ethel Mary Reader née Wood,
    287–288
Sheffield Medical School, 298
Shilling, Beatrice (Tilly), 288
Ships, 317
Shores of Macquarie Island (Bennett), 29
A Short History of Dentistry (Lindsay), 178

Shorten, Monica Ruth, 288–289
Shrimp, 286–287
SIA. *See* Seafish Industry Authority
Sightsavers International, 246
Silversmiths, 72
Singer, Eleanor, 289
Sino-British Science Co-operation Office, 222
Sissinghurst Castle, 275, 276
Skipsey's Marine Band, 79
Sky Roads of the World (Johnson), 154
Slávíkova, Ludmila née Kaplanova, 290
Sleeping sickness, 264
Slit lamp, 195
Slough Blood Supply Department, 319
Smale, Steven, 56
Small Holding Colony, 72
Smallpox, 213–214
SMBA. *See* Scottish Marine Biological
    Association
Smellie, William, 228
Smith, Annie Lorrain, 290
Smith, J. L. B., 73
Smith, Lyman B., 205
Smith, Mrs. E. *See* Holden, Edith Blackwell
Smith, Pamela Jane, 111
Smith, William, 93
Smithsonian Institution, 217
Smits, A., 189
Smollett, Tobias, 228
Smooth Muscle (Bülbring), 50
Smooth muscle research, 49–50
Smuts Readership in Commonwealth Studies,
    261
Snails, 259
*Social Development in Young Children: A Study of
    Beginnings* (Isaacs), 145
"Social Medicine in Developing Countries"
    (Williams), 330
Social Medicine Unit, 299
Social psychology, 147–148
Social reformers, 22
Social Science Association, 26
Social Science Research Council, 147
Social statisticians, 225–227
Société de Biologie, 84
Société de Neurologie, 84
Société Jersiaise, 169
Society for Constructive Birth Control and
    Racial Progress (CBC), 304
Society for General Microbiology, 265, 297
Society for Home Students, 280
Society for Lincolnshire History and
    Archaeology, 113
Society for Research into Higher Education, 1
Society for Social Medicine, 301
Society for the Advancement of National
    Industry, 76

Society for the History of Natural History, 93
Society for the Promotion of Nature Reserves,
    266
Society for the Protection of Birds (SPB), 174
Society for the Study of Inborn Errors of
    Metabolism, 65
Society of Antiquaries of London, 83, 110
Society of Antiquaries of Scotland, 9
Society of Apothecaries, 109
Society of Archaeologists, 277
Society of Chemical Industry, 166
Society of Engineers, 154
Society of Friends, 30, 54, 183, 321, 330, 335
Society of German Chemists, 230
Society of Herbalists, 177
Society of Women Geographers, U. S., 170
Society of Women Veterinary Surgeons, 156,
    313
Sociology, 148–149
Sohonie, Kamala, 291
Soil Association, 16
Sokolovskaya, Z. K., 269
Solar eclipses, 270
Solar spectrum, 140
Soldiers, Sailors, and Air Force Association
    (SSAFA), 121
Solent Air Ferry, 154
Solvay Conference, 77
Some Contemporary Studies in Marine Science (ed.
    Barnes), 202
Some Minute Animal Parasites (Porter and
    Fantham), 251
"Some Points in the Technique of
    Contraception" (Stopes), 304
*Some Tribal Origins, Laws, and Customs of the
    Balkans* (Durham), 89
Some Wild Flowers of Kenya (Adamson), 4
Somerville Club, 257
Somerville Collection, 293
Somerville, Mary Grieg née Fairfax, 291–293
Somerville, William, 292
Sorbonne Museum, 152
Soroptimists, 6, 106
*Sourcebook in the History of Biochemistry, 1740 to
    1940* (Needham), 222
South Africa, 22, 58, 72–73, 96, 159, 282, 332, 333
South African Association for the Advancement
    of Science, 251
South African Geographical Society, 251
South African Museum, 332–333
South America, 184
South India Missionary Association, 286
South, James, 321
South Kensington Museum, 233
Southampton Health Journal, 65
South-east Blood Transfusion Unit, 247
South-Eastern Pricing Bureau, 144

Southern Europe (Newbigin), 224
Southern Television, 139
Southern Wild Flowers and Trees (Lounsberry), 268
South-West London Chemist's Association, 42
Soviet Union, 268–269, 285
Space group theory, 182
Spallanzani, Lazzaro, 23–24
Spam—The Cookbook (Patten), 239
Spanish Society of Physics and Chemistry, 230
SPB. *See* Society for the Protection of Birds
Spencer, Stanley, 15
Sphenodon, 195
Spirostomum ambiguum, 34
The Splendor That Was Egypt (Murray), 219
Sponer, Hertha, 293
Spooner, Malcolm, 294
Spooner, Mary Florence (Molly) née Mare, 293–294
Spooner, William A., 219
"Spore Morphology in British Ferns" (Knox), 162
The Sportophyte, 303
Spreull, Andrew, 80
Squirrel Nutkin (Potter), 254
Squirrels, 289
Squirrels (Shorten), 288
SSAFA. *See* Soldiers, Sailors, and Air Force Association
Standardization, 49
Standing Committee on Postgraduate Medical and Dental Education, 65
Stanier, Roger, 63
Stapledon, George, 277
States of Jersey Nature Conservation Advisory Body, 170
Statistical Society, 160, 226
Statistics, 74–75, 160, 225–227, 249
Staveley, Dulcie, 294–295
Stazione Zoologica, 30
Stearn, U. T., 116
Stephanson, Mary Ann Elizabeth, 295–296
Stephens, James, 233
Stephenson, Marjory, 7, 63, 180, 296–298
Stepping Stones from Alaska to Asia (Hutchison), 142
Stern, Frederick, 290
Stewart, Alice Mary née Naish, 298–301
Stewart, Olga Margaret, 301
Stjernstedt, Rosemary, 301–302
Stoke-on-Trent Association of Engineers, 269
The Stone-Age of Mount Carmel I (Garrod and Bates), 111
Stones, Margaret, 302–303
Stopes, Marie Charlotte Carmichael, 260, 303–305
Storm, Johan, 139

The Story of Gliding (Welch), 325
The Story of West Africa (Kingsley), 159
Strangeway, Tom, 97
Strangeways Laboratory, 124
Strassmann, Fritz, 208
Strickland, L. H., 297
The Structure and Development of the Fungi (Gwynne-Vaughan), 121
"The Structure of Lignite (Brown Coal) and Bituminous Coal in Japan" (Yasui), 339
The Struggle for Happiness (Kovalevskaya), 163
Student's Text-book of English and General History (Beale), 25
Studies in Perinatal Physiology, 327
Study of the Genus Paeonia (Stern), 290
Succinic acid, 182
Sudden infant death syndrome (SIDS), 300
Suffrage, xviii, 13, 25–26, 96, 143, 289
Sun, 2, 270
Superdraft process, 118
Supplement to Elwes' Monograph of the Genus Lilium (Grove and Cotton), 290
"Sur quelques derives d'amylbenzene tertiare," 113
Surgeon's Hall, 152
Surinam, 211
Surrey Flora Committee, 326
Surrey Gliding Club, 325
Susan Isaacs Nursery School, 146
Sutherland, John, 227
Sutton, John, 323
Sverdrup, Jacob, 81
Swainsona, 172
Swedish Atomic Energy Committee, 208
Swedish Chemical Society, 230
Switched Off: The Science Education of Girls (Harding), 125
Symonds, Margaret, 318
The System of the Stars (Clerke), 66

Tablet, 67
Tacconi, Gaetano, 23
Talbot, Lord, 302
Talbot, William Henry Fox, 10, 203
The Tale of Peter Rabbit (Potter), 254
Tammes, Jantine (Tine), 307
Tandem Accelerator Group, 103
Tanks, 225
Tanner's Council of America, 179
Tanzania, 170–171
"The Tarannon Series of Tarannon" (Shakespear), 287
Taraxacum vachellii, 315
Tasma, David, 280
Tasmania, 100
Tasmanian Society for the Reformation of Female Prisoners, 100

Taxonomy, 172
Taylor, Janet, 307–308
Taylor, Mary, 308
Taylor, Robin, 158
Taylor's Scientific Memoirs, 52
Technetium, 230
Tegetmeier, W. G., 234
The Telescope (Ward), 321
Telescope Teachings (Ward), 321
Telescopes, 203
Television, 3, 55, 139
Tempe, I., 229
Terra Nova (ship), 204
Terror (ship), 100
Tetanus, 264
A Text Book of Plant Biology (Rayner), 258
A Textbook of Inorganic Chemistry, 175
Textbook of Zoology (Boss), 161
Textile Institute, 118
Textiles, 118, 210–211
Thames Group, 96
Thames Regional Health Authority, 96
That Why Child (Jeffrey), 149–150
Thatcher, Margaret, 21
The Theory of Series (Bari), 20
The Theory of Sets of Points (Young and Young), 341
"A Theory of the Origin of Monocotyledons Founded on the Structure of Their Seedlings" (Sargant), 279
Things Worthwhile (Cheesman), 59
Thiselton-Dyer, William, 254
Thomas, Hamshaw, 196
Thomas, Meirion, 196
Thompson, Benjamin, 168
Thompson, Joy, 172
Thonless, Robert, 146
Thorium, 175
The Thousand and One Churches (Bell and Ramsey), 27
Through the Badger Gate (Ratcliffe), 258
Tilapias, 184
Time Well Spent (Cheesman), 59
Tito, Marshall Josip Broz, 289
TNT, 299
Tokyo Joshi Koto Shihan Gakko, 164
Tokyo Women's Medical School, 340
Tolstov, S. P., 268
Tonolli, Livia née Pirocchi, 308–309
Tonolli, Vittorio, 309
Torrey Canyon Pollution and Marine Life (Spooner), 294
Toshiyuki, Majima, 164
Trade, Board of, 117
Traité de mécanique céleste (de la Place), 292
Traité de radioactivité (Curie), 78
Traité de zoologie (Grassé), 30

Traité d'horlogerie (Lepaute), 175
Transactions of the Botanical Society of Edinburgh, 55, 191
Transactions of the British Mycological Society, 55, 229, 278
Transactions of the Chemistry Society, 175
Transactions of the Earth Museum, 123
Transactions of the Edinburgh Geological Society, 162
Transactions of the Institute of Mining Engineers, 162
Transactions of the Royal Society of Edinburgh, 91
Translation, 88, 115, 292
Travels in West Africa (Kingsley), 159
Treanor, P., 2
Treatise on Invertebrate Paleontology (Teichert), 133, 217
A Treatise on the Art of Midwifery (Nihell), 228
The Treatment of Inherited Metabolic Disease (ed. Raine), 65
Trematodes, 171, 259, 266
Trendelenburg, Paul, 49
Trewavas, Ethelwynn, 184, 309
Trifolium subterraneum, 5–6
Trilobites, 262
Troup, James MacDonald, 58
The Trout (Brown and Frost), 46, 105
Trypanosoma brucei, 264
Tsetse fly, 209, 264
Tuberculosis, 130, 284–285, 300, 302
Tulse Hill observatory, 140
Turnbull, H. M., 318
Turnbull, Henry, 271
Turner, Emma Louisa, 310
Turner, H. H., 37
Turner, Helen Alma Newton, 28, 310–311
Turner-Warwick, Margaret née Moore, 311–312
Tynemouth Exhibition, 317
Typha, 172
Typhula trifolii, 229
Tyrtov, Professor, 162–163

"Über das Element 93" (Noddack), 230
Uganda, 184, 261, 264
UKAEA. *See* United Kingdom Atomic Energy Authority
UN Fourth World Conference on Women, 102, 125
UNDP. *See* United Nations Development Programme
UNEP. *See* United Nations Environmental Programme
Unifying Concepts in Ecology (Lowe-McConnell and van Dobben), 184
Union of Sign, Glass, and Ticket Writers, 205
United Kingdom Atomic Energy Authority (UKAEA), 117

United Nations, 125
United Nations Development Programme (UNDP), 184
United Nations Environmental Programme (UNEP), 116
Universität Kinderklinik, 60
Universities Federation of Animal Welfare, 314
Universities (Scotland) Act, 153
University Museum, 134, 253
University of London Observatory, 51
University Women's Land Army, 311
The Upper Paleolithic Age in Britain (Garrod), 110
Uranium, 208, 324
Uvarov, Olga Nikolaevna, 313–314

Vachell, Eleanor, 315–316
Val der Pol equation, 56
Van Dobben, W. H., 184
Van Heyningen, Ruth Eleanor née Treverton, 246, 316–317
Vansittart, Henrietta née Lowe, 317
Vaughan, Janet Maria, 247, 317–319
VELA uniform, 173
Venus, craters, 197
Veterinary Record, 80
Veterinary surgery, 79–80, 156, 313–314
Vickery, Joyce Winifred, 319–320
Victoria and Albert Museum, 254
Victoria, Lake, 24
Victoria, Queen, 39, 80, 226, 267, 283
A Victorian Naturalist (Noble, Jay, and Hobbs), 229
Victory (ship), 111
The Victory Cookbook (Patten), 239
Vietnam War, 136
Virchow Archiv, 49
Virchow Hospital, 49
Vitamins, 246
Voltaire, 88

WAAA. *See* Women's Amateur Athletic Association
WAAF. *See* Women's Australian Auxiliary Air Force
WAAF. *See* Women's Auxiliary Air Force
Waddington, C. H., 185
Wade, A. E., 326
Wady el-Mughara caves, 24
Wakefield, Lord, 153–154
Wakefield, Priscilla née Bell, 321
Waldheim, Kurt, 285
Wales, 224
Walpole, Robert, 223
War Office, 11, 143, 226
Ward, Mary née King, 203, 321–322
Warington, Katherine, 322

Warley Garden in Spring and Summer (Willmott), 332
Warley Place, 332
Warnock Commission, 21
Warren, Brian, 21
Warrington Academy, 35
Water, 328–329
Water Gardening (Perry), 243
Water Plants (Arber), 8
Waterhouse, John, 134
Watson, David Meredith Seares, 322
Watson, James, 101
Watson, Janet Vida, 322–324
Watson, Katharine Margarite, 322
Watsonia, 86
Wayfarers' Travel Association, 318
Wayside and Woodland Fungi (Findlay), 254
Webb, Josefine, 300
Webster, Mary McCallum, 302, 324–325
The Weeds of Farmland (Brenchley), 43
Week, 69
Weierstrass, Karl, 163
Welch, Ann Courtenay, 325
Welch, Barbara née Gullick, 325–326
The Welfare of the Expectant Mother (Scharlieb), 283
Wellcome Centre for Cell Matrix Research, 217
Wellcome Institute, 161
Wellcome Research Laboratories, 63
Wells, H. F., 42
Welsh Plant Breeding Station, 277
Werner, Alfred, 141
WES. *See* Women's Engineering Society
West Africa, 159
West African Studies (Kingsley), 159
West End Hospital for Nervous Diseases, 193
West Sutherland Fisheries Trust, 17
West with the Night (Markham), 201
Western, J. H., 277
Western Cerebral Centre, 38–39
Westphal's Comet, 333
WFGA. *See* Women's Farm and Garden Association
WFGU. *See* Women's Farming and Gardening Union
WFOT. *See* World Federation of Occupational Therapists
What Rome Was Built With (Porter), 233
What's Cooking? (Patten), 239
Whetham, Margaret. *See* Anderson, Margaret Dampier née Whetham
Whetham, W. C. D., 7
Whirlpool Nebula, 203
White, Edmund, 42
White, Margaret, 326
Whitehead, Charles, 234
Whiteley, Martha, 252

Whiting, Sarah, 140
Whitley Council, 144
Whitteridge, David, 49
WHO. *See* World Health Organization
Why Not for the World? (Cable, French, and French), 53
WI. *See* Women's Institute
Widdowson, Elsie May, 261, 326–328
Wiggins, Philippa Marion, 328–329
Wijnberg, Rosalie, 329
Wild Birds Protection Act, 204
Wild Flower Diaries (Dent), 85
Wild Flower Magazine, 85
Wild Flower Society, 16, 41, 54, 85, 86, 301, 315, 324, 325, 326
Wild Flowers of Greece (Goulimis), 116
Wild Flowers of Victoria (Rosser), 265
Wildlife in My Garden (Ratcliffe), 258
Wilkins, Maurice, 101
William, Earl of Rosse, 321
Williams, Cicely Delphine, 329–331
Williams, Ethel May Nucella, 144, 331
Willmott, Ellen, 332
Wilman, Maria, 332–333
Wilson, Fiammetta née Worthington, 333
Wiltshire Archaeological and Natural History Magazine, 326
Winch, Hope Constance Monica, 333–334
Windermere and District Angling Association, 105
A Windfall for the Microscope (Ward), 321
Wireless Engineer, 240, 308
Wireless operators, 71, 131
WISE. *See* Women into Science and Engineering
Wise, T. H., 118
Wise, Ursula. *See* Isaacs, Susan Sutherland
Wise Parenthood (Stopes), 304
The Witch-Cult In Western Europe (Murray), 219
Witt, Leslie, 299, 300
Wolf Foundation, 186
Wolf-Rayet stars, 140
Wollaston Fund, 24
Woman Engineer, The, 128
"Women and Original Research" (Sargant), 279
Women in Science and Technology, 64
Women into Science and Engineering (WISE) campaign, 249
Women Pharmacists' Association, 47
Women Returners to Amenity Gardening Scheme (WRAGS), 150
Women's Amateur Athletic Association (WAAA), 240–241
Women's Army Auxiliary Corps, 120
Women's Australian Auxiliary Air Force (WAAF), 37, 131
Women's Australian National Services, 311

Women's Auxiliary Air Force (WAAF), 71, 111, 138
Women's Electrical Association, 287
Women's Engineering Society (WES), 98, 128, 154, 167
Women's Farm and Garden Association (WFGA), 150
Women's Farming and Gardening Union (WFGU), 72, 150
Women's Institute (WI), 84–85, 258
Women's Land Army, 85
Women's Liberal Federation, 84
Women's liberation movement, 260
Women's Medical Association of Japan, 340
Women's National Campaign, 102
Women's National Cancer Control Campaign, 168
Women's National Commission, 168
Women's Royal Air Force, 120
Women's Royal Australian Navy Service (WRANS), 133
Women's Royal Navy Service (WRNS), 219
Women's Suffrage Journal, 26
Women's Suffrage Society, 26
Women's Veterinary Association, xviii
Women's Voluntary Service (WVS), 281
Wood, Audrey, 334–335
Wood, H. M., 79
Wood and Garden (Jekyll), 150
Woodland Whisperings (Rankin), 138
Woolf, Virginia, 234, 318
Woolley, Leonard, 28
Workers' Educational Association, 148
Workman, William Hunter, 192
World College of Obstetricians and Gynaecologists, 21
World Cultural Council, 51
World Federation for Mental Health, 43
World Federation of Occupational Therapists (WFOT), 106
World Health Organization (WHO), 68, 195, 330, 335
The World of the Grey Squirrel (Shorten and Barkalow), 289
A World of Wonders Revealed by the Microscope (Ward), 321
World Peace Council, 156
World Symposium on Warm-Water Fish Culture, 184
World War I, 30, 80, 113, 190, 279, 284
  medical research, 42, 84
  volunteers, 37, 40, 59, 85, 96, 207
  women's medical unit, 143–144
World War II, 18, 34, 38, 63, 117, 118, 132, 135, 166, 224, 239, 288, 295, 319, 342
  aviation, 59, 61
  biological research, 84, 202, 204, 299

blood supply, 318–319
Chemical Defense Research Group, 222
meteorology, 138–139
mustard gas, 10–12, 13
Nazis, 11, 48, 49, 285, 289, 293, 327
Netherlands, 189
Norwegian prisoners, 295–296
nutrition, 60, 327
volunteers, 19, 37, 74, 96, 114, 281, 311, 324
war nurseries, 228–229
women's corps, 37, 59, 71, 111, 120, 131, 133, 322
World's Fair Congress, 181
World's Gliding Championships, 325
Worldwide Standardized Seismographic Network (WWSSN), 173
Worshipful Company of Engineers, 249
WRAGS. *See* Women Returners to Amenity Gardening Scheme
WRANS. *See* Women's Royal Australian Navy Service
Wray Castle, 54, 184, 242
Writers, 46, 69, 92, 210–211, 223–224, 258
  aviation, 15–16, 325
  botany, 22–23
  chemistry, 199
  children's books, 111–112, 253–255, 341
  cooking, 238–239
  electricity, 127–129
  entomology, 59–60
  geography, 32–33
  history of science, 66–67
  home economics, 26–27
  horticulture, 150–151
  meteorology, 138–139
  microscopy, 321–322
  natural history, 263, 321
  nautical writers, 307–308
  nursing, 17–18
  psychoanalysis, 212–213
  scientific writers, 67, 291–293
  translators, 88, 115
WRNS. *See* Women's Royal Navy Service
WVS. *See* Women's Voluntary Service
WWSSN. *See* Worldwide Standardized Seismographic Network

Wyllie, Andrew, 106
X-chromosome inactivation, 185–187
Xenopsylla cheopsis, 266
Xie, Xide (Hsieh Hsi-teh), 337
"The X-Ray Analysis of Complicated Matter" (Hodgkin), 136
X-ray crystallography, 100–101, 134–136, 157–159
X-ray Diffraction Unit (King's College), 101
X-rays, 300

The Yachtsman's Weather Guide (Holford), 139
Yasui, Kono, 339
The Years of the Week (Cockburn), 69
Yonge, C. M., 201–202
Yoshioka, Yoyoi née Washiyama, 340
Young Bears Playing (Holden), 138
Young, Grace née Chisholm, 340–341
Young People's Consultation Centres, 289
Young, S. S. Y., 311
Young Scientists' Section (BAYS), 183
Young, William Henry, 341
Yuasa, Toshiko, 341–342
Yudkin, John, 297
Yugoslavia, 192, 289

Zeisel, Hans, 147
Zernike, Fritz, 38
"Zeros of Integral Functions of Special Types" (Cartwright), 56
Zittel, 115
Zoological Museum (Moscow), 119
Zoological Record, 309
Zoological Society, 59, 60, 91, 115, 195, 198, 251
Zoology, 1–2, 40–41, 91–92, 151, 160–161, 197–198, 209
  crabs, 115, 171
  helminths, 259
  mollusks, 29–31, 103, 171, 181, 203–204
  muscle research, 124–125
  protozoology, 33–34, 54–55, 264–265
  shrimp, 286–287
  squirrels, 289
  See also Biology; Marine biology